Veduta della gran Piazza e Basilica di S. Pietro situata ove erano anticamente il Circo e gl' Orti di Cajo e Nerone nella Valle Vaticana.

Cav. Piranesi F.

LORD HAVE MERCY · AYE GANG WARILY

FIDELITE

WILLIAM EDWARD PETER LOUIS
DRUMMOND·MURRAY OF MASTRICK
SLAINS PURSUIVANT OF ARMS

Nobility
and Analogous Traditional Elites
in the Allocutions of Pius XII

Plinio Corrêa de Oliveira

Nobility
and Analogous Traditional Elites
in the Allocutions of Pius XII

A Theme Illuminating American Social History

Hamilton Press

To my dear and unforgettable mother,
Lucília,
who first taught me to say "Jesus,"
even before "Mamãe,"
and to place devotion to the Catholic Faith
and love of Holy Mother Church
above all earthly goods,
with a gratitude overflowing
with tender memories
and, especially, hope.

Plinio

The author is grateful for permission to include excerpts from the following
copyrighted works: Dixon Wecter, *The Saga of American Society,* Charles
Scribner's Sons, an imprint of the Macmillan Publishing Company with an
introduction by Louis Auchincloss, introduction copyright © 1970 Charles
Scribner's Sons, copyright © 1937 Charles Scribner's Sons, copyright renewed © 1965 Elizabeth Farrar Wecter; Charles M. Andrews, *The Colonial
Period of American History,* Yale University Press, copyright © 1934; Cleve-
land Amory, *Who Killed Society?,* Harper & Bros., copyright © 1934; John
Ingham, *The Iron Barons: A Social Analysis of an American Urban Elite,
1874–1965,* Greenwood Press, copyright © 1978; C. Wright Mills, *The
Power Elite,* Oxford University Press, copyright © 1956; Kenneth Prewitt
and Alan Stone, *The Ruling Elites: Elite Theory, Power, and American
Democracy,* Harper & Row, copyright © 1973; W. Lloyd Warner, *American
Life: Dream & Reality,* University of Chicago Press, copyright © 1962.

Permissions and acknowledgements for other works will be found with their
respective first citation.

Library of Congress number 93–060895
ISBN 0–8191–9310–0

Printed in the United States of America

Front cover: Saint Peter's Basilica, Rome. Pius XII in the *sedia gestatoria,* surrounded by the Noble Guard and ecclesiastical dignitaries.

Facing title page: Saint Peter's Basilica at dusk. In the foreground is the bridge of
Sant'Angelo over the Tiber.

Facing foreword page: A young recruit of the Swiss Guard takes his oath of alle-
giance to the Pope according to ancient ceremony on May 6, 1992, in the patio of
Saint Damasus in the Vatican's Apostolic Palace.

Back cover: The U.S. Marine Corps War Memorial, Arlington, Virginia. The raising of
the flag on Mount Suribachi, Iwo Jima, during World War II.

In 1978 John Paul II was elected
as successor of Saint Peter.
His official title is the
Bishop of Rome,
Vicar of Jesus Christ,
Successor of Saint Peter, Prince of Apostles,
Supreme Pontiff of the Universal Church,
Patriarch of the West, Primate of Italy,
Archbishop and Metropolitan of the Roman Province,
Sovereign of the Vatican State,
Servant of the Servants of God.

The Pope gives his blessing "urbi et orbi," to the city of Rome and the world.

Contents

Part I

Part II

Appendix I

Contents

Plinio Corrêa de Oliveira

Man of Faith, Thought, and Action

*P*linio Corrêa de Oliveira was born in São Paulo, Brazil, in 1908. He descends from traditional families of the State of Pernambuco, where his father, João Paulo Corrêa de Oliveira, an attorney, was born, and of the State of São Paulo, Brazil's most important, where his mother, Lucilia Ribeiro dos Santos, was born.

He completed his high school education at the Colégio São Luiz, of the Jesuit Fathers, in São Paulo. In 1930 he graduated from the Faculdade de Direito, the renowned law school of the same city.

At an early age he became interested in the philosophical and religious analysis of the contemporary crisis.

In 1928 he joined the Marian Congregations of São Paulo and soon became their principal Brazilian leader, distinguishing himself as an orator, lecturer, and man of action.

In 1933 he helped organize the Catholic Electoral League and was elected to the Constitutional Convention. The youngest congressman in Brazil's history, he garnered the largest number of votes and served as a distinguished leader of the Catholic bloc.

On completing his congressional term, he assumed the chair of History of Civilization at the University College of the University of São Paulo Law School and, subsequently, the chair of Modern and Contemporary History at the Pontifical Catholic University of São Paulo's São Bento and Sedes Sapientiae Departments of Philosophy, Science, and Literature.

Professor Corrêa de Oliveira was the first president of the São Paulo Archdiocesan Board of Catholic Action. From 1935 to 1947 he served as director of the Catholic weekly *Legionário*, which attained unparalleled prominence in the Brazilian Catholic press under his tutelage.

In 1951 he began his collaboration with the prestigious monthly *Catolicismo*, and he continues to be the principal contributor to this influential journal.

From 1968 to 1990 he wrote a weekly column for the *Folha de São Paulo*, the largest daily newspaper in the State of São Paulo.

Prof. Plinio Corrêa de Oliveira is the author of fourteen books and numerous essays and articles. His works include:

In Defense of Catholic Action (1943), with a foreword by Archbishop B. Aloisi Masella, Apostolic Nuncio to Brazil and later Cardinal Camerlengo of the Roman Catholic Church. A keen analysis of the first stages of the leftist infiltration of Catholic Action, this work was highly praised in a letter written on behalf of Pope Pius XII by Archbishop G. B. Montini, Substitute Secretary of State of the Holy See, and later Pope Paul VI.

Revolution and Counter-Revolution (1959) is a historical, philosophical, and sociological treatise on the crisis of the West from the advent of Humanism, the Renaissance, and Protestantism to our day. This work demonstrates the cause-and-effect relationship between these movements and the French Revolution of 1789, the Russian Revolution of 1917, and recent transformations in the Soviet empire and the West. Four editions have been published in Portuguese, seven in Spanish, three in Italian, two in English, and two in French.

The Church in the Communist State: The Impossible Coexistence (1963) demonstrates the illicitness of coexistence between the Holy Catholic Church and a government which, while officially recognizing freedom of worship, forbids her to teach that it is morally wrong to abolish private property. Giuseppe Cardinal Pizzardo, Prefect of the Sacred Congregation for Seminaries and Universities, warmly praised the book, declaring the doctrine expounded by its author a "most faithful echo" of pontifical teachings. The work, which has seen 36 printings and editions, has been published in Portuguese, Spanish, French, German, Polish, Italian, Hungarian, and English, and has appeared in 38 periodicals in 13 nations.

Indian Tribalism: Communist-Missionary Ideal for Brazil in the 21st Century (1977) denounces a new onslaught of progressivism in Brazil, the "neo-missiology" of communist-structuralist orientation. It foresaw the principal communist-ecological doctrines and tendencies advanced 15 years later at the 1992 Earth Summit in Rio de Janeiro.

What Does Self-Managing Socialism Mean for Communism? A Barrier or a Bridgehead? (1981). This exposé and analysis of then newly-elected French President François Mitterrand's platform for socialist self-management appeared in 45 major dailies in 19 nations of the Americas, Europe, and Oceania. A summary of the work was published in 49 countries on 6 continents in 13 languages. Altogether, 33.5 million copies were circulated internationally.

Communism and Anticommunism on the Threshold of the Millennium's Last Decade (1990). Published in 58 newspapers in 19 nations, this document is a historic indictment of those in the East and West who contributed to reducing a large bloc of nations to a state inimical to the human spirit. People in the free world who endeavored to subject their own countries to the same captivity are likewise censured.

The preeminent philosopher of the counterrevolutionary doctrine of the TFPs and like-minded organizations, Prof. Plinio Corrêa de Oliveira ranks as an international leader of thought and action in the face of the myriad crises and catastrophes besetting the world.

In the field of action, his greatest accomplishment is the founding of the Brazilian Society for the Defense of Tradition, Family and Property in 1960 and his service as president of the Brazilian TFP since its inception.

Prof. Plinio Corrêa de Oliveira's penetrating treatise *Revolution and Counter-Revolution* has inspired the founding of autonomous TFPs and TFP Bureaus in 25 countries on 6 continents.

NOTE TO THE READER

A compilation of excerpts from the important allocutions of Pope Pius XII to the Roman Patriciate and Nobility was published in 1956 by the highly regarded Brazilian cultural journal *Catolicismo* in its February, March, and April issues. The journal's principal contributor, Prof. Plinio Corrêa de Oliveira, whose intellectual acumen and vibrant action have earned him international acclaim, provided penetrating commentaries on these pontifical texts.

These commentaries reflect not only the author's elevated culture and perception, but also his independence of mind. Faithful to the teachings of the Pontiff's allocutions, he does not hesitate to challenge the prejudice against the nobility that permeates the West. In the 1950s, as today, such resistance to the principles that informed the French and Bolshevik Revolutions was considered iconoclastic by people in the United States and around the globe who idolize egalitarianism.

In his commentaries, Professor Corrêa de Oliveira analyzed all the allocutions Pius XII had delivered to the Roman Patriciate and Nobility up to that time. Now, at the request of the Centro Cultural Reconquista—TFP Lusa,[1] the author has graciously added a commentary on the allocution Pius XII addressed to members of this same distinguished class in 1958. Moreover, in view of contemporary circumstances, he has revised and expanded his previous commentaries and has included excerpts from allocutions of Popes John XXIII and Paul VI on the same subject.[2] Vatican publications provide no reference to documents on the topic by John Paul II.

The manifest relevance of the matter Pius XII discussed in his fourteen allocutions prompted the author to study it not only in the teachings of his successors,

---

[1] The Centro Cultural Reconquista—TFP Lusa, a Portuguese civic association, forms, with its 24 sister Societies for the Defense of Tradition, Family and Property on six continents, the largest network of anticommunist organizations of Catholic inspiration in the world today. In 1990, the TFPs collected a total of 5,218,520 signatures in defense of Lithuania's freedom. The largest petition drive of its kind, it was commended by Lithuania's Foreign Minister, Mr. Algirdas Saudargas, as "one of the best forms of support we have received from the West."

[2] The original texts of all these allocutions may be found in the Vatican's published collections of documents for the respective popes as listed in the Bibliography. Translations of the allocutions of Pius XII are provided in Part III of this work. Footnote references to the allocutions have been shortened to "RPN," followed by the year of the allocution and the page(s) on which they may be found in the collected documents or, when otherwise indicated, in Part III. References to allocutions to the Pontifical Noble Guard have likewise been shortened to "PNG."

but in those of his predecessors as well.

It was impossible for him to engage in a research tracing the subject all the way back to the holy and glorious pontificate of Peter. Due to constraints of time not only on him, but also on readers whose domestic and professional duties demand so much of their attention, the author decided to halt his retrospective study at the justly celebrated pontificate of Pius IX (1846-1878). This pontificate marked the beginning of the reigns of the contemporary Popes, who have governed the Holy Catholic Church since the end of the convulsions stemming from the French Revolution.

A careful reading of the documents of the pontiffs prior and subsequent to Pius XII reveals that he alone treated the issue of the nobility methodically, explaining its nature and its past and present mission. Accordingly, the author deemed it opportune to provide the public with the full texts of Pius XII's allocutions to the Roman Patriciate and Nobility. (They are to be found toward the end of this book.)

Inasmuch as the subject was touched upon in the allocutions delivered to the Pontifical Noble Guard by Pius XII and his successors, selected passages of particular relevance are quoted in the course of this work. A similar procedure was adopted regarding other pontifical documents that address the topic in passing.

The allocution of Pope Benedict XV to the Roman Patriciate and Nobility on January 5, 1920, elaborates on the subject in such depth and with such amplitude as to merit inclusion in the signal collection of teachings Pius XII dedicated *ex professo* to it. Accordingly, its complete text is also herein provided.

Since these allocutions were remarks of gratitude and salutation the Pontiff renewed each time he received New Year's greetings from the Roman Patriciate and Nobility, recurring themes are inevitable. However, Pius XII avoided inconvenient repetition by continually exploring new aspects of his subject, expanding it to its broadest limits and richest depths, as the reader will note should he devote himself to the fruitful task of comparing texts whose themes might seem identical at first.

As the present text unfolds the reader's attention will be drawn naturally to a number of issues related to the subject of the work. These include

— The organic formation of traditional elites analogous to the nobility;

— The revolutionary concepts of "liberty," "equality," and "fraternity" spread throughout the world by the French Revolution, as opposed to the correlated concepts in Catholic doctrine;

— The Catholic doctrine on the monarchical, aristocratic, and democratic forms of government;

— The indispensability of the noble class in an authentically Catholic society.

These and other related issues constitute as it were a crown adorning the book's central topic: the role of the nobility and analogous traditional elites in contemporary society. They too were the subject of enlightening pontifical teachings and historic pronouncements of Saints and Doctors of the Church through the ages. To provide further doctrinal sustenance, the author has enriched his work with a collection of these eloquent documents and perceptive observations.

Struck not only by the clarity and profundity of this historic study but by its evident relevance to the crisis besetting our nation as the Cultural Revolution advances and its errors of egalitarianism are writ ever larger in the citadels of power, the American Society for the Defense of Tradition, Family and Property (TFP) assembled a commission to apply the lens of this analytic masterpiece to a necessarily concise review of the social history of our country. The work of this commission is presented in Appendix I of this book.

While we readily admit that our study cannot match the exceptional character of the greater work from which it draws its inspiration, we trust that it will provide the reader with a frame of reference for reflections on the critical need of an American aristocracy truly faithful to its mission.

Raymond E. Drake
President
The American Society for the Defense
of Tradition, Family and Property (TFP)
New York, March 19, 1993
Feast of Saint Joseph
Prince of the House of David and Worker

Foreword

by Morton C. Blackwell

*A*bout a decade ago I dined one evening with two friends and a guest at Old Europe, a Washington, D.C. restaurant. The guest was a prince, member of a well-known European royal family.

As the prince, then in his early twenties, discussed at our request the many coats of arms of European royalty which adorned the restaurant walls, the elderly German proprietor made his customary round of the tables and introduced himself.

We took the opportunity to introduce our young guest.

The old gentleman was staggered. He actually came very close to dropping to one knee as he said how honored he was to have this young man in his establishment. He left our table and soon returned with an ancient, crumbling guest register, obviously not in current use. He humbly asked our guest to sign it so he could have a record of the visit.

It was an odd sight, this reverence for high nobility in the capital of the United States.

Not that Americans are not interested in royalty and nobility. Supermarket tabloid sales prove they are.

But our country from its founding has officially outlawed hereditary privilege. Although the United States has frequently been allied to monarchies, Americans abroad or at home are often uneasy in the presence of foreign nobility. Should we bow or curtsy? Should we address Queen Elizabeth as "Your Majesty"?

A few years later I was among a group of Americans hosted one evening by the current Duke of Wellington at his country home near London. None of us probably would have considered addressing him as "My Lord," the usual salutation appropriate in Britain for a member of the House of Lords.

The Honorable Morton C. Blackwell is president of The Leadership Institute and the Republican National Committeeman of Virginia. In the Reagan White House, he was Special Assistant to the President for Public Liaison (1981-1984), with responsibility for religious, veteran, and conservative groups. He supervised the youth effort for Ronald Reagan in the 1980 Election Campaign. A leading conservative in the Republican Party, Mr. Blackwell specializes in political education and training.

The Duke's aide suggested we should address him as "Duke" rather than as "Your Grace," the specific form by which dukes are customarily addressed. We Americans appreciated the advice.

For very clear historical reasons, most Americans are uncomfortable with the whole idea of nobility. One friend of mine, a graduate of Harvard, only half in jest says that the French Revolution is an example of the failure of half measures.

So what possible relevance could a book favorable to the nobility and analogous elites have in the United States today?

As it happens, a great deal of relevance.

Originally, this book was written primarily for Catholics. Its author is my friend of a dozen years, Prof. Plinio Corrêa de Oliveira, founder of the Brazilian Society for the Defense of Tradition, Family and Property. Like all the works of the author, it is written elegantly, on a high level, from a devout Catholic viewpoint.

Its clear purpose is to strike at the heart of the deadly leveling tendencies of modern times by making an unassailable case for the legitimacy of elites in human society. What better way to do this among Catholics than to nail it down with the words of modern popes?

Many Catholics will no doubt be surprised at how emphatic the popes have been on this subject.

Many Protestants and others, reading papal documents for perhaps the first time, will be much taken by the clear reasoning of Pius XII and the other pontiffs whose writings and speeches are here well organized and presented.

One does not have to accept papal infallibility to appreciate a case persuasively made. Using theological, moral, and prudential arguments, this book will convince many readers, whatever their faith, that good elites are legitimate, desirable and, yes, necessary.

In Europe, hereditary nobility is not an abstract concept. It is an everyday reality. Such people exist in large numbers, even in countries where they now have no special legal status. Ever conscious of their heritage, European nobility live, work, raise their families and, usually, worship God.

In our era, much of society professes to deplore their existence. But men and women of the noble class and analogous elites are nevertheless objects of much public attention and even admiration.

Measured as a percentage of any population, their importance would be small. But they can and often do lead. Many of them have significant resources and moral authority. Much of the public, not only expatriate restaurateurs, sees them as role models.

What are the duties and responsibilities of such people, born to high status? And how should people not of such status relate to them? These are major topics considered in this book.

From the outset, the author intended that a section of the book would discuss elites in the United States.

On the face of it, our country could seem to be based on the idea that elites are illegitimate. Certainly the example of the United States led many people in other countries to reject the concept of elites.

Yet, as the section on our country in this book demonstrates, the United States has never been without an elite. Political, business and cultural elites have led our society in every period of our history. By and large, this elite has benefited everyone. And quite often these leaders have sprung from the same families over many generations.

Every local community of long duration in our country has its generally recognized "leading families." Especially in the South the histories of family achievements are known and passed down as rich legacies to each succeeding generation. As described in this book, prestigious patriotic societies abound which are based on hereditary descent from American military veterans.

Ferocious egalitarianism has always been alien to American culture. Its early proponent, Thomas Paine, left for what he thought was the greener pasture of revolutionary France. (He barely escaped the guillotine there.)

A clearer understanding of the reality of American elites and their value to our society would go a long way toward rolling back the presumption of many people that there is no legitimate role for elites in our country. This understanding may waken in many people of high status their sense of responsibility to act, may I say, in a more noble way.

Moreover, a better understanding of how so much that is admirable in the United States came to be may alter the common and mistaken view in foreign countries that the relative success of the United States proves all elites elsewhere must be eliminated.

The moral and economic bankruptcy of the communist empire, and its collapse, show what happens when a society turns against tradition, family, and property.

And the dramatic decline in traditional family values has caused most of the disastrous social problems which now beset especially the most prosperous countries, including our own.

I was pleased but a bit surprised when Professor Corrêa de Oliveira asked me to write this Foreword. How often is any Episcopalian, let alone one married to a Southern Baptist, asked to write for a book on papal allocutions?

But my wife and I have been friends of the Societies for the Defense of Tradition, Family and Property for many years. Readers of this book may find it useful to know more about the TFP and how it came to associate with a wide range of conservatives in the United States.

Like me, many American conservatives began their political activity in the upsurge for Barry Goldwater. I was his youngest delegate at the 1964 Republican National Convention.

In those days, conservative interest in the public policy process was focused mainly on anti-communism and economics.

Although Senator Goldwater inspired millions with his principled stands on these issues, he lost the presidential election badly. Americans were not ready to have three presidents in a single year. And liberal elites had convinced many voters that they could deliver something for nothing, that government itself could create a Great Society.

After the 1964 election, a friend told me we should abandon the word *con-*

servative in politics. He thought our views had been so repudiated at the polls that never again in our lifetimes could "conservatives" succeed in the public policy process.

But my friend was wrong.

The liberals went too far. They waked a sleeping giant.

By the early 1980s, a conservative president, Ronald Reagan, had appointed my friend to head a Federal agency and had appointed me to serve on the White House Staff.

Here is what had happened: The liberal elites had politicized traditional values.

In all of 1964 Barry Goldwater probably never was asked his views on abortion. Nor was he asked if he favored bank robbery. Traditional values embedded in our laws were considered settled issues.

Then, with great rapidity in the 1970s, administrative actions, legislation, and especially Federal court decisions by liberal judges overturned generations of custom and law regarding values held dear by millions of Americans.

A powerful movement sprang up and created a new winning majority in American politics, based on conservative principles in both the area of economics and the area of traditional morality.

The story of how that movement grew in numbers and in leadership skills is outside the scope of the present volume. But in this growth process, American conservative leaders came to know the American TFP.

In 1975, about forty leaders of American conservative activity gathered at the Dulles Marriott Hotel near Washington, D.C. The men and women there were veterans of the Goldwater campaign. Each of us had demonstrated to the others both a dedication to conservative principles and an ability to lead. We met to discuss how to beat the liberals.

At the meeting I pointed out that, since the French Revolution, the Left everywhere has been international in scope and interest while conservatives in every country had tended to limit their concerns to national affairs.

I asked if anyone present, for example, knew of a single Canadian leader who shared our general views on economics and social issues. After all, I said, we share a language and one of the longest international borders in the world.

Not one of us knew a potential ally in Canada. In fact, few of us had *any* friends active in the public policy process in any foreign country.

In the next few years, American conservative leaders deliberately reached out to find like-minded people in other countries.

Frankly, the pickings were slim. In the area of traditional values particularly, we found that those who shared our beliefs were hopelessly ineffective. They had not a clue about how to organize or communicate. What is worse, they believed that being right, in the sense of being correct, was sufficient. They considered it beneath their dignity to study how to win.

Then, in 1979, a number of my friends and I met representatives of the new American TFP. From them we received materials about their long-established sister organization in Brazil.

What a pleasant surprise. Here, for the first time, we encountered a foreign group solidly committed to our core values but which had developed impressive skills in organization and communication. Their materials actually looked good and were readable. They knew how to recruit and organize people. They had identified and earned the trust of a strong base of contributors.

My wife and I vacationed in 1981 in Brazil, largely to learn more about the TFP.

What we saw impressed us even more: a busy, well organized headquarters; a network of local centers across the country; a superb, well-used library; lots of young people systematically being taught conservative values and organizational skills; and their founder, Prof. Plinio Corrêa de Oliveira, a remarkably wise man then in his seventies.

Brazil is often compared to the United States. But the countries are quite different in history, religious composition, and culture. So it was to be expected that a large, successful, indigenous conservative organization in Brazil would be unlike conservative organizations in our country.

Indeed their operations were unlike anything I had seen or ever expected to see.

Intensely Catholic, their members receive Communion every day. Although a secular group, in some ways they could be likened to a medieval religious order. They stand opposed to much that has occurred in modern times, which they consider to have commenced at the end of the Middle Ages, a not unreasonable view. They intend to save Western civilization or to die trying.

Since my visit to Brazil, I have taken opportunities to meet national TFP leaders in my travels to half a dozen countries on four continents. Everywhere they are cultured, smart, and working hard in the public policy process for the improvement of their own nations. Many leaders of the American conservative movement, having had similar experiences, share my view of the TFP.

William F. Buckley, Jr. once described the mission of his conservative magazine, *National Review*, as "To stand athwart history and shout, 'Stop!'" Much the same could be said about the TFP.

And just as Buckley's intellectual prowess helped to fuse various conservative elements in the United States into a winning majority here, TFP activity has achieved much against great odds in a number of countries.

If the TFP in the United States still seems small, American conservatives active for traditional values find them time and again to be effective allies and good friends.

The case for nobility and analogous elites is the part of the case against revolution most difficult to be made in the United States, given our history. So perhaps the case made in this book can best be made by a foreign friend of our country.

More than two hundred years ago, a friend of the British colonies, Edmund Burke, strove mightily against the revolutionary rupture of our ties with Great Britain.

In his 1774 *Speech on American Taxation*, Burke reviewed the confluence of ignorance and arrogance which led Parliament to impose unprecedented revenue taxes on the American colonies. "Leave America, if she has a taxable matter in her, to tax herself.... Leave the Americans as they anciently stood..." Burke urged.

In his 1775 *Speech on Conciliation with the Colonies*, Burke discussed the origins and nature of Americans, and then said Americans were

> acute, inquisitive, dexterous, prompt in attack, ready in defense, full of resources. In other countries, the people, more simple, and of a less mercurial cast, judge of an ill principle in government only by an actual grievance; here they anticipate the evil, and judge of the pressure of the grievance by the badness of the principle. They augur misgovernment at a distance, and snuff the approach of tyranny in every tainted breeze.

Burke's eloquent warnings went unheeded. Soon many Americans with every reason to adhere to their traditional government were swept by revolutionary fervor.

Not until the drafting of the Constitution of the United States did American leaders, virtually all of them deeply committed Christians, soberly reflect on how best to apply the accumulated wisdom of history to achieve ordered liberty in self-government. By then, all possibility of a formal, hereditary elite was lost in the United States.

Burke had previously written, "An attempt towards a compulsory equality in all circumstances and an exact practical definition of supreme rights in every case, is the most dangerous and chimerical of all enterprises." He became the intellectual leader of resistance to the French Revolution of 1789.

Burke's 1790 book, *Reflections on the Revolution in France*, cited in this volume, was promptly translated and published widely in Europe. It inspired a principled resistance to the French revolutionaries and their fellow ideologues across the continent.

Although he endorsed the British "Glorious Revolution" of 1688 and made a strong case that British government mistakes caused the American Revolution and even justified it, Burke saw clearly the damage inevitably inflicted by any revolution. In 1791, in his *Appeal from the New to the Old Whigs*, he wrote, "Every revolution contains in it something of evil."

Surely the resulting evil greatly outweighed any good in the Russian Revolution. Almost all American conservative leaders agree with Burke that the same is true of the Revolution of 1789.

In the English-speaking world, Burke still provides a moral and political foundation for dedicated conservatives. Except for his *Reflections*, his work unfortunately has never been widely available elsewhere.

By the way, Burke, a communicant of the Church of England, strongly supported political emancipation of the then-disadvantaged British Catholics.

Our twentieth century dealt fatal setbacks to what has been called Whig theory of history. That nineteenth-century view that civilization inexorably progresses upward in all respects owed nothing to the Old Whig, Edmund Burke. He died fearing the imminent triumph of the ideologues of the French Revolution. He directed that he be buried secretly, lest his bones be disturbed by triumphant revolutionaries.

Yet Burke achieved more than he knew. As Dr. Russell Kirk, I believe, once pointed out, Burke's headstone, if he had one, would still lie undisturbed in its churchyard, in no small measure because of the counter-revolution in thought he fathered.

Modern technology made possible the consummately destructive, anti-religious regimes of Nazi Germany and the Soviet Union, against which Prof. Plinio Corrêa de Oliveira has fought all his life.

How satisfying it would be to those who gave their lives fighting those twin tyrannies if they had lived to our time. Those of us who have fought and lived to see the humiliation of the communist idea may take a little justifiable pride in what we have helped to achieve.

But while socialism and "liberation theology" may be in retreat, much damage has been done. Somehow we must splice together the roots of our civilization and reclaim much lost ground. That is why Professor Corrêa de Oliveira wrote this book.

No society functions without elites. We must systematically develop new, healthy leadership, encourage those who do their duty well, and replace the corrupt elites now poisoning our culture.

If those in a position to do so accept their responsibility and lead, much can be accomplished.

Acknowledgements

The author thanks all the historical societies, research libraries, museums, organizations, and individuals that made available their facilities and talents for the research, translating, editing, illustrating, and typesetting which helped to bring this work to completion. The very large number of these generous contributors makes it impossible to name each of them on this page.

A personal and special word of gratitude, however, is owed to Earl Appleby, who was indefatigable in his editorial assistance; to Marian Horvat for her help in several stages of the work's preparation; to Stephen Sartarelli, who translated the allocutions of Pius XII and Benedict XV from the Italian, and to his wife, Sophie, for her French translations and overall editorial suggestions; to Susan Schiedel for translations from the Latin; and to Alex Alkalay for Spanish translations. The author is also especially indebted to Prof. Gregory W. Sand of East Central College, Missouri, for his precious comments on the work as a whole in conjunction with his historical review of the appendix on America's traditional elites.

Introduction

Preferential option...

The Good Shepherd

Father of the nobility – Father of the poor

Part I

Pope Pius XII

CHAPTER I

Resolving Prior Objections

$\mathcal{W}$hen a train is ready to leave, normal procedure requires both engineer and passengers to be in their proper places and the conductor to signal for departure. Only then can the train begin to roll.

So also, at the outset of an intellectual work it is customary to set forth preliminary principles and explain, if need be, the logical criteria that justify them. Only then may the author pass on to the doctrinal part.

However, if a number of readers are suspicious of the subject to be dealt with, or even have deep-rooted prejudices against it, the situation is like that of an engineer who notices that although the passengers are already seated, the tracks ahead are blocked.

The trip cannot begin without the removal of the obstructions.

In a similar way, the obstacles the present work will encounter—the prejudices that fill the minds of numerous readers regarding the nobility and analogous traditional elites—are so great that the topic can only be treated after their removal.

This explains the unusual title and content of this first chapter.

1. Without Detriment to a Just and Ample Action on Behalf of the Working Class, an Opportune Action in Favor of the Elites

Much is said today about meeting the social needs of workers. In principle, this solicitude is highly commendable and deserves the support of every upright soul.

However, to favor only the working class while neglecting the problems and needs of other classes, often just as harshly affected by the great contemporary crisis, is tantamount to forgetting that society includes not just manual laborers but various classes, each with its specific functions, rights, and duties. The formation of a global classless society is a utopia that has been the unvarying theme of the successive egalitarian movements arising in Christian Europe since the fifteenth century. In our day, this utopia is heralded mainly by socialists, communists, and anarchists.[1]

---

[1] Cf. Plinio Corrêa de Oliveira, *Revolution and Counter-Revolution* (New Rochelle, N.Y.: The Foundation for

The TFPs throughout Europe, the Americas, Oceania, Asia, and Africa support all just improvements for the working class. But they cannot accept the notion that these improvements imply the eradication of other classes or such reduction of their specific status, duties, rights, and functions as would lead to their virtual extinction in the name of the common good. Trying to solve social questions by leveling all classes for the apparent benefit of one class is to provoke genuine class struggle. To suppress all classes for the exclusive benefit of one, the working class, leaves the others no alternative but legitimate self-defense or death.

The TFPs cannot endorse this process of social leveling. In contradistinction to the proponents of class struggle, and in cooperation with the multiple initiatives underway today in favor of social peace through a just and needed advancement of the workers, all conscientious contemporaries must develop an action in favor of social order, opposing the socialist and communist action, which aims to create social friction and, ultimately, unleash class warfare.

The survival of social order requires that the right of each class to what it needs to live in dignity be recognized and that each class be able to fulfill its obligations to the common good.

In other words, action in favor of the workers must be coupled with a complementary action in favor of the elites.

The Church's interest in social questions does not stem from an exclusive love of the working class. The Church is not a labor party. She loves justice and charity more than she loves any specific class, and she strives to establish these virtues among men. For this reason, she loves all social classes, including the nobility, so besieged by egalitarian demagogues.[2]

These reflections naturally lead the reader to the subject of this book. On the one hand, it is evident that Pius XII recognizes that the nobility has a significant and specific mission in contemporary society, a mission shared in considerable measure by the other social elites, as will be discussed later.

This concept is taught in the Sovereign Pontiff's fourteen masterful allocutions delivered in audiences granted the Roman Patriciate and Nobility[3] on the occasion of their New Years' greetings from 1940 through 1952 and again in 1958.[4]

---

a Christian Civilization, Inc., 1980), pp. 28-29, 61-70.

[2]   See Chapter IV, 8, and Chapter V, 6.

[3]   The Roman Patriciate is divided into:

a) Roman Patricians, descended from those who held civil posts in the government of the pontifical city during the Middle Ages.

b) Conscript Roman Patricians, who belong to any of the sixty patrician families recognized as such by the Sovereign Pontiff in a special pontifical bull, which mentioned them by name. They constitute the cream of the Roman Patriciate.

The Roman Nobility is also divided into two categories:

a) Nobles descending from feudatories who had received a fief from the Sovereign Pontiff.

b) Common nobles, whose nobility issued from the appointment to some court office, or directly from a pontifical concession.

[4]   Two of Pius XII's allocutions to the Roman Patriciate and Nobility (those of 1952 and 1958) summarized the others.

In 1944 Pius XII delivered a second allocution to the Roman Nobility on July 11 to thank their families for offer-

On the other hand, no one can ignore the vast and multifaceted offensive underway in today's world to abase and eradicate the nobility and other elites. One need only consider the overpowering, relentless, and pervasive pressures to ignore, contest, or diminish their roles.

In this light, action on behalf of the nobility and the elites is more opportune than ever. Thus we affirm, with serene courage, that in our day and age, when the *preferential option for the poor* has become so necessary, a *preferential option for the nobility* has become indispensable as well. Of course, we include in this expression other traditional elites, which are worthy of support and in danger of disappearing.

This affirmation may seem absurd since in theory the worker's condition is closer to poverty than is the noble's, and since, as is commonly known, many nobles possess large fortunes.

Large fortunes, yes. But these are generally eroded by crushing taxes, giving rise to the distressing spectacle of lords compelled to transform substantial parts of their manors and mansions into museums or inns (while they occupy only a fraction of the family home), where the lord serves as curator and guide, if not bartender, while his spouse feverishly applies herself to often menial chores to keep their ancestral home clean and presentable.

This persecution advances by other means as well, such as the extinction of the rights of primogeniture and the compulsory division of inheritances. Is not a preferential option for the nobility required to counteract this offensive?

If the nobility is regarded as an inherently parasitic class of profligates, the answer is no. However, Pius XII rejected this caricature of the nobility, which is part of the black legend spread by the French Revolution and the revolutions that followed it in Europe and the world. While clearly stating that abuses and excesses deserving history's censure have occurred in noble circles, he nevertheless affirms, in moving terms, the existence of a harmony between the nobility's mission and the natural order instituted by God Himself, as well as the elevated and beneficial character of this mission.[5]

2. Nobility: A Species Within the Genus "Traditional Elites"

The expression "traditional elites" appears frequently throughout this work. We use this term to designate a socioeconomic reality that may be described as follows:

According to the pontifical texts discussed hereafter, the nobility is an elite from every point of view. It is the highest elite, not the sole elite. It is a species within the genus "elites."

---

ing a generous sum of money to help the needy.

Pius XII did not deliver any allocutions to the Roman Patriciate and Nobility between 1953 and 1957. He reestablished the custom with his allocution of January 1958, but died on October 9 of that year.

[5] See RPN 1943, Documents I.

Some elites derive their status from sharing in the specific functions and features of the nobility. Others, although engaged in other functions, also enjoy a special dignity. There are elites, then, that are neither noble nor hereditary *ex natura propria*.

For example, a university professorship in itself introduces its holder into what can be called the nation's elite. The same holds true for a military commission, a diplomatic office, and comparable positions.

While the exercise of these activities is not a privilege of the nobility today, the number of nobles engaged in them is not small. Obviously these nobles do not relinquish their status by doing so. On the contrary, they bring to these activities the excellence of the attributes specific to the nobility.[6]

When enumerating elites one should not overlook those that give impulse to the nation's economy through industry and commerce. These activities are not only legitimate and dignified, but manifestly useful. Their immediate and specific goal, however, is the enrichment of those who practice them. In other words, it is by enriching themselves that these individuals, in a collateral way, enrich the nation. In itself, this is not sufficient to confer nobiliary character. Only a special dedication to the common good—particularly to its most precious element, the Christian character of civilization—can confer nobiliary splendor on an elite.

Nevertheless, this splendor will shine in industrialists or merchants who, in the pursuit of their activities, render noteworthy services to the common good with significant sacrifice of their legitimate personal interests.

Moreover, should the interplay of circumstances enable a non-noble family to render such services for several generations, this alone may well be considered sufficient to elevate that lineage to noble status.

Something of this sort occurred with the Venetian nobility, which was largely made up of merchants. This class governed the Most Serene Republic and, consequently, held in its hands the common good of the State, which it raised to the rank of an international power. It is not surprising, therefore, that these merchants attained the status of nobles. They did this so effectively and authentically that they assimilated the elevated cultural tone and manners of the best military and feudal nobility.

There are, on the other hand, traditional elites based from their onset upon aptitudes and virtues transmitted through genetic continuity, or through the family environment and education.[7]

A traditional elite arises when this transmission bears fruit and, consequently, families—and not rarely large groups of families—distinguish themselves from generation to generation through signal services to the common good. The precious attribute of traditionality is in this way added to the status of this elite. Frequently these elites do not formally constitute a noble class merely because the law in many countries, in accordance with the doctrines of the French Revo-

---

[6]   See Chapter IV, 3 and 7, and Chapter VI, 2 b.

[7]   See Chapter V, 2.

Saint Peter's Square and Basilica on May 10, 1939. The crowd awaits the coronation of Pius XII.

The faithful filling the expanses of Saint Peter's Square and the colonnade of Bernini enthusiastically acclaim Pius XII.

lution, forbids the granting of noble titles by public authority. This is the case not only in certain European countries, but also in the Americas.

Nonetheless, pontifical teachings on the nobility are largely applicable to these traditional elites by virtue of their analogous roles. For this reason these teachings are both important and timely for those who bear authentic and lofty family traditions, even when not adorned by a title. They have a noble mission in favor of the common good and Christian civilization in their respective countries.

The same can be said, *mutatis mutandis*, of the nontraditional elites as they become traditional.

3. Objections to the Nobility Imbued with the Egalitarian Spirit of the French Revolution

Nobility, elites. Why does this book deal only with them? Such will be, no doubt, the objection raised by egalitarian readers, who are ipso facto hostile to the nobility.

Contemporary society is saturated with radically egalitarian prejudices. Sometimes these are consciously or unconsciously harbored even by people belonging to sectors of opinion where one would expect to find unanimity in the opposite vein. Such is the case with members of the clergy who are enthusiasts of the revolutionary trilogy, Liberty, Equality, Fraternity, heedless of the fact that it was originally interpreted in a sense frontally opposed to Catholic doctrine.[8]

If such egalitarian dissonance is found in clerical circles, one should not be surprised that it also occurs among nobles and members of other traditional elites. With the recent bicentennial of the French Revolution fresh in our memories, these reflections readily recall the revolutionary noble par excellence, Philippe Egalité, Duke of Orleans. To this day, his example has not ceased to inspire emulators in more than one illustrious lineage.

In 1891, when Leo XIII published his famous encyclical *Rerum novarum* on the condition of the working class, certain capitalist circles objected that relations between capital and labor, being a specifically economic matter, were no concern of the Roman Pontiff. They suggested that his encyclical encroached on their domain.

Today, some readers might wonder why a pope should concern himself with the nobility and elites, traditional or otherwise. Their mere survival in our changed times might seem to these readers an archaic and useless outgrowth of the feudal era. From this perspective, the nobility and contemporary elites are nothing more than the embodiment of certain ways of thinking, feeling, and acting that man can no longer appreciate or even comprehend.

These readers deem that the few who still value elites are inspired by empty aesthetic or romantic sentiments, and that the people who pride themselves on

---

[8]   See Chapter III, 3 and 4. See also Appendix III for important excerpts from pontifical documents that clarify the issue.

being part of the elites have succumbed to arrogance and vanity. These readers, convinced that nothing will prevent the inevitable march of history from eradicating such obsolete malignancies from the face of the earth, conclude that if Pius XII would not foster the march of history thus understood, at least he ought not put obstacles in its way.

Why, then, did Pius XII address this subject so extensively and in a way so agreeable to counterrevolutionary minds, such as that of this author, who has assembled these teachings, annotated them, and now offers them to the public? Would it not have been better for the Pontiff to have remained silent?

The answer to such egalitarian objections imbued with the spirit of 1789 is simple. People who wish to know the answer can do no better than to hear it from the authoritative lips of Pius XII himself. In his allocutions to the Roman Patriciate and Nobility, Pius XII points out, with an extraordinary gift for synthesis, the profound moral significance of his intervention in the matter, as we shall see.[9] He also highlights the legitimate role of the nobility according to social doctrine inspired by Natural Law and Revelation. At the same time, he describes the richness of soul that became their hallmark in the Christian past. Confirming its continued guardianship of that treasure, the Pontiff proclaims its lofty mission of affirming and radiating this rich legacy throughout the contemporary world. This remains the case despite the devastating effects of the ideological revolutions, world wars, and socioeconomic crises that have reduced many nobles to modest circumstances. Repeatedly the Pontiff reminds them that, much to their honor, their situation is similar to that of Saint Joseph, at once a Prince of the House of David, a simple carpenter, and, above all, the legal father of the Word Incarnate and chaste spouse of the Queen of all Angels and Saints.[10]

4. The Teachings of Pius XII: A Precious Shield Against the Opponents of Nobility

Some readers among the nobility may wonder what the reading of this study can possibly avail them. They might ask themselves, "Have we not already received most of these teachings in the venerable environment of our fathers' homes, rich in elevated traditions of a formative and moral nature? Have we not practiced them throughout our lives, with our gaze set on our forefathers' example?"

We could easily answer this objection by saying that the religious root of these duties and their basis in pontifical documents might not have been clear enough to them. They, in turn, might reply, "How can the knowledge of these teachings be a source of spiritual enrichment for us, since the legacy of our ancestors has proven sufficient to guide our lives in a genuinely aristocratic and Christian way?"

An aristocrat who, alleging these reasons, shuns as useless the study of the

---

[9]   Chapter I, 6.

[10]   See Chapter IV, 8, and Chapter V, 6.

perennial teachings of Pius XII on the Roman Nobility—which are relevant to the entire European nobility—would show signs of superficiality, both of spirit and of religious formation.

If the moral integrity of a Catholic is not based on a lucid and loving knowledge of the Church's teachings, and a deeply rooted adherence to them, it lacks a solid foundation. Thus it risks sudden ruin, especially in today's post-Christian society, so troubled and saturated with incitements to sin and social revolution. To resist the seduction and pressures of this society, the gentle and profound influence of family formation is not sufficient without the support of the teachings of the Faith, observance of the Commandments, steadfast piety, and frequent recourse to the Sacraments.

From this perspective, it is a great encouragement for the truly Catholic aristocrat to know that his traditional way of thinking, feeling, and acting is solidly founded on the teachings of the Vicar of Christ. This encouragement is all the more timely in this age of neopagan "democratism," which victimizes the aristocrat with misunderstanding, criticism, and even sarcasm. This persecution is so persistent that it may expose him to the temptation of feeling ashamed of his noble status. Consequently, the aristocrat can easily harbor the desire of withdrawing from his uncomfortable situation by implicitly or explicitly renouncing his noble state.

The teachings of Pius XII transcribed and analyzed in these pages will serve him as a sturdy shield against his relentless adversaries. They will be forced to admit that a noble who is true to himself, to his Faith, and to his traditions is not an eccentric who simply concocted the convictions and lifestyle that distinguish him. Rather, these will be understood to spring from an immensely more elevated and universal source, the traditional teachings of the Catholic Church.

Although opponents of the nobility may hate such teachings, they cannot reduce them to the category of mere personal speculations of a crank or quixotic paladin of things gone forever.

While this may not convince someone who objects to these ideas, it will curb the boldness and impact of his attack and prove a great polemical advantage to the defenders of the nobility and traditional elites. This is true, above all, when the maligner of the noble class is a Catholic layman or—*pro dolor!*—a priest.

Such opposition is not unlikely, given the tragic crisis affecting the Church.[11]

---

[11] The bibliography on this theme is vast. See especially: Joseph Cardinal Ratzinger, with Vittorio Messori, *The Ratzinger Report* (San Francisco: Ignatius Press, 1985), and Romano Amerio, *Iota unum—Studio delle variazioni della Chiesa Cattolica nel secolo XX* (Milan-Naples: Riccardo Ricciardi Editore, 1985).

See also: Dietrich von Hildebrand, *The Trojan Horse in the City of God* and *The Devastated Vineyard* (Chicago: Franciscan Herald Press, 1967 and 1973, respectively); Rudolf Graber (Bishop of Regensburg), *Athanasius and the Church of Our Time* (Buckinghamshire: Van Duren C.P. Ltd., 1974); Cornelio Fabro, *L'avventura della teologia progressista* and *La svolta antropologica di Karl Rahner* (Milan: Rusconi Editore, both 1974); Anton Holzer, *Vatikanum II: Reformkonzil oder Konstituante einer neuen Kirche* (Basel: Saka, 1977); Wigand Siebel, *Katholisch oder konziliar: Die Krise der Kirche heute* (Munich-Vienna: Langen Müller, 1978); Joseph Cardinal Siri, *Gethsemane: Reflections on the Current Theological Movement* (Chicago: Franciscan Herald Press, 1981); Enrique Rueda, *The Homosexual Network* (Old Greenwich, Conn.: The Devin Adair Company, 1982); Georg May, *Der Glaube in der nachkonziliaren Kirche* (Vienna: Mediatrix Verlag, 1983); Richard Cowden-Guido, *John Paul*

Pius XII's successors also left expressive documents on the nobility's important and undeniable mission today. Paul VI's allocution to the Roman Patriciate and Nobility on January 14, 1964, is noteworthy.

Paul VI receives the Noble Guard on January 7, 1964. From left to right, Prince Alessandro Odescalchi (with the colors of the Corps), Marquis Alessandro Cavalletti, Count Carlo Nasalli Rocca di Corneliano, Marquis Luigi Serlupi d'Ongran, Prince Mario del Drago, Captain General and Commandant of the Guard, Msgr. Nasalli Rocca di Corneliano, Master of the Chamber of His Holiness.

Paul VI referred to this crisis as a "self-demolition," and he expressed his feeling that "Satan's smoke has made its way into the temple of God."[12]

Nor is it unlikely that opponents of the nobility and other traditional or even nontraditional elites may misuse Sacred Scripture to support their argument. In such cases, it is important for nobles and members of other elites to rely on the teachings of Pius XII, his predecessors and successors, thus placing their opponents in the harsh predicament of either recanting their error or admitting that they are in open contradiction with the pontifical teachings cited in this work.

5. Intuitive and Implicit Notions Do Not Suffice—The Wealth of Concepts in Pius XII's Treatment of the Matter

We have enumerated several objections raised today against the nobility as well as arguments the nobles must have honed and ready at hand for their defense.

Proponents and opponents of nobility have some notion, however intuitive and vague, of what the nobility claims to be in view of its essence, *raison d'être*, and fidelity to Christian civilization. But merely intuitive notions, more often implicit than explicit, are insufficient in a serious and conclusive debate. Whence arises the sterility that so often characterizes polemics on the subject.

It should be added in passing that the literature against the nobility is far more abundant and accessible than that in its favor. This explains, at least in part, why the defenders of the nobility are frequently less informed on the subject and, consequently, more insecure and timid than their opponents.

In his allocutions to the Roman Patriciate and Nobility, the memorable Pontiff Pius XII establishes the foundations of a contemporary apologia for the nobility and traditional elites. He does this with an elevation of mind, a wealth of ideas, and a conciseness of style that makes the reading of the present work all the more useful and opportune.

6. Are These Allocutions Merely Social Amenities Devoid of Content, Thought, and Affection?

Some will probably claim, with manifest flippancy, that they are exempted from reading and reflecting on these allocutions of Pius XII, alleging that they were merely

---

II and the Battle for Vatican II (Manassas, Va.: Trinity Communications, 1986).

[12] "The Church today is going through a moment of apprehension. Certain people are engaging in self-criticism, one might even say self-demolition. It is an acute and complex upheaval from within, which no one would have expected after the Council.... The Church is smitten even by those who belong to it" (Speech to the Pontifical Lombard Seminary, December 7, 1968, *Insegnamenti di Paolo VI* [Tipografia Poliglotta Vaticana, 1968], Vol. 6, p. 1188. Cf. *L'Osservatore Romano* [English weekly ed.], December 19, 1968, p. 3). "Referring to the situation of the Church of today, the Holy Father then affirmed that he had the feeling that 'Satan's smoke has made its way into the temple of God through some crack'" (Homily *"Resistite fortes in Fide"* of June 29, 1972, *L'Osservatore Romano* [English weekly ed.], July 13, 1972, p. 6).

given to comply with social courtesy, and therefore lack doctrinal and affective content. Paul VI was of a different opinion, as the following remarks reveal.

> We would like to say many things to you. Your presence provokes much reflection. So it was also with Our venerable Predecessors, especially Pope Pius XII of happy memory. They, on occasions such as this, addressed you with masterful speeches, inviting you in your meditation to consider your own situations and those of our times in the light of their admirable teachings. We want to believe that the echo of those words, like a gust of wind swelling a sail,...still vibrates in your thoughts, filling them with the austere and magnanimous appeals that nourish the vocation preordained for you by Providence and sustain the role still required of you today by contemporary society.[13]

As for their doctrinal content, a reading of the texts and the accompanying commentaries will suffice to demonstrate their relevance and richness. Throughout these pages the reader will see that far from decreasing with time, this relevance has only increased.

A word remains to be said about their affective content. In this regard, it will suffice to quote Pius XII's allocution to the Roman Patriciate and Nobility in 1958.

> You, who at the start of each new year have never failed to come visit Us, must surely remember the careful solicitude with which We endeavored to smooth your way toward the future, which at that time promised to be harsh because of the profound upheavals and transformations in store for the world. We are certain, however, that when your brows too are framed with white and silver, you will yet be witnesses not only to Our esteem and affection, but also to the truth, the validity, and the timeliness of Our recommendations, which We hope are like fruits that have come to you and to society in general.
>
> You will recall to your children and grandchildren how the Pope of your childhood and adolescence did not neglect to point you toward the new responsibilities that the new circumstances of the age imposed on the nobility.[14]

Beyond any doubt, these words show that the allocutions of Pius XII to the Roman Patriciate and Nobility correspond to lofty designs that were clearly defined in the Pontiff's mind and heart. They also show that he expected them to bear lasting and important fruits. This is a far cry from what one would expect from allocutions meant to comply with mere social etiquette and therefore devoid of content, thought, and affection.

The esteem of Pius XII for hereditary nobility shines with particular brilliance in the following words addressed to the Pontifical Noble Guard on December 26, 1942:

---

[13]   RPN 1964, p. 73.

[14]   RPN 1958, p. 708.

None can be envious upon seeing that We bear you such special affection. To whom, in truth, is the immediate protection of Our person entrusted, if not to you? And are you not the first of Our guards?

Guard! What lofty resonance there is in this word: the soul trembles therewith; thoughts take wing. An ardent love for the sovereign and a steadfast reverence to his person and cause vibrate and voice themselves in this name; it sets in motion a tested generosity, an unvanquished constancy and courage in face of the risks met in his service and for his defense; it speaks of virtues which, molding the champion on the one hand, on the other hand evoke from the sovereign sentiments of esteem, affection, and confidence in his guard.

You, the guard of Our person, constitute Our armor, refulgent with that nobility which is the privilege of blood and which shone in you as the pledge of your devotion even before your admission into the Corps, for, as the ancient proverb says, "Good blood cannot lie." Life is the blood that is transmitted from rank to rank, from generation to generation in your illustrious lineages, carrying with it the fire of that devout love for the Church and the Roman Pontiff that neither diminishes nor cools with the changing events, be they joyous or sad. In the darkest hours of the history of the Popes, the loyalty of your ancestors shone brighter and burned more ardently and generously than in the resplendent hours of magnificence and material prosperity....We have no doubt that just as in the past so chosen a tradition of familiar virtues was transmitted from father to son, so will it continue to be transmitted from generation to generation as a patrimony of greatness of soul and most noble merit of one's respective stirp.[15]

7. Documents of Perennial Value

Lastly, some might object that after the death of Pius XII a new era began for the Church, that of the Second Vatican Council. Therefore, the allocutions of the deceased Pontiff to the Roman Patriciate and Nobility fell like dead leaves on the floor of the Church, and Conciliar and post-Conciliar Popes have not returned to the subject.

This is not true, either. As proof, this work cites, *argumentandi gratia*, eloquent documents from the successors of the mourned Pontiff.[16]

We will now proceed to study the allocutions of Pius XII, highlighting their magnificent doctrinal wealth.

---

[15]   PNG 1942, pp. 349-350.

[16]   See Chapter I, 6, and Chapter IV, 11.

*"You, the guard of Our person,
constitute Our armor, refulgent
with that nobility which is the
privilege of blood and which shone
in you as the pledge of your
devotion even before your
admission into the Corps."*

(Words of Pius XII to his Noble Guard)

Above: Christmas 1945. The Pontifical Noble Guard pays homage to the Pope. From left to right: unidentified, Marquis Francesco Theodoli, Prince Giulio Pacelli (the Pope's nephew), noblemen Agostino Sacconi and Angelo Antonucci Lucidi, Count Federico Moroni, and nobleman Fabio Petrucci. Behind the Pope is Prince Francesco Chigi della Rovere, Commandant of the Corps.

Right: Giulio Patrizi di Ripacandida, Duke of Castelgaragnone.

Vatican Museum (Giordani)

**Pontifical Gendarmes in gala uniform.
Saint Damasus patio in the Apostolic Palace.**

CHAPTER II

The Universal Scope of the Allocutions to the Roman Patriciate and Nobility

The Situation of the Italian Nobility in the Pontificate of Pius XII

1. Why Focus Specifically on the Italian Nobility?

In 1947 the constitution of the Italian Republic abolished all titles of nobility.[1] The last blow was thus struck against the juridical status of an age-old class—which lives on today as a social reality—and a problem, complex in all its aspects, was created.

Complexity was already perceptible in the antecedents to the issue. Contrary to what occurs in other European countries—France and Portugal, for example—the makeup of the Italian nobility is highly heterogeneous. Before the political unification of the Italian peninsula in the nineteenth century, the various sovereigns who ruled over different parts of the Italian territory all bestowed titles of nobility. This holds true for the emperors of the Holy Roman Empire; the kings of Spain,

---

[1]   This chapter, dealing particularly with the Italian nobility, is necessary to understand the allocutions of Pius XII commented herein. Still, these allocutions will also interest the aristocracies worldwide, as we have emphasized and shall reaffirm (Chapter I, 2, and Chapter II, 3).

Throughout this work, the author has in mind, in a general way, the nobility and analogous traditional elites of Europe and the Americas. Naturally, he illustrates or documents his assertions with historical examples. Regarding the European nobility, these examples refer more often than not to the nobilities of France, Spain, and Portugal, or—inevitably—to the Roman Nobility. To give examples of every European nobility would greatly overburden the present work. This would be the case even if the author were to limit himself to adding but four nobilities—those of Italy, Austria, Germany, and England—that played roles of primordial importance in European history and culture. Indeed, the admirable plurality of aspects of the European nobilities would demand a special edition of this book for each, containing illustrative examples of their respective origins, development, and decadence. The author may yet undertake this work, if his duties as president of the National Council of the Brazilian Society for the Defense of Tradition, Family and Property (TFP) allow the necessary respite.

of the Two Sicilies, and of Sardinia; the grand-dukes of Tuscany; the dukes of Parma; and still others, including the patriciates of cities such as Florence, Genoa, and Venice. It is principally true—and this is of the utmost interest for the present study—of the Popes. The Popes were temporal sovereigns of the relatively extensive Papal States. They also granted titles of nobility and continued to do so even after the de facto extinction of their temporal sovereignty over these states.

In 1870, when the unification of Italy was consummated with the occupation of Rome by Piedmontese troops, the House of Savoy attempted to amalgamate these various nobilities.

The project failed both politically and juridically. Many noble families remained faithful to the dethroned dynasties from which they had received their titles. Particularly, a considerable part of the Roman aristocracy, maintaining tradition, continued to figure officially in Vatican solemnities. They refused to recognize Rome's annexation to Italy, rejected any rapprochement with the Quirinal, and closed their salons as a sign of protest. To this mourning nobility was given the name "Black Nobility."

Nevertheless, the amalgamation advanced in no small scale in the social sphere through marriages, social relations, and the like. As a result, the Italian aristocracy in our day constitutes a whole, at least from many points of view.

Article 42 of the 1929 Lateran Treaty, however, assured the Roman nobility a special status, since it recognized the Pope's right to grant new titles and accepted those granted previously by the Holy See.[2] Thus the Italian and Roman nobilities, by then already at peace, continued to exist legally side by side.

The Concordat of 1985 between the Holy See and the Italian Republic makes no mention of this matter.

* * *

The situation of the Italian nobility—and of the European nobility in general—did not cease to be complex.

In the Middle Ages the nobility had constituted a social class with specific functions within the State, which entailed certain honors and corresponding obligations.

During modern times this situation had gradually lost its stability, prominence, and brilliance, so that even before the Revolution of 1789 the distinction between the nobility and the people was considerably less marked than in the Middle Ages.

---

[2]   The Treaty of February 11, 1929, specified:

Art. 42 - "Italy will admit, by Royal Decree, the recognition of nobiliary titles conferred by the Supreme Pontiffs, including those granted after 1870, and those to be conferred in the future."

"The cases in which the said recognition will not be subject to the payment of a fee in Italy will be yet defined" (*Raccolta di concordati su materie Ecclesiastiche tra la Santa Sede e le autorità civili* [Tipografia Poliglotta Vaticana, 1954], Vol. 2, p. 102).

The "fee" referred to in this paragraph of the treaty was a symbolic sum that the Italian state required from the nobles of pre-unification states in order for them to obtain recognition of their titles and of their filiation with the nobility. The exemption from such a fee, in certain cases, was the only and very reduced tributary privilege granted the pontifical nobles by the treaty.

Throughout the egalitarian revolutions of the nineteenth century, the position of the nobility suffered successive mutilations of such extent that its political power in the Italian monarchy at the end of World War II survived solely as a prestigious tradition, which was seen, incidentally, with respect and affection by most of society. The republican constitution attempted to deal the final blow to the last vestiges of this tradition.[3]

As the aristocracy's political power declined, its social and economic standing followed the same trend, albeit more slowly. At the turn of the century, the nobles were still at the apex of the social structure, due to their rural and urban properties; their castles, palaces, and artistic treasures; the social renown of their names and titles; and to the excellent moral and cultural values of their traditional household environments, manners, lifestyle, and so on.

The crises resulting from World War I brought some changes to this picture. They deprived part of the noble families of their means of livelihood and forced many of their members to secure subsistence through the exercise of professions at variance, even when honest and worthy, with the psychology, customs, and social prestige of their class.

On the other hand, contemporary society, increasingly shaped by finance and technology, produced new relations and situations as well as new centers of social influence that were usually alien to the aristocracy's traditional surroundings. Thus, a whole new order of things arose alongside the surviving old one, further diminishing the nobility's social importance.

_____

[3] To facilitate the study of the pontifical allocutions herein commented, addressed to the Roman Patriciate and Nobility and, in some way, to the Italian nobility at large, it is useful to say something about the nobility's status in the successive constitutions of unified Italy, both monarchical and republican.

The Albertine Statute, in force until 1947, was the constitution of the kingdom of Sardinia promulgated on March 4, 1848, by King Charles Albert. This statute was successively enforced in all the states annexed by that kingdom and was later adopted as the constitution of unified Italy. Regarding titles of nobility, it established:

Art. 79 - "The titles of nobility of those who have a right to them are hereby upheld. The King may confer new titles."

Art. 80 - "No one may receive decorations, titles, or pensions from a foreign power without the authorization of the King" (*Statuto del Regno,* annotated by Carlo Gallini [Turin: Unione Tipografico Editrice, 1878], p. 102).

The Italian Constitution of 1947, in turn, establishes in its Transitional and Final Provisions:

Art. 14 - "Titles of nobility are not recognized."

"The predicates of those noble titles existent prior to October 28, 1922, are valid as part of the name."

"The Order of Saints Mauritius and Lazarus is preserved as a hospitalary entity and will function in the manner prescribed by law."

"The law orders the suppression of the College of Heraldry" (*Costituzione della Repubblica Italiana, Gazzetta Ufficiale,* no. 298, December 27, 1947, pp. 45-46).

The "predicate" of the title is made up by the name of the old territory appended to the family name (as, for example, Prince Colonna di Paliano). The constitution of 1947 authorizes this compound name to appear in documents as long as it predates fascism.

As far as the author knows, the College of Heraldry of the monarchical era was a specific tribunal for cases of disputed titles, coats of arms, and the like. It has been replaced today by the Italian Nobility Corps, which, without legal force but with great moral and historical authority, has an advisory panel for the admission of members to entities such as the Knights of Malta, the *Circolo della Caccia* (the Hunting Society), the *Circolo degli Scacchi* (the Chess Society), and so on.

No form of political or tax privilege for nobles is recognized, either by the old or the new Italian constitutions since the Albertine Statute recognized the nobility only as a mere reminiscence of the past.

*"From 1485 to today, the designation
of the Corps I was honored to command
changed repeatedly in keeping with
the requisites of the age and
customs of the times: Light Horse Guard,
Knights of Our Lord's Guard, Knights of
the Faith, 'Lance Spezzate' [Broken
Lances Guard], Noble Guard
of the Body of His Holiness,
and Honor Guard of His Holiness.
What never changed was the unbroken
tradition of fidelity to the Pope
which, over centuries, was sealed in blood
and with prison."*

(Words pronounced by the Commandant of
the Noble Guard, Prince Mario del Drago,
at right, in the act of surrendering the
colors of the Corps to the Vatican Secretary
of State on November 14, 1970)

Foto Felici S.d.F. (Rome)

Vatican Museum (Giordani)

The Pontifical Noble Guard was an elite corps comprised exclusively of members of the
Patriciate and Nobility and was assigned to the personal service of the Pope and the
splendor of his temporal principality.

Finally, to all this was added an important ideological factor, also detrimental to the nobility. The worship of technological progress[4] and the equality proclaimed by the Revolution of 1789 tended to create an atmosphere of hatred, prejudice, defamation, and sarcasm against the nobility, which is founded upon tradition and transmitted in a way that egalitarian demagoguery most hates: by blood and cradle.

World War II brought additional and more extensive economic ruin to many noble families, worsening yet further the multiple problems the aristocracy had to face. In this way, the crisis of a great social class became acute and firmly entrenched. It was with this picture before him that Pius XII addressed the current situation of the Italian nobility in his allocutions to the Roman Patriciate and Nobility, which had obvious relevance for all the European nobility.

2. Pius XII and the Roman Nobility

This situation, and particularly the way it affected the Roman Nobility, was known to Pius XII in all its details.

He belonged to a noble family, whose sphere of relations was naturally among the nobility. In 1929, one prominent member of his family was graced with the title of marquis; and the Pope's nephews, Don Carlo Maria, Don Marcantonio, and Don Giulio Pacelli, each received the hereditary title of prince from King Victor Emmanuel III of Italy.[5]

There was something imponderable in that Pope which evoked nobility: his tall, slim bearing, his way of walking, his gestures, even his hands. This Pontiff, so universal in spirit and so friendly to the lowly and poor, was also very Roman and had his attention, consideration, and affection also turned toward the Roman Nobility.

> In the Roman Patriciate and Nobility We see again and love an array of sons and daughters whose pride lies in the hereditary bond and loyalty to the Church and the Roman Pontiff, whose love for the Vicar of Christ arises from the deep root of faith and does not diminish with the passing of the years and the vicissitudes of the ages and of men. In your midst We feel more Roman by custom, by the air We have breathed and still breathe, by the very sky, the very sun, the very banks of the Tiber, on which Our cradle was laid, by that soil that is sacred down to the remotest bowels of the earth, whence Rome draws for her children auspices of an eternity in Heaven.[6]

---

[4]   The expression may appear a bit exaggerated to some readers. They will find it useful to consider the comments of Pius XII regarding this in his 1953 Christmas radio address cited in Chapter V, 3 c.

[5]   Cf. *Libro d'oro della nobiltà Italiana*, 19th ed. (Rome: Collegio Araldico, 1986-1989), Vol. 20.

[6]   RPN 1941, p. 363.

The Noble Guard presents its New Year's greetings to Pope Pius XII. Prince Chigi, Commandant of the Corps, delivers the address.

3. The Universal Scope of the Allocutions of Pius XII to the Roman Patriciate and Nobility

Having thus enunciated the theme, it may seem at first glance that the allocutions to the Roman Patriciate and Nobility are of interest to Italy alone.

In reality, the crisis undermining the Italian nobility also affects, *mutatis mutandis*, all the countries with a monarchical and aristocratic past. It also affects those countries presently living under monarchical regimes whose respective nobilities find themselves in a situation analogous to that in Italy before the fall of the Savoy dynasty in 1946.

Even in countries with no monarchical past, aristocracies were constituted by the natural course of events, in fact if not in law.[7] In these countries, too, the wave of demagogic egalitarianism born of the 1789 Revolution and brought to its height by communism, created in certain environments an atmosphere of resentment and misunderstanding in relation to the traditional elites.

---

[7]   See Chapter V, 1

The allocutions of His Holiness Pope Pius XII thus have a universal scope.

This scope is enhanced by the fact that, in his analysis of the Italian situation, the Pope rises to high doctrinal considerations and, therefore, reaches a perennial and universal dimension. An example of this is his allocution of December 26, 1941, to the Pontifical Noble Guard. From considerations about the nobility, Pius XII ascends to the highest philosophical and religious reflections:

> Yes, faith renders your rank more noble still, for all nobility comes from God, the noblest Being and source of all perfection. Everything in Him is nobility of being. When Moses, sent to deliver the people of Israel from Pharaoh's yoke, asked God atop Mount Horeb what should be the name whereby He would be made manifest to the people, the Lord replied to him: "I am Who am: *Ego sum qui sum.* Thus shalt thou say to the children of Israel: He Who is—*Qui est,* hath sent me to you" (Exod. 3:14). What, therefore, is nobility? "All nobility of any thing," teaches the Angelic Doctor Saint Thomas Aquinas, "appertains to it in accordance with its being; indeed the nobility that man gains from wisdom would be nothing if through such wisdom he were not made wise; and so it is with the other perfections as well. Therefore the measure of a thing's nobility corresponds to the measure in which it possesses being, inasmuch as a thing is said to be more or less noble according to whether its being is restricted to a particularly greater or lesser degree of nobility.... Now God, who is His being, possesses being in accordance with all the virtue of being itself; thus He cannot lack any nobility that belongs to any thing" (*Summa Contra Gentiles,* 1, I, q. 28).
>
> You too have being from God; He it was who made you, and not you yourselves—*"Ipse fecit nos, et non ipsi nos"* (Ps. 99:3). He gave you nobility of blood, nobility of valor, nobility of virtue, nobility of faith and Christian grace. Your nobility of blood you place at the service of the Church and employ in the defense of Saint Peter's Successor; it is a nobility of good works by your forebears, which will ennoble you as well if day by day you take care to add to it the nobility of virtue.... Indeed nobility joined with virtue shines so worthy of praise that the light of virtue often eclipses the glimmer of nobility; and oftentimes in the annals and halls of the great families, the name of virtue alone remains the sole nobility, as even the pagan Juvenal did not hesitate to assert (*Satyr.* VIII, 19-20): *"Tota licet veteres exornent undique cerae atria, nobilitas sola est atque unica virtus"* [Even though old wax figures adorn the palaces of the great families on all sides, their only and exclusive nobility is virtue].[8]

---

[8] PNG 1941, pp. 337-338.

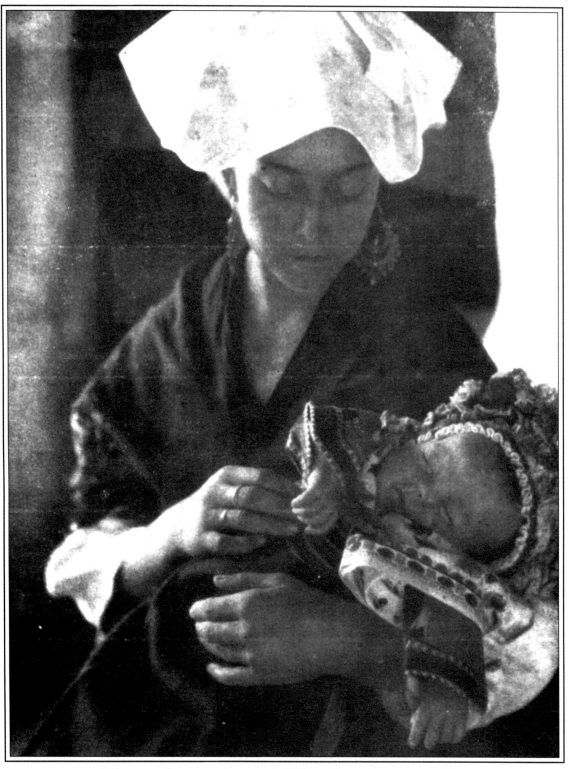

"From the exuberant life of a true people,
an abundant rich life is diffused in the state and all its
organs, instilling into them, with a vigor that is always
renewing itself, the consciousness of their own responsibility,
the true instinct for the common good."
(Pius XII, 1944 Christmas message)

The People and the Masses, Liberty and Equality: Wholesome Versus Revolutionary Concepts in a Democratic Regime

The Teaching of Pius XII

$\mathcal{B}$efore beginning the study of Pius XII's allocutions to the Roman Patriciate and Nobility, it seems useful to forestall any shock that the reading of these commentaries may cause in people influenced by today's radically egalitarian populism. The same shock may also come to others—perhaps even some belonging to the nobility or analogous elites—who fear infuriating the partisans of this populism with the frank and uninhibited assertion of many of the themes articulated in this work. To prevent this, we shall first set forth the true Catholic doctrine on the just and proportioned inequalities in the social and political hierarchies.

1. The Legitimacy and Even Necessity of Just and Proportional Inequalities Among the Social Classes

The Marxist doctrine of class struggle considers all inequalities unjust and harmful. Consequently, it proclaims the legitimacy of the mobilization of the lower classes on a global scale in order to suppress the higher classes. "Workers of the world unite!" is the well-known cry with which Marx and Engels ended the *Communist Manifesto* of 1848.

On the contrary, traditional Catholic doctrine proclaims the legitimacy and even the necessity of just and proportional inequalities among men.[1] Consequently, it

---

[1]   See Documents V.

Miners on strike in Siberia.

"The elementary power of the masses, deftly managed and employed, the state also can utilize; in the ambitious hands of one or several who have been artificially brought together for selfish aims, the state itself, with the support of the masses, reduced to the minimum status of a mere machine, can impose its whims on the better part of the real people.... Liberty, from being a moral duty of the individual, becomes a tyrannous claim to give free rein to a man's impulses and appetites to the detriment of others. Equality degenerates to a mechanical leveling, a colorless uniformity; the sense of true honor, of personal activity, of respect for tradition and dignity—in a word all that gives life its worth—gradually fades away and disappears."
(Pius XII, 1944 Christmas message)

condemns class struggle. This condemnation clearly does not include legitimate attempts—and even struggles—of a class seeking recognition of its rightful position within the social body or the body politic. Catholic doctrine does condemn, however, the degeneration of this legitimate self-defense of a beleaguered class into a war of extermination of other classes or into a denial of their rightful position in society.

A Catholic should desire mutual harmony and peace among the classes and not chronic fighting among them, particularly when such conflict seeks to establish complete and radical equality.

All of this would be better understood had the admirable teachings of Pius XII on "the people" and "the masses" received appropriate dissemination in the West.

"Ah, Liberty, what crimes are committed in thy name!" the notorious French revolutionary Madame Roland allegedly exclaimed shortly before being guillotined by order of the regime of the Terror.[2] Beholding the history of our troubled twentieth century, one could similarly exclaim: "O People, O People, how many insanities, how many injustices, how many crimes are committed in your name by today's revolutionary demagogues!"

The Church certainly loves the people and prides herself on having loved it in a most special manner from the moment of her founding by the Divine Master.

What, however, is the people? It is something quite different from the masses, which are agitated like a churning ocean, an easy prey to revolutionary demagoguery.

Mother that she is, the Church does not refuse her love to these masses as well. Rather, it is precisely because of the love she bears them that she desires, as a precious good, that they be helped to pass from the condition of a mass to that of a people.

Is this assertion a mere play on words? What are the masses? What is the people?

2. The People and the Shapeless Multitude: Two Distinct Concepts

The admirable teachings of Pius XII explain this difference very well, clearly describing the natural concord that can and should exist between the elites and the people, contrary to the assertions of the prophets of class struggle.

Pius XII affirms in his 1944 Christmas radio message:

> The people, and a shapeless multitude (or, as it is called, "the masses") are two distinct concepts.
> 1. The people lives and moves by its own life energy; the masses are inert of themselves and can only be moved from outside.
> 2. The people lives by the fullness of life in the men that compose it, each of

---

2   Cf. Louis Madelin, *Figures of the Revolution* (New York: The Macaulay Co., 1929), p. 168.

whom—at his proper place and in his own way—is a person conscious of his own responsibility and of his own views. The masses, on the contrary, wait for the impulse from outside, an easy plaything in the hands of anyone who exploits their instincts and impressions; ready to follow in turn, today this way, tomorrow another.

3. From the exuberant life of a true people, an abundant rich life is diffused in the state and all its organs, instilling into them, with a vigor that is always renewing itself, the consciousness of their own responsibility, the true instinct for the common good.

The elementary power of the masses, deftly managed and employed, the state also can utilize; in the ambitious hands of one or several who have been artificially brought together for selfish aims, the state itself, with the support of the masses, reduced to the minimum status of a mere machine, can impose its whims on the better part of the real people; the common interest remains seriously, and for a long time, injured by this process, and the injury is very often hard to heal.[3]

3. Natural Inequalities Should Also Exist in a True Democracy

Immediately afterwards, the Pontiff distinguishes between true and false democracy. The former is a corollary of the existence of a true people; the latter, on the contrary, is the consequence of reducing the people to the condition of mere human masses.

4. Hence, follows clearly another conclusion: the masses—as we have just defined them—are the capital enemy of true democracy and of its ideal of liberty and equality.

5. In a people worthy of the name, the citizen feels within him the consciousness of his personality, of his duties and rights, of his own freedom joined to respect for the freedom and dignity of others. In a people worthy of the name all inequalities based not on whim but on the nature of things, inequalities of culture, possessions, social standing—without, of course, prejudice to justice and mutual charity—do not constitute any obstacle to the existence and the prevalence of a true spirit of union and fraternity.

On the contrary, far from impairing civil equality in any way, they give it its true meaning; namely, that before the state everyone has the right to live honorably his own personal life in the place and under the conditions in which the designs and dispositions of Providence have placed him.[4]

This definition of the genuine and legitimate "civil equality," and the correlated concepts of "fraternity" and "union," clarifies, with richness of thought and propriety of expression, the true equality, fraternity, and union according to Catholic

---

[3]   Cf. Vincent A. Yzermans, ed., *The Major Addresses of Pope Pius XII* (St. Paul: North Central Publishing Co., 1961), Vol. 2, p. 81. The numbering and corresponding arrangement in separate paragraphs, here and in subsequent excerpts, were added by this author to facilitate the reader's analysis.

[4]   Ibid., pp. 81-82.

doctrine. This equality and fraternity are radically opposed to those implemented, to a greater or lesser extent, in the sixteenth century by Protestant sects in their respective ecclesiastical structures. They are likewise contrary to the sadly famous trilogy that the French Revolution and its partisans throughout the world hoisted as their motto in the civil and social orders, and which was eventually extended to the socioeconomic order by the Russian Revolution of 1917.[5]

This observation is particularly important since these words are usually understood in the erroneous revolutionary sense when used in everyday conversation or in the media.

4. With the Corruption of Democracy, Liberty Becomes Tyranny and Equality Degenerates into Mechanical Leveling

Having defined true democracy, Pius XII then describes false democracy.

> 6. Against this picture of the democratic ideal of liberty and equality in a people's government by honest and far-seeing men, what a spectacle is that of a democratic state left to the whims of the masses!
>
> Liberty, from being a moral duty of the individual, becomes a tyrannous claim to give free rein to a man's impulses and appetites to the detriment of others. Equality degenerates to a mechanical leveling, a colorless uniformity; the sense of true honor, of personal activity, of respect for tradition and dignity—in a word all that gives life its worth—gradually fades away and disappears. And the only survivors are, on one hand, the victims deluded by the specious mirage of democracy, naively taken for the genuine spirit of democracy, with its liberty and equality; and on the other, the more or less numerous exploiters, who have known how to use the power of money and of organization in order to secure a privileged position above the others, and have gained power.[6]

Many of the teachings in Pius XII's allocutions to the Roman Patriciate and Nobility, and in those to the Pontifical Noble Guard, are founded on these principles of the 1944 Christmas radio message.

From the perspective the Pontiff described so objectively, it is evident that even in our time, in any well-ordered state—be it monarchical, aristocratic, or even democratic—the nobility and the traditional elites are entrusted with an elevated and indispensable mission. We shall now analyze this mission.

---

[5]   Cf. Plinio Corrêa de Oliveira, *Revolution and Counter-Revolution*, pp. 31-32. See also Appendix III of this work.

[6]   Yzermans, *Major Addresses of Pope Pius XII*, pp. 81-82.

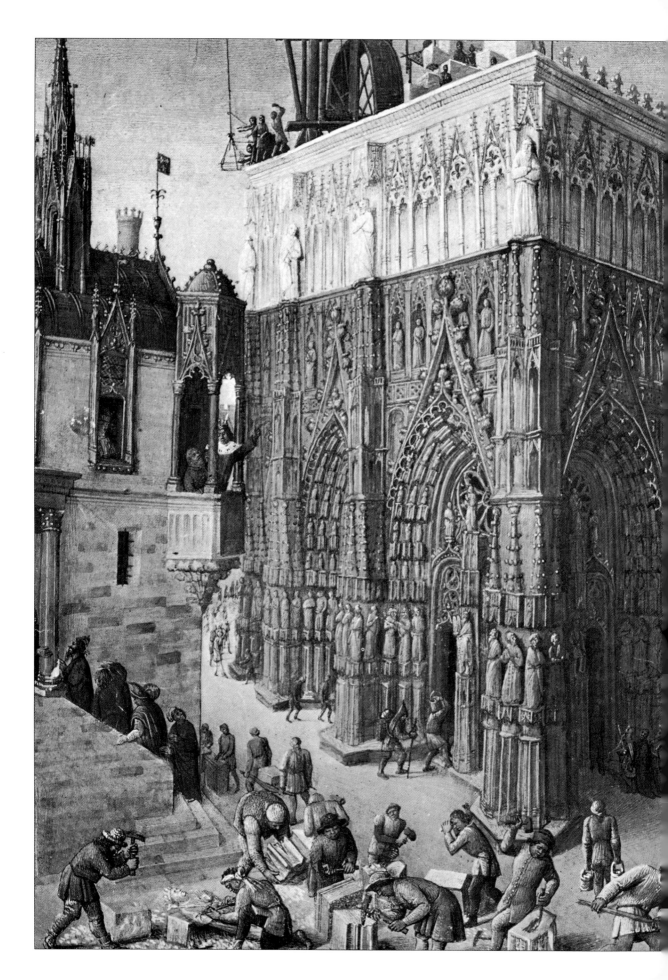

CHAPTER IV

Nobility in a Christian Society
The Perennial Character of Its Mission and Its Prestige in the Contemporary World

The Teaching of Pius XII

1. Clergy, Nobility, and People

In the Middle Ages, society consisted of three classes, the clergy, the nobility, and the people, each of which had special duties, privileges, and honors.

Besides this tripartite division, a clear distinction existed between rulers and those ruled, a distinction inherent to every social group and principally to a country. Not only the king, however, but also the clergy, the nobility, and the people participated in the country's government, each one in its own way and measure.

As is well known, both Church and State constitute perfect societies, each distinct from the other and sovereign in its respective field, that is, the Church in the spiritual realm and the State in the temporal. Nonetheless, this distinction does not prevent the clergy from participating in the government of the State. In order to clarify this point, it is fitting to recall in a few words the specifically spiritual and religious mission of the clergy.

From the spiritual point of view, the clergy is the ensemble of people in the Church who have the mission to teach, govern, and sanctify, while it is for the faithful to be taught, governed, and sanctified. Such is the hierarchical order of the Church. The documents of the Magisterium establishing this distinction between the teaching Church and the learning Church are numerous. For example, Saint Pius X affirms in his encyclical *Vehementer nos*:

> Scripture teaches us, and the tradition of the Fathers confirms the teaching, that the Church is the Mystical Body of Christ, ruled by the *Pastors* and *Doctors*—a society of men containing within its own fold chiefs who have full and perfect powers for ruling, teaching and judging. It follows that the Church is essentially an

unequal society, that is, a society comprising two categories of persons, the pastors and the flock, those who occupy a rank in the different degrees of the hierarchy and the multitude of the faithful. So distinct are these categories that with the pastoral body only rests the right and authority for promoting the end of the society and directing all its members toward that end; the one duty of the multitude is to allow themselves to be led, and, like a docile flock, to follow the pastors.[1]

This distinction between hierarchy and faithful in the Church, between rulers and those ruled, is also affirmed in more than one document of the Second Vatican Council.

> Therefore, by divine condescension the laity have Christ for their brother.... They also have for their brothers those in the sacred ministry who, by teaching, by sanctifying, and by ruling with the authority of Christ so feed the family of God (*Lumen Gentium,* 32).
>
> With ready Christian obedience, laymen as well as all disciples of Christ should accept whatever their sacred pastors, as representatives of Christ, decree in their role as teachers and rulers in the Church (*Lumen Gentium,* 37).
>
> The individual bishops, to each of whom the care of a particular church has been entrusted, are, under the authority of the Supreme Pontiff, the proper, ordinary and immediate pastors of these churches. They feed their sheep in the name of the Lord, and exercise in their regard the office of teaching, sanctifying, and governing (*Christus Dominus,* 11).[2]

Through the exercise of the sacred ministry, the clergy bears the lofty and specifically religious mission of providing for the salvation and sanctification of souls. This mission produces a supremely beneficial effect on temporal society, as it always has and always will until the end of time, since sanctifying souls amounts to imbuing them with the principles of Christian morals and guiding them in the observance of the Law of God. Peoples receptive to this influence of the Church are ipso facto ideally disposed to direct all their temporal activities to the attainment of a high degree of competence, efficacy, and prosperity.

Saint Augustine's famous image of a society whose members are all good Catholics speaks for itself.

> Therefore, let those who say that the teaching of Christ is contrary to the State provide such an army as the teaching of Christ orders soldiers to be; let them provide such governors, such husbands, such wives, such parents, such children, such masters, such servants, such kings, such judges, and lastly such taxpayers and tax collectors as Christian teaching admonishes them to be; and then let them dare to say that this

---

[1]   *American Catholic Quarterly Review*, Vol. 31, no. 122 (April 1906), pp. 213-214.

[2]   *The Documents of Vatican II* (New York: America Press, 1966), pp. 59, 64, 403. Reprinted with permission of America Press, Inc., 105 West 56th St., New York, N.Y. 10019, copyright © 1966 All Rights Reserved.

The Second Vatican Council reiterated the distinction, found in innumerable documents of the Magisterium, between the teaching Church and the learning Church and emphasized the hierarchy's mission to teach, govern, and sanctify.

teaching is opposed to the welfare of the State, or, rather, let them even hesitate to admit that it is the greatest safeguard of the State when faithfully observed.[3]

Under this perspective, it is proper for the clergy to firmly establish and maintain the moral foundations of the perfect civilization, the Christian one. By a natural connection, in the Middle Ages, education and works of public assistance and charity were entrusted to the Church. The Church performed these services, normally the purview of the departments of education and public health in contemporary secular states, without burden to the public coffers.

It is understandable then that the clergy was recognized as the first class in the Middle Ages, due to the supernatural and sacred character of its spiritual mission, and also to the beneficial effects its proper exercise produced in temporal society.

On the other hand, the clergy, in the exercise of its sublime mission, apart from any temporal or terrestrial power, is an active factor in the formation of the nation's spirit and mentality. Between clergy and nation, there normally exists an exchange of understanding, trust, and affection that apportions to the former unmatched possibilities to know and orient the aspirations, concerns, sufferings, in short, the spiritual life of the population, as well as the temporal affairs that are inseparable from it. To accord the clergy a voice and a vote in the great and decisive national assemblies is, therefore, an invaluable way for the State to ascertain the yearnings of its people.

Hence it is understandable that throughout history clerics, although maintaining their alterity in relation to the political life of the country, have frequently been heeded and respected counselors of the public power and valuable participants in the development of certain legislative matters and governmental policies.

But the picture of relations between the clergy and the public power is not limited to this.

The clergy is not a group of angels living in Heaven, but of men who exist and act concretely on this earth as God's ministers. The clergy comprises part of the country's population, before which its members have specific rights and duties. The protection of these rights and the proper fulfillment of these duties are of utmost importance for both Church and State, as Leo XIII eloquently stated in the encyclical *Immortale Dei.*[4]

All this indicates that the clergy is distinct from the other elements of the nation. It is a perfectly defined social class that is a living part of the national

---

[3] *Epist. 138 ad Marcellinum,* Chap. 2, no. 15, *Opera Omnia,* Vol. 2, in J.P. Migne, *Patrologia Latina,* col. 532.

[4] "There was once a time when states were governed by the principles of Gospel teaching. Then it was that the power and divine virtue of Christian wisdom had diffused itself throughout the laws, institutions, and morals of the people; permeating all ranks and relations of civil society. Then, too, the religion instituted by Jesus Christ, established firmly in befitting dignity, flourished everywhere, by the favor of princes and the legitimate protection of magistrates; and Church and State were happily united in concord and friendly interchange of good offices. The State, constituted in this wise, bore fruits important beyond all expectation, whose remembrance is still, and always will be, in renown, witnessed to as they are by countless proofs which can never be blotted out or even obscured by any craft of any enemies" (Rev. John J. Wynne, S.J., ed., *The Great Encyclical Letters of Pope Leo XIII* [New York: Benziger Brothers, 1903], pp. 118-119).

body and, as such, has the right to a voice and a vote in its public life.[5]

After the clergy, the second class was the nobility. Essentially it had a military and warrior character. The nobility was responsible for defending the country against external aggression and for keeping the political and social order. Besides that, in their respective domains, the feudal lords cumulatively exercised, without cost to the Crown, functions somewhat analogous to those of our judges, police chiefs, and city council presidents.

Thus these two classes were essentially ordained toward the common good and, in compensation for their weighty and important charges, they were entitled to corresponding honors and privileges, among which was exemption from taxes.

Lastly, there was the people, a class devoted specifically to productive work. It had, by right, a much lesser participation in war than the nobility and, in most cases, exclusive right to the exercise of the most profitable occupations, such as commerce and industry. Normally its members had no special obligation toward the State. They worked for the common good only in so far as it favored their own personal and familial interests. Thus, this class was not favored with special honors and had to carry the burden of taxes.

Clergy, nobility, and people. This trilogy naturally brings to mind the representative assemblies that characterized many monarchies of the Middle Ages and the Ancien Régime: the Cortes of Portugal and Spain, the Estates General of France, the Parliament of England, and so forth. In these assemblies, there was an authentic national representation that faithfully mirrored social organicity.

During the Enlightenment, other doctrines of political and social philosophy began to conquer several leading sectors of Europe. Under the effects of a mistaken notion of liberty, the Old Continent began to destroy the intermediary bodies and to completely secularize the State and nation. In this way inorganic societies arose, based on a purely quantitative criterion: the number of votes.

This transformation, extending from the last decades of the eighteenth century until our days, perilously facilitated the degeneration of peoples into masses, as Pius XII so wisely pointed out.

2. The Deterioration of the Medieval Order in Modern Times

As explained in Chapter II, the feudal organization of society—at once political, social, and economic—deteriorated in modern times (from the fifteenth to the eighteenth centuries). From then on, the successive political and socioeconomic

---

[5] Another aspect of the clergy's legitimate participation in public life in feudal times was the existence of dioceses and abbeys whose titulars were, at the same time and by the very fact, lords of the respective feudal domains. For example, by virtue of being bishops and regardless of their social origin, the Bishop-Princes of Cologne and of Geneva were princes of their respective cities. Among the latter was Saint Francis de Sales, an eminent Doctor of the Church. Along with the Bishop-Princes there were other ecclesiastical dignitaries on whom titles of lesser rank were conferred. Two examples in Portugal were the Archbishops of Braga, who were also lords of that city, and the Bishops of Coimbra, who were ipso facto Counts of Arganil (ever since Dom Afonso V graced the 36th Bishop of Coimbra, Dom João Galvão, with this title in 1472), whence the title Bishop-Count of Coimbra.

Detail of the altarpiece "São Vicente de Fora," attributed to Nuno Gonçalves, fifteenth century. To Saint Vincent's left are Prince Henry the Navigator, Prince John (later King John II of Portugal), and King Afonso V (kneeling). (Museu Nacional de Arte Antiga, Lisbon)

transformations have tended to meld all the classes and entirely, or almost entirely, deny a special juridical status to the clergy and nobility. This is a difficult contingency to which these classes should not pusillanimously close their eyes, since this would be unworthy of true clerics, as of true nobles.

Pius XII, in one of his masterful allocutions to the Roman Patriciate and Nobility, describes this state of things with noteworthy precision.

> First of all, you must look fearlessly, courageously, at the present reality. It seems superfluous to insist on recalling to your mind what, three years ago, was the object of Our considerations; it would seem vain and unworthy of you to veil it in prudent euphemisms, especially after the words of your eloquent representative have given Us so clear a testimonial of your adhesion to the social doctrine of the Church and to the duties stemming therefrom. The new Italian Constitution no longer recognizes you as possessing, as a social class, in the State and among the people, any particular mission, quality, or privilege.[6]

This situation, the Pontiff observes, is the outcome of a chain of events that creates the impression of following an "irresistible course."[7]

In view of the "very different lifestyles"[8] now emerging in modern society, members of the nobility and traditional elites should not engage in futile lamentation, nor should they ignore reality. Rather, they should take a strong attitude toward it. This is the conduct proper to courageous people: "While the mediocre can only wear a frown in the face of ill fortune, superior spirits are able, according to the classic expression, to prove themselves '*beaux joueurs,*' imperturbably maintaining their noble and untroubled bearing."[9]

3. The Nobility Should Remain a Leading Class in Today's Greatly Changed Social Context

According to Pius XII, "one may think as one wishes"[10] about the new lifestyles. One is not at all obliged to applaud them, but one must accept that they constitute the palpable reality in which we are obliged to live. Just what, then, is the objective and manly acknowledgment of these lifestyles?

Have the nobility and the traditional elites lost their reason for being? Should they break with their traditions and their past? In a word, should they dissolve among the common people, mixing with them, extinguishing everything the noble families preserved in the way of lofty values of virtue, culture, style, and education?

---

[6]   RPN 1952, p. 457; see Chapter II, 1.

[7]   Ibid.

[8]   Ibid.

[9]   Ibid., pp. 457-458. The Pontiff's French expression may be rendered as "good sports."

[10] Ibid.

A hasty reading of the allocution to the Roman Patriciate and Nobility of 1952 would seem to lead to an affirmative answer. This answer, however, would be in patent disagreement with the teachings of analogous allocutions in previous years, as well as with passages from more than one allocution of later pontiffs. This apparent disagreement results especially from the passages quoted above, as well as from others that follow.[11] Yet this is not the teaching expressed by the Pontiff in his 1952 allocution. In his view, the traditional elites should continue to exist and have a lofty mission.

> It may well be that one thing or another about the present conditions displeases you. Yet for the sake and for the love of the common good, for the salvation of Christian civilization, during this crisis which, far from abating, seems instead to be growing, stand firm in the breach, on the front line of defense. There your special qualities can be put to good use even today. Your names, which resonate deeply in the memories even of the distant past, in the history of the Church and of civil society, recall to mind figures of great men and fill your souls with echoes of the dutiful call to prove yourselves worthy.[12]

This teaching is made still clearer in the allocution to the Roman Patriciate and Nobility of 1958, a passage of which was already cited.[13]

> You, who at the start of each new year have never failed to come visit Us, must surely remember the careful solicitude with which We endeavored to smooth your way toward the future, which at that time promised to be harsh because of the profound upheavals and transformations in store for the world. We are certain, however, that when your brows too are framed with white and silver, you will yet be witnesses not only to Our esteem and affection, but also to the truth, the validity, and the timeliness of Our recommendations, which We hope are like fruits that have come to you and to society in general.
>
> You will recall to your children and grandchildren how the Pope of your childhood and adolescence did not neglect to point you toward the new responsibilities that the new circumstances of the age imposed on the nobility; that, indeed, he explained many times how industriousness would be the surest and most worthy way of ensuring yourselves a permanent place among society's leaders; that social inequalities, while they make you stand out, also assign you certain duties toward the common good; that from the highest classes great boons or great harm could come to the people; that transformations of ways of life can, if one so wishes, be harmoniously reconciled with the traditions of which patrician families are the repositories.[14]

---

[11] See Chapter VI, 2 a.

[12] RPN 1952, p. 459.

[13] See Chapter I, 6.

[14] RPN 1958, p. 708.

The Pontiff does not desire, then, the disappearance of the nobility from the profoundly transformed social context of our day. On the contrary, he invites its members to exert the necessary effort to maintain their position as the leading class among the groups that direct the present world. In expressing this wish, the Pontiff includes a singular nuance: The persistence of the nobility among these groups should have a traditional meaning, that is, a sense of continuity, of *permanence*.

In other words, the Pontiff desires fidelity to one of the founding principles of the nobility of former times: the correlation between the "social inequalities" that made them "stand out" and their "duties toward the common good."

Thus, "transformations of ways of life can, if one so wishes, be harmoniously reconciled with the traditions of which patrician families are the repositories."[15]

Pius XII insists on the nobility's permanence in the post-war world, so long as it truly distinguishes itself in the moral qualities it should manifest.

> Sometimes, in alluding to the contingency of time and events, We exhorted you to take an active part in the healing of the wounds caused by the war, in the rebuilding of peace, in the rebirth of the life of the nation, and to refuse all "emigration" or abstention. For in our society there still remained an ample place for you if you showed yourselves to be truly *elites* and *optimates* [aristocrats], that is, exceptional for serenity of mind, readiness to act, and generous adhesion.[16]

4. Through a Judicious Adaptation to the Modern World, the Nobility Does Not Disappear in the General Leveling

In accordance with these observations, an adaptation to the modern world—so much more egalitarian than pre-World War II Europe—does not mean that the nobility should renounce its traditions and disappear in the general leveling. Rather, it means that it should courageously continue a past inspired by perennial principles. The Pontiff emphasizes the highest among these, namely, fidelity to the Christian ideal.

> Also do not forget Our appeals to banish from your hearts all despondency and cowardice in face of the evolution of the times, and Our exhortations to adapt yourselves courageously to the new circumstances by keeping your gaze fixed on the Christian ideal, the true and indelible entitlement to genuine nobility.[17]

---

[15] Ibid.

[16] Ibid.

[17] Ibid.

Such is the courageous adaptation that befits the nobility in face of the evolution of the times.

In consequence, the nobles should not renounce their ancestral glory. Instead, they ought to preserve it for their respective lineages and, even more, for the benefit of the common good as the worthwhile contribution they are still capable of making.

> Yet why, beloved Sons and Daughters, did we express then and do we now repeat these admonitions and recommendations if not to fortify you against bitter disillusionments, to preserve for your houses the heritage of your ancestral glories, and to guarantee for the society to which you belong the valid contribution that you are still capable of making to it?[18]

5. To Fulfill the Hopes Placed in It, the Nobility Should Shine in the Gifts Specific to It

After emphasizing once again the importance of the nobility's fidelity to Catholic morals, Pius XII outlines a fascinating picture of the qualities that the nobility should manifest in order to correspond to the hopes he places in it. It especially interests the present study to note that these qualities should shine in the nobility as a fruit of long family traditions. These traditions are clearly hereditary and comprise something unique to the noble class.

> And yet—you may ask Us—what exactly must we do to achieve so lofty a goal?
> First of all, you must maintain an irreproachable religious and moral conduct, especially within the family, and practice a healthy austerity in life. Let the other classes be aware of the patrimony of virtues and gifts that are your own, the fruit of long family traditions: an imperturbable strength of soul, loyalty and devotion to the worthiest causes, tender and generous compassion toward the weak and the poor, a prudent and delicate manner in difficult and grave matters, and that personal prestige, almost hereditary in noble families, whereby one manages to persuade without oppressing, to sway without forcing, to conquer the minds of others, even adversaries and rivals, without humiliating them. The use of these gifts and the exercise of religious and civic virtues are the most convincing way to respond to prejudices and suspicion, since they manifest the spirit's inner vitality, from which spring all outward vigor and fruitful works.[19]

Here the Pontiff shows his illustrious listeners an adequate way of responding to the invectives of today's vulgar egalitarian, who is opposed to the survival of the noble class.

---

[18] Ibid.

[19] Ibid.

"First of all, you must maintain an irreproachable religious and moral conduct, especially within the family, and practice a healthy austerity in life. Let the other classes be aware of the patrimony of virtues and gifts that are your own, the fruit of long family traditions." (Pius XII, allocution of 1958)

Courtesy of Count Droste zu Vischering

TFP Archive (Felipe Barandiarán)

The lofty values of virtue, culture, refinement, and education found in uncountable noble families have produced praiseworthy fruits of heroism and sanctity throughout the centuries.

Above: Darfeld Castle, the home of the Droste zu Vischering family. This illustrious and ancient Catholic family of Münster, Germany, has distinguished itself since 1271 by services to Church and country.

Just recently, Portugal rejoiced over the beatification of Countess Maria Droste zu Vischering. She spent the last years of her life as a religious in the Bom Pastor convent in Oporto, where she died on June 8, 1899.

6. Even Those Who Show Disdain for
the Old Ways of Life Are Not Totally
Immune to the Splendor of the Nobility

Pius XII emphasizes vigor and fertility of works as characteristic of genuine
nobility and encourages the nobles to contribute such qualities to the common
good.

> Vigor and fruitful works! Behold two characteristics of true nobility, to which
> heraldic symbols, stamped in bronze or carved in marble, are a perennial testimony,
> for they represent as it were the visible thread of the political and cultural history
> of more than a few glorious cities of Europe. It is true that modern society is not
> accustomed by preference to wait for your class to "set the tone" before starting
> works and confronting events; nevertheless, it does not refuse the cooperation of
> the brilliant minds among you, since a wise portion thereof retains an appropriate
> respect for tradition and prizes high decorum, whatever its origins. And the other
> part of society, which displays indifference and perhaps disdain for ancient ways of
> life, is not entirely immune to the seduction of glory; so much so, that it tries very
> hard to create new forms of aristocracy, some worthy of respect, others based on
> vanity and frivolity, satisfied with merely appropriating the inferior elements of the
> ancient institutions.[20]

In this paragraph, Pius XII seems to be refuting an objection possibly raised
by discouraged aristocrats appalled by the egalitarian wave already spread
throughout the modern world. According to these aristocrats, the world scorns the
nobility and refuses to collaborate with it.

Regarding this objection, the Pontiff reasons that one can distinguish two
tendencies in modern society in face of the nobility. One "retains an appropriate
respect for tradition and prizes high decorum, whatever its origins," by which "it
does not refuse the cooperation of the brilliant minds among you." The other
tendency, which consists in exhibiting "indifference and perhaps disdain for
ancient ways of life, is not entirely immune to the seduction of glory." Pius XII
notes expressive evidence of this disposition of spirit.

7. The Specific Virtues and Qualities
of the Nobility Imbue Its Work

The Pontiff continues:

> It is clear, however, that vigor and fruitful works cannot still manifest themselves
> today in forms that have been eclipsed. This does not mean that the field of your
> activities has been reduced; on the contrary, it has been broadened in the total number

---

[20]   Ibid.

of professions and functions. The entire range of professions is open to you; you can be useful and excel in any sector: in areas of public administration and government, or in scientific, cultural, artistic, industrial, or commercial activities.[21]

The Pontiff alludes here to the fact that in the political and socioeconomic regime prevalent before the French Revolution certain professions generally were not exercised by nobles, since these were deemed beneath nobility. Their exercise implied, at times, the loss of noble status. One example was the exercise of commerce, reserved in many places to the bourgeoisie and the common people. These restrictions gradually diminished during the nineteenth and twentieth centuries and have entirely disappeared today.

In this passage, Pius XII seems to have in mind that the disturbances resulting from the two world wars had economically ruined a significant number of noble families. Their members were thereby reduced to exercising secondary activities, inappropriate not only for the nobility but for the high and middle bourgeoisie as well. One could even speak of the proletarianization of certain nobles.

In view of such harsh realities, Pius XII encourages these families not to dissolve in a prosaic anonymity, but rather to practice their traditional virtues and act with vigor and fruitfulness, thus communicating a specifically noble note to any work they exercise either by choice or under the harsh sway of circumstances. In this way they will make the nobility understood and respected, even in the most painful situations.

8. A Sublime Example: The Couple of Royal Lineage in Whose House the God-Man Was Born and Dwelt

This elevated teaching takes examples from the public administration of government and from other offices usually held by the bourgeoisie. But it also brings to mind the couple of the royal line of David in whose house, at once princely and working-class, the God-Man was born and lived for thirty years.[22]

Such a reflection is found in the allocution of Pius XII to the Noble Guard in 1939:

> You were already noble, even before serving God and His Vicar under the gold and white standard. The Church, in whose eyes the human social order rests fundamentally on the family, however humble it may be, does not disdain that family treasure that is hereditary nobility. Indeed, one may even say that Jesus Christ Himself did not scorn it: The man to whom He entrusted the task of protecting His adorable Humanity and His Virgin Mother, was of royal stock: "Joseph, of the house of David" (Luke 1:27). And this is why Our Predecessor Leo XII, in his brief on

[21] RPN 1958, pp. 709-710.
[22] See Chapter V, 6.

reform of the Corps of February 17, 1824, attested that the Noble Guard is "consecrated to render the most proximate and immediate service to Our very Person and constitutes a Corps, which, as much for the end for which it was instituted as for the quality of the individuals composing it, is the first and most respectable of the arms of Our Princedom."[23]

9. The Highest Social Function of the Nobility: To Preserve, Defend, and Spread the Christian Teachings Contained in Its Distinctive Noble Traditions

In his 1958 allocution, the Pontiff mentions the moral duty to resist modern corruption as a general charge to the upper classes, which include the Roman Patriciate and Nobility:

> We would like, finally, for your influence on society to save it from a grave danger inherent in modern times. It is well known that society progresses and raises itself up when the virtues of one class are spread to the others; it declines, on the other hand, if the vices and abuses of one are carried over to the others. Because of the weakness of human nature, more often it is the latter that are spread, with all the more rapidity nowadays, given the greater facility of means of communication, information, and personal contacts, not only among nations, but from one continent to the next. What happens in the realm of physical health is now happening in the realm of morals as well: neither distances nor boundaries can any longer prevent an epidemic germ from quickly reaching faraway regions. The upper classes, of which yours is one, could, because of their multiple relations and frequent sojourns in countries with different and sometimes inferior moral conditions, become easy conveyers of aberrations in customs.[24]

The Holy Father defines this duty of the nobility more specifically: It is a duty to resist, above all in the field of doctrine but also in that of morals. "As for your own task, you must be vigilant and do your utmost to prevent pernicious theories and perverse examples from ever meeting with your approval and sympathy, let alone using you as favorable carriers and hotbeds of infection." This duty is an integral element of "that profound respect for tradition that you cultivate and hope to use to distinguish yourselves in society." These traditions are "precious treasures" that it is important for the noble to "preserve...among the people. This itself may be the highest social function of today's nobility; certainly it is the greatest service that you can render to the Church and to your country."[25]

---

[23] PNG 1939, p. 450.

[24] RPN 1958, p. 710.

[25] Ibid.

View of the audience granted by John XXIII to the Roman Patriciate and Nobility on January 20, 1963.

"The fact of belonging to a particularly distinguished order of society, however, while requiring due consideration, is a call to its members to give more, as befits those who have received more, and who will one day have to render accounts to God for everything."
(John XXIII, allocution of January 9, 1960)

John XXIII with the Noble Guard after his allocution on January 7, 1959.

To conserve, defend, and spread the Christian teachings contained in its distinctive noble traditions: What loftier use can the nobility make of the splendor of past centuries that still illuminates and distinguishes it today?[26]

10. The Nobility's Duty: To Avoid Sinking into Anonymity; To Resist the Influence of Modern Egalitarianism

Pius XII paternally insists that the nobility not let itself be diluted in the anonymity into which the indifference and hostility of many, spurred on by crude modern egalitarianism, seek to drag it. He likewise points out another relevant mission: By cultivating and disseminating its living traditions, the nobility should help preserve the values of each people from a cosmopolitanism that erodes their distinctiveness. "To practice virtue and use the gifts proper to your class for the common good, to excel in professions and activities promptly embraced, to protect the nation from external contaminations: These are the recommendations We feel We must make to you at the start of this New Year."[27]

As he closes this expressive allocution with paternal blessings, the Pontiff makes special mention of the continuity of the nobility. He reminds the noble families present that the grave and honorable duty of continuing the most worthy traditions of the nobility lies with their children: "That the Almighty may strengthen your resolve and fulfill Our desires, answering the prayers We have thus made to Him, We impart to all of you, to your families, and especially to your children, future successors to your worthiest traditions, Our Apostolic blessing."[28]

11. The Nobility: A Particularly Distinguished Order in Human Society—It Will Have Special Accounts to Render to God

An application of these rich and solid teachings to the contemporary condition of the nobility may be found in the allocution of John XXIII to the Roman Patriciate and Nobility on January 9, 1960.

> The Holy Father is pleased to note that the distinguished audience is a reminder of what human society is as a whole: a multiple variety of elements, each with its own personality and efficiency like flowers in the sunlight, and each worthy of respect and honor, regardless of its importance and size.
>
> The fact of belonging to a particularly distinguished order of society, however,

---

[26] Concerning nobility as a factor that facilitates and encourages the practice of Christian virtues, see especially the admirable sermon of Saint Charles Borromeo transcribed in Documents IV, 8.

[27] RPN 1958, pp. 710-711.

[28] Ibid.

while requiring due consideration, is a call to its members to give more, as befits those who have received more, and who will one day have to render accounts to God for everything.

By acting in this manner, you cooperate in the wondrous harmony of the kingdom of Our Lord, with the profound conviction that the things that made the fame of each family in the past must now strengthen its commitment—precisely as dictated by its particular social condition—to the sublime concept of Christian brotherhood and to the exercise of special virtues: sweet and gentle patience, purity of customs, humility, and above all, charity. Only thus will great and undying honor be conferred on individuals!

And from this it follows that, tomorrow, the young scions of today will bless their fathers and demonstrate that Christian thought has been an ideal inspiration and rule of conduct, generosity, and spiritual beauty.

These same dispositions will serve as comfort even in the face of inevitable misfortunes that are never wanting, since the cross resides in every dwelling, from the humblest country house to the most majestic palace. It is nevertheless quite clear and natural that one must pass through this school of pain, of which Our Lord Jesus Christ is the unequaled Teacher.

To fortify the most excellent dispositions of those present the Supreme Pontiff imparts his blessing to each and every family, invoking divine assistance especially where there is suffering and greater need. He adds the paternal wish that you should act in such a manner as not to live *alla giornata* [from day to day] as they say, but should feel and express, in everyday life, thoughts and works in accordance with the Gospel, which has pointed the way along the luminous roads of Christian civilization. He who acts in this way now knows that in the future his name too shall be repeated with respect and admiration.[29]

The specific role of the contemporary nobility is remembered by John XXIII in the allocution to the Roman Patriciate and Nobility of January 10, 1963:

The resolution, expressed on behalf of those present by their authoritative representative, is very reassuring, and its enactment will bring peace, happiness, and blessings.

He who has received most, he who has risen highest, finds himself in the most propitious conditions for setting good example; each must make his contribution: the poor, the humble, the suffering, as well as those who have received numerous gifts from the Lord and enjoy a situation that brings with it particular and serious responsibilities.[30]

---

[29] RPN 1960, pp. 565-566. The Poliglotta Vaticana edition contains only a summary of the allocution.

[30] RPN 1963, p. 348.

Tower of Belém, Lisbon

Elites, Natural Order, Family, and Tradition—Aristocratic Institutions Within Democracies

The Teaching of Pius XII

*T*he previous chapter considered the teachings of Pius XII with respect to the mission of the nobility in our day. We shall now analyze the Pontiff's doctrine concerning the role of traditional elites—the most important being the nobility—in preserving tradition and thereby contributing to progress. We shall also analyze his thinking on the continuity of these elites, and their complete compatibility with true democracy.

1. The Formation of Elites Even in Countries Without a Monarchical or Aristocratic Past

The formation of traditional elites with an aristocratic note is so profoundly natural that it occurs even in countries without a monarchical or an aristocratic past.

> Even in democracies of recent date that have no vestiges of a feudal past behind them, a kind of new nobility or aristocracy has been forming by force of circumstances. It consists of the community of families that by tradition place all their energies at the service of the State, its government, its administration, and whose loyalty it can always count on.[1]

This splendid definition of the essence of nobility reminds us of the great lineages of colonizers, pioneers, and planters who for centuries contributed to the

---

[1] RPN 1947, pp. 370-371.

progress of the Americas, and who, remaining faithful to their traditions, constitute a precious moral resource for their societies.

2. Heredity in Traditional Elites

There is, before all else, a natural fact linked to the existence of traditional elites that needs to be remembered, namely, heredity.

> The nature of this great and mysterious thing that is heredity—the passing on through a bloodline, perpetuated from generation to generation, of a rich ensemble of material and spiritual assets, the continuity of a single physical and moral type from father to son, the tradition that unites members of one same family across the centuries—the true nature of this heredity can undoubtably be distorted by materialistic theories. But one can, and must also, consider this reality enormously important in the fullness of its human and supernatural truth.
>
> One certainly cannot deny the existence of a material substratum in the transmission of hereditary characteristics; to be surprised at this one would have to forget the intimate union of our soul with our body, and in what great measure our most spiritual activities are themselves dependent upon our physical temperament. For this reason Christian morality never forgets to remind parents of the great responsibilities resting on their shoulders in this regard.
>
> Yet of greater import still is spiritual heredity, which is transmitted not so much through these mysterious bonds of material generation as by the permanent action of that privileged environment that is the family, with the slow and profound formation of souls in the atmosphere of a hearth rich in high intellectual, moral, and especially Christian traditions, with the mutual influence of those dwelling under one same roof, an influence whose beneficial effects endure well beyond the years of childhood and youth, all the way to the end of a long life, in those elect souls who are able to meld within themselves the treasures of a precious heredity with the addition of their own merits and experiences.
>
> Such is the most prized patrimony of all, which, illuminated by a solid faith and enlivened by a strong and loyal practice of Christian life in all its demands, will raise, refine, and enrich the souls of your children.[2]

3. Elites: Propelling Forces of True Progress and Guardians of Tradition

There is a link between nobility and tradition. The former is the natural guardian of the latter. In temporal society, the nobility is par excellence the class entrusted with keeping alive the link whereby the wisdom of the past guides the present without, however, paralyzing it.

---

[2] RPN 1941, p. 364.

a. Are elites enemies of progress?

Revolutionary spirits often raise the following objection against the nobility and the traditional elites: Being traditional, they are constantly turned toward the past and have their backs to the future, where true progress lies. They thus constitute an obstacle for any society wishing to pursue progress.

Pius XII teaches us, however, that authentic progress lies only in tradition. Progress is real only if it constitutes a harmonious development of the past, and not necessarily a return to it.[3] Were progress to break with tradition, society would be exposed to terrible risks.

> Things of this earth flow like a river in the course of time: Of necessity the past gives way to the future, and the present is but a fleeting instant joining the former with the latter. This is a fact, a motion, a law; it is not in itself an evil. There would be evil if this present, which should be a tranquil wave in the continuity of the current, became a billow, upturning everything in its path like a typhoon or hurricane and furiously digging, by destruction and ravage, a gulf between what has been and what must follow. Such chaotic leaps as are made by history in its course constitute and mark what is called a crisis, in other words, a dangerous passage, which may lead to salvation, but whose solution is still wrapped in mystery amid the smoke of the conflicting forces.[4]

Societies avoid stagnation, as well as chaos and revolt, through tradition. The guardianship of tradition, to which Pius XII alludes in this passage, is a specific mission of the nobility and the analogous elites.

Some elites neglect this mission by distancing themselves from contemporary life. Others sin by the opposite excess, becoming absorbed in the present and renouncing everything of the past.

Through heredity, the noble prolongs on earth the existence of the great men of the past. "Remembering your ancestors, [you] relive their lives in a way; and your ancestors live again in your names and in the titles they left you through their merits and their greatness."[5]

This confers a very particular moral mission on the nobility and the traditional elites. It is up to them to assure that progress has continuity with the past.

> Is not human society, or at least should it not be, like a finely tuned machine, in which all the parts work together toward the harmonious functioning of the whole? Each part has its own role, and each must apply himself toward the best

---

[3] See Documents VI.

[4] RPN 1944, pp. 177-178.

[5] RPN 1942, p. 345. In this regard, Rivarol, the brilliant French polemicist who opposed the Revolution of 1789, of which he was a contemporary, affirmed, "nobles are like ancient coins that time made into medals" (in M. Berville, *Mémoires de Rivarol* [Paris: Baudouin Frères, 1824], p. 212).

possible progress of the social organism; each must seek to perfect it, according to his strengths and virtues, if he truly loves his neighbor and reasonably strives for the common good and welfare.

Now what part has been assigned in a special way to you, beloved Sons and Daughters? What role has been allotted particularly to you? Precisely that of facilitating this natural development, the role that in the machine is fulfilled by the regulator, the flywheel, the rheostat, which take part in the common activity and receive their part of the motive force so as to ensure the operational movement of the apparatus. In other words, Patriciate and Nobility, you represent and continue tradition.[6]

b. Significance and value of true tradition

Respect for tradition is a very rare virtue in our day. On the one hand, the Revolution[7] turned the craving for novelties and the disdain for the past into common attitudes. On the other hand, the defenders of tradition sometimes understand it in an entirely false manner. Tradition is not merely a historic value, nor is it simply a theme for romantic yearnings for bygone days. It must be understood as an indispensable factor for contemporary life, and not in an exclusively archaeological way. The word *tradition*, says the Pontiff,

resounds disagreeably in many ears, and it is justifiably unpleasant when pronounced by certain lips. Some misunderstand it, others make it the mendacious label of their inactive egotism. Amid this dramatic dissent and confusion, more than a few envious voices, often hostile and in bad faith, more often ignorant or deluded, ask you bluntly: What are you good for? To answer them, you must first come to understand the true meaning and value of this tradition, of which you must of necessity be the principal representatives.

Many minds, even sincere ones, imagine and believe that tradition is nothing more than memory, the pale vestige of a past that no longer exists, that can never return, and that at most is relegated to museums, therein preserved with veneration, perhaps with gratitude, and visited by a few enthusiasts and friends. If tradition consisted only of this, if it were reduced to this, and if it entailed rejection or disdain for the road to the future, then one would be right to deny it respect and honor, and one would have to look with compassion on those who dream over the past and those left behind in face of the present and future, and with greater severity on those who, spurred by less pure and respectable motives, are nothing but derelict in the duties of the now so very mournful hour.

---

[6] RPN 1944, p. 178.

[7] The term *Revolution* is used in this book in the sense attributed it in the study *Revolution and Counter-Revolution*, by the present author. It designates a movement initiated in the fifteenth century which aimed to destroy Christian civilization and to implant a state of things diametrically opposed to it. The Pseudo-Reformation, the French Revolution, and Communism—in its many variations and in its current subtle metamorphosis—are the stages of this process.

But tradition is something very different from a simple attachment to a vanished past; it is the very opposite of a reaction mistrustful of all healthy progress. The word itself is etymologically synonymous with advancement and forward move-ment—synonymous, but not identical. Whereas, in fact, progress means only a for-ward march, step by step, in search of an uncertain future, tradition also signifies a forward march, but a continuous march as well, a movement equally brisk and tranquil, in accordance with life's laws, eluding the distressing dilemma: "*Si jeunesse savait, si vieillesse pouvait!*" [If youth knew, if the aged could]; like that Lord of Turenne of whom it was said: "*Il a eu dans sa jeunesse toute la prudence d'un âge avancé, et dans un âge avancé toute la vigueur de la jeunesse*" [In his youth he had all the prudence of advanced age and in his advanced age all the vigor of youth].[8] By virtue of tradition, youth, enlightened and guided by the experience of elders, moves forward with a surer step, and old age can confidently pass on the plow to stronger hands, to continue the furrow already begun. As the word itself implies, tradition is a gift handed down from generation to generation, the torch that at each relay one runner places in and entrusts to the hand of the next, without the race slowing down or coming to a halt. Tradition and progress complement each other so harmoniously that, just as tradition without progress would be a contradic-tion in terms, so progress without tradition would be a foolhardy proposition, a leap into darkness.

The point, then, is not to go against the stream, to backstep toward lifestyles and forms of activity already eclipsed, but rather to take and follow the best of the past and go out to meet the future with the vigor of unfailing youth.[9]

c. The traditional elites: their importance and legitimacy

The demagogic breath of egalitarianism blowing on the contemporary world creates an atmosphere of antipathy toward traditional elites. This is due, in great measure, to their fidelity to tradition. There is, therefore, a great injustice in this antipathy, so long as these elites understand tradition correctly.

> In this manner, your vocation, grand and laborious, is already radiantly defined, and should win you the gratitude of all and raise you above the accusations that might be leveled at you from either side.
>
> As you prudently seek to help true progress advance toward a saner, happier future, it would be unjust and ungrateful to reproach you and dishonorably brand you for the cult of the past, the study of history, the love of sacred customs, and unshakeable loyalty to eternal principles. The glorious or unhappy examples of those who preceded the present age are a lesson and a light to guide your steps; and it

---

[8] Fléchier, *Oraison funebre*, 1676. The Pope refers to Henri de la Tour d'Auvergne, Viscount de Turenne, Marshall of France (1611-1675).

[9] RPN 1944, pp. 178-180; see Documents VI.

has already been rightly stated that the teachings of history make humanity a man forever moving but never growing old. You live in modern society not like immigrants in a foreign country, but rather as exemplary and illustrious citizens, who want and intend to collaborate with their contemporaries toward the recovery, restoration, and progress of the world.[10]

4. God's Blessing Illuminates, Protects, and Caresses All Cradles, but Does Not Equalize Them

Another factor in the hostility toward the traditional elites lies in the revolutionary preconception that any inequality of origin is contrary to justice. It is generally admitted that one may stand out due to personal merit, but descent from an illustrious family is deemed inadmissible as a special title to honor and influence. In this respect the Holy Father Pius XII teaches us a precious lesson.

> Social inequalities, even those related to birth, are inevitable: Benign nature and God's blessing to humanity illuminate and protect all cradles, looking on them with love, but do not make them equal. Look, for example, at the most inexorably leveled societies. No art has ever been able to work things so that the son of a great chief, the son of a great leader of the masses, should remain in the same condition as an obscure citizen lost among the common people. Yet, although such ineluctable disparities may appear, in a pagan light, to be the inflexible consequence of the conflict between social forces and the power acquired by some people over others, according to the blind laws believed to rule human activity and to make sense of the triumph of some and the sacrifice of others, on the other hand, to a mind instructed and educated in a Christian way these disparities can only be considered a disposition willed by God with the same wisdom as the inequalities within the family. Hence, they are destined to bring men more closely together on the present life's journey toward the Kingdom of Heaven, with some helping others in the way a father helps the mother and children.[11]

---

[10] Ibid., p. 180. The reader should not imagine that with this wise counsel Pius XII overlooks the grave dangers stemming from overrating modern technology. Consider what he has to teach in this respect:

"It seems undeniable that technology itself, which has attained its apogee of splendor and fruitfulness in our century, is in actual circumstances being transformed into a grave spiritual danger. It seems to communicate to modern man, who bows before its altar, a sense of self-sufficiency and satisfaction of his boundless thirst for knowledge and power. With its manifold uses, the absolute confidence it inspires, the inexhaustible possibilities it promises, modern technology unfolds before men of today a vision so vast that it is taken by many to be infinity itself. It is consequently believed to possess an inadmissible autonomy that in turn is transformed, in the mind of some, into an erroneous conception of life and the world that is called the 'spirit of technology.' But of what, precisely, does this consist? It consists in considering that what is of the highest value for humanity and life is the most advantageous exploitation of nature's forces and elements; in setting all the technically possible methods of mechanical production as a goal above all other human activities; and in seeing in these the perfection of earthly culture and happiness" (Christmas message of 1953, *Discorsi e radiomessaggi di Sua Santità Pio XII*, Vol. 15, p. 522).

[11] RPN 1942, p. 347.

5. The Paternal Notion of Social Superiority

The Christian glory of the traditional elites lies in serving not only the Church but also the common good. Pagan aristocracy boasted exclusively of its illustrious lineage. Christian nobility adds to this title another still higher: the exercise of a paternal mission vis-à-vis the other classes.

> The name "Roman Patriciate" awakens in our mind even greater thoughts and visions of history. If the term patrician in pagan Rome, *patricius*, signified the fact of having ancestors and of belonging not to stock of common rank but to a privileged and dominant class, in a Christian light it takes on a more luminous aspect and deeper resonance in that it associates the idea of social superiority with that illustrious paternity. It is a patriciate of Christian Rome, which had its highest and most ancient splendors not in blood but in the honor of protecting Rome and the Church: *patricius Romanorum*, a title carried over from the time of the Exarchs of Ravenna to Charlemagne and Henry III. Through the centuries, successive Popes also had armed defenders of the Church, drawn from the families of the Roman Patriciate; and Lepanto marked and eternalized a great name in the annals of history.[12]

This body of concepts certainly conveys an impression of the paternality permeating the relations between the highest and lowest classes.

Two objections against such an impression readily arise in "modern" minds. First, someone can always be counted on to affirm that frequent oppressive acts committed in the past by the nobility or the analogous elites invalidate this whole doctrine. Others hold that any affirmation of superiority eliminates Christian gentleness, sweetness, and amenity from social relationships. They argue that superiority normally arouses feelings of humiliation, sadness, and sorrow in those over whom it is exercised, and that to arouse such feelings in one's neighbor is opposed to evangelical sweetness.

Pius XII implicitly answers these objections when he affirms:

> If this paternal conception of social superiority has sometimes, in the clash of human passions, driven souls to deviations in the relations between persons of higher rank and those of humbler station, it is no surprise to the history of fallen humanity. Such deviations in no way serve to diminish or obscure the fundamental truth that, for the Christian, social inequalities merge in the great human family; that therefore relations between unequal classes and ranks have to remain regulated by a fair and righteous justice and at the same time be informed by mutual respect and affection, which, while not abolishing the disparities, should diminish the distance and temper the contrasts between them.[13]

---

[12] Ibid., pp. 346-347. The Pope refers at the end of this passage to Marcantonio Colonna, the Younger, Duke of Paliano (1535-1584). Saint Pius V entrusted him with the command of twelve pontifical ships that participated in the battle. He fought with such heroism and ability that he was received triumphantly in Rome.

[13] Ibid., pp. 347-348. By "fallen humanity," the Pontiff alludes to mankind's decadence due to Original Sin.

"Jesus Christ Himself was noble, as were Mary and Joseph, being descendants of royal lineage." (Benedict XV, allocution of January 5, 1917)

Depiction of the Holy Family venerated in the chapel of the national headquarters of the Brazilian TFP in São Paulo. (Anonymous, School of Cuzco, Peru)

Typical examples of this aristocratic gentleness are found in many noble families who know how to be extraordinarily kind toward their subordinates without consenting in any way that their natural superiority be denied or abased.

> In truly Christian families, do we not see perhaps the greatest of patricians being careful and solicitous to maintain toward their domestics and all those around them a comportment which, while surely in keeping with their rank, is always free of haughtiness and expressive of kindness and courtesy in words and actions that demonstrate the nobility of hearts that see these men as brothers and Christians and united to them in Christ by the bonds of charity, of that charity which, even in their ancestral palaces, between the great and humble, always comforts, sustains, gladdens, and sweetens life.[14]

6. Our Lord Jesus Christ Consecrated the Condition of a Noble as well as That of a Laborer

Considering the condition of a noble or a member of the traditional elites in this manner, it is understandable that Our Lord Jesus Christ hallowed it, as was already said,[15] by becoming incarnate in a princely family.

> Although it is true that Christ Our Lord chose, for the comfort of the poor, to come into the world bereft of everything and to grow up in a family of simple laborers, He nevertheless wished to honor with His birth the noblest, most illustrious of the lines of Israel, the House of David itself.
>
> Therefore, loyal to the spirit of Him whose Vicars they are, the Supreme Pontiffs have always held in high consideration the Patriciate and the Roman Nobility, whose sentiments of unalterable devotion to this Apostolic See are the most precious part of the heritage they have received from their forebears and will pass on to their children.[16]

7. The Perennial Character of the Nobility and the Traditional Elites

The dead elements of the past are bound to be blown away by the winds of the Revolution, just like dead leaves caught by the wind. Nevertheless, the nobility, as a species within the genus "elites," can and should survive because it has a permanent reason for being.

> The furious currents of a new age envelop the traditions of the past in their whirlwinds. Yet, more than this, these winds show what is destined to die like

---

[14] Ibid., p. 348.

[15] Chapter IV, 8.

[16] RPN 1941, pp. 363-364; see Documents IV.

withered leaves, and what instead tends with the genuine force of its interior life to stand firm and live on.

A nobility and a patriciate that would, as it were, grow stiff and decrepit by regretting times gone by, would consign themselves to an inevitable decline.

Today more than ever, you are called upon to be an elite, not only by blood and by stock, but even more by your works and sacrifices, by creative actions in the service of the entire social community.

And this is not just a duty of man and citizen that none may shirk with impunity. It is also a sacred commandment of the faith that you have inherited from your fathers and that you must, in their wake, leave whole and unaltered to your descendants.

Banish, therefore, from your ranks all despondency and faint-heartedness; all despondency in the face of the age's evolution, which is bearing away many things that other epochs had built; and all faint-heartedness at the sight of the grave events accompanying the novelties of our age.

Being Roman means being strong in action, but also in support.

Being Christian means confronting the sufferings, the trials, the tasks, and the needs of the age with that courage, strength, and serenity of spirit that draws the antidote to all human fear from the wellsprings of eternal hope.

How humanly great is Horace's proud dictum: *Si fractus illabatur orbis, impavidum ferient ruinae* [Even if the world crumbles to pieces, its ruins would strike him without, however, unsettling him] (*Odes*, III, 3).

Yet how much greater still, how much more confident and exalting is the victorious cry that rises from Christian lips and hearts brimming with faith: *Non confundar in aeternum*! [Let me not be confounded eternally—from the *Te Deum*].[17]

8. The Law Cannot Abolish the Past

Thus we understand why, despite the proclamation of the republic in Italy in 1946, the Holy Father Pius XII upheld the Roman Patriciate and Nobility as a noteworthy remembrance of a past of which the present should conserve elements to assure the continuity of a beneficial and illustrious tradition.

> It is quite true that in the new Italian Constitution "titles of nobility are not recognized" (except, of course, in accordance with Article 42 of the Concordat, as pertains to the Holy See, those titles granted or to be granted by the Supreme Pontiffs);[18] yet not even the Constitution can annul the past, nor the history of your families.[19]

There is no moral judgment in Pius XII's explicit and direct reference to the abolition of nobiliary titles by the Italian Republic. The Pope simply acknowledges

---

[17] RPN 1951, pp. 423-424.

[18] See Chapter II, 1.

[19] RPN 1949, p. 346.

the fact. But *pari passu* he affirms with noble agility that, far from following the example of republican Italy, the Church vindicates the validity of the titles of nobility she has hitherto granted or may come to grant in the future. These titles continued to be valid even in the Republic of Italy in virtue of Article 42 of the Lateran Treaty.[20] This is evident, since an article of the Italian Constitution cannot unilaterally suspend the validity of pontifical titles recognized by a bilateral act such as the Concordat of 1929.[21]

So, the Roman Patriciate and Nobility still have a momentous and magnificent duty, resulting from the prestige that friends and foes alike must acknowledge.

> Therefore even now the people—whether they are favorable toward you or not, whether they feel respectfully loyal or hostile toward you—look at you and see what sort of example you set in life. It is thus up to you to respond to such expectations and show how your conduct and actions are in keeping with truth and virtue, especially in the matters We have just discussed in Our recommendations.[22]

Considering the past of the Roman Nobility and finding therein not something dead but an "impetus for the future," Pius XII, "moved by feelings of honor and loyalty," reserved for it a treatment of special distinction and invited his contemporaries to do likewise.

> In you We hail the descendants and representatives of families long in the service of the Holy See and the Vicar of Christ, who remained faithful to the Roman Pontificate even when it was exposed to outrages and persecutions. Without doubt, over the course of time the social order has been able to evolve, and its center has shifted. Public offices, which once were reserved for your class, may now be conferred and exercised on a basis of equality; nevertheless, such a testimonial of grateful remembrance—which must also serve as an impetus for the future—must also

---

[20] See Chapter II, 1.

[21] Regarding the summary abolition of institutions as old and meritorious as the nobility under the impact of the radical egalitarianism that spread throughout many countries after the two world wars, it is lamentable that Saint Thomas Aquinas' wise teachings were not taken into account. In the *Summa Theologica* (I-II, q. 97, a. 2) under the title "Whether human law should always be changed, whenever something better occurs?" he wrote:

"It is stated in the Decretals: *It is absurd, and a detestable shame, that we should suffer those traditions to be changed which we have received from the fathers of old.*

"As stated above, human law is rightly changed, in so far as such change is conducive to the common weal. But, to a certain extent, the mere change of law is of itself prejudicial to the common good: because custom avails much for the observance of laws, seeing that what is done contrary to general custom, even in slight matters, is looked upon as grave. Consequently, when a law is changed, the binding power of the law is diminished, in so far as custom is abolished. Wherefore human law should never be changed, unless, in some way or other, the common weal be compensated according to the extent of the harm done in this respect. Such compensation may arise either from some very great and very evident benefit conferred by the new enactment; or from the extreme urgency of the case, due to the fact that either the existing law is clearly unjust, or its observance extremely harmful. Wherefore the Jurist says that *in establishing new laws, there should be evidence of the benefit to be derived, before departing from a law which has long been considered just.*"

[22] RPN 1949, p. 346.

Saint Elizabeth of Hungary, Landgravine of Thuringia, used to wash and dress the wounds of persons afflicted with ringworm. (Murillo, 1672, Hospital of Holy Charity, Seville)

command respect and understanding in modern man as well if he wishes to possess just and fair sentiments.[23]

9. Democracy According to the Doctrine of the Church— Archaeologism and False Restoration: Two Extremes to Be Avoided

One might ask if Pius XII with these teachings, uttered in an epoch of overwhelming desire for equality, was attempting to react against this egalitarian tendency by condemning democracy.

In this respect, further considerations may be useful.

The social doctrine of the Church always affirmed the legitimacy of the three forms of government: monarchy, aristocracy, and democracy. It always refused to accept that democracy is the only form of government compatible with justice and charity.

Saint Thomas Aquinas teaches that, in principle, monarchy is a form of government superior to the rest. But this does not mean that particular circumstances may not render aristocracy or democracy more appropriate in one state or another.

Saint Thomas views with singular satisfaction those forms of government in which elements of monarchy, aristocracy, and democracy are harmoniously combined.[24]

Leo XIII, in turn, when explaining the Church's social doctrine on the forms of government, declares: "By giving oneself up to abstractions, one could at length conclude which is the best of these forms, considered in themselves."[25] However, the Pontiff does not affirm which form it is.

Nonetheless, we must note the categorical nature of his affirmation, although it seems at first glance to be conditional: "one could conclude."

In fact, the Pontiff affirms that it is *possible* to determine which form of government is intrinsically better so long as the thinker remains in the realm of abstractions. And so he adds:

> And in all truth it may be affirmed that each of them is good, provided it lead straight to its end—that is to say, to the common good for which social authority is constituted; and finally, it may be added that, from a relative point of view, such and such a form of government may be preferable because of being better adapted to the character and customs of such and such a nation.[26]

---

[23] RPN 1950, p. 357.

[24] For a better understanding of the Church's doctrine and Saint Thomas's thinking on the various forms of government, it is of capital importance to read the pontifical texts and the texts of the Angelic Doctor transcribed in Appendix IV along with the author's commentaries.

[25] Encyclical *Au milieu des sollicitudes*, in Wynne, *Great Encyclical Letters*, p. 255.

[26] Ibid.

One question remains. According to the Pontiff's reasoning, which form of government would be considered better in the realm of mere abstraction?

To answer this we must recall the encyclical *Aeterni Patris* of August 4, 1879, concerning the restoration of Scholasticism according to the doctrine of Saint Thomas Aquinas. Among many other tributes to the work of this great Doctor of the Church we find the following:

> It is well known that almost all the founders and lawgivers of religious orders enjoined upon their members to study and adhere religiously to the doctrines of St. Thomas, warning them that no one of them should with impunity recede, even in the slightest degree, from the teachings of so great a master....
>
> But what is of more importance, the Roman Pontiffs, Our predecessors, extolled St. Thomas with the highest encomiums and distinguished praise....
>
> To the opinions of the greatest Pontiffs, Innocent VI, as if raising a monument to St. Thomas's memory, adds the declaration: "His teaching above all others, the canonical writings excepted, has such an accuracy of expression, such an arrangement of subjects, such a correctness of conclusions, that those who held to it have never been found to depart from the path of truth, and those who opposed it have always been suspected of unsoundness" (Sermon on Saint Thomas).
>
> And it was an honor reserved to St. Thomas alone...that the Fathers of Trent in their Hall of Assembly decided to place upon the altar, side by side with Holy Scripture and the Decrees of the Roman Pontiffs, the Summa of St. Thomas, to seek in it counsel, arguments, and decisions for their purpose.[27]

We must not suppose that in this matter the thinking of Leo XIII would differ from that of Saint Thomas. In this regard, the following sentence of the same Pontiff is worthy of special attention:

> We never intended to add anything either to the opinions of the great scholars on the value of different forms of government, or to Catholic doctrine and the traditions of this Apostolic See on the degree of obedience due to the constituted powers.[28]

Democracy being the government of the people, and the Church's concept of *people* being profoundly different from the current neopagan concept—which equates *people* with *mass*—it follows that the Catholic concept of democracy differs profoundly from what democracy is generally understood to be.[29]

In view of the egalitarian avalanche, and refraining from political preferences, Pius XII seeks to consider the democratic tendency as it exists and to guide it in order to prevent damage to the sociopolitical body.

---

[27] *American Catholic Quarterly Review*, Vol. 4, (October 1879), pp. 753-755 passim.

[28] Letter to Cardinal Mathieu, March 28, 1897, in *La paix intérieure des Nations* (Desclée & Cie., 1952), p. 220.

[29] See Chapter III.

He discloses this design when, during the reorganization of post-war Italy, he gave the Roman Nobility the following counsel:

> Everyone generally admits that this reorganization cannot be conceived as a pure and simple return to the past. Such a step backward is not possible. The world, despite its often disorderly, disconnected, fragmented, and incoherent movements, has continued to move ahead; history does not stop, it cannot stop; it is forever advancing, following its course, whether straight and orderly or twisted and confused, toward progress or toward an illusion of progress.[30]

When reconstructing a society, as when reconstructing a building, there are two extremes to avoid: one, merely archaeological reconstruction; the other, construction of an entirely different edifice, in which case it would not really be a reconstruction. The Pontiff says:

> Just as one could not conceive of reconstructing a building required to serve modern-day needs in the same manner as one would conceive of an archaeological reconstruction, likewise such rebuilding would not be possible following arbitrary designs, even if these were theoretically the best and most desirable. One must always bear in mind inescapable reality, the entire sweep and scope of reality.[31]

10. Highly Aristocratic Institutions Are Also Necessary in Democracies

Now, if the Church does not intend to destroy democracy, she certainly does desire that it be well understood and that the distinction between the Christian and revolutionary concepts of democracy be clear. It is timely to remember, in this vein, what Pius XII teaches about the traditional character and the aristocratic tone of a true Christian democracy.

> On another occasion, We spoke of the conditions necessary for a people to be ripe for a healthy democracy. Yet who can raise and nurture this state of ripeness? No doubt the Church could draw many lessons in this regard from the treasury of its experiences and its own civilizing activities. Yet your presence here today brings to mind one particular observation. As history will testify, wherever true democracy reigns, the life of the people is permeated with sound traditions, which it is not legitimate to destroy. The primary representatives of these traditions are the ruling classes, or rather, the groups of men and women, or the associations, which set the tone, as we say, for the village or the city, for the region or the entire country.
> Whence the existence and influence, among all civilized peoples, of aristocratic institutions, aristocratic in the highest sense of the word, like certain academies of

---

[30] RPN 1945, p. 274.

[31] Ibid.

Highly aristocratic institutions are also necessary in democracies.

West Point United States Military Academy.

widespread and well-deserved renown. And the nobility is in that number too. Without claiming any privilege or monopoly, it is, or ought to be, one of these institutions. It is a traditional institution, founded on the continuity of an ancient education. Of course, in a democratic society, which our own wishes to be, the mere title of birth no longer suffices to command authority or esteem; therefore, in order to preserve in worthy fashion your elevated station and social rank, indeed to increase it and raise it, you must truly be an elite, you must meet the conditions and fulfill the indispensable demands of the epoch wherein we live.[32]

The milieu of a true nobility or traditional elite is as it were a breeding ground where elevated qualities of intelligence, will, and sensibility are formed, thereby increasing its prestige with the merit of each successive generation. For Pius XII, this type of nobility or traditional elite is not a heterogeneous and contradictory element within a truly Christian democracy, but rather a precious element of it. Thus we perceive how different an authentically Christian democracy is from the egalitarian democracy proclaimed by the Revolution. For the latter, the destruction of all elites—and especially the nobility—is deemed an essential condition for democratic authenticity.[33]

---

[32] RPN 1946, pp. 340-341.

[33] On the legitimacy and necessity of the nobility's existence in an authentically Catholic society, see the substantial outline published under the title "Aristocracy" in an important homiletic work elaborated under the direction of Angel Cardinal Herrera Oria. It is transcribed and analyzed in Appendix V of this book.

CHAPTER VI

The Meaningful Contribution of the Nobility and Traditional Elites to the Solution of the Contemporary Crisis

The Teaching of Pius XII

*H*aving seen the legitimacy and necessity of the existence of traditional elites, we shall now present Pius XII's teachings on how these elites should act as leaders of society, through the qualities and virtues proper to them. Indeed, they have no right to exempt themselves from this responsibility.

1. Christian Virtue:
The Essence of Nobility

Today's noble should be, above all, a man in whom spiritual qualities shine. Christian virtue and the Christian ideal are part of the very essence of nobility.

> Lift your gaze and keep it fixed on the Christian ideal. All those upheavals, those evolutions and revolutions, have left it untouched. They can do nothing against what is the inner essence of true nobility, that which aspires to Christian perfection, the same that the Redeemer pointed to in the Sermon on the Mount. Unconditional loyalty to Catholic doctrine, to Christ, and to His Church; the ability and the will to be also models and guides for others.... You must present to the world, even to the world of believers and of practicing Catholics, the spectacle of a faultless conjugal life, the edification of a truly exemplary domestic hearth.[1]

Pius XII then calls the nobility to a holy intransigence.

---

[1]   RPN 1952, p. 458.

You must build a dike against every infiltration, into your home and your circles, of ruinous ideas, pernicious indulgences and tolerances that might contaminate and sully the purity of matrimony and family. Here indeed is an exemplary and holy enterprise, well suited to ignite the zeal of the Roman and Christian nobility in our times.[2]

a. The spiritual qualities of the contemporary noble

To overcome the grave obstacles that hinder the perfect fulfillment of his duty, a member of the nobility or traditional elites should be a man of valor. This is what the Vicar of Jesus Christ expects of him.

Therefore, what We expect of you is above all a strength of soul that even the harshest trials cannot vanquish; a strength of soul that should make you not only perfect soldiers of Christ for yourselves, but also, as it were, instructors and supporters for those who might be tempted to doubt or give in.

What We expect of you is, secondly, a readiness to act that is not daunted nor discouraged by any anticipation of sacrifice that might be required for the common good; a readiness and a fervor that, in making you swift to carry out all your duties as Catholics and citizens, should keep you from falling into an apathetic, inert "abstentionism," which would be a grievous sin at a time when the most vital interests of religion and country are at stake.

What We expect of you, lastly, is a generous adhesion—not under your breath and for the mere sake of formality, but from the bottom of your hearts and carried out without reservation—to Christian doctrine and the Christian life, to the precept of brotherhood and social justice, the observance of which cannot fail to ensure you spiritual and temporal happiness.

May this strength of soul, this fervor, this brotherly spirit guide every one of your steps and reaffirm your path in the course of the New Year, which has been so uncertain in its birth and almost seems to be leading you toward a dark tunnel.[3]

The Pontiff develops these concepts even more in his allocution of 1949.

All are in need of *strength of soul*, but especially so in our times, in order to bear the suffering bravely, to overcome life's difficulties victoriously, to constantly perform one's duty. Who does not have some reason for suffering? Who does not have some cause for sorrow? Who does not have something to fight for? Only he who surrenders and flees. Yet your right to surrender and flee is much less than that of others. Suffering and hardship today are commonly the lot of all classes, all social stations, all families, all persons. And if a few are exempt, if they swim in

---

[2]   Ibid.

[3]   RPN 1948, pp. 423-424.

The *trombettieri* of the Pontifical Noble Guard.
Their famous silver trumpets announced the arrival of the
Supreme Pontiff at Saint Peter's Basilica.

Vatican Museum (Giordani)

superabundance and enjoyment, this must spur them to take the miseries and hardships of others upon themselves. Who could find contentment and rest, who, rather, would not feel uneasy and ashamed, to live in idleness and frivolity, in luxury and pleasure, amid almost universal tribulation?

Readiness to act. In this moment of great personal and social solidarity, everyone must be ready to work, to sacrifice oneself, to devote oneself to the good of all. The difference lies not in the fact of obligation, but in the manner of fulfilling it. Is it not true that those who have more time and more abundant means at their disposal should be more assiduous and more solicitous in their desire to serve? In speaking of means, We are not referring only nor primarily to wealth, but to all the gifts of intelligence, culture, education, knowledge, and authority, which fate does not grant to certain privileged individuals for their exclusive advantage or to create an irremediable inequality among brothers, but rather for the good of the whole social community. In all that involves serving one's neighbor, society, the Church and God, you must always be the first. Therein lies your true rank of honor, your most noble preeminence.

Generous adhesion to the precepts of Christian doctrine and the Christian life. These are the same for all, for there are not two truths, nor two laws; rich and poor, big and small, noble and humble, all are equally expected to submit their intellects through faith in the same dogma, their wills through obedience to the same morals. Divine justice, however, will be much more severe toward those who have been given more, those who are better able to understand the sole doctrine and to put it into practice in everyday life, those who with their example and their authority can more easily direct others onto the road of justice and salvation, or else lose them on the fatal roads of unbelief and sin.[4]

These last words show that the Pontiff does not accept a nobility or a traditional elite that is not effectively and unselfishly apostolic. A nobility living for profit and not for Faith, without ideals and like the bourgeois (in the pejorative sense sometimes attributed to this word), is not a true nobility but a mere corpse thereof.[5]

b. Aristocratic chivalrousness: a bond of charity

The effective and enduring possession of these virtues and spiritual qualities naturally breeds chivalrous and distinguished manners. Does a noble, gifted with such qualities and manners, constitute an element of division among the social classes?

No. Far from being a divisive factor, a well-understood aristocratic chivalrousness is truly an element of union that gracefully penetrates the relationships be-

---

[4] RPN 1949, pp. 346-347.

[5] In this regard, see Saint Charles Borromeo's homily in Documents IV, 8.

tween the nobles and the members of the other social classes with whom they deal because of their occupation or activities.

This chivalrousness maintains the distinction of classes "without confusion or disorder,"[6] that is, without egalitarian leveling. Quite the contrary, it establishes friendly relations among them.

2. The Nobility and the Traditional Elites as Guides of Society

The spiritual qualities and chivalrous manners that derive from Christian virtues qualify the noble to exercise the mission of guiding society.

a. Guiding society: a form of apostolate

Today's multitudes need competent guides.

> The numberless, anonymous multitude is easily provoked to disorder; it surrenders blindly, passively, to the torrent that carries it away or to the whims of the currents that divide and divert it. Once it has become the plaything of the passions or interests of its agitators, as of its own illusions, it is no longer able to take root on the rock and stabilize itself to form a true people, that is, a living body with limbs and organs differentiated according to their respective forms and functions, yet working all together for its autonomous activity in order and unity.[7]

It is the responsibility of the nobility and the traditional elites to guide society, thereby accomplishing a brilliant apostolate.

> You could well become this elite. You have behind you an entire past of age-old traditions that represent fundamental values for the healthy life of a people. Among these traditions, of which you are rightfully proud, you number religiousness, the living and working Catholic faith, as the most important of all. Has history not already cruelly proved that any human society without a religious foundation rushes inevitably toward its dissolution and ends up in terror? In emulation of your ancestors, you should therefore shine in the eyes of the people with the light of your spiritual life, with the splendor of your unshakeable faith in Christ and the Church.
>
> Among these traditions is also the inviolate honor of a profoundly Christian conjugal and familial life. In all countries, or at least in those of Western civilization, there rises now a cry of anguish about marriage and the family, a cry so piercing it is impossible not to hear it. Here too, with your exemplary conduct you must put yourselves at the head of the movement for the reform and restoration of the domestic hearth.

---

[6] RPN 1945, p. 277.

[7] RPN 1946, p. 340; See Chapter III.

It also shows itself in what can be called humanism, that is, the presence, the intervention of the complete man in all the manifestations of his activities, even if specialized, in such a way that the specialization of his ability should never hypertrophy, should never atrophy, never becloud the general culture, just as in a musical phrase the dominant should never break the harmony nor burden the melody.

It is also made manifest in the dignity of one's entire bearing and conduct—a dignity that is not imperious, however, and that, far from emphasizing distances, only lets them appear when necessary to inspire in others a higher nobility of soul, mind, and heart.

Lastly, it manifests itself above all in the sense of lofty morality, or righteousness, honesty, and probity that must inform every word and every deed.[11]

Aristocratic refinement, so inherently worthy of admiration, would be useless and even harmful were it not based on a higher moral sense.

An immoral or amoral society that no longer distinguishes between right and wrong in its conscience or in its outward actions, that no longer feels horror at the sight of corruption but rather makes excuses for it, adapts to it indifferently, woos it with favors, practices it with no misgivings or remorse, indeed parades it without blushing, thereby degrading itself and making a mockery of virtue, is on the road to ruin....

True nobility is another matter altogether: In social relations it lets shine a humility filled with greatness, a charity untouched by any egotism or concern for one's own interest. We are not unaware of the tremendous goodness, gentleness, devotion, and self-abnegation with which many, and many among your number, have in these times of endless suffering and anguish bent down to aid the unfortunate and have been able to radiate about themselves the light of their charitable love, in all its most progressive and efficacious forms. And this is another aspect of your mission.[12]

"Humility filled with greatness": What an admirable expression, so opposed to the vain style of the jet set and to the vulgarity of today's supposedly democratic and modern manners, lifestyles, and way of being!

c. Elites with a traditional upbringing are profound observers of reality

A noble, gifted with a profoundly traditional spirit, can find in the experience of the past that lives in him the means to understand current issues better than many other people. Far from being on the fringes of reality, he is a subtle and profound observer of it.

There are ills in society, just as there are ills in individuals. It was a great event

---

[11]   Ibid., p. 276.

[12]   Ibid., pp. 276-277.

in the history of medicine when one day the famous Laennec, a man of genius and faith, anxiously bending over the chests of the sick and armed with the stethoscope he had invented, performed auscultation, distinguishing and interpreting the slightest breaths, the barely audible acoustic phenomena of the lungs and heart. Is it not perhaps a social duty of the first order and of the highest interest to go among the people and listen to the aspirations and malaise of our contemporaries, to hear and discern the beatings of their hearts, to seek remedies for common ills, to delicately touch their wounds to heal them and save them from the infection that might set in for want of care, making sure not to irritate them with too harsh a touch?

To understand and love in Christ's charity the people of your time, to give proof of this understanding and love through actions: This is the art and the way of doing that greater good that falls to you, doing it not only directly for those around you, but also in an almost limitless sphere. Then does your experience become a benefit for all. And in this area, how magnificent is the example set by so many noble spirits ardently and eagerly striving to bring about and spread a Christian social order![13]

Moved by Faith, the authentic and, therefore, genuinely traditional aristocrat, while preserving himself as such, can and must love the people, over whom he should exercise a truly Christian influence.

d. The authentically traditional aristocrat: an image of God's providence

But, someone might ask, will not the nobility belittle itself by assuming today's leadership posts? And will its love of the past not constitute an obstacle to the exercise of present activities? In this respect Pius XII teaches:

No less offensive to you, and no less damaging to society, would be the unfounded and unjust prejudice that did not hesitate to insinuate and have it believed that the patricians and nobles were failing in their honor and in the high office of their station in practicing and fulfilling their duties and functions, placing them alongside the general activity of the population. It is quite true that in ancient times the exercise of professions was usually considered beneath the dignity of nobles, except for the military profession; but even then, once armed defense made them free, more than a few of them readily gave themselves over to intellectual works or even manual labor. Nowadays, of course, with the changes in political and social conditions, it is not unusual to find the names of great families associated with progress in science, agriculture, industry, public administration, and government—and they are all the more perceptive observers of the present as well as confident and bold pioneers of the future, since with a steady hand they hold firm to the past, ready to take advantage of the experience of their ancestors but quick to be wary of the illusions and mistakes that have been the cause of many

---

[13]   RPN 1944, pp. 180-181.

"However horrible the incidents of war may be, the soldier who is called upon to offer and to give his life for his country is the noblest development of mankind."

(From a speech of General Douglas MacArthur at West Point)

false and dangerous steps.

As custodians, by your own choosing, of the true tradition honoring your families, the task and honor of contributing to the salvation of human society falls to you, to preserve it from the sterility to which the melancholy thinkers jealous of the past would condemn it and from the catastrophe to which the reckless adventurers and prophets dazzled by a false and mendacious future would lead it. In your work, above you and as it were within you, there shall appear the image of Divine Providence which with strength and gentleness disposes and directs all things toward their perfection (Wis. 8:1), as long as the folly of human pride does not intervene to thwart its designs, which are, however, always above evil, chance, and fortune. By such action you, too, shall be precious collaborators of the Church, which, even amid the turmoil and conflict, never ceases to foster the spiritual progress of nations, the city of God on earth in preparation for the eternal city.[14]

e. The aristocracy's mission among the poor

One aspect of the traditional elites' participation in the direction of society is their educational and charitable action. This is admirably described by Pius XII.

But, like every rich patrimony, this one brings with it some very strict duties, all the more strict as this patrimony is rich. There are two above all:

1) the duty not to squander such treasures, to pass them on whole, indeed increased, if possible, to those who will come after you; to resist, therefore, the temptation to see in them merely the means to a life of greater ease, pleasure, distinction and refinement;

2) the duty not to reserve these assets for yourselves alone, but to let them generously benefit those who have been less favored by Providence.

The nobility of beneficence and virtue, dear Sons and Daughters, was itself conquered by your ancestors, and bearing witness to this are the monuments and houses, the hospices, asylums, and hospitals of Rome, where their names and their memory bespeak their provident and vigilant kindness to the needy and unfortunate. We are well aware that in the Patriciate and the Roman Nobility this glory and challenge to do good, inasmuch as they have been in a position to do good, has not been lacking. Yet at this present, painful hour, in which the sky is troubled by watchful, suspicious nights, your spirit, while maintaining a noble seriousness, indeed a lifestyle of austerity that excludes all trifles and frivolous pleasures, which for every genteel heart are incompatible with the spectacle of so much suffering, feels all the more keenly the urge for charitable works impelling you to increase and multiply the merits you have already achieved in the alleviation of human misery and poverty.[15]

---

[14] Ibid., pp. 181-182.

[15] RPN 1941, pp. 364-365.

3. The Absent Leaders—
The Harm of Their Absence

a. Absenteeism and omission:
sin of the elites

Unfortunately, not a few members of the nobility and the traditional elites have a tendency to isolate themselves from contemporary life. Imagining themselves to be protected from the uncertainties of life by a secure patrimony and absorbed in memories of bygone days, some of them estrange themselves from real life. They shut themselves off from the outside world and let the days and years elapse in a careless, quiet life with no definite earthly objective.

Search for their names in apostolic works, in charitable activities, in diplomacy, in academia, in politics, in the arts, in the armed forces, in the financial world. It will be in vain. Save for some exceptions, they will be absent. Even in social life, where it would be natural for them to shine, their role is at times null. We may even witness the situation of a country, province, or city where everything happens as if they did not exist.

Why this absenteeism? The cause lies in a mixture of qualities and defects. If we were to examine closely the lifestyle of these elites, more often than not we would find it dignified, honest, even exemplary, because it is inspired by noble reminiscences of a profoundly Christian past. This past, however, seems not to have any meaning except for themselves. They cling to it with exacting obstinacy and alienate themselves from contemporary life. They do not perceive that among those reminiscences, there are elements that are no longer applicable to our day.[16] Nevertheless, that past still holds certain values, inspirations, propensities, and directives that could favorably and deeply influence the ''very different lifestyles'' of the ''new chapter [that] has begun.''[17]

This precious ensemble of spiritual, moral, cultural, and social values—of great importance both in the public and private spheres—is tradition, a life born of the past to lead the future. Upholding the permanence of tradition, the nobility and the analogous elites should exercise a profound and co-directive action of presence in society for the common good.

b. The absence of leaders:
a virtual complicity

One thus comprehends even better the moral irresponsibility implicit in the omissions of the perpetually absent elites.

---

[16] ''A page of history has been turned; a chapter has ended. A period has been placed, indicating the end of a social and economic past'' (RPN 1952, p. 457).

[17] Ibid.

Less difficult, on the other hand, is the task of determining, from the various options open to you, what should be your mode of conduct.

The first of these modes of conduct is unacceptable: that of the deserter, of him who was incorrectly called the *"emigré à l'intérieur"*;[18] it is the abstention of the angry, resentful man who, out of spite or discouragement, makes no use of his qualities or energies, participates in none of his country's and his epoch's activities, but rather withdraws—like Achilles in his tent, near the swift-moving boats, far from the battles[19]—while the destinies of the fatherland are at stake.

Abstention is even less appropriate when it is the result of an indolent, passive indifference. Indeed, worse than ill humor, worse than spite and discouragement, would be nonchalance in the face of a ruin into which one's own brothers, one's own people, were about to fall. In vain would it attempt to hide behind the mask of neutrality; it is not at all neutral; it is, like it or not, complicit. Each light snowflake falling softly on the mountain's slope and adorning it with its whiteness plays its part, while letting itself be dragged along, in turning the little clump of snow that breaks away from the peak into the avalanche that brings disaster to the valley, crushing and burying peaceful homes. Only the solid mass, which is one with the rock of the foundation, can victoriously resist and stop the avalanche, or at least diminish its destructive course.

In this same way the man who is just and firm in his desire for good, the man of whom Horace speaks in a famous ode (*Carmen Secularae*, III, 3), who does not let himself be moved in his unshakeable thought by the furor of the citizens who give criminal orders nor by the tyrant's menacing scowl, but remains undaunted, even should the universe crumble over his head: *"si fractus inlabatur orbis, impavidum ferient ruinae."* Yet if this just and strong man is a Christian, he will not content himself with standing erect and impassive amid the ruins; he will feel duty-bound to resist and prevent catastrophe, or at least to limit its damage. And if he cannot contain its destructive force, he will be there again to rebuild the demolished edifice, to sow the devastated field. That is what your conduct should rightly be. It must consist—without having to renounce the freedom of your convictions and your opinions on human vicissitudes—in accepting the contingent order of things such as it is, and in directing its efficiency toward the good, not of a specific class, but of the entire community.[20]

With these last words the Pope insists on the principle that, as long as it fulfills its duty, a traditional elite benefits the whole social body.

---

[18] "Emigrant to the countryside": The Pontiff borrows the French political expression of the 1830s used to designate the nobles who left Paris after the accession of the Duke of Orleans to the throne as "King of the French." Not agreeing with his accession, in which they saw a revolutionary usurpation, these nobles went to live in their respective castles in the countryside.

The expression highlights the contrast between the attitude of these aristocrats, who "emigrated" without leaving the national territory, and their predecessors of 1789, who preferred to rally outside the country, in order to prepare an attack against the French Revolution.

[19] According to the narration in Homer's *Iliad*, Achilles, the most famous hero of the Trojan War, enraged with Agamemnon, the leader of the Greek army, withdrew to his tent, thus nearly causing the loss of the war.

[20] RPN 1947, pp. 368-369.

4. Another Way to Shirk One's Mission:
To Allow Oneself to Be Corrupted
and Debased

The nobility and the traditional elites can also sin against their mission by allowing themselves to deteriorate through impiety and immorality.

> The French high society of the eighteenth century was one tragic example of this, among so many others. Never was a society more refined, more elegant, more brilliant, more fascinating. The most varied pleasures of the mind, an intense intellectual culture, a very refined art of pleasure, and an exquisite delicacy of manners and language predominated in that outwardly so courtly and gracious society, and yet everything in it—books, stories, images, furniture, clothing, hair-styles—encouraged a sensuality that penetrated one's veins and one's heart, and even marital infidelity scarcely surprised or scandalized anyone anymore. Thus did that society work toward its own downfall, rushing headlong toward the abyss it had dug out with its own hands.[21]

When they become corrupt like this, the nobility and the traditional elites exert a tragically destructive action upon society, which should see in them an example and an incentive for the practice of virtue and goodness. In the contemporary crisis, they therefore have the duty of making reparation for their destructive action in the past and at present.

History is forged principally by the elites. Because of this, if the action of the Christian nobility in the past was highly beneficial, the paganization of the nobility was one of the sources of the catastrophic contemporary crisis.

> It is useful, however, to recall that this movement toward unbelief and irreligion found its starting point not from below but from above, that is to say, in the ruling classes, in the upper tiers of society, the nobility, the thinkers and philosophers. We do not, mind you, mean all the nobility, much less the Roman nobility, which has greatly distinguished itself for its loyalty to the Church and to this Apostolic See— and the eloquent and filial expressions We have just heard are yet another luminous demonstration thereof—but rather, the nobility of Europe in general. Does one not clearly perceive in the Christian West in the last few centuries a spiritual evolution which, horizontally and vertically, breadthwise and lengthwise, so to speak, has been progressively undermining and demolishing the Faith, leading to that devastation visible today in the multitudes of men without religion or hostile to religion, or at least animated and confused by a profound and ill-conceived skepticism toward the supernatural and Christianity?
>
> The vanguard of this evolution was the so-called Protestant Reformation, during whose vicissitudes and wars a large part of Europe's nobility broke away from the

---

[21]   RPN 1945, pp. 276-277.

Foto Felici S.d.F. (Rome)

"You have behind you an entire past of age-old traditions that represent fundamental values for the healthy life of a people. Among these traditions, of which you are rightfully proud, you number religiousness, the living and working Catholic faith, as the most important of all. Has history not already cruelly proved that any human society without a religious foundation rushes inevitably toward its dissolution and ends up in terror? In emulation of your ancestors, you should therefore shine in the eyes of the people with the light of your spiritual life, with the splendor of your unshakeable faith in Christ and the Church.

"Among these traditions is also the inviolate honor of a profoundly Christian conjugal and familial life. In all countries, or at least in those of Western civilization, there rises now a cry of anguish about marriage and the family, a cry so piercing it is impossible not to hear it. Here too, with your exemplary conduct you must put yourselves at the head of the movement for the reform and restoration of the domestic hearth." *(Pius XII, allocution of 1946)*

Catholic Church and appropriated her possessions. But unbelief properly speaking spread in the age that preceded the French Revolution. Historians note that atheism, even in the guise of deism, had become widespread at that time in high society in France and elsewhere; belief in a God who was Creator and Redeemer had become, in that world given over to all the pleasures of the senses, something almost ridiculous and unseemly for cultivated minds avid for novelty and progress. In the greater number of the salons of the greatest and most refined ladies, where the most arduous questions of religion, philosophy, and politics were tossed about, literati and philosophers, champions of subversive doctrines, were considered the finest, most eagerly sought ornaments of those worldly meeting-places. Impiety was fashionable in the high nobility, and the writers most in vogue would have been less audacious in their attacks on religion if they had not enjoyed the approval and incitement of the most elegant high society. Not that all the nobility and all the philosophers set their sights on the immediate de-Christianization of the masses. On the contrary, religion was supposed to remain, for the simple people, as a means of governance in the hands of the State. They, however, felt themselves and thought themselves to be above faith and its moral precepts, a policy that very quickly proved to be deadly and shortsighted, even when considered from a purely psychological perspective. With inexorable logic, the people, powerful in goodness and terrible in evil, always know how to draw practical conclusions from their observations and judgments, however well-founded or mistaken they may be.

Take the history of civilization of the last two centuries: It clearly reveals and demonstrates the damage to the faith and morals of nations wrought by bad examples being set and handed down from above, the religious frivolity of the upper classes, the open intellectual struggle against the revealed truth.[22]

5. For the Common Good of Society: Preferential Option for the Nobility in the Field of Apostolate

Much is said about the apostolate on behalf of the masses and its corollary, preferential action in favor of their material needs. But it is important not to be one-sided in this matter and never to forget the great importance of the apostolate to the elites and, through them, to the whole social body. It is likewise necessary never to lose sight of the importance of a related apostolic preference for the nobles. In this way, with great benefit to social concord, a preferential option for the poor will be harmoniously complemented by a preferential option for the nobles and for the analogous elites. Pius XII states:

> Now, what conclusion are we to draw from these lessons of history? That today salvation must begin there, at the place where the perversion had its origin. It is not in itself difficult to maintain religion and sound morals in the people when the

---

[22] RPN 1943, pp. 358-360.

upper classes set a good example and create public conditions that do not make a Christian education immeasurably onerous, but rather promote it as something sweet and to be imitated. Is your duty not the same, beloved Sons and Daughters, you who, by the nobility of your families and the offices you often hold, belong to the ruling classes? The great mission which to you and to very few others has been assigned—that is, first to reform and perfect private life in yourselves and in your homes, and then to apply yourselves, each in his place and in his share, to bring forth a Christian order in public life—does not admit postponement or delay. It is a most noble mission, rich with promises, especially at a moment when, in reaction to a devastating, demoralizing materialism, a new thirst for spiritual values has been emerging in the masses, and minds are opening up to religious things, in a move away from unbelief. These developments allow one to hope that the lowest point of spiritual decline has by now been left behind. To all of you, therefore, falls the glory, by the light and appeal of good examples raising themselves above all mediocrity, of working together to make these initiatives and aspirations to religious and social good achieve their happy fulfillment.[23]

The specific apostolate of the nobility and of the traditional elites continues, therefore, to be of the greatest importance.

---

[23] Ibid, pp. 360-361.

Statue of Saint Louis IX,
King of France, in
Saint Louis, Missouri.

CHAPTER VII

Genesis of the Nobility
Its Past and Present Mission

Pius XII's Main Emphasis

𝒯he study of the allocutions of Pius XII to the Roman Patriciate and Nobility arouses the curiosity of the average person, especially because the public is often surprisingly uninformed about the nobility, its origins, its role, and the various traits it has assumed throughout the ages.

His curiosity, however, may not be wholly satisfied by reading these allocutions. In them, the Pontiff did not comment on the nobility in all its aspects. This is not surprising, since he was addressing nobles, naturally acquainted with many doctrinal and historical facts concerning the nobility. This may not be the case with readers of this work.

To satisfy the curiosity of many intelligent but incompletely informed readers, this chapter presents a compilation of facts about the nobility that may be difficult to find readily available in a single work.

Containing multiple considerations on diverse themes, this chapter is naturally one of the book's longest. In order not to extend it, the number of citations has been limited to an indispensable minimum.

1. The Private Sphere and the Common Good

a. Human groups—leaders

In any human group existing in the private sphere, the exercise of authority confers a certain prominence. This is the case of a father—and, in participation with him, his wife—the president of an association, a professor, the coach of an athletic team, and so on.

1) Intellectual requisites of a leader

The exercise of authority requires certain qualities. In the first place, the leader must have a clear and firm notion of the objective and the common good of the group he directs. Then he needs a lucid knowledge of the means and procedures to attain this good.

These intellectual qualities, however, do not suffice.

The leader must also be able to communicate his knowledge and, as much as possible, persuade those who differ. However broad his powers, however drastic the penalties imposed on those who disobey, however honorable and generous the rewards conferred on those who do obey, these factors are not enough for the leader to make himself obeyed.

A profound and stable consensus must exist between his subordinates and him regarding his objectives and methods. His subordinates must also have earnest confidence in his capacity to employ these methods correctly and achieve these goals, all in view of attaining the common good.

2) Requisites of the will and the sensibility

Moreover, it is insufficient for the leader merely to persuade through flawless logical argumentation. Other attributes are also necessary. These lie in the realm of the will and the sensibility.

Above all, the leader must be gifted with a penetrating psychological sense. This quality requires the simultaneous exercise of the intelligence, will, and sensibility. A very intelligent but weak-willed and unperceptive person ordinarily lacks the psychological sense needed to fathom even elementary aspects of his own mentality. How much less can he fathom that of others, such as his spouse, children, students, and employees. For a leader lacking psychological sense it is difficult not only to persuade the minds of subordinates but also to unite their wills for a common action.

Not even this psychological sense, however, suffices. The leader must also be endowed with a sensibility rich enough to suffuse whatever he says with the flavor of reality, honesty, authenticity, and a touch of interest and inspiration that prompts those who should obey him to follow joyfully.

In brief, these are the qualities without which someone who presides over a private social group will lack the conditions to fulfill his mission in ordinary circumstances.

3) The leader in exceptional circumstances, whether favorable or adverse

However, exceptional circumstances, whether favorable or adverse, occasionally alter the normal order in any private group.

Unable to rise to the occasion, the average leader risks losing the excellent opportunities that he either fathoms incompletely or misses altogether. In this way, he lets them slip by, taking either partial advantage of them or no advantage at all.

Should he prove incapable of discerning danger when it appears on the horizon, evaluating the threat it poses, and devising means to eliminate it as quickly as possible, he risks seriously harming the group under his direction and even causing its ruin.

When confronted with exceptional occasions, whether favorable or unfavorable, a good leader is stimulated by them and grows in his qualities in proportion to the exceptional nature of the circumstances, thereby proving himself superior to them.

4) The usefulness and timeliness of
   systematizing these concepts

None of this is new. However, since these commonsense ideas have become blurred in many minds in our confused times, a succinct systematization has become necessary for easily understanding what follows.

b. The superiority and nobility of the common good—its distinction from the individual good—private organizations whose common good has a transcendent character, whether regional or national

Regarding groups of any kind in the private sector, we can say that since the common good of the group—in other words, its general good—is higher than the individual good of its members, it is ipso facto nobler.

1) The importance of private-sector
   organizations for the common good of the
   region, the nation, and the State

At times the common good of a private organization transcends itself, rising to another level.

We will illustrate this point with the following example:

A private university—of which there are so many in America and Europe—frequently develops its own style of researching, thinking, and teaching. Its intellectual achievements are molded by this style and corresponding religious, patriotic, artistic, and cultural impulses. Having distilled an enduring set of values, the university perfects and transmits it from one generation of teachers and students to the next. This tradition constitutes a precious boon for the successive generations of academics. It deeply marks the lives of the graduates and creates a human type that can influence the character of the city around or near the university. It is obvious that this institution, although private, constitutes a common good for the region and, depending on the case, the whole country.

Private institutions like this university enable us to understand better the regional or national common good. Their excellence brings them closer to this common good, and thus they acquire a certain nobility that is not to be confused with the dignity, indeed authentic, of institutions limited to the private sector.

2) The family: a special private society

Of all these private institutions, none is as fundamental as the family: the greatest source of authentic and dynamic life for the nation and the State. It will be discussed in section two of this chapter.

* * *

Thus we see how the impact and influence of private institutions can deeply mark the political life of a nation, and even the international order, and thus safeguard the country from cliques of adventurers. This impact and influence result largely from the intensity, vitality, and cohesion of these institutions, and from the continuous striving for improvement that animates them.

c. The nation and the State are born from the private sphere—the plenitude of the common good

1) The formation of nations and regions

A nation is born when an ensemble of people, social groups, and associations dedicated to the private good—or cumulatively to the private and the common good—coalesce into a whole that is clearly distinct from everything outside it. It becomes a closed circuit of an ethnic, cultural, social, economic, and political character, and does not allow itself to be included or federated into any larger whole. The common good of this nation, which constitutes a state when politically organized, hovers above the good of each of the constituent groups. The latter, in turn, hovers over the good of each individual.[1]

An analogous affirmation could be made with regard to a region. A region is a territorial reality with an ensemble of constituent elements similar to those of a nation. It differs from the nation in that it does not embrace all the constituent elements of a nation, but only a significant part of them. The difference between the various regions of a nation results from the fact that the constituent elements usually vary from one region to another.

A comparison may clarify this point. Regions differ from each other and from

---

[1] The term *hovers* requires an explanation. It suggests a superiority that exists for the benefit of the successively lower orders. The State is at the summit of this social structure; at times it is like a roof that weighs upon the walls but at the same time protects them from inclement weather; at times it is like a tower that hovers over a group of buildings, adding beauty to them, serving as a bridge between the earthly and the heavenly, inspiring enchantment, enthusiasm, and elevation of spirit in those over whom it hovers.

Like a roof or a tower, the state structure should have all the necessary solidity, combined with the maximum lightness: one pound less than necessary may cause its downfall; one pound more than necessary may impart a certain ungraceful and oppressive aspect to the structure.

the nation as a whole like different carvings in the same stone. Nations differ from one another like one statue from another.

Sovereignty is proper to nations; autonomy is proper to regions. An example of this is found in federal states, which are sovereign and composed of autonomous federated units.

2) The State as a perfect society—
its sovereignty and majesty—
its supreme nobility

The common good in this sense encompasses all subordinate goods without absorbing or repressing them. This encompassing gives the State a supremacy of mission, power, and, therefore, intrinsic dignity, which is adequately expressed by the word *majesty*.[2] A nation normally constitutes a complete and *perfect*[3] society. Regardless of its form of government, this society is sovereign and majestic.

Its majestic power is supremely noble. By virtue of being sovereign, that is, supreme, it has an intrinsic natural nobility superior to that of the intermediate bodies between the individual and the State.

Everything said before corroborates this.

2. The Family Vis-à-vis the Individual, the Intermediate Bodies, and the State

At this point several questions arise. What is the family's relationship to the bodies that mediate between the individual and the State? More specifically, what is its relationship to these bodies according to their various connections to the common good? Above all, what is its relationship to the body that encompasses, unites, and governs all the other bodies, that is, the State and its supreme directive organ, the government?

We have already referred to the family as one of the intermediate bodies. We may add here that its situation vis-à-vis these other bodies is entirely unique. While the latter tend to differ from each other, the family, for its part, tends to permeate them all. None of these bodies can exercise over the family an influence equal to that which the family can exercise over them.

---

[2] The Latin *majestas* derives from *major*, the comparative form of *magnus*, which means *great*, both in the physical and moral senses. It often includes the accessory meaning of force, power, and nobility. This makes *magnus* an honorific or laudatory epithet in elevated language. The same meaning extends to its derivatives and composites. (Cf. A. Ernout and A. Meillet, *Dictionnaire etymologique de la langue latine—Histoire des mots*, 4th ed., [Paris: Editions Klincksieck, 1979], p. 377.)

[3] From the Latin *perfecta*, which means completed, finished, terminated.

a. From the individual to the family, from the family to the *gens*, and finally to the tribe—the process toward the foundation of the *civitas*—the State is born

Marriage is the common state of man. Therefore, it is as a member of his family that a man joins the great fabric of families that make up the social body of a country.

The social body is also formed of other intermediate groups such as guilds, universities, and local governments. An individual's admission into one of these groups is also a means of integration into the social body.

When we consider the State's origin, we see that, in one way or another, it arose from entities whose "raw material" was the family. The family had given rise to large family blocs that the Greeks termed *génos* and the Romans *gens*. The *gens*, in turn, formed larger blocs still of a familial nature, but whose genealogical correlations tended to be diluted and lost in the night of time. These were the *phratries* of the Greeks and the *curiae* of the Romans. "The association," explains Fustel de Coulanges, "naturally continued to grow larger in the same manner. Many curiae or phratries grouped together and formed a tribe."[4] Later, the ensemble of tribes formed the city, or better, the *civitas*; and with it the State.[5]

b. The main elements of the common good of the intermediate bodies, the region, and the State are already present in the individual and the family— the fruitful family: a small world

Experience shows that a family's vitality and unity are usually in direct proportion to its fecundity.

In large families, the children normally look up to the parents as leaders of a sizeable community, given the number of its members as well as the considerable religious, moral, cultural and material values inherent to the family unit. This surrounds parental authority with prestige. The parents are, in a way, a common good of all the children. Thus, it is normal that none of the children try to monopolize all the parents' attention and affection, making of them a merely individual good. Jealousy among siblings finds scant favorable ground in large families. On the contrary, it can easily arise in families with few children.

Tension between parents and children is also frequent in small families and tends to result in one side tyrannizing the other. For example, parents can abuse their authority by absenting themselves from the home in order to spend their

---

[4]   Numa Denis Fustel de Coulanges, *La Cité Antique* (Paris: Hachette, n.d.), bk. 3, p. 135.

[5]   On this theme, see the texts of Fustel de Coulanges, Frantz Funck-Brentano, and Msgr. Henri Delassus in Documents VII, VIII, and IX, respectively.

free time in worldly entertainments, leaving the children to the mercenary care of baby-sitters or scattered in the chaos of turbulent boarding schools devoid of any real affection. Parents can also tyrannize their children through various forms of family violence, so cruel and so frequent in our de-Christianized society.

In larger families, these domestic tyrannies become less likely. The children perceive more clearly how much they weigh upon their parents, and therefore tend to be grateful, helping them reverently, and, at the appropriate time, sharing the burdens of family affairs.

On the other hand, a large number of children brings to the home liveliness and joy, and an endless creative originality in ways of being, acting, feeling, and analyzing reality both inside and outside the home. Family conviviality becomes a school of wisdom and experience made up of a tradition solicitously communicated by the parents and prudently renewed by the children. The family thus constitutes a small world, at once open and closed to the influences of the outside world.

The cohesion of this small world results from all the aforementioned factors. It is strengthened mainly by the religious and moral formation given by the parents in consonance with the parish priest, and by the harmonic convergence of inherited physical and moral qualities that contribute to model the personalities of the children.

c. Families: small worlds that interrelate like nations and states

The characteristics that differentiate the small world of one family from that of another bring to mind the differences between regions of a country or between countries in the same area of civilization.

A family constituted in this way usually has a common temperament as well as common yearnings, tendencies, and aversions. It has its own way of living together, resting, working, solving problems, facing adversities, and profiting from favorable circumstances. In all these fields, large families show patterns of thought and behavior reinforced by the example of ancestors who are frequently idealized by nostalgia and the passing of time.

d. The family and the world of professional or public activities—lineages and professions

Continually enriched by new aspects modeled by a tradition that is admired, respected, and loved by all family members, this incomparable school of continuity greatly influences individuals in their choice of a profession or charge to be exercised in favor of the common good.

As a result, it frequently happens that members of a family choose the same profession, forming professional lineages. In this way, the family's influence permeates the professional world. In this consortium between the professional or public world on the one hand and the family on the other, the former also influences the latter. A natural and highly desirable symbiosis is thus established. However, it is important to note that, by the very nature of things, the family's influence on the extrinsic activities is normally greater than the influence of these activities on the family.

When the family is authentically Catholic, its natural and spontaneous cohesion is enhanced by the supernatural strength of mutual charity derived from grace. In such conditions, the family is optimally poised to influence all, or almost all, the intermediate bodies between the individual and the State, and finally the State itself.

e. Family lineages form elites even in the most plebeian professional groups or milieus

With these considerations, we can see how the presence, in all social classes, of lineages filled with tradition and creative force is a precious and irreplaceable ordering factor in individual life, the private sector, and public life.

We can also see why the administration of some private bodies customarily ends up in the hands of lineages that prove to be the most gifted in understanding and coordinating the social group, to which they impart a robust tradition and a vigorous impulse toward continual improvement.

In view of this it is legitimate that a para-nobiliary elite or dominant para-dynastic lineage arise within some of these groups. Its appearance contributes to the formation, in rural sub-regions and regions, of local "dynasties" analogous to a family endowed with royal majesty.

f. Human society is hierarchical and, as such, participative—kingly fathers and fatherly kings

In this light, a nation is an ensemble of social bodies. At times these are likewise constituted by gradually lesser bodies, down to the individual.

If we follow the inverse order, we will clearly perceive the gradational and, as such, hierarchical character of the bodies between the individual and the highest level of government.

Since the social fabric is an extensive network of individuals, families, and intermediate bodies, we may conclude that, from a certain viewpoint, it is also an ensemble of diverse hierarchies that coexist, collaborate, and intertwine. Above them hovers, in the temporal sphere, the majesty of a perfect society, the State; and in the spiritual sphere (the highest one) the majesty of the other perfect society, the Church.

This society of elites is highly participative. In it, refinement, influence, prestige, wealth, and power are shared from top to bottom in diverse ways according to each degree by bodies with particular characteristics. Thus in the past it could

Charlemagne, crowned emperor on Christmas Day of the year 800 by Pope Saint Leo III, profoundly marked the outlook of all succeeding generations.
Even today his great role in history is recalled with admiration and reverence.

be said that in the home, even the most modest home, the father was the king of his children, while at the summit the king was the father of fathers.[6]

3. Historical Origins of the Feudal Nobility—The Genesis of Feudalism

In this context, it is easier to understand what the nobility is. It is the class that, unlike others, does not merely have elements of nobility, but is fully noble, entirely noble; it is noble par excellence.

A word about its historical origins is appropriate here.

a. The class of landowners constitutes a military nobility and a political authority

The grand Carolingian empire had been reduced to rubble. Devastating incursions of barbarians, Normans, Hungarians, and Saracens preyed upon its ruins. Attacked on all sides and unable to resist with recourse to the greatly weakened central power of the kings, the populations naturally turned to their respective landowners, demanding that they command and govern them in such calamitous circumstances. Heeding their request, the landowners built fortifications for themselves and for their own.

True to the profoundly Christian spirit of the time, "their own" paternally included not only family members, but the manorial society, formed by the domestic servants, manual workers, and their respective families living on the lord's lands. All received shelter, food, religious assistance, and military leadership in these fortifications that, with time, became imposing seignorial castles, of which so many still remain. Within these fortifications, peasants safeguarded the movable goods and livestock they had managed to save from the invaders' greed.

In military action, the landowner and his family were the foremost combatants. Their duty was to command, to be in the vanguard, leading the most daring offensives and the most determined resistance. The condition of military leader and hero was now added to the condition of landowner.

Quite naturally, these circumstances translated during the intervals of peace into local political power over the surrounding lands. This made the landowner a lord, *dominus*, in the full sense of the word, with the duties of lawmaker and judge. As such, he became a link of union with the king.

---

[6]   It is interesting to mention the commentary contained in Frantz Funck-Brentano's *L'Ancien Régime* which quotes the memoirs of the peasant Retif de la Bretonne: "The State is a large family composed of all the private families, and the Prince [that is the monarch] is the father of all the fathers."

About this close link between the condition of a king and that of a father, Saint Thomas Aquinas declares: "He who rules a home is called a father of a family, not a king. Still, he bears a certain resemblance to a king, on account of which, kings are sometimes called the fathers of peoples" *(On the Governance of Rulers* [London: Sheed and Ward, 1938], p. 39).

Saint Paul magnificently teaches us about the sacred character of paternal authority: "For this cause I bow my knees to the Father of Our Lord Jesus Christ, of whom all paternity in heaven and earth is named" (Eph. 3:14-15).

See also the text by Msgr. Henri Delassus in Documents IX.

b. The noble class: subordinate participation in royal power

Thus, the noble class developed as a subordinate participation in the royal power.

This noble class oversaw the common good of the private sphere, that is, the preservation and improvement of agriculture and livestock raising, from which both nobles and plebeians lived. As the king's representatives in the area, they were also responsible for the common good of the public sphere. More elevated and universal than the private common good, the public common good was intrinsically noble.

The nobility also participated in the central power of the monarch. The higher nobles were frequently royal councillors. Most of the ministers, ambassadors, and generals were members of the nobility, which thus held posts indispensable to the exercise of the supreme government of the country.

The link between high public office and the nobiliary condition was such that, when the common good required that plebeians be elevated to these posts, they were usually ennobled, frequently with hereditary titles.

Endowed by circumstances with a mission higher than mere farming—namely, the partial overseeing of the *salus publica* in war and peace—the landowner found himself invested with local powers that normally belonged to the government. Hence he automatically rose to a higher condition. He became a miniature of the king, since his mission was an intrinsic participation in the nobility of the royal mission itself.

From the spontaneous circumstances of history the figure of the landowner-lord emerged. His mission, at once private and noble, was gradually broadened as Christian Europe, increasingly free of afflictions and external threats, enjoyed longer periods of peace. It did not cease to expand for a long time.

c. The regions are defined—the regional common good—the local lord

This new situation enabled people to expand their horizons, thoughts, and activities to gradually vaster fields. Regions were born, shaped by local factors such as geographic characteristics, military necessities, commercial interests, and the influx of pilgrims to popular shrines, students to renowned universities, and merchants to famous fairs.

Psychological affinities also contributed to the formation of these regions. These affinities resulted from a long past of fighting common enemies, a similarity of language, customs, artistic expressions, and so on.

The regional common good thus encompassed the several local common goods, and was therefore higher and nobler.

The direction of this regional common good naturally befell some higher lord, owner of vaster dominions, more powerful, more representative of the whole region, and therefore more capable of uniting the various areas without harm to their autonomies, whether for reasons of war or peacetime pursuits.

The regional lord was a miniature of the king in the region. His station entailed rights and duties intrinsically nobler than those of the landowner-lord, a miniature of the king in the locale. Therefore, the feudal lord (the noble landowner-lord whose numerous workers participated in his property rights through a link similar to today's emphyteusis[7]) owed the regional lord a vassalage analogous to that rendered by the regional lord to the king. This resulted in the formation of a nobiliary hierarchy at the top of the social hierarchy.

d. The medieval king

Of course, in principle none of this existed independently of or in opposition to the king, the supreme symbol of the people and the nation. On the contrary, it existed under his tutelar aegis and supreme power in order to preserve on his behalf this great organic whole of autonomous regions and locales that was the nation.

Even when the de facto royal power was at its weakest, the unitary monarchical principle was never contested. A nostalgia for royal unity—and even, in many places, for the Carolingian imperial unity, which embraced all of Christendom— never ceased to exist throughout the Middle Ages. As the kings gradually recovered the means to exercise a power that effectively encompassed the whole realm and represented its common good, they did so.

This immense consolidation, definition, and organization, first at the local level and then at the regional level, followed by a no lesser re-articulation of the national unity and authority, did not occur without strife. Here and there excessive claims, formulated in a unilateral and passionate way, were made both by representatives of legitimate autonomies and by promoters of necessary unifications. This generally led to feudal wars that, at times, were long and intertwined with international conflicts.

Such was the heavy price men paid because of Original Sin, actual sins, and softness or complacency, when not surrender, in the struggle against the spirit of evil.

Despite these obstacles, the profound meaning of the history of feudalism and the nobility cannot be understood without considering what was said above. This is how the society and state of the Middle Ages were modeled.

In some places the origin and development of the feudal regime varied according to the local circumstances. The exemplification above, therefore, does not apply to all European states. Many of its elements, however, are present in the history of kingdoms that did not have a feudal regime in the full sense of the word, as, for example, Portugal and Spain.[8]

---

[7] A juridical term meaning a perpetual right to the use of land that is the property of someone else.

[8] Cf. José Mattoso, *A Nobreza Medieval Portuguesa* (Lisbon: Editorial Estampa, 1981), pp. 27-28, and *Enciclopedia universal ilustrada*, Espasa-Calpe, Vol. 21, pp. 955, 958, and Vol. 23, p. 1139.

The Gothic Chapel at
The Cloisters museum
in New York City.

e. The feudal regime: a factor of unity or division?—The experience of contemporary federalism

Many historians see the feudalism of certain regions of Europe and the para-feudal agrarian arrangements of others as dangerously divisive.

Experience shows, however, that autonomy per se is not necessarily a factor of disunity.

No one today sees divisive factors in the autonomy of the states forming the federal republics on the American continents. On the contrary, one sees flexible, resilient, and fruitful relationships. One sees an intelligently planned union. Regionalism does not mean hostility among the parts, or between the parts and the whole, but harmonious autonomy and spiritual and material richness, both in the features common to all the regions and in the peculiarities of each.

4. The Mutual Shaping of the Noble and the Nobility

a. Genesis—a process based on custom

Seeing the nobility as it existed at its peak in medieval and post-medieval Europe, and also the image its admirers form of it today—whether in Europe or in the nations born of the Discoveries, the organizational genius of the European peoples, and the missionary zeal of the Church—we notice that it is rooted in certain coherent principles. These constitute a doctrine that has remained essentially the same *semper et ubique*, albeit with notable variations according to time and place.

We can discern the germination of this doctrine in the mentality of the European peoples of the early Middle Ages as they shaped the nobiliary institutions, usually by way of custom. Historically, this doctrine reached its widest and most logical application at the height of the Middle Ages. This occurred in step with the full and harmonious expansion of feudalism and its ramifications in the political, social, and economic fields.

We must emphasize that this theoretical-consuetudinary elaboration was carried out simultaneously and harmoniously not only by the noble families but by the rest of the social body as well, notably the clergy, universities, and other intermediate bodies. From intellectuals exploring the highest regions of human thought, down to modest bourgeois and simple manual laborers, everyone contributed to the process.

This process is so natural that it continues in several fields even in our troubled century.

b. Some examples

Before the First World War, the German army was largely modeled by the idea that public opinion, deeply influenced by Prussian militarism, had of it. An analogous process had shaped the gestalt of Kaiser Wilhelm II, symbol of the army and the nation. A similar affirmation could be made (with less of a military note) about the idea public opinion in other countries had of their respective monarchs and armed forces, as, for example, Franz Josef in Austria and Edward VII in England.

We use these historical examples because they are indisputable... if anything is indisputable in these matters.

As for the perenniality of this process, it suffices to mention the marriage ceremony of Charles and Diana, the Prince and Princess of Wales. The ancient and resplendent ceremony caused a universal wave of enthusiasm, which, in turn, strengthened the already classic psychological and moral profile expected of an heir apparent and his wife by the age-old yearnings of England. The ceremony also revealed the incidental modernizations the country wants to introduce into this profile and, therefore, into the general physiognomy of the nation.

These examples illustrate how a whole nation, with little clash among its currents, can gradually and prudently shape institutions like the nobility through a force of custom that is spontaneous, creative, conservative and restorative.

5. Absolute Monarchy: Hypertrophy of Royalty Leading to the Populist Totalitarian State

The harmonious result attained in feudal society began to crumble with the dissemination of the principles of the legists[9] and other factors. From then until the Revolution of 1789, royal power in Europe tended to absorb the ancient autonomies and to become ever more centralizing.

a. The absolute monarchy absorbs the subordinate bodies and powers

The absolute monarchy spreading throughout Europe was very different from the system of superposed elites, noble or otherwise, which had existed in so many nations. The powers formerly spread among the various levels were gradually concentrated in the hands of the king, who increasingly identified himself with the State. Whence the famous phrase attributed to Louis XIV: *"L'Etat, c'est moi."*

In contrast to the feudal monarch, the absolute monarch of modern times was surrounded by a nobility that accompanied him day and night, serving him mainly as an ornamental element without any effective power. In this way, the absolute king found himself separated from the rest of the nation by a deep trench, or better, an abyss. Such was the case in the modern French monarchy, for example, which had in Louis XIV, the Sun King, its most complete model.[10]

---

[9]   *Legist*: name given to royal counselors at the end of the Middle Ages who, drawing on ancient Roman Law, strove to develop royal absolutism and to oppose feudalism.

[10]   The absorption of nobility by centralization and the hypertrophy of royal power did not equally affect the nobilities of every country and every region within a country.

With greater or lesser eagerness, most late eighteenth-century monarchs tended to adopt this model. At first glance, they impressed by their omnipotence. The appearance of unlimited power, however, was merely superficial and only partially veiled the profound impotence in which the absolute kings put themselves by their isolation.

b. The only solution for the absolute monarchy was to support itself with civil and military bureaucracies, the heavy "crutches" of absolute monarchy

By becoming increasingly detached from the intermediate bodies that constituted the nation, absolute monarchs either lost or weakened their natural supports through the suffocation produced by their own absolutism.

Unable to stand, walk, and struggle alone, and deprived of their natural constituent elements (the intermediate bodies), absolute monarchs were forced to support themselves with ever larger bureaucracies. These bureaucratic networks became the heavy crutches, brilliant but fragile, of this late eighteenth-century monarchy. The larger a bureaucracy is, the heavier it is. The heavier it is, the more it burdens those obliged to carry it.

Through this process, absolute and bureaucratic royalty began to devour the paternal, familial, and organic state.

We shall mention a few historical examples to illustrate how this process occurred in some European countries.

c. The centralization of power in France

1) Under the kings

In France the great fiefs were gradually reabsorbed by the Crown, particularly through marriage alliances between members of the Royal House and heiresses to great feudal units. Meanwhile, a kind of centripetal force concentrated the realm's main levers of command and influence in Paris. Louis XIV pursued this policy to its extreme.

A typical example of a nobility that resisted this destructive influence of the absolute monarchy was that of Vendée, in France. This region later became a focus of resistance to the French Revolution.

Regarding the resistance of the Vendean nobility to the central power, the renowned historian Georges Bordonove relates:

"The nobility of Vendée forms a caste, not shut in idle remembrances, but animated by its own dynamism. The existence of Versailles has not weakened it in the least, either physically or morally. Save exceptions, the influence of the new ideas, the thought of the philosophers and rhetoricians of the Age of Enlightenment, leave it indifferent. On the other hand, it has only too great a tendency to remember the role it played in past centuries, the power and the fortune it possessed, the past greatness and the preeminence of Poitou. It suffers, undoubtedly, from the diminishing of the nobility in benefit of the centralizing power of the State. It has never entirely forgiven Richelieu for having demolished its feudal castles, nor the Sun King for his haughty absolutism" (*La vie quotidienne en Vendée* [Paris: Hachette, 1974], p. 49).

To better understand the Vendean nobles' reservations about royal absolutism (against which, in turn, the revolutionaries of 1789 so furiously and profusely cried) we must bear in mind that the throne had no more ardent defenders than they, nor did the revolutionaries find more heroic and lofty opponents.

The last feudal territory absorbed by the French Crown was the duchy of Lorraine, incorporated through diplomatic negotiations that still retained aspects of a familial arrangement. The Treaty of Vienna (1738) between France and Austria established that Lorraine would belong during his lifetime to Stanislaw Leszczynski, the dethroned king of Poland and father of Queen Marie Leszczynska, wife of Louis XV. When Stanislaw died, the duchy of Lorraine would automatically be incorporated into the kingdom of France. So it happened.

2) Weakness of the ostentatious Bonapartist "omnipotence"

The ostentatious and ominous archetype of this bureaucratic monarchy, which no longer had anything paternal about it, was Bonaparte's entirely military, financial, and administrative state.

After defeating the Austrians at Wagram (1809), Napoleon occupied Vienna for a few months. When the French troops finally left, Emperor Francis I of Austria returned to his capital. The Viennese offered him a festive reception to console him for the crushing defeat and the misfortunes he and the country had suffered.[11] It is reported that, upon hearing this news, the Corsican despot could not help exclaiming, "What a strong monarchy!" Thus did he term the Hapsburg monarchy, perhaps the most paternal and organic of Europe at that time.

History proved Bonaparte right. When he was definitively crushed at Waterloo at the end of the Hundred Days, no one in France thought of offering him a festive homage in reparation for the immense tragedy that had befallen him.

On the other hand, when the Count of Artois, the future Charles X, entered Paris for the first time since the Revolution as official representative of his brother Louis XVIII, a grand celebration was held to acclaim the legitimate dynasty returning from exile without the laurels of any military victory, but with the prestige of an immense misfortune borne with majestic dignity.[12]

After his second and definitive abdication, Napoleon, isolated in defeat, was reduced to such an impotence that he was forced to request shelter from one of his archenemies, the King of England. Not even the prospect of his imminent downfall aroused in his closest followers the filial love of loyal subjects for their monarch and the courage to undertake some guerrilla action or revolution on his behalf.

On the contrary, guerrilla actions and revolutions did break out in Vendée and the Iberian Peninsula, where people were inspired by loyalty to their legitimate princes.[13] Also, the steadfast loyalty of the brave peasants of the Tyrol is legen-

---

[11]   See Documents X.

[12]   The magnificent reception the Parisians gave their future king is described with exemplary fidelity by the aforementioned historian Georges Bordonove in his work *Les Rois qui ont fait la France—Charles X*. Passages of this description are transcribed in Documents X.

[13]   Beyond suspicion of any bias on this point, the renowned Austrian historian Johann Baptist Weiss narrates the epopee of the Portuguese patriotic reaction against the Napoleonic troops, unsuccessfully commanded, consecutively, by three of the Corsican's most outstanding generals: Junot, Soult, and Massena. He writes about the early successes of the national reaction against Junot and his troops:

dary. Led by Andreas Hofer, they rose up against Napoleon in the name of the Catholic Church and the House of Austria.

These defenders of the Faith—as well as of the Portuguese and Spanish Crowns and independence, the French throne, and the Hapsburgs—shed their blood for dynasties that still bore considerable traces of the fatherliness of bygone days. In this and in many other ways, these dynasties differed radically from the harsh and arrogant despotism of Napoleon Bonaparte and the weak and cowardly despotism of his brother Joseph, whom he brashly promoted from "king" of Naples to "king" of Spain.

Except for the Hundred Days' adventure, the French army accepted Napoleon's fall with discipline. However epic and brilliant may have been the memories that united it to the Corsican, they did not have the force of cohesion of familial ties. Napoleon could not say of his armies what Queen Isabella of Castile affirmed, not without a certain envy, of the loyal and bellicose Portuguese people. The secret of their loyalty and dedication, she said, was that the brave Portuguese combatants "are all sons, not subjects" of their king.[14]

d. The dissolution of the Holy Roman Empire

The throne of the Holy Roman Empire, elective from its origins, became de facto hereditary in 1438, when Albert II, the Illustrious, from the House of Austria, was elected. From then on the college of Electoral Princes always chose the head of this House for the imperial throne. The election of Francis of Lorraine in 1745 was only an apparent exception, since he had married the heiress of the House of Austria, Archduchess Maria Theresa of Hapsburg. The house of Hapsburg-Lorraine thus came into being as the legitimate continuer of the House of Austria at the head of the Holy Roman Empire.[15]

"The Portuguese unfurled their national flag at the tolling of bells, amid festive joy and fireworks, in the city [of Oporto]. The movement spread throughout the country like fire on dry grass. On June 11, 1808, the old governor of Trás-os-Montes proclaimed the Prince Regent as sovereign and called the inhabitants to arms. In the cities and towns the people responded: 'Long live the Prince Regent! Long live Portugal! Death to Napoleon!'

"On June 17 the same acclamation resounded in Guimarães, on the 18th in Viana; on the 19th the Archbishop of Braga reinstated the prerogatives of the royal House of Braganza, with great affluence of people; he kissed the old flag and blessed the people, who sang the *Te Deum*. A junta was then elected, with the Archbishop as president.

"In Coimbra the university students rebelled in support of their country's liberation, and their temple of learning was transformed into an arsenal of war. Gunpowder was prepared in the chemistry laboratory. The students went throughout the towns, inciting the laborers to arm themselves; they were received with the tolling of bells, fireworks, and joyful cries. Everyone armed himself; the workers brandished their scythes and dug up cannons buried after the last war with Spain; friars went at the head of the troops with crucifixes in their hands. The clergy was all fire and flames for the national uprising, but it prevented the cruelties that were committed in Spain against the French.

"The situation of the Bonapartist troops became difficult. Junot clearly perceived the tremendous danger. He could receive no help from France, either by sea, because the English warships dominated it and kept watch along the coast, or by land because Spain was in arms and all mail was intercepted. With 24,000 men he could not dominate the uprising of a whole people" (*Historia Universal* [Barcelona: Tipografia la Educación, 1931], pp. 262-263).

[14]   Elaine Sanceau, *The Reign of the Fortunate King* (Hamden, Conn.: Archon Books, 1970), p. 123.

[15]   An earlier exception was that of Charles Albert, Elector of Bavaria, who received the imperial crown after the death of Charles VI, the father of Archduchess Maria Theresa. With the name of Charles VII, he occupied the imperial throne for a very short period (1742-1745), and his death opened the way for the election of Francis of

Franz Josef I, Emperor of Austria and King of Hungary, receives Kaiser Wilhelm II and other sovereign princes of the German Empire.

Nonetheless, the strongly federative character of the Holy Roman Empire lasted until its dissolution in 1806, when Napoleon forced Emperor Francis II (Francis I of Austria) to abdicate. With his imposition of the Confederation of the Rhine that same year, the Corsican drastically reduced the number of sovereign principalities in the Empire.

The subsequent German Confederation (1815-1866), which had the emperor of Austria as its hereditary president, represented a conservative interim in this centripetal march. It was, however, dissolved after the Austro-Prussian war and the battle of Sadowa (1866). The North German Confederation was then formed under Prussian hegemony. Austria and the states of southern Germany were excluded.

After the defeat of Napoleon III in 1870, this confederation became the German Reich, which was much more centralized and recognized only twenty-five member states as sovereign.

Lorraine. The latter's ascension to the supreme dignity of the Holy Roman Empire in itself constituted a proof of the political power of the House of Austria. Francis of Lorraine was elected emperor at the request of Maria Theresa, who thereby obtained for her spouse the highest nobiliary title of Christendom, proportioning the marriage of the illustrious heiress of the Hapsburgs with someone who had been merely duke of Lorraine and grand duke of Tuscany.

The centripetal impulse did not stop here. The *Anschluss* of Austria and, shortly thereafter, the annexation of the Sudetenland to the Third Reich (1938) carried this impulse to an extreme and resulted in the Second World War. The nullification of these centripetal conquests of Adolf Hitler and the recent incorporation of East Germany into the present German state may mark the final point of these successive modifications of the German map.

e. Absolutism in the Iberian Peninsula

1) Before the French Revolution

The march toward royal absolutism in Portugal and Spain followed a similar pattern.

With the decline of the Middle Ages, the political and socioeconomic organization tended to become centralized in both Iberian kingdoms. This tendency was shrewdly exploited by their respective monarchs, with the aim of broadening and consolidating the Crown's power over the various bodies of the State, especially the high nobility. When the French Revolution erupted, the power of the kings of Portugal and Spain had reached its historical apex.

Of course this did not take place without much friction between the kings and the nobility.

This tension provoked dramatic episodes in Portugal. During the reign of John II (1481-1495), the Duke of Braganza and other great nobles were executed. The Duke of Viseu, the Queen's brother, was stabbed in the monarch's presence. In the reign of Joseph I (1750-1777), the Duke of Aveiro and some of the most outstanding figures of the aristocracy—among whom were members of the illustrious house of Távora—were publicly executed.

In Spain, this centralizing tendency was already noticeable in several monarchs of the House of Trastamara. It grew throughout the following reigns, becoming fully defined during the reign of Ferdinand of Aragon and Isabella of Castile. It reached its apex with the kings of the House of Bourbon in the eighteenth century.

Among the initial measures taken by Ferdinand and Isabella were the demolition of many castles, the prohibition of building new ones, the curtailing of nobiliary privileges, and the transfer of seaport administration to the Crown. These measures diminished the power of the nobility. Concomitantly, the mastership of the main military orders was incorporated into the Crown.

At the end of this evolution—prior to 1789—the historical nobility was increasingly inclined to gravitate around the monarch and reside in the capital, frequently in the royal palaces themselves. In this way its members imitated the nobility of other European countries, following the trend established by the Sun King and his successors amid the unparalleled magnificence of Versailles.

These nobles held high positions at court. Court life absorbed a great part of their time and demanded a luxurious lifestyle that exceeded the revenues of their patrimonial lands. Consequently, the kings remunerated many of these nobles for their services at court. Even then, however, this remuneration and the patrimonial revenues were often insufficient. In more than one court, nobles incurred crushing debts, at times paid off through mésalliances with the upper bourgeoisie or with subsidies granted by the king as a favor.

2) The consequence of absolutism: the weakening of the nobility and the royal power itself

After the ill-fated Napoleonic invasions of Portugal (1807-1810) and Spain (1808-1814), both monarchic regimes became increasingly liberal. These Crowns thereby lost not only political but also socioeconomic influence. The growing largess with which the Portuguese and Spanish monarchs granted titles of nobility, on the other hand, brought many plebeians into the nobility. They were ennobled because of mere personal preference of the monarch, or for services rendered to the State or society in various fields.[16]

Although this expansion of the nobility corresponded to reasonable demands of socioeconomic transformations by recognizing the value of these services to the common good, at times it lacked discretion and discernment, thus depreciating the prestige the nobility enjoyed. As a result, the reward received by authentic promoters of the common good became increasingly less meaningful. The nobility can only suffer by such a lack of discreet and discerning selection, since nobility and selection are correlated concepts.

After the proclamation of the republic in Portugal, in 1910, the nobiliary titles, honorific distinctions, and rights of the nobility were abolished.[17]

The proclamation of the republic in Spain in 1873 and again in 1931, with the successive monarchic restorations, twice led to the abolition and subsequent restoration of the nobility's rights and privileges. All this had a traumatic effect on the institution of the nobility.

---

[16]   Perhaps no monarch was more inclined to make the nobility an open class than King Charles III of Spain (1759-1788). See section 9 c of this chapter.

[17]   With regard to the situation of titled nobles under the republican regime, Dr. Rui Dique Travassos Valdez explains: "The article of the Constitution of 1911 that abolished nobiliary distinctions in the country was later modified, based on the consideration of acquired rights. Nobles whose title had been personally granted during the monarchy, and who had paid the necessary fees, were thereby legally authorized to use their title, with the condition that their civil name precede it....

"During the exile of King Manuel II, many approached the sovereign, as head of the nobility (the Miguelistas, for their part, approached the leader of their Cause), requesting from him authorization to use their title. This authorization was usually deferred...and had more the character of a promise of official renewal in the event of a restoration of the monarchy.

"When the King died, Duarte Nuno, Duke of Braganza, was recognized by most of the Portuguese monarchists as uniting in himself the dynastic rights of the two branches of the House of Braganza. A Commission of Verification and Registry of Titles was established, followed by the Nobiliary Council, an organ to which this Prince granted powers to deal with these issues.

"None of these organs has legal standing in the State. However, it is noteworthy that several titled nobles, whose titles were only recognized by one of the aforementioned bodies during the republican regime, were designated by their title (always preceded by their civil name) in the 'Diário do Governo,' as is the custom with those who had a decree in their favor" ("Títulos Nobiliárquicos," in *Nobreza de Portugal e do Brasil* [Lisbon: Editorial Enciclopédia, 1960], Vol. 2, pp. 197-198).

f. The super-powerful bourgeois state—
the omnipotent communist state

Concerning the present status of this centralizing process, it should be noted that already in the nineteenth century the super-powerful bourgeois state was beginning to take shape in various nations, some residually monarchical, others triumphantly republican.

Throughout the *Belle Epoque*—as during the period between the Wars and in the aftermath of World War II—more and more crowns fell as the super-powerful democratic state paved the way for the omnipotent proletarian state.

A history of the absolutism of the proletarian state, the furious maligner yet remote continuator of the Enlightenment's royal absolutism, is clearly outside the scope of this work. So is a history of the rise of perestroika, glasnost, and socialist self-management—reactions that malign yet perpetuate proletarian absolutism.

6. The Genesis of the Contemporary State

a. The decline of regions—the march toward
the hypertrophy of royal power

As stated in the previous section, at the outset of modern times the feudal system entered a process of political decadence. Royal power gradually consolidated, reaching a state of hypertrophy in the seventeenth and eighteenth centuries. The contemporary state began to appear, based ever less on the rural aristocracy and the autonomous and creative impulse of regions, and ever more on bureaucratic organs, through which the action of the State extended to the whole nation.

Concurrently, the means of communication gradually improved and were secured from the endemic banditry of previous centuries. This favored multiple exchange between the regions of the country. The expansion of commerce and the rise of new industries standardized consumption. Regionalism waned as the increasingly larger cities began to shift the nerve centers from micro-regions to macro-regions and then to national metropolises.

More than ever, the capital of each country became the great pole of attraction of its centripetal energies and the source of the irradiation of the Crown's power. *Pari passu*, the court drew more and more of the nobility, until then predominantly rural. The nobility flocked around the king, who determined the direction of everything done in the country.

b. Royal absolutism became state absolutism
under the democratic regime

This gradual yet relentless centripetal process had continuity in the successively more absorbing types of state born in the nineteenth and twentieth centuries. The republican and bourgeois state of the nineteenth century, despite its liberal democratic aspects, was more centralizing than the monarchical state of the previous phase. In it, an undeniable process of democratization[18] opened all the doors of power to the non-noble classes, but gradually excluded the noble classes from this same power—a rather debatable way of practicing equality. Liberty, in turn, became more and more restricted as a growing mass of laws began to weigh on the citizen.

c. Centripetal pyramidization— super-pyramidization—two examples: large banks and the mass media

For a global idea of the decline of liberty throughout the nineteenth century, we must take into account the tendency to pyramidization that manifested itself in the field of private enterprise. A gradual intertwining of companies formed increasingly larger blocs, which tended to absorb any autonomous unit reluctant to join its respective pyramid. Obviously, at the peak of these pyramids were (and still are) super-fortunes controlling the progressively smaller fortunes. As a result, owners of small and medium-sized businesses lost much of their freedom of action in face of the competition and pressures of macro-capitalism.

By the very nature of things, this group of pyramids was in turn capped by even more powerful institutions; for example, the banking system and the mass media.

This process accelerated in our century due to the new inventions and the continual progress of science and technology.

Besides diminishing the freedom of small business owners, this concentration of the private capital in the hands of a few holders of large fortunes can have another consequence, affecting the position of macro-capitalism vis-à-vis the State.

A strange inversion of values began to occur in the liberal-democratic bourgeois world—ever more democratic and leveling from one point of view, and ever less liberal from another. Consider large banks and the mass media. These institutions are usually privately owned, yet, incidentally, often wield in our days more power than the nobility in the nineteenth century, or even before the French Revolution. More importantly, they frequently have more power over the State than the State has over them. Large banks and the mass media have more means to influence the filling of elective offices in most modern democracies than the State has to influence the selection of top executive officers for these institutions. This is so notorious that the State at times feels handicapped if it does not assume the role of a large banking or media enterprise. It therefore invades the private sphere—itself an invader of the State's sphere.

Is this convergence? No. It is a road to chaos.

From the point of view of freedom of action and progress, this confrontation between the State and macro-capitalism brings no economic or political advantage to the average citizen.

Consider an election-day scenario. People are lined up at the voting booths. Standing in line like any other citizen is a magnate of the "antithetical nobility"[19]

---

[18] The word *democratization* is used here in the revolutionary sense of democracy, which, as we have seen, is not the only sense it can be given. See Chapter III, 3.

[19] The expression denotes the class of persons whose circumstances could approximate them to the nobility,

of the twentieth century. He enters the booth and casts his ballot, aware that it is worth as much or as little as the vote of the most obscure citizen.

The next day, he comments on the electoral results at his club as if he had influenced them no more than any other voter. However, which of his listeners who knows that he owns a large newspaper chain, which can sway the vote of today's amorphous and disoriented masses, will entertain such an illusion?

d. State capitalism: continuation of the centripetal and authoritarian trend— the tomb of all that came before

What changes did state capitalism bring to the countries where it was implemented? It heightened *ad infinitum* the preceding centripetal trend. It turned the State into a Leviathan, whose omnipotence dwarfed the powers of the kings and nobles of earlier eras. In its craving to centralize, state collectivism absorbed absolutely everything. It thereby buried in the same abyss, in the same nothingness, as in a tomb, kings, nobles, and, not much later, the "antithetical aristocrats," who had by then reached the height of their historical march.

All this happened through the influence—at times direct, at times remote—of the ideology of 1789.[20]

e. One tomb—two trilogies

Were these the only victims of this collectivist gangrene?

No. The successively inferior levels of the bourgeoisie were also victimized. The Leviathan's collectivist absorption did not spare a single individual, nor a single individual right. In the unfortunate countries it tyrannized, collectivism violated even the most elementary rights of man, those that stem not from any state law, but from the natural order of things, expressed with divine wisdom and simplicity in the Ten Commandments.

This sinister panorama of collectivism was made evident to the whole human race with the fall of the Iron Curtain. Even the right to life had been absorbed by the collectivist state, which thereby denied man what the contemporary ecological trends strive to guarantee to the most fragile bird and to the smallest and most repugnant worm. In this way, the workers, the lowest servants of the State, became the most recent occupants of this tomb.

Were the tombstone to bear a general epitaph for these victims of yesteryear, yesterday, and today, it might well read:

TRADITION—FAMILY—PROPERTY

---

but whose egalitarian prejudices lead them to repudiate this possibility. See section 8 f of this chapter for a fuller explanation.

[20] Cf. Plinio Corrêa de Oliveira, *Revolution and Counter-Revolution*, pp. 31-32.

These are the three great principles that collectivism denied. Their denial provoked the intrepid and combative reaction of the largest group of anticommunist organizations of Catholic inspiration in the modern world.

According to certain popular legends, over the tombs of the victims of blatant injustice flutter multitudes of confused and tormented evil spirits. We could imagine, therefore, another trilogy, hovering over this agitated, feverish, and noisy swirl:

MASSIFICATION—SERVITUDE—HUNGER

f. What remains of the nobility today?
The answer of Pius XII

At this point it is fitting to ask what remains of the nobility, now that revolutionary totalitarianism has destroyed the autonomies and the growing egalitarianism of our age has abolished the special offices and related privileges that made the nobility, in the Middle Ages and still in the Ancien Régime, a defined social and political body.

Pius XII categorically answers: "A page of history has been turned; a chapter has ended. A period has been placed, indicating the end of a social and economic past."[21]

From this class, to which nothing palpable remains, the Pontiff still expects the exercise of a high function for the common good. He describes this function with precision and evident satisfaction in his various allocutions, including those of 1952 and 1958, the year of his death. His thought clearly lives on in the allocutions of John XXIII and Paul VI to the Roman Patriciate and Nobility and to the Pontifical Noble Guard.

To fully understand this delicate, subtle, and important matter, we must first consider the historical panorama explained herein, analyzing the events from a specific angle.

7. The Moral Profile of the Medieval Noble

In every social body constituted by professionals in the same field, we easily notice how much the profession influences the mentality and the intellectual and moral profile of its members, and, consequently, the domestic and social relationships extrinsic to their professional sphere.

In the Middle Ages and the Ancien Régime, the condition of a noble could not be equated to a mere profession. In a sense, it was a livelihood, but it was also much more. Consequently, it profoundly marked the noble and his family, through which the noble condition was to be transmitted to future generations. The title was incorporated into the family's name and sometimes subsumed it. The coat of arms was the family's emblem. And the land over which the noble

---

[21] PNR 1952, p. 457.

exercised his power usually bore his own name, and when it did not, its name was incorporated into his title.[22]

a. In war as in peace,
the example of perfection

Two essential principles defined the physiognomy of the noble:

1. In order to be the exemplary man placed at the summit of the fief as the light atop a chandelier, the noble had to be, by definition, a Christian hero disposed to endure any sacrifice on behalf of the good of his king and his people. He had to be the armed defender of the Faith and Christendom in the frequent wars against pagans and heretics.

2. In every field, he and his family had to give a good example—or better, an excellent example—to their subordinates and peers. In virtue as in culture, manners, taste, the decoration of the home, and celebrations, their example had to motivate the whole social body so that everyone would improve in every field.

b. The Christian gentleman
and the Christian lady

These two principles had an admirable practical scope, as we shall see. During the Middle Ages, they were lived with authenticity of conviction and religious sentiment. In this manner, the physiognomy of the Christian gentleman and the Christian lady appeared in European and, later, in Western culture. *Gentleman* and *lady*: two concepts that, throughout the ages and despite the successive dilutions inflicted by the gradual secularization in the Old Regime, always designated the excellence of a human standard. Even in our time, in which both titles have lamentably become obsolete, they nevertheless continue to designate this excellence.

Even when the nobility lost everything we mentioned, not only in Italy (which Pius XII had particularly in mind) but in other countries as well, its elevated human standard remained. This standard, the supreme and last treasure of the nobility, cannot be fully understood without taking into account why and how it was formed through the creative process of feudalism and the feudal hierarchy.

---

[22] This mutualism among man, function, and land was expressed in a touching way by Paul Claudel in *The Hostage*: "Coufontaine—As the earth gives us her name, so do I give her my manhood. Thanks to her we still have roots, and through me and the grace of God, she is not without seed. I am her lord. And that is why, above all others, I bear her name, her name to which the title is prefixed; the title of *de*! My fief lies within my kingdom as within a smaller France. The earth is of me, and my race becomes gentle-blooded and noble: a thing which cannot be bought" (In *Three Plays*, transl. by John Heard [Boston: John W. Luce Co., 1945], p. 18).

c. Sacrifice, good manners, etiquette, and protocol—simplifications and mutilations imposed by the bourgeois world

Sacrifice. The word deserves to be emphasized, for it had a central importance in the life of the noble. It was present even in his social life in the form of an ascesis that deeply marked it. Indeed, good manners, etiquette, and protocol were developed according to standards that demanded from the noble a continual repression of what is vulgar, rough, and even offensive in so many of man's impulses. Social life was, in some aspects, a perpetual sacrifice that became more demanding as civilization progressed and refined itself.

This statement may elicit a skeptical smile from some readers. However, if they wish to see how true it is, let them consider the mitigations, simplifications, and mutilations that the bourgeois world, born of the French Revolution, has gradually imposed upon the etiquette and ceremony that have survived to our days. Without exception, all these changes were introduced to offer ease, insouciance, and bourgeois comfort to the nouveaux riches bent on conserving as much as possible, in the midst of their recently-acquired opulence, the vulgarity of their previous lifestyle.

Thus, the erosion of good taste, etiquette, and good manners resulted from a spirit of laissez-faire, a desire to "unwind," and the prevalence of the spontaneous and extravagant whims of "hippieism," which reached an apex in the unbridled rebellion of the Sorbonne in 1968 and in subsequent youth movements such as "punkism."

d. Harmonious diversity in the practice of virtues: through self-denial in the religious state; amid grandeur and splendor in temporal society

At this point we should mention a trait of soul that stands out in many members of the nobility.

Many saints of noble birth renounced their social condition to practice the perfection of virtue in the earthly self-denial of the religious state. How splendid were the examples they gave to Christendom and the world!

Other noble saints, however, remained amid the splendors of temporal life. With the prestige of their station, they stressed in the eyes of the other social classes the magnificence of the Christian virtues, and set a good moral example to the collectivity they headed. They did this to the advantage, not only of the salvation of souls, but of temporal society too. In this sense, nothing is more beneficial to the State and society than having in its highest ranks persons shining with the sublime respectability that emanates from the saints of the Catholic Church.

Moreover, these saints—so worthy of reverence and admiration because of their elevated station—were especially loved by the multitudes due to their constant and exemplary practice of Christian charity. Indeed, there are innumerable beatified and canonized nobles who, without renouncing the earthly honors of their rank, stood out for their particular love for the needy. They earnestly practiced a *preferential option for the poor.*

Many nobles who chose the admirable self-denial of religious life also shone in this solicitous service to the needy. They became poor with the poor to lighten the earthly crosses of the destitute and prepare their souls for heaven.

It would unduly prolong this work to mention the numerous nobles of both sexes who, for love of God and neighbor, practiced the Evangelical virtues amid the grandeur and splendor of temporal society, as well as those who practiced them in the self-denial of religious life.[23]

e. How not to govern—how to govern

To govern is not only, nor principally, to make laws and penalize transgressors, compelling the population to obey by means of an extensive bureaucracy and a coercive police force. At best, one can govern a prison in this way, but not a people.

As we said in the beginning of this chapter, to govern men it is first necessary to gain their admiration, confidence, and affection. This requires a profound consonance of principles, aspirations, and rejections, and a body of culture and traditions common to those governing and those governed. Feudal lords generally achieved this objective in their fiefs by continually stimulating the people toward excellence in every field.

Even when trying to obtain a popular consensus in favor of wars resulting from the conditions of the time, the nobility used suasive means. In doing so it was expected to give priority to the ecclesiastical hierarchy's preachings on the moral circumstances that might justify a war, whether for religious or temporal reasons.

f. The *bonum* and *pulchrum* of just war—
The knight felt it to the depths of his soul

The nobility made the *bonum* of just war shine together with its *pulchrum*[24] through the expressiveness of its military ceremonial, the beauty of its arms, the caparison of its horses, and so on.

A noble viewed his participation in just war as an immolation for the glorification of the Church, the spreading of the Faith, and the common good of the temporal sphere. He was ordained toward this immolation, as, in an analogous way, the clergy and religious were ordained toward the spiritual immolation inherent to their respective state.

---

[23]   Regarding the number of nobles elevated by the Church to the honors of the altar, see Documents XII.

[24]   *Bonum* and *pulchrum*, good and beauty, respectively, are used here in their philosophical senses as attributes of being. Good is that which is suitable or befitting a thing; beauty denotes that which pleases upon being seen or heard because of its integrity, proportion, and clarity.

The Battle of Rocroy.
The victorious Prince of Condé
shows clemency to the heroic defeated army.

Knights—who were not always nobles—felt the *bonum* and the *pulchrum* of this immolation to the depths of their souls. They went to war with this state of spirit. The beauty with which they surrounded military activity was far from a mere means of enticing plebeians into accompanying them to war. This was, however, the effect this beauty produced in the spirit of the people. (Let it be said in passing that the commoners of the time were not subject to compulsory draft.)

Of course, in that age of ardent Faith, the teachings of the Church had a much greater effect upon the people than did these brilliant appearances. These teachings left no doubt about the fact that a holy war, more than being simply legitimate, could be a duty for all Christians, nobles and plebeians alike.[25]

8. The Nobility of Our Time— The Magnitude of Its Present Mission

a. The essence of all nobilities, whatever their nationality

What is the substratum of the human type that characterizes the nobility? To answer this question, historical scholarship has accumulated data on the origin of this class, its political, social, and economic roles throughout the ages, its influence on morality, fashions, and social customs, and its patronizing of the arts and culture.

What is a noble?

A noble is a member of the nobility. This membership implies that he corresponds to a certain psychological and moral type which, in turn, wholly shapes him. However profound the transformations endured by this class throughout the ages, however numerous the varieties it presents according to different nationalities, the nobility is always one. For this reason, however much a Hungarian magnate might differ from a Spanish grandee, or a French duke and peer from a British, Italian, German, or Portuguese duke, a noble is always a noble in the public's eyes. More specifically, a count is always a count, a baron always a baron, a *hidalgo* or gentleman always a *hidalgo* or gentleman.

The historical vicissitudes the nobility endured modified its situation dramatically. While some nobles still remain at the summit of wealth and prestige, others are in the abyss of poverty, forced to do hard and humble labor to earn a living, and looked upon with sarcasm and contempt by many contemporaries imbued with the egalitarian and bourgeois spirit spread by the French Revolution. Still others are bereft of any goods, downtrodden and reduced to a proletarian condition by communist regimes from whose despotic domination they were unable to escape in time.

---

[25] The teachings of popes, saints, doctors, and theologians about the conditions for a just war can be found in Documents XI.

b. Nobility: a standard of excellence— the impulse to all forms of elevation and perfection

Deprived of any political power in contemporary republics, the nobility retains mere shreds of it in monarchies. It has a scant representation in the world of finance, when it has any. In diplomacy, as well as in the world of culture and the patronage of the arts, its role is much less evident than that of the bourgeoisie. In most cases, the nobility today is little more than a residue. Notwithstanding all this, it is a precious remnant that represents a tradition essentially consisting of a human type.

How can this human type be defined?

The very course of events made the nobility a standard of excellence that would edify all men and, in a certain sense, give all excellent things the prominence they deserve.[26] When we say that something is noble and aristocratic, we stress that it is excellent in its kind. This is so even in our society intoxicated with egalitarianism, vulgarity, and base moral corruption.

Even down to the first decades of our century, temporal society, at least in its general lines, still tended to continuously improve in the most varied fields. As far as public or private religiousness and morality are concerned, this statement would need to be strongly nuanced.

Today, on the contrary, there is an omnifarious tendency toward vulgarity and extravagance, and at times even toward the brutal and insolent triumph of ugliness and obscenity. In this sense, the revolution of the Sorbonne in 1968 was an explosion of universal scope that ignited evil tendencies long incubated in the contemporary world. These phenomena brought with them a pronounced proletarianization, in the most pejorative sense of the word.

Nevertheless, the old impulse toward elevation and perfection, born in the Middle Ages and developed, in certain aspects, in the following centuries, has not died. On the contrary, it still checks, to some extent, the expansion of the proletarianizing impulse. In some ambiences, it even has a certain dominance.

In the past, the nobility as a social class had the mission of cultivating, nourishing, and spreading this impulse toward perfection throughout society. It was preeminently oriented toward this mission in the temporal sphere, as was the clergy in the spiritual order.

The noble was a symbol of this impulse, its very personification. He was like a living book in which all of society could read everything our elders, eager for elevation, yearned for and were gradually attaining. Such was the noble.

Of everything he was, this precious impulse is perhaps the best he retains. Little wonder that men of our time, in growing numbers, turn to him and ask with mute anxiety if the nobility will preserve this impulse and even expand it courageously, and thus help save the world from the chaos and catastrophes into which it is sinking.

---

[26] Regarding the nobility as a social factor in the propulsion of society toward all forms of elevation and perfection, see also Appendix V.

Should the twentieth-century noble remain aware of this mission and, animated by Faith and love for a well-understood tradition, do everything to fulfill it, he will achieve a victory of no less grandeur than that of his ancestors when they held back the barbarians, drove Islam beyond the Mediterranean, or smashed through the gates of Jerusalem under the command of Godfrey of Bouillon.

c. Pius XII's main emphasis

Of everything the nobility was or possessed in former times, the only thing left is this multifaceted excellence, along with a residual ensemble of indispensable conditions that prevent it, most of the time, from falling to a proletarian or proletarianizing situation.

We said "only." Indeed, how little this is in relation to what the nobles once were and had! But how much better this is when compared with the insolent and boastful vulgarity of so many of our contemporaries! How favorably this remnant of excellence among the true aristocrats compares with the vulgar corruption among the moneyed jet set, the extravagance of more than one surviving tycoon, the unrestrained self-indulgence and Sancho Panza-like security of certain middle and lower bourgeois!

This excellence is the main emphasis of Pius XII's allocutions to the Roman Patriciate and Nobility. The Pontiff shows the illustrious members of this class, and through them the whole world, that the excellence inherent to nobility confers on them an unequivocal place among the leading classes emerging from the new conditions of life; a place of clear religious, moral, and cultural significance, which makes the nobility a precious shield against the torrential decadence of the contemporary world.

d. The nobility: leaven and not mere dust from the past—the priestly mission of the nobility to elevate, purify, and pacify the world

On January 5, 1920, shortly after the First World War, Benedict XV (1914-1922) addressed the Roman Patriciate and Nobility. He uttered words of ardent praise for their dedicated and heroic conduct during the dramatic days of the conflict, while emphasizing the importance of the mission that lay before them in the ensuing period of peace.

On that occasion the Pontiff spoke of a "priesthood much like the Priesthood of the Church: that of the nobility."

The Pontiff was not only alluding to the good example set by the Roman patricians and nobles during the war. With loftier considerations, he affirms that at the core of the nobility's mission there is something priestly. Coming from a Pope, this eulogy of the nobility could not be greater.

Of course, the Pontiff does not intend to equate the condition of a noble with that of a priest. He does not affirm an identity between the two missions, only a strong similarity. He develops this principle with quotations from Saint Paul, as we shall see.

When stressing the importance and authenticity of the noble's duties in the field of Faith and morality, the Pontiff's teaching takes on a superb force of expression.

> Alongside the *"regale Sacerdotium"* of Christ, you too, My Children, rose up as society's *"genus electum,"* and your task was that which above all others resembled and emulated the task of the clergy. While the clergy aided, supported, and comforted with words, example, courage, and the promise of Christ, the nobility also performed their duty on the field of battle, in the ambulances, in the cities, in the countrysides; and, in fighting, assisting, striving, and dying, they remained true— old and young, men and women—true to the traditions of their ancestral glories and to the obligations that nobility entails.
>
> If, therefore, it pleases Us to hear praise given to the priests of our Church for the work done during the painful period of the war, it is also right that We should give due praise in turn to the priesthood of the nobility. Both of these priesthoods serve as the Pope's attendants, for in the darkest hours they have well interpreted his sentiments.[27]

Benedict XV then speaks about the duties of the nobility in the period of peace that was beginning.

> Should We not, therefore, say that the priesthood of the nobility, like the priesthood that will continue its good works even in peacetime, will be viewed by Us with especial benevolence? Indeed, from the zealous ardor displayed in times of misfortune We are pleased to infer the constancy of purpose with which the patricians and nobles of Rome will continue to carry out, in happier days, the holy tasks on which the priesthood of the nobility lives.
>
> St. Paul the Apostle admonished the nobles of his day, that they might be, or become, what their station required of them. [He was] not satisfied with having said that they too should present themselves as models of good action, in doctrine, in integrity, in seriousness of purpose: *"in omnibus te ipsum praebe exemplum bonorum operum; in doctrina, in integritate, in gravitate"* (Titus 2:7). Saint Paul was thinking more directly of nobles when he wrote to his disciple Timothy to admonish the wealthy *"divitibus huius saeculi praecipe,"* that they might do good and become rich with good works: *"bene agere, divites fieri in bonis operibus"* (I Tim. 6:17-18).
>
> One can rightly say that the Apostle's admonitions are admirably applicable as well to the nobles of our times. You too, O beloved Children, the higher your station, the greater your obligation to lead others by the light of your good example: *"in omnibus te ipsum praebe exemplum bonorum operum."*[28]

---

[27] *L'Osservatore Romano*, January 5-6, 1920.

[28] Ibid.

Some readers might object: Do these duties also apply to the nobility in our days, so different from those of Benedict XV? Would it not be more objective to say that these duties now belong as much to any citizen as to the nobles? The teachings of Benedict XV run counter to these objections. The Pontiff continues:

> In all ages nobles have been duty-bound to assist in the teaching of the truth, *"in doctrina"*; today, however, when the confusion of ideas, companion to the revolution of the people, has in so many places and in so many minds made the true notions of right, justice, charity, religion, and fatherland disappear, it has become all the more imperative for the nobility to strive to restore to the intellectual patrimony those sacred notions that should guide them in their daily activities. In all ages nobles have been duty-bound to allow nothing indecent to enter their words and their actions, that their own license might not become an incitement to the vices of their subalterns, *"in integritate, in gravitate."* Yet, this duty too, Oh how urgent and weighty it has become, because of the bad habits of our time! Not just the gentlemen are beholden, however; the ladies, too, are obliged to join together in the holy struggle against the extravagancies and obscenities of fashion, distancing themselves from, and not tolerating in others, what is not permitted by the laws of Christian modesty.
>
> And coming to the application of what Saint Paul advised directly to the nobles of his day,...to Us it is enough that the patricians and nobles of Rome continue, in peacetime, to shape themselves by that spirit of charity of which they have given such wonderful proof in times of war....
>
> Your nobility, then, will not be seen as a useless relic of times gone by, but as a leavening to resurrect corrupt society; it will be a beacon, a preserving salt, a guide for wanderers; it will be immortal not only on this earth where everything, even the glory of the most illustrious dynasties, fades and vanishes, but will be immortal in heaven, where everything lives and is exalted in the Author of all things beautiful and noble.[29]

When giving the Apostolic blessing at the end of the allocution, the Pontiff manifests his desire that "each might cooperate with the priesthood proper to his class toward the elevation and purification of the world and, by doing good to others, ensure entry for himself as well into the kingdom of eternal life—'*ut aprehendant veram vitam!*'"[30]

e. Present admirers of the nobility

Even when scorned and despised, the noble who remains worthy of his forebears is always a noble. He is the object of special attention, and not rarely even courtesy, on the part of those with whom he comes into contact.

An example of the interest aroused by the nobility is the fact that today, even

---

[29] Ibid.

[30] Ibid. For the full text of this allocution, see Documents II.

Pope Benedict XV, at the end of the First World War, warmly eulogized the Roman Patriciate and Nobility's dedication and heroism in the dramatic days of war, mentioning "another priesthood much like the Priesthood of the Church: that of the nobility."

more than in preceding decades, there is in every society a growing number of people who admire the nobility with great respect and a moving, almost romantic, interest. A list of facts proving the presence in our days of this compact vein of admirers would be endless.

Two facts speak for themselves. One, already mentioned, is the joyous and admiring enthusiasm with which countless multitudes throughout the world accompanied, via television, the marriage ceremony of the Prince of Wales and Princess Diana. Another is the constant growth of the Parisian magazine *Point de Vue—Images du monde*, which is dedicated to news concerning the aristocratic segments of the population around the world, be they in monarchies or republics. The circulation of *Point de Vue*, around 180,000 copies in 1956, grew to 515,000 in 1991.[31]

f. The nobility: thesis and antithesis

At this point we should include some considerations on those moneyed elites that, instead of striving to cultivate qualities appropriate to their high economic station, pride themselves on maintaining their vulgar habits and lifestyles.

Individual property tends to remain within the lineage of its owner. The family institution leads to this in a powerful way. This has resulted, at times, in the formation of commercial, industrial, and publishing lineages, or even "dynasties." Each of these family groups can exert over political events an incomparably greater power than the common voter, although all citizens are equal in the eyes of the law...

Do these lineages constitute a new nobility?

From a strictly functional point of view, perhaps they do, but this is not the only point of view, nor even necessarily the main one. Concretely, this new "nobility" frequently is not, nor could it be, a true nobility, foremostly because a great part of its members do not wish to be noble.

In fact, egalitarian prejudices, which so many of these lineages cultivate and flaunt since their origin, lead them to differentiate themselves progressively from the old nobility, become insensible to its prestige, and, not infrequently, downgrade it in the eyes of the world. This is done not by a forced elimination of the characteristics differentiating the old nobility from the masses, but by this new "nobility's" ostentation of a characteristic willingly cultivated for demagogic purposes. This characteristic is vulgarity.

While the historical nobility was and wanted to be an elite, this modern antithesis of the nobility frequently prides itself in not differing from the masses. It strives to camouflage itself with the ways and habits of the masses, purportedly to escape an impending vengeance of the demagogic egalitarian spirit. This spirit is usually fanned by the mass media whose owners and top executives paradoxically often belong to this same antithetical nobility.

---

[31] We read in *Dictionnaire encyclopedique QUID* in the section "Les journaux se racontent" (Robert Laffont, 1991, p. 1218): "The history of *Point de Vue* is that of a magazine which, without financial aid or advertising, managed year after year to rank among the top illustrated French periodicals of international class." This happened, we add, despite its being controversial in more than one circle of the French elite.

As the head with the body, the nobility naturally forms an organic whole with the people. Conversely, this antithetical nobility tends to avoid this vital differentiation as much as possible, striving—at least in appearance—to integrate itself into that great amorphous and lifeless whole which is the masses.[32]

It would be exaggerated to affirm that all contemporary plutocrats are this way. But many of them undeniably are. This is especially true of some of the richest among them, to whom, by the way, an attentive observer will not deny notability by their dynamism, their power, and the archetype of their characteristics.

9. The Flourishing of Analogous Elites— Contemporary Forms of Nobility?

In speaking of the bourgeois society and its peculiarities, we do not intend to include those families of the bourgeoisie in whose bosom, down through the generations, flourished a genuine family tradition, rich in moral, cultural, and social values.

Contrary to the antithetical nobility, these families' fidelity to tradition and their desire for continual improvement make them true elites.

In a social structure open to everything that enriches it with true values, these families little by little become an aristocrat-like class. They gradually and smoothly blend into the aristocracy or, by force of custom, become a new aristocracy with its own characteristics alongside the old aristocracy.

Whoever is simultaneously at the summit of political power and social influence— as is the case of monarchs—must know how to preside in a kind, prudent, and tactful way over these highly respectable betterments of the sociopolitical structure. He must be more concerned with sounding out the yearnings that animate the wholesome social transformations and identify the aspirations of an organic society than with geometrically setting a course for the nation through decrees.

Far from jealously and narrow-mindedly hindering the full flourishing of other elites, the existence of aristocratic elites is a standard for fruitful analogies and a stimulus for fraternal improvements.

The pejorative sense of the term *bourgeoisie* is applicable to the sectors of this social category that are uninterested in forming their family traditions, or in maintaining and improving them through successive generations, and instead concentrate on pursuing the most outlandish modernity. Even when their families have lived in opulence or easy comfort for several generations, these bourgeois still choose to resemble a group of parvenus—parvenus in a state of permanent mutation caused by their self-destructive determination not to refine their habits over time!

a. A matter the Pontiffs did not treat: Are there updated forms of nobility?

The preceding considerations lead to an aspect of this question that Pius XII, his predecessors, and successors did not deal with, perhaps for reasons of prudence.

---

[32] See Chapter III.

As shown throughout these chapters, Pius XII attributes an important role to the nobility of our time. In view of this role, the Pontiff wishes to conserve the nobility as one of the leading classes of the modern world. Thus he strives to open its eyes to what it retains of the past, and to the use it should make of this remainder as a means of survival and action, not only to preserve its present situation successfully, but perhaps to recover a broader place for itself at the summit of today's society.

But the nobility's acknowledged role is so important that its fulfillment requires more than this paltry and indeed contested residue. Means should be found to expand the nobility's base of action. What would be the desirable way of doing this? To what extent would this "desirable" also be viable in modern conditions?

Why not consider, for example, a society that would generously provide a framework of support for the nobility's existence and the plenitude of its benefic action? This framework could eventually take on "updated" forms, consisting of more than just urban or rural property. For example, why not officially recognize the nobility as the bearer of the precious boon of tradition and as a counselor to be heeded and respected by those who hold the levers of power in today's world?

We should not exclude the hypothesis that Pius XII seriously considered this possibility, even though, for prudential reasons, he did not express the conclusions he may have reached.

Since he analyzed the modern problems of the nobility with such solicitous attention, nothing would have been more natural than for him to have pondered what follows.

b. Authentic, if less brilliant, nobilities—historic examples

With time, especially from the late Middle Ages on, new nobilities came into existence. Although less brilliant, they were no less authentic than the nobility par excellence: the warrior, rural, and seignorial nobility. Examples of these new nobilities abound in Europe.

In Portugal the doors of the nobility were opened to intellectuals. Anyone who graduated from the famous University of Coimbra in theology, philosophy, law, medicine, or mathematics became noble, although without a hereditary title. If three successive generations of a family graduated at Coimbra in one of these fields, all their descendants, even if they did not study at this university, became hereditary nobles.[33]

In Spain, the investiture in certain civil, military, or cultural offices, and even the exercise of certain forms of commerce and industry particularly useful to the nation, automatically conferred either a personal lifetime nobiliary status or a hereditary one.[34]

---

[33] Cf. Luiz da Silva Pereira Oliveira, *Privilégios da Nobreza e Fidalguia de Portugal* (Lisbon: Oficina de João Rodrigues Neves, 1806), pp. 67-81.

[34] Through the exercise of their office, the following persons could become nobles: "the high servants of the

In France, beside the *noblesse de robe* (nobility of the robe), composed of magistrates, there was the *noblesse de cloche* (nobility of the bell). This latter name refers to the bell used by the authorities of small towns to summon the people. This *noblesse de cloche* was customarily formed by bourgeois families who had distinguished themselves in the service of the common good of small urban communities.[35]

c. Nouveaux riches, *nouveaux nobles*

These ennoblements did not occur, however, without giving rise to noteworthy problems. Certain historic episodes illustrate this clearly.

For example, King Charles III (1759-1788), contrasting the new industrial progress of some European nations with the painful backwardness of Spain in this field, decided to stimulate the establishment of industries in his kingdom through the Royal Decree of March 18, 1783. Among other measures, he decided to ele-

---

Royal Household; the governesses and wet nurses of the Royal Infantes; the *alcaldes de Casa y Corte*; presidents, councillors, and justices of the Royal Chanceries" (Vicenta María Márquez de la Plata and Luis Valero de Bernabé, *Nobiliaria Española—origen, evolución, instituciones y probanzas* [Madrid: Prensa y Ediciones Iberoamericanas, 1991], p. 15). In this work, adopted as a manual by the Escuela de Ciencias Nobiliarias, Heráldicas y Genealógicas of Madrid, can be found a comprehensive and didactic overview of this topic.

With regard to the nobility acquired by the exercise of military offices, we cite the following illustration: "In the Royal Decree of August 20, 1637, Philip IV rules that an officer who serves in war for one year enjoys the nobility of privilege, and one who does so for four years may transmit this nobility to his heirs....

"Personal nobility is recognized to all army officers by the Royal Decree of April 16, 1799; and that of May 18, 1864, ordains that the title of Don and Noble be given to the sons of captains and higher officers, to the grandchildren of lieutenant-colonels, and to well-known hidalgos who serve in the army" (Vicente de Cadenas y Vicent, *Cuadernos de doctrina nobiliaria* [Madrid: Instituto Salazar y Castro, C.S.I.C.—Asociación de Hidalgos a Fuero de España, Ediciones Hidalguia, 1969], no. 1, p. 28).

Among other privileges granted to people dedicated to culture, the *Codigo de las siete partidas* of Alphonsus X, the Wise (1252-1284), conferred the title of Count on the Masters of Jurisprudence who exercised the office for more than twenty years. (Cf. Bernabé Moreno de Vargas, *Discursos de la nobleza de España* [Madrid: Instituto Salazar y Castro, C.S.I.C., Ediciones Hidalguia, 1971], pp. 28-29.)

Cadenas y Vicent summarizes the criteria of ennoblement in his important work *Apuntes de nobiliaria y nociones de genealogía y heráldica*:

"The priesthood, the performance of honorable offices, the military career, the humanities, the bestowal of a title, matrimony, being born in certain cases of a noble mother, or in certain territories, having rendered great services to mankind, the country, or the sovereign, having sacrificed oneself or one's goods for great ideals, etc., always were, and should continue to be, just causes for acquiring nobility, since the universal tendency is to broaden the base of the noble class, the most cultured and sacrificed of those that compose the nation, to take advantage of its virtues in benefit of the community" (*Primer curso de la Escuela de Genealogía, Heráldica y Nobiliaria*, 2d ed. [Madrid: Instituto Luis de Salazar y Castro, C.S.I.C., Ediciones Hidalguia, 1984], p. 30).

Ennoblement through the exercise of industrial activities will be mentioned in the next section, 9 c.

[35] In fact, nobility could also be acquired through the exercise of other offices and functions, such as military commissions, royal household offices (high offices at court, the office of secretary and notary of the king), financial offices, university posts, and so on.

There is a widespread conviction in France that it is very difficult to draw up a complete list of the ennobling offices and functions of the Old Regime. In the book *La noblesse*, from which this enumeration is taken, Philippe du Puy de Clinchamps goes so far as to affirm that "in the history of the nobility there is no chapter more entangled than that of ennoblement through the holding of an office" (Collection *Que sais-je?* [Paris: Presses Universitaires de France, 1962], pp. 20, 22).

There does not seem to be a censure in this affirmation, but merely the registering of a fact, since everything organic and living tends to be complex, and at times even complicated. This differs greatly from the many cold and rigid bureaucratic cadres devised by state capitalism and by certain pyramidal clusters of private macro-capitalism.

vate almost automatically to nobiliary status those subjects who, with advantage to the common good, successfully invested capital and effort to establish industries or develop those already existing.[36]

Many candidates to the nobility became industrialists as a result of this resolution. However, as we have seen, the authenticity of the noble condition consists not only in the use of a title conferred by royal decree, but also—and notably—in the possession of what could be called the characteristic moral profile of the aristocratic class. It is understandable that certain nouveaux riches becoming *nouveaux nobles* by the royal decree might have found it very difficult to acquire this moral profile. This profile is only acquired through a long family tradition, which the nouveaux riches and the *nouveaux nobles* usually lack. Important elements of this tradition can be found, however, in less affluent traditional bourgeois elites.

The injection of this new blood into the traditional nobility could, in certain cases, increase its vitality and creativity. However, it could also introduce certain traces of vulgarity and *arrivisme* disdainful of old traditions, with evident harm to the integrity and coherence of the aristocratic profile. The very authenticity of the nobility could thus be impaired.

Similar situations in more than one European country had an analogous result. In general, though, it was circumscribed by various factors.

First of all, the aristocratic influence was still profound in European society. The *nouveau noble*-nouveau riche felt ill at ease in his new social condition if he did not strive to assimilate, at least in part, its profile and manners. He rarely gained easy admittance to many of the salons. This exerted an aristocratizing pressure upon him that was reinforced by the attitude of the common people.

The people perceived the comic situation of the brand-new count or marquis and made him the target of unpleasant mockery. Far from opposing the environment in which he was heterogeneous, then, the new noble generally strove in earnest to adapt himself to it. Above all, he did his best to give his children a genuinely aristocratic education.

These circumstances facilitated the absorption of the new elements by the old nobility to such an extent that, after one or more generations, the differences between the traditional and new nobles disappeared. The new nobles ceased to be "new" with the mere passing of time. The marriage of young nobles, bearers of historic names, to daughters or granddaughters of nouveaux riches-*nouveaux nobles* enabled them to avoid economic decadence and to give new luster to their coats of arms.

To some extent this continues today. However, due to the strongly egalitarian tone of modern society and to other factors mentioned in this book, an almost automatic ennobling, such as that instituted by King Charles III, would demean the nobility much more than it would serve it, since the nouveaux riches are less and less inclined to become new nobles.

---

[36]   Cf. Cadenas y Vicent, *Cuadernos*, pp. 35-38.

d. Are there means, within the present political framework, of creating new forms of nobility?

The question remains: Are there means today of establishing new nobilities—with new hierarchies and modalities that correspond to new functions—so long as they aim to attain some degree of that plenitude of excellence linked to hereditary continuity, which characterizes the nobility still recognized as such today?

On the other hand, what means are there within the present political framework, and independently of hereditary succession, to admit new forms of nobility for people who have rendered distinguished services to the common good, either because of outstanding talent, salient personality, heroic self-denial and chivalrous courage, or great capacity of action?

In the Middle Ages and in the Old Regime, there was always room to receive into the nobility people who, although born in the humblest plebeian home, nevertheless gave incontestable proofs of possessing these attributes in a heroic or excellent degree. This was the case of some soldiers who distinguished themselves in war by their courage or tactical skill.

e. A new hierarchical step in the social ladder

These considerations broaden the perspective and give a new flexibility to the distinction between nobility and bourgeoisie, paving the way for a nobiliary *tertium genus*. This would be a nobility *diminutae rationis*, like the nobility of the robe and the nobility of the bell in Old France.

A question arises here about the use of the word *nobility*.

Just as the fruitful vitality of a country's social body can give rise to new nobilities, so it can also spark the formation of new non-noble levels within lower classes. This is happening among blue-collar workers today. Modern technology's demand for highly skilled and responsible manpower is creating a third category of worker, midway between the intellectual and the manual worker.

This picture places the reader before a blossoming of new situations. Only with the utmost tact and the intelligent caution intrinsic to organic societies will it be possible to develop, with firmness of principles, justice, and objectivity, new levels in the social hierarchy.

There is yet another question: In view of this rousing "hierarchical" work that the course of events is demanding from the principled men of today, what do we mean by *noble*? In other words, what characteristics should a new level in the social scale have to merit the qualification of noble? And what characteristics would bar title to this illustrious qualifier?

The question covers so many complex situations in constant change that it is impossible to provide a quick and simple answer at this time. This is especially true if we consider that problems of this nature are better solved through the joint effort of thinkers and the consuetudinary evolution of society than through the lucubrations of mere theorizers, technocrats, and the like.

Merely touching upon this interesting question, we must say that the qualifier *noble* can only be granted to social categories that maintain significant analogies with the nobility's original and archetypical standard, which was born in the Middle Ages. It continues to be the standard of true nobility down to our times.

Among the factors whose felicitous convergence favors the formation of new types of nobility we may mention the vigorous and close link between the purpose of the social class and the regional or national common good; the distinctive willingness of its members to disinterestedly sacrifice personal rights and interests for the sake of this common good; the excellence attained by its members in their daily activities; the consequent and exemplary elevation of the human, moral, and social standards of its members; a correlated lifestyle made possible by the special gratitude with which society reciprocates this dedication to the common good; and, finally, sufficient economic means to confer adequate preeminence to the condition resulting from these factors.[37]

f. The hope that the way indicated by Pius XII not be forgotten

These reflections, prompted by the attentive study of the allocutions of Pius XII on the nobility, express hope—yes, hope that the way shown by this Pontiff be neither forgotten nor underestimated by the nobility, nor by the authentic but not specifically noble social elites existing not only in Europe, but also in the three Americas, Australia, and elsewhere.

May the closing words of this chapter express hope therefore and not merely legitimate nostalgia.

---

[37] Appendixes I and II of this work provide examples of the formation of analogous traditional elites and new forms of aristocracy in the New World.

At the Apogee of Today's Religious, Moral, and Ideological Crisis: A Propitious Moment for the Action of the Nobility and the Traditional Elites

*D*espite the stupendous vitality the European peoples displayed in facing the havoc wreaked by the two world wars, one must admit that the reconstruction in the aftermath of the last conflict demanded considerable effort and much time.

Throughout the period when Pius XII pronounced his allocutions to the Roman Patriciate and Nobility (1940-1958), the postwar economic recovery of Europe was progressing slowly. The Pontiff's paternal concern naturally led him to make many references to this critical situation in these memorable allocutions.

In the following decade, however, the rate of the economic recovery increased appreciably, resulting in famous "economic miracles" like the "German miracle" and the "Italian miracle." This series of "miracles" has not ended. The present economic prosperity of Spain and Portugal—little-favored nations until now—can still be somehow included in it.

This surge of prosperity—the apogee of which Pius XII (who died in 1958) did not see, but to which the Conciliar constitution *Gaudium et Spes* sang a hymn of salutation and joy in 1965—noticeably modified the European scene.

History will one day give a detailed account of the role played by the nobility and other traditional elites in this recovery. This account will perhaps permit an assessment of the repercussion of Pius XII's notable directives on the conduct of these classes as they helped in Europe's economic recovery. Without venturing a precise judgment, it seems that this role was considerable, albeit proportional to the means of action available to the aristocracy and the elites of each country.

One thing is certain. When the tragic extent of the failure of state capitalism and the dictatorship of the proletariat in Soviet Russia and Eastern Europe began to be patent in 1989, the western European countries, the United States, and other nations promptly sent enormous sums to their aid—for which little or no repayment may be expected. Thus did the great democratic nations, oriented and enriched by free enterprise, implicitly show mankind the triumphant contrast between West and East.

Nevertheless, how mistaken are those who imagine that this reacquired prosperity solved the crises inherited by the Western nations in previous decades and worsened by new factors. The misconception that prosperity is always the mainstay of the order and well-being of nations, and that poverty is the principal cause of crises is clearly disproved by events in postwar Europe.

The process of healing and reflourishing on the Old Continent was well advanced in 1968 when the terrible Sorbonne crisis erupted. This crisis revealed the tumultuous and destructive influence on the youth of philosophies previously considered extravagant manifestations of certain "beautiful people" in cultural and worldly circles.

The extensive reverberations of the Sorbonne phenomenon among avant-garde youth in Europe and elsewhere revealed the depth of this opened chasm. The general deterioration of customs, already deplored by Pius XII, found favorable grounds in this milieu of wealth and extravagance, prompting a moral and cultural crisis that plunged the free world into a situation that was graver than previous crises, which had been merely or predominantly economic. The spreading of prosperity was rightly seen by lucid and well-documented observers as an important factor in this tragic worsening of the moral crisis.[1]

This situation was exacerbated by a crisis of totally unprecedented magnitude that afflicts the Catholic Church, the pillar and foundation of morality and the good order of society.[2]

Two important events subsequently influenced these perspectives: the Gulf War and the victorious stand of the Baltic peoples—notably the glorious resistance of the heroic Lithuanian people—in favor of their independence. It would be a serious error to underestimate the importance of this latter event. Involving fundamental principles of morality and international order, it caused a just and emphatic disturbance in the conscience of peoples, as was shown by the brilliant petition drive promoted by the TFPs in 26 countries, which attained the impressive total of 5,218,520 signatures.[3]

* * *

As this work draws to a close, grave unknowns beset mankind.

The world situation described by Pius XII has changed considerably, mainly thanks to the economic improvement resulting from Europe's aforementioned "miracles."

---

[1] TFP-Covadonga's *España, anestesiada sin percibirlo, amordazada sin quererlo, extraviada sin saberlo: La obra del PSOE* (Madrid: Editorial Fernando III El Santo, 1988), pp. 109-113, described the phenomenon as it happened in Spain. Summaries of this book were published in several languages by other TFPs.

[2] See Chapter I, 4.

[3] On December 4, 1990, a delegation of eleven members from various TFPs, led by Dr. Caio V. Xavier da Silveira, Director of the TFP Bureau in Paris, went to Vilnius, the capital of Lithuania, to deliver personally the microfilms of these signatures to President Vytautas Landsbergis. Going on to Moscow, the delegation delivered a letter in the Kremlin offices of Mikhail Gorbachev on December 11. The letter stated: "In the name of over five million signers, we formally ask you to remove all the obstacles to Lithuania's total independence. World public opinion and History will be grateful for this action."

May Our Lady of Fatima, the special patroness of this agitated contemporary world, help the nobility and like elites to heed the wise teaching Pius XII bequeathed them.

Since then, however, two great crises have become more pronounced. One is the internal crisis in the former empire behind the Iron Curtain; the other is the crisis within the Catholic Church.

This latter painful crisis is related to the very essence of the issues discussed herein. We nevertheless will refrain from analyzing it, for its gravity and amplitude would demand a separate work, probably of many volumes.

The general features of the former crisis are well known throughout the world. At the moment of this writing, the nations that constituted the U.S.S.R. have separated. Frictions among them are increasing, deepened as they are by the fact that some of these nations have the means to unleash an atomic war.

It is not improbable that an armed conflict within the former U.S.S.R. would lead to the involvement of major Western nations, with consequences of apocalyptic dimension. One of these consequences could easily be the migration of entire populations pressed by fear of war and actual famine to Central and Western Europe. This migration could assume a critical character of unpredictable scope.

What effects would this exodus have on nations until recently under Soviet domination, such as those on the Baltic Sea? What effects would it have on other countries, such as Poland, the Czech Republic, Slovakia, Hungary, Rumania, and Bulgaria, about which it would be very daring to affirm that they have entirely escaped the communist yoke?

To complete this panorama, we should consider the possible reaction of the Maghreb in face of a Western Europe enmeshed in problems of this magnitude, as well as developments throughout northern Africa and the profound impact of the immense fundamentalist wave sweeping the peoples of Islam, of which the Maghreb is an integral part. Who can predict with certainty the extremes to which these factors of instability will bring the world, and especially the Christian world?

For the time being, the latter is not engulfed in the triple drama of a seemingly peaceful invasion from the East, a probably less peaceful invasion from Africa, and an eventual worldwide conflagration. However, the fatal outcome of the long revolutionary process whose outline was summarized in the last chapter of this work is already within sight.

This process has advanced relentlessly, from the waning and fall of the Middle Ages to the initial joyful triumphs of the Renaissance; to the religious revolution of Protestantism, which remotely began to foment and prepare the French Revolution and, even more remotely, the Russian Revolution of 1917. So invariably victorious has been its path despite uncountable obstacles that one might consider the power that moved this process invincible and its results definitive.

These results seem definitive indeed if one overlooks the nature of this process. At first glance it seems eminently constructive, since it successively raised three edifices: the Protestant Pseudo-Reformation, the liberal-democratic republic, and the Soviet socialist republic.

The true nature of this process, however, is essentially destructive. It is Destruction itself. It toppled the faltering Middle Ages, the vanishing Old Regime, and the apoplectic, frenetic, and turbulent bourgeois world. Under its pressure the former U.S.S.R. lies in ruins—sinister, mysterious, and rotten like a fruit long-since fallen from the branch.

Hic et nunc, is it not true that the milestones of this process are but ruins? And what is the most recent ruin generating but a general confusion that constantly threatens imminent and contradictory catastrophes, which disintegrate before falling upon the world, thus begetting prospects of new catastrophes even more imminent and contradictory. These may vanish in turn, only to give way to new monsters. Or they may become frightful realities, like the migration of Slavic hordes from the East to the West, or Moslem hordes from the South to the North.

Who knows? Will this actually happen? Will this be all? Will it be even worse than this?

Such a picture would discourage all men who lack Faith. Those with Faith, however, can already hear a voice coming from beyond this confused and grim horizon. The voice, capable of inspiring the most encouraging confidence, says: "Finally, my Immaculate Heart will triumph!"[4]

What credit can be placed in this voice? The answer, which it gives, is but a sentence long: "I am from heaven."[5]

So there are reasons for hope. Hope for what? For the help of Providence in any work performed with vision, rigor, and method to defend the world from the threats hanging over mankind like so many swords of Damocles.

It behooves us, then, to pray, confide in Providence, and act.

To develop this action, it is fitting to remind the nobility and analogous elites of their special and, indeed, primordial mission in the present circumstances.

May Our Lady of Fatima, the special patroness of this agitated contemporary world, help the nobility and like elites to heed the wise teachings Pius XII bequeathed them. These teachings direct them to a task that Pope Benedict XV had expressively termed the "priesthood" of the nobility.[6]

Should they dedicate themselves entirely to this extraordinary task, they and their descendants will one day be amazed at the vastness of the results they will have obtained for their respective countries, for mankind, and, above all, for the Holy Catholic Church.

---

[4] Words of Our Lady at Fatima in the apparition of July 13, 1917 (*Memórias da Irmã Lúcia*, 3d ed. [Fatima, Portugal: Postulação, 1978], p. 150).

[5] Ibid., p. 146.

[6] See Chapter VII, 8 d.

Part II

With gratitude, the TFP dedicates this study to the memory of two eminent examples of the American elite, Mrs. Virginia Hallinan Tatton and Mrs. Mary O'Connor Braman, who were united in the course of a long existence by cordial family ties and by the profession of the same Catholic Faith.

They understood and admired the work of the TFP and supported it with a distinguished generosity.

The United States:
An Aristocratic Nation
Within a Democratic State

This Appendix provides an analysis of American social history from the perspective of the thesis on the nobility and analogous traditional elites expounded by Prof. Plinio Corrêa de Oliveira in Part I of this book. This Appendix was prepared by a commission of the American Society for the Defense of Tradition, Family and Property (TFP). The research and work of this commission were done under the general guidance and coordination of Professor Corrêa de Oliveira.

The Church teaches us to love

The rays of the Sun of Divine predilection shone with touching splendor on this genuine poor man, who was born a slave. Endowed with a great soul, he showed a gentleman's dedication and magnanimity to his masters even—and especially—when misfortune cast them into poverty. They rewarded his generosity, giving him his deserved freedom and loving him as a devoted son.

Providence also displayed its preferential option on behalf of this authentic American lady, linked by marriage to the Scottish nobility and by blood to the genuine analogous elites of our country when it was splendidly beginning its great trajectory.

Saint Elizabeth Ann Seton (1774-1821): Born an Episcopalian to one of New York's most distinguished families, the Bayleys, she was the first native-born American to be elevated to the honors of the altar. She married William Seton, from whose family, of noble Scottish descent, Mary Stuart, Queen of Scots and brave Catholic martyr, had chosen a lady-in-waiting more than two hundred years earlier. He was also one of New York's wealthiest importers. His health having deteriorated due to tuberculosis, in a last attempt to stave off death, he decided on a sea voyage to Leghorn, Italy, and there he died. In the aristocratic Filicchi family of Leghorn, Mrs. Seton found assistance in her woes. These truly Christian nobles did a marvelous apostolate with her and acquainted her for the first time with the truths of the Faith.

Not long after, returning to New York, she announced to her family and friends that she was thinking of becoming a Catholic and was met with shocked disbelief. There was a rush to prevent her from joining the Church of the "offscoured" Irish and German immigrants, and upon her final submission to the Catholic Church she became the object of suspicion and ridicule, and was disowned by most of her family.

After much prayer, she left for Baltimore with her five children, where she founded her first school. The hope of establishing a religious community was apparent from the beginning. With a donation from a wealthy convert, she established a community of sisters in Emmitsburg, Maryland, where she also founded the first parochial school in the United States. Although dying at the age of 47, she lived to see her work flourish.

Servant of God Pierre Toussaint (1766-1853): Born to slavery in Saint Domingue (present-day Haiti), Toussaint came to New York in 1789 with his master, Jean Bérard du Pithon, a French noble and prosperous planter who was fleeing the turmoil unleashed in Saint Domingue by the French Revolution. Two years later, his master died without having been able to recover the family fortune, thus leaving Madame Bérard in poverty. Distressed at the plight of his mistress, Toussaint did not allow her poverty to come to light. He provided for the table by applying his skills as a fashionable hairdresser for the ladies of New York's high society, served dinners to his mistress and her guests elegantly dressed as butler, and entertained everyone after the meals with the music of his violin.

Given his freedom in 1807, he married in 1811. Because of his virtue, discretion, and admirable wisdom, many people of the upper class brought him their troubles, seeking his advice. His generosity and dedication seemed unlimited, and he became the unknown benefactor of many who had fallen on hard times. He died in 1853, having profoundly marked New York society. Throngs of grateful people, white and black, high and low-born, filled Old Saint Peter's Church for his funeral. His remains lie today in the crypt of Saint Patrick's Cathedral, where they gloriously await the day of resurrection and, we hope, the day when he will be honored with the glorious title of "saint."

Introduction

$\mathcal{T}$he main text of this book established the legitimacy, utility, and role of the nobility and other traditional elites within contemporary society. Special attention was placed on the traditional nobility in the European context, that is, the military nobility of rural origin.

In his memorable allocutions to the Roman Patriciate and Nobility, the inspiration for the present book, Pius XII addressed not only the nobility of the Eternal City, but the entire European nobility of his time. Thus the themes he treated were not restricted to problems specific to the Roman aristocracy.

Moreover, in various allocutions the Pontiff referred to the elites analogous to the nobility and to their function within contemporary society.[1]

This provided ample justification for including analogous elites in the present study of the nobility. Just as the development of social life in the Middle Ages led naturally to the formation of its historical nobility, later social processes legitimately gave rise to family lineages of long history and elevated culture in the fields of teaching, law, public administration, commerce, and industry. Through the process of social evolution these families and their descendants came to constitute a privileged body alongside the historical nobility in the nations of the West. They became, in a word, analogous elites.

This form of nobility was neither military nor rural in origin, but rather of a cultural and administrative nature, rising from a hereditary tradition of public service or corporate leadership.

The development of analogous elites refutes the persistent myth that the European nobility was a closed caste, inaccessible to those outside its ranks, and raises questions of special interest to the United States today. If the formation of traditional elites analogous to the nobility occurred in Europe amid well-known ideological, social, and economic circumstances, we may ask if analogous circumstances existing in North America from the colonial period onward also produced such elites. We may further ask whether these elites were sufficiently well-estab-

---

[1] Regarding the traditional elites and their mission in contemporary society according to the allocutions of Pius XII, see Part I, Chapter V, 1, 2, 7, 9, 12, and Chapter VI, 3. Regarding traditional elites as new types of nobility, see Part I, Chapter VII, 9.

Meeting of Columbus with the Catholic Kings after his discovery of America. Oil by García Ibañez. (Museo del Ejército, Madrid)

The great Queen Isabella's effort to obtain the means for Columbus to accomplish his mission of discovery brought the light of her presence to the fountainheads of the history of the three Americas. She even pawned the jewels of the Crown of Castile to furnish the funds needed by the daring Genoese navigator.

The missionary purpose ranked foremost in the endeavors of the Queen, who, along with her husband, King Ferdinand of Aragon, prostrated the remnants of Moorish power in Spain and victoriously entered Granada.

Today, an important and growing worldwide movement is beseeching John Paul II for the canonization of Isabella the Catholic. The postulator of her cause is the illustrious theologian and canonist Father Anastasio Gutiérrez, C.M.F.

lished and stable to qualify as traditional. Finally, we may inquire into their place and function in democratic American society.

This organic process of forming analogous elites continues to this day, even amid enormous social, political, economic, and cultural transformations. This point is critical, since the very concept of a nobility seems archaic to many contemporary readers. For such mentalities, devoting an entire book to the study of this subject contradicts a deeply rooted principle of the modern age, embodied in the mercantile aphorism, Time is money. Such a book might seem a waste of time, devoid of any practical benefit.

We have no intention of excavating a stagnant nobility from dusty archives or museum showcases. Rather, we seek to show that a sound society must develop in such a way that traditional and emerging elites are able to exercise their beneficial directive function.

That this process continues in countries that still have monarchies—even when constitutional—comes as no surprise. But, someone might ask, does this also take place in democratic societies which, by definition, are based on the negation of hereditary privileges? In fact, contemporary studies have shown that social stratification is natural and useful in any form of government and that the organic process of forming elites has existed in all human societies, whatever their nature.[2]

Even unhealthy societies generate elites—unhealthy elites. In contrast to healthy societies, they generate monsters. Such is the case of the communist *nomenklatura* and other forms of discriminatory and oppressive elites that arose from the morbid inequalities that the communist regime inevitably created.

An analysis of the development of analogous elites across the contemporary world would be an interesting study, though impractical within the scope of a single book. Such a monumental work would require a multi-volume encyclopedia.

The present book documents the development of these elites in the New World, not only those born of the Catholic and Latin-Iberian tradition, but those of predominantly Protestant and Anglo-Saxon origin as well.

In Brazil, for example, the process occurred spontaneously, giving rise to a varied aristocracy that eventually constituted a true landed gentry with its own traditions and privileges.[3] In Hispanic America, the formation of a local aristocracy had a more institutional character, frequently established by royal decree or by processes governed by positive law.[4] These aristocracies contributed to the development of the cultures in their respective countries, gradually differentiating themselves from the aristocracies of their mother countries and other colonies.

Did something similar take place in the United States of America? According to conventional wisdom, no other country in history has had more innovative conditions than the United States. It was born of a revolution that sought a *novus ordo seclorum*, severed from the great tradition of European civilization, which it

---

[2] See Chapters I-III of this Appendix.

[3] See Appendix II.

[4] See Appendix II.

denigrated as old and decadent, victim of the defects supposedly typical of aristocratic societies.[5]

The United States is universally considered the republic par excellence, whose very Declaration of Independence consecrated the principle that "all men are created equal." It is the nation of "self-made men," where anyone can rise "from rags to riches"; the nation of individual liberties, where authority and hierarchy are viewed with suspicion; the New World where the Old-World elegance of aristocratic ceremony gives way to the unrestrained simplicity of democratic manners; the nation where pragmatism and "common sense" take precedence over aesthetic and spiritual considerations.

The enormous influx of immigrants, coming from virtually every corner of the globe, further accentuated these characteristics and seemed to definitively bury any residual hope of forming local traditional elites.

The very words "American nobility" might seem incongruous.[6] However, since nobility and analogous elites appeared in the Latin American countries, countries born of egalitarian revolutions largely inspired by the French Revolution, cannot one also legitimately ask if there could have been an American aristocracy?[7] We speak of aristocracy, not nobility, because in the United States there was no titled nobility outside the colonial period.[8]

The question about the existence of elites in the United States is of fundamental importance for our day. A positive response to this inquiry would demand a profound and objective revision of not a few cliches about this great nation should

---

[5] Describing the differences between the New and Old Worlds, historian Gordon Wood writes: "Throughout the eighteenth century European liberal intellectuals had put together from the diffuse political thought of the day an image of the New World that contrasted sharply with the Old. Mired in what the Enlightenment believed to be a decadent feudal society debilitated by oversophistication and cultivation, the European illuminati came to see in the Americans, 'this enlightened people.'... The New World seemed uniquely free of the constraining distinctions of social rank—a naturally egalitarian society, young, rustic, energetic, sometimes even frighteningly and fascinatingly barbarous, but at any rate without the stifling and corrupting refinement of the Old World. In the minds of many of the French philosophers America had become a 'mirage in the West,' a symbol of their dreamed-of new order" (Gordon Wood, *The Creation of the American Republic, 1776-1787* [Chapel Hill: Univ. of North Carolina Press, 1969; W. W. Norton & Co., 1972], p. 98. Used with permission.)

[6] Sociologists Kenneth Prewitt and Alan Stone comment: "The word *elite* grates on the ears of most Americans. Like *racism* or *socialism*, *elite* is too harsh and un-American a term to gain wide acceptance. It is to be expected that the term infrequently appears in political reporting and political speeches. To use a phrase such as 'political elite' is to come too close to denying that all men are created equal, and this is to deny the founding charter itself" (Kenneth Prewitt and Alan Stone, *The Ruling Elites: Elite Theory, Power and American Democracy* [New York: Harper and Row, 1973], p. 2). Prewitt and Stone are professors at the University of Chicago and Rutgers University, respectively.

[7] Because of an analogy between the elites in the three Americas and those of Europe, the authors, for convenience of expression, chose to call certain traditional elites of the United States "aristocracy." Clearly, the human groups encompassed by this denomination are very different from each other. These differences, naturally, can be observed not only among the several American elites that could be called aristocracy, but also between these and their Latin American and European counterparts.

[8] It is well known that in the period shortly before independence, the English Crown had begun to consider granting titles of nobility to prominent citizens of the American colonies in order to form a local titled aristocracy and thereby provide a solution to the chronic instability of colonial society. This, indeed, was one of the factors that precipitated the American Revolution, because the revolutionaries did not want this solution. (Cf. Wood, *The Creation of the American Republic*, pp. 111-112.)

the facts prove them obsolete. The United States would appear in a different light. The mirage of the "American way of life," created especially by Hollywood, would fade in the light of evidence that in the United States, as in all societies, an elite-forming process exists, perhaps even more marked in certain ways than in many Latin American societies.

Such a finding would have an impact not only in the United States, but throughout the world. For no one will deny that the fascination with the Hollywood myth of the American way of life lies at the root of profound psychological, cultural, and social transformations in Europe, Latin America, and other parts of the world where the influence of American culture has made itself felt. Under the illusion that this myth opened the road to the future, countless people adapted their mentalities, ideas, and ways of being to it, often abandoning the traditions and customs of their own cultures. The deleterious effects of this veritable cultural revolution, under the aegis of the American liberal myth, should not be underestimated.

The present study intends to offer support for a more realistic view of the United States, thus correcting distortions that have steered so many countries in the wrong direction.

On the other hand, the problem of analogous elites in the United States has a special doctrinal interest. Such a study would indicate how elites were formed in the spontaneity of an entirely liberal society, through a type of social free enterprise.

We will not attempt to find in the United States a medieval military nobility, nor its descendants brought to American soil by misfortune or adventure. Rather, we will seek to establish the existence of elites analogous to the nobility in the United States and their important role in the political, economic, social, and cultural life of the country.

This seems a particularly opportune moment to raise the question of the existence of analogous elites in the United States, for important sectors of the American middle class have become a fertile ground for the germination of these elites since the end of World War II.

A key characteristic of American society is a desire, an impetus for self-improvement, which manifests itself in the immense majority of its people in a multitude of ways. This desire for the advancement of each individual, family, and class motivates them to seek all possible means of improving their knowledge, status, and wealth. From this it follows that the lower levels of the middle class are able to enjoy a standard of living that, a generation before, belonged to higher classes.

Another characteristic that can be observed at other levels of the middle class, especially in the more intellectualized sectors, is a desire for a greater culture, due in part to the presence at American universities of European professors, who enhance the already-improving cultural level of these institutions. In addition, many Americans have traveled to Europe and other countries to pursue advanced studies and degrees in science, literature, history, and other fields.

This elevation of the intellectual level and standard of living in sectors of the middle class clashed with existing democratic and egalitarian habits. Egalitarianism exuded a certain vulgarity within this class. Intellectual improvements, however, rebuffed this vulgarity and elevated American culture. The triumph of culture over egalitarianism would turn these sectors of the middle class into an ever more fertile ground from which analogous elites could arise.

How, then, does one approach the issue of elites analogous to the nobility within the United States? The present study is written with the objective of contributing to an adequate response to this important question.

CHAPTER I

Social Stratification in the United States

1. A Unilateral Picture of the United States

a. The influence of the American myth

Throughout the last century and the first half of the present one, historical literature regarding the United States reflected diverse interpretations of the American myth.[1] According to the more radical interpretations of this myth, the United States is the "redeemer nation,"[2] entrusted with the "manifest destiny" of spreading the dominion of liberal democracy, "liberating" the nations of the world from "oppressions" reminiscent of the austere and hierarchical European civilization that originated in the Middle Ages, thereby ushering in a new era for mankind.[3]

The impressive territorial expansion and, especially, the formidable economic

---

[1]   The expression "American myth" designates a certain egalitarian and liberal way of perceiving the American spirit. This stems more from ideological preconceptions of Enlightenment and rationalist origin, characteristic of certain currents of thought, than from an objective vision of the American situation. The religious repercussions of this myth were condemned by Pope Leo XIII in his Apostolic Letter *Testem benevolentiae* of 1899. Cf. Thomas McAvoy, *The Americanist Heresy in Roman Catholicism, 1895-1900* (Notre Dame, Ind.: Univ. of Notre Dame Press, 1963).

[2]   Cf. Ernest Lee Tuveson, *Redeemer Nation: The Idea of America's Millennial Role* (Chicago: Univ. of Chicago Press, 1968); Conrad Cherry, *God's New Israel* (Englewood Cliffs, N.J.: Prentice-Hall, 1971); and A. Frederick Merk, *Manifest Destiny and Mission in American History* (New York: Alfred A. Knopf, 1963).

[3]   An affirmation of this myth in its fanaticism is contained in the words of Senator Albert Beveridge, historian and political leader, in 1897: "God has not been preparing the English-speaking and Teutonic peoples for a thousand years for nothing but vain and idle self-contemplation and self-admiration. No. He made us master organizers of the world to establish system where chaos reigned. He has given us the spirit of progress to overwhelm the forces of reaction throughout the earth. He has made us adept in government that we may administer government among savage and senile peoples. Were it not for such a force as this the world would relapse into barbarism and night. And of all our race He has marked the American people as His chosen nation to finally lead in the redemption of the world" (quoted in Tuveson, *Redeemer Nation*, p. vii).

Such thinking still prevails in broad political and cultural sectors of the country, though rarely in such terms. Applied to the arena of international politics, it is called the "missionary" concept of the vocation of American democracy. Its opposite is, of course, isolationism.

We use the expression "liberal democracy." As this book clearly demonstrates, democracy is in itself legitimate and in accordance with the natural order. Liberal or revolutionary democracy, however, is egalitarian and destroys the sound traditions of the people. It is in this sense that the expression is used here.

and military development of the United States—which from the original thirteen colonies grew to be the fourth largest country in the world and the greatest temporal power in history—seemed to confirm this "manifest destiny."

Obviously, this manifest destiny would make no sense unless such a democracy thrived first within the country itself. Influenced by this myth in its various interpretations, many American historians and sociologists dedicated themselves almost exclusively to emphasizing the liberal, democratic, and egalitarian aspects of our country. Frequently sacrificing scientific rigor to an apologetic spirit in defense of this myth, they virtually ignored the existence of elites, aristocratic institutions, and institutions with aristocratic aspects analogous to those of the Old World.

As a result, a unilateral interpretation of the American situation was elaborated. This interpretation not only influenced the United States, but its diffusion throughout Europe facilitated the enthusiastic acceptance of revolutionary democratic ideas on that continent.

b. Alexis de Tocqueville: one source of this unilateral vision

Part of this unilateral interpretation of the American reality comes from the exegesis liberal scholars made of the work of Alexis de Tocqueville (1805-1859). This young French aristocrat visited the United States between 1831 and 1832. In 1835 he published his celebrated work *Democracy in America*, which quickly became the classic reference book for any analysis of American democratic society.

As historian Edward Pessen of the City University of New York has said, Tocqueville's work is the most influential and enduring analysis ever written about American democracy of that time. While other works have been largely laid aside, the interpretation of Tocqueville continues to enjoy widespread acceptance.[4]

The Viscount of Tocqueville unabashedly proclaimed himself an aristocrat: "I am an aristocrat by instinct." Sadly, however, he was persuaded that aristocracy had had its day and that he could not have "any natural affection for it, since that aristocracy had ceased to exist, and one can be strongly attached only to the living."[5]

This pessimism proceeded from his peculiar historical vision. "The nations of our time," he wrote, "cannot prevent the conditions of men from becoming equal."[6] The French aristocrat lamented this march toward equality, but saw it as historically inevitable and futile to resist: "Mankind today is impelled by an unknown force that moves it, at times gently, at times violently, toward the destruction of aristocracy.

[4]   Cf. Edward Pessen, *Riches, Class and Power Before the Civil War* (Lexington, Mass.: D.C. Heath & Co., 1973), p. 1. Pessen is Distinguished Professor of History at Baruch College at the City University of New York and a specialist in the pre-Civil War era.

[5]   Quoted in David Brudnoy, "'Liberty by Taste': Tocqueville's Search for Freedom," in *Modern Age—The First Twenty-Five Years: A Selection*, George Panichas, ed. (Indianapolis: Liberty Press, 1988), p. 157.

[6]   Alexis de Tocqueville, *Democracy in America* (New York: Vintage Books [1945] 1990), Vol. 2, p. 334. Copyright © 1945 and renewed 1973 by Alfred A. Knopf, Inc. Reprinted by permission of the publisher.

Alexis de Tocqueville

We may try to regulate or to slow down this force, but we cannot vanquish it."[7] He even contended that this process was willed by Providence: "To attempt to check democracy would be in that case to resist the will of God."[8]

Resigned to this course of events, Tocqueville devoted his immense intelligence and insight to trying "to regulate or to slow down" the revolutionary march toward total egalitarianism. He did so by defending the values of "liberty" as a means to prevent it from ending up in state despotism or mob rule. "It depends upon [the nations] themselves," he warned, "whether the principle of equality is to lead them to servitude or freedom, to knowledge or barbarism, to prosperity or wretchedness."[9]

When Tocqueville toured the United States in 1831, he thought he had found a society that had made the transition from the Old Regime based on aristocracy to a new order based on equality without succumbing to despotism or mob rule. In America, he contended, "a state of equality is perhaps less elevated, but it is more just; and its justice constitutes its greatness and its beauty."[10]

Tocqueville returned to France determined to provide his fellow countrymen and Europeans an example of a modern society in which equality had triumphed without encroaching on liberty. This was the origin of his perceptive *Democracy in America*. This goal, more apologetic than scientific, made Tocqueville concentrate his attention almost exclusively on the democratic and dynamic aspects of the country, while overlooking the strong aristocratic elements that still existed. The result was a penetrating but one-sided picture of the United States which served as the source of much of the liberal scholarship regarding the American system.[11]

Tocqueville's work presented Europe—then in revolutionary turmoil—with a fascinating vision of a prosperous and almost totally democratic country, where family, aristocratic and hereditary values had been virtually extinguished.

> In America the aristocratic element has always been feeble from its birth; and if at the present day it is not actually destroyed, it is at any rate so completely disabled that we can scarcely assign to it any degree of influence on the course of affairs. The democratic principle, on the contrary, has gained so much strength by time, by events, and by legislation, as to have become not only predominant, but all-powerful. No family or corporate authority can be perceived; very often one cannot even discover in it any very lasting individual influence.[12]

---

[7] Tocqueville, *L'Ancien Régime et la Révolution* (Paris: Gallimard, 1967), p. 50.

[8] Tocqueville, *Democracy in America*, Vol. 1, p. 7.

[9] Ibid., Vol. 2, p. 334.

[10] Ibid., p. 333.

[11] Tocqueville also inspired conservative scholarship. His *Democracy* was addressed to the Americans as much as to the Europeans. He pointed to those pitfalls that could derail the American experiment, and called for the preservation of certain values, particularly religion and family, as a means of keeping the experiment within proper bearings. For a conservative interpretation of Tocqueville, see Russell Kirk, *The Conservative Mind: From Burke to Elliot*, 6th rev. ed. (South Bend, Ind.: Gateway Editions, 1978), pp. 178-195.

[12] Tocqueville, *Democracy in America*, Vol. 1, pp. 52-53.

According to Tocqueville's interpretation, in the first half of the nineteenth century the United States was a society dominated by the masses. There were few very rich men but also few very poor ones. The rich were almost all "self-made men" of humble origin, their wealth not extending to the third generation. It was a dynamic and mobile society, with the rich and the poor rising and falling within the social kaleidoscope. In this society, social differences were insignificant. The word *servant* was taboo, prisoners shook hands with their wardens, workers dressed like the bourgeois, politicians, even those from patrician families, flaunted humble origins, and the general vulgarity of manners testified to the predominance of the lower classes.[13]

Tocqueville summarizes his ideas:

> Among the novel objects that attracted my attention during my stay in the United States, nothing struck me more forcibly than the general equality of condition among the people.... [This equality] gives a peculiar direction to public opinion and a peculiar tenor to the laws.
>
> ...The more I advanced in the study of American society, the more I perceived that this equality of condition is the fundamental fact from which all others seem to be derived and the central point at which all my observations constantly terminated.[14]

As one can deduce from this synthesis of Tocqueville's thinking regarding American society, he did not escape falling prey to the American myth. As Edward Pessen points out, "Tocqueville does not always make clear whether it is the *American* democratic society or an abstract democratic model of his own devising that underlies some of his imaginative flights."[15]

Various interpretations of this unilateral vision largely dominated American historiography and sociology until the middle of the present century. Sociologists labeled this vision the "pluralist school" because its adherents emphasize the horizontal, ecumenical and dynamic aspects of American society, neglecting factors of social stratification. Modern scholarship, however, has rectified this vision. "This charming canvas of a crude but exhilarating social democracy," explains Pessen, "has been largely demolished by modern research."[16] This is what we shall now expound.

---

[13] Cf. Pessen, *Riches, Class and Power Before the Civil War*, pp. 2-3.

[14] Tocqueville, *Democracy in America*, Vol. 1, p. 3.

[15] Pessen, *Riches, Class and Power Before the Civil War*, p. 2.

[16] Edward Pessen, "Status and Social Class in America," in *Making America: The Society and Culture of the United States*, Luther S. Luedtke, ed. (Washington, D.C.: U.S. Information Agency [1987] 1988), p. 276.

2. The Elitist School

a. The discrediting of the liberal myth

Influenced by this American myth, sociologists and historians formerly simply closed their eyes to the existence of elites in our country. Vance Packard, one of the oldest representatives of what came to be known as the elitist school, writes:

> Until recently, even sociologists had shrunk away from a candid exploration of social class in America. Social classes, they realized, were not supposed to exist. Furthermore, Karl Marx had made class a dirty word. As a result the social scientists, until a few years ago, knew more about the social classes of New Guinea than they did of those in the United States of America.[17]

Philip Burch, Rutgers University political science professor, pursues a similar vein in his detailed study on American elites. Regarding elite family ties, he observes: "This area has long been overlooked by American social scientists, perhaps because the very concept runs counter to the nation's democratic ethos."[18]

In fact, an implicit censure was imposed on those who dared to raise the subject of elites in the United States. Such studies were belittled as the fruit of dreamers, and discredited in "serious" academic milieus. "To propose that American society is almost as class-based as British society pushes one to the fringes of social respectability," noted Peter Cookson and Caroline Hodges Persell.[19]

However, by the mid-1930s the egalitarian interpretation of the American democratic experience began to reveal serious deficiencies. Growing numbers of sociological, historical, and psychological studies began to demonstrate not only the existence of defined and cohesive elites in American society, but also that the history of the elites is the principal essence of the history of the country. Professors Thomas Dye and L. Harmon Zeigler write:

> The pluralist ideology went unchallenged for a number of years, not only in American government texts, but also in the general literature of political science. Recently, however, several scholars have challenged the pluralists' claims to empirical validity and, therefore, undermined their claim to normative prescription as well. These scholars [are] sometimes referred to as neo-elitists.[20]

---

[17] Vance Packard, *The Status Seekers* (New York: David McKay Co., 1959), p. 6.

[18] Philip Burch, *Elites in American History* (New York: Holmes & Meier, 1980), Vol. 3, pp. 3-4.

[19] Peter W. Cookson, Jr., and Caroline Hodges Persell, *Preparing for Power: America's Elite Boarding Schools* (New York: Basic Books, 1985), p. 16.

[20] Thomas R. Dye and L. Harmon Zeigler, *The Irony of Democracy*, 2d. ed. (Belmont, Calif.: Duxbury Press, 1972), p. vii. Copyright © 1972 Wadsworth, Inc. Reprinted by permission of the publisher.

Confronted with the reality of the existence in the United States of elites analogous to the nobility and of their important role in the social, cultural, political, and economic life of the country, this nucleus of scholars (often of disparate political and social ideologies) began the enormous task of reexamining concepts that had dominated American historiography and sociology. A revisionist school was thus born, and soon acquired the name "elitist" because of its emphasis on the historical role of the elites.

The appearance of this elitist school coincides with and at a certain point relates to the post-World War II "conservative revival." Galvanized by a group of thinkers at the end of the 1940s, this current sought to revive conservative and traditional thinking in face of the growing debility of the dominant liberal doctrines. A fruit of this revival was a multiform conservative movement that continues to this day. One of its leading figures is the political thinker Dr. Russell Kirk.[21]

The elitist school deems the stance of the egalitarian pluralist school flawed because it is derived from presuppositions proven false by sociological, historical, and psychological research. After demonstrating the inconsistency of the rationalist bases of liberal democracy, the prominent elitist scholar C. Wright Mills concludes: "But now we must recognize this description [of democratic society] as a set of images out of a fairy tale."[22]

Analyzing the scientific and doctrinal bankruptcy of other sociological schools (among which were the Marxist and pluralist schools and that of Max Weber), Michael Burton and John Higley reached the same conclusions.

> Political sociology is currently without a dominant or leading paradigm. Pluralism has been largely displaced, but nothing has taken its place....
>
> We think elite theory may be able to step into this gap.... Even though much debate about their detailed formulation and application could be expected, the broad contentions of elite inevitability, elite variability, and elite-nonelite interdependence are consonant with the thinking of many political sociologists today. Indeed, over the last decade or so political sociology has experienced a noticeable, albeit implicit, convergence in the direction of elite theory....
>
> The field of elite studies is now rather enormous. Since Putnam's (1976) authoritative survey of some 650 works in English alone, nearly half that number have been published (the Social Science Index lists nearly 250 articles on elites appearing between 1976 and 1984).[23]

---

[21] Cf. Kirk's *Conservative Mind*, already noted, and *The Portable Conservative Reader* (New York: Penguin, 1982).

[22] C. Wright Mills, *The Power Elite* (New York: Oxford Univ. Press, 1956), p. 300.

[23] Michael G. Burton and John Higley, "Invitation to Elite Theory: The Basic Contentions Reconsidered," in *Power Elites and Organizations*, G. William Domhoff and Thomas R. Dye, eds. (Newbury Park, Calif.: Sage Publications, 1987), pp. 235-237. Burton is a professor of sociology at Loyola College, Baltimore. Higley is a professor of government and sociology at the University of Texas at Austin.

Of fairly recent origin, the elitist school has yet to develop fully its doctrines and their consequences. There seems to be room for development in the area of the moral influence of social elites—as, for example, their role as models for society. The elitist school focuses its analysis particularly on the political and sociological elements of the elites. In this it differs from the perspective of the author of this book, who bases his analysis of the social hierarchy on principles of religion, morality, and natural law.

The application of the principles of Pius XII regarding the existence and function of elites in modern society, that is, the use of religious criteria for analyzing a subject not customarily considered religious, is sound and advantageous. Considering the large number of Catholics in the world and the resulting influence of a Pontiff's thinking, an understanding of such papal teaching is a matter of great public interest, even for those who are not Catholics.

One cannot, however, deny the objective validity of the findings of the elitist school, which belie many preconceptions inherent in the liberal democratic vision and which present a more faithful picture of the social and historical reality of the United States as—in many ways—an aristocratic nation living within a democratic state.

b. Major themes of the elitist school

Dye and Zeigler point out key notions regarding elites and elitism.

> Elites are not necessarily conspiracies to oppress or exploit the masses....
> Elitism asserts that society is divided into the few who have power and the many who do not. According to elite theory, elites—not masses—allocate values for society....
> Elites, not masses, govern America. Especially in this industrial, scientific, and nuclear age, life in a democracy, just as in a totalitarian society, is shaped by a handful of men....
> Elitism does not mean that public policy will ignore or be against the welfare of the masses but only that the responsibility for the mass welfare rests upon the shoulders of elites, not upon the masses.
> ...Elitism contends that the masses have at best only an indirect influence over the decision-making behavior of elites.[24]

Burton and Higley synthesize the essential notions of the classical elite theorists under three major headings:
— Elites are an inevitable feature of all societies.
— It is the elites, and not the masses, who generally constitute the decisive factor in determining the direction of the social body.
— The movement of the social body is determined by a necessary interdependence between elites and nonelites.[25]

---

[24] Dye and Zeigler, *The Irony of Democracy*, pp. 3, 7, 343.

[25] Cf. Burton and Higley, "Invitation to Elite Theory," p. 220. By affirming this third major theme, the theore-

c. Elites, stratification, and social inequalities
are indispensable in an organic society

Many American sociologists emphasize that social stratification is normal and inherent to all societies, as it has existed in all times and places. The American myth of liberalism notwithstanding, United States is no exception to the rule.

Refuting the egalitarian myth, sociologist Pierre van den Berghe writes, not without a certain irony:

> That all men are created equal may have seemed a self-evident truth to the amiable optimist who signed the United States Declaration of Independence, but it flies in the face of all evidence. That all men should be treated as if they were equal is a rather exotic and recent idea born in Western culture a little over two hundred years ago.
>
> In the majority of societies for nearly all of human history, inequality has been treated as axiomatic, and human relations have been ordered on the premise that any two people are seldom if ever equal.... Egalitarianism may be good rhetoric, but it is bad sociology and, empirically, rank nonsense....
>
> ...All human societies are stratified.... A hierarchical order [is] evident in the human family, the smallest and most universal form of human social organization.[26]

The same idea is expressed by Robert Nisbet, who says that hierarchy arises from the "functional requirements of the social bond. There is no form of community that is without some form of stratification of function and role. Wherever two or more people associate, there is bound to be some form of hierarchy."[27]

In the same vein, Robin Williams of Cornell University states: "All known societies have some system of ranking their constituent members or groups along some kind of superiority-inferiority scale.... The differential valuation of men as individuals and as members of social categories is a universal, formal property of social systems."[28]

Analyzing social stratification in greater detail, Seymour Martin Lipset and Reinhard Bendix observe:

> In every complex society there is a division of labor and a hierarchy of prestige. Positions of leadership and social responsibility are usually ranked at the top, and positions requiring long training and superior intelligence are ranked just below. The number of leaders and highly educated individuals constitutes everywhere a small

---

ticians of the elites effectively refute the Marxist myth of class struggle, that is, the myth of a necessary antagonism between elites and nonelites.

[26] Pierre L. van den Berghe, *Man in Society: A Biosocial View* (New York: Elsevier, 1978), pp. 137-138.

[27] Robert Nisbet, *Twilight of Authority* (New York: Oxford Univ. Press, 1975), p. 238.

[28] Robin M. Williams, Jr., *American Society: A Sociological Interpretation* (New York: Alfred A. Knopf, 1960), p. 88.

minority. On the other hand, the great majority is made up of persons in the lower strata who perform manual and routine work of every sort and who command scant rewards and little prestige.[29]

Suzanne Keller, sociology professor at the City University of New York, conveys her decisive conclusions regarding the indispensable existence of inequalities in a social order:

> The existence and persistence of influential minorities is one of the constant characteristics of organized social life. Whether a community is small or large, rich or poor, simple or complex, it always sets some of its members apart as very important, very powerful, or very prominent. The notion of a stratum elevated above the mass of men may prompt approval, indifference, or despair, but regardless of how men feel about it, the fact remains that their lives, fortunes, and fate are and have long been dependent on what a small number of men in high places think and do.[30]

Nisbet affirms categorically: "Here we are brought face to face with the universal fact of *hierarchy*.... No society has ever existed, nor in all probability ever could exist, without inequality."[31]

Dye and Zeigler write:

> Elitism is a necessary characteristic of *all* societies....
>
> Inequalities among men are inevitable.... Men are not born with the same abilities, nor can they acquire them by education. Modern democrats who recognize that inequality in *wealth* is a serious obstacle to political equality propose to eliminate such inequality by taking from the rich and giving to the poor, to achieve a "leveling" which they believe is essential to democracy.... But *even if* inequalities of *wealth* were eliminated, differences among men in intelligence, organizational skills, leadership abilities, knowledge and information, drive and ambition, and interest and activity would remain. Such inequalities are sufficient to assure oligarchy, even if wealth were uniform.[32]

Sociologist Joseph Fichter writes compellingly: "The aspiration for complete democracy or for perfect equality among people is without scientific validity. Similarly, the promotion of an ideal of a classless society is both unrealistic and impossible."[33]

---

[29]   Seymour Martin Lipset and Reinhard Bendix, *Social Mobility in Industrial Society* (Berkeley and Los Angeles: Univ. of California Press, 1967), p. 1.

[30]   Suzanne Keller, *Beyond the Ruling Class: Strategic Elites in Modern Society* (New York: Random House, 1963), p. 3.

[31]   Robert A. Nisbet, *The Social Bond: An Introduction to the Study of Society* (New York: Alfred A. Knopf, 1970), p. 53. Copyright © 1970 Alfred A. Knopf, Inc. Reprinted by permission of the publisher.

[32]   Dye and Zeigler, *The Irony of Democracy*, pp. 363-364.

[33]   Joseph Fichter, *Sociology* (Chicago: Univ. of Chicago Press, 1957), p. 49.

The constant presence of social elites in society was explored in the nineteenth century by the Italian sociologists Gaetano Mosca and Vilfredo Pareto, and by the German sociologist Robert Michels. Commenting on their works, Burton and Higley observe:

> Mosca and Pareto surveyed history widely to demonstrate the inevitability of elites; Michels showed that even in an avowedly democratic and egalitarian organization such as the German Social Democratic party before World War I the emergence of an elite was unavoidable.
>
> Three-quarters of a century later, the inevitability contention stands unrefuted. The many dramatic upheavals and changes that have occurred since the classical theorists wrote have nowhere produced a modern society without elites.[34]

Indeed, the foundation of elitism cannot be denied, as it is based on a universal empirical finding. As van den Berghe notes:

> The sociological "left wing" has argued that stratification is "dysfunctional," while the "right wing" has held that it is "functional," meaning "good" for society. Whether good or bad, inequality undeniably exists in all human societies.... Other than liking or disliking it, there is not much we can do about it.[35]

3. The Elites in the United States

a. American society is hierarchical

American society, as all others, is hierarchical. It could not be otherwise, since the existence of elites is not only a natural occurrence in every organized social body, but constitutes an element essential to its proper functioning.

According to William Domhoff, professor of psychology at the University of California at Santa Cruz, "scholars also have done away with the classless society myth.... [America's] social structure is made up of strata that shade off one into the other until we arrive at the highest level."[36]

W. Lloyd Warner further explains:

> It is clear to those of us who have made studies in many parts of the United States that the primary and most important fact about the American social system is that it is composed of two basic, but antithetical, principles: the first, the principle of equality; the second, the principle of unequal status and of superior and inferior rank....

---

[34]   Burton and Higley, "Invitation to Elite Theory," pp. 220-221.

[35]   Van den Berghe, *Man in Society*, p. 169.

[36]   G. William Domhoff, *The Higher Circles* (New York: Vintage Books, 1970), pp. 73-74. Copyright © 1970 G. William Domhoff. Reprinted by permission of Random House, Inc.

>...Status systems must always exist.... The only possible choice for Americans is not between their status system and a perfect system of equality but between their kind of hierarchy and some other.[37]

Herbert von Borch, an author of German origin, comments on the less than accurate European perception of the United States as a democratic and egalitarian country:

>To the foreign observer, American life appears at first sight as egalitarian. He sees a colorful, vital, mobile surface, as compared with the old incrustations of European societies.... Under the surface, then, there unfolds a fascinating patchwork of consciously cultivated group distinctions, involving...deeper forces of separation.[38]

The presence of hierarchical social classes in the United States is stressed by Pessen: "Yet for all the undeniable singularity of American history, the evidence is abundant that classes, class lines, and distinctions of status do exist and have always existed here, as elsewhere in the modern world."[39]

Such class distinction does not restrict itself to persons and families of great fortune, but touches all of American society. As C. Wright Mills explains:

>In every town and small city of America an upper set of families stands above the middle classes and towers over the underlying population of clerks and wage workers. The members of this set possess more than do others of whatever there is locally to possess; they hold the keys to local decision; their names and faces are often printed in the local paper; in fact, they own the newspaper as well as the radio station; they also own the three important local plants and most of the commercial properties along the main street; they direct the banks. Mingling closely with one another, they are quite conscious of the fact that they belong to the leading class of the leading families....
>
>...So it has traditionally been, and so it is today in the small towns of America.[40]

We have, then, a society which, while not using titles of nobility, is no less hierarchical than European society. This social differentiation is obvious, for example, in New England, the original nucleus of English colonization, which remains the center of some of America's oldest traditions.

---

[37] W. Lloyd Warner, *American Life: Dream and Reality*, rev. ed. (Chicago: Univ. of Chicago Press, 1962), pp. 127, 129.

[38] Herbert von Borch, *The Unfinished Society* (Indianapolis: Charter Books, 1963), pp. 228-229. Copyright © 1962 by R. Piper & Co., Verlag, Germany.

[39] Pessen, "Status and Social Class in America," p. 270.

[40] Mills, *The Power Elite*, p. 30. Mills's testimony is above suspicion. A leftist by tendency (whom some consider a precursor of the New Left of the 1960s), Mills studied the elites in the United States not to defend them, but to denounce them. Nor is he the only elite theorist of this orientation. His sociological descriptions, nonetheless, coincide with those of all authors of this school in affirming the empirical fact of the hierarchical character of American society.

The Biltmore Estate in
Asheville, North Carolina.

In his analysis of social classes in this important region, W. Lloyd Warner writes:

> Studies of communities in New England clearly demonstrate the presence of a well-defined social-class system. At the top is an aristocracy of birth and wealth. This is the so-called "old family" class.... The families into which they were born can trace their lineage through many generations participating in a way of life characteristic of the upper class....
>
> The new families, the lower level of the upper class, came up through the new industries—shoes, textiles, silverware—and finance.... Except that they aspire to old-family status, if not for themselves then for their children....
>
> Below them are the members of the solid, highly respectable upper-middle class.... They aspire to the classes above and hope their good deeds, civic activities, and high moral principles will somehow be recognized.... Such recognition might increase their status and would be likely to make them members of the lower-upper group....
>
> These three strata, the two upper classes and the upper-middle, constitute the levels above the Common Man. There is a considerable distance socially between them and the mass of the people immediately below them.[41]

In the absence of titles of nobility, other expressions were coined to designate the Old Families in various cities and states. We have, for example, the Boston Brahmins, the Proper Philadelphians, the Knickerbockers or the Metropolitan 400 of New York, the Proper San Franciscans, the Genteel Charlestonians, the First Families of Virginia, the California Dons (designating families of old Spanish aristocracy), and so on. Many of these families still own their original ancestral mansions.[42]

In conclusion, these sociologists affirm that it is impossible to understand American society without considering its hierarchical character, as these words of Warner indicate:

> It is impossible to study with intelligence and insight the basic problems of contemporary American society and the psychic life of its members without giving full consideration to the several hierarchies which sort people, their behavior, and the objects of our culture into higher and lower social statuses. They permeate every aspect of the social life of this country.[43]

---

[41] W. Lloyd Warner, *Social Class in America: A Manual of Procedure for the Measurement of Social Status* (Chicago: Science Research Associates, 1949; New York: Harper Torchbooks, 1960), pp. 11-13.

[42] In 1981, the Preservation League of New York included thirty-seven great manors of the Hudson Valley among the most "significant properties" of the United States. Of these, twenty-two still remained in the hands of the original families. (Cf. Christopher Norwood, "The Last Aristocrats," *The New York Times Magazine*, November 16, 1981, p. 40.)

In Natchez, Mississippi, one of the centers of high social life in the South, the same phenomenon occurs. Robert de Blieux, ex-curator of the historical sites of the city, says: "Most of the cherished Natchez mansions have been owned by the same families for generations. They are the 'old-line Natchez people'" (cited in Casey Bukro, "Deep South Ambiance is Alive, Well in Natchez," *The Sacramento Bee*, March 1, 1992).

[43] Warner, *American Life: Dream and Reality*, p. 68.

b. The history of the United States is the history of its directing elites

After establishing the normative existence of elites in all societies, including the United States, the sociologists of the elitist school proceed to the next logical conclusion. Contrary to the egalitarian myth that social transformations are initiated by the masses, they affirm that it is the elites, not the masses, who establish the tone of national life. Every transformation in the elites has repercussions throughout the social body of the country. Kenneth Prewitt and Alan Stone write:

> The history of politics is the history of elites. The character of a society—whether it is just or unjust, dynamic or stagnant, pacifistic or militaristic—is determined by the character of its elite. The goals of society are established by the elites and accomplished under their direction.
>
> The elite perspective does not deny social change; even radical transformations of society are possible. The elitists only point out that most change comes about as the composition and structure of the elite is transformed.[44]

In no society are any of the classes that compose it habitually and necessarily deprived of all influence, however small. At any moment, even if only by omission, a class with little can exercise co-directive action on the social destiny of the nation. This truth is either expressed or implied in the thinking of countless authors, from the remotest past, who have analyzed this issue. We have, for example, the famous analogy between society and the human organism attributed to Menenius Agrippa.[45]

However, when the influence of one social class becomes almost exclusively preponderant, it is legitimate to affirm that the influence of this class is exclusive. The true meaning underlying this simplified language will not escape an astute reader.

With these premises in mind, the elitist scholars undertook the study of American history, not from the standpoint of the masses (that of the mythological historiography) but from that of the elites and their dominant social position. As Prewitt and Stone declare:

> American history is popularly portrayed in texts and politicians' speeches as if mass participation...has been of major political significance.... Despite the popularity of this interpretation of American history, many scholars...have reached quite different conclusions. This re-examination of American history (known as *revisionism*) is

---

[44] Prewitt and Stone, *The Ruling Elites*, p. 4.

[45] Menenius Agrippa was Roman consul in 503 BC. He defeated the Sabines and Samnites and was a great orator. In order to quell a conflict that had risen between the plebes and the Senate, he elaborated an apology, "The Members and the Stomach," which showed that, just as the revolt of some organs against others led to the organism's death, the same would occur with society if harmony among the social classes did not prevail. The conflict was resolved with the creation of the tribune of the people in the Senate.

still taking place.... However, enough studies have been made to cast considerable doubt on the conventional view of American history and to convince the reader that popular participation in political decision-making has usually been of minor importance.[46]

Such scientific studies analyzing the history of the power structure invariably reach the same conclusion, that the United States is not governed by masses, but by elites.[47] Dye and Zeigler state:

> In an influential book on power in Atlanta, Georgia, sociologist Floyd Hunter describes a pyramidal structure of power and influence, with most of the important community decisions reserved for a top layer of the business and financial leaders....
> Hunter's findings in Atlanta...are discomforting to those who wish to see America governed in a truly democratic fashion. Hunter's research challenges the notion of popular participation in decision making...it raises doubts as to whether cherished democratic values are being realized in American community life.[48]

The directive role of elites in the United States is not restricted to the political and economic spheres, but also extends significantly, even principally, to the social and cultural realm. American cultural life would be far different were it not for the tradition of generous patronage of the upper classes. In her book on wealthy classes in the United States, Charlotte Curtis explains:

> By giving millions to found and support art galleries, museums, operas, symphonies, hospitals, medical research, parks, educational institutions and a wide variety of charities, they popularize one cause over another, affecting local and national cultural, health and educational priorities in ways no ordinary person or few groups can.[49]

The attitudes of upper class women strongly influence national life, even when they do not hold public offices. Comments William Domhoff:

> The women of the upper class are fashion leaders, patrons of culture, directors of social welfare, and sustainers of the social activities that keep the upper class a social class.
> ...they participate in a great many activities which sustain the upper class as a social class and help to maintain the stability of the social system as a whole.[50]

The directive role of the elites is at times imponderable. Consider the influence

---

[46] Prewitt and Stone, *The Ruling Elites*, p. 31.

[47] A notable work dealing with this field is Philip Burch's three-volume study *Elites in American History*, from which we have already quoted.

[48] Dye and Zeigler, *The Irony of Democracy*, pp. 13, 14.

[49] Charlotte Curtis, *The Rich and Other Atrocities* (New York: Harper & Row, 1973), p. x.

[50] Domhoff, *The Higher Circles*, pp. 33, 56.

President Washington with the first Cabinet of the United States.
Left to right: Henry Knox, Thomas Jefferson, Edmund Randolph,
Alexander Hamilton, and George Washington.

of elites on the tastes of the public at large. As Charlotte Curtis notes: "By wearing the newest fashions, decorating and redecorating their several houses, demanding exquisite foods from their personal chefs,...they create taste in this country."[51]

Dye and Zeigler conclude:

> Mass governance is neither feasible nor desirable. Widespread popular participation in national political decisions is not only impossible to achieve in a modern industrial society, it is incompatible with the liberal values of individual dignity, personal liberty, and social justice. Efforts to encourage mass participation in American politics are completely misdirected....
>
> Elitism is a necessary characteristic of *all* societies.... There is no "solution" to elitism, for it is not *the* problem in a democracy.... The question, then, is not how to combat elitism or empower the masses...but rather how to *build* an orderly, humane, and just society.[52]

4. The American Paradox

American society is oriented by two fundamental but antithetical principles, the principle of equality and the principle of inequality.[53]

The coexistence of a commonly held democratic and egalitarian mythology with the commonly lived hierarchical reality creates a dilemma, which the simple affirmation of the inevitable existence of inequalities does not eliminate.

Such a dichotomy between ideology and lifestyle has been a constant feature of the American elites. As Warner points out: "Their official ideology is always heavily democratic and equalitarian, but their behavior and their values tend to separate them out as being superior to, and different from, the classes below them."[54]

This clash of principles restrains the elites from their natural expansion. They remain, to use the French expression, *coincées*, that is, pressed into the farthest corner, without the power needed to benefit society as they ought.

To the detriment of our country, many of the elite are convinced, at least in theory, that they should not exist. This shameful conviction impedes their expansion toward their natural destiny. It is as if some disease were acting upon a tree to prevent the growth of its branches.

The phenomenon of elites, as all that is under man's domain, is susceptible to exaggeration and excess, but the fear of one excess should not result in its opposite. In the present case, one can easily go from one excess to another. The fear of exaggerating the role of the elites can easily lead to their atrophy and the tragic consequences attendant thereto.

---

[51] Curtis, *The Rich and Other Atrocities*, p. x.

[52] Dye and Zeigler, *The Irony of Democracy*, p. 363.

[53] Cf. Warner, *American Life: Dream and Reality*, p. 20.

[54] Warner, *American Life: Dream and Reality*, p. 116.

One of the fruits of the elite is the production of a superior human type. However, as this superiority collides with democratic preconceptions, many members of the elites conceal their superiority; for example, corporate managers who wield a colossal power yet strive with an equal zeal to assume the habits of those of lower social status.

Therein lies the fundamental paradox of a society whose ideology is dominated by democratic and egalitarian principles and whose organic social constitution is governed by its natural hierarchies. As Joseph Fichter writes: "We have here apparently a peculiar combination of an actual stratified society and a general unwillingness of most Americans to admit the presence of stratification."[55]

In his introduction to Dixon Wecter's book on the history of elites in the United States, Louis Auchincloss states: "The very existence of a fashionable world has seemed to many the perpetuation of an arch heresy in the shrine of democracy, a vulgar noise breaking the hushed silence of the American dream."[56]

Origins and effects of the American paradox

The American paradox was born with the republic itself. Consistent with the republican ideology, the Founding Fathers of the new nation developed a legal and institutional framework that provided no place for aristocratic privilege. The first article of the Constitution, for example, prohibits the republican government from granting any titles of nobility; nor can titles from sovereigns or foreign governments be accepted by those who hold public office.[57] Other legal supports for a hereditary aristocracy, such as entail laws and primogeniture, were abolished in the first decades of the republic.

Nonetheless, aristocratic sentiments have persisted throughout the history of the country. Deprived of the traditional examples of social hierarchy, Americans, inspired by the organic vigor of society, searched for other role models.

According to David Potter, they rejected hereditary but not acquired social status. Since everyone needs a social identity and status, Americans were compelled to seek their own identities and to compete to elevate their social standing as "self-made" men. Such competitiveness for success inevitably generates pressures and tensions that for many, as Potter notes, are intolerable. It is not surprising that the most characteristic forms of mental illness in the United States are those originating in a sense of personal inadequacy and insecurity brought on by an implacable competitive system in all spheres of life.[58]

---

[55] Fichter, *Sociology*, p. 75.

[56] Louis Auchincloss, introduction to Dixon Wecter, *The Saga of American Society: A Record of Social Aspiration 1607-1937* (New York: Charles Scribner's Sons [1939] 1970), p. xiv.

[57] "No title of nobility shall be granted by the United States: and no person holding any office of profit or trust under them, shall, without the consent of the Congress, accept of any present, emolument, office, or title, of any kind whatever, from any king, prince, or foreign state" (Constitution of the United States of America, Article I, Section 9).

[58] Cf. David Potter, *Freedom and Its Limitations in American Life* (Stanford: Stanford Univ. Press, 1976), pp. 28-29.

The same phenomenon is reported by Lipset and Bendix.

> In cultures which accept the idea of aristocracy, and which explicitly recognize
> the existence of classes, it may be possible for an individual to ignore distinctions
> of status in a number of social contexts without feeling that he has thereby jeop-
> ardized his social or economic position.[59]

Thus, the United States presents the curiosity of a society with a directive elite
earnestly cultivating distinctions of status and, at the same time, theoretically convinced
that elites should not exist. Pessen notes this "paradoxical scene in which most of the
people seem altogether oblivious to the significance, even to the very existence, of the
class distinctions that in fact play so central a part in American life."[60]

5. Status in American Society:
Its Concept and Sources

Social hierarchy in the United States is comprised of many factors, some well
defined, others imponderable and inexpressible.

The term *status* is often used to designate this combination. As described by
Joseph Fichter, "social status is the position, or rank, which the person's contemporaries objectively accord to him within his society."[61]

Thus, everyone has a status, that is, a place in society, which stems from the
perceptions of others within society. Nonetheless, the expression is used more
frequently to refer especially to high social status, that is, to situations proper to
the upper classes. Richard Coleman and Lee Rainwater describe the elements that
delineate social status in the following terms:

> When Americans describe how they rank people they know and where they place
> themselves socially, they talk not just of income, or of income plus education plus
> occupation. They bring many more things to bear—most prominently moral stand-
> ards, family history, community participation, social skills, speech, and physical ap-
> pearance—few of which are measurable or ever have been measured in quantitative
> studies of status factors. These we will call the *finer points* in social standing.[62]

Among the sources of social status in the United States, sociologists include
wealth, lineage, education, club and association membership, occupation, and
authority.

---

[59] Lipset and Bendix, *Social Mobility in Industrial Society*, p. 48.

[60] Pessen, "Status and Social Class in America," p. 279.

[61] Fichter, *Sociology*, p. 41.

[62] Richard Coleman and Lee Rainwater, *Social Standing in America: New Dimensions of Class* (New York: Basic Books, 1978), p. 22.

a. Wealth

Wealth, past or present, contributes to social status.

> Even where wealth is not a direct and immediate condition of high status, not a means by which high status may be achieved directly, the presence of wealth or the fact that one's lineage was at one time connected with wealth is taken commonly as a manifestation of high status.... So is our own age in the United States and much of Western Europe. For some time now wealth, measured either as annual income or as fixed capital, has been a major criterion used in the ranking of status in the social order.[63]

However, not all wealth confers equal social status. Warner distinguishes various types of wealth, each conferring a successively lower level of social status. Inherited wealth carries the most prestige, because it signifies that the family has been rich for several generations. Wealth acquired through business, which permits its possessor to live from its revenue, characterizes the next level of social status. The lowest level is of those who must work to earn a living.[64]

Coleman and Rainwater confirm that inherited wealth confers the most prestige: "This was true up and down the social ladder; *inheritors at all economic levels were named by their acquaintances as examples of persons standing socially higher....* Nowhere is this more so than in Upper America."[65]

Sources of wealth can make a substantial difference in status. As Robert Bierstedt, a sociology professor at the University of Virginia, comments:

> Even if wealth is earned in legal and ethical ways, there are additional differences to be noted. Money acquired in laxatives, depilatories, cosmetics, gadgets, patent medicines, motion pictures, or retail trade may not have the "rank" attributed to money acquired in steel, railroads, lumber, shipping, finance, or heavy industry.[66]

Sociological studies show that those who steer the ship of American society are generally from the wealthier classes. Prewitt and Stone affirm:

> The tiny group, consisting primarily of men, that directs the political economy of the United States is overwhelmingly recruited from the wealthier families of society. Few persons reach elite positions in political and economic life unless they are born to wealth, acquire it fairly early in life, or at least have access to it....
> ...It is not wrong, however, to claim that the wealthiest strata of the population supply a very disproportionate number of those recruited into the elite. Top positions

[63] Nisbet, *The Social Bond*, pp. 191-192.

[64] Cf. Warner, *Social Class in America*, pp. 139-142.

[65] Coleman and Rainwater, *Social Standing in America*, p. 50.

[66] Robert Bierstedt, *The Social Order*, 4th ed. (New York: McGraw-Hill, 1974), p. 469. Copyright © 1974. Reproduced with permission of McGraw-Hill.

are nearly always held by men from prosperous business or professional families, or by men who themselves have become leading businessmen and professionals.[67]

However, one should not make the mistake of overestimating the importance of wealth as a criterion of higher social status in the United States. As Vance Packard points out:

> These people of the real upper class would have you believe that wealth has little bearing on their social preeminence. Rather, it is the gracious, leisurely way of life they have achieved as a result of their innate good taste and high breeding. In smaller communities, "old" family background is especially important.[68]

b. Lineage

Perhaps no other criterion is as important in determining social status as that of family. Kingsley Davis explains:

> One of the family's main functions is the ascription of status.... Children are said to "acquire their parents' status," with the implication that the two parents have a common status to transmit and that the child gets this status automatically as a member of the family.[69]

Renowned sociologist Max Lerner clearly illustrates the importance of the family in attaining high social status in the United States.

> Somewhere in between an aristocracy of blood and land and a power elite of acquired wealth there is the domain that the American newspapers call "Society." Wealth alone does not open the portals of this domain, as a number of rich men and their wives have ruefully learned in studying the "Social Register." Birth and family are the key to entrance, although a number have declassed themselves by marrying below their station.... In communities such as the old New England cities, only the "old families" hold the top social positions. The "new families," while they may belong to the plutocracy and command much greater wealth, do not carry the same charismatic quality.[70]

Robert Nisbet, who has undertaken noteworthy studies on the family in modern American society, comments:

---

[67] Prewitt and Stone, *The Ruling Elites*, pp. 136-137.

[68] Packard, *The Status Seekers*, p. 39.

[69] Kingsley Davis, *Human Society* (New York: The Macmillan Co., 1949), p. 364.

[70] Max Lerner, *America as a Civilization*, 30th anniv. ed. (New York: Henry Holt & Co., 1987), p. 481. Copyright © 1957 by Max Lerner. Copyright renewed © 1985 Max Lerner. Reprinted by permission of Simon & Schuster, Inc.

Thomas Lee

Richard Henry Lee

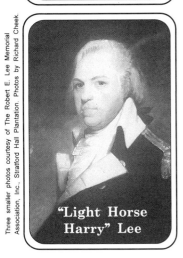

"Light Horse
Harry" Lee

General Robert E. Lee

Several generations of a distinguished family of Virginia.

Even in contemporary American democracy, however, we find sections of the country in which family descent is vital to social status. We know these sections best perhaps in certain areas of the South and of New England—the so-called First Families of Virginia, the Cabots, Lowells, and Lodges of Massachusetts, et al. But there are still other sections in the Midwest and West that contain communities in which family line, irrespective of anything else, can grant one high status.[71]

Like the European nobility, members of elite American families marry among themselves, having great consideration for the interests of the clan, making alliances with other powerful families, forming networks that tend to dominate the economic and social life of the country.

Stephen Birmingham, well-known historian of the American traditional upper class, writes, under the expressive title "Royal Marriage":

Marriage—that was what propelled a dynasty, a family empire, just as it does today, as prominent family joined prominent family at the altar in mergers of both romance and power, weaving a web of privacy and privilege over the years that would be almost impenetrable to outsiders...confounding genealogists.[72]

Similar conclusions are reached by William Domhoff: "First Families in Boston have tended toward marrying each other in a way that would do justice to the planned marriages of European royalty."[73]

The successive marriages between persons of the upper class resulted in the formation of a social network based on the family, wherein persons acquire status not just as individuals, but also as members of families or clans. In this respect, Nathaniel Burt, historian of Philadelphia's upper classes, notes: "As important as being an actual member of a Family, perhaps more important, is being caught in the Web."[74]

In some regions of the United States, especially in the South and in New England, one can find veritable patriarchal families, which tend to include even the manorial society, that is, servants and dependents, as did the aristocratic families of old Europe. According to Mills:

In New England and in the South more families than in other regions are acutely conscious of family lines and old residence, and more resistant to the social ascendancy of the newly rich and the newly arrived. There is perhaps a stronger and more embracing sense of family, which, especially in the South, comes to include long faithful servants as well as grandchildren. The sense of kinship may be extended even to those who, although not related by marriage or blood, are considered as "cousins" or "aunts" because

---

[71] Nisbet, *The Social Bond*, p. 196.

[72] Stephen Birmingham, *America's Secret Aristocracy* (Boston: Little, Brown & Co., 1987), p. 23.

[73] Domhoff, *The Higher Circles*, p. 77.

[74] Nathaniel Burt, *The Perennial Philadelphians* (Boston: Little, Brown & Co., 1963), p. 42.

they "grew up with mother." Old upper-class families thus tend to form an endogenous cousinhood, whose clan piety and sense of kinship lead to a reverence for the past and often to a cultivated interest in the history of the region in which the clan has for so long played such an honorable role.[75]

Such clans tend to keep the patrimony within the family, thereby forming true dynasties not unlike the European aristocratic ones. Talcott Parsons writes:

> In these "family elite" elements the symmetry of the multilineal kinship structure is sharply skewed in the direction of a patrilineal system with a tendency to primogeniture—one in many respects resembling that historically prevalent among European aristocracies, though considerably looser. There is a tendency for this in turn to be bound up with family property, especially an ancestral home, and continuity of status in a particular local community.[76]

Max Lerner demonstrates that even within the administrative structure of large corporations the most important decisions are made by those who belong to traditional families.

> It must be added, however, that the new people, who come up from the lower middle classes, usually do not have final control over corporate decisions even though they are in the managerial posts. That decisive and final control often remains in the hands of those who, by the fact of being a birth elite and having money and power over generations, have the prestige that adds weight to their functional qualities and equities within the corporation.[77]

c. Education

A proper education normally confers social status in the United States. While not a guarantee, "the correlation between education and social status in contemporary American society is nevertheless a very high one," Nisbet affirms. "Of all means of rising in the social scale, educational achievement has been historically one of the most effective."[78]

Members of the American elites distinguish themselves from other classes by their education. William Domhoff relates:

> From infancy through young adulthood, members of the upper class receive a distinctive education. This education begins early in life in preschools that frequently

---

[75] Mills, *The Power Elite*, p. 32.

[76] Talcott Parsons, "The Kinship System of the Contemporary United States," *American Anthropologist*, n.s. Vol. 45 (1943), p. 29.

[77] Lerner, *America as a Civilization*, pp. 480-481.

[78] Nisbet, *The Social Bond*, p. 194.

Georgetown University

are attached to a neighborhood church of high social status. Schooling continues during the elementary years at a local private school called a day school. The adolescent years may see the student remain at day school, but there is a strong chance that at least one or two years will be spent away from home at a boarding school....

The linchpins in the upper-class educational system are the dozens of boarding schools that were developed in the last half of the nineteenth and the early part of the twentieth centuries.... Baltzell concludes that these schools became "surrogate families" that played a major role "in creating an upper-class subculture on almost a national scale in America."[79]

Public schools were set up in the last century to give free education to the masses of immigrants. Zealous to preserve their manners and traditions, the upper classes established their own private educational institutions. Their boarding schools were inspired by English elite schools, such as Eton and Harrow, that have educated the British elites for centuries.[80]

According to John Ingham, these private schools fulfilled four social functions:

> First, they isolated the children of older upper-class families into homogeneous environments where they did not have to mix with those from other social environments. Second, they "served the latent function of acculturating the members of the younger generation, especially those not quite to manor born, into an upper-class style of life." Third, these schools provided a convenient means for upper-class children from one city to meet and form lasting friendships with their upper-class counterparts in other cities. Finally, these schools, isolated in small towns and rural environments, provided an insulation from the increasingly urban and heterogeneous nature of their home communities.[81]

Mills succinctly concludes:

> Like the hierarchy of clubs for the fathers—but in more important and deeper ways—the private schools do perform the task of selecting and training newer members of a national upper stratum, as well as upholding the higher standards among the children of families who have long been at the top.[82]

---

[79] G. William Domhoff, *Who Rules America Now?* (New York: Simon & Schuster, Inc., 1983; Touchstone, 1986), pp. 24-25, quoting E. Digby Baltzell, *Philadelphia Gentlemen: The Making of a National Upper Class* (New York: The Free Press, 1958), p. 339. Copyright © 1983 by Simon & Schuster, Inc. except for the quotation of Baltzell. Reprinted by permission of Simon & Schuster, Inc. This and subsequent quotations of Baltzell used with his permission.

[80] Cf. Packard, *The Status Seekers*, p. 237.

[81] John Ingham, *The Iron Barons: A Social Analysis of an American Urban Elite, 1874-1965* (Westport, Conn.: Greenwood Press, 1978), p. 93, quoting James McLachlan, *American Boarding Schools: A Historical Study* (New York: Scribners, 1970), p. 280. Copyright © John N. Ingham except for quote of James McLachlan. Greenwood Press is an imprint of Greenwood Publishing Group, Inc., Westport, Conn. Reprinted with permission.

[82] Mills, *The Power Elite*, p. 64.

Domhoff writes in a similar vein.

> This separate educational system is important evidence for the distinctiveness of the mentality and lifestyle that exists within the upper class, for schools play a large role in transmitting the class structure to their students. Surveying and summarizing a great many studies on schools in general, sociologist Randall Collins concludes: "Schools primarily teach vocabulary and inflection, styles of dress, aesthetic tastes, values and manners."[83]

d. Clubs and associations

"The social club in America has done a great deal to keep alive the gentleman in the courtly sense," Dixon Wecter observes, "providing asylum from the pandemonium of commerce, the bumptiousness of democracy, and the feminism of his own household.... Every American city with a vestige of tradition has one eminently respectable men's club."[84] But Packard emphasizes that not all clubs are equal.

> Every city has its elite clubs and its waiting-room clubs. In fact, there is usually a well-understood hierarchy of clubs....
>
> ...Most of the current aristocrats or their families belonged to waiting-room clubs during their rise to power, and may or may not continue membership in them, along with their membership in the elite clubs.[85]

In his classic study of the upper class in the United States, Digby Baltzell writes: "In most major American cities there are one or two distinguished metropolitan men's clubs whose members dominate the social and economic life of the community."[86]

Some clubs are very old, such as the Philadelphia Club, which dates from 1830; New York's Union and Century Clubs, founded in 1836 and 1847 respectively; the Sommerset of Boston, founded in 1851; and the Pacific Union of San Francisco, founded in 1852.

These clubs are as important for the formation of adults of the upper class as the boarding schools are for their children. Comments Domhoff:

> Just as private schools are a pervasive feature in the lives of upper-class children, so, too, are private social clubs a major point of orientation in the lives of upper-

---

[83] Domhoff, *Who Rules America Now?*, p. 24, quoting Randall Collins, "Functional and Conflict Theories of Educational Stratification," *American Sociological Review*, Vol. 36, 1971, p. 1010. In their study on upper class boarding schools, Cookson and Persell "document how the philosophies, programs, and lifestyles of boarding schools help transmit power and privilege and how elite families use the schools to maintain their social class" (Cookson and Persell, *Preparing for Power*, p. 4).

[84] Wecter, *The Saga of American Society*, pp. 253, 266.

[85] Packard, *The Status Seekers*, pp. 179-180.

[86] Baltzell, *Philadelphia Gentlemen*, p. 336.

class adults. These clubs also play a role in differentiating members of the upper class from other members of society.[87]

Like the schools, these clubs fulfill an important social function by placing members of elites from various parts of the country in contact with each other.

The clubs of the upper class are generally exclusive and often so closed that they pass largely unperceived by members of other classes. On this point, Mills makes the following observation:

The exclusive Century Club in New York City.

It is not unusual for gentlemen to belong to three or four or even more [clubs]. These clubs of the various cities are truly exclusive in the sense that they are not widely known to the middle and lower classes.... They are of and by and for the upper circles, and no other....

To the outsider, the club to which the upper class man or woman belongs is a badge of certification of his status; to the insider, the club provides a more intimate or clan-like set of exclusive groupings which places and characterizes a man.[88]

Finally, as Mills says, these clubs serve to introduce the new rich into upper class circles according to the precise cadence their assimilation demands.

Membership in the right clubs assumes great social importance when the merely rich push and shove at the boundaries of society.... Clubs are important rungs in the social ladder for would-be members of the top status levels; they are status elevators for the

---

[87] Domhoff, *Who Rules America Now?*, p. 28.

[88] Mills, *The Power Elite*, p. 61. Some of these clubs are so exclusive that even persons of the upper classes have difficulty becoming members, as Cleveland Amory writes in a book on the Boston upper class: "So severe are Boston's leading clubs that even blue bloods have had to watch their step to gain admission" (Cleveland Amory, *The Proper Bostonians* [New York: E.P. Dutton & Co., 1947], p. 358).

new into the old upper classes; for men, and their sons, can be gradually advanced from one club to the next, and so, if successful, into the inner citadel of the most exclusive. [89]

Members of the upper classes are not alone in seeking membership in exclusive clubs in order to maintain their character and identity. There are clubs that bring together persons of the middle classes, as Ingham notes. "Below the level of these aristocratic strongholds in each city are a series of lesser clubs which follow a fairly uniform pattern from city to city."[90]

Professional associations form elites within their own spheres. Sociologist Michael Powell shows how the elitist character of the Association of the Bar of the City of New York (ABCNY) was created and maintained "as a patrician legal association with membership requirements akin to those of the upper-class clubs with which they were so familiar. Holding to patrician notions of professionalism, and generally opposed to democratic tendencies within the bar, they advocated higher entry standards."[91]

e. Rank and authority

"Our occupational rank looms as a powerful factor in fixing our status in the public's mind," notes Packard. After analyzing the various elements that confer social prestige on an occupation, he lists sixty-one professions and offices in decreasing order of their prestige in the eyes of the American public. At the top are judges, bishops, business executives, high-ranking military officers, and such representatives of the liberal professions as doctors and lawyers. At the bottom are maids, miners, street cleaners, and other representatives of service jobs.[92]

Robert Bierstedt observes:

> Those who have high rank or status in their occupational associations will also, with some exceptions, have high-ranking status in their communities.... A bishop of the Episcopal Church, for example, may have only a small income, relatively speaking, but the status of bishop confers the prestige that supports a high rank on the class scale.... On the other hand, the incomes of entertainers and professional athletes

---

[89]   Mills, *The Power Elite*, pp. 61-62. Commenting on the social ascension of families, Warner notes: "A family often is considered to be in the top level of the upper-class group only if it has participated in this upper-class behavior for several generations. The members of the lower-upper group...achieve final acceptance as solid members of the top level only through the passage of time, often three or more generations" (Warner, *American Life: Dream and Reality*, pp. 116, 117).

[90]   Ingham, *The Iron Barons*, p. 97.

[91]   Michael Powell, *From Patrician to Professional Elite: The Transformation of the New York City Bar Association* (New York: Russell Sage Foundation, 1988), p. 226. Pressured by profound cultural and social changes, the ABCNY has been forced to admit a greater variety of members since the 1960s. Its elitist character, however, persists, as Powell demonstrates.

[92]   Packard, *The Status Seekers*, p. 93. Cf. also pp. 112-113.

sometimes reach astronomical proportions—or so it seems to the rest of us—without contributing very much to the enhancement of their class positions.[93]

Positions of authority in society confer status, as Nisbet affirms:

> Possession of authority has always been an indicator of status that is distinguishable from each of the others we are describing. Irrespective of amount of wealth, of advancement of education, or of family origin, the position of authority one holds, the degree of influence he exerts over others, is sufficient to rank him fairly high.[94]

In the United States many offices of authority are filled by self-made men who reach their positions in politics, industry, commerce, finance, and the like by their own merits and work, and thereby become part of the governing elites, acquiring a social status in keeping with their position.[95]

Thus we conclude that the free enterprise system as it exists in the United States presents a broad array of ways for an individual to acquire social status, which usually results from a combination of several of the above-mentioned factors.

6. Inherited Social Status Tends to Form an Aristocracy

Sociologists attest that acquired status naturally tends to diffuse itself, beginning with the family. By virtue of the family's organic structure, when one of its members acquires a distinguished status through his merit, family members participate in this status, thereby making it part of the family patrimony. In this way, social status naturally tends to become hereditary.

"What is entirely neglected is the hereditary character of status," notes Prof. Egon Ernest Bergel in a study on social stratification. "Even in our extremely mobile system ascribed, that is, inherited, status is the rule, achieved status the exception."[96]

Bierstedt also comments on this point.

> Societies regard the unity of the family as a matter of extreme importance, since societal survival depends, to some degree at least, upon a family system.... To wives is ascribed the status of their husbands, to children the status of their parents. In this way the stratification of statuses comes to be a family and, therefore, a group phenomenon. Later on this status ascribed to the family becomes hereditary.[97]

---

[93]   Bierstedt, *The Social Order*, p. 471.

[94]   Nisbet, *The Social Bond*, p. 192.

[95]   Cf. Frederic Cople Jaher, *The Urban Establishment: Upper Strata in Boston, New York, Charleston, Chicago, and Los Angeles* (Urbana, Ill.: Univ. of Illinois Press, 1981), pp. 718-719.

[96]   Egon Ernest Bergel, *Social Stratification* (New York: McGraw-Hill, 1962), p. 265.

[97]   Bierstedt, *The Social Order*, pp. 453-454. An example of this is the transmission of position from father to

Social anthropologist Ralph Linton makes the same claim.

> Even when the social divisions originate in individual differences of ability, there seems to be a strong tendency for such divisions to become hereditary. The members of a socially favored division try to transmit the advantages they have gained to their offspring.... In many cases these tendencies result in the organization of the society into a series of hereditary classes or castes. Such hereditary units are always used as reference points for the ascription of status.[98]

When this transmission of status occurs within family lineages of the upper class, they begin to constitute—despite the democratic framework of the State—the foundation for a true aristocracy, as Lipset and Bendix observe.

> Men and women occupying positions of high status generally endeavor to preserve their privileges for their kin and heirs; indeed, a "good" father is one who tries to pass the status he enjoys on to his children, and in many societies he will try to extend it to near and distant relatives as well. Hence, in every stratified, complex society there is, as Plato suggested, a straining towards aristocracy and a limitation of mobility.[99]

According to Nathaniel Burt, the transmission of merit is hereditary. This establishes the prestige of a family, and confers on American society a vibrant past and a present permeated with good manners and tradition. These are elements, he affirms, not of a democracy, but of an aristocracy.[100]

The formation of such an aristocracy is further favored by the natural tendency of families of a similar social level to socialize and marry among themselves. These hereditary groups, made up of persons of the upper class, are in the United States an elite analogous to the European titled nobility. Bierstedt states:

> When class endogamy—that is, marriage within one's own stratum—is encouraged and customarily practiced, class status can be perpetuated over relatively long periods. In some societies it is symbolized by titles of rank and perpetuated by a hereditary nobility. The importance of family or kin as a criterion of class is not the same in all societies, but it is a criterion that plays some part in the total picture. In the United States, for example, one need only mention the Adams and the Lowell families in Massachusetts and the Byrd and the Randolph families in Virginia.[101]

---

son in the industrial and commercial sectors. Sociologists have noted that in a majority of cases, businesses are passed from father to son, thus establishing a family continuity. Cf. also Robin Williams, *American Society*, p. 117.

[98] Ralph Linton, *The Study of Man*, student's ed. (New York: Appleton-Century-Crofts [1936] 1964), pp. 126-127.

[99] Lipset and Bendix, *Social Mobility in Industrial Society*, p. 2.

[100] Cf. Nathaniel Burt, *First Families: The Making of American Aristocracy* (Boston: Little, Brown & Co., 1970), p. 431.

[101] Bierstedt, *The Social Order*, pp. 469-470.

Let us conclude with Martin Stansfeld, who does not hesitate to speak of an aristocracy in the United States.

> Some people think American aristocracy died out two hundred years ago when inherited titles were banned by the Constitution, but that is definitely not so. There are no inherited American titles, but aristocracy in every other sense—people of substance, education, influence and wealth—goes all the way back to the George Washingtons and the Thomas Jeffersons. It is very much alive and growing in this country today.[102]

7. Hereditary Transmission of Qualities and Merit as Family Patrimony

As we have seen, the hereditary transmission of status through the family has been studied and verified by many sociologists. In addition to status, qualities can also be transmitted by the family. Each generation transmits to the next its moral and cultural values. This transmission of qualities within a family throughout generations is affirmed by Burt, who acknowledges that this is a normal occurrence in American society.

> This succession of merit [from one generation to another]...is hereditary. It most certainly keeps families going, it most certainly establishes family prestige, it most certainly adds to American society a strong past and present tinge of birth, gentility, tradition, and what have you; all those things which are the appendages if not the crude essence of aristocracy.[103]

In turn, Walter Muir Whitehill observes that

> many families of high social status have maintained an extraordinary level of national distinction, generation after generation. This is the American version of aristocracy, an aristocracy of accomplishment, achieved rapidly by conspicuous and intelligent effort, but imposing upon succeeding generations a responsibility quite as binding, and sometimes as hindering, as the traditional aristocracies of Europe.[104]

In one of his allocutions to the Roman Patriciate and Nobility, Pius XII refers specifically to the transmission of moral and spiritual qualities of a family from one generation to another.[105]

The hereditary transmission of merit, while intimately related to the transmission

---

[102] Martin Stansfeld, "American Aristocracy is Very Much Alive and Growing," *U.S. News and World Report*, December 12, 1983, p. 64.

[103] Burt, *First Families*, p. 431.

[104] Walter Muir Whitehill, "The New Aristocracies of Success," in *American Civilization*, Daniel J. Boorstin, ed. (London: Thames & Hudson, 1972), p. 165.

[105] See Part I, Chapter V, 2.

King Charles II

of status described in the previous section, has received little attention, and may appear strange to many. But it has been studied by sociologists like Bernard Farber, who admits the hereditary transmission of something beyond mere material patrimony.

> Possibly the most valuable property of a kin group aside from wealth is its position among other kinship units in terms of honor and status, a position defined by the content of the symbolic estate [in other terms a moral patrimony] that the kinship group possesses. This symbolic estate includes the achievements and honors of those individuals, both living and dead, related to the kinship group. More generally, families may become known by a great ancestor (real or fictitious), wealth, or personal achievements. One role of kinship groups in social differentiation is to perpetuate and enhance these symbolic estates, which become an important part of the family culture.[106]

From the perspective of a democratic mentality, which recognizes reward only for personal merit, the hereditary transmission of merit is one of the great injustices of an aristocratic regime, for it enables a privileged few to be born into an advantageous position, that is, a status inherited from their ancestors.

Nevertheless, if many deny that merit can be inherited, many find it reasonable that gratitude can be manifested not only directly to the benefactor, but also to his descendants.

In this way, when someone receives a great favor from another person, the former can repay the latter in the form of a reward to his son. For example, if a man in a difficult situation receives help from another person, once he has overcome the trial it would make perfect sense for him to express his gratitude to the benefactor's son.

This derives from the principle that all of the father's patrimony is hereditary, including his moral patrimony, that is, the favors and benefits the father bestowed upon other people or the State.

In his son, the father loves a projection of his own personality. He considers a favor done to his son as a favor to himself. To show the son gratitude owed to the father is to recognize in the former an extension of the latter, a hereditary link between the two.

This may apply as well between an individual and the State, where the State is the beneficiary of a meritorious action and the individual the benefactor.

For example, a man who renders notable services to a king becomes the creditor of the king's affection, a purely moral good, which cannot be appraised in material terms. As the creditor of the king's affection, he becomes the creditor of his rewards. Should the king be unable to repay this moral debt to his benefactor, he can repay it to his sons.

An interesting example of this occurred in American colonial history. William Penn received the colony of Pennsylvania from King Charles II in gratitude for the services that his father had rendered the Stuarts. Historian George Tindall describes the transaction.

---

[106] Bernard Farber, *Kinship and Class* (New York: Basic Books, 1971), p. 8.

William Penn, Lord Proprietor of the lands that became Pennsylvania and Delaware.

> Upon his father's death he [Penn] inherited the friendship of the Stuarts and a substantial estate, including a claim of £16,000 his father had lent the crown.... He got from Charles II in 1681 proprietary rights to a tract extending westward from the Delaware for five degrees of longitude and from the "beginning" of the forty-third degree on the north to the "beginning" of the fortieth degree on the south. The land was named, at the king's insistence, for Penn's father: Pennsylvania.[107]

A great man who has rendered illustrious services to his country, by his courage, zeal, dedication, and competence in the military, political, diplomatic, or cultural spheres, may have the gratitude that is his due manifested to his descendants as well. This gratitude should be acknowledged not simply by the State, but also by the people.

For example, it is undeniable that the simple fact of being a descendant of George Washington would make one an object of special consideration and elevate one's status in American society. This increased social standing does not derive from personal merits but from the merits of the ancestor and from the nation's gratitude for his service.

The legitimacy of this kind of hereditary debt is sanctioned by God Himself in various passages of Scripture. On several occasions He withheld punishments or granted favors to His Chosen People because of the merits of their great ancestors, such as Abraham, Isaac, Jacob, and David.[108]

Popes and saints have likewise affirmed the transmission of merits and qualities of ancestors to their descendants. In his allocutions to the Roman Patriciate and Nobility, and in those to the Pontifical Noble Guard, Pius XII refers to it.[109]

---

[107] George Tindall, *America: A Narrative History* (New York: W. W. Norton & Co., 1984), Vol. 1, p. 78.

[108] Referring to the patriarchs of old, the book of *Ecclesiastes* declares: "Let us now praise men of renown, and our fathers in their generation.... And their children for their sakes remain forever: their seed and their glory shall not be forsaken" (Eccl. 44:1,13). And further on: "Abraham was the great father of a multitude of nations, and there was not found the like to him in glory, who kept the law of the most High, and was in covenant with him. In his flesh he established the covenant, and in temptation he was found faithful. Therefore by an oath he gave him glory in his posterity.... And he did in like manner with Isaac for the sake of Abraham his father" (Eccl. 44:20-22, 24).

[109] "You too, remembering your ancestors, relive their lives in a way; and your ancestors live again in your names and in the titles they left you through their merits and their greatness.... Social inequalities, even those related to birth, are inevitable.... No art has ever been able to work things so that the son of a great chief, the son of a great leader of the masses, should remain in the same condition as an obscure citizen lost among the common people" (RPN 1942). "In you We hail the descendants and representatives of families long in the service of the Holy See and the Vicar of Christ, who remained faithful to the Roman Pontificate even when it was exposed to outrages and persecutions.... Such a testimonial of grateful remembrance—which must also serve as an impetus for the future—must also command respect and understanding" (RPN 1950). "You placed the nobility of blood at the service of the Church and in the guard of the Successor of Saint Peter; nobility of the splendid works of your elders, which ennobles you as well, if day by day, each of you takes care to augment in himself the nobility of virtue" (PNG 1941).

In like manner, saints such as Charles Borromeo have made it very clear that the inheritance of the merit and qualities of ancestors is legitimate: "For, if that person is to be considered noble who traces his origins from illustrious ancestors, how great is the nobility of Mary, whose filiation traces from Kings, Patriarchs, Prophets, and Priests of the Tribe of Judah, to the seed of Abraham, and to the royal stirp of David?... In first place, the splendor of the blood and the virtue and famous deeds of the ancestors have a marvelous effect in disposing the noble, virile man to follow in the footsteps of those from whom he descended" (Sermon on the birthday of Our Lady, September 8, 1584). The entire text of this sermon, so rich in other matters, may be read in Documents IV of this work.

CHAPTER II

Authentic and Inauthentic Elites

*I*n the preceding chapter we examined some basic tenets of the elitist school of sociology, whose extensive research confirms the existence of stable and thriving elites in the Unites States. We shall now broaden our concept of elite.

1. Elites

a. Local elites

In its first sense, an elite[1] is a group of select persons who stand out as individuals from the mass of people constituting a community. Isolated individuals, unrelated among themselves, do not constitute an elite. Rather, we speak of an elite only when its constituents interrelate with sufficient vitality and diligence so as to create a common primary psychological and intellectual milieu.

An elite, therefore, is not a mere juxtaposition of preeminent persons. It is formed when such persons develop a relationship among themselves in which there is a mutual exchange of values. This relationship gradually constitutes a particular culture synthesizing the intellectual and moral values of all its members.

This distillation is done especially through informal conversation. The persons who constitute an elite need not necessarily be drawn together by a concrete theme, but rather by an admixture of subjects introduced spontaneously through the art of good conversation. The result is a natural conviviality wherein each personality contributes to the development of an elite culture.

This type of conversation broadens horizons in an unfettered atmosphere in which unexpected and unforeseen topics both appear and disappear. Such free mingling of ideas and impressions gives life to conversation and constitutes the charm and cultural importance of this type of discussion, which is a cherished pastime among elites.

Take, for example, a great diplomat, a renowned financial expert, an eminent

---

[1] We use the word *elite* throughout this work in its social sense as defined by *Webster's Third New International Dictionary*: "The choice part or segment: Flower, Cream, Aristocracy: as, a segment or group regarded as socially superior...a minority group or stratum that exerts influence, authority, or decisive power."

writer, a distinguished doctor, and a prominent lawyer. Let us say these men gather once a month to converse for half an hour. This would be a group of eminent persons, but it would not constitute an elite.

This group would constitute a true elite only if its members conversed more frequently and for longer periods of time—and without a fixed schedule. They might discuss various issues, exchanging ideas and values, which would ultimately create a specific atmosphere that gives rise to an elite culture.

This exchange of ideas and values would be more complete and successful if the spouses of these men were to make up an informal social circle in which a similar process could take place. Spontaneity would provide authenticity for this type of relationship, which should be born freely from the natural interplay of human affairs.

From this perspective, one can better understand the innate creativity of an elite. Only when it generates a way of thinking and a culture common to its constituents does it deserve to be called a true elite.

This, then, is a first way to conceive of an elite: a group of people who constitute the best within their locality. They excel in their respective activities, which are also the most important activities, and they generate an elite culture through their informal social interrelations.

A second, more restricted concept is that of an elite composed exclusively of those persons of exceptional importance who transcend the scope of the city's elect. They are an elite in another sense of the word. Small in number, they do not properly represent the cultural elite of the city, but rather transcend it.

b. National and international elites

The elite of the nation is formed by people who excel at the national level. It is composed of the exceptional figures of the nation, who are representative of its highest sectors of activity and who have corresponding relationships. Such an interrelation is manifested, for example, when a president invites outstanding figures in the fields of politics, economics, and culture to a ball or banquet at the White House.

Most will not achieve international renown. Those who do achieve international stature, without ceasing to belong to the national elite, constitute within it, so to speak, an elite of elites.

Below this national elite are successive layers of lesser elites in which this interrelation repeats itself, until we finally reach the local elites described above.

Consider a city which boasts a military academy, a theological institute, and an art school. The prominent people of the city entertain the higher academic staff of these schools in their homes, thus forming a local elite, whose conviviality, while not as elevated as our previous example, is analogous to it.

A hierarchy is formed through this process. Beginning with the local elites, it extends through successively higher circles to the most quintessential elites. This graduated and continuous scale of elites constitutes the structure of a healthy elitist society, wherein the highest circles develop a lifestyle and a human type that harmonically influence the lower levels.

Historically, this is the type of elitist society formed in the West in the mold of Christian civilization.

This hierarchy implies two continual movements. One is in a vertical direction, whereby people of real merit can rise from one level to another. The other is in a horizontal direction, whereby people of the same level complement each other from moral, cultural, and other points of view. This double process attains a notable richness in countries with an authentically Christian civilization. This is because Christian charity, with its clearly supernatural mark, has a peerless efficacy in fraternally uniting men.

c. Traditional, aristocratic, and authentic elites

The word *elite* is usually accompanied by qualifiers, such as professional, cultural, moral, ethnic, and so forth. For this reason, it is useful to describe the meaning of three frequent qualifiers of the word: traditional, aristocratic, and authentic.

A professional elite can be traditional without being aristocratic. It can, for example, be made up of the best fishermen who have practiced their profession along the New England coast for many generations.

An aristocratic elite is composed of members who exercise an activity compatible with the aristocratic condition. It also must be rooted in tradition, that is, to have existed for a period of time adequate to confer upon it a traditional character.

The authenticity of an elite, both traditional and aristocratic, comes from the excellence of its activities and lifestyle. It also arises from the fact that its members are truly what they claim to be. An elite of costume jewelry makers, however qualified and old, is not authentic if its members define themselves as fine jewelers.

d. The elite and the upper class

What is the difference between the elite and the upper class?

The elite is the source of the upper class.

Let us return to the example of a small city to facilitate understanding the difference between the two. As noted, the elite of a city is formed by those who exercise prestigious activities and who are preeminent within their fields. But this still does not necessarily constitute a social class.

A social class is constituted when these individuals and their descendants acquire stability in their prominent positions. Such habitual eminence shapes them, and forms them into a single class. On the other hand, an elite is an informal group of individuals. We can only speak of a social class if the respective families also interrelate among themselves.

In short, the upper class is formed by a group of families who attained a certain degree of perfection by which they are molded and through which they became established.

e. Refinement of the elites

The previous considerations presuppose a process of refinement and cultivation of those persons and families who aspire to become members of the elite. Without this refinement, they can be rich, even very rich, but they will not be an authentic traditional elite.

How does this process work? A man becomes rich, and a desire for prestige is born in him. To attain such prestige he feels the need to have certain noticeable qualities that distinguish him from the common man: more culture, better education, greater refinement, and the like. He feels the need to adopt a lifestyle that corresponds to the idea that the public has regarding what a man of prestige should be. Moved by this desire for prestige, he begins to refine himself according to this model.

When this process of refinement began in the United States, American cultural life did not offer adequate national archetypes. As Richard Bushman points out, the republic stunted American culture, depriving it of its highest human models, that is, those of the aristocracy.

> Americans in the nineteenth century faced a number of perplexing difficulties growing out of the contradictions in their culture. Among the discomforts and embarrassments, they were left with a truncated culture whose zenith and ultimate realization lay outside their borders. Republicanism cut off the top of American society by forbidding an American aristocracy. Aristocratic bloodlines, traditionally the bearers of the highest culture, could not be tolerated.... It meant that the best people and the best circles, the models for others to follow, were always elsewhere.
>
> Even the best societies of the greatest cities lived in the shadows of still more refined aristocratic society in Europe....
>
> ...[Therefore], the genteel lived by a standard outside themselves and their own circle. They could not break the colonial and provincial habit of looking upward and outward for leadership.[2]

Those aspiring to be part of the elite were obliged to imitate European models, principally English, the natural archetype for Americans. As a result, they thought that living in the manner of an English gentleman would confer social prestige. And since the English generally acknowledged the superiority of French fashions, the wives of these Americans began to adopt certain French styles in order to have prestige among the American public.

In this way, rudimentary elites acquired in two or three generations an authenticity that made them capable of being assimilated by the older elites.

In a well-constituted society, such a process of refinement would take place in all social classes, not just in the highest. For underneath this process lies man's innate desire for perfection. We shall return to this point later.

---

[2] Richard L. Bushman, *The Refinement of America* (New York: Alfred A. Knopf, 1992), pp. 413-414.

2. Inauthentic Elites

Any study on elites in the United States encounters a problem. Elites are, by nature, the result of a process of refinement in society and should thus represent the best and most elevated the country has to offer. However, it is undeniable that numerous persons within the elite have a blatantly revolutionary mentality, and that certain groups of the elite are the paladins of transformations of a liberal and socialist character in various spheres. It is also undeniable that these persons and groups frequently assumed an attitude of sympathy toward international communism.

A group may control a sizable patrimony or hold extensive power; nevertheless, if it has not had sufficient time or the will to develop the excellence proper to authentic elites, it cannot claim to be such. It lacks the horizons, refinement of style and manners, and the delicacy of sentiments that distinguish the authentic elites.

In other cases, it may have acquired the qualities of an authentic elite. Moved by ideological preferences or other factors, however, it chooses to adopt—along with its refined manners, high education, and aristocratic habits—a revolutionary ideology or, at least, a liberal democratic mentality that favors a welfare state that is detrimental to the intermediate bodies of society.

One could ask, then, if a generic defense of elites favors even implicitly the destructive action of these liberal elites.

a. The "toads"

In addressing the question of elites in the United States, we should distinguish between authentic and inauthentic elites. Inauthentic or artificial elites do not have a natural affinity with the best traditions and the deepest yearnings of the American people; indeed, at times, they oppose them.

As indicated in the sociological studies previously cited, traditional elites continue to exercise influence over American society, especially at the grassroots level.

However, the directive posts in government, politics, finance, industry, the media, and important foundations and cultural organizations are frequently occupied by persons who belong, not to authentic elites, but to a genre of counter-elites, whose principles, ideas, and lifestyles often conflict with the general way of thinking and acting of the majority of the population.

These inauthentic elites, far from representing the nation, constitute an almost foreign body grafted onto it. Yet they appear more frequently and brilliantly before the public eye than do the traditional elites, as they receive excessive and sympathetic media attention. For this reason, countless Americans regard the pseudo-elites as the only elite. From this misconception, an unjust antipathy toward elites arises.

To symbolize the moral and psychological profile of the human type of these inauthentic elites, the word *toad* and its plural *toads* for the collective body have become common coin in the TFPs.[3] Generally speaking, the toad is a son of the

---

3   The appellation was first used by Prof. Plinio Corrêa de Oliveira when, writing in the daily newspaper *Folha*

Industrial Revolution, the offspring of an industrial economy that has accorded him a fortune out of proportion to the patrimonies of his countrymen. Such fortunes can be in industry, finance, or even arts and athletics, as is the case with certain film, television, and sports figures. There is such a lack of equilibrium between the toads and other economic levels of the population that the former seem to live in a stratosphere, isolated from the rest of society, leading lives economically and socially disproportionate to their origins and cultural level.

b. Harmful character of the toads

Under these conditions, the toads are virtually a cancer within the social body. Far from crowning a harmonic hierarchy of elites, they build their own structure of power, influence, and prestige, without overlapping with the other levels of elites. The dynamism of their anti-natural structure ultimately harms the political, economic, social, and cultural life of the nation.

Just as the top rung of a ladder should be in proportion to the rungs below it, the true elite should be proportional to the other elements of the social body. A ladder with an inordinately high last step would be unusable.

In modern industrial societies, this disproportionately high last rung is often constituted by enormous fortunes, entailing inordinate power, influence, and media coverage. The holders of such fortunes, individual or corporate, possess property and interests throughout the country and even in diverse parts of the globe. Transgressing the natural and sound limits of private property, they practically constitute states within the State.

In time, this unnatural situation produces a mentality in the members of these counter-elites that tends toward a doctrinal skepticism that scorns the ideas, manners, and traditions of Christian civilization, and leads to an almost exclusive preference for the power and status that the mega-fortunes confer as a means of exercising an almost tyrannical action over the nation.

This conglomerate of super-national individual and corporate toads form a trans-elite at the summit of economic life that more closely resembles a *nomenklatura* than an authentic elite.

c. Toads and communism

Observing the attitude of these toads toward the communist world, we witness a perplexing fact. Far from being in the vanguard of a broad action against international communism, as their privileged station would seem to demand, many toads promoted conciliation, ever ready to negotiate with and extend Western credit to the communists and their allies.

This conciliatory attitude was one of the most shocking aspects of the counter-

---

de São Paulo on June 25, 1969, he applied the term to the members of the pseudo-elite with a liberal or socialist mentality.

elite, which was frequently willing to prevent the collapse of regimes that presented themselves as the arch-enemies of capitalism. Such was the case, for example, with American investors who showered the U.S.S.R. with money, even during periods of great tension between the two states, thereby providing the Soviets with economic resources indispensable for their survival.

A comprehensive explication of this phenomenon is beyond the scope of this work. However, the similarity between the role of the toads in the capitalist states and that of the *nomenklatura* in the communist regimes is revealing. In reality, the overwhelming state power of the communists enabling them to interfere in all spheres of life has much in common with the overwhelming economic power of the counter-elite capitalists. In sum, the *nomenklatura* is an image of the toads.

Accordingly, it is not surprising ideological barriers were easily crossed between these analogous counter-elites ostensibly antithetical.[4]

d. The jet set

The jet set constitutes yet another inauthentic elite. The expression indicates the very wealthy who live to spend money and enjoy life traveling between the most fashionable places. It includes the most disparate persons: a royal princess, a high-rolling gambler, a famous jockey, a scandal-ridden movie star. The criteria for membership are wealth, a taste for extravagance, and a passion to appear in the public eye. In sum, Money + Desire to Spend + Passion for Publicity = Jet Set.

Here, too, the deleterious effect of the media is noticeable. The spotlights of publicity that do not shine benignly on traditional elites are favorably focused on the jet set. For example, if a member of the jet set is present at the marriage of a couple belonging to a traditional elite, the media will highlight the jet-setter, while largely ignoring the traditional guests.

The jet set is a caricature of an authentic elite, as its decor, ambience, and fashion, profoundly marked by a desire to display wealth rather than taste, evidence. The garish and demagogic tone of the jet-set ambiences has nothing aristocratic about it.

3. The Different Roads of the Authentic and Inauthentic Elites

When a person acquires a fortune, whether by his own merit or inheritance, two roads lie before him: He can take the arduous road to secure for himself, or his descendants, an entrance into the traditional elites; or he can take the easy path, becoming a toad.

---

4   William Domhoff points to factors that led to this common *Weltanschauung*: "Internationalism, acceptance of big government, and acceptance of the welfare state are three characteristics of present-day big business thinking which lead ultra-conservatives to compare a corporate America with the realities of Soviet Russia. There is a final rough similarity. The big businessman of today does not have a religious outlook on the world.... He has a secular view of the world, based upon his liberal and scientific education" (Domhoff, *The Governing Class in America*, p. 295).

a. The road of assimilation into the traditional elites

Along this high road one finds the person who is not overly concerned with increasing his fortune. Instead, he strives to assimilate the values of European tradition and culture, with a view to attaining appropriate social status. The prudent and judicious management of his patrimony permits a refined lifestyle analogous to that of the aristocracy. As long as his patrimony suffices to maintain his acquired status, and as long as he upholds cultural values corresponding to his position, he feels satisfied. His prestige derives more from his social status after all, not his bank account. Accordingly, he is largely independent of the maxims governing a revolutionary society, the impositions of high finance, the imperatives of certain extravagant styles, and the "hype" of media propaganda. He can perfect himself to the point of assimilation into the traditional elites, whether at the regional or national level.

b. The road of the toads

Others take the low road of revolutionary pragmatism, despising tradition and, above all, striving to acquire ever more disproportionate temporal treasures and ever more monopolistic economic power.

Their fixed idea is that money is the sole source of prestige, and they drive themselves to acquire it at all costs, recklessly launching themselves into the world of international finance and heedlessly breaking the ties that bind them to the nation's traditions. Entirely absorbed with business, they lack that spirit of equanimity proper to authentic aristocracy.

Nonetheless, the descendants of toads can acquire an aristocratic spirit if they abandon this superficial appetite for wealth and pleasure and strive to desire spiritual and cultural goods.

4. Social Classes

a. The concept of perfection applied to individuals and families

The concept of perfection is readily understood. Perfection is the state of a being that contains all the necessary attributes for its own integrity. For a rational being, perfection implies the ability to discern one's ends and to possess the means to realize them.

Perfection admits several degrees. First, there is a minimal perfection, which consists of the possession of those attributes in a merely adequate number and quality. A higher degree consists of the possession of these attributes in a sufficiently ample number and quality to allow for a certain liberality or abundance. The highest degree of social perfection consists in possessing these attributes to a degree and profusion sufficient to distinguish their holder in a prestigious and even glorious way in the judgment of his fellow men.

This scale involves an unsurpassable limit. A man cannot go beyond what the natural capacity and elasticity of his being permit. For example, through prodigious effort, a person may raise himself to the condition of an average musician who can entertain a small audience. However, he may never rise to the level of a naturally gifted composer with the extraordinary facility and prodigious talent of a Mozart.

The ascension through the various degrees of perfection is usually arduous. And if it is true that all just men tend toward their perfection, it is usually true that few manage to reach the pinnacle of this steep ascent.

A family can be characterized by the natural participation of its members in the same perfection to different degrees. Not infrequently, if its members strive to attain this perfection with noble tenacity and fraternal support, at least some of them will manage to achieve it in an eminent degree.

b. All classes should tend to perfection

It is proper for everything that has a sound and healthy existence to tend continually toward perfection. This natural tendency should also manifest itself in the social classes.[5]

Perfection has degrees, as we have noted. From this perspective, a social class is a group of families that has achieved a degree of perfection proper to its level.

It is natural for parents—be they workers, bourgeois, or nobles—to desire to provide their children with the same standard of living they themselves enjoy. This continuity is just but insufficient. As much as possible, parents should desire to bequeath a higher standard of living to their children. This does not necessitate that a laborer's son become a lawyer. The condition of workers may be greatly perfected and their cultural level appreciably augmented in the course of generations without their ceasing to be workers.

Another area capable of perfection is that of virtue. For example, there can be progress in conjugal love, in maternal and paternal love, and in so many other virtues. Such moral progress is necessarily accompanied sooner or later by artistic and cultural progress. This does not necessarily imply a change of social status, but a perfecting of the class as a whole.

A result of this perfecting in the lower classes within Christian civilization was the appearance of popular art that produced true masterpieces by artisans and peasants. This art was not learned in a school of fine arts, but conceived and executed as an expression of elevated qualities of soul.

This is not to say that it would be illicit for a person to rise from one class to another. This can be healthy and good when someone appears with special

---

[5]   We understand class in its social sense as defined in *Webster's Third New International Dictionary*: "**a:** one group of a usually society-wide grouping of people according to social status, political or economic similarities, or interests or ways of life in common **b:** social rank, especially: high social rank **c:** an economic or social rank above that of the proletariat."

talents that justify, and even demand, such a rise. But this should be an exception rather than the rule, even while avidly supported.[6]

A person who proves to be an exception to the rule should not be rejected by the upper classes as a subversive element that will upset the social equilibrium. If someone with great talent appears, the doors of the upper classes should be open to him. Someone who rises like this is not spearheading a revolution, but rather participating in genuine progress. In fact, if he refines himself to the level of his new class, his children will already be born into that class.

Part of the process toward perfection, this must take place in all classes, but especially in upper class families, since they should provide an example for the rest of society.

The journey through the various degrees of perfection constitutes the harmonic and authentic progress of society. Herein resides the central thesis of Christian civilization: The entire society walks toward a common ideal, realized in its own way by each class.

c. Our Lord Jesus Christ: the perfect human type

In their journey toward perfection, the different classes naturally develop human types proper to each, gradually approximating an ideal type.

This model, the ideal human type for all classes, this personification of perfection, is not a theoretical model, but a historic reality. The human type par excellence is the person of Our Lord Jesus Christ, the God-Man. The ascending march of humanity is a march toward Our Lord Jesus Christ, who realized the perfect human type in His humanity.

In Our Lord Jesus Christ, the perfection of human nature is elevated to a degree superior to itself through the Hypostatic Union with the Divine nature. In Our Lord Jesus Christ all the human virtues are present harmonically and supremely. They build upon each other in a perfect way, revealing, as the lamp shade reveals the light, the Divine Perfection itself, the God-Man.

A society committed to assimilating what could be called the human type of Our Lord Jesus Christ will continuously rise toward perfection. In this lies all genuine progress.

---

[6] This exceptionality, contrary to the prevailing myth, is observed in American society, as sociologist Paul Mott affirms: "The most obvious fact about mobility in our society is that the son is very likely to have the same occupational position as his father, or to be one rank above or below him. Movement from one extreme of the occupational status to the other is very unlikely" (Paul Mott, *The Organization of Society* [Englewood Cliffs, N.J.: Prentice-Hall, 1965], p. 204).

Le Beau Dieu d'Amiens.
Stone statue of Our Lord Jesus Christ
at the entrance of the Cathedral of Amiens, France.

5. Aristocracy

a. Christian aristocracy

Aristocracy[7] is the class in which the distilling of this ideal human type, the quest for this perfection toward which all society should tend, was more complete. In other words, it fell to the aristocracy to realize the most perfect, the most elevated, and the most noble human type.

Hence, the human type of Our Lord Jesus Christ is at the heart of the Western concept of aristocracy.

In effect, the West developed its political, social, and cultural standards within the flux of Christian civilization.[8] The human type of the Christian gentleman, the model and prototype of Western aristocracy, had as its first and supreme ideal the imitation of the perfections of Our Lord Jesus Christ.

In fact, the virtues that compose the moral profile of the Christian aristocrat (honor, abnegation, courage, magnanimity, respect, honesty, and so on) were inspired by the example and teachings of Our Lord Jesus Christ, in whom they are found in a supreme and divine degree.

In conclusion, a true aristocracy is one which, seriously and enthusiastically, strives to realize the model of perfection of Our Lord Jesus Christ. It withers and fades to the degree that it strays from this high ideal.

b. Aristocracy and sanctity

It should not be deduced from the preceding that the condition of aristocrat is synonymous with sanctity. For it cannot be denied that there have been many saints who were not aristocrats and many aristocrats who were not saints.

But if aristocracy is not to be confused with sanctity, neither can it be entirely dissociated from it. A person might be a saint but not realize in his personality all the temporal reflections that sanctity can yield. There can be saints whose virtues are not permeated with the qualities that distinguish the aristocrat because this is not within their vocation.

Some aristocrats limit themselves to guaranteeing the solidity and strength of the temporal order. Others strive to go further and to achieve the highest standards of beauty and perfection in this order. This course can make the aristocrat a saint.

---

[7] We use the term *aristocracy* in its social sense as defined in *Webster's Third New International Dictionary*: "**1**: government by the best individuals or by a relatively small privileged class **2a**: a form of government in which the power is vested in a minority consisting of those felt to be best qualified to rule...**3**: a governing body made up of those felt to be outstanding citizens, especially nobles or others of high rank: an upper class usually made up of an hereditary nobility; a patrician order **4**: the aggregate of those felt to be superior."

[8] The later division of Europe—and subsequently the Americas—into Catholic and Protestant blocs is beyond the scope of this study, which is sociological and historical, not religious, in nature. It is undeniable, however, that the foundations of the Western order, and more concretely of the social types it created, came from the great tradition of Christian civilization, and that this Christian civilization was based on the person of Our Lord Jesus Christ, as its name indicates.

Following his God-given vocation, he strives to make his qualities, especially the temporal ones, flourish and rise to the highest peaks. In so doing, he strives to see the relation between temporal things and the goods of the spirit and God Himself.

In those who are not aristocrats, sanctity does not necessarily tend toward aristocracy. It undoubtedly favors the realization, in an excellent way, of what is inherent to the condition of the person. Sanctity, therefore, elevates the individual within his condition, but not necessarily to a higher one.

c. The aristocracy synthesizes the perfections of the community

The reflections above consider the aristocracy from the point of view of the pole of perfection toward which it should tend. But the aristocracy can be considered further as expressing the collective perfection of a city or region.

In effect, every city or region has what could be called a collective personality or a "common soul" that, in a certain sense, is worth more than the sum of its individual personalities. This "common soul" is a synthesis of the perfections toward which its individuals, families, and classes tend. It is the collective product of their march toward perfection.

The aristocrat best expresses this "common soul." By elevating himself to a standard above the community, he becomes its embodiment. For this reason, he has the mission of representing its particular spirit. The superior task of the aristocrat is to conserve that spirit, elevate it, and make it progress. Thus his vocation is turned toward the common good.

d. Aristocracy and grandeur

The aristocrat will only fulfill his vocation when he has a clear idea of the grandeur of his country and is willing to represent it in his person.

Many historical facts serve to symbolize American grandeur. One is the famous flag-raising at Iwo Jima. We may also point to such embodiments of grandeur as generals George Patton and Douglas MacArthur.

However, to fully realize the ideal of grandeur to which the United States is called, the families of her traditional elites must develop the distinctive features and aristocratic profile of this grandeur.

In principle, in every elite family there exists a "dream" that contains a germinative idea of the grandeur their nation is called to achieve. It is their duty to realize this "dream," a quest gravely hindered by the pressures of the egalitarian myth. Thus, we witness the telling division between those Americans enthralled with quantitative grandeur (economic productivity) and those inspired by qualitative grandeur (the honor and glory of the nation).

Beautiful uniforms, gleaming weapons, great parades, and endless applause of enraptured crowds would amount to nothing more than theatrics were it not for authentic and proven courage such as that shown by U.S. Marines at Iwo Jima.

CHAPTER III

Sentimentalism: An Explanation for the Egalitarian Mentality

1. A Misconception of Compassion

Not a few Americans have an aversion to social and economic inequalities. This repulsion arises not so much from philosophical convictions as from a temperamental disposition at the heart of which lies a serious misconception about the nature of compassion.

Such mentalities believe that inequalities, particularly those of a social or economic character, invariably cause suffering in those of lower status. According to this misperception, even those with the means to lead a comfortable life suffer from the fact that others are richer than they. Behind this attitude, one perceives the unspoken presence of a philosophy of envy.

This attitude results from an erroneous interpretation of true Christian compassion in the face of socioeconomic inequalities.

Christian compassion does not oblige one to feel sorry for someone who has what he needs to live in a manner suited to his social level. Christian compassion simply elicits the desire to help those who lack the means to lead a dignified life according to the demands of human nature and their status. Accordingly, there is no reason for someone to feel guilty simply because he is richer or has a higher social standing than others. Nor does having less than others make the upright man suffer; rather, he is satisfied at seeing that others have more than he.

The erroneous interpretation of compassion affects some members of the traditional elites in a curious manner. They deem it their duty to disguise their high station, education, and splendor. In doing so they misguidedly believe they are fulfilling their Christian duty to prevent others from suffering the humiliation of seeing people who are higher than themselves.

The precise opposite is true. The higher classes have the duty to shine in the eyes of the lower classes. The latter have the right to contemplate the splendor of the higher classes and to be inspired by it. In effect, the condition of the higher classes should stimulate members of the lower classes to improve their own situations. The contemplation of the higher classes can inspire members of the lower classes who are gifted with exceptional talents to aspire legitimately to a higher condition.

This desire must not be confused with the reprehensible "coveting of thy neighbors' goods" prohibited by the tenth Commandment. Such coveting occurs when someone becomes envious because another person is or has more than he; or when he comes to hate his neighbor and is consumed with a passion to deprive him of what is justly his. Base sentiments like these should not be confused with the noble desire to equal, or even surpass, through diligent effort, the situation one admires in another.

It cannot be denied that there are situations in which it is understandable for an aristocracy to retire from public view. If, for example, the upper classes perceive that the splendor of their social lives will be misunderstood and maliciously manipulated against them, they have the right to maintain a more discreet position in society in accordance with their good judgment.

2. A Liberal, Reformist, and Egalitarian Philanthropy

Moved by such false compassion, many wealthy people believe that their own happiness will not be complete as long as others suffer from having less.

This attitude leads them to philanthropic sentimentalism. They feel a certain personal well-being in materially helping not only the truly needy, but all those less fortunate than themselves. To assure their own happiness, they become philanthropists.

In turn, this philanthropic sentimentalism prompts them to desire the elimination of the supposed root of "unhappiness," that is, social and economic inequalities. In this way, a reformist tendency, fundamentally liberal and egalitarian, to transform society in a revolutionary way is born.

This inclination manifests itself, for example, in American foreign policy, which is frequently oriented by liberal principles. This policy strives to impose liberal democracy which, according to its mentors, is the magic answer to the woes of poorer countries.

In the United States, liberal and egalitarian reforms of a socialist nature often come from the revolutionary elements of the higher classes, and not from the working classes.

CHAPTER IV

The Juridical-Social Structure of Colonization

$\mathcal{T}$he first colonizers of North America were Spanish Catholics. Almost a century before the English colonists, they had explored the continent to its heart, establishing colonies, founding cities, and evangelizing the Indians.

The French began their epic exploration of the North American continent in the first half of the sixteenth century, but due to internal convulsions on the European continent, they established their first permanent colony only in the following century, with the founding of Quebec in 1608. Throughout the seventeenth century, French Canadian colonizers and missionaries explored the length of the Mississippi.

It was the English colonization, however, that prevailed and gave the United States its dominant character. The first English colony, Jamestown, was founded in 1607.

This study does not intend to narrate a complete history of the English colonies in North America. So many were the differences between the various colonies, each of which was a politically independent entity, that each would require a separate study. However, they share at least one common feature: All developed local aristocracies that can be considered a true landed gentry.

1. The English Social Structure in the Colonial Period: An Overview

To understand the character of the aristocracy in the North American colonial period, it is necessary to consider the model that inspired the colonizers: the English society of the day. England was undergoing profound religious, political, social, and economic changes that were in the process of overthrowing many of the institutions of the Middle Ages that yet remained.

The old nobility had been decimated by the War of the Roses, in which the partisans of the Houses of York and Lancaster confronted each other in a ferocious civil war that lasted thirty-five years (1450-1485), causing the extinction of many noble houses of medieval origin and profoundly weakening the reigning feudal system. Less than a century later, the Anglican revolution further aggravated the situation. The English Protestant sovereigns introduced the custom of compensating persons who had supported them in the revolt against Rome with land grants and riches—often derived from spoils taken from the Church—and with titles of nobility.

In this way there arose a titled oligarchy without historical ties to the land granted to it or to its tenants. This oligarchy largely replaced the old medieval nobility, without managing to command the respect it enjoyed.

Despite the rapid transformations taking place throughout the sixteenth and seventeenth centuries, England remained a predominantly agrarian nation, where land, not commerce, and rural, not urban life, most strongly influenced the upper classes. It was land possession that conferred status and social position on the proprietor.

England was distinctive in having a large class of country gentry, known as squires, or simply, gentlemen. In contrast to the absolute monarchies of continental Europe, where the respective aristocracies no longer governed, the members of this rural aristocracy had become the governing class of the country. Many squires had even obtained coats of arms from the royal College of Arms, and, with them, a state of recognized nobility.

The landed gentry had jurisdiction over tracts of land, called manors. In each manor were one or two small towns or villages. Part of the manorial lands—the demesne—came under the direct and exclusive proprietorship of the lord; the rest were under the freeholders, the proprietors whose rights derived from custom and who paid the lord a sum akin to a tax.

The freeholders belonged to the social category of yeomen, small rural or industrial proprietors whose status was above that of the manual worker, but below that of the gentry. Some yeomen managed to attain wealth, and, by acquiring more lands, to rise to the level of gentlemen and even obtain a coat of arms.

In addition, there were the copyholders, whose rights and duties upon the land were stipulated by a contract with the lord, and not by the customs of the manor.

Such manors possessed certain feudal characteristics. However, the feudal forms of economic relationships that still existed in law were abolished and replaced in 1660 with a fixed tax, the quitrent,[1] and an oath of submission to the king. While still maintaining much of the feudal form in its social aspects, this change allowed for a simplified and more flexible method of conserving rural proprietorship in accordance with social and economic transformations of a capitalist nature then taking place.

In short, the manor constituted the foundation of stability in rural English life. It defined the basic relationships among the social classes.

Enjoying ample prestige and power, the country gentry, and not the old titled nobility, controlled public administration and the House of Commons in Parliament, thereby directing colonial policy up to the time of American independence.

The Crown left the government of the counties largely in the hands of these

---

[1] The quitrent is of medieval origin. It was a tribute paid by the subject of a lord to exempt himself from some service due.

The arrival of Spanish colonizers at Monterey.

gentlemen, who exercised political and juridical power in their lands and in the small cities of their regions. In exchange for services rendered, some received titles of knight or baronet, thus joining the lower nobility. Some were raised to the peerage of the Realm.

Despite the many factors that undermined this social order and transformed the lord of the manor into a mere rural proprietor, the gentry remained the foundation of the social order, the very epitome of rural, genteel, and aristocratic England.

With the growth of mercantilism in the seventeenth century, many businessmen who had made their fortunes in commerce and industry penetrated the ranks of the gentry.[2] Having earned sufficient money and desiring a more honorable lifestyle, these merchants would buy land and move to the countryside, living like gentlemen, often even filling the social gaps left by the eradication of the feudal nobility.[3]

This slow and gradual process of interpenetration, favoring the nascent urban and industrial society, constituted the predominant aspect of English social life at the time of the colonization of America. It continued until the middle of the nineteenth century, when the power of the rural aristocracy was broken amid the transformations produced by the Industrial Revolution.

Historian Charles Andrews summarizes the transformations that took place in the English social order.

> Thus the old relationship between lord and tenants, which had been determined by ties that were personal and social and only in a lesser degree economic, was passing away. The old manor as a collective unit, bound by custom and long standing usages, was already disintegrating; the old lordship was becoming a capitalistic affair, a matter of finance and administration, and social standards were influenced rather by money than by "ancientry."[4]

Referring to the changes in the status of various social groups, Andrews continues:

> Thus while the old manorial system was undergoing important modifications in its internal structure and in the status of its villagers and tenants, the lord himself was losing his seignorial trappings and becoming the head of a landed estate. In common parlance he was still the lord of the manor, the owner of freehold and copyhold, and the receiver of rents from his tenants.... England of the seventeenth

---

[2]   In contrast to other countries, England regarded commerce and industry as honorable professions to which nobles could dedicate themselves without tarnishing their image or position.

[3]   "In England in the later seventeenth century the ambition of a prosperous tradesman was to become a country gentleman. To retire from a place behind the shop-counter or from a seat at the clerk's desk to a spacious manor house in the midst of broad acres—this was the daydream of the rising middle class" (Daniel J. Boorstin, *The Americans: The Colonial Experience* [New York: Random House, 1958], p. 99). Copyright © 1958 Daniel J. Boorstin. Reprinted by permission of Random House, Inc.

[4]   Charles M. Andrews, *The Colonial Period of American History: The Settlements* (New Haven: Yale Univ. Press, 1934), Vol. 2, p. 218.

and eighteenth centuries, though rather aristocratic than seignorial, was still proprietary and manorial.[5]

In broad strokes, this was the English social structure at the time of American colonization.

2. The First English Colonizers and Settlers in the New World: The Beginning of a Native Colonial Aristocracy

The people who landed on American shores were, for the most part, of bourgeois or popular origin: businessmen, weavers, artisans, public functionaries, and workers.

While relatively few titled nobles emigrated to the New World, the number of younger sons of gentlemen and squires who came to America and spread throughout the colonies was not insignificant, especially in Virginia, Maryland, and the Carolinas.[6] Deprived of inheritance by the entail laws of Europe, many tried their luck in the New World. With them, notes historian Louis Wright, came something of the spirit of the gentry and, notably, the desire to make a fortune to reacquire the status of their ancestors. "We are likely to forget," writes Louis Wright, "that a considerable number of the seventeenth-century settlers did come from families of the gentry—enough, perhaps, to serve as leaven for the developing aristocracy."[7]

After becoming wealthy rural proprietors, these immigrants—sons of the gentry and more humble classes alike—adopted the English gentleman as a model for their new social status.[8] Hence, from the initial mass of immigrants, a local aristocracy began to arise. "By far the larger part were humble people," notes historian Thomas Jefferson Wertenbaker, adding, "Out of this mass gradually emerged an aristocracy."[9]

Particularly interesting is the case of the Cavaliers who arrived in Virginia in the middle of the seventeenth century. "Cavaliers" was the name acquired by the partisans of King Charles I in the war against the sectarian Parliamentarians of Oliver Cromwell (1642-1649). With the defeat of the Royal party, many Cavaliers—avowed monarchists—preferred to go into exile in the North American colonies than to suffer

---

[5]   Ibid., p. 216.

[6]   Frederic Jaher states that families of minor gentry, comfortable yeomen, merchants, and sea captains were the main source for the upper class of the early Carolinas (cf. *The Urban Establishment*, p. 321).

[7]   Louis B. Wright, *The First Gentlemen of Virginia* (Charlottesville: The Univ. of Virginia Press, 1964), p. 40. Reprinted with the permission of the publisher.

[8]   Clifford Dowdey makes the following comment regarding colonial Virginia: "This country gentry, not the nobility, was the class which formed the model for the emigrants who succeeded in the Virginia Colony" (Clifford Dowdey, *The Virginia Dynasties* [Boston: Little, Brown & Co. 1969], p. 13).

[9]   Thomas Jefferson Wertenbaker, *The Old South: The Founding of American Civilization* (New York: Cooper Square Publishers, Inc., 1963), p. 21.

Defeated in the Civil War that devastated seventeenth-century England, many Cavaliers (left) fled to Virginia. Cromwell's Roundheads (right) pursued them, however, and eventually forced them to surrender.

the Puritan despotism of Cromwell. Even though many were not nobles, their monarchical militancy helped to consolidate aristocratic sentiments in Virginia. "The coming of the 'cavaliers' in a formative state of the Colony gave color to Virginia's unquestionably Royalist sympathies," writes Clifford Dowdey.[10]

In the absence of a titled and hereditary nobility, but in the persistence of a vibrant tradition of social hierarchy carried over from Europe, the English colonies in North America created social and economic conditions that favored the gradual formation of a local elite based on the customs and mentality prevailing in England.

As in Europe, in the colonies land ownership was the surest and swiftest means to attain social status and thereby enter the ruling circles of society. It was not long before groups of families, interrelated by marriages, were recognized as local authorities. "In all the colonies, the Councils were almost totally comprised of members of these small aristocracies," notes historian James T. Adams.[11]

Little by little this elite acquired prestige, wealth, and power. Concomitantly, it refined its tastes and manners, acquiring culture and that sense of public duty and noblesse oblige proper to the upper classes. In this way a local aristocracy was born.

Testimony regarding the formation of this colonial aristocracy

Historians T. Harry Williams, Richard Current, and Frank Freidel show that the colonists tended to emulate the English gentleman.

> From England, the colonists derived their conceptions of the proper relationship of man to man in society. They accepted the English ideal of the gentleman as a person above but not apart from the rest of humanity, a person with special privileges, but also special obligations, including the obligation of serving the public and helping the less fortunate.... Neither in England nor in the colonies did Englishmen believe in social equality.[12]

From the beginning the tendency to form a social hierarchy was evident, and, as these same authors state, "class consciousness and class distinctions were quite noticeable in colonial America."[13] They go on to describe this general process of social stratification.

> A colonial class system grew up. Once social differentiation was well developed, as it was by the middle of the eighteenth century, the upper classes in the colonies

---

[10]   Dowdey, *The Virginia Dynasties*, p. 17.

[11]   James T. Adams, *Provincial Society* (New York: Macmillan Co., 1927), p. 66.

[12]   T. Harry Williams, Richard N. Current, and Frank Freidel, *A History of the United States (to 1876)* (New York: Alfred A. Knopf, 1962), pp. 22, 73.

[13]   Ibid., p. 73.

consisted of the royal officials, the proprietary families, the great landholders in the North and the planters in the South, and the leading merchants....

...All except the slaves could aspire to a higher place for themselves or at least for their children. Once a man had made a fortune, he was accepted readily by those who theretofore had considered him their social inferior.... Afterwards his descendants were inclined to forget the humble and even grubby origins of the family fortune and to think of themselves as thoroughgoing aristocrats.[14]

Historian Louis Hartz calls attention to the aristocratic style of life cultivated by the early American elite, distinct from, though analogous to, the European nobility.

One can point to the great estates of New York where the Patroons lived in something resembling feudal splendor. One can point to the society of the South where life was extraordinarily stratified with the slaves at the bottom and a set of genteel planters at the top. One can even point to the glittering social group that gathered about the royal governors in the North.[15]

During the colonial period, a local aristocracy arose and became firmly established in all regions. Social historian Edward Pessen emphasizes this often overlooked fact:

It is commonplace among historians of colonial America that, notwithstanding dissimilarities in the lives and institutions of the people in the three great geographical sections (New England, the ''Middle Colonies,'' and the South), society in each area was vitally affected by class and class differences. An upper crust emerged, whatever the topography, the crops, the labor system, or chief industries of a locale or region.... The upper crust came close to monopolizing positions of influence, whether in the governors' councils or legislative assemblies of the colonies or in the lay groups, such as the vestries in Virginia, that shaped the policies of the then extremely influential church bodies....

...Throughout the society class distinctions were explicitly manifest in such disparate matters as appropriate dress, forms of address, or seating arrangements in church....

...The leaders of colonial society continued to think...that the few with a special or large ''stake in society'' could alone be counted on to rule responsibly.[16]

The social order and aristocratic elites varied from one colony to another according to local conditions. In the South, the aristocratic elites were comprised

---

[14] Ibid., pp. 73, 72.

[15] Louis Hartz, *The Liberal Tradition in America* (San Diego: Harvest/Harcourt Brace Jovanovich, 1955), p. 52.

[16] Pessen, *Status and Social Class in America*, pp. 273-275.

mainly of planters, whereas in the North, great proprietors and businessmen predominated. Louis Wright describes this diversity:

> Many families in Virginia, Maryland, New England, New York, New Jersey, Pennsylvania, and the Carolinas had been there for several generations. They farmed the land, sailed the seas, fished commercially, and engaged in many businesses, crafts, and trades. A few acquired great fortunes and established themselves as a proud and aristocratic gentry....
>
> All the colonies developed an upper crust of wealthy planters, merchants, or shippers who quickly assumed the airs and trappings of an aristocracy. The planter aristocracy of the agrarian colonies approximated English country families more nearly than any other social group in America, but the merchant grandees of New England were fully as proud of their accomplishments and status.[17]

By the time of American independence, a well-established aristocracy, constituting the social, cultural, political, and military leadership, could be found in all colonies. Arthur Schlesinger, Jr., writes:

> By 1776 the colonial aristocracy had endured for more than a century and a half in the oldest regions, for over a century in others, and had sunk deep roots elsewhere. With the passage of time, it had consolidated its position and constantly replenished its vitality with transfusions of new blood. Its members had not, moreover, used their station exclusively for self-aggrandizement and worldly display, but, as a class, had considered themselves trustees for the common good, identifying their welfare with that of the community at large....
>
> In all the colonies men of quality occupied responsible posts in every sphere of official activity: the executive department, the provincial and local lawmaking branches, the armed forces, the judiciary.... In no less degree they provided the cultural leadership.[18]

3. The Juridical Structure of the American Colonies Favored the Development of Elites

The English Crown did not participate directly in the initial colonization of North America, which was carried out almost entirely by private initiative. Marshall Harris, a student of historical and current aspects of land ownership in the United States, writes:

> Not one of the thirteen original colonies was settled by the Crown. As a consequence, all of their governments originally were either corporate or proprietary in

---

[17] Louis B. Wright, *The American Heritage History of the Thirteen Colonies* (New York: American Heritage Publishing Co., 1967), pp. 299, 311.

[18] Arthur M. Schlesinger, Jr., *The Birth of the Nation* (New York: Alfred A. Knopf, 1968), p. 145.

nature. The three Puritan colonies were settled by chartered corporations, while the early governments of the other ten colonies were strictly proprietary, except perhaps for New York and Virginia.[19]

When America was discovered, Europe was still strongly influenced by the socioeconomic system that had flourished during the Middle Ages.

> So far as Western society is concerned, the frame of reference for all these [socioeconomic] contrasts is the transition from medieval to modern Europe. It is the social structure of the Middle Ages, real or imagined, that has provided the common point of departure for the most diverse interpretations.... It must be our point of departure also.[20]

Despite its decline in the European world, the feudal system continued to provide a framework to regulate land ownership and other socioeconomic relations in the New World. Historian Everett Dick observes:

> Although the feudal system was on the decline in the Old World, it was the basis for early land-tenure policies in America. The king made land grants, and although the term "baron" or "lord" was not used, the feudal idea prevailed nevertheless. Whether a man came as an employee of a trading company, as a settler upon the land of a proprietor, or as a newcomer upon the land of the king in a royal colony, there was at first no thought of the common man actually owning the soil he tilled.[21]

Regardless of the forms of land ownership that took root during the early colonization of America, much remained of the feudal order already waning in the Old World. Historian Louis Hartz observes: "'Feudalism' refers technically to the institutions of the medieval era, and it is well known that aspects of the decadent feudalism of the later period, such as primogeniture, entail, and quitrents, were present in America even in the eighteenth century."[22] These feudal aspects helped preserve the economic base of the great families of the colonial era.

As the colonies took shape, three basic types of government were established: royal government, government by corporation, and government by proprietor.

a. Royal colonies

A royal colony was governed by the King through the intermediary of a governor appointed by him. The King also could name a council that would serve

[19] Marshall Harris, *Origin of the Land Tenure System in the United States* (Ames, Iowa: Iowa State College Press, 1953; reprint, Westport, Conn.: Greenwood Press, 1970), pp. 76-77.

[20] Robert Nisbet, *The Quest for Community* (New York: Oxford Univ. Press, 1953), p. 79.

[21] Everett Dick, *The Lure of the Land* (Lincoln, Neb.: Univ. of Nebraska Press, 1970), pp. 2-3.

[22] Hartz, *The Liberal Tradition in America*, p. 3.

as a consulting organ to assist the governor.[23] The King retained full executive powers to grant lands to individuals, create proprietorships, and regulate all the administrative aspects of colonial life. The proprietors paid taxes on their lands to the Crown.

b. Corporate colonies

In the corporate colonies of New England, Massachusetts, Rhode Island, and Connecticut, the systems of land ownership differed significantly in origin. Their differences can be partly attributed to the strong religious convictions of their first colonizers, reflected in the corporate organizations they formed. These were corporations of a political and commercial nature, which were granted charters by the Crown that allowed them extensive privileges, broad rights over the land, great power in the government of the colony, and the right to elect their own governor.

These colonies were to be governed according to their charters, which defined the powers of government. In these colonies all free men received a parcel of land and were exempt from feudal obligations. They also periodically elected representatives to an assembly that had general rights over the land and controlled its distribution.

c. Proprietary colonies

In this type of colony the right to promote colonization and distribute lands was granted by the King to the lord proprietors, who had extensive rights of jurisdiction over the territories they received (proprietorships).

As in feudal England, where the lords who protected the borders of the kingdom had special privileges and exercised quasi-royal authority, these proprietors were granted rights and privileges that virtually made them supreme lords of the land. This authority was an incentive to assure the difficult and hazardous task of colonizing a distant land.

The proprietorships were vast expanses of land granted by the King to important persons for services rendered the Crown. Among the first proprietors were nobles who had distinguished themselves in the struggle to restore the Stuart dynasty. These nobles became lords of these lands, where their broad exercise of governmental powers was restricted only by their duties as subjects of the King and the respect they owed English laws.

Notable examples of proprietorships are the colony of Maryland, granted to Lord Baltimore by King Charles I in 1632; the colonies of Pennsylvania and Delaware, granted in 1681 and 1682 to William Penn by King Charles II and by the Duke of York; the Fairfax family estate in the colony of Virginia, which

---

[23] The institution of governor and council persists in the United States to this day, e.g., in the state of New Hampshire.

comprised almost half a million acres; and the Carolinas, granted to a group of eight proprietors.

An understanding of this form of government and land ownership is crucial since it prospered in the initial phase of colonization in nearly all the colonies.

During the colonial period the Crown transformed seven proprietorships into royal colonies by revoking their charters, refusing to renew them, or acquiring the proprietary rights. However, even after the establishment of royal government, the system of land ownership remained intact.

The lord proprietors—nobles or members of the gentry—rarely lived in the colonies, but administered their lands through agents. They had the important task of peopling and developing the colony; in recompense, they received the rents and taxes. Within their territory they sold parcels of land according to practices that varied from colony to colony. There arose in this way large, medium, and small rural proprietors, dependent on the lord proprietor, to whom they owed an annual tribute, the quitrent, normally paid in cash. At other times, the proprietors leased lands, often eventually ceding ownership of them in recompense for some beneficial act, such as engaging in frontier warfare against the Indians. In turn, the land proprietors dependent upon the lord proprietor could sell or grant lots to third parties, who became immediately dependent upon these proprietors.

Testimony regarding proprietary government in the colonies

Commenting on the broad governmental powers granted to lord proprietors, Charles Andrews notes:

> The greater number were at the outset proprietary in form and manner of government, the patentees of which often enjoyed by virtue of their charters prerogatives more absolute even than those of the grantor, the king of England himself.... The colonial proprietors, most of whom never visited their possessions and in only a few instances attempted to govern their people in person, demanded from the beginning full recognition of their proprietary rights in the soil and, to a greater or lesser extent, varying with the different colonies, exacted bonds of obedience and fidelity to themselves as the absolute governing lords of the territory.[24]

James Adams, who traces the development of the colonial system of government and land ownership, emphasizes:

> The colonial land system was thus mainly feudal in character but by the end of the seventeenth century the strictly feudal tenures with the personal service exacted from tenant to lord had largely disappeared and the quitrent had come to be the measure and fulfillment of most of the tenant's obligations. Although its payment

---

[24] Andrews, *The Colonial Period of American History,* Vol. 2, p. 197.

was acknowledgment that the actual title to the property lay in the overlord and not in the tenant, nevertheless, this did not in the least limit the latter's entire freedom to sell or bequeath his acres provided he had fulfilled his obligations to the overlord.[25]

Despite variations from colony to colony, save for the three New England colonies, full property rights belonged either to the King or to the lord proprietor. Adams points out that throughout the different colonies, "no land anywhere was held under any form of tenure save that from an overlord, either the king or proprietors to whom the Crown had granted the lands which they in turn either sold or leased to the settlers."[26]

Marshall Harris explains:

> The proprietary governments were established under charters that granted powers of government from the Crown to one or more persons as proprietary or proprietaries. The proprietary possessed almost the same authority that the Crown maintained over the royal colonies. However, proprietors Baltimore and Penn had more rights in the establishment of tenures in their colonies than the king had regarding the land of England.... The proprietary or proprietaries invariably provided for assemblies to be selected from the freemen of their colony, but maintained, with few exceptions, exclusive executive prerogatives, appointed judicial officers, and convened or dismissed the assemblies at will.[27]

4. Feudalism in the United States

a. The manors

As previously noted, in medieval England the manor was a unit with a social, juridical, economic, and administrative organization that included rural properties under the governance of a lord who retained feudal rights over its inhabitants. Transformations during this period of colonial expansion eliminated many of its feudal aspects. In the New World, the term *manor* came to have a more flexible meaning, designating similar, though distinct, systems.

As a juridical system of land ownership, the manors were only established enduringly in Maryland and in certain areas of New York, where the term *manor* signified a para-feudal system of land ownership rather than a simple private rural estate. In other colonies, such as Virginia or the Carolinas, *manor* designated a great rural estate with its ancestral mansion, its lands, and the relationship that organically existed between the owner and his subordinates, without, however, having legal entailments. Despite such diversity, the term denoted a social system

---

[25] Adams, *Provincial Society 1690-1763*, p. 12.

[26] Ibid.

[27] Harris, *Origin of the Land Tenure System*, p. 76.

Oaklyn Plantation, South Carolina:
a symbol of Southern tradition.

favorable to the development of an aristocratic elite.

From a legal standpoint, the manors were those properties granted by the king, proprietor, or governor. The grant vested the owner with the attributes proper to a feudal lord. He had the right to govern the lands, administer justice, levy taxes, maintain his own army, and direct an administrative body similar to a small court with constables, judges, and so forth. In turn, he promised to cultivate and populate the region, keep order, and maintain the roads and bridges. This owner received the title "Lord of the Manor."

Like the proprietor, the lord of the manor could grant parcels of land to third parties. Some grants involved ceding possession, in which case the grantee would depend only partially on the lord, to whom he owed the payment of the quitrent. There were also grants without land possession, where the grantee was more dependent on the lord. All, however, remained under the administrative and juridical authority of the lord, and they could not transfer the land without a prior agreement with him. This favored the rise of numerous small proprietors and tenants whose relations with the lord were inspired, to a greater or lesser degree, by the feudal system.

At the base of this social pyramid were salaried workers and indentured servants. The latter were immigrants whose passage was paid and whose lodging and sustenance were assured by a landlord or the local government. The indentured servant, in return, worked without remuneration to repay the cost of the trip, usually for a period of four to seven years. At the end of this time, indentured servants often bought or even received a parcel of land and agricultural tools, and thereby became small proprietors. The slaves would only come in great numbers at a later period.

In time, the manors were gradually transformed into mere rural estates of a commercial nature, cultivated by slaves or rented to third parties.

b. Transformation of the manors in the Southern colonies into a plantation society

The system of proprietorships and manors was an attempt to transplant the English juridical order to the colonies. Due to conditions peculiar to each of the colonies and to socioeconomic transformations that occurred during this period, this system did not endure. Yet it was the seed of a new social order that flowered later, one more organically nourished and adapted to local conditions. In the South, this was the society of the great plantations, whose most dynamic human element was made up of the great planter-merchants and the social hierarchy that developed around and under them.

Various factors led to this transformation in the Southern colonies.

In the first place, the existence of large frontier areas, with fluid social structures, did not facilitate the full application of the rights of the proprietors and lords of the manor. The quitrent was often paid irregularly, and the fulfillment of the tenants' duties could not always be demanded. Living on the frontiers of civilization, in an environment that required initiative and autonomy, tenants often acted with great independence. Moreover, the landlords, wishing to obtain renters for unoccupied lands, offered more liberal contracts.

At the end of the seventeenth century, to remedy the lack of European immigration, the farmers began to import black slaves, with obvious economic advantage to the planters. This contributed significantly to transform the social organization of the manor into plantations whose more business-like character, commercial and capitalist, eroded the personal and organic relationship between the lord and his subordinates.

Curtis Nettels explains this transformation in Maryland:

> However, workers could not be obtained who would place themselves permanently in the dependent status of tenants, and the early manors were forced to rely upon indentured servants and Negro slaves; in consequence the manor was converted into a plantation of the Virginian type, although the name survived.[28]

Throughout the South, the model of the Virginia plantation came to dominate economic and social life. Jackson Turner Main writes:

> The commercial farm type of society therefore had come to predominate in all of the southern states except North Carolina. As region after region was opened up, the great planters purchased large tracts which were developed with slave labor or rented to tenants. Only gradually did the tenants acquire property and become free farmers.[29]

The introduction of large scale slave labor increased the area the planter could cultivate and the value of the land, stimulating the formation of great monoculture properties of a commercial nature focused on international markets.[30]

---

[28] Curtis P. Nettels, *The Roots of American Civilization* (New York: Appleton-Century-Crofts, 1963), p. 306.

[29] Jackson Turner Main, *The Social Structure of Revolutionary America* (Princeton: Princeton Univ. Press, 1965), pp. 44, 45.

[30] Regarding slavery, a salient aspect of colonial society, it is important to note that it was the usual condition of a great part of mankind when the Church was founded two thousand years ago. With time, however, the gentle influence of the Gospel loosened the cruel bonds of slavery as it existed in the Roman Empire. By the Middle Ages, slavery had been eradicated from Christian Europe. Lamentably, as a consequence of its fascination with all things Greek and Roman, the Renaissance revived slavery among Europeans. The Popes raised their voice to condemn it repeatedly throughout the three or so centuries it lasted in the New World. The measures taken by the Popes include:
—Paul III's excommunication in 1537 of those who enslaved the Indians of America (Denziger 1495).
—Gregory XVI's brief of December 3, 1839, in which he encouraged the bishops of the world to use their best efforts to 1) alleviate the hardships of slaves, 2) stop the slave trade, and 3) end slavery (cf. *Acta Gregorii Papae XVI*, ed. Bernasconi [Rome: S.C. de Propagande Fide, Typographia Polyglotta Vaticanae], Vol. 2, pp. 387-388).
—Pius IX's strong words against slavery when beatifying Saint Peter Claver in 1850 (cf. *Pii IX Pont. Max. Acta*, Part I, p. 645 ff.).
—Leo XIII's letter to the bishops of Brazil on May 5, 1888, recalling the Church's indefatigable efforts against slavery and expressing his joy at its abolition by the "Golden Law" in this country (cf. *Acta Leonis XIII* [Rome: Typis Polyglottis Vaticanae], Vol. 8, pp. 169-192).

The influx of slaves—the coup de grâce to the manor system—had a detrimental effect on the small tenants of the rural middle class. "The influx of slaves not only put almost a complete end to the importation of white servants," writes Wertenbaker, "but it reacted disastrously upon the Virginia yeomanry."[31]

Another factor transforming the social structure was the nearly unlimited availability of virgin land, there for the taking, as the saying went.

Immigrants who could easily acquire their own land did not need to subject themselves to the patronage of lords and great proprietors. Wertenbaker writes:

> With the cost of land very low, with the means of earning the purchase price so readily in hand, with the conditions for an independent career all so favorable, it was not to be expected that the freedman should content himself permanently with the status of a hired laborer. Nor was there any reason why he should become a tenant.[32]

With the decline of the manors and the development of the plantation system in the Southern colonies, along with the concomitant rise of a commercial class in the Northern colonies, the two regions began to follow divergent paths. As will be seen, this divergence grew sharper until it reached its tragic zenith in the Civil War of 1861-1865, called by Southerners the War Between the States. While the North embraced a mercantilist, industrial, banking order, the South continued as a rural, agrarian, patriarchal society. This difference was embodied in their respective elites. The North saw the rise of a rich mercantile class, and later, an industrial and banking class, which subsequently tended to develop an aristocracy. The South conserved a predominantly rural aristocracy marked by the lifestyle of the English country gentry.

---

[31] Thomas J. Wertenbaker, *The Planters of Colonial Virginia* (New York: Russell & Russell, 1959), p. 137.

[32] Ibid., p. 44.

CHAPTER V

The Formation of a Colonial Aristocracy in Various Regions

1. The Colonial South: Virginia, Maryland, and the Carolinas

a. Virginia: aristocracy of the great planters

1) The early years

Founded in 1607, the colony of Virginia was the first permanent English settlement in the New World, the point of departure for colonial expansion into the heart of the North American continent, and the model for other regions, especially Maryland.

The first English colony on American soil was the work of the Virginia Company of London, a commercial enterprise of nobles, gentlemen, and tradesmen whose objective was colonization. The Company's charter, granted by King James I, gave it proprietary rights over the colony. Later, in 1624, the company ceded these rights to the Crown.

The initial years of the colony were unstable. The first settlers did not come to work and cultivate the land. Rather, they were adventurers, moved by the hope of finding gold and making a quick fortune, not by the prospect of cultivating and colonizing the wilderness. Nevertheless, the colony quickly grew in population and stability with the arrival of further settlers more interested in agriculture than in adventure.

To increase the settled area and its population, the Company issued property titles to those willing to occupy the land and populate it with their families and servants. More than forty such titles were granted to individuals or groups to constitute rural estates, manors, or plantations of considerable size.[1]

Vested with broad privileges and governmental powers over their tenants, the

---

[1] Cf. Andrews, *The Colonial Period of American History*, Vol. 1, pp. 128-129.

lords of many of these manors were virtually independent. By the middle of the seventeenth century, however, the majority of Virginia's manors had lost their autonomy as a rudimentary social order, quite fluid at first, gradually appeared in the colony. It was based on land ownership and had the English gentry as its model. "They would become landed proprietors as much as possible like the country gentry of England," notes Louis Wright, "but they would adapt their 'gentility' to the requirements of new conditions. And, whatever their background, that is what they did."[2]

An abundance of natural resources and a great social mobility facilitated the acquisition of wealth and social status. Historian Daniel Boorstin describes the process.

> In the earliest years of colonial Virginia the opportunity to rise into the ranks of the gentry was not uncommon.
> Many Virginia families were founded by tradesmen or artisans, men of extraordinary talents, prosperity, or good luck, who acquired broad acres and soon could afford the style of life appropriate to a country gentleman.[3]

2) An aristocracy is born

In the decades that followed 1620 many men of fortune and high social standing immigrated to the colony. These included the younger sons of English gentry and traders, well-to-do yeomen, and merchants. Andrews states that "there were not many men of the better class in proportion to those of humble birth," but "the control of government was in the hands, almost entirely, of men of rank, of influence and good social standing." He says also that there were numerous merchants and that "they and their descendants became men of wealth and the founders of some of the best known of Virginia's colonial families."[4] These men were called "founders of dynasties."

Dowdey describes the rise of a rural aristocracy in colonial Virginia.

> The myths of the Virginia "aristocrat" began when the personal attributes of the established English aristocracy were imputed to the men and women who ventured to Virginia and, in building a colonial ruling class, founded an aristocracy of their own. In time the social attributes associated with an aristocracy would be developed, along with a graceful and elegant style of life which characterized the society. But this was the evolution of a colonial order founded by ambitious emigrants whose traits are not usually associated with the "aristocrat" in the social meaning.... They came to better their fortunes in a new land and, by circumstance and coalescence, at first formed an aristocracy only in the formal meaning of government by a few....
> ...In Virginia the first families to win position laid the framework of a ruling

---

[2] Wright, *The First Gentlemen of Virginia*, p. 46.

[3] Boorstin, *The Americans: The Colonial Experience*, p. 100.

[4] Andrews, *The Colonial Period of American History*, Vol. 1, pp. 208-209.

order, which the second and third generations evolved into a ruling class, or aristocracy.[5]

On the same subject, Wright observes:

> The great day of the Virginia landed aristocracy came in the eighteenth century, but before 1700 many families who would be important in later generations were already established.... [having] already laid the foundations of dynasties that would grow in wealth and influence in the next century.[6]

The initial phase of Virginia's colonization ended in 1641 with the arrival of Sir William Berkeley as governor. The next phase would be marked by the establishment of a social order based on the class of great planter-merchants. According to Boorstin, by the end of the seventeenth century,

> Virginia had become an aristocracy.... Most of the families which were to rule Virginia later in the century had already laid the foundations of their fortunes in vast land grants acquired before 1700. The "best" families tended to intermarry and by mid-century probably not more than a hundred families controlled the wealth and government of the colony.[7]

3) The plantations

After a period of sustenance farming within a closed economy, the colonizers discovered an extremely lucrative crop, tobacco. An export product that generated great profits, it permitted landholders to amass great wealth and acquire vast tracts of land for cultivation by a large number of slaves. This development favored westward expansion into lands where the planters could freely grow tobacco. It also favored the appearance of a new agrarian structure—the plantations, characterized by large farms, monoculture farming, slave labor, and a symbiosis with the overseas markets. The plantation system, developing without large urban centers, became consolidated and led to the dominant political and social role of the planter class. Boorstin describes these self-sufficient Virginia plantations.

> Life on a large plantation was far from that in a simple agrarian economy. There were hundreds of slaves, white craftsmen, overseers, stewards, and traders who were producing tobacco as a money-crop, raising food, and manufacturing tools, farm instruments, and clothing for their own use and for sale in local and foreign markets to which they were sometimes carried in the planter's own ship.[8]

---

[5] Dowdey, *The Virginia Dynasties*, pp. 9, 14.

[6] Wright, *History of the Thirteen Colonies*, pp. 174-175.

[7] Boorstin, *The Americans: The Colonial Experience*, p. 103.

[8] Ibid., p. 108.

Renowned Southern scholar Richard M. Weaver comments on aspects of the plantation society.

> With such diversity of occupation, there was a task adapted to everyone, and when a worker grew too old for a certain kind of employment, he would be shifted, in paternalistic fashion, to another better suited to his condition. The strong sense of particularism which developed in these communities derived principally from the circumstance that everyone had his place. The feeling of being bound to a locality, which has been almost wholly lost by the deracinated population of the modern metropolis, was a part of the plantation dweller's daily consciousness and an important factor in his self-respect.[9]

Describing the para-feudal aspects of the Southern plantations, the same author maintains that the props of Southern feudalism were

> the relative self-sufficiency of the plantation; the *noblesse oblige* of its proprietor; the social distinctions among those who dwelled upon it, which had the effect of creating respect and loyalty instead of envy and hatred; the sense of kinship with the soil, present too in its humbler inhabitants.... [The plantation] possessed stability, an indispensable condition for positive values: it maintained society in the only true sense of the term, for it had structure and articulation, and it made possible a personal world in which people were known by their names and their histories.[10]

Social historian Jack Greene points out that the plantations were "diversified and, in a few cases, perhaps even almost self-sufficient communities that quickly became the 'principal symbol of Chesapeake society.'"[11]

4) An aristocracy of planter-merchants

The greatest planters in the Southern colonies were not merely large-scale farmers, but planter-merchants who traded directly with the mother country. They had their own warehouses, ships, and ports—important maritime centers that became the pulsating hubs of commerce in the region.

In *The Virginia Dynasties*, Clifford Dowdey illustrates the organic development of the country gentry in Virginia. The Virginia aristocracy was not formed by aristocratic elements coming from the English nobility, as we have seen, but from local elements who were not noble by birth. They were proprietors of large plantations, owners of large expanses of land, or merchants. Through their competence,

---

[9]   Richard M. Weaver, *The Southern Tradition at Bay: A History of Postbellum Thought* (New Rochelle, N.Y.: Arlington House, 1968), p. 52.

[10]   Ibid., pp. 58-59.

[11]   Jack P. Greene, *Pursuits of Happiness* (Chapel Hill: Univ. of North Carolina Press, 1988), p. 92.

they ended up constituting a social and economic elite that formed the "nobility of Virginia." Having assumed political power, they gradually became aristocratic in their manners, education, and social relations.

This "nobility," comprised of planter-merchants and large farmers, did not take the titled nobility of England as its model, but looked more keenly to the country gentleman as a prototype. "This country gentry, not the nobility," affirms Dowdey, "was the class which formed the model for the emigrants who succeeded in the Virginia Colony."[12]

Apart from land ownership, the planters acquired social status through their military efforts in fighting the Indians. Wright notes that the circumstances of colonial life impelled these families of the rural elite to assume the social obligations and responsibilities characteristic of an aristocracy: "The independence of plantation life, the responsibilities for the direction of affairs, and the necessary social obligations in the community served to make leaders of the larger landowners.... They soon occupied the position of country gentlemen, whatever their fathers had been in the mother country."[13]

5) The political power of the landed gentry

The summit of the social pyramid in Virginia consisted of a strongly inter-related group of families and planters of great fortune and prestige who exercised political power in the colony in a virtually hereditary way.

> Virginia had no titled aristocracy, but it had an equivalent in the great ones who sat in the Council of State.
>
> By the later years of the seventeenth century, the evolution of a Virginia aristocracy had progressed to a point where a small ruling class not only monopolized public offices but also, by that very fact, dominated the economic life of the colony.[14]

These planters had various responsibilities in their exercise of power. They served in numerous civil and military leadership positions, and they dominated the parochial councils of the Anglican churches.[15] They constituted the colonial legislature, which met four times a year, and served as advisers to the governor.

Wright describes how the landed aristocracy monopolized economic and political power.

---

[12] Dowdey, *The Virginia Dynasties*, p. 13.

[13] Wright, *The First Gentlemen of Virginia*, p. 57.

[14] Ibid., pp. 54-55.

[15] As in England, the official religion of the colony of Virginia was Anglicanism. However, its organization was considerably less hierarchical, since the true power of decision in administrative and disciplinary matters was more often found in the hands of the laymen. "The Church of Virginia,..." explains Boorstin, "was a group of independent parishes, governed in temporal matters by the House of Burgesses and in doctrinal matters by no central authority at all." Each parish had power "through its vestry to choose its own minister and retain him only so long as he satisfied them" (Boorstin, *The Americans: The Colonial Experience*, p. 127).

The great planters, possessing sometimes thousands of acres, developed a landed aristocracy that succeeded in monopolizing much of the economic and political power.... They served as justices of the peace, sheriffs of the counties, colonels of the militia, members of the Council of State [which advised the governor], and members of the House of Burgesses. At meetings of the council and the House of Burgesses the flower of this planter aristocracy gathered in the little capital of Williamsburg to attend to political business and to enjoy social contacts that they missed on distant plantations.[16]

Wertenbaker emphasizes the aristocratic structure of the society.

Society was aristocratic rather than democratic. Wealth, education, political power were concentrated in the hands of a comparatively small group who monopolized the seats in the Council of State and the General Court, and to a large extent in the Lower House of Assembly, filled the vestries, held all the important commands in the militia, built stately mansions, employed tutors for their children, owned each several plantations in addition perhaps to tens of thousands of unoccupied acres in the Piedmont or the Valley of Virginia. Next in order, and far more numerous were the yeomanry—owners of little plantations of from fifty to two hundred acres. Prosperous, intelligent, self-reliant, jealous of their rights in the seventeenth century, they were the backbone of the region and their influence counted heavily in the General Assemblies.... But they looked to the aristocracy for leadership in both political and economic matters.[17]

This social class considered the exercise of public power something that unquestionably belonged to it. Boorstin writes:

Perhaps never in recent times has a ruling group taken a more proprietary attitude toward public office. During the years of the Revolution and the first decades of independence, the burgesses selected (almost exclusively from their own membership) the Virginia governors, council members, judges, military officers, and delegates to Federal conventions. Their personal knowledge of each member of the Virginia ruling class qualified them to distribute public dignities and burdens with an impressive, if not infallible, wisdom.[18]

6) The military role of the colonial elite

The colonial militia was an important institution on the frontier, where incursions of hostile and bellicose Indians posed a constant threat, and where intermittent conflicts with the Spanish and French colonies invariably accompanied the European wars.

[16] Wright, *History of the Thirteen Colonies*, pp. 309, 310.

[17] Wertenbaker, *The Old South*, pp. 10-11.

[18] Boorstin, *The Americans: The Colonial Experience*, p. 112.

Colonel Washington assumes command as Major General Edward Braddock falls mortally wounded in the French and Indian War.

In the Southern colonies, where the aristocratic tradition was more pronounced, militia leadership fell upon the civic leaders, the planters, who assumed the highest positions of command in the colonial militia. According to a 1989 United States Army study, rank in the militia in the colonial era generally corresponded to social position in the community.[19]

Although they were not specialists in military strategy, the planters were generally named colonels of the local militia.

The chief planter in each county was designated commander over military and naval forces in his jurisdiction and given the title of "colonel." Not merely was he

_____

[19] Cf. *American Military History* (Washington, D.C.: Center of Military History of the United States Army, 1989), p. 28.

responsible for drilling the militia in time of peace and leading it in time of danger, but also, among other things, he was entrusted with some of the duties of law enforcement.[20]

Dowdey notes: "By no means an empty title, 'colonel' was a designation of high rank, and the proper title was as carefully used in addressing a colonel as in addressing a lord."[21]

7) The planters' sense of social obligation

Besides exercising political power, the planter aristocracy had an acute sense of its social and civic obligations as the ruling class of the colony. This disposed its members to serve the public good, which they often did without remuneration and even to the detriment of their personal interests.

This fact belies the myth that the planters were greedy tyrannizers who were chiefly interested in seizing the power of colonial government without contributing to the common good. Wright sets the record straight:

> The notion sometimes expressed by cynics that the wealthy planters monopolized all the civil and military power exclusively for their personal aggrandizement is demonstrably false. They had inherited from an earlier period a sense of obligation to serve the state, and they often filled tedious and unremunerative public offices without complaint. When militia duty was required, they served as a matter of course, even when it meant personal hardship and loss of valuable time.[22]

In his analysis of Chesapeake society, Carl Bridenbaugh presents the sense of social obligation and aristocratic spirit, the sense of *noblesse oblige*, as one of the aristocracy's most salient features.

> *Noblesse oblige* was as much a part of the creed of the Chesapeake gentry as it was of the old regime in France. The inferior and middling sort of people generally found the owner of the big estate courteous, kind, and the fair and understanding judge on the quorum, ready to extend a helping hand before his aid was sought. A gentleman knew his neighbors of every rank and called them by name. Above all, the leading planters were imbued with the belief that they constituted a class whose obligations to serve and to govern well must be fulfilled in return for the privileges which were their birthright.[23]

---

[20]   Wright, *The First Gentlemen of Virginia*, pp. 52-53.

[21]   Dowdey, *The Virginia Dynasties*, p. 44.

[22]   Louis B. Wright, *The Cultural Life of the American Colonies 1607-1763* (New York: Harper & Row, Publishers, 1957), p. 6. Copyright © 1957 by Harper & Row, Publishers, Inc. Reprinted by permission of Harper Collins Publishers, Inc.

[23]   Carl Bridenbaugh, *Myths and Realities: Societies of the Colonial South* (Westport, Conn.: Greenwood Press [1952] 1981), p. 16.

In sum, their privileged position as new elites imposed on the planters a sense of social obligation. So Wright observes: "Many of the self-made aristocrats in the colonies, both in New England and the South, had a keen sense of social obligation and a belief that privilege carried with it responsibility."[24]

8) Social life and aristocratic tone

To alleviate their isolation, Southern aristocrats developed the custom of visiting each other's plantations, giving rise to an ample and elegant social life, centered almost exclusively on the plantations themselves. From this grew the proverbial Southern hospitality that lives on even to this day.

> The amenities of plantation life encouraged the cultivation of the social graces expected of the gentry. Gentlemen and ladies followed the traditional training that would develop in them the art of pleasing. They were expected to pay proper attention to their manners, to learn the technique of polite compliment and pleasant conversation, to be graceful in dancing, and to be at least moderately conversant with music and polite letters.[25]

The Virginia aristocrats looked to Europe for their models and, frequently, for their education.

> America, without the cult of the Virginia planter in the eighteenth century, would have been appreciably more gray and barren. For one thing, with all his vanities he had taste. Frequently he had gone to Eton, Winchester, Oxford, Cambridge, or the Middle Temple for his schooling...and perhaps he had taken in Paris and Rome on the Grand Tour.[26]

Among this upper class there was an irresistible desire to possess a coat of arms duly conferred by the royal College of Arms of London in the name of the King. "Having acquired the estate and dignity of country gentlemen, Virginia planters soon began to yearn for coats of arms," Wright reports. "The eagerness of the Virginia gentry for coat armor is significant of their desire to be of the gentry, to be like the aristocracy in the mother country." He says further: "According to one Virginia antiquarian, over one hundred and fifty colonial families had a 'vested right' to [coats of arms]."[27]

The planters exercised a social function proper to the nobility: the leadership of cultural and social life. As Dowdey notes, the large plantation owners became archetypal figures: "The big planters were the models who...established the customs and the values, the styles and the tastes, and, most of all, the attitudes."[28]

---

[24] Wright, *History of the Thirteen Colonies*, pp. 313-314.

[25] Wright, *The First Gentlemen of Virginia*, p. 79.

[26] Wecter, *The Saga of American Society*, p. 24.

[27] Wright, *The First Gentlemen of Virginia*, p. 60, citing Brock, *The Colonial Virginian*, p. 12.

[28] Dowdey, *The Virginia Dynasties*, p. 124.

These planters adopted yet another aristocratic hallmark: the building of family manors that served as dynastic seats. "The construction of manorial mansions," says Dowdey, "was part of a movement begun in the 1720s to erect dynastic seats following the style of the English higher gentry. Most of the new dynastic seats...combined indigenousness with grandeur, and the center house was usually flanked by outbuildings in a formal design."[29] Wertenbaker also describes this trend: "So there arose on the banks of the James or the Potomac or the Severn a series of mansions which in dignity, in correctness of proportion, in charm of detail, would have done credit to England itself."[30]

Deprived of frequent contact with centers of culture, the planters constructed enormous and elegant libraries which were often the centers of their mansions. Reading and conversation became daily pastimes, greatly favoring the enrichment of cultural and social life. Wertenbaker justly describes the aristocracy of the South as an "educated, cultured, widely read wealthy class, whose interests varied from statecraft to astronomy, from music to philosophy, from medicine to gardening."[31] Wright affirms that the Virginian aristocracy "had been educated in the humanistic tradition, and they had the wisdom of the ancients, as well as the resources of their own heritage."[32]

Wertenbaker sees the half century before independence as the apogee of this splendor of social life and nobility of the Virginia planters.

> They extended their holdings over one plantation after another, doubled and tripled their stock of slaves, acquired vast tracts of land in the Piedmont region, built their stately homes on the banks of the James, the Potomac and the Severn, filled them with costly furniture and silver, laid out their formal gardens, entertained with the lavish hospitality of English noblemen.[33]

In their passion for elegance, the aristocracy of Virginia was surpassed only by the French nobility.[34]

By the end of the colonial period, this aristocracy of planters had conferred on Southern society a brilliance that profoundly marked its life. Dixon Wecter points out:

> The quarter-century from 1740 to 1765 saw the greatest florescence of luxury which this land had ever known—silks, jewels, gold and silver plate, French and Spanish wines, portrait-painting, carriages from London, horse-racing for high stakes, fox-hunts, concerts, balls and plays in the theatres.... People of means felt no need

---

[29] Ibid., p. 368.

[30] Wertenbaker, *The Old South*, pp. 47-48.

[31] Ibid., p. 70.

[32] Wright, *The First Gentlemen of Virginia*, p. 350.

[33] Wertenbaker, *The Old South*, p. 27.

[34] Cf. Thomas Jefferson Wertenbaker, *Patrician and Plebeian in Virginia* (New York: Russell and Russell, 1959), p. 111.

to affect that later republican simplicity which became fashionable and perhaps expedient, after revolutions in America and France.[35]

9) Change of attitude

With time the planters had acquired the habits and manners of the aristocracy. This led to a change in attitude toward commerce, which they came to regard as something proper to an inferior social status. "The Virginia planter aristocrat, despite some family alliances, in time began to consider the merchants a somewhat inferior class and the mercantile pursuit not entirely in keeping with the character of a 'gentleman,'" writes Wertenbaker.[36]

The great proprietor, established as a lord on his plantation, had become accustomed to a position of direction, authority, and responsibility in relation to the community. This conferred on him a greater chivalrous spirit, while he lost something of the mercantile instinct that had marked prior generations.

> The economic and political conditions in the colony were destined to work a change in this as in other things in the Virginia planter. The gradual loss of the mercantile instinct, the habit of command acquired by the control of servants and slaves, and the long use of political power, the growth of patriotism, eventually instilled into him a chivalric love of warfare not unlike that of the knights of old....
>
> ...It is clear that at this period the old customs had passed away; that there was a new atmosphere in Virginia; that the planter was no longer a merchant but a Cavalier. The commercial spirit had become distinctly distasteful to him.[37]

The planter's change in attitude was manifested by an increased patriarchal sense proper to the feudal spirit.

> Cut off from his neighbors, the planter spent his life in isolation almost as great as that of the feudal barons of the Middle Ages. The plantation was to him a little world whose activities it was his business to direct and this world molded his character far more than any outward influence.[38]

The words of William Byrd of Virginia, spoken at the beginning of the eighteenth century, are quite significant: "Like one of the patriarchs, I have my flocks and my herds, my bond-men and bond-women, and every sort of trade amongst my own servants, so that I live in a kind of independence of everyone but Providence."[39]

---

[35] Wecter, *The Saga of American Society*, pp. 22-23.

[36] Thomas Jefferson Wertenbaker, *The Golden Age of Colonial Culture* (Ithaca, N.Y.: Cornell Univ. Press, 1970), p. 11.

[37] Wertenbaker, *Patrician and Plebeian in Virginia*, pp. 73, 102.

[38] Ibid., p. 54.

[39] Cited by Jan Lewis, *The Pursuit of Happiness* (Cambridge: Cambridge Univ. Press, 1983), p. 12.

10) Social mobility

A final observation regarding the aristocratic order in Virginia pertains to its social mobility. Small landholders could increase their possessions and eventually be assimilated into the rural aristocracy. In the same way, through poor administration or the squandering of wealth and possessions, families of this aristocracy could fall to a lower social status. Wright describes this:

> Although the higher planter group soon became acutely conscious of class distinctions, in pre-Revolutionary days they never developed into a true caste. As in England, there was a constant ebb and flow in the ranks of the upper class, as small planters grew prosperous and worked themselves into a better station, or as old planters fell on evil days and lost their possessions.[40]

This social and political arrangement conferred a peaceful and stable character on the colonial South, where social conflict was virtually unknown. The people of Chesapeake, says Carl Bridenbaugh,

> succeeded in achieving a stable agrarian society in which there was no unrest. Equilibrium based on a widely recognized and quietly accepted class structure in which the aristocracy was completely dominant was evident to all observers....
>
> The genius of this people lay in agriculture and politics; it displayed itself to the world as *noblesse oblige*, gracious hospitality, zest for living, effortless courtesy—all forms of action befitting their way of life. The Chesapeake society produced a unique bourgeois aristocracy with more than its share of great and noble men; they were, however, men of intellect, not intellectuals.[41]

b. Maryland

1) A Protestant revolt against a Catholic lord proprietor

In 1632 King Charles I granted a charter to a Catholic nobleman, George Calvert, the first Lord Baltimore, conceding to him the territory that later became the state of Maryland, and delegating him powers similar to those of a local sovereign, including the right to grant titles of nobility and to distribute lands and honors. Calvert wanted the colony to be a refuge for Catholics persecuted in England, since the charter granted liberty to all religions.

The actual colonization, however, fell to George Calvert's son Cecil and to his descendants. In 1634 the second Lord Baltimore sent to the colony a group of

---

[40]   Wright, *The First Gentlemen of Virginia*, p. 48.

[41]   Bridenbaugh, *Myths and Realities*, p. 51, 53.

Portrait of GEORGE CALVERT,
the first Lord Baltimore,

sixteen to twenty gentlemen, most of them Catholic, and two to three hundred settlers, predominately Protestant.

In its first decade, colonial life was prosperous and peaceful. Soon, however, the political and religious strife that had erupted in England extended to her colonies. With the victory of Cromwell's Puritan sectarians over the royalists, convulsions of a religious, social, and political nature shook Maryland as well. The Puritan majority revolted against the Catholic proprietor and the lords of manors, plundering and wreaking havoc in the name of the English Parliament dominated by Puritan revolutionaries.

In 1654, the Puritan faction of Maryland revolted against the policy of religious toleration for Catholics and demanded that the anti-Catholic statutes in force in the mother country be applied in the colony. Overthrowing the lawful government of the proprietor, they suppressed the religious liberty of Catholics.

Sydney Ahlstrom, professor of history at Yale, writes: "The victorious Puritans then outlawed Roman Catholicism, plundered the estates of the Jesuits, forced all priests into exile, and executed at least four Roman Catholics. Lord Baltimore regained his proprietary privileges in 1657 only on condition that Josias Fendall, a Protestant, serve as governor."[42]

The restoration of the Stuarts to the throne with Charles II in 1660 brought the restoration of the former governors in the colonies. The Calverts regained their proprietary rights, but life in the colony remained agitated because of the Protestant animosity toward Catholics. The period of agitation undermined the stability of the manor system and resulted in a tendency toward revolutionary democracy in the political structures of the colony.

In 1689, one year after the deposition of James II, the authority of the Catholic proprietors was again usurped by a Protestant revolt. In 1691, William III revoked the charter granted to Lord Baltimore by Charles I, and Maryland temporarily became a royal colony with Anglicanism as its official religion. Only in 1715 were the Calverts reinvested with their proprietary authority—after they had agreed to renounce the Catholic Faith.

2) Feudal character of the Maryland manors

The brilliance of the social life of the rural aristocracy in Maryland rivaled that of Virginia. Because of their similarity, the societies of the two colonies formed a single whole that various authors have called the "Chesapeake society." Having examined the juridical-social structure of Virginia, we limit ourselves to noting some distinguishing characteristics of the aristocracy of Maryland, and describing its para-feudal system of manors.

The most complete and vigorous attempt to implant the English system of manors in the colonies, with its personal bonds and feudal hierarchy, took place

---

[42] Sydney E. Ahlstrom, *A Religious History of the American People* (New Haven: Yale Univ. Press, 1972), p. 335.

in Maryland during the first half century of its colonial life. In a work on colonial life in the lower Potomac region, Paul Wilstach writes: "The development of such plantations, in Maryland called Manors on account of the land tenure established there and of the domestic and social life which flourished on them and the great personages they produced, is one of the absorbing features of the story of tidewater Potomac."[43]

One of the reasons for the success of early Maryland was that the family charged with governing the colony actually resided there, and not in England. Provided with the broadest of powers, the Calverts, in the words of Dixon Wecter, "always looked upon themselves as feudal lords, the planters as their barons, and the laboring classes as their tenantry."[44]

The proprietorship of Maryland, contrary to tendencies already in vogue in England, established a feudal system of government and land ownership, manors, manorial courts, and secondary bonds. This system flourished for more than a half century. Richard Weaver comments:

> Politically the feudal structure was desirable because by making the owner of broad acres true lord of the domain it simplified administration. Lord Baltimore recognized this when in Maryland he offered manorial powers to those able to take up large holdings. Some three score estates were granted on such terms and were run more or less in the fashion of an English medieval manor until in the course of time they were turned into its American counterpart, the Southern plantation.[45]

The success of the Calverts in repeating in the New World the system that had been in force for so long in England was such that Paul Wilstach affirms: "An analogy has been drawn between the Lord Proprietor, the Lords of the Manors, and the freeholders of the Potomac colony on the one hand, and the King, the Barons and the gentry of England on the other."[46] According to Marshall Harris, "the authority and power conferred upon Cecil Calvert was truly royal, while nothing of significance, except general sovereignty, was reserved to the king. Maryland was a feudal seigniory of the medieval vintage."[47] Andrews terms Maryland a great palatinate, that is, an area where a feudal lord exercised his sovereignty, and explains the feudal relations that existed in the colony in this period.

> The entire area was a palatinate or great barony, within which, standing in a feudal relationship with the proprietor, were the lords of the manors and the freeholders with their tenements.... They set the stamp of a decentralized and rural

---

43   Paul Wilstach, *Potomac Landings* (Garden City, N.Y.: Doubleday, Page & Co., 1921), p. 65.

44   Wecter, *The Saga of American Society*, p. 29.

45   Weaver, *The Southern Tradition at Bay*, pp. 48-49.

46   Wilstach, *Potomac Landings*, p. 66.

47   Harris, *Origin of the Land Tenure System*, p. 121.

Evergreen House in Baltimore:
an example of an aristocratic Maryland mansion.

plantation system upon the colony, organized on a manorial plan and imitating as nearly as possible the features of an English barony.[48]

To be lord of a manor, the landowner needed to be invested as such by the lord proprietor or governor and to possess at least a thousand acres of land. The mere possession of the land did not automatically make someone lord of a manor, for manorial rights could only be conceded by charter. In this way, a lord of a manor distinguished himself from the planter aristocracy that was developing in parallel.

"Maryland had an upper planter class much like that of Virginia," Wright points out, "some of whom acquired great tracts of land and established family dynasties of power and continuing influence."[49]

Throughout the course of the seventeenth century, the Calverts established more than sixty manors, not including those that belonged to themselves and their relatives. This helped to create a defined social hierarchy, distinguishing the nobility from the rest of the population, marking the social life in the colonial period and even beyond. As Andrews observes: "At the beginning Maryland was no mere palatinate on paper; it was a land of actual manors, demesne lands, freehold tenements, rent rolls, and quitrents."[50]

The same author goes on to show how the social distinctions were reflected in the political field.

> By order of the proprietor the eight councillors...who were themselves always lords of manors, were to be supplemented by seven others, each of whom had to be a manorial lord in order to qualify for the position. These fifteen councillors formed an upper house of assembly, which composed as it was of the "ablest planters" came as near as did an upper house in any colony to being a house of lords.[51]

In the middle of the seventeenth century, Maryland had lords of manor who presided over minor courts, with barons, officers of justice, colonels, tenants, and peasants. Following the feudal model, justice was administered by those lords through two courts, the Court Baron and the Court Leet. The disputes that arose in the territory of the manor were judged according to its own laws, customs, and regulations. In these courts the tenants and peasants also swore fidelity to their lords in feudal terms, promising to be honest and faithful. Although the Court Baron and the Court Leet were a source of great power and advantage for the lord of the manor as long as he held jurisdiction, this judicial system gradually weakened and soon ceded place to an elective system of judges for county courts.[52]

---

[48] Andrews, *The Colonial Period of American History*, Vol. 2, p. 293.

[49] Wright, *History of the Thirteen Colonies*, p. 310.

[50] Andrews, *The Colonial Period of American History*, Vol. 2, p. 297.

[51] Ibid., p. 329.

[52] Cf. Wiltach, *Potomac Landings*, p. 68; and Wertenbaker, *The Founding of American Civilization*, pp. 309-310.

c. The Carolinas

1) The aristocratic constitution

In 1663 Charles II granted the Carolinas to a group of eight lord proprietors, among whom were some of the most celebrated nobles of the time who had distinguished themselves in the efforts to restore the Stuarts to the throne. Since the area of the Carolinas was a contested region, the object of Spanish claims, it represented an outpost of the growing English empire in America.

After a difficult beginning, the colony developed rapidly with the planting of rice. In this initial period, one of the lord proprietors, the Earl of Shaftesbury, promulgated the celebrated Fundamental Constitutions of Carolina. This document was intended "to avoid an excessive democracy" and to create an "hereditary nobility" based on land ownership.

In his history of South Carolina, Wright describes the Fundamental Constitutions. "An odd mixture of medieval ideas and advanced concepts of toleration, the Fundamental Constitutions prescribed a hierarchical society with a landed nobility consisting of 'landgraves' and 'caciques' at the top; next would come commoners who might be lords of manors, followed by freeholders and yeomen."[53]

The Constitutions created a bicameral parliament, with the juridical and administrative powers residing in the upper house, as well as the power to approve or reject the laws passed by the lower house.

In commenting on the Fundamental Constitutions, historians often emphasize the fact that the colony never managed to completely implement the social system it so carefully detailed. Indeed the nobiliary system was only partially and temporarily applied. In 1721 the Crown reacquired its rights over the Carolinas, nullifying the decrees of the Constitutions. However, by this time many large landowners had already solidly established themselves, laying the foundation for an aristocratic order that would continue until the Civil War.

"Although a noble order failed to survive, by the 1690s gentry appeared in the coastal parishes," explains Frederic Jaher. "A large proportion of its land and power remained in the hands of direct descendants until the Civil War."[54]

Wright concurs. "Despite the collapse of the scheme for a nobility, the acquisition by colonial families of large tracts of land worked by black slave-labor in effect established an aristocracy of sorts that persisted for nearly two centuries."[55]

The lord proprietors of the Carolinas had less success in their attempt to establish a lasting government than their counterparts in Maryland and Pennsylvania. Nevertheless, during their government—at times turbulent, particularly in its final phase—the colony survived and prospered.[56]

---

[53] Louis B. Wright, *South Carolina: A Bicentennial History* (New York: W. W. Norton & Co., 1976), p. 40.

[54] Jaher, *The Urban Establishment*, p. 320.

[55] Wright, *South Carolina: A Bicentennial History*, p. 41.

[56] Cf. ibid., p. 62.

2) The colonial aristocracy

Frederick P. Bowes, a specialist on the colonial period of the Carolinas, points out that a significant consequence of the Fundamental Constitutions was the establishment of an aristocratic social order.

> By far the largest element in the governing elite were the rich landowners whose broad plantations covered the low country around Charleston. Land was the chief source and form of wealth in the colony, and the proprietary policy of making lordly grants to favored individuals gave rise to a clique of wealthy landowners who before long had secured title to almost all the best lands in the Charleston area.... These landowners, many of them councillors and assemblymen, took advantage of the interim between the fall of the proprietary regime and the purchase of the colony by the Crown to appropriate some 800,000 additional acres of valuable low river lands under old patents that had been granted by the proprietors.[57]

Wright compares the colonial aristocracy of South Carolina to that of Virginia, noting that both colonies developed aristocracies in the colonial period which bore some resemblance to the English gentry, although the upper classes in the two colonies differed markedly.

> The great Virginia families who came over earlier in the seventeenth century were more conscious of an ancient tradition of gentility and were more deliberate in their efforts to reproduce patterns of life similar to those of the county families in the home country. Many Virginia immigrants brought along Renaissance books on the rationale of behavior; their libraries revealed immense interest in the heritage of the past going back to Greece and Rome; and their correspondence discloses profound concern for the lessons that the classics and the writers of the Renaissance had to teach.
>
> The great families of South Carolina were founded by men who came later in the seventeenth and early in the eighteenth centuries.... This is not to say that the South Carolina gentry were less conscious of status than their Virginia brethren, or less concerned to assert their privileges and to display the outward manifestations of an upper class. But they reflected the social patterns of the London of Queen Anne and the Georges, rather than the older traditions of English county families.[58]

Although younger than its counterparts in Virginia and Maryland, the Carolina aristocracy grew to form a cultured and influential gentry of greater wealth than the Virginian aristocracy. Bridenbaugh describes it as follows:

> During the pre-Revolutionary decades the Carolina Society was taking form with inordinate rapidity. Newness and wealth were its outstanding characteristics. In forty years

---

[57]   Frederick P. Bowes, *The Culture of Early Charleston* (Chapel Hill: Univ. of North Carolina Press, 1942), pp. 115-116.

[58]   Wright, *South Carolina: A Bicentennial History*, pp. 102-103.

or less, a planting plutocracy arose on the basis of fortunes amassed in rice and indigo or in trade and sought to transform itself into an aristocracy after the Old World pattern."[59]

Wright describes the role of the planter-merchants in the formation of an aristocratic elite in South Carolina at the end of the colonial period.

> South Carolina had an upper class whose fortunes came from rice planting, sometimes combined with trade and merchandising.... Many of the prominent aristocrats at the end of the colonial period traced their origins back to simple workmen who managed to capitalize upon opportunities to buy land and make a profit from trade.... South Carolina grandees of the tidewater region combined trade and farming.[60]

Frederick Bowes's work on the colonial times of South Carolina provides a detailed account of the development of an aristocratic style of life among the planters and merchants, who formed a solid class on the basis of rice planting and commerce.

> It was in every sense an aristocracy, for to power, wealth and privilege were added in time education, manners and refinement to further elevate its members above the common level. The intermarriage of wealthy families and the formation of exclusive clubs and societies knit ever more closely the bonds uniting this class.[61]

In the Carolinas the upper classes displayed a strong sense of civic duty. In 1770 the Governor of South Carolina, William Bull II, stated that many took upon themselves "a gratuitous execution of many branches of Power under a desire of shewing a public spirit and easing the public expences."[62]

Of special interest in the early history of South Carolina was the immigration of numerous Huguenots who fled France after the revocation of the Edict of Nantes by Louis XIV. The majority of these immigrants were skilled artisans and persons of an elevated professional and social background. Many became rich and rose rapidly on the social ladder, marrying into the better families and becoming distinguished members of the local aristocracy.

3) Charleston: a brilliant social life

When speaking of the Carolinas, a word must be said about Charleston. It was the only city of true importance in the region until well after the War of Independence. No other city of the South shone with such social brilliance. Situated at a site where the Ashley and Cooper Rivers meet, it attracted an aristocracy

---

[59] Bridenbaugh, *Myths and Realities*, p. 116.

[60] Wright, *History of the Thirteen Colonies*, pp. 310-311.

[61] Bowes, *The Culture of Early Charleston*, p. 115.

[62] Quoted in Jaher, *The Urban Establishment*, p. 329.

comprised of great planters and merchants who dominated the economic and political life of the coastal region of the Carolinas.

Wright's history of South Carolina compares the ruling class of Charleston to that of Venice.

> Charleston, like Venice in its heyday, was a city-state, ruled by an intelligent and cultivated oligarchy of great families who managed to monopolize control, generation after generation.... Whatever their beginnings, the rich and powerful very early gained control of the colonial government; and for more than a century they concentrated all political power of the colony in Charleston.[63]

Bridenbaugh describes "Charles Town" as the

> great center for the beneficiaries of the Carolina Society.... [The city] provided the delightful vision of the elegant life, elevated above the common sphere, "glittering like the morning-star, full of splendor, vitality, gaiety." There the rice and indigo gentry displayed and consumed their wealth.... "It was [a society] circumscribed by a still powerful aristocratic tradition.... Here was the only leisure-class Society of colonial America; here, the only people among whom "the unbought grace of life"—enjoyment, charm, refinement—became the *summmum bonum*.[64]

Wecter refers to the renowned writer and conservative English philosopher Edmund Burke who "by hearsay...reported that of all the American cities, Charleston 'approached more nearly to the social refinement of a great European capital.'" Wecter also notes Crevecoeur's comparison of Charleston's role in North America to what Lima's had long been in South America.[65]

Regarding this remarkable colonial city, Wright observes:

> Possessed of the greatest per capita wealth of any city in North America, Charleston did its best to imitate the *beau monde* of Augustan London. Its leading citizens kept up with the fashions and the news of the English metropolis, and by the middle of the eighteenth century their punctiliousness of manners gave them an air of gentility hardly equaled by the English aristocracy in the same period.... Wealthy families hired tutors and governesses for their children and frequently sent them to England or the Continent to finish their education. When they returned, insofar as they could, they tried to make Charleston a replica of the London of the Hanoverians. They established and supported a theater, they imported and read the latest books from London, and they organized concert groups and enjoyed music; in short, they established an urban culture of polish and sophistication.[66]

---

[63]   Wright, *South Carolina: A Bicentennial History*, p. 100.

[64]   Bridenbaugh, *Myths and Realities*, pp. 116-117.

[65]   Wecter, *The Saga of American Society*, p. 32.

[66]   Wright, *The Cultural Life of the American Colonies*, p. 19.

We close with Wertenbaker's lively description of the refinement of the planter aristocracy of the Carolinas that made Charleston the center of its social life.

> Charleston, then, became the center of a refined society which delighted in laying out its wealth in beautiful houses, stately balls, in luxurious gardens, in costly dinners, in musical entertainments, in the theater, in portraits, in literary clubs, in fine furniture and silver. Drawing their inspiration from the English squires, the Charlestonians vied with them in all the amenities of life and the graces of the cultured gentleman. Although wealth was the basis of this refined society, in time wealth alone was not sufficient to admit one to it.[67]

2. New England: Massachusetts, Connecticut and Rhode Island

a. Early period: the religious society of the Puritans

In 1620 the *Mayflower* landed off the coast of New England, bringing the first group of English emigrants. They were the Pilgrims, members of a Protestant sect that recognized neither the Anglican Church nor the King as a religious head. They came generally from the more modest classes. "Most of the Separatists who came to America in the *Mayflower*," observes Charles Andrews, "had had little or no education."[68]

Of the forty-one men who signed the Mayflower Compact, only eleven could use the title "Mr." before their names, and none could be qualified as a gentleman. "A group of English emigrants more socially insignificant could hardly be imagined," remarks Wecter in describing this assemblage.[69] Because of their singularly sectarian character, these Pilgrims did not mix with the other emigrants who later came to New England.

In 1629 the Great Puritan Migration began. Large numbers of English Calvinist Puritans, who opposed the hierarchy, doctrines, and rites of the Anglican Church, but retained some strong features of Christian morality, came to the New World to found a society organized on their egalitarian religious principles. These principles proposed a church without hierarchy, pomp, ceremonies, and adornment, a church governed by the biblical interpretations and laws emanating from its theologians and "divinely" illuminated ministers.

Abandoning the idea of "purifying" the Church of England, they felt that by virtue of their special "alliance" with God, they were providentially charged with the mission of founding a Calvinist Jerusalem in the New World, where they would be unhampered by any interference from the Anglican hierarchy or state.

---

[67] Wertenbaker, *The Golden Age of Colonial Culture*, p. 129.

[68] Andrews, *The Colonial Period of American History*, Vol. 1, p. 274.

[69] Wecter, *The Saga of American Society*, p. 37.

These Puritan emigrants were much better off socially and economically than their Pilgrim predecessors. The Great Puritan Migration was organized and directed by wealthy and influential men of England's middle class who were well-educated and had political experience.

Andrews describes them in the following terms:

> First, [there were] a few of high rank, connected with the peerage. Secondly, a few substantial English squires, influential but not numerous, always called "Misters." Thirdly, yeomen, goodmen and their wives of the middle class but below the squires, who were as a rule small farmers or tradesmen, law abiding, and religiously minded, migrating for land and homes...or, in the case of artisans and tradesmen, for freer opportunities to carry on their work. Fourthly, lesser tenantry from the English demesnes, most of whom were of peasant stock, inferior in position, intelligence, and education...who had probably come in many cases as groups following a leader.[70]

Their religious outlook dominated the first years of colonial life. Based on the Calvinist doctrine of the "theology of the Alliance," the Puritans attempted to construct a temporal order that conformed to their religious conceptions and to establish a state governed by a religious oligarchy. "The New World Canaan commenced as an ordered agricultural village whose civil and spiritual governance devolved upon an oligarchy of magistrates and ministers," notes Jaher.[71]

The social order in the primitive Puritan community was one of "hierarchical communalism."[72] The political, social, and economic life of the community centered far more on each city or town, than on the colony as a whole.

At the same time, residual aspects of the old manor system, especially the more communal ones, persisted. As Williams, Current, and Freidel point out:

> In New England the early settlers usually took up land in groups, each member receiving a village lot of his own, sharing the "common" as pasture and timberland, and tilling the strips assigned to him in the outlying fields. This township system was a relic of the manorial system, but here the town proprietors took the place of the feudal lord.[73]

Thus in the early decades of colonization, New England was characterized—from a religious, political, and social point of view—by dogmatic and even intolerant governments, even in relation to other Protestant groups. In this society, the elites were more intellectual and were formed principally by elements from the class of liberal professionals, the Puritan clergy, and a nascent merchant class.

---

[70] Andrews, *The Colonial Period of American History*, Vol. 1, p. 502.

[71] Jaher, *The Urban Establishment*, p. 15.

[72] E. Digby Baltzell, *Puritan Boston and Quaker Philadelphia* (New York: The Free Press, 1979), p. 124.

[73] Williams, Current, and Freidel, *A History of the United States*, p. 60.

The Mayflower

In effect, the Puritans erected a religious state, excluding or ostracizing those who refused an oath of adherence to their Calvinist doctrines. They placed the government of the community in the hands of a Puritan social and religious elite. According to Andrews, Puritan leader John Winthrop, one of the principal founders of the colony of Massachusetts Bay and its first governor, was profoundly convinced that

> it was for the good of all that power should be kept in the hands of those whose Christian calling it was to govern and that their number should remain as small as possible. He always stood in dread of a plebeian tyranny—control by the inferior sort—and was convinced that the "people" were not to be trusted with the election of so important an official as the governor.[74]

Lacking a central religious authority, it soon became impossible to maintain religious and social unity. By 1640 the growing Puritan community faced increasing numbers of dissident and schismatic groups, which formed new colonies. This contributed to diminishing the social status and influence of Calvinist ministers in colonial life. The religious break-up of the Puritan community transformed it "into unrelated, often irreconcilable parts."[75]

The 1660s witnessed the further decline of the sense of the Puritan religious mission, and the peculiar religious aspect of the colony "lost its former preeminence in community life."[76]

b. An urban and mercantile elite

As the religious factor waned, the character of colonial life in the Puritan communities changed, making way for the values of mercantile individualism that had triumphed in England. The Puritan elites turned their energies toward commerce, and undertook the new challenge of building the kingdom of mammon with the same self-confident zeal with which they had purported to build the kingdom of God. The Crown assumed control of the colony in 1684. This "effectively shattered 'any lingering sense among the colonists that they formed a special, divinely chosen community,'" as Greene notes.[77] At the same time, it accelerated the formation of new elites.

In the colonies of New England, geographic, economic and social conditions did not favor the cultivation of vast properties. There was no class of large planters as in the South. Although society remained predominantly agricultural, economic development around 1650 gave rise to a mercantile elite, whose wealth came principally from commerce and shipbuilding.

---

[74] Andrews, *The Colonial Period of American History*, Vol. 1, pp. 438-439.

[75] Greene, *Pursuits of Happiness*, p. 60.

[76] Ibid., p. 61.

[77] Ibid., p. 60, quoting Robert Pope, "New England versus the New England Mind: The Myth of Declension," *Journal of Social History*, Vol. 3 (1969-70), p. 105.

This elite grew and prospered in many coastal cities of New England and came to dominate the social, political, and economic life of the larger urban centers of the region. It gradually fused with the Puritan political and religious elite, becoming an aristocracy quite different from that of the planters in the South. Wertenbaker writes:

> It was the rather sterile soil of New England which gave her a small farmer class instead of a planter aristocracy, her forests which made possible her shipbuilding industry, the great schools of cod and herring which made Gloucester, Salem, and Marblehead fishing centers; her many fine harbors stimulated trade and created her merchant aristocracy. This aristocracy was largely responsible for much of what is distinctive and charming in colonial New England culture.[78]

Jaher adds:

> A rapid emergence of mercantile leadership in such port towns as New Haven, Salem, Newburyport, Beverly, and Boston inhibited the realization of a Godly community. Virtually from Boston's initial settlement, a commercial enclave exerted considerable influence over town affairs. This elite assumed authoritative social roles, commanded essential community resources, and developed a collective identity....
>
> ...At an early date prominent traders constituted a multidimensional elite which supported key communal enterprises and occupied important public offices.[79]

Homer Carey Hockett, a former history professor at Ohio State University, also points out the status acquired by this class of merchants: "The growth of commerce introduced a new class into the social grouping of New England. Before Boston was ten years old, merchants began to bid for a share of the influence enjoyed by the gentry."[80]

Regarding the Boston merchant class, Bridenbaugh writes: "The number and importance of Boston merchants increased with the trade of the port until by 1690 they had attained the dignity of an economic and social class that challenged the supremacy of the Puritan priesthood."[81]

Curtis Nettels mentions the rise of this mercantile elite that would become characteristic of and predominant in the society of the Northern states.

> In the northern towns the growth of merchant capitalism had produced, by 1700, the nucleus of an upper class.... When a merchant acquired extensive property and devoted his time to its general supervision rather than to routine business, and when his income was

---

[78]   Wertenbaker, *The Golden Age of Colonial Culture*, pp. 8-9.

[79]   Jaher, *The Urban Establishment*, pp. 15, 16.

[80]   Homer Carey Hockett, *Political and Social Growth of the American People, 1492-1865*, 3d ed. (New York: The Macmillan Co., 1940), p. 73. In New England, the name "gentry" was attributed to the class made up of Puritan magistrates and ministers, of whom many descended from the English gentry.

[81]   Carl Bridenbaugh, *Cities in the Wilderness* (New York: Alfred A. Knopf [1938] 1966), p. 38.

derived primarily from his investments, he had attained a distinctly upper-class standing.[82]

c. An opulent aristocracy exercising political leadership

It was not long before the commercial elite began to acquire definite aspects of a mercantile aristocracy, as Wright relates.

> Within two generations after the settlement of Boston, Newport, New York, Philadelphia, and other towns, merchants and traders were adding ships and warehouses to their possessions, accumulating working capital, building comfortable and sometimes imposing houses, and establishing family dynasties. They were the mercantile aristocracy, a powerful and proud group, who would grow in greatness throughout the colonial period.... Some of them developed a pride of family and place that equaled if it did not exceed the pretensions of the planter aristocracy in the southern colonies.[83]

The wealthiest and proudest of this developing aristocracy were, according to Wright, the great ship-owning merchants, who "became the aristocrats of the colonial business world."[84]

Jack Greene depicts the opulent lifestyle of this mercantile elite:

> If few New Englanders enjoyed such impressive wealth, those who did, aspired, as did the Chesapeake gentry, to recreate the genteel culture of contemporary Britain. To that end, they built larger and more commodious houses and filled them with English and Continental furnishings and other fashionable consumer items, made charitable bequests, filled their towns with impressive public buildings, created a host of urban voluntary associations, and otherwise sought to reproduce the urban amenities of British provincial cities.... Everywhere, however, elite behavior in New England was calculated to reinforce the traditional prescriptive association among wealth, social status, and political authority.[85]

As the eighteenth century unfolded, the wealthy families of New England came to constitute a leading urban elite, as Greene describes:

> Towns with more developed economic structures showed a powerful tendency toward oligarchy, with a handful of wealthy and prominent families...dominating both appointed and elective offices. In most towns, these family political dynasties were based on long association with the town's history.[86]

---

[82] Nettels, *The Roots of American Civilization*, p. 309.

[83] Wright, *The Cultural Life of the American Colonies*, p. 30.

[84] Ibid., p. 34.

[85] Greene, *Pursuits of Happiness*, p. 70.

[86] Ibid., pp. 70-71.

Lyndhurst: one of many mansions along the Hudson.

Arthur Schlesinger emphasizes the political leadership exercised by the elites.

> Social and political leadership in New England belonged as a matter of custom to the "well-born"—the clergy, the professional classes, and the wealthier merchants. Seats in the meeting-houses, places at the table and in processions, were regulated with a nice regard for social differentiation.[87]

Bridenbaugh confirms this role of the elites: "In each community a small group of men arose, some of them 'damnable rich,' who gathered into their hands the control of colonial commerce, and with it political power and social prestige."[88]

By the end of the colonial period, the political role of the mercantile and professional elites in New England was comparable to that exercised by the planters in the South. As Nettels states, "the northern merchants also matched the southern planter class in political influence. They generally controlled the governor's council and the local governments of their towns."[89]

3. New York

a. Dutch patroons and English manors

New Netherland, later to become New York, was founded in 1624 by the Dutch as a commercial outpost on the Hudson River for fur trading. A charter issued in 1629 enabled emigrants with sufficient capital to acquire large tracts of land, and systematic colonization began. The first steps toward the establishment of a semi-feudal system of manors ensued, as each manor was granted to a lord, who received broad powers and rights to govern his lands.

"The grantee, known as a patroon, had rights similar to those exercised by an English lord of a manor.... He could impose regulations with the force of law, hold manorial courts...collect rents, and dispose of his grant by sale or bequest."[90]

In 1664 a fleet sailing under authority of the Duke of York conquered New Netherland. It was renamed New York, and the Duke became its lord proprietor. Later, after he was crowned the king of England, New York became a royal colony.

Williams, Current, and Freidel describe the continuity of the colony's social structure during its transition from Dutch to English control.

> New York, formerly New Netherland, already the property of the Duke of York and renamed by him, was his to rule as virtually an absolute monarch. Instead of going to America he delegated his powers to a governor and a council. He confirmed the Dutch patroonships already set up...and he gave away comparable estates

87 Arthur Meier Schlesinger, *New Viewpoints in American History* (New York: The Macmillan Co., 1922), p. 73.

88 Bridenbaugh, *Cities in the Wilderness*, p. 38.

89 Nettels, *The Roots of American Civilization*, p. 311.

90 Wright, *History of the Thirteen Colonies*, p. 129.

to Englishmen so as to create a class of influential landowners loyal to him.[91]

In her study on colonial life in the Hudson River Valley, historian Maud Goodwin describes the development of a gentry based on the system of land grants and manors.

> When the English took possession of New Netherland in 1664, the old patroonships were confirmed as manorial grants from England. As time went on, many new manors were erected until, when the province was finally added to England in 1674, "The Lords of the Manor" along the Hudson had taken on the proportions of a landed aristocracy.[92]

Toward the end of the seventeenth century, the English government provided a new stimulus for the development of large rural properties similar to the Dutch patroonships. As Marshall Harris notes, "the large manorial estates created by subsequent English grants were hardly distinguishable from their earlier cousins, the Dutch patroonships." He states further that "this strong feudal aristocracy left a marked impression upon the subsequent social and political life of the colony."[93]

This aristocratic social order would endure for many generations. It produced an affluent class of landed lords and a class of tenants, who worked the land.

Often challenged by local governments, the lords of manors in New York were constantly obliged to defend their manorial rights. Although many lords managed to retain their property rights, by the end of the first quarter of the eighteenth century, feudal-like differences between manors and large rural properties had almost disappeared, yet the manorial designation remained.[94]

Even with the diminution of their legal rights and jurisdiction, this landed gentry maintained its social status. As Sung Bok Kim, a specialist in New York's colonial history, reports:

> The manorial proprietors were still predominant in their respective domains, not because of their legal power,...but because of their status as landlords. The owners of these manors...referred to themselves as "lord" or "lord proprietor," drawing on their ancient patent title, but the title had lost its substantive meaning.[95]

This aristocracy also retained political power. Kim writes:

> It would be a mistake, however, to suppose that the castration of the manor lordship left the proprietors politically powerless.... The mere fact that these men owned vast tracts of land and had great wealth put them at the top of the provincial

---

[91]   Williams, Current, and Freidel, *A History of the United States*, pp. 43, 44.

[92]   Maud Wilder Goodwin, *Dutch and English on the Hudson* (New Haven: Yale Univ. Press, 1919), p. 47.

[93]   Harris, *Origin of the Land Tenure System*, pp. 93, 97.

[94]   Cf. Sung Bok Kim, *Landlord and Tenant in Colonial New York* (Chapel Hill: Univ. of North Carolina Press, 1979), p. 87.

[95]   Ibid., p. 122.

class hierarchy and brought them a variety of respectable public offices, which in turn gave them considerable influence.[96]

b. A leading class formed by landholders, merchants, and lawyers

The social elites in the colony of New York reflected aspects of the rural aristocracy of the Southern colonies and the commercial and professional urban elites that predominated in New England. It was therefore a particularly brilliant aristocratic society.

At the turn of the eighteenth century, New York had a landed gentry constituted by lords of manors and large landholders, many of whom had been merchants in the city. Notes Wright:

> Merchants, who had gained wealth in trade carried on through the growing port of New York, eagerly sought land in the interior, and many of them put together vast baronial estates. Toward the end of the century, the royal governors designated some of these estates as manors and invested the owners with the privileges accorded lords of manors in England. These great landowners constituted an aristocracy that monopolized both power and privilege in the province. The names of many of them are written large in the history of New York.[97]

These manor lords and land barons of New York had much more in common with the Southern elites than with the Puritan political and commercial elites. Jaher comments:

> The early patriciate resembled the southern gentry rather than the Puritan merchants, magistrates, and ministers who ruled seventeenth-century Massachusetts Bay Colony. Huge land grants in the Hudson Valley enabled estate proprietors to live in baronial splendor that rivaled the planters of Virginia and South Carolina and rarely existed in relatively egalitarian New England. Primogeniture and entail sometimes kept large concentrations of real property in eighteenth-century New York and the South from being divided or alienated, thus preserving inherited economic and social position.[98]

Despite the mercantilist dynamism of the commercial elites in New York City, colonial "pre-eminence belonged to the landed gentry, living in feudal elegance on their great estates along the Hudson, and dominating the affairs of the province by the aid of their connections, through business or marriage, with the wealthy merchant families of New York city."[99]

---

[96] Ibid., p. 107.

[97] Wright, *History of the Thirteen Colonies*, p. 165.

[98] Jaher, *The Urban Establishment*, p. 160.

[99] Schlesinger, *New Viewpoints in American History*, p. 73.

Wright cites the relationships between the landed gentry and the commercial elite of New York: "New York had an aristocracy of wealthy and influential families, some of whom held vast tracts of land, while others depended upon the Indian trade and a variety of commercial activities.... Wealthy families frequently intermarried and consolidated fortunes already substantial."[100] New York's rural and mercantile elites thus formed a colonial upper class with exceptional importance and influence. "The mercantile elite merged with the landed gentry, making the colony a city-state with a more powerful and cohesive aristocracy than emerged from the interior village and port-town elites in Massachusetts Bay," writes Jaher.[101]

These elites came to hold almost complete political and economic power in colonial New York. As Jaher notes: "They controlled land patents, high military and civil offices, and mercantile regulations and operations, and achieved wealth, social standing, and influence with the royal administration. Each facet of their leadership reinforced the others, and the whole was fortified by intermarriage."[102] Due to the common interests of rural life and commercial activities, no real stigma was attached to these activities, particularly when family interests were involved. "Virtually every great landed clan also ranked among the foremost mercantile families of the province," asserts Jaher.[103]

Prominent lawyers joined the large landholders and wealthy merchants to constitute a leading class united by common interests and family ties, as Wright reports: "Large landholders, prosperous merchants, and influential lawyers made up the ruling aristocracy in New York. There was constant intermarriage in these groups and many of the leading families had members in all three categories."[104]

Historian Virginia Harrington likewise affirms this union.

> Socially, economically and politically, the landholders, lawyers and merchants formed a single, privileged, ruling class as against the rank and file of small freeholders, tenant-farmers, shopkeepers, artisans and laborers. Generations of inter-marriage had welded these first three groups into a large, interrelated clan whose interests could not be far separated.[105]

By the middle of the eighteenth century, the New York Bar Association had become an exclusive association of wealthy and educated family heads who participated in the leading class. "The distinction among landlord, lawyer, and merchant was blurred," points out Milton Klein. "The three groups formed a single privileged, ruling class, and there was scarcely a prominent lawyer in the colony

---

[100] Wright, *History of the Thirteen Colonies*, p. 313.

[101] Jaher, *The Urban Establishment*, p. 170.

[102] Ibid., p. 160.

[103] Ibid., p. 161.

[104] Wright, *Cultural Life of the American Colonies*, p. 41.

[105] Virginia D. Harrington, *The New York Merchant on the Eve of the Revolution* (New York: 1935; Gloucester, Mass.: Peter Smith, 1964), p. 11.

who was not related by ties of blood or marriage to one of the great landed or mercantile families.''[106]

c. Political control by the colonial elite in New York

During the colonial period, the large landholders assumed important government functions, both in the colony and in the counties. They, or one of their loyal tenants, frequently occupied public offices, such as justice of the peace.

> A manor proprietor might be nominated as a commissioner of the highways running through his district, and find himself with the responsibility of laying out and maintaining roads. He might be consulted by the government about the appointment of militia officers and justices of the peace in his district, and be given a rank sufficiently high to hold the command of its militia. He could be called upon by a justice of the peace and the inhabitants in his bailiwick for aid and counsel in minor local, familial, and personal disputes. These functions and roles were aristocratic obligations more than solicited offices.[107]

Nettels confirms the political dominion of the leading class throughout the colony.

> Politically the magnates dominated local government through the sheriffs, their allies; they dispensed justice among their tenants, and in the provincial legislature they acted after 1693 chiefly through the elected house—entitled in some instances to representatives for their estates, and always dominating elections in their districts.[108]

According to Jaher, "New York politics, dominated by city merchants and great landlords, was also more elitist than the Massachusetts government."[109]

Some manors had the special privilege of a seat in the state legislature. Such places were normally filled by the lord of the manor himself, a member of his family, or someone he named. Kim describes the situation:

> Manorial seats in the assembly were generally monopolized by the proprietors and their relatives throughout the colonial period, provoking one unhappy provincial official to remark that they "are become Hereditary Members."... For a manor district to elect a representative other than the landlord himself or his nominee would have seemed downright absurd to the landlord and probably to his tenants as well.

---

[106] Milton M. Klein, "From Community to Status: The Development of the Legal Profession in Colonial New York," in *Business Enterprise in Early New York*, Joseph R. Frese, S.J., and Jacob Judd, eds. (Tarrytown, N.Y.: Sleepy Hollow Restorations, Inc., 1979), p. 183.

[107] Kim, *Landlord and Tenant in Colonial New York*, p. 123.

[108] Nettels, *The Roots of American Civilization*, p. 309.

[109] Jaher, *The Urban Establishment*, p. 160.

A VIEW OF NEW YORK IN 1775

From an Aquatint in The Atlantic Neptune
Published in 1781 for the use of the Royal Navy.
Engraved for the Society of Iconophiles

The Bettmann Archive

This was particularly true in a political society in which the representative system was territorial in nature and a stake in property was considered the precondition for political participation.[110]

This author also relates that these manorial representatives became the greatest opponents of royal prerogatives:

> Without exception, manorial representatives, initially attached to the governors' interests in the 1720s and 1730s, later became the most outspoken antiprerogative and whiggish members, constituting a force that the conservative elements in the province endeavored to suppress in subsequent years, particularly during the Revolutionary era. Thus, ironically, the manorial privileges originally granted to enhance the Crown's prerogative ultimately produced a force against this very prerogative.[111]

4. From Pennsylvania Quakers to Philadelphia Gentlemen

a. An egalitarian utopia with a religious base

In 1681 the aristocrat William Penn, son of an eminent royalist who had fought for the restoration of the Stuarts, received a charter from King Charles II that named

---

[110]   Kim, *Landlord and Tenant in Colonial New York*, p. 118.

[111]   Ibid., p. 116.

him lord proprietor of the lands that would later be Pennsylvania and Delaware. He made these lands a refuge for the Quaker sect, to which he belonged and which was being persecuted in England for religious and political reasons.

The Quaker sect was a religious movement of protest against the Anglican Church and state in the seventeenth century. Because of its radical egalitarianism, it represented the extreme left of the Protestant revolution in England. Quaker egalitarianism was founded on the doctrine of the divine immanence and the "interior light" in each person. Tolerant of doctrinal divergences, Quakers believed all men were essentially good and equal because each had a fragment of the divine essence. None of the religious groups that sought refuge in America was more insistent than they in the belief in equality and communal democracy. The Quaker sect, notes Boorstin, was "notorious for its contempt of forms and hierarchies, for its fluidity, and for its antipathy to dogma."[112]

William Penn envisioned an austere, simple, and egalitarian society minus the luxury and opulence of an aristocracy. Theaters, music, fine furniture, and fancy dresses: all were to be banished.

However, despite these egalitarian beliefs and customs, a society without class distinctions, based only on fraternal love, soon proved utopian. In the actual society founded by the Quakers in the New World, a differentiation of classes and social groups was quickly established.

In fact, because of the rapid influx of immigrants of various ethnic origins, the Quakers soon became a minority in their own colony. Philadelphia, the capital and most important city, became cosmopolitan, "a highly mobile society of laymen— merchants, scientists, doctors, reformers, artists, and craftsmen—drawn from all social classes and from many parts of the New and Old Worlds."[113]

Despite this heterogeneous population, the Quakers were able to maintain the reins of government during the greater part of the colonial period, and eventually assumed the social preeminence and authority that they had purported to despise so thoroughly in the Old World. Faced with the actual task of governing and constructing a society, "the Quakers," Boorstin observes, "realized that their religious doctrines, if construed strictly, would put difficulties in the way of their running a government. It was one thing to live by Quaker principles, quite another to rule by them."[114]

b. Material progress tends to form aristocratic elites

Despite difficulties in the political order, Pennsylvania enjoyed a prosperous first half-century, which saw "the center of American Quaker life...shift 'from Meetinghouse to Counting-house.'"[115] In the measure that people grew in wealth and social position, a

---

[112] Boorstin, *The Americans: The Colonial Experience*, p. 41.

[113] Baltzell, *Puritan Boston and Quaker Philadelphia*, p. 143.

[114] Boorstin, *The Americans: The Colonial Experience*, p. 43.

[115] Quoted in Boorstin, *The Americans: The Colonial Experience*, p. 43.

Philadelphia in colonial days.

mercantile elite began to form. "In Philadelphia it was the broad Delaware, bringing the largest ocean ships to her wharves, together with the rich agricultural back
country, which built up the merchant aristocracy," Wertenbaker points out.[116]

The acquisition of wealth and establishment of a defined social hierarchy "sof-
tened in some degree the Quaker resolution to adhere to a simple life," Wright
observes. "Under the impact of prosperity Quaker merchants built commodious
houses, furnished them luxuriously, and lived in much the same style that other
grandees affected."[117]

At the end of the seventeenth century, writes E. Digby Baltzell,

> a small group of men held most of the important positions, were related by marriage
> one with another, and made their fortunes over the seas, as daring merchants and
> traders, or inland with the Indians, whom they treated well from the very start.
> These early Quaker Grandees were a pious group who collected books and libraries
> and built fine formal gardens.[118]

---

[116]   Wertenbaker, *The Golden Age of Colonial Culture*, p. 9.

[117]   Wright, *Cultural Life of the American Colonies*, p. 43.

[118]   Baltzell, *Philadelphia Gentlemen*, p. 79.

c. Social, economic, and
cultural brilliance of Philadelphia

Philadelphia was in many ways the preeminent American city during this period, as Wright and others attest. "Philadelphia in the eighteenth century surpassed Boston and New York as a center of commerce, and near the end of the colonial period, when it had become the second city of the British Empire, it boasted some of the most powerful commercial families in America."[119] "Philadelphia was the second largest English city—only London surpassed it in numbers," states Lipset. "Philadelphia and other colonial American capitals were centers of relatively high culture at this time: they had universities and learned societies, and their elite was in touch with, and contributed to, the intellectual and scientific life of Britain."[120]

Baltzell, well-known scholar of Philadelphia's colonial social structures and a descendent himself of one of its traditional families, likewise affirms: "Philadelphia was the largest city in the new nation and contained perhaps the wealthiest, most successful, gayest, and most brilliant elite in the land."[121]

This elite assimilated the latest styles and most fashionable currents of thought. "In the middle decades of the eighteenth century, the values of the French Enlightenment—secular, rational, humane, democratic, egalitarian, and individualistic—were brought to America through the thriving city of Philadelphia," writes Baltzell.[122] Many of the ideas that later fueled the American Revolution were cultivated in the grand halls of its aristocracy. Baltzell states in another work:

> Proper Philadelphia's Golden Age spanned the last twenty-five years of the eighteenth century. This was also the city's most prolific First Family founding era. Many of the inner circle of Proper Philadelphians in the middle of the twentieth century, men who dominate the Philadelphia Club, the First City Troop, and the ancient Assembly Balls, as well as the banks, had prominent ancestors during the Revolutionary period.[123]

5. Georgia: The Failure of
a Philanthropic Scheme

Although the social elite of Georgia was still developing at the end of the colonial period, this colony deserves mention. The colony was established on utopian ideas of a philanthropic nature, rather than the religious inspiration of the Quakers and Puritans.

Founded in 1732, half a century after Pennsylvania, Georgia was the last of the English colonies established on America's East coast and was intended to prevent Spanish expansion into empty territories claimed by both nations.

---

[119] Wright, *Cultural Life of the American Colonies*, p. 42.

[120] Seymour Martin Lipset, *The First New Nation* (New York: Basic Books, 1963), pp. 92-93.

[121] Baltzell, *Puritan Boston and Quaker Philadelphia*, p. 4.

[122] Ibid., p. 143.

[123] Baltzell, *Philadelphia Gentlemen*, p. 81.

A royal charter was granted for a period of twenty-one years to a group of twenty-one proprietors led by James Oglethorpe. He and his associates founded the colony as a purely philanthropic enterprise, without a view to profit. One of its principal aims was to offer opportunity to individuals who had fallen into debt or poverty, or who had come into some conflict with the stringent English laws of the time. The colony was to be a refuge for, in Oglethorpe's terms, "such as were most distressed, virtuous and industrious,"[124] and was to provide them an opportunity to obtain sustenance for themselves and their families.

From the beginning, the colonizers were given no voice in the government. All decisions, even those referring to the slightest details in the community's life, were made in London. Individual initiative was stifled to such an extent by the fantasy of these distant proprietors that Boorstin was led to write: "Such provisions for the emigrants to Georgia have more the ring of a well-run jail or of a mercenary army than of a colony of free men seeking their fortune in a new world."[125]

Oglethorpe's philanthropic endeavor established a totally artificial system of land ownership in Georgia similar to the socialist utopian schemes attempted elsewhere during the next century. This forced egalitarianism had disastrous economic consequences.

Each settler was given fifty acres of land, and the maximum amount of property an individual could hold was set at 500 acres. Moreover, a property could not be abandoned or divided, and could only be bequeathed in a will to a masculine heir. In the absence of such, the property reverted to the company. This system stifled the formation of a local elite. The opportunity that existed in other colonies to acquire more land and rise in the social scale was not afforded to the colonizers of Georgia. By establishing this static system, the proprietors of the philanthropic company impeded the social, economic, and political development of the colony.

Boorstin remarks about the trustees of the Georgia colony that "their sin was not so much that they were ignorant, but that they acted as if they did know, and by their laws imposed their ignorance upon the settlers."[126]

As the colony stagnated, many of those who felt constrained by the utopian regulations concocted in London resolved to abandon Georgia and try their luck elsewhere. "It is uncertain just how much of the population had deserted Georgia for the freer opportunities of Carolina and the other colonies by the middle of the century," observes Boorstin. But many had left, and "Georgia was on the way to becoming a deserted colony."[127]

With the failure of the experiment, the philanthropic company returned its patent to the Crown in 1752. Georgia ended its first discouraging stage as a royal colony; only then did it set out on its pathway to progress and take its first steps toward the development of a local elite.

---

[124] Boorstin, *The Americans: The Colonial Experience*, p. 79.

[125] Ibid., p. 87.

[126] Ibid., p. 81.

[127] Ibid., p. 95.

6. Anti-Catholicism During the Colonial Period

The religious struggles that shook Europe from the sixteenth century onward were reflected in the colonies of the Americas, especially in the English colonies where Protestantism was dominant in its diverse forms.

With the exception of Maryland, the elites of these colonies were formed by members of Protestant denominations whose degree of adhesion to the egalitarian principles of their religion resulted in a greater or lesser animosity to the hierarchical Catholic Church. This animosity was fueled, especially in New England, by the continuous and bloody fights against the French Catholics of Quebec and their Indian allies.

The widespread anti-Catholic spirit in the colonial era is described by historian Sydney Ahlstrom:

> Colonial history is full of overt and explicit anti-Catholicism.... American Catholics faced disabilities in every colony, even Maryland.
>
> [Moreover,] the development of the idea of equality during the American Revolution produced further moderating effects. Even so, seven of the original thirteen colonies carried some kind of anti-Catholic legislation into the national period, the Bill of Rights notwithstanding.[128]

Catholics were persecuted less in Pennsylvania than in other colonies, so a greater number of them settled there. However, during the time of Queen Anne even this colony was obliged to apply the English laws that deprived Catholics of their right to vote and hold public offices. These laws remained in effect in all the colonies until the end of the colonial period.

After the fall of the Stuarts and the coming of William of Orange, the liberty of Catholics in New York was suppressed. In 1701, they were deprived of the right to vote and to hold public offices. During the administrations of more than thirty governors of that colony, up until Independence, the situation of Catholics saw no improvement. Catholic priests were forbidden to enter the colony. For more than seventy-five years, Catholics were not allowed even one public church for their worship, although Mass was occasionally celebrated in secret.

"Outside of Maryland and Pennsylvania, where small islands of Roman Catholicism managed to survive either in public view or half in secret," states Ahlstrom, "Roman Catholic church history in the later colonial period is little more than a matter of rumor, unsubstantiated 'tradition,' and cautious inference."[129]

This deprived the colonial elites of the precious contribution the Catholic spirit could have furnished for their social and cultural formation and for the flourishing of a more fully Christian and aristocratic human type.

---

[128] Ahlstrom, *A Religious History of the American People*, pp. 558-559. See also William Reichley, *Religion in American Public Life* (Washington, D.C.: The Brookings Institution, 1985).

[129] Ahlstrom, *Religious History of the American People*, p. 341.

CHAPTER VI

The American Revolution, Independence, and the Constitution

1. Colonial Elites in the Revolutionary Period (1763-1781)

The American Revolution—that is, the revolutionary movement that resulted in the independence of the thirteen English colonies in America—had various causes. It would be simplistic to attribute it only to the radical political ideas of the English Whigs[1] or merely to the influence of John Locke and other Enlightenment philosophers over cultured sectors of American public opinion.

In his work on the American Revolution, Gordon Wood refers to the causes that converged to produce the Revolution.

> By drawing on the evidence of antiquity and their own English past as transmitted to them through the radical Whig tradition the colonists sought to formulate a science of politics and of history that would explain what was happening to England and to themselves—an explanation that when joined with a complicated medley of notions taken from Enlightenment rationalism and New England covenant theology possessed revolutionary implications.[2]

When one considers the complexity of the factors that led to American independence, one fact stands out: the popular myth of a kind, virtuous, and free people led to revolt by the tyranny of an implacable monarch does not correspond to reality.

Contrary to prevailing mythology, Americans as a whole enjoyed more rights than the majority of nations at that time. Wood affirms: "There was none of the legendary tyranny of history that had so often driven desperate people into rebel-

---

[1] "Whig" was the name given to one of the two large parties in England during the seventeenth and eighteenth centuries. The Whigs endeavored to limit the power of the kings and strengthen that of Parliament. They were at times linked to dissident religious groups.

[2] Wood, *Creation of the American Republic*, p. 17.

lion. The Americans were not an oppressed people; they had no crushing imperial shackles to throw off.... The objective social reality scarcely seemed capable of explaining a revolution."[3]

Recent studies, then, have begun to dispel this myth of a people oppressed by tyranny. They show that the movement that led to the American Revolution, far from arising from a mere dispute over concrete political or economic matters, was rooted in a manifestly revolutionary ideology like the one that would soon triumph in France. This ideology's effect on the life of the American traditional elites, although less immediate and extreme than its French counterpart's, was very profound.

There were, indeed, conflicts of interest between the mother country and the colonies. The decade preceding the Revolution was characterized by a growing effort on the part of the English Crown to implement a standardized imperial policy in the colonies, accustomed to more laissez-faire governments. At the same time, Parliament was trying to promote a mercantilist policy detrimental to the interests of the colonial elites. These elites firmly opposed the royal and parliamentary pretensions, which encroached on their rights and traditional customs.

Such differences would normally have been resolved peacefully. However, flames of controversy were fanned by radical elements who transformed this discontent into an attitude of defiance to British policy. "The continuance of agitation after 1770, then, was due to radicals who aimed at reforms both in British and domestic relations," writes Hockett.[4]

The ideological impetus for independence was first and foremost the work of radical elements. Nowhere is this manifested more clearly than in the wave of revolutionary rhetoric that swept the country, changing the colonists' principles, opinions, sentiments, and desires.

a. From personal resentment to the desire for an aristocratic republic

During this period of increasing intervention by Crown and Parliament, a type of discontent toward the English government, more personal than political, revealed itself. The numerous moderate Whigs among the colonial elites constantly complained, says Wood, of "the abuse of royal authority in creating political and hence social distinctions, the manipulation of official appointments that enabled those creatures with the proper connections, those filled with the most flattery...to leap ahead of those equally—if not better—qualified into lucrative positions of power and prestige."[5]

Despite this discontent, the furthest thing from their minds was the desire to destroy the established social hierarchy with the introduction of the republic. These elites

---

[3]   Ibid., pp. 3, 4.

[4]   Hockett, *Political and Social Growth of the American People*, p. 180.

[5]   Wood, *Creation of the American Republic*, pp. 79-80.

were "acutely conscious of degrees of rank and sensitive to the slightest social insult," comments Wood. Oblivious to the inevitable leveling effect of revolutionary republicanism, they sought only the crushing of the "parasitic sycophants of the Crown."[6]

Succumbing to the revolutionary appeal to build a new society based on a "natural equality" governed by a "natural aristocracy," the colonial elites never intended to abandon the upper strata of the social scale. They wanted merely to free themselves from the "artificial distinctions" granted arbitrarily by the Crown or resulting from privileges unrelated to merit. Wood describes the concept revolutionary colonial elites had of a "natural aristocracy."

> The ideal, especially in the southern colonies, was the creation and maintenance of a truly natural aristocracy, based on virtue, temperance, independence, and devotion to the commonwealth....
>
> The Revolutionaries were generally confident that there existed in the community a "Senatorial part," a natural social and intellectual elite who, now that the Crown was gone, would find their rightful place in the upper houses of the legislatures....
>
> ...It was much more subtle than the mere possession of wealth; it was a deeper social feeling, a sense of being socially established, of possessing attributes—family, education, and refinement—that others lacked, above all, of being accepted by and being able to move easily among those who considered themselves to be the respectable and cultivated.[7]

The Southern planters or the New England gentlemen-lawyers undoubtedly longed for an eminent position in this republican order.

b. The American Revolution: the work of elites

What had started as nonconformity with the imprudent demands of Parliament and the Crown had, within a decade, erupted into a genuine revolutionary movement.

The American Revolution was definitely a phenomenon of the elites. The march toward independence was possible due to a solidarity within sectors of the upper classes from all the colonies. It was the aristocrats who masterminded it from their mansions on the banks of the Potomac, the James, the Hudson, and elsewhere. "Some of them were deists and freethinkers as well, and on their library shelves could be found the works of Voltaire, Volney, Hume, Gibbon, and Tom Paine's *Age of Reason*," notes Clement Eaton.[8]

According to von Borch, it was a colonial aristocratic elite espousing republican principles that articulated the revolt against England:

---

[6]   Ibid., pp. 71, 72.

[7]   Ibid., pp. 71, 209, 497.

[8]   Clement Eaton, *The Growth of Southern Civilization, 1790-1860* (New York: Harper & Bros., 1961), p. 13.

The Founding Fathers at the Constitutional Convention.

Here we have what is, perhaps, the most deep-seated paradox in the emergence of America. The "Virginia dynasty" of the first presidents of the independent federal State—Washington, Jefferson, Madison and Monroe—came from precisely this planter aristocracy. Within that aristocracy there developed the powers and the ideas which made the colonies independent of England and gave them a free, if conservative, domestic regime. The revolution against England was planned on the dignified estates on the banks of the Virginia streams....

...The self-assured lords of the plantation style of living were the leaders of the anti-English revolt.[9]

Deep within the man of the revolutionary elite was a dichotomy between aristocratic habits and republican ideas. This dichotomy has become a characteristic of American elites, a legacy from their Revolutionary past. Wood comments on this interior tension.

A New England lawyer and a Virginia planter both could fill their diaries with their private struggles between the attractions and repulsions of the world of prestige and social refinement. This kind of tension and ambivalence of attitude, when widespread, made for a painful disjunction of values and a highly unstable social situation.[10]

[9]   Von Borch, *The Unfinished Society*, p. 216.

[10] Wood, *Creation of the American Republic*, p. 75.

Summing up the social, political and economic effects of the revolutionary movement, Edward Pessen states:

> The American Revolution did not undermine the class system nor did it weaken the barriers between the classes that had been erected during the colonial era. Indubitably, a new and more democratic political order did emerge on both the national and state levels.... [However], actual political power continued to be largely concentrated in the hands of small numbers of individuals, who were themselves of or beholden to the monied men in their states and localities. Insofar as wealth is a clue to class, wealth tended to become more unequally distributed after the Revolution than it had been before. New wealth holders did not supplant so much as they supplemented the accumulators of the earlier time.[11]

c. The division of colonial society in face of the Revolution

Colonial society, including the elites, was divided into two factions: the Whigs, a liberal and reformist party controlled by a minority of radical elements who wanted independence from England; and the Loyalists, or Tories, the majority and "status quo" party—at times active, at times passive—which felt there were certain justified complaints against England but rejected separation, preferring reconciliation.

"No leader, not even the most outspoken American partisan, was anti-British when the long evolution of events that culminated in revolution first began," affirms historian Pauline Maier in her important work *From Resistance to Revolution.*[12]

Before 1775 few American colonists actually realized the far-reaching consequences of colonial resistance. Radical leaders had to overcome the ponderous weight of loyalist sentiment among the public and, accordingly, moderate their propaganda to suit the public mood. As late as 1774, Thomas Jefferson confessed that, "the leap" to independence was "too long as yet for the mass of our citizens."[13]

The fact that loyalty to the Crown was the prevailing public sentiment right up to the eve of the Revolution is confirmed by Claude H. van Tyne, who writes that "loyalty was the normal condition" in face of the existing government.[14] He observes that the radical Whigs needed to change the opinion of the colonists so that they would follow a new revolutionary order that they neither comprehended

---

[11]   Pessen, *Status and Social Class in America*, p. 275.

[12]   Pauline Maier, *From Resistance to Revolution* (New York: Random House, Inc., 1972), p. xi.

[13]   Quoted by Merrill D. Peterson, *Thomas Jefferson and the New Nation: A Biography* (New York: Oxford Univ. Press, 1970), p. 71.

[14]   Claude H. van Tyne, *The Loyalists in the American Revolution* (Gloucester, Mass.: Peter Smith [1902] 1959), p.2.

nor naturally embraced.

In the North, many merchants of New England, New York, and Pennsylvania numbered among the Loyalists. In the South, the planters as a whole constituted a class of moderate Whigs dominated by radical leaders, but there were numerous small farmers in the frontier regions who leaned strongly toward the Loyalists.

Hockett cites the organization of the Whigs as a factor in the revolutionary success.

> The Loyalists were numerous and of the most prominent class; but they agreed only in fearing that resistance to England might be carried too far. Lack of a positive program reduced their weight to the minimum. On the other hand the Whigs were active and well knit. Their local committees suppressed the utterance of Loyalist opinions.[15]

Revolutionary committees literally brought the Revolution to every door, demanding conformity at the price of ostracism, disrepute, and even physical violence.

During the course of the Revolution, the struggle took on clear aspects of a civil war, with violent differences between the Whigs and Loyalists. During the conflict, many Loyalists of all classes sought refuge in England or Canada: "The revolution was one of the great upheavals on this continent," states Canadian professor Hereward Senior of McGill University. "It drove about 80,000 into exile out of a population of 2,000,000."[16] Schlesinger confirms this:

> When the armed conflict came, thousands of men and women, bearing the stigma of "Tory," were forced to flee their native land, many of them settling in Canada.... Their estates and fortunes were confiscated by the revolutionary state governments; and decrees of proscription were issued against their possible return.... But other members of the upper class, like the landed gentry of the South and some of the great Quaker merchants, cast their fate with the revolutionists, although many of them seriously disapproved of the extremist doctrines advocated by the popular leaders.[17]

2. The Declaration of Independence (1776)

In May of 1775, the Continental Congress met for the second time in Philadelphia. This assembly of representatives from the colonies met to propose retaliations against English colonial policy. By the end of that same year, almost all hope of reconciliation had been extinguished.

The radical faction saw its opportunity to push harder toward a rupture, not

---

[15] Hockett, *Political and Social Growth of the American People*, pp. 190-191.

[16] Hereward Senior, *The Loyalists of Quebec, 1774-1825* (Montreal: Price Patterson Ltd., 1989), p. 3.

[17] Schlesinger, *New Viewpoints in American History*, p. 77.

only with the English Parliament, but with the Crown itself, in order to form thirteen independent republican states. By 1776, the radical elements were openly and unrestrainedly demanding a declaration of independence.[18]

On July 2, 1776, after frenetic pressure had been exerted by the radical patriots, the final and definitive step toward total independence was taken when the Continental Congress approved the Declaration of Independence, written by an aristocratic planter and radical republican, Thomas Jefferson.

The Declaration of Independence approved was actually a declaration by "thirteen united States of America" proclaiming that as "Free and Independent States they have full power to levy war, conclude peace, contract alliances, establish commerce, and to do all other acts and things which independent States may of right do."[19]

Thus, impelled by liberal philosophical principles and supported by revolutionary propaganda manipulating public opinion, the radical faction took an unprecedented step: the founding of a new nation. Von Borch writes:

> In 1776...a colonial venture was transformed into a free, independent society by a deliberate and well-pondered act of will, and because the Union was not so much born as made, America more than any other historical entity can be identified with a particular philosophy. Its Utopia, which the Founding Fathers wished to achieve for all time on North American soil, flowed from...that fusion of ideas and sentiments known to the history of philosophy as enlightenment, rationalism, optimism or deism.[20]

The Declaration adopted liberal democratic principles for its government and society, breaking with the political and religious traditions of the colonial past. "Its message is the eighteenth-century message of the unlimited capacity of man, as a free being, to create his own social system and to recreate it as often as it fails to satisfy the two values which Jefferson considered paramount—freedom and happiness," von Borch comments.[21]

By adopting the Declaration of Independence as its fundamental doctrine, the Continental Congress united the revolutionary liberal philosophy to the colonial revolt, and transformed a rebellion inside the British Empire into a symbol of liberation for all humanity.

A detailed examination of the elements contained in the Declaration of Independence reveals the simultaneous presence of two distinct actions:

1) The rupture of the thirteen colonies with the English Crown. Considered in itself, this rupture would have resulted only in the political birth of thirteen small nations, not only independent from their former mother country but also from each other.

---

[18] Cf. Maier, *From Resistance to Revolution*, p. 266.

[19] Wood, *Creation of the American Republic*, p. 356.

[20] Von Borch, *The Unfinished Society*, p. 12.

[21] Ibid., p. 13.

2) The formation of a bond between these thirteen separate entities. This bond united them as a bloc to make war or peace with England, settle an alliance with France, and eventually open up peaceful negotiations with other nations. The co-ordination of the simultaneous action of these thirteen allied entities was placed in the hands of the Continental Congress, that is, of a pan-American assembly.

A complete description of the next step requires mention of several elements, which, although not properly political, are of great importance and rich in dynamic implications.

For example, the thirteen states officially professed one and the same ensemble of principles of political philosophy, proclaiming them as "self-evident truths" that should guide the lives of all the states. The confessional nature of the state of the previous era would be replaced by this ensemble of deist philosophical principles. At a more universal level, this would make the country a paradigm to be imitated by all the nations of the world. The diffusion of this model would bestow a missionary character on the newly founded republic.

By proclaiming these philosophical principles as a model for mankind, the bloc of states assumed the role of a herald calling out to "convert" all nations to a *novus ordo seclorum*. One can see from this that, since its inception, the federation revealed tendencies that were later transformed into a system of thought and a plan of action.

From this came the formation of a state that, although officially federative, would become not only strong but eventually the greatest power in the world. Incorporating the thirteen original colonies, it would add new territories until it reached the fifty states of today.

The prevalence of the philosophical-religious principles—or more precisely, the secularist-philosophical principles—of the Declaration of Independence continues to our day. These principles conferred a democratic secular-humanist missionary thrust of international scope on the new nation; in turn, this gave rise to one of the most important controversies of American history: isolationism versus expansionism.

3. The Years Following Independence (1781-1787)

When hostilities ended in October of 1781, the thirteen newly independent colonies formed a loose central government regulated by the Articles of Confederation, which had been drafted by the Continental Congress. The Articles provided for a limited central power, especially regarding foreign policy, declaration of war, foreign commerce, and so on. However, it had little authority within each state. There was no head of state nor common judiciary power.

Immediately following independence, a movement began within the state assemblies that aimed to eliminate social privileges and achieve the greatest possible leveling in both the legislative and economic spheres. The ultimate goal of this movement was to undermine the economic base of the aristocratic elites and to diminish or even eliminate their predominance in society. Within the first fifteen years, all the state assemblies had, as Williams, Current, and Freidel point out, "eliminated the legal rights of primogeniture and entail, which before the war had helped to maintain a landed aristocracy by transferring an entire estate to the oldest son (when a man died without a will) and by keeping the estate intact from generation to generation."[22]

The American Revolution was, therefore, the first step toward the gradual destruction of the great rural properties, the economic base of the patrician families of the colonial era. Lands belonging to the Crown, the lord proprietors, and the Loyalists were expropriated or confiscated and divided into smaller farms. With the passing of subsequent generations, the large properties that still remained were also parceled out with the application of laws against primogeniture and entail. "Except in the South," says von Borch, "the upper class began to sever its ties with the soil and take on the leadership of an industrial and financial, economic society."[23]

The formation of a confederation of American states at the end of the War of Independence did not bring the desired peace and social harmony. "By the fall of 1786," historian Minor Myers notes, "...many came to see the Articles of Confederation as a plan for anarchy rather than government."[24]

All the states, from New England to South Carolina, experienced the negative effects of the egalitarian atmosphere spread by the Revolution's rhetoric, which sought to eliminate all superiorities based on any circumstances other than merit. Republican aversion to inherited inequalities was fully vented in a general denunciation of all inequalities or differences, be they economic, social, intellectual, or professional. Radical republicans attacked any manifestation of social superiority or refinement as contrary to the spirit and principles of the Revolution. Even simple references to degrees of respectability concealed an aristocratic tone for the most radical egalitarian republicans.[25]

The highest positions of political life, vacated by Loyalists who had gone into exile, were occupied by a new political and economic elite that, unknown a decade before, now filled the assembly seats. "The most pronounced social effect of the Revolution was not harmony or stability but the sudden appearance of new men everywhere in politics and business," writes Wood. "'men, respectable neither for their property, their virtue, nor their abilities,' were taking a lead in public affairs."[26]

John Jay, a renowned member of the traditional elites in New York, complained that the new authorities "are giving rank and Importance to men whom Wisdom would have left in obscurity." The "state legislatures were being filled and yearly refilled with different faces, often with 'men without reading, experience, or principle,'" as the future president James Madison lamented.[27]

---

[22] Williams, Current, and Freidel, *History of the United States*, p. 143.

[23] Von Borch, *The Unfinished Society*, p. 217.

[24] Minor Myers, Jr., *Liberty Without Anarchy* (Charlottesville, Va.: The Univ. Press of Virginia, 1983), p. 70.

[25] Cf. Wood, *Creation of the American Republic*, pp. 399, 400, 402.

[26] Wood, *Creation of the American Republic*, pp. 476-477, quoting "Sober Citizen," To the Inhabitants of the City and County of New-York, Apr. 16, 1776 (N.Y., 1776).

[27] Quoted in Wood, *Creation of the American Republic*, p. 477.

Many, especially in the South, had hoped that the Revolution would reduce social instability. Yet the exact opposite took place. "Equality was not creating harmony and contentment after all," comments Wood. "Indeed, it was noted, equality had become the very cause of the evils it was designed to eliminate."[28]

When the state constitutions were developed, the prevailing mood was based on the revolutionary principle of transferring sovereignty to the "people." Its immediate consequence in the political life of several states was turmoil. Riots, electoral rallies, popular conventions to manifest the will of the "people" in the smallest aspects of public life became widespread. According to Wood, in all the states, "an excess of power in the people was leading not simply to licentiousness but to a new kind of tyranny, not by the traditional rulers, but by the people themselves—what John Adams in 1776 had called a theoretical contradiction, a democratic despotism."[29] Further on, Wood adds:

> Americans thus experienced in the 1780's not merely a crisis of authority—licentiousness leading to anarchy—which was a comprehensible abuse of republican liberty, but also a serious shattering of older ways of examining politics and a fundamental questioning of majority rule that threatened to shake the foundations of their republican experiments.[30]

The utopia of a "natural aristocracy"—that is, nonhereditary social elites—exercising a salutary influence over a virtuous and reflective people, as purposed by the theoreticians of republicanism, proved a pipe dream. As Wood points out, "the revolution seemed to be having precisely the opposite effect: enabling socially insignificant men...to gain positions of dominance without passing through the social ranks and acquiring the recognizable dignities of social leadership."[31]

By making incapable men leaders, the people flaunted their power, turning against the whole patrician class. It was not what the traditional elites had expected. Wood notes, "the planters [in the South] found themselves confronted with widespread challenges to their authority that they had never anticipated in 1776."[32]

Lacking a strong executive power and with the legislative assemblies overwhelmed by parochial disputes, many states sank into a turbulent situation wherein government became next to impossible. Some of them were victims of violent popular explosions, making any type of effective federal government virtually nonexistent.

All these factors appeared to many to foreshadow the failure of the revolutionary experiment. Obviously, some type of social control and centralized government was necessary to resolve the crisis. "The growing radicalism in the states

---

[28] Wood, *Creation of the American Republic*, p. 398.

[29] Ibid., p. 404.

[30] Ibid., p. 411.

[31] Ibid., p. 481.

[32] Ibid., p. 482.

was intimidating the propertied classes, who began to suggest that a strong central government was necessary to insure 'domestic tranquillity,' guarantee 'a republican form of government,' and protect property 'against domestic violence.'"[33]

"The Declaration notwithstanding," Edward Pessen concludes, "the leaders of colonial society continued to think, after the Revolution as before, that the few with a special or large 'stake in society' could alone be counted on to rule responsibly."[34]

4. The Constitution—Its Authors and Its Goals (1787-1788)

a. The Founding Fathers: a national aristocratic elite

In 1787 representatives of twelve states met in Philadelphia to amend the Articles of Confederation. They ended up drafting a constitution for a federative republic destined to replace the free confederation of the thirteen newly independent states.

This elite group of merchants, lawyers, and planters—who to a large extent represented the aristocratic element of post-revolutionary American society—met in a closed session. Significantly, the more radical revolutionary leaders were either abroad or refused to participate.

This self-selected group of eminent men took upon themselves the task of drafting a federal constitution. Presiding over the session was George Washington "with consummate grace, born of both his personal and his class charisma."[35] The authority of their social class and the prestige of their family pasts conferred distinction on this group, which represented the best of colonial tradition. It was, in fact, upon this group of aristocrats that the enduring legend of the Founding Fathers was built.[36]

Dye and Zeigler describe this distinguished group:

> Those 55 men who wrote the Constitution of the United States and founded a new nation were a truly exceptional elite, not only "rich and well-born" but also educated, talented, and resourceful. When Thomas Jefferson, then serving as the nation's minister in Paris, first saw the list of delegates to the Constitutional Convention of 1787, he wrote to John Adams, who was the minister to London: "It is really an assembly of demigods."[37]

---

[33] Dye and Zeigler, *The Irony of Democracy*, p. 32.

[34] Pessen, *Status and Social Class in America*, p. 275.

[35] Baltzell, *Puritan Boston and Quaker Philadelphia*, p. 187.

[36] Seymour Martin Lipset points out that one of the legitimizing factors of the post-revolutionary government was the personal charisma of its leaders. See *The First New Nation*, p. 18.

[37] Dye and Zeigler, *The Irony of Democracy*, p. 27.

*John Jay, first Chief Justice
of the United States Supreme Court.*

This assembly of "demigods" that set the course of the American republic for future generations represented diverse levels of prestige and authority, as Baltzell notes: "These fifty-five individuals provide a classic example of leadership by men of long established class authority. Two of them, Washington and Franklin, were of world renown, a dozen or so were national figures, the rest were more or less established local leaders."[38] In sum, the Founding Fathers inspired respect and confidence; they possessed that moral authority that belongs only to an authentic elite.

> The 55 men who met in the summer of 1787 to establish a new national government were the most prestigious, wealthy, educated, and skillful group of "notables" ever to be assembled in America for a political meeting. The Founding Fathers were truly the elite of elites—an elite both willing and able to act with creative boldness in establishing a government for an entire nation.
>
> ...The Founding Fathers were aware that elites are most effective in negotiation, compromise, and decision making when operating in secrecy.
>
> ...Only men self-confident of their own powers and abilities, men of principle and property, would be capable of proceeding in this bold fashion.[39]

Louis Wright describes the aristocratic origin of these revolutionary leaders: "From the ranks of the men who had used their leisure to cultivate their minds came leaders who shaped the destinies of the country in 1776 and in 1787. The Federal Constitution was the work of gentlemen cognizant of their duty to serve the highest interests of the state."[40] Indeed, "planter-aristocrats ruled Virginia as by prescriptive right, and from the ranks of their descendants came statesmen who helped weld thirteen rebellious colonies into a nation."[41]

Contradicting the democratic myth of the popular origins of America's republic, Dye and Ziegler attest:

> The Constitution of the United States was not "ordained and established" by "the people." Only a small fraction of "the people" participated in any way in the adoption of the Constitution. The Constitution was prepared in Philadelphia by a small, educated, talented, wealthy elite, representative of powerful economic interests—bondholders, investors, merchants, real estate owners, and planters.[42]

This elite, comprised of family men with property, gathered in Philadelphia to elaborate a constitution that would permit the survival of the New World's first experiment in republican government based on revolutionary principles.

---

[38] Baltzell, *Puritan Boston and Quaker Philadelphia*, p. 186.

[39] Dye and Ziegler, *The Irony of Democracy*, pp. 34-35.

[40] Wright, *The First Gentlemen of Virginia*, p. 350.

[41] Ibid., p. 2.

[42] Dye and Ziegler, *The Irony of Democracy*, p. 56.

b. The Constitution: a step backward

Many radical leaders of the time, as well as liberal historians of later times, saw an incompatibility between the "democratic" ideas represented in the Declaration of Independence and the hierarchical political and social structures established and protected by the Constitution. When they viewed the Declaration and the Constitution, they saw "the one devoted to the rights of man and the other to the rights of property, the one looking to Jefferson and the other to Hamilton."[43]

Although most delegates to the Philadelphia Convention were aristocrats and some even had monarchical sentiments, the majority favored a republican form of government and wanted to retain it as a base to stabilize the social order the Revolution had subverted. Dye and Zeigler write: "By 'republican government' they meant a representative, responsible, and non-hereditary government. But by 'republican government' they certainly did not mean mass democracy, with direct participation by the people in decision making.... Decision makers themselves should be men of wealth, education, and proven leadership ability."[44]

For the Founding Fathers, equality did not mean that men were equal in birth, wealth, intelligence, talent, or virtue. Countering the myth of America's egalitarian roots, Dye and Zeigler assert:

> Inequalities in society were accepted as a natural product of diversity among men. It was definitely not the function of government to reduce these inequalities; in fact, "dangerous leveling" was a serious violation of man's right to property, his right to use and dispose of the fruits of his industry. On the contrary, it was the very function of government to protect property and to prevent "leveling" influences from reducing the natural inequalities of wealth and power.[45]

Seen in this light, the Constitution, while ideologically liberal, was a document that favored social inequalities and sought to attenuate the egalitarian impulses aroused by the democratic rhetoric that stimulated popular passions at the time of the Revolution. It served as an instrument to restore and sustain the traditional influence of the elites in politics that had been undermined by the social transformation after the Revolution. "The Constitution was intrinsically an aristocratic document designed to check the democratic tendencies of the period," Wood affirms.[46]

The goal of the Constitution was to create a stable national government. With this end in mind, convention delegates endeavored to "bring the natural aristocracy

---

[43] James L. Bugg, ed., *Jacksonian Democracy: Myth or Reality?* (New York: Holt, Rinehart and Winston, 1962), p. 34. Alexander Hamilton was a federalist leader and George Washington's secretary of the treasury. He was an active proponent of an aristocratic government and even advocated a constitutional monarchy for the United States. He helped to imbue the presidency with ceremonies and pomp reminiscent of European courts.

[44] Dye and Zeigler, *The Irony of Democracy*, p. 39.

[45] Ibid., pp. 38-39.

[46] Wood, *Creation of the American Republic*, p. 513.

back into use and to convey 'authority to those, and those only who by nature, education, and good dispositions, are qualified for government,'" Wood points out.[47] This was the essential problem that the federal Constitution was designed to solve.

From a broader perspective, the Constitution can be seen as a political document inspired by the social powers of the time. Those aspects that favored a hierarchical social order and a federalist regime provoked a division among the elites themselves. Even though the majority of them favored a republican form of government, they differed among themselves regarding the political and social orientation of the republic.

5. Federalists and Anti-federalists

When the Constitution was submitted to the states for ratification or rejection, the country was divided politically. "The Constitution being the program of the old dominant class," notes Hockett, "the question of ratification produced for the first time a nationwide division along lines of cleavage which had hitherto been only local."[48]

Those who favored its adoption called themselves "Federalists," emphasizing the federative aspect of the new plan of government that would establish a central government empowered with enough authority to prevent the disintegration of the country. "It was impossible for him [the Federalist]," writes Claude Bowers, "to conceive of a strong and capable government over which the aristocracy did not have sway."[49] Those opposed to the Constitution were called "Anti-federalists" and disfavored a centralized government because they saw in it an aristocratic manifestation of the leading elites. Instead, they supported fortifying local governments of a more popular character. The struggle to shape the cultural and political profile of the nation hinged on this division.

"Both the proponents and opponents of the Constitution focused throughout the debates on an essential point of political sociology that ultimately must be used to distinguish a Federalist from an Anti-federalist. The quarrel was fundamentally one between aristocracy and democracy," asserts Wood.[50] However, men belonging to the various local aristocracies were found on both sides of the political line. This division, therefore, demonstrates that it was not a clear-cut fight between the elites and the rest of the social classes. Rather there were factions among the elites themselves, one preferring a quicker pace in the implementation of the revolutionary ideas, and the other a slower pace.[51]

---

[47]   Ibid., p. 510, quoting Jonathan Jackson, *Thoughts Upon the Political Situation of the United States* (Worcester, 1788).

[48]   Hockett, *Political and Social Growth of the American People*, p. 298.

[49]   Claude G. Bowers, *Jefferson and Hamilton: The Struggle for Democracy in America* (New York: Houghton Mifflin Co., 1925), p. 29.

[50]   Wood, *Creation of the American Republic*, pp. 484-485.

[51]   Cf. Plinio Corrêa de Oliveira, *Revolution and Counter-Revolution*, p. 47.

The Anti-federalists opposed the ratification of the Constitution because they suspected an aristocratic plot to overturn the principles of popular government proclaimed in the Declaration of Independence and to transfer the power "from the many to the few."[52]

They considered themselves the true champions of revolutionary, democratic, and egalitarian principles against the colonial traditional elites that formed the government. These opponents of the Constitution considered it a threat to "the genius of democracy" to establish a government with central powers and an upper house dominated by the aristocracy. For them, this was a repudiation of all they had fought for in 1776. "They charged that the new Constitution created an aristocratic upper house and an almost monarchial presidency," note Dye and Zeigler.[53]

The obstacles to the ratification of the Constitution raised by the powerful Anti-federalist faction were effectively removed, however, by the Federalists' persuasive arguments in support of a powerful central government. The Federalist propaganda, disguised in revolutionary rhetoric and principles, effectively dismantled the opposition's weaker front and persuaded public opinion that the Federalist plan contained in the Constitution was the most reasonable path to follow.

A common desire to prevent a failure of the republican experiment eventually, if temporarily, united the principal leaders of both factions around the Constitution, even though each faction continued to interpret it differently. The Federalists, although retaining obvious aristocratic and in some cases even monarchical propensities, in the end supported the republic. Notwithstanding the anti-egalitarian aspects of the Constitution, its authors adopted the democratic rhetoric of the Revolution, deeming the "people" the exclusive source to "ordain and establish the Constitution of the United States of America."

The road was thus opened for establishing a unified American political doctrine that would progressively become a dominant democratic and liberal ideology. Wood writes:

> The Federalists in 1787 hastened the destruction of whatever chance there was in America for the growth of an avowedly aristocratic conception of politics and thereby contributed to the creation of that encompassing liberal tradition.... By attempting to confront and retard the thrust of the Revolution with the rhetoric of the Revolution, the Federalists fixed the terms for the future discussion of American politics. They thus brought the ideology of the Revolution to consummation and created a distinctly American political theory but only at the cost of eventually impoverishing later American political thought.[54]

By adopting the democratic rhetoric of the Revolution, the Federalists were

---

[52]   Wood, *Creation of the American Republic*, p. 516.

[53]   Dye and Zeigler, *The Irony of Democracy*, p. 54.

[54]   Wood, *Creation of the American Republic*, p. 562.

Alexander Hamilton

able to use the Constitution in a way that permitted the elites to govern the new republic without an abrupt rupture with the past and, at the same time, without abandoning the core of its revolutionary doctrines. For the Federalist leaders who formulated the Constitution, says Wood,

> the move for the new central government became the ultimate act of the entire Revolutionary era; it was both a progressive attempt to salvage the Revolution in the face of its imminent failure and a reactionary effort to restrain its excesses.... They did not see themselves as repudiating either the Revolution or popular government, but saw themselves as saving both from their excesses. If the Constitution were not established, they told themselves and the country over and over, then republicanism was doomed, the grand experiment was over, and a division of the confederacy, monarchy, or worse would result.[55]

This conservative reactionary movement never really contested the radicalism of the post-independence period. Many constitutional clauses were inspired by the revolutionary principles manifest in the Declaration of Independence. However, in the concrete order, conservative measures were established that preserved inherent rights to legitimate social inequalities, private property, and free enterprise.

The Founding Fathers, although strongly imbued with aristocratic habits, by accepting the principles of liberal democracy, left the way open for future transformations of a more gradual evolution in that direction rather than for radical changes of a revolutionary nature.

6. Aristocratic and Monarchical Tendencies at the Time of Independence and the Constitution

As already noted, at the beginning of the revolutionary process that effected the independence of the thirteen colonies, the majority of the colonists sought neither separation from England nor a change in the form of government. Almost until the end of the process that led to armed revolt, Americans merely claimed rights and liberties considered common to all Englishmen, intending to remain faithful to the British Crown.

For this reason, the majority of the inhabitants did not perceive the issue as one involving a dramatic change from a monarchic colony to an independent republic. In their view, independence was not equivalent to establishing a republican government. "The Americans were not dedicated to overthrowing the King's authority at the outset," confirms Maier.[56]

Nevertheless, the radicalization of the confrontation in its final phases, as well as the drafting of the Declaration of Independence and the constitutions of the

---

[55] Ibid., pp. 475, 517.

[56] Maier, *From Resistance to Revolution*, p. 161.

various states, made it quite clear that the conflict had assumed larger objectives; the revolt had transcended guaranteeing the constitutional liberties that all English subjects should enjoy and had acquired an ideological nature: It had become a republican revolution, "sustained by a powerful, even millennial, creed by which Americans saw themselves no longer merely contending for the protection of particular liberties but on the verge of ushering in a new era of freedom and bliss."[57]

The concept of a republican form of government was unclear to the American people. Not even those who desired to implant it could formulate the concept in a viable way. "The very word [republic] inspired confusion," notes Maier, "such that John Adams, perhaps the country's most learned student of politics, complained that he 'never understood' what a republican government was and believed 'no other man ever did or ever will.'"[58]

Indeed, even after the exodus of politically active Loyalists, monarchist manifestations in many sectors of the population revealed the existence of strong monarchist tendencies, latent or patent, which the republican revolutionaries were obliged to repress energetically, contradicting their own liberal principles.

Not only were these tendencies not extinguished with independence, they remained dynamic throughout the first and crucial period of national life. They showed themselves to be particularly strong in the armed forces of the new nation, the Continental Army. Washington himself commented, notes Myers, "that he had been pressed to assume a crown on *more* than one occasion."[59]

During the administrations of Washington and Adams, the presidency was permeated with an aura of pomp and ceremony reminiscent of the European royalty. Revolutionary sensibilities particularly bristled when the head of state was transported in an elegant carriage pulled by six white horses with uniformed postillions and footmen. Even more offensive to the ears of Democratic-Republicans was the proposal presented in the Senate to give the president the title of "His Highness, the President of the United States of America."

"Government was inevitably imbued with the tone of society," explains Merrill Peterson. "Adams, with many others, thought that some of the pomp and majesty of Old World courts was needed to impress the people with the dignity and authority of the new government. The flavor of a court, albeit a republican one, was everywhere."[60]

Striking evidence of the pervasiveness of these aristocratic sentiments and monarchical tendencies can be found in the private correspondence of Thomas Jefferson, a Democratic-Republican leader who strongly opposed this attitude. Returning to the American capital in 1790 to assume the position of secretary of state in Washington's administration, Jefferson described the prevailing monarchist sentiment in the federal government of the time:

[57] Wood, *Creation of the American Republic*, p. 44.
[58] Maier, *From Resistance to Revolution*, p. 287.
[59] Myers, *Liberty Without Anarchy*, p. 84.
[60] Peterson, *Thomas Jefferson and the New Nation*, pp. 405, 406.

"Lady Washington's Reception," by Huntington.

I found a state of things, in the general society of the place, which I could not have supposed possible. Being a stranger there, I was feasted from table to table.... The revolution I had left, and that we had just gone through in the recent change of our government, being the common topics of conversation, I was astonished to find the general prevalence of monarchical sentiments, insomuch that in maintaining those of republicanism I had always the whole company on my hands, never scarcely finding among them a single coadvocate in that argument.... The furthest that any one would go, in support of the republican features of our new government, would be to say, "the present Constitution is well as a beginning, and may be allowed a fair trial; but it is, in fact, only a stepping-stone to something better."[61]

---

[61] Quoted in Schlesinger, *New Viewpoints in American History*, p. 82.

The existence of these monarchist propensities was recognized by Washington himself. Regarding a letter of Washington to Madison on March 31, 1787, Myers observes:

> Having said that monarchy was contrary to the American psyche, Washington then went on to make an astounding observation. "I am also clear, that even admitting the utility; nay the necessity of the [monarchic] form, yet that period is not yet arrived for adopting the change without shaking the Peace of this country to its foundation." That is, Washington's objections were to the timing, not the *idea* of monarchy. The time for monarchy had simply "not yet arrived." [62]

---

[62] Myers, *Liberty Without Anarchy*, p. 85.

CHAPTER VII

The Republic up to the Civil War

1. The Aristocratic Republic (1788-1828)

The four decades following the ratification of the federal Constitution could well be called an aristocratic era when the presidency was occupied by a succession of gentlemen, whether Virginia planters or Massachusetts lawyers. As the new republic took on an aristocratic cultural character, criticisms against the aristocratic form of government waned and tolerance for elites grew. This was a victory for the aristocracy, which was able to imprint an aristocratic note on political and social life.

In the decade following the Constitution's ratification, the Federalist elite that had devised it dominated the public, social, and economic life of the new country. In this period defiance of federal authority was greatly diminished and a solid national government was established.

According to Arthur Schlesinger, "the government of wealth and intelligence, as carried on by the Federalists, bore fruit in an unparalleled crop of constructive legislation under Washington and Adams."[1]

The Federalist program was largely oriented toward the interests of the financial and mercantile elites of the North. This prompted opposition among Southern planters and other rural proprietors, who became allies of the Anti-federalists, or Democratic-Republicans, as this latter faction came to be called.

At the end of the eighteenth century the country was politically divided between these two competing parties: the Federalists and the Democratic-Republicans.[2]

---

[1]   Schlesinger, *New Viewpoints in American History*, p. 83.

[2]   The outbreak of the French Revolution gave new impetus to this division: "The strains endemic in the establishment of a new structure of authority were increased by the fact that the nation and the embryonic parties were divided in their sympathies for the two major contestants in the European war, Revolutionary France and Great Britain" (Lipset, *The First New Nation*, p. 39).

In Jefferson's words, "The form our own government was to take depended much more on the events of France than anybody had before imagined" (quoted in Daniel Sisson, *The American Revolution of 1800* [New York: Alfred A. Knopf, 1974], p. 167).

The period of the Terror in France was particularly feared and rejected by the Federalists, since it appeared

The Democratic-Republicans were quick to "develop party organizations...to organize an opposition based on popular support."[3] Through these organizations, they undermined the grassroots of the Federalist leaders, who nevertheless maintained dominion over the trades and public offices. This emerging sector of Republicans, says William Chambers, was "'going to the people' in a virtually unprecedented attempt not only to represent popular interest and concerns, but to monopolize popular opposition to those who held power."[4]

Instead of attacking the Constitution, as their Anti-federalist predecessors had done, the new Democratic-Republican party entered the political foray parading its democratic interpretation of the Constitution.

The Federalists, in turn, adhered to a more traditional idea of party structure. Members of the Federalist party were linked among themselves only by a commitment to a common program; they did not bother with any party mechanism working at a local level in close contact with the people. To obtain votes, the Federalist candidates counted on their social influence and prestige in their communities.

This blunder in strategy brought about the victory of the Democratic-Republicans in the elections of 1800. Such was the import of the Federalist defeat of 1800 for the course of American political culture that it has often been referred to as the Second American Revolution. The presidency was successively occupied by three representatives of Virginia's traditional elites—Jefferson, Madison, and Monroe[5]—the so-called Virginia Dynasty. These men, although aristocrats by family and by custom, were leaders of the Democratic-Republican party. This resulted in a virtual single-party government that lasted until 1825.

Defeated for the presidency in 1800, the Federalists never were able to regain office on a national scale and virtually disappeared after the War of 1812.[6]

According to Lipset, one of the causes of this demise was the Federalists' "unwillingness or inability to learn how to perform as an opposition party in an egalitarian democracy. Some historians suggest that they failed basically because, as men convinced of their 'natural' right to rule, they did not believe in parties which appealed to the people."[7] Former Federalists joined forces as best they

---

to confirm their worst apprehensions regarding government by the masses. On the other hand, the revolutionary Terror was initially applauded by many Republicans. "Americans adopted different views about the events in France, the Federalists denouncing and the Republicans applauding them. Indeed, many of the Republicans imitated the French radicals (the Jacobins) by cutting their hair short, wearing pantaloons, and addressing one another as 'Citizen' Smith or 'Citizeness' Jones. Thus, for a time, it was possible to tell a man's party by his manners and appearance, for the Federalists kept the old-fashioned long hair or powdered wig, knee breeches, and traditional etiquette of the gentleman" (Williams, Current, and Freidel, *A History of the United States*, pp. 193-194).

[3]   Lipset, *The First New Nation*, p. 33.

[4]   William N. Chambers, *Parties in a New Nation* (New York: Oxford Univ. Press, 1963), p. 65.

[5]   Thomas Jefferson was president from 1801 to 1809; James Madison, from 1809 to 1817; James Monroe, from 1817 to 1825. They were succeeded by John Quincy Adams, who served from 1825 to 1829.

[6]   Cf. *The First New Nation*, p. 40.

[7]   Ibid., p. 40. Cf. William O. Lynch, *Fifty Years of Party Warfare 1789-1837* (Indianapolis: Bobbs Merrill, 1931), pp. 122-123.

The signing of the Louisiana Purchase.
Left to right: Monroe, Livingston, and Marbois.

could with the democrats or retired from active political life.

As for the Democratic-Republican party, once in power it for the most part continued the policy of its predecessors; nevertheless, it did dispense with much of the formality and ceremony of the Federalist era. Republican "simplicity" became the norm, and the elaborate rules of etiquette the Federalists had introduced as part of the president's ceremonial were largely suppressed. This did not mean, however, that the air of gentility and distinction proper to Southern planters was altogether absent from the governmental milieu of Washington. Schlesinger comments on this supersedence of elites:

> In the retrospect of history it is clear that political power had shifted from a mercantile aristocracy built on English models to a landed aristocracy fully acclimated to the American environment. The great planters of the South supplied the atmosphere of gentility in which the federal administration at Washington moved and had its being.[8]

Lipset notes that Jefferson, Madison, and Monroe were all aristocrats and enjoyed a prestige that stemmed from their role in the founding of the country and their leadership in the all-powerful Democratic-Republican party. They used their personal power and class influence to legitimize the national authority and the democratic government.[9]

The aristocratic republic was a regime in which influence and power were shared by the old aristocrats and the new elites. The old aristocracy dominated in some sectors while representatives of the new elites predominated in others. The latter, however, having risen on the social scale in the name of equality, paradoxically aspired to enter the higher classes and distance themselves from those below. The aristocratic republic was also fruit of a revolutionary colonial elite. When it disappeared, a new era opened in the life of America. It is usually referred to as the "Era of the Common Man."

The transformation of the country in this period

During the four decades of national life under the Constitution which ended with the election of Andrew Jackson to the presidency in 1828, the country underwent great transformations. From an insular society, predominantly agrarian and strongly rooted in family and interpersonal communitarian ties, it became a society of continental proportions marked by a great urban and industrial development that weakened the family and caused social instability. During the colonial period, the peopling and colonizing effort had rarely extended beyond a few hundred miles inland. In the first half century after independence, eleven new states were

---

[8] Schlesinger, *New Viewpoints in American History*, p. 84.

[9] Cf. Lipset, *The First New Nation*, p. 44.

added to the Union, and vast territories were conquered or acquired, soon extending the country's boundaries from the Atlantic to the Pacific. The population quadrupled, and the influx of immigrants grew enormously.

The new social conditions brought about by industrialization, urbanization, and immigration caused profound changes in lifestyles. The growing influence of the democratic ideology in all social classes stimulated these changes.

2. The Parallel Stages of an International Revolution

Throughout the colonial period of the three Americas, the respective mother countries were governed by a regime that, some differences aside, is known generically as the Old Regime. This was the system European countries implanted in their colonies.

With the successive proclamations of independence by the American nations, this regime ceased to exist in the New World. In effect, the several independence movements worked as so many "French Revolutions," for they almost entirely demolished the Old Regime in the Americas. To a greater or lesser degree, the Old Regime was supplanted by regimes with goals and "ideals" stemming from the French and the American Revolutions.

It is illusory to think that these movements in the colonies sought only to proclaim independence from their respective mother countries. They also intended to make the Revolution,[10] which was not merely a revolution for independence but the egalitarian Revolution for the overthrow of the Old Regime and the installation of egalitarian democracies in every country.

A widespread myth exists in the Americas that at a certain moment fiery explosions of republican and egalitarian sentiment erupted spontaneously, consuming the last remnants of colonial traditions. This is obviously an exaggeration.

Clearly, there was a common revolutionary ideology behind these revolutions. Clearly, they exerted an influence on each other. A victorious revolution in one nation heightened the conviction that a similar movement could succeed elsewhere and imparted an élan to revolutionaries, a precious factor in their ultimate victory.

It would be a mistake, however, to think that this revolutionary conflagration flamed across the hemisphere without resistance. On the contrary, important points of resistance often forced revolutionary movements to abandon the direct path in favor of a circuitous route replete with twists and turns, and even surprises.

As we have noted, such a course can be observed in the early history of the United States, the model democratic country of the Americas, where strong monarchist and aristocratic resistances forced the egalitarian republican movement to advance with prudence and to implement its more radical goals only gradually.

Such gradualism is evidenced in the French Revolution's three successive phases:

---

[10] This term is used here in the wide sense given it by Prof. Plinio Correa de Oliveira in the essay *Revolution and Counter-Revolution* to designate a process that through the centuries has been destroying the Christian civilization built in the Middle Ages.

Though horrified at the cruelties and other excesses of the Terror, many Americans toasted to the French Revolution's motto, Liberty, Equality, Fraternity.

1) Absolute monarchy until 1789 (Estates General);

2) Increasingly radical revolutionary government until the abolition of royalty in 1792 (Constitutional Assembly and Legislative Assembly);

3) Radical revolutionary republican government (Convention and Terror).

Similar phases can be observed in many of the egalitarian revolutions of the New World.

Another myth is that the revolutions of the Americas were sparked by class struggle. The opposite is true. Not infrequently, the initial revolutionary impulse took on an aristocratic character and strived to gain the support of the aristocracy. The presence of numerous aristocrats at the forefront of the revolutionary movements in many American countries is noteworthy. The republican revolutions often succeeded precisely because they were led by men who enjoyed the public's confidence as aristocrats. The people trusted these men not only because of their social status and influence, but because of the tone of seriousness and morality that they assigned to public life. This respectability predisposed the people to accept a populist democracy in the United States and other countries of the Western Hemisphere. Moreover, in the revolutionary ferment, many of the aristocrats themselves became accustomed to a state of affairs that led them to voluntarily and even happily relinquish their privileges.

3. The Jacksonian Era
of Popular Democracy

Andrew Jackson, elected president in 1828, was the first president of the United States who did not come from the traditional elites. His rise to the presidency marked the end of the aristocratic republic, and the beginning of a broader and more profound diffusion of the democratic ideology into the country's political, social, and cultural life. Indeed, Jackson is the symbol around which the myth of American democratic equality crystallized, the myth, as we have already seen, formulated in the writings of Alexis de Tocqueville.

Andrew Jackson was a man with a strong personality, a self-made man transformed into a hero, the incarnation of the American ideal of a common man who overcame the unjust aristocratic domination of American political, economic, and social life. According to social historian James Bugg, "Jackson, the hero of the age, symbolized for Americans all those characteristics that made them a chosen people, set apart to convert and save the world.... There were in reality two Jacksons, one the historical figure, and the other the symbol in the American myth."[11]

Richard Hofstader comments on the implications of the Jackson movement: "With Old Hickory's election a fluid economic and social system broke the bonds of a fixed and stratified political order. Originally a fight against political privilege, the Jacksonian movement had broadened into a fight against economic privilege, rallying to its support a host of 'rural capitalists and village entrepreneurs.'"[12]

The years between the election of Jackson and the Civil War saw a gradual transformation in the very nature of American republicanism. During this period, notes Robert Remini, a leading authority on Andrew Jackson, the country went from a government regarded, in Madison's words in the *Federalist*, as "'the medium of a chosen body of citizens' whose wisdom, patriotism, and love of justice would best discern what was in the country's genuine interests" to a government of popular majority. "By 1837 the word *democracy* had largely supplanted the term *republicanism* in national discourse."[13]

Just as during the Virginia dynasty there had been a revolutionary attempt to establish political equality, Jacksonian democracy also attempted "the realization of social equality, so that the actual condition of men in society shall be in harmony with their acknowledged rights as citizens."[14]

Showing their true ideological inspiration, the Jacksonian democrats applauded

---

[11] Bugg, *Jacksonian Democracy*, p. 107.

[12] Richard Hofstader, *The American Political Tradition and the Men Who Made It* (New York: Alfred A. Knopf, 1949), quoted in Bugg, *Jacksonian Democracy*, p. 7.

[13] Robert Remini, *The Legacy of Andrew Jackson* (Baton Rouge: Louisiana State Univ. Press, 1988), pp. 24, 8.

[14] Arthur M. Schlesinger, Jr., "Jacksonian Democracy as an Intellectual Movement," in Bugg, *Jacksonian Democracy*, p. 77.

the riots and revolts that were shaking Europe at that time, and considered themselves part of the same worldwide revolutionary movement. As Schlesinger relates:

> The Jacksonians watched with keen interest the stirrings of revolt abroad. Jackson and his cabinet joined in the celebrations in Washington which followed the Revolution of 1830 in France.... Lamennais, the eloquent voice of French popular aspirations, was read in Jacksonian circles....
>
> Jacksonians everywhere had this faith in the international significance of their fight. America was the proving ground of democracy and it was the mission of American Democrats to exhibit to the world the glories of government by the people.[15]

a. Political, economic, and social consequences for the traditional elites

One of the more immediate consequences of Jackson's populist government was the establishment of a political machine to mobilize the masses by stirring up resentments through the rhetoric of class struggle decrying aristocratic privilege and lifestyles. Under this violent attack, the traditional elites (with the exception of those in some Southern states) began to retreat from public life. Although they still occupied high offices and had significant influence in state governments, the perspective of a governmental class formed by "natural aristocrats" and based on personal merit, social preeminence, and family distinction was vanquished. Leadership no longer depended on personal status, class, or education. Political life was no longer a setting wherein the natural aristocrat represented the best of society. "Winning elections became to an unprecedented degree the business of professionals who managed powerful machines," notes Marvin Meyers.[16] Victor M. Lidz observes:

> All but a handful of the "aristocrats of talent and virtue" had retreated from public life, frustrated that their standards of personal honor inhibited them from playing the sorts of political roles that were necessary to gain election. They had been replaced by a new group of "professional politicians" whose claims to office were closely tied to their experiences in operating political parties.[17]

Before the advent of popular democracy, politics demanded a certain honorability and respectability, and allowed for their increase. Indeed, it was almost a spiritual exercise. With the transition from the aristocratic republic to the populist Jacksonian republic, political leadership largely slipped from the hands of the traditional families.

---

[15] Ibid., pp. 81, 82.

[16] Marvin Meyers, *The Jacksonian Persuasion: Politics and Belief* (Stanford, Calif.: Stanford Univ. Press [1957] 1960), p. 7.

[17] Victor M. Lidz, "Founding Fathers and Party Leaders," in Harold J. Bershady, ed., *Social Class and Democratic Leadership* (Philadelphia: Univ. of Pennsylvania Press, 1989), p. 268.

With this, political leadership itself lost most of its social prestige, as nonintel-
lectual adventurers and unscrupulous demagogues entered the political center stage.
What the new political class conquered became debased in their own hands. However,
the social influence of the traditional elites remained strong.

From the moment the political scene was abandoned by men for whom honorability was an indispensable predicate for victory, the role and nature of politics
began to change, and democracy was frequently distorted. Politics ceased to be
the vehicle through which public opinion effected democracy and instead became
a huge enterprise for the manipulation of public opinion, which was no longer
expressed in its noble spontaneity.

Politics was reduced to an activity manipulated by electoral machines with no
other end than winning elections. The electoral process began to require increasing
capital for the propaganda that had become one of its essential components, calling for the participation of great businessmen to supply the capital and of specialists to raise and administer the money and run the complex political machin-
ery.[18] As money became ever more necessary in the electoral process, moneyed
interests became ever more influential in fabricating public opinion.[19]

All this carried the electoral process far from the idealized democracy of eighteenth-century philosophers, where each voter was an independent and disinterested
political thinker.

b. The new leaders

Victor Lidz, in his study on the Founding Fathers and party leaders, states:

> The Jacksonian period, represented a deep-seated shift in the social composition
> of the nation's leadership. Without changing the words, it brought a newly demo-
> cratic meaning to America's republican Constitution, a meaning the Founding Fathers
> hardly anticipated and would certainly have reproved.[20]

"It had become politically fatal to be labeled an aristocrat," says George Tindall.[21] In response, the traditional elites retreated from public view to cultivate
an aristocratic lifestyle in their private milieu, the upper society, and their exclusive clubs. They exerted their influence through their economic power and philanthropic organizations. No political party or anyone with political pretensions
dared to openly represent the interests of the aristocratic elites.

The democratic rhetoric of the times fostered social divisions, always portraying

---

[18] Later, funds provided by powerful labor organizations and even the government also came to be used for
electoral propaganda.

[19] This influence manifested itself in this period through the press, and in our century also through radio, television, and other propaganda means.

[20] Lidz, "Founding Fathers," pp. 266-267.

[21] Tindall, *America: A Narrative History*, Vol. 1, p. 388.

Equestrian statue of Andrew Jackson in Lafayette Square, across from the White House.

The White House

such clashes as "a struggle of honest workers against corrupt aristocrats, between the many and the few."[22]

This violently activist social philosophy "was stated and restated," says Schlesinger, "on every level of political discourse from presidential messages to stump speeches, from newspaper editorials to private letters."[23]

The populist democratic language was one of conflict and antagonism. It spoke of disputes between the productive and nonproductive classes, between farmers on the one hand and financiers and businessmen on the other, all within a context of growing animosity toward the hereditary wealth of the Southern gentlemen and the traditional mercantile elites. This animosity boasted of being a struggle for liberty against domination; of possessing the moral superiority of the self-made man over the idle corruption of the traditional elites.

In short, Jacksonian rhetoric helped to enkindle a fundamental opposition, "the great struggle between people and aristocracy for mastery of the republic.... There is for Jackson a whole body, the sovereign people, beset with aristocratic sores," comments Meyers.[24]

The democratizing of the economy displaced the traditional elites from their near total control of the banks and capital markets. Bray Hammond presents the conflict of that period as a struggle between the new elites and the traditional ones, an inevitable fact, as he sees it, in a country experiencing rapid expansion. He states that the economic policy of the time was by no means a "blow at capitalism or property."

> It was a blow at an older set of capitalists by a newer, more numerous set. It was incident to the democratization of business, the diffusion of enterprise among the mass of people, and the transfer of economic primacy from an old and conservative merchant class to a newer, more aggressive, and more numerous body of businessmen and speculators of all sorts.[25]

Douglas Miller adds:

> Despite these democratizing factors, certain prestigious families preserved distinguished reputations into the age of the common man.... In fact virtually every community from Portland, Maine, to New Orleans had its local elite, whether landed or mercantile. Many such families intermarried and were very exclusive in their social life.[26]

---

[22] Remini, *The Legacy of Andrew Jackson*, p. 21.

[23] Schlesinger, "Jacksonian Democracy as an Intellectual Movement," p. 72.

[24] Marvin Meyers, "Restoration of the Old Republic Theme in the Jacksonian Persuasion," in Bugg, *Jacksonian Democracy*, p. 112.

[25] Bray Hammond, "The Jacksonians," in Bugg, *Jacksonian Democracy*, p. 94.

[26] Douglas T. Miller, *The Birth of Modern America: 1820-1850* (New York: Pegasus, 1978), pp. 119-120.

4. The Antebellum Elites

a. The North: rise and assimilation
of the nouveaux riches

The years preceding the Civil War saw the emergence of private institutions devised by the upper classes as a defense mechanism or social barrier against the brashness and ostentation of the nouveaux riches. At the same time, these institutions afforded a means of the latter's assimilation into the ranks of the traditional upper classes.

In the North, new economic opportunities generated new wealth and a new wealthy class. New elites of manufacturing enterprises arose alongside the old families of the mercantile elite who still retained their position and prestige. The nouveaux riches were gradually assimilated by these older, more respectable elites through marriages.

The laws against primogeniture and entail had produced their effects: the traditional rural elite was in economic decline, although their social status remained untouched. As Douglas Miller points out, "numerous new opportunists flooded the ranks of the rich, making it difficult for the established families of colonial times to preserve their preeminence."[27]

Miller says further on:

> There was a marked tendency in the seaboard states for great landed properties to decline....
>
> However, respectable old families could and often did preserve themselves by uniting with the parvenu in marriage—trading respectability for money....
>
> Arranged marriages between rich but new families and threadbare but respectable old families became more and more frequent during the 1830s and 1840s.[28]

While the Southern elites maintained their traditional social structures and agrarian-based economy, the Northern mercantile and rural traditional elites maintained their status by diversifying their investments in industrial enterprises. Regarding the North, Miller writes:

> The industrial revolution, in conjunction with gains in commercial wealth and urban land values, was creating a powerful and prestigious class of financial magnates in the midst of democratic America. A limited group in most areas was acquiring wealth, social recognition, and a good deal of control over the nation's manufacturing, transportation, and commercial facilities....
>
> ..."Everywhere growth and expansion intensified earlier stratification."[29]

---

[27]   Ibid., p. 119.

[28]   Ibid., pp. 120-121.

[29]   Miller, *The Birth of Modern America*, pp. 133-134, quoting Richard Wade, *The Urban Frontier* (Chicago: 1964).

The old elites not only adapted to the new economic conditions, but stimulated them. The new industrialists, joined to the traditional mercantile elite by marriage and business interests, furnished them the means to sustain their old standard of living within the changing climate. In reference to this process in Boston, Jaher writes:

> They became the new economic core of blueblood Boston, but virtually every distinguished family furnished shareholders and officers. The industry, owned and managed by interconnected families, was a community enterprise which kinship succession kept in upper-class hands for the rest of the century....
>
> ...In addition to controlling these institutions, bluebloods were officers and major stockholders in five of the seven largest Boston banks. Command over the major sources of capital in Massachusetts permitted the upper class to exercise financial dominion over the state.[30]

In New York, the rural aristocracy waned, as the new plutocracy waxed.

> Aristocracy in New York was in a state of transition. The class of gentry was declining, but the rise of the wealthy capitalists more than offset this....
>
> ...In the North, and particularly in New York, the wealthy classes were beginning to exercise a power and an influence far greater than had ever been possessed by any earlier American elite....
>
> ...The image of the aristocrat had changed from the traditional patriarchal squire to the wealthy plutocrat—the city-centered merchant or industrialist more concerned with drawing rooms and counting houses than manors and tenants. Unlike the landed aristocrats, whose position as an elite group steadily declined before the forces of democracy, capitalist-aristocrats thrived under the laissez-faire economic conditions prevalent in Jacksonian America.[31]

b. The lifestyle of the Northern traditional elites

During this period the traditional elites played a less important role in politics than before, but they continued to exercise their influence in the large cities through private philanthropic groups.

> New York City, Brooklyn, Boston, and Philadelphia were hardly governed by a "patriciate" in the decades before 1850. Instead the elite of the great northeastern cities governed the hundreds of voluntary associations that complemented, and in some cases surpassed, in importance the work done by municipal political bodies.

---

[30] Jaher, *The Urban Establishment*, pp. 51, 53.

[31] Douglas T. Miller, *Jacksonian Aristocracy* (New York: Oxford Univ. Press, 1967), pp. 80, 181, 70.

Politics were left to men of wealth, but not the greatest wealth, and to a sprinkling of elite family representatives.[32]

Pessen describes the elites in large Northern cities of the time.

> The elite of a city typically numbered several hundred families of great prestige; many of them had been eminent since the seventeenth century, but a surprising number were renowned only since the middle of or late in the eighteenth. These families moved in a restricted social orbit, maintaining exclusive relationships both on a formal and informal level, attending the same dinner parties and balls, active in the same clubs and voluntary associations, living in residential enclaves populated by their own sort, marrying by a rule of social endogamy, and usually—although not invariably—possessing great wealth.[33]

In pre-Civil War Boston, for example, there was a strong traditional elite that descended from old families of colonial times and which formed the core of its upper social class.

> Dozens of the richest Bostonians of the 1830s and 1840s were descendants of families that had migrated from England to Massachusetts two centuries earlier, attaining prominence immediately on arrival or soon after and maintaining it almost unbroken thereafter.[34]

The great wealth of these Bostonian elites provided a philanthropic impetus and favored their social and cultural improvement. "Charitable and cultural activities were conducted along overlapping lines characteristic of patrician enterprises," Jaher writes. "Early retirement from business, inherited wealth, and increased emphasis upon culture stimulated social activity. Salons appeared, intellectual gatherings multiplied."[35] And Miller writes: "Philadelphia and Baltimore societies were similar to Boston's in that they too were tightly knit and dependent on both birth and wealth."[36]

Pessen remarks that the backgrounds of the Philadelphia rich of the early nineteenth century were similar to those of the New York City and Boston elites.

> As in its great urban rivals to the north, the most prestigious families were, with few exceptions, the oldest families; these had either accompanied William Penn on the *Welcome*...or arrived soon enough afterwards to be associated with the city's beginnings.... Wealthy Philadelphians of the 1840s were descendants of what Cleveland Amory

---

[32] Pessen, *Riches, Class and Power Before the Civil War*, p. 294.

[33] Ibid., p. 283.

[34] Ibid., p. 111.

[35] Jaher, *The Urban Establishment*, pp. 63, 66.

[36] Miller, *Jacksonian Aristocracy*, p. 133.

has described as "perhaps the most aristocratic of all Philadelphia families."[37]

In New York certain private clubs and organizations, with membership based on ancestry, became focal points for the city's aristocracy. The membership roles of exclusive clubs included descendants of the most traditional elites in the city and state. "Social life in New York revolved around elegant parties and formal balls, both privately given or run by subscription."[38] "New York City had more social clubs during the era than did its great urban rivals. Some of these associations were dedicated to nothing more than assuring greater exclusivity to their elite memberships in their leisure-hour activities."[39]

During the years before the Civil War, the traditional elites in the North were obliged to accept many newly rich families into their ranks. The patrician families eventually took a greater part in the liberal professions even while they relinquished their direct participation in political life. Social leadership remained a patrimony of the traditional elites, whose lifestyle the nouveaux riches endeavored to imitate.

This new aristocracy formed by the fusion of the old traditional elites with the new plutocratic elites was destined to become the standard of a new American upper class emerging after the tragic years of the Civil War. Says Schlesinger: "Contemned by the southern patricians as nouveaux riches, this aspiring group were destined to be the forerunners of the class that was to supplant the southern aristocracy in the period after the Civil War and become the modern conservators of the aristocratic tradition."[40]

c. The South: the planter, a social apex and a human type

Before the Civil War, Southern society was imbued with an attitude closely linked to rural life and social hierarchy. The impulse toward industrialization was less pronounced, political divisions were more superficial, and democratic tendencies less marked than in the North or the West.

> Southern civilization was ordered and orderly. Class organization was sharply but not rigidly defined; some groups occupied higher positions than others, but each held a status with which it was largely satisfied. As a result, class competition was at a minimum.... [Moreover the standard of living was generally comfortable and more relaxed than in the industrial North.] All classes (or almost all) enjoyed a comfortable life (some more than others) without having to work too hard.[41]

---

[37] Pessen, *Riches, Class and Power Before the Civil War*, p. 120.

[38] Miller, *Jacksonian Aristocracy*, p. 77.

[39] Pessen, *Riches, Class and Power Before the Civil War*, p. 225.

[40] Schlesinger, *New Viewpoints in American History*, p. 92.

[41] Williams, Current, and Freidel, *A History of the United States*, p. 474.

Dumas Malone and Basil Rauch describe the values prized by Southern society.

> The virtues most praised were not those of the world of commerce but those of the landed gentry of the Old World and the vanished age of chivalry—not efficiency, shrewdness, and aggressiveness but honor, generosity, and good manners. By and large the leading Southerners found their models in the past, while the Northerners looked forward to a new age of business and boundless progress.[42]

The South "subscribed to the democratic myth, but more than any other section it glorified aristocratic leadership. Its agricultural system was commercial and specialized, and thus in harmony with modern trends, but many of its social institutions were more feudal than modern."[43]

The social structure of the South revolved around the planters. They set the tone of the economic, social, and political life of the society. "Planters were acknowledged as the social models and natural leaders of society by consensus," affirms Tindall.[44] Wecter states: "At the top were the plantation aristocrats, comprising the approximately one thousand families.... In the ranking class belonged some of the old eighteenth century grandees...who had salvaged enough despite laws against entail to keep the family name in style."[45] Below them were the smaller planters and numerous farmers, professionals, and merchants.

The qualifications necessary to be considered a planter were fluid and defined according to the time and place. A hierarchy existed within the planter class itself. The large planters—generally those who owned plantations of over 800 acres with 40 or more working slaves—were at the peak of the social pyramid.

> The major planters represented the social ideal of the South. Enriched by vast annual incomes, dwelling in palatial homes, surrounded by broad acres and many slaves, they were the class to which all Southerners paid a certain deference and to which every ambitious Southerner aspired. Enabled by their wealth to practice the leisured arts, they cultivated gracious living, good manners, learning, and politics. Their social pattern determined to a considerable degree the tone of all Southern society.[46]

The Southern planters constituted the closest parallel in the United States to the social situation of the European nobility. The plantation country gentry preserved the traditions of the English aristocrat, such as the sense of noblesse oblige, the rendering

---

[42]   Dumas Malone and Basil Rauch, *Crisis of the Union 1841-1877* (New York: Appleton-Century-Crofts, 1960), p. 98

[43]   Williams, Current, and Freidel, *A History of the United States*, p. 476.

[44]   Tindall, *America: A Narrative History*, Vol. 1, p. 551.

[45]   Wecter, *The Saga of American Society*, p. 104.

[46]   Williams, Current, and Freidel, *A History of the United States*, p. 478.

of public services, the practice of hospitality, and strict adhesion to the gentle-man's code. It especially valued the idea of personal dignity and honor. Referring specifically to the social life of South Carolina's country gentry, historian Clement Eaton notes that it was "a well-knit ruling class, whose power and prestige had been diminished by the Revolution, but who nevertheless retained great vitality even after the rise of Jacksonian democracy in the 1820's."[47]

While the Northern traditional elites consolidated their economic situation by fusing with nouveau-riche merchants and industrialists, often withdrawing from direct participation in political life, the Southern planters maintained their social preeminence and political leadership, although they adopted a democratic rhetoric. As Miller points out, "the planters themselves made the concession of adopting a democratic political style, but their leadership was never seriously at issue."[48] The South democratic rhetoric clothed an aristocratic order. "Though the South continued to speak of common-man democracy, the vital reform movements sweeping the North in these years were absent."[49]

Noting the uncontested leadership exercised by the class of planters in Southern society, Williams, Current, and Freidel write:

> The planters exercised a dominating leadership because the great majority of whites desired them to execute such a function. As the planters were the models of social aspiration in the section, so they also appeared to the masses as the natural leaders of Southern life.... Because their wealth gave them leisure, they were able to cultivate the arts of leadership and, what was very important, spend time being leaders, time which lesser people often could not afford.[50]

The Southern patrician class resisted the unrestricted admission of the new wealthy elites into their ranks much more effectively than the mercantile elites of the North. The parvenus were only absorbed by traditional society after they had adopted refined patrician manners and lifestyles as well as conservative atti-tudes. Lawyers, doctors, soldiers, and politicians were linked both by family ties and economic interests to the class of planters; the merchant class also aspired to the acquisition of prestige that money could not buy. In the period prior to the Civil War, the business class was stationed below the planters, politicians, soldiers, and liberal professionals. Except in a few urban centers, a work-capital relationship did not develop between employees and employers. The predominance of the agrarian ideal was manifested in the aspiration of businessmen to become planters.[51]

The cultivation of cotton as a commercial product enriched many Southern

---

[47] Eaton, *The Growth of Southern Civilization*, p. 1.

[48] Miller, *The Birth of Modern America*, p. 136.

[49] Ibid., p. 137.

[50] Williams, Current, and Freidel, *A History of the United States*, p. 479.

[51] Cf. ibid., p. 480.

planters and stimulated southwestward territorial expansion. Many old families of Virginia and the Carolinas colonized and developed the frontier region with the agility and efficiency proper to those accustomed to leadership and sufficient capital. Contrary to popular myth, "it was never the poor man's frontier."[52]

The aristocratic lifestyle introduced in this region served as a model for the new planters, who aspired to attain the social prestige associated with the traditional planters. "The ideal of the country gentleman was carried by emigrating Virginians and Carolinians to remote corners of the South," notes Eaton.[53]

The cotton culture served to stimulate the traditional Southern concepts of distinction and values. Schlesinger states:

> The vast expansion of cotton culture from 1800 to 1830 gave a new dignity and importance to this high-toned gentry. The few thousands of "first families," who lived upon the incomes of plantations and formed the upper-crust of southern society, spent their winters in New Orleans, their springs in Charleston and their summers at the Virginia springs.... The personal ideal of this aristocracy was summed up in the term "chivalry," an expression denoting the virtues of gallantry toward women, courtesy to inferiors, a mettlesome sense of honor, and a lavish hospitality.[54]

Southern aristocrats inherited an appreciation for the military spirit and a sense of chivalry from the authentic European nobility. Jaher writes: "Southern patricians shared with the European gentry and nobility an inclination for military training, a legacy of the age of chivalry notably absent in northern and western urban commercial elites.... In accord with the European aristocratic tradition, southerners constituted a majority of the cavalry officers."[55]

Although this aristocracy adhered to some revolutionary concepts, as a whole it remained more conservative than its Northern progressivist counterpart in the decades prior to the Civil War.

The Old South, despite its defects, was a civilization with a peculiar charm, a wholesome sense of reality, and a stable economy with well-distributed property; it constituted an authentic people living together harmoniously, bound by certain spiritual values. The social order was generally accepted. Immoderate profit and competition were restrained by an ethic that prized leisure as much as work. It was a society that looked toward its future without rejecting the values of the past, thus fostering a high sense of aesthetics expressed in the art of living: attire, conversation, manners, meals, hunts, and political and religious oratory. Historian I. A. Newby sums up the values of the Old South as those that characterize a "good society": deep roots, a religious sense, a strong urban base, conservative policies and a decentralized government. Its people were loyal to their families,

---

[52] Eaton, *The Growth of Southern Civilization*, p. 18.

[53] Ibid., p. 2.

[54] Schlesinger, *New Viewpoints in American History*, pp. 90-91.

[55] Jaher, *The Urban Establishment*, p. 386.

Generals Lee and Grant at Appomattox. Dignity in adversity is a characteristic of the true elites.

classes, and local societies.

> Only its religion had been wrong: the Old South had been Protestant when by everything in the Agrarian prescription it should have been Catholic. Protestantism was the religion of individualism and liberal capitalism, not traditionalism and authority, or as [Allen] Tate put it, "hardly a religion at all, but a result of secular ambition." The Old South had thus been an anomaly, "a feudal society without a feudal religion," which was one of the reasons its way of life had not survived military defeat.[56]

Only in the decade immediately prior to the Civil War did the elites begin to lose ground to the democratic trends of the time. But it was the War itself that struck the mortal blow at the Southern aristocracy and its way of life. The South's thwarted attempt to separate from the North and form a nation of confederate states with an agrarian and traditional civilization had serious implications in the ideological context of the times. Schlesinger writes:

> The Civil War dealt a body blow to the most exclusive aristocracy our country has ever known. The former master class issued from the conflict with the stigma of unsuccessful revolutionists; they had lost the flower of their manhood and most

---

[56]   I. A. Newby, *The South: A History* (New York: Holt, Rinehart and Winston, 1978), p. 451.

of their wealth.... The aristocracy of the old South, which had played so large a part in the history of the nation and had produced many of its greatest men, was annihilated, to live no more except as a splendid and romantic memory of the days "before the war."[57]

Newby points out the conservative nature of the Confederate movement for independence: "The Confederates were attempting an anomaly, a conservative revolution, a political change to prevent social and economic change. Unlike other modern movements for independence and nationhood, theirs was conservative and counterrevolutionary rather than radical and revolutionary."[58]

At the end of the Civil War, in contrast to what might be expected, the country was not shaken by a confrontation of a principally ideological and doctrinal character between the partisans of an aristocratic regime and those favorable to a democratic regime. Rather, there was a certain ideological numbness within American society. Neither the more intelligent minds, the first-rate scholars, and the most capable individuals, nor the more influential newspapers, explored or seriously examined monarchy-aristocracy-democracy as a principal topic for writing and conversation.

There was only an oblique and vague concern for this issue. The ideological clash was thus largely muffled, even by those who had clear convictions on it.

5. Anti-Catholicism in the Period Before the Civil War

At least officially, the American Revolution, the Declaration of Independence, and the Constitution opened the nation's social and political life to Catholics by granting them previously denied political rights. In practice, however, the results of this movement were not as positive or encouraging as the application of liberal principles might suggest. Outside of Maryland and Louisiana, where the presence of traditional Catholic elites had been felt since colonial times, Catholics remained a small sociopolitical sub-class.

With the enormous Catholic immigration in the decades prior to the Civil War, the Catholic Church grew from a virtually nonexistent institution to the largest religious group in the country. The First Provincial Council in 1829 was a response to this rapid growth. In this situation, anti-Catholicism revived under a form—nativism—that found ample adherence in all social classes.

The hostility of American Protestants of all denominations swelled to the point of fomenting a "Protestant crusade" against the growing Catholic influence in the country. The Pope, the Jesuits, and the Catholic hierarchy were accused of forming a "Holy Alliance" to promote the immigration of Catholics, and thereby subvert democracy in America. Catholic Emancipation in England in 1829 provoked a

---

[57] Schlesinger, *New Viewpoints in American History*, p. 93.

[58] Newby, *The South: A History*, p. 211.

Saint John Neumann, Bishop of Philadelphia,
indefatigably strove to maintain the faith of his flock.

flood of anti-Catholic literature, which overflowed into the United States, further exciting anti-Catholic sentiments.

Anti-Catholicism was not limited to defamatory literature. Anti-Catholic preaching fueled the animosity until it exploded in riots in several cities. In Boston, for example, mobs set fire to a convent and a Catholic school. A decade later, violence broke out in Philadelphia, where two Catholic churches and dozens of homes of Irish Catholic immigrants were burnt down. The final toll was thirteen dead and fifty wounded. A few days later, similar violence was threatened against the Catholics of New York. The bishop of the city, John Hughes, responded with decisive action; the strongly-armed Catholics he stationed around the churches dampened the bellicose fervor of the nativists.

The nativist phenomenon was not restricted to mass agitation. Anti-Catholicism fused with the nativist rejection of immigration, spreading a subtle bias throughout sections of the upper class. As Sidney Ahlstrom points out, "anti-Catholic sentiment broadened out through the middle and upper classes of 'American' ancestry, becoming diluted but not disappearing as it blended with vague feelings of Anglo-Saxon pride and class consciousness."[59]

The nativist movement spawned a secret political society: the "Know-Nothings." Its members swore to oppose the election of immigrants and Catholics to public office and to remove them whenever possible. In 1854 and in subsequent years, they achieved spectacular victories in local and state elections throughout the country. They seemed on their way to dominating Congress and even obtaining a victory in the presidential elections when debates over slavery and secession divided their political base. According to Ahlstrom, just as the nativist movement and anti-Catholicism constituted powerful social influences prior to the Civil War, "so it would be after the Civil War. Against a background of rapid social change, both nativism and anti-Catholicism...would again become ugly realities."[60]

In large regions where Protestant fundamentalism was strong and Catholics were few, it may be said that Catholics had almost no social status. The Catholic families in such communities lived apart from the main social structure of the region. Where Catholics were more numerous, they were more easily admitted into the social system, but always precariously and to the extent they practiced their faith privately and unobtrusively. Thus, because of their religion, Catholics tended to constitute a group apart from the main social body.[61]

---

[59]   Sydney E. Ahlstrom, *A Religious History of the American People*, p. 564.

[60]   Ibid., p. 568.

[61]   Cf. John L. Thomas, S.J., *The American Catholic Family* (Englewood Cliff, N.J.: Prentice-Hall, 1958), pp. 139-140.

CHAPTER VIII

The Elites After the Civil War

1. Social Revolution
Following the Civil War

The Civil War was a turning point in American life. The North's victory definitively shaped what would be the profile of the national elite. The war accelerated the process of industrialization and profoundly transformed the face of the nation.

The war was a social revolution, a collision of two ways of life, of two frames of mind. It subjugated the planter class inclined toward a traditional social order and imposed industrial capitalism as the socioeconomic regime that would determine the lifestyles of subsequent American elites. Above all, the war strongly influenced the formation of the human type that would become the model for future elites.

Overshadowing the war's economic consequences was the demoralization of the prototypical planter, the dissolution of his lifestyle, and the disintegration of the power and influence of the traditional elites in the South. Jaher asserts:

> Old South patriciates encountered an abrupt disaster in the Civil War. Military tradition, the cavalier myth, determination to defend southern civilization, and elitist attitudes emphasizing special obligations to protect the social order, lead in battle, and face danger prompted bluebloods to volunteer for armed service.... A large portion of the gentry that might have provided leadership and sustained the class in subsequent decades disappeared in the prime of life. Aside from a high mortality rate, extensive property destruction as a result of the conflict being fought mostly in the South traumatized the upper class and prevented a postwar patrician restoration.[1]

Despite the humiliation and other painful consequences of defeat, the customary deference to the old planter class persisted within local communities. "'Every community,' Union officer John DeForest noted in postwar South Carolina, 'had its great man, or its little great man, around whom his fellow citizens gather

---

[1]   Jaher, *The Urban Establishment*, p. 398.

when they want information, and to whose monologues they listen with a respect akin to humility.'"[2]

Notwithstanding local custom, however, the Southern traditional elites occupied a secondary position in relation to the Northern industrial and financial elites. "The Civil War strongly reinforced the power of the Northern aristocracy," notes Miller, "and gave to the Northern elite a greater degree of national political power than it had hitherto enjoyed."[3]

Victorious in the War, the North accelerated the drive toward industrial capitalism. The economic and social transformation of the United States into an industrialized nation dominated by urban and industrial elites of that region was already well under way before 1860, but it reached its height in the second half of the nineteenth century.

> The importance of the Civil War for America's elite structure was the commanding position that the new industrial capitalists won during the course of the struggle.... When the Southern planters were removed from the national scenario, the government in Washington became the exclusive domain of the new industrial leaders.[4]

2. The Nouveaux Riches and the Traditional Elites

Industrialization and economic growth propelled a large number of the nouveaux riches into the ranks of the elites in the half century following the Civil War. These new elites often commanded dazzling wealth, but social precedence remained with the old families.

> The old families, whose wealth dates back before 1860, and which have therefore been wealthy for three or four generations, enjoy undisputed social precedence. The very great fortunes, which made some Americans the richest men on earth, were only made with the industrialization of the country on a continental scale between the Civil War and the First World War.[5]

Supplied with seemingly limitless fortunes and desiring the lifestyle and status of the traditional elites, the nouveaux riches of the time staged unprecedented spectacles of ostentation and dissipation. Their proliferation as a result of the triumph of industrialism effected a reshaping of America's upper class, not by leveling the social stratification, but by giving rise to new elites more in accord with industrial society.

---

[2] Tindall, *America: A Narrative History*, Vol. 1, p. 715.

[3] Miller, *Jacksonian Aristocracy*, p. 180.

[4] Dye and Zeigler, *The Irony of Democracy*, p. 73.

[5] Von Borch, *The Unfinished Society*, p. 217.

After the Civil War, America's eastern seaboard provincial and familial aristocracies were eventually replaced by an exclusive and competitive associational plutocracy, rooted in the "Gilded Age" and continuing to the present day. As with so much else in American life, the 1880's witnessed a turning point in the structure of the upper class.[6]

Baltzell explains that what occurred was not properly a replacement of elites, but rather a fusion of the two elites.

In metropolitan America in the last two decades of the nineteenth century, local aristocracies of birth and breeding (old money) merged with that new and more conspicuously colorful world known as "Society." As millionaires multiplied and had to be accepted, as one lost track of "who" people were and had to recognize "what" they were worth, the *Social Register* became an index of a new upper class in metropolitan America.[7]

Max Lerner describes how the new national elites of the large cities dominated the elites of the small cities.

The rise of an upper class of newly rich families has transformed the upper American social status, both in small and large cities, and has introduced a ferment of new moral standards. The earlier America had a number of cities, each of which boasted its "old families" and its inner circles of blood and standing.... But increasingly this local "society" has been subordinated to the power groups and social sets of the big metropolitan centers, where celebrities cluster and the Social Register operates, and men make decisions affecting the whole nation.[8]

3. The Industrial Revolution

a. The Industrial Revolution in the United States

In the years following independence, the sociopolitical and economic life of the nation was marked by a continuous debate among the American elites over the path the new republic should follow in its development. Some defended an industrial and commercial economy, while others proclaimed that the well-being of the nation depended on having a predominantly agrarian society wherein self-sufficient producers would comprise the majority.

Although in the first half of the nineteenth century both the North and the South were affected by the forces that gave rise to the Industrial Revolution, the

---

[6] Baltzell, *Philadelphia Gentlemen*, p. 18.

[7] E. Digby Baltzell, "Who's Who in America and the Social Register," in *Class, Status, and Power: Social Stratification in Comparative Perspective*, Reinhard Bendix and Seymour Martin Lipset, eds. (New York: The Free Press, 1966), p. 274.

[8] Max Lerner, *America as a Civilization*, p. 482.

Top left: The Breakers of Newport, Rhode Island, is an outstanding example of the many magnificent and splendorous mansions built around the turn of the century in America.

Bottom left: The Music Room at the Breakers. Distinction, refinement, and charm are evident in this aristocratic mansion.

Above: Medieval banquet hall at Biltmore House, Asheville, North Carolina.

social and economic life of those regions reacted differently. The North had turned increasingly toward progress and material satisfaction, urbanization, industrialization, and a diversified economy. In the South, on the other hand, the economy had remained largely rooted in the plantation regime. It was an agricultural economy that produced raw material for domestic and foreign markets and that developed an almost complete self-sufficiency in articles of daily use. This type of production was situated outside the modern market economy, but with the profits from the sale of agricultural products, the planters were able to buy from the North or from Europe luxury items that the South did not produce. The Southern cities, unlike those of the North, were "appendages of the plantation regime, not independent centers of social and economic innovation."[9]

The aftermath of the Civil War, however, imposed the socioeconomic model of the Industrial Revolution on the whole country. The migration of a large number of rural inhabitants to the cities, together with an influx of foreign immigrants, transformed the customs and shook the foundations of an economy almost exclusively based on rural life.

b. A new attitude

The Industrial Revolution also prompted the appearance of a secularist and pragmatic attitude focused on comfort and material progress. This change of attitude implied an entirely new conception of ideological and religious issues. In fact, the mentors of the Industrial Revolution promoted the idea that the country's highest interest would best be served by rapid and vibrant material progress through industrialization. A boundless scientific and technological progress would relegate discussions and disagreements on ideological and religious issues to a secondary plane. They argued that these issues only caused misunderstandings and divisions among the population, to the detriment of the common good. The worship of the machine—a symbol of material progress and wealth—was to be promoted as the best way to maintain social peace and harmony among the classes. Thus material progress would achieve what theretofore had been attained through morality and religion.[10]

Merely secular material progress uproots religious sentiment. The secularization of the temporal order—in reality its gradual sinking into atheism—produces a profound transformation of the moral and religious order of any society. As Italian sociologist Sabino S. Acquaviva notes, a religious crisis always accompanies the process of industrialization.[11]

---

[9]   Newby, *The South: A History*, p. 126.

[10]   Christopher Lasch writes: "The idea of progress, according to a widely accepted interpretation, represents a secularized version of the Christian belief in Providence.... 'It is no accident,' Carl Becker wrote in 1921, 'that the belief in Progress and a concern for 'posterity' waxed in proportion as the belief in Providence and a concern for a future life waned'" (Lasch, *The True and Only Heaven: Progress and Its Critics* [New York: W. W. Norton & Co., 1991], p. 40).

[11]   Cf. Sabino S. Acquaviva, *The Decline of the Sacred in Industrial Society* (New York: Harper & Row, 1979), p. xi.

The new working class, integrated into the industrial system, is profoundly influenced by an environment dominated by secularistic and materialistic values. The industrial world forms a complex network of psychological relationships, supported by science, machines, technology, and the new urban and depersonalized conditions of mass living that have a desacralizing effect on society. This took place not only in the United States but in other Western countries as well. Interests of a material order subjugated religious sentiments and principles everywhere.[12]

Indeed, the ephemeral material progress achieved by these means can be termed false when it undermines the foundation of a social edifice built on the moral and spiritual values of Christian civilization. Promotion of this false material progress could only lead to moral and religious crises resulting in a situation even more revolutionary than the Industrial Revolution itself. This is why noted conservative scholar Russell Kirk affirms that "modern industrialism, in Britain and America and most of western Europe, smashed the economic defenses of conservative society.... Industrialism was a harder knock to conservatism than the books of the French equalitarians."[13]

c. Super-production and super-consumerism— Balance and temperance

Among the negative consequences of the economic order generated by the Industrial Revolution are super-production and super-consumerism. No one can deny the existence today, especially in what are called "first-world countries," of an over-production of foodstuffs and consumer goods. This over-production resulted in good measure from the idea that to produce five hundred is always better than to produce five. The problem of what to do with the five hundred was only of secondary importance. This attitude ignores the whole idea of balance: that there should be neither misery nor over-production.

Such balance was present in economic systems preceding the Industrial Revolution, but progressively waned with its advent. A traditional rural property produced not only goods harvested directly from the land, but also textiles, furniture, and handicrafts. Production was sufficient to provide leisure and even a certain abundance. Unnecessary or even detrimental over-production was unknown. This, however, did not preclude the exportation of the principal products of the region, whose profits could be used to import desired articles.[14]

Balanced consumerism controlled the quantity and the quality of production. It

---

[12] Cf. ibid., p. 151.

[13] Kirk, *The Conservative Mind*, pp. 197, 199.

[14] In the United States, the Southern planters came closest to this system. However, rural near self-sufficiency was widespread throughout the nation. "Americans were wedded to the self-sustaining family farm as the norm of social and economic organization and the locus of public virtue. Such a people had an understandably difficult time accommodating the system of production, labor, and rewards that came with the factory" (Michael Brewster Folsom and Steven D. Lubar, eds., *The Philosophy of Manufactures* [Cambridge: MIT Press, 1982], pp. xxii-xxiii).

impeded the formation of mega-cities and mega-industry. As the agrarian-based system of economy considered the well-being of the spirit as well as that of the body, production was calm and balanced, not frenetic. The virtue of temperance, instilled by a religious formation, assured man a sense of proportionality that made him desire what was reasonable and balanced.

This desire for balance was characteristic of the spirit of the medieval man. However, with the advent of Humanism and the Renaissance, this frame of mind changed dramatically. Men, spurred on by the desire for fortunes and roles that were disproportional to their nature, lost their sense of balance. This disordered appetite is at the root of excess production and consumerism, and of unbridled desire for pleasure. At the same time, spiritual, religious, moral, and cultural values became increasingly scorned and relegated to oblivion.

d. The myth of the self-made man

Along with the proliferation of new millionaires resulting from the Industrial Revolution, there arose a myth that the majority of them were self-made men. Inherent in this myth was the idea, trumpeted throughout the world, that most of the successful businessmen in the United States, from the second half of the nineteenth century onwards, came from poor families of the lower social strata or were immigrants' sons. Through sheer will power and hard work and, of course, the opportunities afforded by a democratic and egalitarian society, they supposedly were able to make fortunes and rise to the highest rungs of the social and economic ladder.

Recent research refutes this sociological notion, conclusively showing that while this type of social ascension did exist, it was the exception rather than the rule. John Ingham states that the new economic and industrial elites "came from generally upper-middle-class, white Anglo-Saxon Protestant households."[15]

> Although it is often comforting to think of the "rags to riches" millionaires, the fact remains that the vast majority of those who held executive positions in the nineteenth century, and who continued as part of a wealthy and powerful upper class in the twentieth century, were those who were originally from the proper kinds of family and cultural backgrounds.[16]

Referring to the iron and steel millionaires created by the industrialization of the past century, he affirms:

> Although Pittsburgh's iron and steel entrepreneurs differed little from those in Philadelphia, or from American businessmen generally, there had long been a stereotype about these Pittsburgh steelmen. This view saw the city as the seedbed of

---

[15] Ingham, *The Iron Barons*, p. 1.

[16] Ibid., p. 222.

Andrew Carnegie, "self-made" industrialist.

"shirtsleeve millionaires," of barefoot boys from poor families who amassed great wealth and power by dint of their own work and intelligence. Yet, as this study will show, Pittsburgh iron and steel men were largely the sons of businessmen, from upper-middle-class and upper-class backgrounds.[17]

Sociologist Robin Williams reached a similar conclusion in his analysis of mobility in American society:

> Vertical occupational movement largely occurs step by step—unskilled to skilled laborer, clerk to manager, and so forth—rather than by the spectacular ascent of the Horatio Alger myth or of the latter-day Hollywood success story....
>
> More recent studies show that since the beginning of the nineteenth century, American business leaders have come for the most part from economically well-off families and that the proportion so derived has remained fairly stable (between three fifths and three fourths) for a long time. Less than one fifth of the business elite come from the ranks of laborers, craftsmen, small entrepreneurs, lower white-collar employees, or farmers.[18]

Von Borch affirms that the twentieth century has followed and even intensified this same pattern:

> Wealth is coming to be founded increasingly on inherited wealth. And it is becoming increasingly unusual for anyone to rise to the millionaire class from the very bottom. At the present time, "self-made men" constitute only nine per cent of the highest income group; twenty-three per cent come from the middle class, and sixty-eight per cent from an upper class that has long been wealthy.[19]

Pessen, drawing on other research, affirms:

> Modern studies of the family status and backgrounds of five hundred big business leaders of 1900 and the 1870s disclose that they were overwhelmingly of high status and from unusually successful families. Discovering that "poor immigrant boys and poor farm boys actually made up no more than three per cent of the business leaders" of 1900 whose backgrounds he studied, William Miller concludes wryly that poor boys "who become business leaders have always been more conspicuous in American history books than in American history."[20]

---

[17] Ibid., p. 5.

[18] Williams, *American Society*, pp. 117, 123. He refers specifically to studies of Seymour Martin Lipset and Reinhard Bendix, *Social Mobility in Industrial Society* (Berkeley and Los Angeles: Univ. of California Press, 1959), pp. 122-127.

[19] Von Borch, *The Unfinished Society*, p. 219.

[20] Pessen, *Riches, Class and Power Before the Civil War*, p. 79.

Domhoff affirms:

> The work of historian William Miller and his associates in the Research Center for Entrepreneurial History at Harvard has shown that important business leaders and corporation lawyers from the 1870's on have been native-born Anglo-Saxons of "high-status" Protestant religions...who were the well-educated sons of native-born businessmen and professionals.... The few cases of rags to riches which were trumpeted by publicists and uncritically accepted by some historians of an earlier generation were the rare exceptions rather than the rule.[21]

Seymour Martin Lipset and Reinhard Bendix also demonstrate that this mobility in the United States has actually proven to be little different from that observed in industrial societies of other countries such as those of Western Europe.[22]

4. Private Institutions—Preservation and Assimilation

In the reorganization of the upper-class social structure, the old customs and lifestyles of the traditional elites became institutionalized in associations and groups wherein the traditions of the older upper classes continued to shape the lifestyles and aspirations of the newer elites. These institutions "structured this process of assimilation by providing ways and means for the old and new rich to play and learn and worship together."[23]

Ingham describes the emergence of upper class institutions that served to incorporate and assimilate the nouveaux riches.

> A series of upper-class institutions emerged for this purpose—from neighborhood and religion, which had earlier antecedents, to education and social clubs, which were relatively new to the upper-class scene. These formal institutions were united with an older, informal institution—marriage—to establish a complex yet reasonably logical system whereby the new elites were sorted, tagged and ranked according to status. The system also marked clear steps and stages (a series of hurdles perhaps) that the new elite had to scale before being allowed that most intimate area of social assimilation—marriage into the oldest and "best" families.[24]

Baltzell explains how the traditional upper classes transmitted their way of being through private educational institutions.

---

[21] Domhoff, *The Higher Circles*, pp. 72-73.

[22] Cf. Lipset and Bendix, *Social Mobility in Industrial Societies*, p. 13.

[23] Baltzell, *Philadelphia Gentlemen*, p. 10.

[24] Ingham, *The Iron Barons*, pp. 84-85.

> In the course of the twentieth century...the New England Episcopalian boarding schools and the more fashionable Eastern universities began to educate an inter-city and national upper class. These fashionable family-surrogates taught the sons of the new and old rich, whether from Boston, Baltimore, Philadelphia, or San Francisco, the subtle nuances of an upper-class way of life.[25]

Thus, though the traditional elites no longer had their prior political influence, their social influence continued thanks to the educational institutions they founded.

> The upper-class colonial gentry of the Northeast had retreated from direct political rule by the mid-nineteenth century, but they came to dominate the educational institutions that socialized later generations of elites of different origins. In this way, they continued to leave their mark on the elites of the industrial age.[26]

a. Family trusts and foundations

Many of the old families protected their patrimonies from disintegration through a system of trusts whereby the family's wealth was preserved intact and administered to benefit the family members. Such trusts, first used by the traditional elite of Boston in the 1820s, were fully developed by the 1880s. They became an important instrument for providing the financial security of many families of the traditional upper class amid the transformations of the industrial era. They still endure, permitting generation after generation to maintain the family's cohesion and economic status and, consequently, its traditions.

> The family, organized bureaucratically by trusts, was now subordinated as a social unit to the institutions that it created and that assumed its functions. Trusts and fiduciaries preserved organized families, but moved them as units to the sidelines of activity, while freeing their personnel to take up professions and to occupy leadership positions in the new complex of cultural and business institutions.[27]

To some degree, the prevalence of the family trust invalidated the notion that the great fortunes of the country are in the hands of individuals.[28]

The philanthropic foundation, unlimited in its duration and enjoying tax exemption, also provided a framework for many modalities of public service and for the "moral legitimization" of the family dynasties. Says Marcus: "The phil-

---

[25]   Baltzell, *Philadelphia Gentlemen*, p. 10.

[26]   George F. Marcus, *Elites: Ethnographic Issues* (Albuquerque: School of American Research, Univ. of New Mexico Press, 1983), pp. 42-43.

[27]   Ibid., p. 238. Cf. also p. 230.

[28]   Cf. Michael Patrick Allen, *The Founding Fortunes* (New York: E. P. Dutton; Truman Talley Books, 1987), p. 103.

anthropic foundation, which supported the professions and education, became the organizational niche in which the perpetuation of particular families could be realized."[29]

With its patrimonies safeguarded in family trusts and administered by professionals, this upper class came to enjoy an undeniable continuity.[30] This continuity, a fruit of the efficacy of its institutions, afforded this class increasing influence and prestige in a world marked by democratic egalitarianism.[31] Domhoff, referring to the more recent phases of the evolution of American upper classes, observes that "'the rich' in the United States are not a handful of discontented eccentrics, jet setters, and jaded scions who have been pushed aside by the rise of corporations and governmental bureaucracies. They are instead full-fledged members of a thriving social class which is as alive and well as it has ever been."[32]

---

[29]   Marcus, *Elites: Ethnographic Issues*, p. 239.

[30]   This is not to say that there have not been many cases of philanthropic foundations slipping from the control of the founders' descendants and engaging in activities far from the founders' intentions.

[31]   The popularity of local and regional dynasties was illustrated in the cover article "The Rich in America" (Paul Glastris, *U.S. New and World Report*, November 18, 1991): "Yet while tycoons of distant Wall Street might be reviled, the dynasties of provincial cities tend to inspire awe, respect—even affection. The Danielses of Raleigh, the Haases of San Francisco and the Lykes of Tampa may not be as 'colorful' as the Bushes. Nor are they household names across the country. But in their hometowns they are celebrities with unparalleled local power."

[32]   G. William Domhoff, *The Powers That Be* (New York: Random House, 1978), p. 4.

CHAPTER IX

Traditional Elites
in Contemporary America

$\mathcal{T}$he present study examined the existence of social classes, the beneficial and necessary role of a leading elite, and the fact that—contrary to certain historical literature—American society is based on a class system.

It proceeded to a brief sketch documenting the existence of aristocratic elites in America from colonial times, showing their origins, apogee, and subsequent evolution in the republican state.

We shall now examine some aspects of these traditional elites within the context of the modern democratic state that deprives them of the opportunity to display their aristocratic mien in its full measure.

1. Traditional Elites in the Upper Class

We must first establish that traditional elites have survived as an integral part of the upper class in contemporary America. Referring to the place of distinction they occupy within this class, sociologist Lloyd Warner asserts:

> The class systems of the communities in the several regions of the United States are basically similar....
>
> On the eastern seaboard of New England there are six recognizable class levels. The upper class is divided into a new and old aristocracy. The so-called "old-family" level at the top provides the keystone to the status arch. Immediately beneath it are the people called the "new families," who are new to the status rather than to the community. They are the fortunate mobile people who have climbed to a level where they participate with the top group in their clubs and cliques. These lower-upper-class people recognize that they are below those born to high position with lineages of several generations. The old families hold their position by virtue of inheritance, validated by the possession of a recognized social lineage.[1]

---

[1] Warner, *American Life: Dream and Reality*, p. 74.

It is these "old families" that, principally, determine the character of the most refined sectors of the upper class, infusing them with wholesome traditions. The inter-relationship between the upper class and the traditional elites in contemporary society is also affirmed by Lucy Kavaler, who quotes a gentleman bearing "one of New York's oldest names" as saying that "a real social register would have to be compiled from the membership lists of the hereditary organizations."[2]

On the other hand, students of the upper class in American society show that the present-day criteria used to acknowledge someone as a member of the upper class coincide, to a great extent, with traditional standards used to determine membership in an aristocratic elite. Domhoff, for example, considers the upper class as constituting a group of families of high social position, great fortune, and unique lifestyle, whose members socialize and marry among themselves. He says further: "The social upper class can be defined as people who are listed in certain social registers and blue books, people who attend certain private schools, and people who belong to certain exclusive social clubs."[3]

2. Traditional Elites in Other Social Categories

But the upper class is not exclusive in harboring people belonging to the traditional elites. These can also be found in other social categories:

a) Descendants of notable figures in military, government, or economic spheres who have promoted the common good of society and etched their moral profiles on a city, region, or the country. In this group figure descendants of officers who commanded troops in war, of distinguished diplomats or politicians, and of entrepreneurs who forged the economic power of the country.

b) Families who have remained faithful to their hereditary past. Also in this category are families who no longer enjoy the status of illustrious ancestors but preserve their memory and maintain customs worthy of their traditions. When, however, a family breaks with its past or ceases to vigorously transmit its spirit to its descendants, it ceases to be part of the traditional elites.

c) Descendants of European nobles who emigrated to the United States and preserved the notion of the dignity proceeding from their ancestors' deeds and traditions.

---

[2] Lucy Kavaler, *The Private World of High Society* (New York: David McKay Co., 1960), p. 7. Hereditary organizations are examined in sections 3 and 4 of this chapter.

[3] Domhoff, *The Higher Circles*, p. 32.

Consuelo Vanderbilt,
Duchess of Marlborough,
dressed for the coronation
of Edward VII.

3. Hereditary Associations

a. Their aristocratic character

The traditional elites in the United States, to preserve their aristocratic character in a world where non-aristocratic habits increasingly prevailed, formed exclusive associations in the intimacy of which they could leisurely display their high bearing and traditional customs. Writing in 1960, social historian Cleveland Amory explained:

> In our own day the Aristocrat can best be found, in sizable numbers, if not in Society at least in *a* Society—in particular, in the Aristocrat's all but patented patriotic Societies like the Cincinnati, Colonial Dames, Colonial Wars, D.A.R., etc. For, while these are, as we have seen, not necessarily today's "Society," they are assuredly, indeed even genealogically, yesterday's—which makes them, of course, today's Aristocracy.[4]

These associations vary in origins, purposes, and admission requirements. Some perpetuate the memory of ancestors who distinguished themselves in battle. Others remember ancestors who were founders or settlers in colonial times or in the nineteenth-century period of territorial expansion, or who occupied prominent positions in colonial or republican government. Membership in these groups generally requires proof of one's descent from such personages and a vote of acceptance by a committee or even all the association's members.

Other organizations unite descendants of the European nobility who settled in America, while yet others cultivate elevated manners, organizing social events that reflect an urbane taste and style.

Since not a few of these associations, whatever their nature, include patriotic activities among their objectives, they are viewed by many people merely as patriotic societies. Yet there is more to them than patriotism. There is exclusiveness based on descent—which would seem to contradict the democratic inclusiveness that supposedly characterizes modern republican institutions. Herein lies a paradox pointed out by Wallace Davies in his work on the origins of American hereditary associations:

> But even an upsurge of patriotic feeling and an absorption in the American past fail to explain the hereditary form of these societies. Indeed, a renewed interest in republican institutions and the ideals of democracy...would seem offhand inconsistent with such imitation of Old World aristocracy and position based upon pedigree.[5]

As we saw in Chapter I, the founders of the United States proscribed an official

---

[4]   Cleveland Amory, *Who Killed Society?* (New York: Harper & Bros., 1960), p. 67.

[5]   Wallace Evan Davies, *Patriotism on Parade* (Cambridge: Harvard Univ. Press, 1955), p. 47.

nobility with titles and political rights. Even though they were themselves aristocrats, they generally sanctioned an aristocratic culture only in the private sphere.
One can surmise that, to overcome this constraint, the founders of the oldest
hereditary associations aimed to obtain for these an official recognition, which
would have made of them something similar to the European nobility. They went
as far as the laws and culture of the United States would allow. This ultimate
intent reflects in the aristocratic nature of the associations they founded.

Simple membership in an hereditary association does not make a person aris
tocratic, especially since not all of these associations possess characteristics that
could be said to render one aristocratic ipso facto. What is of interest here are
the psychological motivations—not always explicit—that gave rise to many of
these associations and that are generally analogous to those observed in a titled
aristocracy.

We must also highlight the cultural relevance of these associations. Their salutary, although often little recognized, contribution to the cultural life of the United
States continues in our day. Following the example of their predecessors who
served the *res publica*, members promote the common good of society by means
of diverse works such as endowing museums and libraries, restoring historic
monuments, and supporting scholarly works on the history of the country, regions,
and illustrious families. In this way they preserve and foster the cultural inheritance and traditions of the United States.

b. Their private character

Lamentably, the aristocratic nature of these groups does not extend its influence
to the public at large. The general public is more often than not unaware of their
very existence, since most associations are careful to avoid the limelight. A few
do not even publicize their existence. Moreover, they do not accept in their midst
anyone outside a select milieu of society, precisely in order to distinguish themselves in a nonegalitarian way.

This selective criterion generates—depending on the degree of exclusiveness—
concentric circles of groups composed of traditional families, from the most to
the least exclusive. While some have less rigid requirements, others are difficult
or almost impossible to enter. Amory provides an example.

> Probably the most difficult of all patriotic Societies to enter is the Order of the
> Founders and Patriots...because of what, genealogically, is demanded. The member must
> descend from a "Founder," a person living in the Colonies prior to 1700, and descend,
> in the same line, from a "Patriot," a man who fought in Washington's army.[6]

Other associations, such as the Philadelphia branch of the General Society of
Colonial Wars, not only have strict genealogical requisites, but limit membership

---

[6]   Ibid., p. 70.

to a certain number.

Many of these associations, both in the North and the South, were founded in the years between the Civil War and the First World War, which corresponded to the surge of industrialization, the consequent creation of new fortunes and the waves of immigration. This was a time of profound social and economic transformations that greatly diminished the status of the pre-war elites. In order to safeguard their situation, the traditional families felt the need to build protective walls of social exclusion around themselves. Among these were many hereditary associations, whose stringent membership requirements proved to be an almost unsurmountable barrier for the new millionaires attempting to enter the upper social circles.

Ingham describes the situation: "The older upper classes had constructed a web of tradition and manners which did much to keep out the uncouth and to temper the aspirations of the impetuous."[7]

In these private associations, the traditional elites found some protection against those whose only distinction was the possession of wealth. The nouveau riche families who—after several generations—managed to penetrate the ranks of these associations first had to pay homage to tradition, and not assume a haughty demeanor of one flaunting wealth before the impoverished aristocrats.

In the end, this enhanced the very respectability of the nouveaux riches who were admitted into the traditional social class, since to acquire the status of this class they had to respect its way of life and emulate its customs. Warner sums up the social distinction between the American traditional elites and the parvenus:

> A family often is considered to be in the top level of the upper-class group only if it has participated in this upper-class behavior for several generations. The members of the lower-upper group, having moved up socially very often through money and its "correct" use in imitation of upper class behavior, achieve final acceptance as solid members of the top level only through the passage of time, often three or more generations.[8]

Today, many descendants of last century's new millionaires already belong to some of these associations, having been accepted into the upper circles through assimilation and marriage. Baltzell describes this process:

> In an age which marked the centralization of economic power under the control of finance capitalism, the gentlemen bankers and lawyers...sent their sons to Groton, St. Paul's, or St. Mark's and afterwards to Harvard, Yale, or Princeton.... These young men from many cities, educated together, got to know one another's sisters at debutante parties and fashionable weddings.... After marriage, almost invariably within this select circle, they lived in these same suburbs and commuted to the city

---

[7] Ingham, *The Iron Barons*, p. 20.

[8] Warner, *American Life: Dream and Reality*, pp. 116-117.

where they lunched with their peers and their fathers.... Several generations repeat the cycle, and a centralized business nobility thus becomes a reality in America.[9]

This process of assimilation of the nouveaux riches to the lifestyle of the traditional upper class is also emphasized by Jaher in his detailed study of urban elites in the United States.

> In fact, the newcomers felt that their own elevation in status depended in part upon learning the style of their forerunners. And who could teach them better than the offspring of the old families! Accordingly, the recently endowed sought to join prestigious social clubs, to serve on boards of distinguished benevolent and cultural institutions, to be present at exclusive dinners and dances, and to send their children to proper preparatory schools and colleges.[10]

This phenomenon reveals one of the most significant forces of social conservatism and stability in the United States.

4. Some Examples of Associations

a. Patriotic associations of a hereditary character

The 1986 *Hereditary Register of the United States* lists 109 hereditary associations, the oldest one founded in 1637 and the most recent one in 1976. Of course, some are more dynamic than others. They are normally described as cultural, historical, preservationist, and the like.

From a certain point of view, the most important of these hereditary associations is the Society of the Cincinnati. Members must be descendants of officers who fought at least three years in the War of Independence or who remained in the army to the end of the war. Moreover, in many states only one member from each qualifying family can belong to the society.

The society, composed of officers of the Continental Army, was organized in 1783. Major General Henry Knox was its principal founder, and Major General Baron von Steuben presided at early organizational meetings. The society was named after the illustrious Roman Quinctius Cincinnatus, who left his farm to assume temporary leadership of the Roman army to save Rome when it was threatened by its enemies; after the victory, he relinquished his post and returned to his lands. George Washington was voted the first president general of this society, which had King Louis XVI as its patron in France.

In the early years of Independence, the society was known for the monarchical sympathies of some of its founders and members. According to various authors,

---

[9]   Baltzell, "Who's Who in America and The Social Register," pp. 274-275.

[10]   Jaher, *The Urban Establishment*, p. 11.

they wanted to establish a military nobility in the country.[11]

Its membership represented distinguished families of the period. Myers relates that "several members came from the top ranks of wealth and social prominence.... Whether they saw themselves as a nascent or established aristocracy, there was a quality of grandeur—their critics thought pomposity—about many Cincinnati."[12]

At its very inception, the society was furiously opposed by liberals like Jefferson, Samuel Adams, and Franklin. The French revolutionary Mirabeau wrote to caution the American liberals against the society's aristocratic tone. According to Wood,

> the ferocious attacks on the Order of the Cincinnati in the 1780's actually represented only the most notable expression of...egalitarian resentments. Because this "Barefaced and Arrogant" attempt by former Revolutionary army officers to perpetuate their honor was considered by men like Aedanus Burke, James Warren, and Samuel Adams to be "as rapid a Stride towards an hereditary Military Nobility as was ever made in so short a Time."[13]

Thomas Jefferson repeatedly denounced the monarchical tendencies of the Cincinnati. The ultimate purpose of the Society of the Cincinnati, Jefferson contended, was "to 'ingraft' onto 'the future frame of government' a 'hereditary order.'" Historian Daniel Sisson comments, "Jefferson, it seemed, always feared the latent monarchical tendencies in America."[14]

Lacking official recognition of the republican government, the society retreated to the private sphere. As a rule, members only wore the badge of the society in public when they traveled abroad.[15]

"In the postwar years the Cincinnati served as a model for many other hereditary societies," writes Myers. "By the end of the nineteenth century there were dozens of them, commemorating ancestors from all periods of America's history. All were a distant reflection of the Cincinnati, and high society...moved discreetly, to find spots in the 'right' societies."[16]

One of the associations inspired by the Cincinnati in our century is the Military Order of the Stars and Bars. Candidates to membership must be male descendants of a commissioned officer of the armed forces of the Confederate States honorably separated from service. They must be members in good standing of the Sons of

---

[11] Cf. Myers, *Liberty without Anarchy*, p. 94.

[12] Ibid., p. 128.

[13] Wood, *Creation of the American Republic*, pp. 399-400.

[14] Sisson, *The American Revolution of 1800*, pp. 127-128.

[15] "It is likely no Englishman feels a greater sense of pride in being a Knight of the Garter, or Scotsman, a Knight of the Thistle, than an American feels in being a member of the Society of the Cincinnati" (*The Hereditary Register of the United States of America* [Phoenix: The Hereditary Register Publications, 1981], p. 21). As the title suggests, this work is a directory of associations such as those discussed here. Unless otherwise noted, our descriptions of each of these associations are based largely on their respective entries in the *Register*.

[16] Myers, *Liberty without Anarchy*, p. 229.

George Washington playing the flute accompanied by his step-daughter, Nelly Custis.

Confederate Veterans.

Other associations gather descendants from families who participated in the founding events of their respective states. Few states are without their exclusive hereditary associations to celebrate their "first families."

One of the most notable of these associations is the Order of First Families of Virginia. This society was instituted in 1912 with the specific purpose of commemorating and preserving the singular distinction of descendants of Virginians of "dignity and consequence." In addition to sponsoring social functions, the group studies the genealogies of these families and publishes their findings. Admission is restricted to persons who are direct descendants of settlers of Virginia.[17]

Another group with special significance is the Order of Colonial Lords of Manors in America, founded in 1911 by John Henry Livingston, a descendant of one of the most eminent American lineages of lords of manors who played an important role in the history of the United States. Writing the history of his renowned family, Edwin Livingston has harsh words for those members who "through a false idea of modesty, or through ignorance, repudiate that nobility to which [they] are fully and legally entitled."[18]

[17] Cf. *The Hereditary Register*, p. 181.

[18] Quoted in Clare Brandt, *An American Aristocracy: The Livingstons* (New York: Doubleday & Co., 1986), p. 210.

These are but a few examples of the many patriotic and hereditary associations existing in the United States.

b. Family associations

The associations of descendants of certain historic figures and the societies devoted to perpetuating a family name are equally worthy of mention. Such groups were started to commemorate the deeds and the spirit of the founders of families, thus maintaining the familial *esprit de corps* through the generations. They also act as a social unit ready to assist less fortunate members and help them to maintain their family status. More than two thousand family associations of varying types exist in the United States.[19]

A characteristic example of a remarkably aristocratic family institution is the National Society Washington Family Descendants. Founded in 1954, it aims to cherish, maintain, and fortify family ties and to perpetuate the memory of George Washington. To gain admission, a person must show that he descends directly and legitimately from George Washington's family, on either the masculine or feminine side, and must be approved by all the society's members. Her Majesty Queen Elizabeth II numbers among its honorary members.

c. Associations of descendants of the European nobility

American descendants of European noble or royal families have also formed associations in a land where the attraction to the mystique of nobility has always been strong. Proof of this attraction is the avid interest a large segment of the American public exhibits in following the activities of the royal families throughout the world, especially that of England, as well as the cordial reception American society offers to many members of the titled European nobility who visit the country.[20]

The Association of the German Nobility in North America, the Polish Nobility Association, and the Russian Nobility Association in America are examples of groups in this category. Their membership requirements are often more restrictive than those of the associations previously discussed.

d. Debutante balls and other social pageantry

Notable in the social life of America's upper class is the series of events that lead to the annual debutante balls, a custom with roots in Old Regime pageantry.

---

[19] Cf. *Family Associations, Societies and Reunions* (Munroe Falls, Ohio: Summit Publications), 1991-1992 edition.

[20] When Lord Fairfax visited the United States in 1986, for example, his itinerary included Fairfax County, Virginia, which had been a fief of his family in colonial times. He was enthusiastically received by the people of the county.

Debutante ball, Astor Hotel ballroom, New York City.

The debut ritual involves a long and arduous process that prepares new generations for the social exigencies of the traditional upper-class lifestyle. The debut itself is only the final step on a long road, a whole education in etiquette, bearing, and good manners that begins quite early, even in infancy, and continues through a girl's youth and adolescence until she reaches the age to qualify as a subdebutante. This is followed by the traditional "coming out" into society life. At some balls the custom has been established of inviting members of the European nobility to receive the debutantes into society. Domhoff comments:

> The debutante season is a series of parties, teas, and dances, culminating in one or more grand balls. It announces the arrival of young women of the upper class into adult society with the utmost of formality and elegance. These highly expensive rituals, in which great attention is lavished on every detail of the food, decorations, and entertainment, have a long history in the upper class. Making their appearance in Philadelphia in 1748 and Charleston, South Carolina, in 1762, they vary only slightly from city to city across the country.[21]

Describing the social function of this ball, Baltzell affirms that it is "a *rite de passage* which functions to introduce the post-adolescent into the upper-class adult world, and to insure upper-class endogamy as a normative pattern of behavior."[22]

In 1960, Lucy Kavaler listed 155 debutante balls in 31 states, all modeled after the balls of New York, Philadelphia, Charleston, and Baltimore. Kavaler described their inestimable social significance: "To millions of Americans the debut stands as the ultimate in social recognition. Today, presentation at one of the major debutante balls has come to be *the* criterion by which a girl becomes known as a member of society. And this acceptance carries over to her family as well."[23]

Charleston's St. Cecilia Society provides an example of this. Founded in 1737 as a concert society, this group holds an annual ball that only its members and special guests may attend. The full list of prerequisites for admission of new members has never been published; however, they are known to be very strict. Traditionally, neither actors nor actresses were permitted to attend the ball; this prohibition also held for divorced and remarried people. A member's daughter who marries a non-member may still be present at the ball, but she cannot be accompanied by her husband or children.[24]

The Philadelphia Assembly, first held in 1748, has been ranked among the most aristocratic balls in the United States, and it always gathered the best of Philadelphia's upper society. Historian Nathaniel Burt states:

---

[21] Domhoff, *Who Rules America Now?*, p. 32.

[22] Baltzell, *Philadelphia Gentlemen*, p. 60.

[23] Kavaler, *The Private World of High Society*, pp. 131-132.

[24] Cf. Amory, *Who Killed Society?*, pp. 90-91, and Birmingham, *America's Secret Aristocracy*, pp. 149-152.

> [The] Philadelphia Assembly...is probably still the most august of America's so-
> cial occasions.... Admission to the Assembly is, or is supposed to be, strictly he-
> reditary in the male line. That is, sons and daughters of members are eligible, though
> not automatically, when they reach a proper age. If a daughter marries out of the
> Assembly, she stays out. A son however can marry anybody and stay in.[25]

The 1793 assembly was held in George Washington's honor, giving rise to one of the Assembly's longstanding traditions: a toast to the Father of our Country.

In Baltimore, soon after the war of 1812, when the city's great patrician fami-lies were at their apex, the Bachelors Cotillon was born, an annual affair directed by the men of the city's most traditional circles. The Bachelors Cotillon—one of the country's oldest debutante balls—has been a model for similar cotillions in other cities and states.

In New York, the social affairs of the city form a kind of pyramid structure at whose peak are the most exclusive social events of the old families, while the less elevated levels in the upper class have their own balls. In addition to the New York families of the "Old Guard" who stage their own exclusive balls for the presentation of debutantes, some of the patriotic and hereditary associations, such as the Saint Nicholas Society of the City of New York and the General Society of Mayflower Descendants, present members or members' daughters at annual balls and dinners.

Balls promoted by similar associations revolve around the traditional elites of each region and highlight the social life of many cities like Atlanta, Fort Worth, St. Louis, New Orleans, Los Angeles, and Chicago.

e. Traditional associations of other ethnic groups

As we have seen, the traditional elites in American society are largely made up of the old families, which, in ethnic terms, signifies families of European, predominantly Anglo-Saxon, origin.

As might be expected, families of a more recent immigration and of different ethnic origins adopted American customs and styles through the generations and gradually became integral elements of the American elites. In addition to this, within their own communities they established their own social hierarchy.

Few people realize, for example, that among black Americans there flourishes an elite with its own intense social life, debuts, clubs, and old families, which plays within its own milieu a role equivalent to that of the traditional elites in American society as a whole.

---

[25] Burt, *The Perennial Philadelphians*, pp. 95, 278.

Lifting Our Gaze Toward the Alienated Elites

Purely ideological debates on the issues of equality and inequality—and especially on the subject of monarchy-aristocracy-democracy—have not customarily occupied center stage in the United States. Only in the years immediately following independence did a debate of this nature have some import in American political life. An example of this was the controversy between Jefferson and Adams over the correct interpretation of the American Revolution. While the former adopted a position more akin to the Jacobin faction of the French Revolution, the latter upheld the more moderate principles of the English Enlightenment.[1]

After a consensus was reached on the republican and democratic form of government, the focus of American political debate shifted to other areas, whose ideological nature was more implicit than explicit, such as taxation, administration, regional disputes, territorial expansion, and so forth. These issues only indirectly reflected the aristocracy-democracy controversy, which still continued to hold center stage in Europe's political debate as well as in its intellectual and cultural life. The only issue with a more clear-cut ideological nature that sparked a passionate debate in the United States was slavery.

One effect of this ideological vacuum was that Americans increasingly began to consider political life, and the State itself, as merely a means to promote the material progress and well-being of the population. The ideological foundation of policy was seldom considered.

As this pragmatic politics became the norm, social life was relegated to a secondary plane, since it was not considered important for the nation's progress, but merely a question of etiquette, gallantry, and honor. A dichotomy was created between political life and social life. The same men who would violently disagree in the political arena could live together amenably in the social sphere.

After the Second World War both the general public and intellectuals began to show growing interest in the subtleties and complexities of social life. Numer-

---

[1]   Cf., for example, Peterson, *Thomas Jefferson and The New Nation*, p. 443.

ous books and essays highlighted the importance of these questions. This revival of interest in social issues coincided with a growing public discontent regarding political life. Gradually, the politician lost his status as an authentic representative of the people and increasingly came to be seen as an opportunist. Large sectors of public opinion formed the conviction that the democratic system had become flawed since the dominant parties no longer represented the people's true sentiments and interests.

This frustration with the political class is escalating and expresses itself by pointing out the moral or financial scandals of elected officials. But the deeper issue of this discontent lies in the contrast between the democratic myth Americans learn from elementary school and the real situation they are confronted with every day.

Americans are indoctrinated with a notion of direct democracy drawn from the democracy that flourished in Athens, where the great orators debated the current issues before the whole people, who would later vote to decide the destiny of the city-state. This notion is reinforced by an idealized vision of the town-hall meetings in the small villages of New England in the colonial period, where the citizens participated fully in public life by casting their votes in the local assemblies. But few Americans believe that today's democracy corresponds to this idealized notion. Somewhere along the course of American history this ideal democracy seems to have been derailed.

In face of this overwhelming disillusionment with political life, a growing number of discerning Americans are turning their eyes toward the elites who still thrive in the nation's social life. They see them as a sector from which hope may yet come. For these people, the authentic elites better embody the aspirations of America and are thus more capable of providing adequate solutions to the nation's quandary.[2]

This concern and the hopes it generates could still change the course of American history. May this work serve as a contribution to this process, that it may find its proper course and produce the desired solutions.

---

[2] This return of the social sphere to the center stage of American life may take surprising twists. For example, who would imagine that a vanguard leftist magazine like the *Utne Reader* would encourage its readers throughout the country to establish conversation salons in the manner of the old literary salons of the upper society of Paris and New York? In an article published by the *New York Times* on April 13, 1992, Jonathan Rabinovitz reports that the *Utne Reader* sees these salons as a means to realize a social movement in the spirit of the 1990s. The idea has been well received. To date, more than five hundred salons have been organized by readers of the magazine. Thus the salons, which served so well to foment and spread revolutionary ideas in eighteenth-century France, are now being revived with similar goals in contemporary America. This indicates a new appetite for conversation within a context that is more social than political, and could considerably influence the very structure of American democracy.

Genesis, Development, and Twilight of the "Nobility of the Land" in Colonial, Imperial, and Republican Brazil

The Importance of the Incorporation of Analogous Elements into the Original Nobility

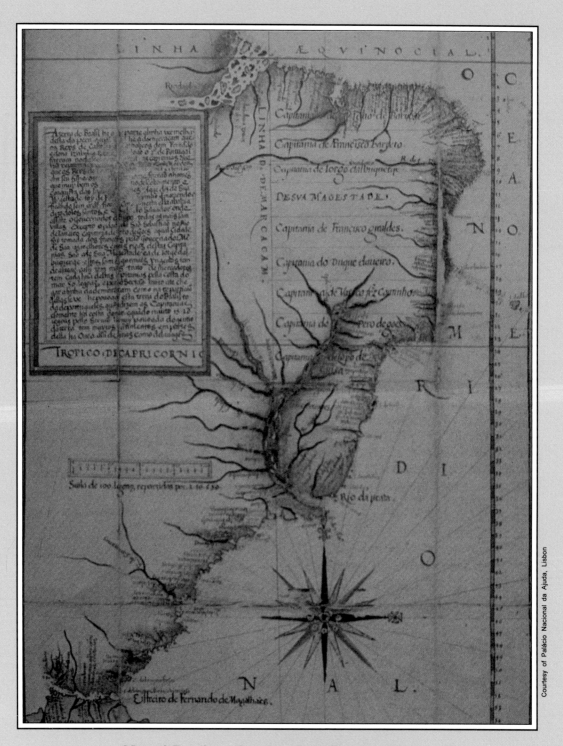

Map of Brazil attributed to Luis Teixeira, 1586.
(Biblioteca da Ajuda, Lisbon)

Introduction

$\mathcal{T}$he study of elites analogous to the nobility is of interest to both Europe and the New World. This interest may be even greater in the latter. In some parts of the Americas, as in Europe, there was a defined noble class with juridical status; however, this class did not exercise as dominant a role in the history of any American nation as the nobility did in the Old World. For a long period, the propelling role in society belonged rather to the aristocratic elites formed organically in America, which incorporated nobles from Europe.

These traditional elites had a dominant role because of their number, their social and economic functions, and their generally harmonious relationship with the lower classes.

For those interested in the study of aristocracy, the subject of analogous elites provides a good starting point for useful considerations on the types of nobility that could come into existence in contemporary society. These types could arise if a monarchical government were to dedicate itself to forming new variations of nobility around the historical nobility. Because of their traditional outlook, these new variations would not be a perch for social climbers. In this way, innovative forms of nobility would appear. They would coexist harmoniously with the original nobility or eventually become part of it. This development is all the more possible today since there is much talk of restoring monarchy in several countries.

By way of example, some brief historical data about the formation of such analogous elites in Brazil is presented here.

The reader will thus become acquainted with the organic formation of early elites in the states of Pernambuco and Bahia and, to a certain extent, in other regions of northeastern Brazil, during the so-called sugarcane socioeconomic cycle.

To stimulate the planting of sugarcane, and thereby consolidate the colonization of the land and increase economic production, the Portuguese Crown granted some nobiliary privileges to planters who owned sugar mills (*engenhos*). These planters, called *senhores de engenho* (sugar mill lords), formed an aristocratic class, a de facto nobility.

Among the rural elite, there were also aristocratic Portuguese families who had emigrated to the thriving South American colony. As the area of cultivated land expanded, new landowners who did not belong to the initial elite appeared.

These different categories of landowners naturally blended into a single elite. This elite gradually prospered, raised its standard of living and refined its manners.

Urban elites spontaneously formed through an analogous process. The number of villages in Brazil was growing, and many of them were steadily on the way to becoming cities. An original elite formed in these urban centers. It was mainly comprised of officials occupying high civil or military posts, which at that time conferred nobility. They were joined by a number of Portuguese nobles or *fidalgos*[1] who had moved to the Colony.

At the same time, the demands of urban life led to the arrival of professionals (such as doctors and merchants) whose civil status and economic level were clearly distinct from those of manual laborers. They formed a category known as *homens novos* (new men). In the restricted circles of relationships in the villages and cities of the time, these people frequently dealt with members of the elite. The contact between them naturally led to a gradual fusion of the two into an urban aristocracy.

Together with members of the rural aristocracy, the urban aristocrats formed the leading class in the area, and therefore usually held the main public offices. The members of this leading class were called *homens bons* (good men).

Subsequent socioeconomic cycles—the gold, precious stones, and coffee cycles—saw similar processes. The similarity was due not to imitation, but to an easily understandable analogy of circumstances.

Brazilian society and the emerging nation needed the impulse of leading elites, whose qualitative and numerical growth was furthered by the gradual assimilation of analogous elements. Clearly, the formation of such analogous elements and their assimilation by the elites were in the interest of the common good.

The formation of nobility and analogous elites in Spanish America differed from that in Brazil. The complexity of the problems encountered in the formation and expansion of elites throughout Latin America and the originality of the solutions were prodigious.

* * *

These notes on the Brazilian nobility in colonial, royal, and imperial times are intended to show the profoundly natural way in which the nobiliary class was formed, especially in the early period of Brazil's history. They also serve to illustrate the organic process that shaped elites analogous to the nobility and provided natural access to the nobility.

There is no intention to present here a full picture of the Brazilian or Luso-

---

[1]   *Fidalgos* are the sons of nobles who do not themselves inherit a title.

Brazilian nobility as it was at the time of Brazilian independence (1822) nor all the modifications suffered by this class due to subsequent imperial legislation, which was strongly influenced by the spirit of the French Revolution.[2]

---

[2] Regarding the Brazilian nobility, see, for example, António José Victoriano Borges da Fonseca, *Nobiliarchia Pernambucana* (Rio de Janeiro: Biblioteca Nacional, 1935); Carvalho Franco, *Nobiliário Colonial*, 2d ed. (São Paulo); Fernando de Azevedo, *Obras Completas*, 2d ed., Vol. 11, *Canaviais e Engenhos na Vida Política do Brasil* (Edições Melhoramentos); Gilberto Freyre, *Interpretação do Brasil* (Rio de Janeiro: José Olympio Editora, 1947); Lt. Col. Henrique Wiederspahn, "A Evolução da Nobreza Cavalheiresca e Militar Luso-Brasileira desde o Descobrimento até a República," in *Boletim do Colégio de Armas e Consulta Heráldica do Brasil*, no. 1, (1955); J. Capistrano de Abreu, *Capítulos da História Colonial (1500-1800)*, 4th ed. (Sociedade Capistrano de Abreu, 1954); Luís Palacin, *Sociedade Colonial—1549 a 1599* (Goiânia: Universidade Federal de Goiás, 1981); Manoel Rodrigues Ferreira, *As Repúblicas Municipais no Brasil (1532-1820)* (São Paulo: Prefeitura do Município de São Paulo, 1980); Nelson Omegna, *A Cidade Colonial* (Rio de Janeiro: José Olympio Editora, 1961); Nelson Werneck Sodré, *Formação da Sociedade Brasileira* (Rio de Janeiro: José Olympio Editora, 1944); Nestor Duarte, *A Ordem Privada e a Organização Política Nacional* (São Paulo: Companhia Editora Nacional, 1939); F. J. Oliveira Vianna, *Instituições Políticas Brasileiras* (Rio de Janeiro: José Olympio Editora, 1955); Rui Vieira da Cunha, *Estudo da Nobreza Brasileira* and *Figuras e Fatos da Nobreza Brasileira* (Rio de Janeiro: Arquivo Nacional, 1966 and 1975, respectively).

The discovery of Brazil. Painting by B. Calixto.
(Museu Paulista, São Paulo)

CHAPTER I

How Elites Were Formed in Colonial Brazil

1. The First Settlers

a. The lower classes

For the most part, the settling of Luso-America was done by members of the humble classes of Portugal. F. J. Oliveira Vianna describes them as

> plebeians, tillers from Minho, Trás-os-Montes, the Beiras, or Estremadura—sober and honorable men, although of modest means, "men with qualities," as can be read in some of the letters from the *sesmarias*[1]—who request lands. Taking their large and small cattle, in obscurity and silence they gradually settle the fields and woods of the hinterland.[2]

These humble classes were not exclusively peasant. Alfredo Ellis, Jr., affirms: "When colonizing Brazil, Portugal sent over bourgeois, with urban or semi-urban commercial backgrounds and without ties to the soil."[3]

Among the first settlers there were also a number of exiles, but they were far from being a majority. Oliveira Lima writes:

> The legend that Brazil was colonized by exiles has already been disproved. Nor were exiles necessarily criminals, in the modern sense. Offenses that were not ignominious, and even simple misconduct by good people, were often punished with banishment. Portugal's two greatest poets, Camões and Bocage, were both exiled to India.[4]

---

[1] A *sesmaria* was uncultivated or abandoned land which the kings of Portugal granted to farmers, *sesmeiros*.

[2] F. J. Oliveira Vianna, *Populações Meridionais do Brasil*, 3d ed. (São Paulo: Companhia Editora Nacional), Vol. 1, p. 15.

[3] Alfredo Ellis, Jr., "Amador Bueno e Seu Tempo," in *Colecção História da Civilização Brasileira*, Vol. 7, no. 86 (São Paulo: Universidade de São Paulo, 1948), p. 61.

[4] Oliveira Lima, *O Movimento da Independência—1821-1822* (São Paulo: Companhia Melhoramentos de São Paulo, 1922), pp. 28-29.

There were also some fugitives who found sanctuary in the New World from punishment for illegal actions committed in Portugal, since King John III had determined that "whoever settles here shall not be prosecuted for crimes committed elsewhere."[5]

Over the centuries, Christianized Indians joined the new social context, usually as manual laborers, since the Church relentlessly opposed their enslavement. Besides the Indians, there were black slaves from Africa. Numerous in Brazil, they were also to be found in one or another Spanish colony.

b. The aristocrats and the men of letters

During the colonization, people belonging to higher levels of society also came over. On account of their learning or birth, they were better suited to public office, whether civil or ecclesiastical. They imparted elements of culture to the rustic atmosphere of the new colony.

Among them ranked the governors-general, the provincial governors, and the viceroys, as well as the lord proprietors of the original *capitanias*[6]—all nobles—who actually lived on their lands for a time: Duarte Coelho, of Pernambuco, Martim Afonso de Sousa, of São Vicente, and others.

Referring to the first settlers of the *capitania* of Pernambuco, Carlos Xavier Paes Barreto asserts that "the settlers of northeastern Brazil were not exclusively from the ignorant masses.... Many of those who landed in New Lusitania were descendants of accomplished magistrates and statesmen."[7] Historian Alfredo Ellis adds:

> It was only natural that Portugal would send over people from all social levels. While the bourgeoisie predominated in the settling of Brazil, it is evident that members of the old aristocracy also came over in the early days; these were men with coats of arms who easily found their stirps represented in the [royal palace's] *sala de Cintra*.[8]

Regarding these Portuguese nobles, Oliveira Lima emphasizes that "it was not the great nobles, the powerful representatives of high lineages...who crossed the ocean. It was the representatives of the lesser nobility, the *fidalgos*, the military class."[9] As Oliveira Vianna writes: "It was precisely this lesser nobility that most contributed to the formation of the Brazilian and the Spanish-

---

[5] Pedro Calmon, *História do Brasil* (Rio de Janeiro: Livraria José Olympio Editora, 1959), Vol. 1, p. 170.

[6] *Capitanias*: vast land grants from the Portuguese Crown, analogous to the proprietorships granted by the English Crown in North America.

[7] Carlos Xavier Paes Barreto, *Os Primitivos Colonizadores Nordestinos e Seus Descendentes* (Rio de Janeiro: Editora Melso, 1960), p. 20.

[8] Ellis, "Amador Bueno e Seu Tempo," p. 62.

[9] Oliveira Lima, *O Movimento da Independência*, p. 27.

American nobilities. Poorly off when not impoverished, they emigrated to 'make it in America,' hoping to remedy the poverty they endured on the [Iberian] Peninsula."[10]

c. The Faith: a requirement

Some commentators of Brazilian history allege that the Portuguese colonization was motivated predominantly by economic interests and that the evangelizing ideal was very secondary or even mere lip-service to religious traditions with remnants of influence in Portugal.

This was not so. The missionary effort was given great importance by the kings of Portugal and the entire Portuguese nation. The Royal Decree of December 17, 1548, given to Tomé de Sousa by John III, states: "The main reason that led me to order the colonization of the lands of Brazil was [the desire] that its people convert to our holy Catholic Faith."[11] That is why all the early colonizers—whether plebeians, bourgeois, or nobles—were required to profess complete adherence to the Catholic Faith, even if they were not Portuguese.

> The colonizers of Brazil were not concerned about unity or purity of race. Throughout most of the sixteenth century the Colony was open to foreigners, and the only thing that mattered to the colonial authorities was that they belong to the Catholic Faith or Religion. Handelmann notes that the main prerequisite for admission as a settler in sixteenth-century Brazil was adherence to the Christian religion: "only Christians"—which in Portugal meant Catholics—"could obtain *sesmarias*."...
>
> During certain colonial periods it was common for a friar to board every ship that docked at Brazilian ports to examine the conscience, faith, and religion of the newcomers. Immigrants were barred only for heterodoxy, for the stain of heresy in the soul and not for a deformity of the body. Religious health was what mattered.... The friar would board the ship to interrogate individuals about orthodoxy, as today one inquires about health and race....
>
> "The Portuguese disregards race and considers as his equals those who profess the same religion as he."
>
> This solidarity lasted gloriously throughout our whole colonial period. It united us against French Calvinists, Dutch Reformists, and English Protestants. That is why *Brazilian* and *Catholic* are so difficult to separate. Catholicism was really the bond of our unity.[12]

---

[10]   Oliveira Vianna, *Instituições Políticas Brasileiras*, p. 174.

[11]   John III, *Regimento de Tomé de Sousa* (Biblioteca Nacional de Lisboa, Arquivo da Marinha), Book I (dispatches).

[12]   Gilberto Freyre, *Casa-Grande & Senzala*, 5th ed. (São Paulo: Editora José Olympio, 1946), Vol. 1, pp. 121-123.

Martim Afonso de Sousa,
Lord Proprietor of São Vicente.
(Museu Paulista, São Paulo)

Founding of São Vicente. Painting by B. Calixto.
(Museu Paulista, São Paulo)

2. Genesis and Development
   of the Colony's First Elites

The interaction of these factors slowly and organically formed a select group composed of diverse elements. Rustic and unrefined in most of its members, this elite—or rudiment of an elite—mirrored the early living conditions on this lush and wild continent.

The members of this initial elite maintained a certain equality in their social relationships and living standards. This is not surprising, given their small number and the psychological pressure of the adverse living conditions imposed by a nature barely touched by man. With the successive generations, differentiation occurred and the elite became stratified.

a. Ennoblement in recognition
   of military feats

The cream of this elite included the individuals who had shown outstanding military courage in the fights against the Indians or in the wars against foreign heretics—mainly Dutch and French[13]—who had come over with both mercantile and religious intentions.

Generally speaking, this was the characteristic of the nobility on the Old Continent. The military class par excellence was that of the feudal lords. They, more than any of their countrymen, shed their blood for the spiritual and temporal common good. This immolation placed the nobles in a position analogous to that of the martyrs. The heroism they usually displayed proved the integrity of soul with which they accepted their immolation. Consequently, they were entitled to exceptional privileges and honors.

The elevation of a plebeian combatant to the nobility or the promotion of a noble combatant to a higher degree of nobility was therefore a just and appropriate reward for military valor.

Naturally, this conception of the military class was reflected in the way Brazilian colonial society was formed. According to Oliveira Vianna, many of those who requested *sesmarias* would justify their claims by

---

[13] In the sixteenth and seventeenth centuries, Protestants had a marked influence in what is today Holland and part of Belgium. Due to Catholic expansion in Holland over the last decades, many people do not realize it once was a great international Protestant bulwark: a fact that must be kept in mind if one is to understand the Dutch invasions of Brazil.

Something similar can be said of France, where Protestantism was not as dominant but was still a significant power. Louis XIV sought to neutralize it with the revocation of the Edict of Nantes in 1685 and with his famous *dragonades*. Neither measure succeeded in exterminating Protestantism in France. Nevertheless, by forcing the nonconforming Protestants to leave the country *en masse*, he dealt Protestantism a heavy blow from which it never recovered. Protestantism (especially Calvinism) was reduced to a totally secondary position in that country. But the situation was still very different when Villegagnon attacked Rio de Janeiro.

The French attempt to land in Maranhão, however, was of a completely different nature. The invaders were Catholics, and to them is owed the fact that the state capital of Maranhão is named São Luis.

showing their wounds, their mutilations, their body cut by the sword of a Norman, a Breton, or a Fleming, or pierced by the arrow of an Indian. With this they entered into *possession of the land*, which was the principal nobility.... It was military bravery that dignified the person and assured him access to the nobility and aristocracy.[14]

b. Ennoblement in recognition of acts of bravery in pioneering

While some distinguished themselves by their military courage, others stood out for their bravery in other fields. As Oliveira Vianna explains, "in colonial society, as in the Middle Ages, selection is...on the basis of bravery, valor, and 'virtue' in the Roman sense of the word."[15] Therefore, those who had a prominent role in the arduous task of pioneering our immense uncultivated territory also belonged to the highest level of society. L. Amaral Gurgel praises

> those Titans of the colonial period; that notable race whose sons, with their fierce countenances, leather clothes, and strong arms, shouldering the conquering blunderbusses, explored the inhospitable territories of the north and south; who, in the words of Taunay "pushed the meridians of Alexander VI and of Tordesillas practically to the foothills of the Andes by crossing the harsh jungle fraught with dangers and mysteries."[16]

c. Ennoblement in recognition of lordship over land and people

As Brazil's population increased, farming and ranching expanded in the large tracts of land granted as *sesmarias* by the Portuguese kings. These activities also called for heroism.

> During the colonial period, the taming of the land is an essentially military undertaking. An arduous military ordeal precedes the clearing of every latifundium, the settling of every *sesmaria*, the building of every corral, the construction of every sugar mill. From north to south, the first steps of agriculture and ranching are taken with a sword in hand.
>
> The usual process of taming the land begins with a "settlement." This means clearing the land, fending off Indians, hunting down wild beasts, tilling the land, and starting herds. Only then can the settler claim the *sesmaria*.[17]

---

[14] Oliveira Vianna, *Instituições Políticas Brasileiras*, pp. 177-178.

[15] Oliveira Vianna, *Populações Meridionais do Brasil*, Vol. 1, p. 102.

[16] L. Amaral Gurgel, *Ensaios Quinhentistas* (São Paulo: Editora J. Fagundes, 1936), p. 174.

[17] F. J. Oliveira Vianna, *O Povo Brasileiro e a Sua Evolução* (Rio de Janeiro: Ministério da Agricultura, Indústria, e Comércio—Directoria Geral de Estatística, Tipografia da Estatística, 1922), p. 19.

The large landowners then appeared. Developing thriving and profitable estates, they built homes for their families in the country and in the city. Their dwellings were often luxurious, and at times, like medieval castles, served as fortresses.

These landowners were patriarchs at the head of a numerous progeny. They had seignorial rights over an impressive number of subordinates, both slaves and freemen, and often held some powers inherent to the State.

João Alfredo Corrêa de Oliveira,[18] describing his uncle and father-in-law, the Baron of Goiana, writes in this regard:

> He belonged to the affectionate generations that paid homage to these memories; those strong generations that loved the land, in which they saw their liberty and independence glitter like gold, and whence they reaped the twin harvest of riches and virtues. To live by one's own efforts and the grace of God; to accumulate wealth through wise economy and wholesome sobriety; to follow a profession that does not seek another's money nor depend on deceit and fallacy; to feel oneself firmly established on indestructible property, which remains when others devaluate and pass away; to own an inexhaustible source of subsistence, which is the well-cultivated soil; to acquire from it energy, perseverance, and patience—all this seemed to them, and is, the most secure and dignified position. For these generations, inherited land was a family entail and a coat of arms that, like honor, was dearer than life.[19]

The moral profile and the juridical status of the great planters were similar to those of feudal lords. This is why historians have compared the socioeconomic structure of colonial Brazil to feudalism.

Very understandably, this category was incorporated to the dominant social elite, as Oliveira Vianna emphasizes. When describing "what occurred across the country in the colonial centuries," he quotes an author from northeastern Brazil: "To own inherited lands was a sign of nobility. This ownership was supposed to continue undivided in the hands of descendants."[20]

---

[18] Councillor João Alfredo Corrêa de Oliveira, born on December 12, 1835, was familiar with the situation he describes here. His family was among the most eminent sugar mill families of Goiana and was related to almost all the seignorial families of Pernambuco. Exceptionally intelligent, he graduated from the Olinda Law School and embarked on a brilliant political career in which he attained the highest posts in the Imperial government. He served as a senator, a member of the Emperor's council, and prime minister. He was one of the most active leaders of the abolitionist movement and as prime minister signed with Princess Isabel, the Regent of the Empire, the Golden Law of May 13, 1888, which abolished slavery in Brazil. When the Republic was proclaimed in 1889, he remained faithful to the monarchical ideals, becoming a member of the Monarchical Directorate, to which Princess Isabel entrusted the task of guiding the action of Brazilian monarchists. He died in Rio de Janeiro on March 6, 1919.

[19] João Alfredo Corrêa de Oliveira, "O Barão de Goiana e Sua Época Genealógica," in *Minha Meninice & Outros Ensaios* (Recife: Editora Massangana, 1988), p. 56.

[20] Oliveira Vianna, *Instituições Políticas Brasileiras*, Vol. 1, pp. 256-257.

d. Ennoblement in recognition of the exercise of civil and military authority

With time, other categories of people would enter the elite in another way.

Exercising command, even in the private sphere, has always been considered intrinsically honorable, since there is greater honorability in the function of directing than in that of obeying or serving.

When a person designated by a superior authority exercises command in the public sphere in name of the State, he is like a personification of public authority. He should receive proportional honors, for he is like a projection of the holder of supreme power. His preeminence lasts as long as he holds office. When divested of his office and reduced to the condition of a private person, he is left in a situation of *capitis deminutio.* He becomes a detached and incomplete person, like a clam wrenched from its shell. His life becomes a melancholic wait for death, as it were.

However, in Europe—from which we received our Faith and civilization, and with them our ways of feeling and acting—public offices were frequently held for life when the nature of their exercise demanded all the activity and thought of the holder. The holder became one with his position. Dedicated to the office in this way, he was able to consecrate the best of himself to it. The office was not divorced from his personal interests, unlike what usually happens in today's systems of government and administration. Life-terms created ideal conditions for honesty and dedication in office.

Applying these considerations to the higher offices, which gradually became more important and complex in the small but growing state apparatus of colonial Brazil, it is not difficult to understand why their holders naturally became part of the elite. Commenting on the qualities and offices that the inhabitants of the cities and towns had to have in order to be considered nobles, Nelson Omegna mentions that "public servants and the military numbered among the best classes."[21]

Even when an important office was temporary, something of its inherent distinction remained with its former holder. Along with his wife and children, he could continue to belong to the social elite, in keeping with the saying, "A king never loses his majesty."

e. The familial essence of the elites

The previous sections described the different ways in which individuals distinguished themselves by their personal qualities and thereby entered the social elite that would later form the Brazilian nobility.

Since the aristocracy is essentially a familial institution, the social promotion attained by an individual was ipso facto extended to his spouse. *"Erunt duo in*

---

[21]   Omegna, *A Cidade Colonial*, p. 124.

carne una"—"they are two in one flesh" (Matt. 19:6), says the Gospel of husband and wife. It is natural that the children would also belong to the same elite. Families, then, more than a group of individuals, were the seed of the future Brazilian nobility. "The family," Gilberto Freyre points out, "and not the individual, the State, or any merchant company, has been the main colonizing force in Brazil since the sixteenth century,...constituting the most powerful colonial aristocracy of America."[22]

3. The "Nobility of the Land"

a. Constitutive elements and formation

The colonial elite was formed by the inter-marriage of the descendants of the first settlers adorned with the prestige of being founders of the New World; the valiant and often heroic pioneers; the heroic defenders of the land against foreigners and heretics; the early farmers and ranchers, who established the foundations of a more stable economy and were influential by the wealth of their patrimonies; and the holders of high- and medium-level administrative offices, respected because of the very nature of their powers. These descendants began to live in spacious mansions, often decorated with objects from Portugal or its colonies in India or the Far East. These mansions were built in constantly growing cities that were embellished by churches of great artistic merit, especially in the states of Bahia, Pernambuco, and Minas Gerais.

The arts and culture of the Brazilian colony were enriched by Brazilians who studied at Coimbra and other European universities. They made possible the founding of similar educational institutions in Brazil. This amounted to a true cultural emancipation.

This elite assumed so many characteristics of an aristocracy in the making, or already made, that it was commonly called the "nobility of the land." Brandonio, author of *Diálogo das Grandezas do Brasil*, describes this elite-forming process when he answers the objection that there could not be a true nobility in Brazil since most of the first colonizers were not noble.

> You should know that these first settlers in Brazil soon became rich due to the abundance of the land. With their wealth, they gradually abandoned the rustic nature their poverty in Portugal had imposed on them. Enthroned on this wealth and this lordship over the land, their children shed the old skin as a snake does and acquired most honorable manners. Many high nobles and *fidalgos* also came to this country and married into this class, in such a way that all came to have a common blood that is truly noble.[23]

---

[22] Freyre, *Casa-Grande & Senzala*, p. 107.

[23] Brandonio, *Diálogo das Grandezas do Brasil* (Rio de Janeiro: 1943), p. 155.

Commenting on the formation of this elite in Brazil, Luís Palacin concludes: "With the adoption of common lifestyles and ideals and the holding of the same privileges, already by the end of the sixteenth century an authentic colonial nobility had taken shape from the fusion of such varied elements."[24] According to Palacin, this nobility

> comprised the high-ranking public servants and their families, the sugar mill lords and the great landholders, the most important merchants, and the first settlers. This group, which in time would tend to progressively close itself off, but which was then still sufficiently open due to the conditions of the new settlement, was known as the *homens bons* [good men], who were registered at the town hall.[25]

This organic process of class differentiation in colonial society was stressed by Fernando de Azevedo when he referred to the social organization, which was

> separated into classes, or better, into strata, not necessarily defined by law but regulated by tradition and customs. The upper level was constituted by the rural aristocracy. This aristocracy had privileges such as private jurisdiction, and immunities, principally exemption from taxes. It was above the bourgeoisie (merchants and artisans), the tillers, and the slaves. This feudal style of organization was not transplanted from the motherland, but was born spontaneously in the Colony as a result of the peculiar conditions of the colonization of these newly-discovered lands.[26]

b. Characteristics that distinguished the Brazilian nobility from the European nobility

Thus was formed the nobility of the land, the apex of the social structure during the Brazilian colonial period.

Like Europe of the time, the new colony rightly believed that the leadership of progress and the choice of direction for the country belonged to the elites. It was imperative, therefore, that the elites be constituted in an authentic and vigorous way so that their leadership would be vigorous and their choice of direction wise.

The very haste in forming this elite led an initial group of settlers to assimilate others, who for various reasons already enjoyed merited distinction and therefore could join the initial group without depreciating or degrading it. This embryonic nobility of the land grew to its proper dimensions by incorporating persons and families that, under various titles, were on par with it.

---

[24] Luís Palacin, *Sociedade Colonial—1549 a 1599* (Goiânia: Editora da Universidade Federal de Goiás, 1981), p. 186

[25] Ibid., p. 181.

[26] Azevedo, *Canaviais e Engenhos*, p. 86.

Organically chosen in view of local needs, this means of expansion differed from that in several European countries, where parallel elites long remained distinct from the nobility. Later, some of them did become authentic nobilities, yet they merely paralleled the nobility par excellence, which continued to be the military nobility.

The rise of non-noble elites in Europe could be divided into three stages:

1. Elements of the common people who shared a certain preeminence formed a group that gradually became a class;

2. This class built a tradition of abnegated and successful service to the spiritual or temporal common good. It grew continuously in distinction and respectability;

3. Already akin to the nobility, it became, by force of custom or by law, a nobility *diminutae rationis*, as the French *noblesse de robe* (nobility of the robe) was for a long time.

Social relationships, common lifestyles, and marriages strengthened the ties between the two nobilities.

Then came the Revolution of 1789. It is difficult to know what the outcome of this development would have been if this hecatomb had not destroyed both nobilities. Most probably they would have blended.

This historical march, dictated by the specific social and political circumstances of European development, is appreciably different from the process that led to the formation of Brazil's nobility of the land.

* * *

To what degree was this nobility of the land an authentic nobility, recognized as such by the public authorities in Lisbon, the kingdom's capital, during the whole colonial period? And what effect did the presence of the Portuguese Court in Brazil from 1808 to 1821 have on this order of things? How was the nobility of the land affected by independence and by the Empire that followed? And what about the Republic? These are additional questions this overview raises. Some of them will be dealt with now.

The *bandeirante* António Raposo Tavares.
(Museu Paulista, São Paulo)

The Socioeconomic Cycles of Brazil and the History of the Nobility of the Land

*B*razil's socioeconomic history is divided into several cycles. While not all authors agree on a criterion for this division, some point to four cycles: the brazilwood cycle, the sugarcane cycle, the gold and precious stones cycle, and the coffee cycle.

Each cycle is named after the commodity that was the mainstay of the national economy in a given period. This does not mean that when a cycle began, the exploitation of the previously dominant commodity automatically ceased, but simply that it was no longer the main source of income for the country. On the other hand, this division does not exclude the existence of other commodities that marked Brazil's economy; for example, cattle, cacao, tobacco, and rubber.

What most characterizes these cycles is not the systems and techniques of production and exploitation of the land, nor the conditions of the environment where they developed, but rather their influence on society. Fernando de Azevedo affirms:

> These cycles encompassed enough factors to deserve the name "agrarian civilizations," such as those of sugar and coffee, each "civilization" referring both to natural conditions and human history. Each of these agricultural systems or regimes...not only profoundly influenced the institutions, but also tended to forge a particular lifestyle and mentality.... The full understanding of the structure of an agrarian system [requires] a penetrating inquiry into the principles or norms that govern a rural community, the types of social relations and the juridical framework that, having been created for them, consolidates tradition, laws, and customs.[1]

1. The Brazilwood Cycle and the *Capitanias*

Trade in brazilwood began three years after the discovery of Brazil. This wood was to be found on the Brazilian coast and was prized in European markets for

---

[1] Azevedo, *Canaviais e Engenhos*, p. 65.

the red dye extracted from it. The Portuguese manning the trading posts were in charge of felling the trees and stacking the wood in places convenient for shipping. This exploitation, done mostly by natives equipped with machetes and other tools provided by contractors, did not result in colonization.

Concerned with the defense of Brazil, John III decided to promote colonization by establishing the regime of hereditary *capitanias*, for which he chose "people willing to live in Brazil and rich enough to colonize it."[2] The king issued the first land grant on March 10, 1534, to Duarte Coelho. There were twelve initial *capitanias*, which the king of Portugal wanted to grant to "the best kind of people: old navigators, military leaders, personages of the Court."[3] This regime was "a type of feudalism."[4] Nestor Duarte affirms:

> On account of the tendency and development of their purpose, the *capitanias* are a feudal organization. The feudal institution is characterized in relation to the royal power by two features: full and hereditary land ownership, and the merging of sovereignty and property....
>
> These are mentioned in the charters completing the land grants. Therein is defined the economic hierarchy, for they are "a contract of perpetual emphyteusis by which the leaseholders who receive *sesmaria* lands agree to become perpetual tributaries of both the Crown and the lord proprietors, the *capitães-mores*." This is the feudal hierarchy, with the king at the top, the territorial lords below him, and the leaseholders (*sesmeiros*) and the peasants at the bottom.[5]

According to Rocha Pombo, in the *capitania* regime, the lord proprietor—who had the titles of Captain and Governor—was a deputy of the king. In the charter, the monarch granted him a portion of the *capitania* as full, immediate, and personal property. He was entitled only to the usufruct of the remaining land. He received the fruits of the fief the sovereign had given him. These fruits—the titles and benefits derived from the possession of the *capitania*—were inalienable and all of them were inherited by the eldest son. The younger sons came next in the line of succession, the legitimate sons taking precedence over any illegitimate ones.

Within the laws of the kingdom and the terms of the charter, the lord proprietor had rights of sovereignty. He had full jurisdiction over the civil and criminal courts; he nominated the *ouvidor*[6] and all court officials; he presided at the election of judges and aldermen, either in person or through the *ouvidor*.

The *capitão* also had the right to establish towns at his discretion and to dis-

---

[2] Calmon, *História do Brasil*, Vol. 1, p. 170.

[3] Ibid.

[4] Ibid.

[5] Nestor Duarte, *A Ordem Privada e a Organização Política Nacional*, pp. 42, 44.

[6] An *ouvidor*, in colonial days, was a justice of the peace appointed and maintained on their properties by the owners of land grants.

tribute lands to anyone (his wife and successor excluded) regardless of their social position, as long as they were Christians. All the salt works and all the water mills, as well as any other mills built in the *capitania*, belonged to him. He was entitled to a twentieth of all profits on the sale of brazilwood and fish, to a tithe on all the treasury's revenues, to a toll on the rivers, and to an annual pension of 500 *reis* to be paid by the village and town notaries in the *capitania*.

There was free commerce, both with Portugal and other countries, although the latter was subject to the royal tithe.

The settlers' rights and duties were stated in the charters. Justice as well as civil and political status were assured them by the laws and customs of the motherland. They were guaranteed the right to request and receive *sesmarias*, exemption from any tax not stipulated in the charter, complete freedom of commerce, and privilege over foreign merchants. Together with their people—sons, hired hands, and slaves—the settlers were obliged to follow the *capitão* in wartime.

The Crown retained a monopoly on brazilwood, spices, and drugs; a tithe on harvests and fishing; and a fifth on all precious stones and metals (after the *capitão*'s tithe).

The king assumed all the expenses of religious worship.[7]

Thus began the systematic occupation and colonization of the Brazilian soil. Pedro Calmon relates that when Duarte Coelho, the first *capitão*, "came to reside in his domains, he followed Martim Afonso's wise procedure in São Vicente: the village was founded, the cane planted, the sugar mill built, an understanding reached with the peaceful Indians, and a harsh chastisement inflicted on those who engaged in hostilities."[8]

2. The Sugarcane Cycle

The planting of sugarcane and the building of the sugar mill of which the historian speaks constituted the nascent agriculture that bound the people to the land.

So it was in the feudal setting of the *capitanias* that the sugarcane cycle began. "The planting of sugarcane brought from Madeira became the main activity in São Vicente, Espírito Santo, Bahia, Pernambuco, Ilhéus, and Itamaracá, as recommended and stipulated in the grants of the *capitanias* of Brazil.... The first planters were the lord proprietors themselves."[9]

At first, sugarcane planting was generally done by paid hands, for "the scarcity of imported black labor made it difficult for newcomers to build a sugar mill. The mills were few, then, and belonged to a territorial nobility related by marriage. This nobility developed slowly in poor surroundings where activity was necessarily tranquil."[10]

[7] Cf. Rocha Pombo, *História do Brasil* (Rio de Janeiro: W. M. Jackson Editores, 1942), Vol. 1, pp. 131-133.

[8] Calmon, *História do Brasil*, Vol. 1, p. 172.

[9] Ibid., Vol. 2, pp. 355, 356.

[10] Ibid., p. 358.

Vitoria do Paraguassu sugar mill. Engraving, ca. 1850.

Mataripe sugar mill. Watercolor, ca. 1875.

a. The rise of the "sugar mill lords"

Pedro Calmon refers to the "territorial nobility." Indeed, when the Crown exempted sugar from Portuguese port taxes, plantations and mills multiplied, creating a solid economic base. This consolidated the colonization and shaped the Brazilian social organization of the time by giving rise to a rural aristocracy.

> The prestige of their familial, economic, and religious organization—mansion, sugar mill, and chapel—and the power they acquired on their lands, make the great proprietors of the fertile coastal lands an agrarian aristocracy. Those "of good birth," the "fidalgos" of the time, either are or become sugar mill lords.[11]

Another author affirms that the most important social consequence of the Brazilian sugarcane cycle "was undoubtedly the emergence of the sugar mill lord and the clan that formed around him."

> A brief sketch of this seignorial influence begins with the ownership of the land. It soon brings us to the cultivation of the cane fields, whether in partnership or directly by the entrepreneurs. In the first case, we have the *sesmarias*; in the second we have the cooperation of poor neighbors, the "work gangs" and "helping hands" of true colonization. Both are based on slavery, however. The setting up of a sugar mill is more complicated. Wood has to be obtained for the fire and for the crates. Shipping is needed for bay, river and sea transportation. Then there are dealings with shippers, middle men, and, not rarely, international financiers. Once the production and population center is established, with its natural leaders and the consecutive grouping of human elements come the consequences of miscegenation, of seignorial omnipotence, of opulence or at least abundance that generally characterizes the regime....
>
> In short, this is what the sugarcane cycle meant for the development of Brazil. The first agricultural and industrial activity, it quickly became the dominant one in the first two centuries of national life, and characterized a whole region of the country during the Empire.[12]

b. The ambiances and customs of the sugar mill lords

Like the lord at the time of early feudalism in Europe, the mill lord originally led an austere and dangerous life that called for much courage. A description of the mill lord's house, a mixture of home and fortress like the feudal castle, illustrates this point: "The Great House [the name usually given the mill lord's manor] was also a military stronghold." In Mem de Sá's inventory, it is described

---

[11] Azevedo, *Canaviais e Engenhos*, p. 107.

[12] Hélio Vianna, *Formação Brasileira* (Rio de Janeiro: Livraria José Olympio Editora, 1935), pp. 36, 38, 39.

as "a newly built fortress-house, constructed with stone and lime, newly roofed and half floored, surrounded by wood for building porches, which are also to be floored." There was also a "covered bulwark surrounded with wattle and daub."[13]

Theodoro Sampaio, referring to the first century of colonization, writes: "The ranches were like armed camps. The landholders used to protect their dwellings and manors with a double row of heavy stakes like the gentile. Guarded by servants, dependents, and Indian slaves, the defenses were also a refuge for neighbors suddenly attacked by Indians."[14]

The subsequent economic progress made possible the building of more beautiful and comfortable homes.

> Manor houses with chapels, overlooking the tile-covered shed and the slave quarters, bear witness to the solidity of their owners' fortunes.... Successive generations knew how to maintain them within the tranquility of agricultural life, under the shadow of institutions that guaranteed the stability and continuity of the sugar mill, in a defensive isolation where the lords' sense of class, nationality, and autonomy developed with discreetness and dignity.[15]

To the mill lords' patriarchal authority and to their power and wealth, corresponded

> a grandeur and magnificence that were not overlooked by the chroniclers of the time and that deeply impressed foreign visitors. Everything in their vast and solid homes—some of stone and lime, others of adobe and bricks—denoted, along with wealth, the discretion and hospitality of the old patriarchal families, whose religious spirit is recorded in their ornamental crosses, oratories, and chapels.[16]

These seignorial residences were so splendid that when Labatut[17] was crossing the fields of Recôncavo on his way to lay siege to the city of Salvador and saw some of them in the distance, he exclaimed: "They look like principalities!"[18] This opulence was accompanied by a hospitality and abundance that impressed the Jesuit Father Fernão Cardim, who wrote:

> One thing that I really marveled at on this trip was the great ease with which they entertain guests. No matter what time of night or day we arrived, they quickly prepared food for the five of us (not counting the youths).... Their houses are so

---

[13] Pedro Calmon, *História do Brasil*, Vol. 2, p. 360.

[14] Freyre, *Casa-Grande & Senzala*, Vol. 1, p. 24.

[15] Calmon, *História do Brasil*, Vol. 3, p. 916.

[16] Azevedo, *Canaviais e Engenhos*, p. 80.

[17] Labatut was a French officer contracted by the government of the first Empire to command the Brazilian forces in the fight for the consolidation of independence.

[18] Azevedo, *Canaviais e Engenhos*, p. 48.

well stocked with everything that in their abundance they are like counts.[19]

The refinement of the residences was matched by the apparel of the ladies and gentlemen and by the splendor of their recreation. Oliveira Vianna writes:

> In *Valeroso Lucideno*[20] we read that any noble of seventeenth-century Pernambuco who did not own silver plate was considered destitute, and that the ladies' dress and adornment were so rich that "pearls, rubies, emeralds, and diamonds seem to have showered on their heads and necks."[21]

The same historian adds:

> The aristocrats of Pernambuco maintained the equestrian traditions from the time of Dom Duarte, the Knight King.... They loved bullfights, horse races, and cavalcades. They were superb horsemen, graceful and audacious; they excelled in the elegance and gentleness of their mounts, in the richness of their harnesses (all covered with silver), in their skill at bullfighting, in their distinction during jousts, ring tourneys, and other riding feats.[22]

These traditions and entertainments were much to the taste of the Portuguese nobility.

The testimony of João Alfredo Corrêa de Oliveira is also significant:

> The sugar mill lords were a grave, united, beneficial, and hospitable class; they had good manners; they rode sturdy horses with fine harnesses; they were accompanied by pages dressed in laced uniforms; they were esteemed and reverently greeted by the people; in town they donned dress coats for religious celebrations, council meetings, jury duty, and elections.[23]

c. Military role of the sugar mill lords

The life of nobles in the Middle Ages and in the Old Regime was by no means limited to the enjoyment of luxury at home and the splendor of social recreations. War imposed by the conditions of the time was an important part of their lives.

The same can be said of the Brazilian "homens bons" and nobles of old. The

---

[19] Father Fernão Cardim, S.J., *Tratados da Terra e Gente do Brasil* (Belo Horizonte: Livraria Itatiaia Editora), pp. 157-158.

[20] *Valeroso Lucideno*, a work published in Lisbon in 1648, recounts the epic uprising in Pernambuco against the Dutch heretics. It was written between battles by Friar Manuel Calado, also known as Friar Manuel of the Savior, one of the heroes of this insurrection.

[21] Oliveira Vianna, *Populações Meridionais do Brasil*, Vol. 1, p. 7.

[22] Ibid., p. 9.

[23] Corrêa de Oliveira, *Minha Meninice & Outros Ensaios*, p. 71.

The Battle of Guararapes, won against the Dutch by João Fernandes Vieira, André Vidal de Negreiros, Henrique Dias, and Filipe Camarão.

João Fernandes Vieira rejects the gold with which the Dutch tried to buy his honor.

sugar mill lords were the great power that opposed the invading Dutch, French, and English—enemies of the Faith and His Majesty—and repelled the attacks of savages averse to the evangelizing action of the missionaries. This rural aristocracy thus reinforced its noble character by military heroism, the most essential and archetypical aspect of the nobiliary class.

> The organization of the sugar mill, at the same time factory and fortress...notably aided the defense of the coastline. A factory-fortress with a large population of slaves and rural workers, the manor of the sugar mill lord was the focus of the most tenacious resistance to the Dutch. This feat is intimately linked to the history of the sugarcane cycle, with which was erected the first milestone of our civilization. The fertile, clayish soil along the coast made possible the building of the sugar mills, in whose manors, walled and built like fortresses to resist Indian attacks, were forged, with organization and discipline, the weapons needed for the defense of the Colony against the ships of the corsairs and the invasions of the Dutch.[24]

Gilberto Freyre describes the fundamentally religious character of these military actions.

> In America, the Portuguese scattered throughout a vast territory repeated the process of unification the Iberian peninsula had undergone: Christians versus infidels. Our Indian wars were never wars of whites against redskins, but of Christians against pagans. Our hostility to the English, French, and Dutch always had the character of a religious prophylaxis: Catholics against heretics.... It is not the foreigner who is denied entry to the Colony, but rather sin, heresy, and infidelity. When an Indian was treated like an enemy, it was because he was an infidel, and not because he was of a different race or color.[25]

3. The Gold and Precious Stones Cycle

After colonizing the coast, the Portuguese set out to conquer the hinterland. This marked the beginning of the gold and precious stones cycle, in which the *bandeirantes* (armed explorers) played a key role and, in this way, added a new element to the Brazilian rural aristocracy.

a. *Entradas* and *bandeiras*

To understand the importance and timeliness of the *bandeiras* (groups of *bandeirantes*), it is necessary to bear in mind that the Portuguese colonization of Brazil was initially limited to the extensive coastal region. Beyond the coast there

---

[24] Fernando de Azevedo, *A Cultura Brasileira: Introdução ao Estudo da Cultura no Brasil*, 3d ed. (São Paulo: Editora Melhoramentos), p. 154.

[25] Freyre, *Casa-Grande & Senzala*, Vol. 1, pp. 350-351.

was an immense hinterland yet to be explored, tamed, and used.

Both the Crown and private enterprise mobilized for this endeavor. Usually, the pioneering expeditions undertaken by the Crown through the local authorities were called *entradas*, and the private expeditions were called *bandeiras*. The latter attained better results, both in terms of lands discovered and of wealth acquired. Even at that time private enterprise was much more efficient...

According to Rocha Pombo, the first *bandeiras* were "headed by Martim de Sá, Dias Adorno, and Nicolau Barreto." Pombo also says that "the mission of these first expeditions was to open wide paths into the heart of this immense continent, along which the vigor of the seaside settlements could be continuously channeled deep into the hinterland."[26]

Historian Almir de Andrade highlights the conquering and pioneering side of the *bandeiras*:

> By their adventuresome nature, the *bandeiras* tended to expand rather than settle, to explore rather than produce. They were the conquering arm that stretched frontiers, and not the everyday hoe working steadfastly from sun to sun, upon which our social structure was built. This social structure came from the north, through the influence of the cultural centers of Bahia and Pernambuco.[27]

Undoubtedly the *bandeiras* pursued financial gain, but it would be a great mistake to think that this was their only goal.

> The cause of the *bandeiras* was essentially moral, though it was also tied to individual ambition for treasures, and to the Paulista[28] dream of conquering for their king...an immense empire whose frontiers would be clearly natural borders: the Atlantic, the Plate, the Paraná, the Paraguay, the Andes, and the Amazon.[29]

Nor can it be affirmed that most *bandeirantes* had absolutely no desire to spread the Faith. Evangelization was an inevitable consequence of their pioneering and the settling of baptized populations in the territories they placed under the authority of the kings of Portugal. For these monarchs the spreading of the Faith was always one of the main objectives of the epopee of the Discoveries, and it was in this light that they viewed the *entradas* and *bandeiras*.

> The first public building to rise amid the confusion of the Discoveries was the rustic chapel, a bamboo and clay structure with a thatched roof. Any place was

---

[26] Pombo, *História do Brasil*, Vol. 2, p. 293.

[27] Almir de Andrade, *Formação da Sociologia Brasileira*, Vol. 1, *Os Primeiros Estudos Sociais no Brasil* (Rio de Janeiro: Livraria José Olympio Editora, 1941), p. 100.

[28] *Paulista*: from the state of São Paulo.

[29] F. Contreiras Rodrigues, *Traços da Economia Social e Política do Brasil Colonial* (Ariel Editora, 1935), p. 181.

suitable: sometimes atop a hill, flanked by a roughly-hewn cross, dominating the rugged scenery; sometimes at the bottom of a deep valley....

If the hopes came true and gold was found in abundance along the river, the primitive camp filled with people, huts multiplied, paths began to resemble streets, and the little chapel was enlarged, reinforced, or even rebuilt. Many of these first chapels, some probably dating to the late seventeenth century, are still found today on the outskirts of some cities and mining towns. Though at times disfigured, they bear witness to the first phases of spiritual life on Brazilian soil.[30]

To appreciate the elevated spirit that characterized the people of colonial São Paulo, it suffices to consider

how many inhabitants belonging to the best lineages of Piratininga abandoned their homes and belongings to aid the Northeasterners against the Dutch invaders, the Cariri and Gueren tribes, or the Blacks of Palmares.... To São Paulo we owe the first weaving of our nationality, for it never begrudged its protection to any part of the Colony that needed it.[31]

b. *Bandeirantes* and the Nobility of the Land

We shall now focus on the role of the *bandeiras* in the formation of the territorial nobility.

At a time when "São Paulo had the Atlantic and the Andes for outskirts, and the Amazon and Plate rivers for avenues,"[32] to use the expression of Jaime Cortesão, it was mainly "good men" who filled the ranks of the *bandeiras*. Most of the remaining personnel eventually became part of this class since "in those times, bravery was the main criterion for gaining social prestige."[33] This led Oliveira Vianna to affirm:

The nobility of São Paulo was, before all else, a warrior nobility.... The title of nobility was won by feats of pioneering....

This aspect of the *bandeiras* and of the São Paulo society in the sixteenth and seventeenth centuries must be understood clearly. What took place then was identical to what occurred during the first phase of the medieval period.... We know that in the early Middle Ages the social status of a man was gained by bravery, that is, by warrior merit.... Admittance to the aristocracy depended on this.[34]

---

[30] Afonso Arinos de Melo Franco, *A Sociedade Bandeirante das Minas* in *Curso de Bandeirologia* (Departamento Estadual de Informações, 1946), p. 90.

[31] Rodrigues, *Traços da Economia Social e Política do Brasil Colonial*, p. 190.

[32] Jaime Cortesão, *Raposo Tavares e a Formação Territorial do Brasil* (Rio de Janeiro: Imprensa Nacional, 1958), p. 135.

[33] Oliveira Vianna, *Instituições Políticas Brasileiras*, Vol. 1, p. 170.

[34] Ibid., pp. 170-171.

4. The Nobility of the Land in Relation to the King and the Portuguese Nobility

What was the attitude of the kings of Portugal, the Court, and the Portuguese nobility toward the "good men" and the nobility of the land taking shape in the Colony? Was it a whole-hearted acceptance tending to a complete assimilation, even when it was not a question of rewarding heroic deeds?

a. The sugar mill lord: a noble condition

Quoting the *Diálogo das Grandezas do Brasil*, Pedro Calmon states:

"The richer people own sugar mills and bear the title of lords, which His Majesty grants them in his letters and regulations. The others own sugar cane fields...." The status of a sugar mill lord was therefore equivalent to a feudal nobiliary "lordship." It denoted magnificence. Such were the Brazilian *fidalgos*, who, as Father Fernão Cardim notes, "treated each other like counts."[35]

Fernando de Azevedo categorically states: "*Sugar mill lord* was a noble title among the *fidalgos* of the Realm."[36] Luís Palacin echoes this:

The title of sugar mill lord sufficed to introduce its holder into the nobility.... Antonil[37] compared the sugar mill to a European fief: "Many aspire to the title of sugar mill lord.... The condition of sugar mill lord is coveted in Brazil as much as nobiliary titles are among Portuguese *fidalgos*."[38]

The distinguished historian of the Jesuits in Brazil, Father Serafim Leite, citing a 1614 letter of the Jesuit Henrique Gomes of Bahia, says:

Sugar mill lord, "a title presented...by the grandees of Brazil when requesting ennoblement. In fact, most of them are nobles on account of it." Ennoblement based on the cultivation of sugar cane and the ownership of a sugar mill is mentioned by all observers of Brazil's social life. The Jesuit's observation in 1614 is a good proof of this because of its content and epoch.[39]

This fact led Carlos Xavier Paes Barreto to assert the following about the

---

[35] Calmon, *História do Brasil*, Vol. 2, p. 358.

[36] Azevedo, *Canaviais e Engenhos*, p. 88.

[37] Pen name of João António Andreoni, a Jesuit who was in Brazil in 1711. He wrote *Cultura e Opulência do Brasil por Suas Drogas e Minas*.

[38] Palacin, *Sociedade Colonial*, pp. 181-182.

[39] Father Serafim Leite, *História da Companhia de Jesus no Brasil* (Rio de Janeiro: Instituto Nacional do Livro, 1945), Vol. 5, p. 452.

Town Hall of Ouro Preto, Minas Gerais, Brazil.
Municipal government was a privilege of the rural aristocracy.

sugar mill lords: "Nobility was linked to the land.... While the planters, unlike the ancient Romans, did not have their names inscribed in marble in the amphitheaters, they did have all the prerogatives of the nobility."[40]

There is a nuance to what these respected authors affirm. In other words, the reader should not infer that the condition of sugar mill lord was as precise and unequivocal as the Portuguese nobility's when it came to nobiliary status or public offices.

---

[40] Paes Barreto, *Os Primitivos Colonizadores Nordestinos*, p. 127.

b. "Honorable men" and "good men"

Luís Palacin points out that documents of early colonial Brazil undoubtedly include

> the terms of nobility used to qualify important personages: *fidalgo*, *knight*, and *noble*. But these titles are rare. Normally, a more generic title is used for all those who tended to form a single class on account of their fortune, authority, and social prestige: *principal man of the land*, *powerful man*, and *great man* are some of the titles used. However, the most common title is *honorable man*, which denotes the nobiliary character of the possession of authority and wealth in colonial society.
>
> It is not easy to outline precisely this ideal of an honorable life. It is certainly rooted in the knightly aspirations of the medieval nobility.[41]

The designation *good men* likewise encompassed not only the several social categories that constituted the nobility of the land, but also other categories with social prominence in colonial life. Alfredo Ellis explains: "Each village had its 'good men,' who were the principal men in the land either by birth or wealth, or by the reputation earned in struggles against the gentile, the invader, or the hardships of the surroundings."[42]

According to Oliveira Vianna, "the names of these 'good men' were listed in the *Registers of Nobility* kept in the Town Hall.... To be included in the *Registers* as a 'good man' was a clear sign of nobility, as shown in the 'certificate of lineage' issued to those interested."[43]

c. Privileges of the nobility of the land—municipal government

As already seen, the elites comprising the nobility of the land gave ample proof of courage in defending the Brazilian coastline against foreign invasions, especially of the French and Dutch, and in the pioneering and fighting necessary to begin the settlement of the hinterland.

For such outstanding services, the King granted these elites privileges, rewards, and honors. One of these privileges, the government of the municipal councils, should be emphasized. Actually, this benevolent attitude of the Crown toward the Brazilian society and state, which were gradually being structured, did not manifest itself only in the reward of military heroism.

Rocha Pombo relates that the aristocrats of Pernambuco, rendered famous by their victorious battles against the Dutch Protestants, claimed certain privileges from the metropolis. "The mother country," he writes, "was most receptive to

---

[41]   Palacin, *Sociedade Colonial*, p. 184.

[42]   Alfredo Ellis, Jr., *Resumo da História de São Paulo* (São Paulo: Tipografia Brasil, 1942), p. 109.

[43]   Oliveira Vianna, *Populações Meridionais do Brasil*, Vol. 1, p. 162.

the requests of the people of Pernambuco. It granted many concessions, answered every complaint, and transferred the administration and government of the land to the heroes who had liberated it."[44] Alfredo Ellis confirms this: "Municipal authority was exercised by the legitimate conquerors, and defenders of the land against its external and internal enemies."[45]

In fact, the mother country was always inclined to favor the proportional autonomies of the colonial populations. That is why municipal council members, for example, were elected, not appointed. However, their election should not be confused with the modern electoral process.

> In the colonial period, our towns were not governed democratically in the modern sense of the word. At that time, only people enjoying active and passive electoral rights could vote and be elected. They constituted a select class, a nobility: the nobility of the "good men." It was a true aristocracy, in which figured only people of noble lineage who had come over or had immigrated and settled here, their descendants, the rich sugar mill lords; the Colony's upper civil and military bureaucrats and their descendants. This nobility was joined by elements from another class: the "new men," bourgeois who had become rich through commerce, and who, by their conduct, lifestyle, fortune, and services to the local community or city, had penetrated the social circles of this nobility of lineage or office.[46]

Alfredo Ellis confirms the existence of this privilege, whereby "municipal authority was exercised by the 'good men,' that is, the nobility of the land."[47]

The Brazilian communist Caio Prado, Jr., hardly a person to favor the nobility, also stresses that municipal government was a privilege of the rural aristocracy: "Only the 'good men,' the nobility, as the landowners were called, voted in the elections for municipal administrative offices. They zealously defended this privilege."[48] Manoel Rodrigues Ferreira likewise affirms:

> The names [of those elected] were brought to the *ouvidor geral*,[49] who after examining them issued a document called "certificate of confirmation of usages," or simply "certificate of confirmation," whereby the choice was ratified and the elected persons allowed to take office....
> The "certificates of confirmation of usages"...were justified because only the "good men" of the village or city, that is, the local nobility, could be elected.[50]

---

[44] Pombo, *História do Brasil*, Vol. 3, pp. 179-180.

[45] Ellis, "Amador Bueno e Seu Tempo," p. 66.

[46] Oliveira Vianna, *Populações Meridionais do Brasil*, Vol. 1, p. 162.

[47] Ellis, *Resumo da História de São Paulo*, p. 107.

[48] Caio Prado, Jr., *Evolução Política do Brasil e Outros Estudos*, 7th ed. (São Paulo: Editora Brasiliense, 1971), p. 29.

[49] An *Ouvidor geral* was a special magistrate in colonial days.

[50] Manoel Rodrigues Ferreira, *As Repúblicas Municipais no Brasil* (São Paulo: Prefeitura do Município de São

5. A "Brazilian Feudalism"

The facts cited until now show the birth and development of the local powers and elites in the settlements of colonial Brazil. As stated, they present many traces of feudalism.

There is a longstanding and widespread idea that the Americas are solidly democratic continents where monarchies and aristocracies are unable to flourish. This idea was, for example, a leitmotiv of the republican propaganda in Brazil that toppled the throne of the Braganzas. Therefore, before describing the decline of Brazilian "colonial feudalism," it does not seem superfluous to mention some opinions of historians on the nature of Brazil's "feudalism," which is analogous to Europe's.

Gilberto Freyre affirms: "The people [the Portuguese] that, according to Herculano, barely knew feudalism, regressed in the sixteenth century to the feudal era, reviving its aristocratic methods in the colonization of America. It was a kind of compensation for or rectification of its own history."[51]

Nestor Duarte writes: "The first century of our Colony was termed by Silvio Romero our feudal century, our Middle Ages. With well-founded criticism, Martins Junior rectifies his assessment, affirming that these Middle Ages, this feudalism, continued well into the second and third centuries."[52]

Charles Morazé adds: "These powerful landholders organized themselves into a feudal authority. They supported themselves on the patriarchal family, whose tradition lives on in modern Brazil."[53]

Stressing the role of the family as the foundation of feudal organization, Duarte remarks that "transplanted from Portugal, the family structure was reborn here in circumstances highly favorable to its primitive prestige and strength in the origins of human societies. It was a true revival of heroic times or, if you prefer, of feudal times."[54]

While Brazil's feudalism had similarities with Europe's, it also had original elements. These should not be overlooked. One of the more noticeable elements of this originality was the great importance municipalities had in this feudal context. They enjoyed specific liberties, and their organization was eminently aristocratic. Morazé stresses that "at a time when Louis XIV was centralizing power in France, municipal authority in Brazil maintained a strictly feudal organization throughout the country."[55] He adds that municipal political life in Brazil revealed

---

Paulo, 1980), pp. 45, 46.

[51] Freyre, *Casa-Grande & Senzala*, p. 347.

[52] Duarte, *A Ordem Privada e a Organização Política Nacional*, p. 82.

[53] Charles Morazé, *Les Trois Ages du Brésil: Essai de Politique* (Paris: Librairie Armand Colin, 1954), p. 65. Morazé, formerly professor of political science at the College of Philosophy, Sciences and Literature of the University of São Paulo, is now a professor at the Institute of Political Studies of the University of Paris.

[54] Duarte, *A Ordem Privada e a Organização Política Nacional*, p. 126.

[55] Morazé, *Les Trois Ages du Brésil*, p. 65.

The Rua do Rosário in São Paulo, by José Wasth Rodrigues, 1858.
(Museu Paulista, São Paulo)

Passage of the Emperor through the Rua Direita in Rio de Janeiro.
Engraving by Rugendas.

"a marked originality which completely distinguished it from the municipal political life of European countries in that period."[56]

Nestor Duarte states: "In the council of the feudalized municipality sat the
sugar mill lords, the nobility of the land, who vindicated the privilege of being
the only holders of office."[57]

In his turn, Oliveira Vianna affirms: "Especially in the colonial period, the
office of alderman...could only be exercised by nobles or qualified people." The
latter "belonged to lineages of nobles, office-holders, or wealthy entrepreneurs
(for example), merchants, on the condition that they live according to the 'law
of the nobility,' in other words, like old Portuguese *fidalgos*."[58]

6. The Centralization of Power and the Curtailment of the Privileges of the Nobility of the Land

a. The offensive of the legists and the loss of municipal autonomy

Around the end of the eighteenth century, this structure, which to a large degree
had been shaped by custom in a way pleasing to the Portuguese Crown, became
the target of an offensive from outside the Colony and began to decline. Pedro
Calmon describes this process.

> The administrative and political evolution of the mother country was repeated in
> America. The martial phase of the arbitrary *capitães-generais* and *capitães-mores*
> was succeeded by the civil and scholarly era of the *juiz de fora* [a circuit judge
> appointed by the king] and the *corregedor* [a magistrate appointed by the king].
> Bachelors of law came (or returned) from the University of Coimbra with the pre-
> eminence they had in Portugal. Their jurisdiction extended beyond the limits of the
> court of justice to encompass the order of the entire municipal government.... They
> abolished the residual privileges of the nobility (the local potentates) just as King
> John II's *corregedores* in Portugal had overcome the resistance of the great titled
> lords: by inflexibly exercising their judicial powers.
>
> Deep down they were legists.... More than just agents of a dogmatic law, they
> were, above all, instruments of State unification.
>
> The centralizing and paternalistic tendency of the monarchy began by interfering
> in the municipal councils.[59]

[56]   Ibid., p. 66.

[57]   Duarte, *A Ordem Privada e a Organização Política Nacional*, p. 143.

[58]   Oliveira Vianna, *Populações Meridionais do Brasil*, Vol. 1, p. 165.

[59]   Calmon, *História do Brasil*, Vol. 3, pp. 892-893.

b. The withdrawal of the nobility of the land
from the cities to the countryside

With the development of the major urban centers, an increasing number of families of "good men" and nobles of the land had moved to the cities, with their beautiful churches of great artistic value, imposing public buildings such as town halls, and luxurious residences. The convergence of these people in urban centers, the family entertainments, and the frequently splendorous religious ceremonies favored social relations among members of the same class. These relations, in turn, resulted in engagements and marriages.

However, the legists' influence frequently excluded from the municipal political scene the nobles of the land and the "good men," who had previously governed it with considerable autonomy. They tended, therefore, to leave the cities for their plantations, where they had unlimited space to expand their agricultural and ranching activities.

This tranquil and dignified rural life still brought significant benefits to the common good. As Oliveira Vianna explains: "Removed from the higher offices of colonial government, the nobles of the land modestly retreated to the rural shadows, where they tended herds, produced sugar, and mined gold. In this way, they expanded the settlement and cultivation of the hinterland as they cleared lands and multiplied their corrals."[60]

The rural elites thus increased their estates. This allowed them to display an even greater luxury, not so much in the isolated and unpretentious everyday life on the plantation, as in the cities, where all the members of the upper class met on occasion. At least temporarily, then, the aristocratic class gained in social prestige what it had lost in political power.

c. The decline of aristocratic influence

But there should be no illusions regarding this. Far from the coast—where commerce unloaded the latest merchandise inspired by the changing fashions of Europe, as well as the latest furniture and goods for personal use—the nobility of the land ceased to improve its lifestyle and customs. Inevitably, this stagnation led it to assimilate some local customs and ways of being. In short, traces of rusticity appeared in the aristocratic personality of these country elites.

Oliveira Vianna points out the dilemma of the nobility of the land:

> Either they choose the countryside, where their main interests lie, or the city, the center of entertainment and dissipation. With time they opt for the countryside, as is to be expected, and slowly sink into the obscurity and silence of rural life.
>
> This withdrawal, this retreat, this migration of the colonial nobility to the countryside, is well described by the Count of Cunha, our first Viceroy. In a letter to

---

[60] Oliveira Vianna, *Populações Meridionais do Brasil*, Vol. 1, p. 34.

the King, in 1767, he writes:

"...These people, who were the ones who could shine and figure in the city, which they ennobled by their presence, are now dispersed in the remotest districts, far from each other, and totally isolated; many of them do not marry well, some leaving only illegitimate mulatto children as heirs...."

...In the nineteenth century, our territorial nobility has become almost completely rural in its habits and customs, and especially in its spirit and character. Nothing is left of the traditions of the old Portuguese nobility, save the gentlemanly respect for family and honor.[61]

7. The Move of the Portuguese Court to Brazil

This period of bucolic tranquility was brought to an end by an unexpected consequence of the great wars and revolutions that had been shaking Europe since 1789, namely the arrival of Prince John, Regent of Portugal, who also held the title of Prince of Brazil, since he was heir to the Portuguese throne and exercised the royal power because of the dementia of his mother, Queen Maria I.

Oliveira Vianna comments on this event:

> This great historic accident marks the beginning of a decisive era of considerable transformation in the social and political life of our territorial nobility.
>
> Our colorful rural patriciate from Minas, São Paulo, and the interior of the Province of Rio commences its descent on Rio de Janeiro, where the head of the new Empire is. Its best elements, the cream of its aristocracy, begin to frequent this tropical Versailles located in São Cristóvão.[62]

In Rio de Janeiro they encounter, "on the one hand, a brand-new bourgeoisie of merchants enriched by the commercial boom following the opening of the ports; and on the other hand, an aristocratic multitude of Portuguese *fidalgos* who had come with the King."[63]

It is not surprising that this encounter of heterogeneous elements caused friction. Oliveira Vianna continues:

> In the intimacy of the Court, right next to the King, these three distinct and hostile classes confront each other: the opulent nobles of the land, with their sugar mills and plantations, and their historic disdain for peons and merchants; the merchants, conscious of their wealth and strength, and peeved by this offensive disdain; and the Portuguese immigrants, with the arrogance of their *fidalgo* lineages and the impertinent haughtiness of civilized people visiting heathen lands.[64]

---

[61] Ibid., pp. 18, 23.

[62] Ibid., pp. 34-35.

[63] Ibid., p. 35.

[64] Ibid.

The coronation of Dom Pedro I as Emperor of Brazil, December 1, 1822.
Engraving by J. B. Debret.

The solemn landing of Archduchess Leopoldine of Austria in Rio de Janeiro,
November 6, 1817. The Archduchess married Crown Prince Dom Pedro of
Portugal, future Emperor of Brazil.

This historical overview of the nobility of the land in the colonial period can be concluded with these words of Oliveira Vianna: "As can be seen, these family-based organizations, powerfully supported on the mass of their feudal clans, crossed the three colonial centuries displaying prestige and might in public, private, and administrative life."[65]

8. Titles of Nobility in the Brazilian Empire

What effects did the creation of titles of nobility during the Empire have on the nobility of the land? Very few. One would almost say none.

The Brazilian Imperial Constitution of 1824 did not recognize privileges stemming from birth: "All privileges not deemed essentially and strictly linked to public offices are hereby abolished."[66] As a consequence of this article of the first imperial constitution, the titles of nobility granted by the Emperor were not recognized as hereditary.

This measure reflected the influence of the individualism and liberalism that swept Europe and America throughout the nineteenth century and that continues in many institutions, laws, and customs. The rationale was that titles of nobility would only be compatible with progress if they rewarded personal achievement. By no means should the merits of an ancestor benefit his descendants, so titles were not hereditary.

Merely a reward, the title could not confer specific jurisdiction over any portion of the national territory, especially over lands belonging to the titled person. This scrupulous disassociation of private property from political power was considered essential for a regime imbued with the principles of the French Revolution not to be confused with feudalism, which was still being fought by liberal factions. In this regard, Oliveira Lima conclusively states:

> The Brazilian Empire was democratic in more than just name. This was so much so that when it organized its nobility it did not make it hereditary, which is essential for continuity. The monarchical Constitution of 1824 did not recognize privileges of birth: the aristocracy of the time was formed by rewarding personal merits and services; part of it represented wealth, one of the mainstays of the State and an area for private initiative.[67]

Among the Imperial nobility, there were cases in which father and son had the same title. Sometimes, the title would differ even though the toponym or the family name was the same. This did not mean, however, that the title was hereditary, since it was bestowed on the father and the son personally as a reward for their individual merits.

---

[65] F. J. Oliveira Vianna, *Instituições Políticas Brasileiras*, 1st ed. (1949), Vol. 1, p. 270.

[66] *Constituição Política do Império do Brasil*, Art. 179, no. xvi.

[67] Oliveira Lima, *O Movimento da Independência*, pp. 29-30.

This was the case of the Viscount of Rio Branco, Prime Minister of the Empire in 1871, and his son, the celebrated Baron of Rio Branco, an accomplished diplomat who distinguished himself in the drafting of the treaties that definitively established the borders between Brazil and her many neighbors.

The Baron of Rio Branco only became famous when serving as foreign minister of the Republic during the first decade of this century. The Emperor had granted him the title before the fall of the monarchy, undoubtedly to please his father.

On the other hand, the descendants of some titled nobles of the Empire whose title was linked to a toponym (Viscount of Ouro Preto, Marquis of Paranaguá) adopted the place-name in lieu of their family name, without, however, using the title itself (José de Ouro Preto, Maria de Paranaguá). This procedure, which might not have been strictly legal, did not mean that the title was hereditary.

It is clear that these non-hereditary titles, granted merely as personal rewards, could not form a social class in the strict sense. A social class has proper conditions for existence only when it is composed of families and not of mere individuals. Thus, as previously stated, these titles had little or no bearing on the nobility of the land.

Emptied of its historical content, an Imperial title conferred on a noble of the land was not much more than a badge of honor. It might make him more prominent within his class, but this had much less meaning than a concession of lordship over lands by the kings of Portugal, especially since Emperors Peter I and Peter II granted titles not only to lords of land, but also to Brazilians of any social extraction they deemed worthy of this distinction in view of services to the country.

9. Parliamentary Monarchy and the Nobility of the Land

a. The electoral clans

The declaration of Brazil's independence in 1822 introduced a parliamentary monarchy and with it a representative electoral system. The political scene was thus profoundly transformed.

Given the new situation and the non-hereditary character of the few titles granted in the Empire to nobles of the land, one could think this nobility would fade away as a historical relic no longer linked to the present.

This did not happen.

Faced with these transformations, the nobility of the land did not remain idle. It strived to perpetuate its political power in the new conditions resulting from the establishment of a crowned democracy in Brazil.

In the democratic system, sovereignty lies entirely, or almost entirely, with the people. Therefore, whoever has influence over the electorate holds the power. Now, with some exceptions in really important cities, it was the nobles of the land who had this influence. Most electoral results depended on the nobility of the land, which wielded its power through the political parties. A political party depends on its electoral strength, and this was in the hands of the nobility of the land.

The way they organized themselves to preserve their prestige was unexpected and picturesque. Oliveira Vianna writes:

> These rural lords—until then dispersed and autonomous in their self-sufficient condition—were now together and organized.... They formed two large groups, each with an ostensive leader. In the municipality, they were the government and authority and everyone obeyed them.... All of them were now united under party labels.... They were either Conservatives or Liberals.[68]

It is not surprising that the nation's political scene underwent noteworthy transformations, especially during the first decades of the Empire. Oliveira Vianna describes them:

> We term these new and small local structures, originating in the nineteenth century, electoral clans, because of their similarity to feudal and family clans.... They had the same structure, make-up, and purpose. The only difference was that they had a larger geographic base, encompassing the whole municipality and not just the limited area of the fief (sugar mill or plantation). After 1832, these small local groups affiliated themselves with broader associations, first the provincial political parties, then the national ones: the Conservative and Liberal Parties, with headquarters in the Empire's capital and with provincial leaders, the "provincial presidents."[69]

b. The National Guard and the Nobility of the Land

The Law of August 18, 1831, abolished the old military institutions of the Colony (the militia corps, the municipal guards, and the men-at-arms) and created

---

[68] Oliveira Vianna, *Instituições Políticas Brasileiras*, 1st ed., Vol. 2, p. 279.

[69] Ibid., p. 280. The same author explains that these electoral groups, formed at the municipal level and run by the rural aristocracy, began to appear after the Law of 1828 reorganizing the municipalities, and took definite shape with the 1832 promulgation of the Code of Process.

"This code, with its municipalist democracy, obliged, and even *forced*, these rural lords to reach understandings and make arrangements among themselves to elect local authorities—such as justices of the peace (who had police functions), municipal judges (who were criminal judges and also had certain police functions), aldermen, and officers of the National Guard. These offices or positions were elective and also entailed certain police and peace-keeping functions" (ibid., p. 281).

Oliveira Vianna describes the consolidation of the electoral clans: "This consolidation was first centered on the provincial authority (with the *small centralization* that resulted from the Additional Act). It began in 1835 and continued until the Law of December 3, 1841. Then came the *great centralization*, the centralization of the Empire, which lasted until 1889, when the Republic was proclaimed. This process brought about the *national* consolidation of these clans.... The 'electoral clans' of the municipalities then became mere sections of one of the two great national parties, the Conservative and the Liberal" (ibid., pp. 281-282).

the National Guard.

In this two-party system, where local authorities were appointed by the central power instead of being elected as before, the aristocratic class of electoral clan leaders strove to gain the sympathy of the provincial presidents, "who submitted names to the Center, not only to fill the extremely important National Guard posts, but also to be included in the Empire's nobility."[70] So it is important to understand the relations between the National Guard and the nobility of the land.

> One cannot overemphasize the role of the National Guard in the constitution of the electoral clans. The National Guard officer corps was the focal point of the rural nobility....
>
> During the Empire, an officer of the National Guard held a local position equivalent to that of a colonial *juiz de fora* or *capitão-mor regente*. He was part of a highly-qualified local nobility.
>
> The title of "colonel" or "lieutenant-colonel"—later vulgarized by the Republic—was the highest distinction granted a planter in the municipality. The modest title of *alferes* [second-lieutenant] was only conferred on important local authorities....
>
> This was the political function of the National Guard: to enable the richest or most powerful lord to direct the other feudal and seignorial clans. He was able to do this thanks to the protection of the governor, who granted him control over recruitment, the civil and military police, and the municipal council with its inspectors.[71]

Rui Vieira da Cunha in turn affirms:

> The National Guard is of capital importance for a proper understanding of the social structure of the Empire. Power and influence flowed into it, making it aristocratic at a time when the titles of nobility were being democratized and reduced to mere honorific awards.
>
> The systematic interpretation of the articles of the Law creating the National Guard...leads to the following conclusion: "The officers of the National Guard are as noble as the Army's."[72]

10. The Coffee Cycle

The coffee cycle had begun in the mid-1700s, giving a new aspect to the nobility of the land with the emergence of the "coffee aristocracy." The prestige

---

[70] Ibid., p. 283.

[71] Ibid., pp. 284-285.

[72] Rui Vieira da Cunha, *Estudo da Nobreza Brasileira (Cadetes)* (Rio de Janeiro: Arquivo Nacional, 1966), p. 42.

1889-1922. Exiled by the Republic, the Imperial Family kept in touch with their numerous friends in Brazil. Above: A card from Princess Isabel (Head of the Imperial Family since the death of her father, Dom Pedro II), and her consort, Prince Gaston of Orleans, Count d'Eu, to Dona Gabriela Ribeiro dos Santos, Prof. Plinio Corrêa de Oliveira's maternal grandmother. The message from the Imperial Couple (pictured) to this close friend reads: "All our dedication and friendship in Jesus and Mary! In union of prayers! August 18, 1920."

After the Republic was proclaimed in 1889, Princess Isabel nominated Councillor João Alfredo Corrêa de Oliveira (the author's paternal great-uncle, left) member of the Monarchical Directorate, to which she entrusted the task of guiding the action of Brazilian monarchists. As Prime Minister, Councillor João Alfredo had signed with Princess Isabel, at the time Regent of the Empire, the Golden Law of May 13, 1888, which gave freedom to all slaves.

and influence of this aristocracy marked, above all, the life of the Empire. It would also mark the first decades of the Republic. On this subject, Roger Bastide declares:

> The sugar and gold civilizations were followed by the coffee civilization....
>
> This civilization extends from the Empire's splendors to Getúlio Vargas's death [1954]. Coffee created an aristocracy and later destroyed (or at least transformed) it.
>
> Coffee is inseparable from the history of the nineteenth century and the early twentieth century.
>
> ... In the province of São Paulo, coffee gave rise to a patriarchal society identical to those of Bahia and Pernambuco two centuries earlier. According to [Freyre], the coffee barons continued and reproduced the sugar aristocracy.[73]

a. The rural aristocracy and the proclamation of the Republic

The political influence of the families stemming from the old nobility of the land did not disappear with the proclamation of the Republic in 1889, and their social prestige remained predominant. They refined their ways and customs, avidly assimilating the manners and splendor of the social life of Europe's upper class. The testimony of Georges Clemenceau in this regard is noteworthy. Writing about his 1911 visit to Brazil, this world-renowned politician who was France's prime minister during the First World War commented:

> Concerning the social elite...we must always return to the starting point: a feudal oligarchy, the focus of culture and refinement.... It is on the plantation, the center of his domains, that we find the planter. A refined feudal type, imbued with European thought, open to all the lofty sentiments of social generosity that characterized our eighteenth-century aristocracy at a certain point,...he is infinitely superior to most of his European counterparts born of tradition or created by the happenstance of democracy.... He is so different from satire's depiction of him that in Paris you will cross paths with this dominator without realizing it. He is so modest in speech and simple in figure....
>
> The city of São Paulo is so curiously French in some of its aspects that not once during a whole week did I have the sensation of being in a foreign country.... São Paulo society...has a dual tendency: While it resolutely orients itself by the French spirit, it develops in parallel all the aspects of Brazilian individuality that determine its character. Be sure that the Paulista is Paulista to the depth of his soul, whether he is in Brazil, France, or anywhere else. This said, tell me if there ever was a Frenchman with more courteous manners, more agreeable conversation, and

---

[73] The term *aristocracy* is used *lato sensu*. It does not designate a social class created and recognized by law, but one born from the course of events and, therefore, less defined. Roger Bastide, *Brasil Terra de Contrastes*, 4th ed. (São Paulo: Difusão Europeia do Livro, 1971), pp. 127-128, 129-130.

Even after the proclamation of the Republic in 1889, the families that descended from the old "nobility of the land" continued to refine their lifestyle and customs, assimilating the manners and splendor of social life of the best European ambiences. Georges Clemenceau, who travelled to Brazil in 1911, wrote in this regard that the city of São Paulo, without

losing any of its Brazilian character, "is so curiously French in some of its aspects that not once during a whole week did I have the sensation of being in a foreign country." "Tell me," he continued, "if there ever was a Frenchman with more courteous manners, more agreeable conversation, and more aristocratic delicacy of spirit [than a Paulista]."

more aristocratic delicacy of spirit in the figure of a businessman who is prudent yet audacious, and who knows how to value coffee.[74]

However, the general social transformations in the West, whether during the Empire or the first decades of the Republic, inevitably influenced Brazilian society, to the detriment of the old rural elites. The increasingly easy communications with Europe and the United States disseminated in Brazil the ever more radical egalitarian thinking that was widespread in the Old World and in the young and energetic United States. This thinking was hostile to any kind of aristocracy or social elite.

Most of the more cultured elements of Brazilian society were inclined to follow the trends from the main world centers. They viewed with increasing antipathy the contradiction between the fictitious democracy in Brazil and the democracy implemented in the more prestigious nations. The political power of the agricultural class seemed to them an imposture, a falsification of the democratic regime.

> The liberal ideas spread with education.... With the rise of the coffee aristocracy, they began to reign in the corridors of the law school of São Paulo among the planters' sons, leading to the triumph of abolitionism, the Republic, and the revolt against the political monopoly of the rich "colonels."[75]

Newspapers were being founded throughout the country. The majority of them favored what they called "authentic democracy."

To the left of the Republican Party, the discreet but powerful defender of the status quo, rose the Democratic Party, the voice for political change.

b. The Coffee Crisis

In the late 1920s, a formidable crisis shook the coffee industry, based mostly in the states of Minas Gerais, Rio de Janeiro, and São Paulo. The crisis was provoked by the inept policy of the republican government regarding a coffee production level that exceeded demand on the world market. This unforeseen crisis struck when many coffee-planters were deeply in debt. Some had taken out loans to increase already excessive production; others, to build or remodel residences in the main cities.

Indeed, with the expansion of the rail and road systems, coffee planters had begun building their urban residences in the main cities instead of in the small towns near their plantations. In the large cities, now easily accessible, the planters could lead a brilliant social life and obtain an excellent education for their sons and daughters in schools run by religious orders, most of which had come from

---

[74] Georges Clemenceau, "Notes de Voyage dans l'Amerique du Sud—XIII," *L'Illustration*, April 22, 1911, pp. 310, 313.

[75] Bastide, *Brasil Terra de Contrastes*, p. 139.

Europe. Furthermore, they could oversee the higher education of their sons in the universities that were opening. Indebted and impoverished—in part due to lack of prudence and foresight—the class of great coffee planters suffered a blow that considerably diminished its social prestige and especially its political clout.

Long before these developments occurred in southern Brazil, the sugar mill lords of Pernambuco and other northeastern states had begun to decline.

> This was due to the rise of industry. Its large sugar mills eliminated the small ones and concentrated their dependents (the rural workers) around the factory. The aristocratic cycle of the sugar mills had ended. The *lord* was replaced by the *company* (which at times was organized in England and bore an English name), while zone monopoly supplanted the resilient initiative of the old owners.[76]

The profits of many traditional sugar mills dropped to the point of barely providing enough for the lord to live on.

c. The Revolution of 1930 and the end of the traditional rural elites in Brazil

The course of events was generating new circumstances that would result in the virtual extinction of the rural aristocracy. "This rural aristocracy had provided leadership for Brazilian society for centuries, but finally lost control of the nation in 1930."[77]

The Revolution of 1930 toppled President Washington Luiz, a symbol of the flagging old order, and placed Getúlio Vargas in the presidency. This revolution initiated fifteen years of nearly continuous dictatorship that, while proclaiming itself anticommunist, supported the social transformations demanded by the Left. "Getulism" inaugurated a populist republic.

In it, the class of landed lords was reduced to scattered remnants "*rari nantes in gurgite vasto*,"[78] sparse pieces of wreckage floating in a Brazil that was constantly growing in population, urbanization, and industrialization; with immigrants from all corners of the earth whose sons were working their way up the social ladder and acquiring plantations that the old landowners, weak and impoverished, could no longer maintain.

The old class, ever less defined, sank almost to a man into partial or total anonymity amid the tumult of a Brazil that grew ever richer and ever more different.

---

[76] Calmon, *História do Brasil*, Vol. 7, p. 2300.

[77] Robert J. Havighurst and J. Roberto Moreira, *Society and Education in Brazil* (Pittsburgh: Univ. of Pittsburgh Press, 1969), p. 42.

[78] Virgil, *Aeneid*, I, 118.

The execution of Louis XVI

APPENDIX III

The Revolutionary Trilogy
Liberty, Equality, Fraternity

In the Words of Various Popes

By coincidence, the writing of this book began in the bicentennial year of the French Revolution. Many obstacles caused long and numerous interruptions for the author, so the book was only finished four years later.

This coincidence is propitious, however. Many of the issues discussed herein were preponderant elements of the ideas and goals of the revolutionaries of 1789. These ideas and goals were clearly reflected in their acts of violence, their injustices, and their tumultuous reforms.

The commemorations of the French Revolution's bicentennial considerably awakened the remembrance of this great convulsion throughout the world. Some echoes still linger today, affording the theme of this book greater relevance than it might have had before the bicentennial.

Thus, it will not be surprising if during a perusal of this book the French Revolution came more than once to the minds of readers who enjoy history. Among other issues, then, the famous revolutionary trilogy Liberty, Equality, Fraternity will have crossed their minds.

To satisfy the possible desire of these readers to delve deeper into the matter, we have transcribed some pontifical texts concerning this trilogy that complement the text already cited.[1]

1. Omnifarious Liberty and Absolute Equality: Foolish and Even Monstrous Concepts

In the decretal of March 10, 1791, to the Cardinal de la Rochefoucauld and

---

[1] Part I, Chapter III, 4.

to the Archbishop of Aix-en-Provence, Pius VI expressed himself concerning the principles of the Civil Constitution of the Clergy.

For indeed, that Assembly [the French Constituent Assembly] has decreed that it was laid down in natural law that a man established in society should rejoice in every sort of liberty, so that he surely ought not to be disturbed about religion, having as he does the authority to think, to say, to write, and even to print and publish whatever he wishes concerning the proof of religion itself. These marvels it has declared to be derived from and to emanate from the equality of human beings among themselves and from the liberty of nature. But what more insane thing can be imagined than to set up such equality and liberty among all, so that nothing is attributed to reason, with which the human race has been especially endowed by nature, and by which it is distinguished from all other living creatures? When God had created man and had placed him in the Paradise of pleasure, did He not at the same time impose a penalty of death on him if he should eat from the tree of the knowledge of good and evil? Did He not immediately by this first command restrict his liberty? Did He not subsequently, when man had made himself guilty through disobedience, add more commands through Moses? And although He had "left him in the hand of his own counsel," so that he might be able to deserve well or ill, nevertheless "He added His commandments and precepts" so that "If thou wilt keep the commandments...they shall preserve thee" (Eccl. 15:14-16).

Where, then, is that liberty of thinking and of acting that the decrees of the Assembly attribute to man established in society, as if it were an immutable law of nature itself?... It will have been necessary already from the beginning for a man to be made subject to his elders, so that he might be guided and instructed by them and might be able to align his own life in accord with the norm of reason, humanity, and religion; certainly from the origin of each and every individual, it is obvious that the equality and liberty boasted of among human beings is vain and empty. "Wherefore be subject of necessity" (Rom. 13:5). Therefore, in order that human beings might be able to come together into civil society, a form of government had to be constituted, in which those natural rights of liberty were assigned to a position below the laws and the supreme power of the rulers; from which it follows, as Saint Augustine teaches: "Indeed, the general agreement of human society is to obey its rulers" (*Confessions*, Book III, Chapter 8, pt. 1). Wherefore, this power ought to be traced back not so much to a social contract as to God himself, the Author of what is right and just.[2]

---

[2] *Pii VI Pont. Max. Acta* (Rome: Typis S. Congreg. de Propaganda Fide, 1871), Vol. 1, pp. 70-71.

2. The Liberty and Equality Spread by the French Revolution: Fallacious Concepts Disseminated by Most-Perfidious Philosophers

Pius VI repeatedly condemned the false concept of liberty and equality. In the Secret Consistory of June 17, 1793, quoting the words of the encyclical *Inscrutabile Divinae Sapientiae* of December 25, 1775, he declared:

> "The most perfidious philosophers go farther. They dissolve all those bonds by which human beings are joined to one another and to their rulers and by which they are maintained in their sense of duty; they keep screaming and proclaiming to the point of nausea that human beings are born free and not subject to the rule of anyone, and that society is therefore a multitude of foolish human beings whose stupidity prostrates them before priests, by whom they are deceived, and before kings, by whom they are oppressed; to such a point that concord between the priesthood and the empire is nothing other than a giant conspiracy against man's innate liberty."
>
> To this false and mendacious name of *liberty*, those vaunted patrons of the human race have added the equally deceptive name of *equality*, as if among human beings who have come together in civil society, although they are subject to various emotions and follow diverse and uncertain impulses according to their individual whims, there ought not be one who by means of authority and force might prevail upon, oblige, moderate, and recall them from their perverse ways of acting to a sense of duty, lest society itself, from the reckless and contrary impetus of many desires, should fall into anarchy and be utterly dissolved. It is like harmony, which derives from the agreement of many sounds and which, if it does not consist of a suitable combination of strings and voices, disintegrates into a disturbed and clearly dissonant clatter.[3]

3. The Abuse of *Liberty* and *Equality* Leads to Socialism and Communism

In his encyclical *Nostis et nobiscum* of December 8, 1849, Pius IX denounces a false understanding of these words.

> As regards this teaching and these theories [about distancing the peoples of Italy from obedience to the Pope and the Holy See], it is now generally known that the special goal of their proponents is to introduce to the people the pernicious fictions of Socialism and Communism by misapplying the terms *liberty* and *equality*.[4]

---

[3] Ibid., Vol. 2, pp. 26-27.

[4] Claudia Carlen, *The Papal Encyclicals 1740-1878* (Raleigh, N.C.: McGrath Publishing Co., 1981), pp. 298-299.

4. Christian Equality Does Not Suppress the Differences Among Men, but Makes of the Variety of Conditions an Admirable Harmony

From Leo XIII's encyclical *Humanum genus* against Freemasonry of April 20, 1884, we draw the following passage:

> Not without cause do We use this occasion to state again what We have stated elsewhere, namely, that the Third Order of Saint Francis...should be studiously promoted and sustained.
>
> Among the many benefits to be expected from it will be the great benefit of drawing the minds of men to liberty, fraternity, and equality of right; not such as the Freemasons absurdly imagine, but such as Jesus Christ obtained for the human race and Saint Francis aspired to: the liberty, We mean, of sons of God, through which we may be free from slavery to Satan or to our passions, both of them most wicked masters; the fraternity whose origin is in God the common Creator and Father of all; the equality which, founded on justice and charity, does not take away all distinctions among men, but, out of the varieties of life, of duties, and of pursuits, forms that union and that harmony which naturally tend to the benefit and dignity of the State.[5]

5. A Philosophy the Church Is Far From Celebrating

In the apostolic letter *Notre charge apostolique* of August 25, 1910, which condemns the French Catholic leftist movement known as *Le Sillon* of Marc Sangnier, Saint Pius X analyzes the celebrated trilogy.

> The *Sillon* is nobly solicitous for human dignity; but it understands that dignity in the manner of certain philosophers of whom the Church does not at all feel proud. The first element of that dignity is liberty, understood in the sense that, except in the matter of religion, each man is autonomous. From this fundamental principle it draws the following conclusions: today the people are in tutelage under an authority distinct from themselves; they ought to free themselves from it: *political emancipation*. They are dependent upon employers who hold their instruments of labor, exploit them, oppress them and degrade them; they should shake off the yoke: *economic emancipation*. Finally, they are ruled by a caste, called the directing caste, to whom their intellectual development gives an undue preponderance in the direction of affairs; they must break away from their domination: *intellectual emancipation*. The leveling down of conditions from this triple point of view will establish equality amongst men, and this equality is true human justice. A political and social

---

[5]   Wynne, *The Great Encyclical Letters of Pope Leo XIII*, p. 103.

organization founded upon this double basis, liberty and equality (to which will soon be added fraternity)—this is what they call democracy....

First of all, in politics, the *Sillon* does not abolish authority; on the contrary, it considers it necessary; but it wishes to divide it, or rather to multiply it in such a way that each citizen will become a kind of king....

Proportions being preserved, it will be the same in the economic order. Taken away from a particular class, the mastership will be so well multiplied that each workingman will become a sort of master....

We come now to the principal element, the moral element.... Snatched away from the narrowness of private interests, and raised up to the interests of the profession, and, even higher, to those of the whole nation, nay, higher still, to those of humanity (for the horizon of the *Sillon* is not bounded by the frontiers of the country, it extends to all men, even to the ends of the earth), the human heart, enlarged by the love of the common welfare, would embrace all comrades of the same profession, all compatriots, all men. Here is human greatness and nobility, the idea realized by the celebrated trilogy, *liberty, equality, fraternity....*

Such, in short, is the theory—we might say the dream—of the *Sillon.*[6]

In this manner, Saint Pius X continues in the footsteps of his predecessors who, since Pius VI, condemned the errors implied in the motto of the French Revolution.

6. The Revolutionary Principles of 1789 Contained the Synthesis of All the Teachings of the False Prophets

When promulgating the decree on the heroic virtue of Blessed Marcellin Champagnat[7] on July 11, 1920, Benedict XV pronounced an allocution from which we borrow the following passages:

One need only turn one's thoughts to the early nineteenth century to recognize that many false prophets appeared in France at that time, and from there aimed to spread abroad the maleficent influence of their perverse teachings. They were prophets who posed as vindicators of the rights of the people, predicting the coming of an age of liberty, fraternity, and equality. Who fails to see that they were disguised as sheep, *"in vestimentis ovium"*!

Yet the liberty predicted by those prophets opened the door not to good but to evil; the fraternity foretold by those prophets did not hail God as the sole Father of all brothers; and the equality proclaimed by the would-be prophets rested not on the identical nature of our origins, nor on our common redemption, nor on the shared destiny of all men. These, alas, were prophets who preached an equality

---

6   *American Catholic Quarterly Review*, Vol. 35 (October 1910), pp. 697-698.

7   Blessed Marcellin Joseph Benoit Champagnat, founder of the Society of the Marist Brothers, was born on May 20, 1789. He died on June 6, 1840, and was beatified by Pius XII on May 29, 1955.

meant to destroy the distinction of class willed by God for our society; prophets who called all men brothers in order to eradicate the idea of the subjection of some men to others; prophets who proclaimed the freedom to do evil, to call darkness light, to confuse falsehood with truth, to prefer the former to the latter, to sacrifice the right and reason of justice and truth to error and vice. It is not difficult to see that these prophets, who presented themselves in sheep's clothing, were inwardly, in reality that is, ravening wolves: *"qui veniunt in vestimentis ovium, intrinsecus autem sunt lupi rapaces!"* And little surprise that against these false prophets resounded a terrible word: Beware! *"Attendite a falsis prophetis!"*

Marcellin Champagnat heard that word; indeed, he understood that it was said not only for his sake, and he decided to echo that same word among the sons of the people whom he knew to be most vulnerable to falling prey to the principles of 1789 because of their inexperience and the ignorance of their parents in matters of religion....

"Attendite a falsis prophetis"—these are the words that were virtually repeated by those who wished to stem the torrent of errors and vices which, thanks to the French Revolution, were threatening to flood the entire earth. *"Attendite a falsis prophetis"*—these are the words that explain the mission embraced by Marcellin Champagnat, the words that must not be consigned to oblivion by those given to studying his life.

It is not without interest to observe the fact that Marcellin Champagnat, born in 1789, was destined to combat the practical application of the very principles that from the year of his birth were given a name and gained an unfortunate and painful celebrity.

To justify his work he needed only continue his reading of today's Gospel, for a brief glance at the wounds opened by the principles of 1789 in the breast of civil and religious society would have shown that those principles contained the sum of the teachings of false prophets: *"ex fructibus eorum cognoscetis eos."*...

Not irrelevant to the expansion of the houses of the Little Brothers of Mary and to the good guidance of the young people welcomed therein, was the Most Holy Virgin herself in the form of an image that first appeared, then disappeared, then was found again. That first expansion was certainly wondrous and found its explanation only in the subsequent expansion which by the tenth lustrum after its foundation saw the day when five thousand religious of the new institute were giving salutary instruction to a hundred thousand children scattered over every region of the globe.

If the Venerable Champagnat, by the light of prophecy, could have seen so extraordinary a result, he might perhaps have lamented the still excessive number of children left in the shadow of death and ignorance; he might indeed have deplored not having been better able to prevent the nefarious growth of the worst seed scattered by the French Revolution; nevertheless, a feeling of dutiful gratitude to God for the good achieved by the Congregation founded by him would have obliged him to admit that, just as from the bad fruit of the teaching of certain prophets of his time he had deduced the falsity thereof, so from the good fruit stemming from his works he could deduce the goodness: *"Igitur ex fructibus eorum cognoscetis eos."*[8]

---

[8] *L'Osservatore Romano*, July 12-13, 1920, 2d ed.

7. Christian Concepts That Assumed an Anti-Christian, Secular, and Irreligious Banner

During a visit to Frascati on September 1, 1963, Paul VI, referring to Saint Vincent Pallotti's work in that city, presented the following considerations on the French Revolution and its motto Liberty, Equality, Fraternity:

> It was the period following the French Revolution, with the many disasters and the disordered and chaotic, yet excited and even hopeful, ideas which that revolution awoke in men of the past century. There was great need to set that period in order, one could say to stabilize it, to make it as sound as it should be.
>
> At the same time one could note the ferment that accompanies something new; there were vital ideas afoot, there was a combination of the great principles of the revolution that had done nothing more or less than appropriate to itself certain Christian concepts—fraternity, liberty, equality, progress, the desire to lift up the lower classes. All this was Christian, but now it had taken up as its own a banner that was anti-Christian, secularistic, irreligious; that tended to pervert that feature of the Gospel heritage that was aimed at setting a higher and nobler value on human life.[9]

8. At Heart, These Were Christian Ideas; But Those Who First Formulated Them Made No Reference to the Alliance Between Man and God

In the homily of the Mass at *Le Bourget* airport in Paris on June 1, 1980, John Paul II affirmed:

> What have the sons and daughters of your nation not done for the knowledge of man, for the expression of man in the formulation of his inalienable rights! Everyone knows the role played by liberty, equality and fraternity in your culture and in your history. At heart, these are Christian ideas. As I say all this I am well aware that those who were the first to formulate these ideas, this ideal, were not referring to the alliance of man with Eternal Wisdom. They wanted to act for man.[10]

9. A Historical Movement Stirred by an Impetuous Wave of Violence and Religious Hatred

In the audience in which he received pilgrims of Angers on the occasion of

---

[9]   *The Pope Speaks*, Vol. 9, no. 2, p. 176.

[10]   *Insegnamenti di Giovanni Paolo II* (Libreria Editrice Vaticana, 1980), Vol. 3, no. 1, p. 1589.

the beatification of Guillaume Repin and his companions, on February 20, 1984, John Paul II affirmed:

> I know that the French Revolution—especially during the period known as the Terror—took many other victims from you in the west, thousands who were guillotined, shot, drowned, or who died in the prisons of Angers. God alone knows their merits, their sacrifice, their faith. The diocese and the Holy See could only examine a number of cases, in which the evidence of martyrdom was better known and its religious motivation more obvious....
>
> [The] arrest and condemnation [of Blessed Repin and his ninety-eight companions] certainly were situated in a political context of opposition to a regime which at that time rejected so many religious values. Even if this historic movement had been inspired by generous sentiments—liberty, equality, fraternity—and by a desire for necessary reforms, it found itself swept into a wave of reprisals, violence, and religious hatred. This is a fact. It is not for us to judge this political evolution here. We leave to the historians the task of qualifying its excesses.[11]

* * *

The reader might notice here and there in these texts an apparent contradiction among the pronouncements of the different popes who dealt with the trilogy Liberty, Equality, Fraternity.

This impression fades the more the reader bears in mind that, properly considered in themselves—and therefore in the light of Catholic principles—each of these words designates concepts worthy of approval. This is what some popes sought to stress.

As a rule, however, the thinkers and writers who laid the groundwork for the French Revolution, the men of action who contrived the tremendous sociopolitical commotion that shook France after 1789, and also the pamphleteers and demagogues who carried it to the streets, prompting so many injustices and such terrible crimes, did not understand these words in this light. Rather, they hurled themselves as one to the demolition of Religion, to the hatred of all legitimate authority, and to the furious denial of all inequalities, even when just and necessary.

To praise the trilogy Liberty, Equality, Fraternity in itself does not imply approval of the radical and absurd errors that the revolutionaries, as a group, inferred therein. The full meaning of these errors was revealed in the final and extreme thrust of the French Revolution: the communist insurrection of Babeuf.[12] This

---

[11]   Ibid. (1984), Vol. 7, no. 1, pp. 447-448.

[12]   François Noël Babeuf (1760-1797). This French revolutionary led the "Conspiracy of the Equals," which was active in the winter of 1795-96 and constituted "the first attempt to realize communism." His "Plebeian Manifesto" advocated community of goods and duties. It was "the first form of the revolutionary ideology of the new society born of the Revolution itself. Communism, until then a utopian dream, became with Babeufism an ideological system; through the Conspiracy of the Equals it entered political history" (Albert Soboul, *La Revolution Française* [Paris: Gallimard, 1962], Vol. 2, pp. 216, 219).

Regarding the role played by Babeuf in the continuity of the revolutionary spirit, Marx wrote in a work that

insurrection showed the extent to which the 1789 Revolution bore the seeds of communism—synthesis of religious, philosophical, political, social, and economic errors—that caused the unspeakable moral and material misfortunes confronting Eastern European peoples today.

One of the most successful ruses of the French Revolution consisted in sowing confusion among many simple and unsuspecting people by labeling a monstrous mass of doctrinal errors and criminal events with honest and even commendable words. Many such people were led to think that at root the doctrines of the French Revolution were good even though most of its events were severely reprehensible. Others understood that the principles which produced such events could not be less censurable than the results, and therefore deduced that the trilogy preached as the synthesis of these perverse principles deserved the same rejection.

Although it is slowly being dispelled, this harmful confusion persists.

Some popes, addressing a public that included many such-minded people, strove to correct unilateral and overly severe opinions regarding this astutely manipulated trilogy. Other popes endeavored to prevent the intrinsic innocuousness of the trilogy's terms from leading people to overlook the French Revolution's essential perversity, which traversed the last century and most of our own using the labels of socialism or communism, and which, in its most genuine content, is now agonizing in Eastern Europe. Or, to put it better, it is undergoing a metamorphosis, searching for new words, new formulas, new wiles to attain its goals, which are radically atheistic when not pantheistic and, at any rate, absolutely and universally egalitarian.

---

he blasphemously titled *The Holy Family*: "The revolutionary movement that began in 1789 in the social circle—which during its evolution had as its principal representatives Leclerc and Roux and which temporarily collapsed with Babeuf's conspiracy—was already spreading the communist idea that Babeuf's friend Buonarroti would reintroduce into France after the revolution of 1830. This idea, developed in all its consequences, marks the beginning of the modern world" (quoted in François Furet, *Dictionnaire Critique de la Revolution Française* [Paris: Flammarion, 1988], p. 199).

The Directory opposed Babeuf's movement. He was imprisoned and executed in 1797.

Forms of Government in the Light of the Church's Social Doctrine

In Theory and in Practice

A. Pontifical and Other Texts on the Forms of Government: Monarchy, Aristocracy, and Democracy

1. The Monarchic Regime: The Best Form of Government

In his allocution to the Secret Consistory on June 17, 1793, concerning the execution of King Louis XVI of France, Pius VI stated: "After having abolished the monarchical form of government, which is the best, it [the Convention] transferred all public power to the people."[1]

2. The Church Is Not Opposed to Any Form of Government that Is Just and Serves the Common Good

Leo XIII says in his encyclical *Diuturnum illud* (June 29, 1881):

> There is no question here respecting forms of government, for there is no reason why the Church should not approve of the chief power being held by one man or by more, provided only it be just, and that it tend to the common advantage. Wherefore, so long as justice be respected, the people are not hindered from choosing for themselves that form of government which suits best either their own disposition, or the institutions and customs of their ancestors.[2]

---

[1] *Pii VI Pont. Max. Acta* (Rome: Typis S. Congreg. de Propaganda Fide, 1871), Vol. 2, p. 17.

[2] Rev. Joseph Husslein, S.J., *Social Wellsprings* (Milwaukee: Bruce Publishing Co., 1940), Vol. 1, p. 51.

View of the Altar of the Confession, in Saint Peter's Basilica.
In right foreground, an ancient statue of the first Pope.

In his encyclical *Immortale Dei* (November 1, 1885), the same Pontiff states:

> The right to rule is not necessarily, however, bound up with any special mode of government. It may take this or that form, provided only that it be of a nature to insure the general welfare....
>
> If judged dispassionately, no one of the several forms of government is in itself condemned, inasmuch as none of them contain anything contrary to Catholic doctrine, and all of them are capable, if wisely and justly managed, of insuring the welfare of the State.[3]

In these texts, Leo XIII supposes the case of a nation that, without violating the principle of authority or acquired rights, has to choose between the existing form of government and some other.

These teachings are also applicable, *mutatis mutandis*, to a person who, as a private individual, is faced with this choice, as for example, when he votes in a plebiscite to opt for a monarchy, an aristocratic republic, or a democratic republic; or when he chooses political party affiliation.

3. A Form of Government May Be Preferable, Because It Is Better Suited to the Character or Customs of the People for Which It Is Intended

In his encyclical *Au milieu des sollicitudes* (February 16, 1892), Leo XIII writes:

> Various political governments have succeeded one another in France during the last century, each having its own distinctive form: the Empire, the Monarchy, and the Republic. By giving oneself up to abstractions, one could at length conclude which is the best of these forms, considered in themselves; and in all truth, it may be affirmed that each one of them is good, provided it lead straight to its end—that is to say, to the common good for which social authority is constituted; and finally, it may be added that, from a relative point of view, such and such a form of government may be preferable because of being better adapted to the character and customs of such or such a nation. In this order of speculative ideas, Catholics, like all other citizens, are free to prefer one form of government to another precisely because no one of these forms is, in itself, opposed to the principles of sound reason nor to the maxims of Christian doctrine.[4]

---

[3] Wynne, *The Great Encyclical Letters of Pope Leo XIII*, pp. 109, 126-127.

[4] Wynne, *Great Encyclical Letters*, p. 255.

4. The Error of *Le Sillon*: Only Democracy Will Usher in the Reign of Perfect Justice

Saint Pius X says in the apostolic letter *Notre charge apostolique* (August 25, 1910):

> The *Sillon*[5]...therefore, sows amongst your Catholic youth erroneous and fatal notions upon authority, liberty and obedience. The same is to be said with regard to justice and equality. It strives, it says, to attain an era of equality, which, owing to that fact alone, would be an era of greater justice. Thus to it every inequality of condition is an injustice or, at least, a diminution of justice! A principle supremely contrary to the nature of things, productive of envy and injustice and subversive of all social order. Thus democracy alone will inaugurate the reign of perfect justice! Is it not an insult to the other forms of government, which are thus degraded to the rank of wretched incapables? Moreover, the *Sillon* goes contrary to this point in the teaching of Leo XIII. It could have read in the encyclical on political government already quoted that "justice safeguards: it is not forbidden to the people to choose for themselves the government which corresponds best with their character or the institutions and customs that they have received from their ancestors," and the encyclical alludes to the well-known triple form of government. It supposes, then, that justice is compatible with each one of them. And does not the encyclical on the condition of the workers affirm clearly the possibility of restoring justice in the actual organization of society, inasmuch as it indicates the means of doing so? Without any doubt, Leo XIII meant to speak not of any justice, but of perfect justice. Therefore, in teaching that justice is compatible with the three forms of government referred to, it taught that in this respect democracy does not enjoy a special privilege. The Sillonists who contend to the contrary either refuse to hear the Church or form to themselves a conception which is not Catholic with regard to justice and equality.[6]

5. The Catholic Church Finds No Difficulties in Adapting to the Various Forms of Government

Pius XI writes in the encyclical *Dilectissima nobis* (June 3, 1933):

> The Catholic Church is never bound to one form of government more than to another, provided the Divine rights of God and of Christian consciences are safe. She does not find any difficulty in adapting herself to various civil institutions, be they monarchic or republican, aristocratic or democratic.[7]

---

[5] *Le Sillon* claimed Christian inspiration. Founded in 1894 by Marc Sagnier, it disappeared in 1910 after having been condemned by Saint Pius X. Nevertheless, it had already paved the way for the Christian Democratic Parties of Europe (cf. *Le Petit Larousse* [Paris: Larousse, 1992], s.v. *Sillon*, p. 1681).

[6] *American Catholic Quarterly Review*, Vol. 35 (October 1910), pp. 700-701.

[7] *Catholic Mind*, Vol. 31 (July 1933), p. 242.

6. True Democracy Is Not Incompatible with Monarchy

In his 1944 Christmas message Pius XII says:

> Democracy, taken in the broad sense, admits of various forms, and can be realized in monarchies as well as in republics....
>
> The democratic state, be it monarchical or republican, should, like any form of government, be entrusted with the power to command with real and effective authority.[8]

7. The Catholic Church Accepts Any Form of Government that Does Not Oppose Divine and Human Rights

In an allocution to the extraordinary Secret Consistory of February 14, 1949, Pius XII affirms:

> [The Catholic Church] admits any and every form of civil government provided it be not inconsistent with divine and human rights. But when it does contradict these rights, bishops and the faithful themselves are bound by their own conscience to resist unjust laws.[9]

8. To Determine the Political Structure of a Country It Is Necessary to Take into Consideration the Circumstances of Each People

In the encyclical *Pacem in terris* (April 11, 1963), John XXIII says:

> It is impossible to determine in all cases what is the most suitable form of government, or how civil authorities can most effectively fulfill their respective functions, i.e., legislative, judicial, and executive functions of the State.
>
> In determining the structure and operation of government which a State is to have, great weight has to be given to the circumstances which will vary at different times and in different places.[10]

---

8   Yzermans, *The Major Addresses of Pope Pius XII*, Vol. 2, pp. 80, 82.

9   *The Catholic Mind*, Vol. 47 (April 1949), p. 253.

10   *Peace on Earth* (Boston: Daughters of St. Paul, n.d.), p. 22.

9. The Church Does Not Manifest Any Preference for Political Systems or Institutional Solutions

John Paul II says in the encyclical *Sollicitudo rei socialis* (December 30, 1987):

> The Church does not propose economic and political systems or programs nor does she show preference for one or another, provided that human dignity is properly respected and promoted, and provided she herself is allowed the room she needs to exercise her ministry in the world.[11]

In the encyclical *Centesimus annus* (May 1, 1991), John Paul II states:

> The Church respects the legitimate autonomy of the democratic order and is not entitled to express preferences for this or that institutional or constitutional solution. Her contribution to the political order is precisely her vision of the dignity of the person revealed in all its fullness in the mystery of the Incarnate Word.[12]

10. The Fundamental Structure of the Political Community: A Fruit of Each People's Genius and History

The constitution *Gaudium et spes* (1965) of the Second Vatican Council says:

> Individuals, families, and various groups which compose the civic community are aware of their own insufficiency in the matter of establishing a fully human condition of life. They see the need for that wider community in which each would daily contribute his energies toward the ever better attainment of the common good. It is for this reason that they have set up the political community in its manifold expressions.
>
> Hence the political community exists for that common good in which the community finds its full justification and meaning, and from which it derives its pristine and proper right....
>
> The practical ways in which the political community structures itself and regulates public authority can vary according to the particular character of a people and its historical development. But these methods should always serve to mold men who are civilized, peace-loving, and well disposed toward all—to the advantage of the whole human family.[13]

---

[11] *Origins*, Vol. 17, no. 38 (March 3, 1988), p. 655.

[12] Ibid., Vol. 21, no. 1 (May 16, 1991), p. 18.

[13] *The Documents of Vatican II*, pp. 283-284, 285.

11. The Monarchy Is in Itself the Best Regime, for It Is the One that More Easily Favors Peace

To the pontifical texts quoted in testimony of the Church's social doctrine on this subject, it is fitting to add some representative texts of Saint Thomas Aquinas, given the prominence of his thinking in traditional Catholic teaching.

In *De Regimine Principum*, "having set forth these preliminary points" (that it behooves men to live in society and therefore it is indispensable that they be correctly governed by some ruler), Saint Thomas goes on to say.

> We must now inquire what is better for a province or a city: whether to be ruled by one man or by many. Now this may be considered from the very purpose of government. For the aim of any ruler should be directed towards securing the welfare of whatever he undertakes to rule. The duty of the pilot, for instance, is to preserve his ship amidst the perils of the sea and to bring it to the port of safety.
>
> Now, the welfare and safety of a multitude formed into a society is the preservation of its unity, which is called peace, and which, if taken away, the benefit of social life is lost and moreover the multitude in its disagreement becomes a burden to itself.
>
> The chief concern of the ruler of a multitude, therefore, should be to procure the unity of peace: and it is not legitimate for him to deliberate whether he shall establish peace in the multitude subject to him, just as a physician does not deliberate whether he shall heal the sick man encharged to him. For no one should deliberate about an end which he is obliged to seek, but only about the means to attain that end. Wherefore, the Apostle, having commended the unity of the faithful people, says: "Be ye careful to keep the unity of the spirit in the bond of peace" (Eph. 4:3). The more efficacious, therefore, a government is in keeping the unity of peace, the more useful it will be. For we call that more useful which leads the better to the end. Now, it is manifest that what is itself one can more efficaciously bring about unity than several: just as the most efficacious cause of heat is that which is by its nature hot. Therefore the rule of one man is more useful than the rule of many.
>
> Furthermore, it is evident that several persons could by no means keep a multitude from harm if they totally disagreed. For a certain union is necessary among them if they are to rule at all: several men, for instance, could not pull a ship in one direction unless joined together in some fashion. Now several are said to be united according as they come closer to being one. So one man rules better than several who come near being one.
>
> Again, whatever is in accord with nature is best: for in all things nature does what is best. Now, every natural governance is governance by one. In the multitude of bodily members there is one which moves them all, namely, the heart; and among the powers of the soul one power presides as chief, namely, the reason. Even among the bees there is one queen and in the whole universe there is One God, Maker and Ruler of all things. And this is reasonable. For every multitude is derived from unity. Wherefore,

artificial things imitate natural things and since the work of art is better according as it attains a closer likeness to what is in nature, it necessarily follows that it is best, in the case of a human multitude, that it be ruled by one person.

This is also evident from experience; for provinces or cities which are not ruled by one person are torn with dissensions and are tossed about without peace so that the complaint seems to be fulfilled which the Lord uttered through the Prophet: "Many pastors have destroyed my vineyard" (Jer. 12:10). But, on the contrary, provinces and cities which are ruled under one king enjoy peace, flourish in justice and delight in prosperity. Hence, the Lord by His prophets promises to His people as a great reward that He will give them one head and that one Prince will be in the midst of them.[14]

The eminent Thomist, Fr. Victorino Rodríguez, O.P.,[15] adds the following comment to this explanation of the Angelic Doctor, which he enriches with other texts of Saint Thomas:

On preferring monarchy to preserve the peace of society—It is undeniable that peace, in the positive, dynamic sense of "tranquil liberty" (Cicero, II *Philipp.*, chap. 44) or "tranquility of order" (Saint Augustine, *De Civitate Dei*, Book 19, chap. 13, 1), is the single most important factor for the common good, if not a synthesis of all its constituents, and the aspiration of any honest government. Now then, insofar as peace partakes of order or unity, in and of itself it has a more direct and straight connection with a unitary or monarchic form of government than with other more pluralist or dispersed forms. This is one aspect of government that is stressed in these chapters: for intrinsic reasons of unity, through analogy with the natural order, from the lessons of history, and because it is in accord with theocratic government. Later we will see also how a democratic government offers advantages for the peace of society.

On the aspect underscored here, he [Saint Thomas] left us another splendid page in the *Summa Theologica*, I, q. 103, a. 3:

"Now the best government is government by one. The reason of this is that government is nothing but the directing of the things governed to the end; which consists in some good. But unity belongs to the idea of goodness, as Boethius proves (*De consolatione*, iii.) from this, that all things desire good, so do they desire unity; without which they would cease to exist. For a thing so far exists as it is one. Whence we observe that things resist division, as far as they can; and the dissolution of a thing arises from some defect therein. Therefore the intention of a ruler over a multitude is unity, or peace. Now the proper cause of unity is one.

---

[14] Saint Thomas Aquinas, *On the Governance of Rulers*, Gerald Phelan, trans. (London: Sheed and Ward, 1938), Book I, chap. 2, pp. 40-42.

[15] A faithful disciple of the renowned Father Santiago Ramirez, O.P., his master in scholastic philosophy, Father Rodríguez has published more than 250 articles and books on philosophical and theological subjects. Outstanding among these are *Key Issues of Christian Humanism* and *Studies in Theological Anthropology*.

Father Rodríguez is Prior of the Monastery of Santo Domingo el Real, in Madrid, former professor at the Theology School of San Esteban in Salamanca, and professor at the Pontifical University of the same city. He is presently a professor in the Superior Council of Scientific Investigations in Madrid, a member of the Royal Academy of Doctors of the same city, and a member of the Roman Pontifical Academy of Theology.

For it is clear that several cannot be the cause of unity or concord, except so far as they are united. Furthermore, what is one in itself is more apt and a better cause of unity than several things united. Therefore a multitude is better governed by one than by several."[16]

12. The Best Way to Moderate and Fortify Monarchy Is to Surround It with Aristocracy and Democracy

Commenting on the thinking of Saint Thomas Aquinas regarding the mixed form of government, Father Rodríguez writes.

> On mixed regimes, theoretically the optimum form of government—In this work [*De Regimine Principum*], and more specifically in this seventh[17] chapter, following an analysis of the three kinds of governments (monarchy, aristocracy, democracy), Saint Thomas leans toward the monarchical form, albeit one having moderated power so as to avoid tyranny: *"Simul etiam sic eius temperetur potestas, ut in tyrannidem ne facili declinare non possit"* [Its power should be tempered so that it may not easily deteriorate into a tyranny].
>
> This idea of restraining the monarch's power led him, in later works, to shape the theory of the mixed regime as the optimum form of government: The best way to restrain the monarchy and to make it effective is to surround it with aristocracy and democracy. I limit myself to transcribing only the two texts that seem fundamental and that are sufficiently clear in this regard.
>
> "It is incomprehensible that an optimum government can emerge from the two terrible forms of government (tyranny and democracy[18] or demagogy). A far better procedure is that in which they who form the city's government use various correct forms of government, since the more mixed it be, the better, as more citizens participate in governing the city" (in *II Politicorum*, lect. 7, no. 247).
>
> "Some say that the best city government is the one that is a type of mixture of the aforementioned systems (monarchy, aristocracy, democracy). The reason is that, in this way, one system is held in check by the presence of the other. This leaves less room for rebellion, since everyone participates in the governance of the city, with the people ruling in some things, the aristocracy in others, and the king in yet others" (ibid.).[19]

---

[16] *El Régimen Político de Santo Tomás de Aquino* (Madrid: Editorial Fuerza Nueva, 1978), pp. 37, 39. Translation of *Summa* excerpt from R. & T. Washbourne, London, 1912, Vol. 4, p. 370.

[17] Chapter 6 in Phelan's English translation.

[18] Regarding the term *democracy*, Father Victorino writes: "This pejorative sense of democracy in *De Regimine Principum* is upheld in the commentaries on Aristotle's *Ethics* and *Politics*, wherein it is also called 'plebeian' government, 'popular' government, government of the 'poor,' wherein a numerical majority of citizens reigns over a more qualified minority and, consequently, oppresses it unjustly (hence the pejorative sense of this democracy).... Nevertheless, in the *Summa Theologica*, when the forms of government are alluded to (e.g., I-II, q. 95, a. 4; II-II, q. 61, a. 2), only tyranny appears as an incorrect form of government, and neither oligarchy nor democracy, which can be more or less correct" (Father Rodríguez, *El Régimen Político*, pp. 31, 33).

[19] Father Rodríguez, *El Régimen Político*, pp. 61, 63.

Apotheosis of Saint Thomas Aquinas, by Francisco de Zurbarán.
(Museo de Bellas Artes, Seville)

13. A Democratic Constitution Should Assume and Protect the Values of the Christian Faith, Without Which It Will Not Be Able to Survive

In view of the peculiar circumstances of our day, it is opportune to quote a judicious analysis of Joseph Cardinal Ratzinger, Prefect of the Congregation for the Doctrine of the Faith, in an interview to the newspaper *El Mercurio* of Santiago, Chile (June 12, 1988):

> Some 150 years ago, Alexis de Tocqueville pointed out that democracy can continue to exist if it be preceded by a specific ethos. The mechanisms of democracy work only if this is clear and not subject to debate, and only then can such mechanisms be turned into instruments of justice. Majority rule is tolerable only if the majority is not entitled to act exclusively at its own discretion, since both majority and minority must be united in mutual respect for a system of justice that is binding on both. Consequently, there are fundamental elements prior to the existence of the State that are not subject to bargaining between majority and minority and that must be inviolable for all.
>
> The question is: Who defines these "fundamental elements"? And who protects them? As Tocqueville was to remark, this issue did not arise as a constitutional problem in the first American democracy, that of the United States, because there was a certain basic Christian consensus—Protestant—that no one questioned and everyone considered obvious. This principle was nourished by the common conviction of the citizens, a conviction that was beyond debate. But what happens when such convictions no longer exist? Will it be possible to declare, by majority decision, that something considered unjust until yesterday is now right, and vice versa? In the third century, Origen declared in this regard: "If injustice should become law in the land of the Scythians, then the Christians living there would be acting in violation of the law." This is easily translated to the twentieth century: When the national-socialist government declared injustice to be the law, for the duration of that state of affairs a Christian was forced to violate the law. "Obey God, rather than men." But how do we incorporate this factor into the concept of democracy?
>
> In any event, it is evident that a democratic constitution, in its foundations, must take precautions with regard to the values proceeding from the Christian Faith, declaring them inviolable, precisely in the name of liberty. Such safeguarding of the law will persist of course only if protected by the conviction of a large number of citizens. This is why it is of supreme importance for the preparation and conservation of democracy to preserve and strengthen those basic moral convictions, without which democracy could not survive.

B. Forms of Government:
Abstract Principles and Their Influence
in the Formation of a Political Mentality

It seems particularly fitting to raise some considerations regarding the pontifical documents and teachings of Saint Thomas on the forms of government included in this work.

1. The Concrete Usefulness of
the Abstract Principles

First, a reflection: These documents enunciate mainly abstract principles. Yet, many people today consider abstractions to be useless in political, social, or economic matters. They question, or simply deny, the relevance of the cited documents. Even a cursory observation of reality, however, shows clearly that the opposite is true.

For example, abstract principles have a very marked and at times even preponderant influence on the great majority of our contemporaries when they opt for one of the three forms of government. So we see that:

* Of the three forms of government (monarchy, aristocracy, and democracy) pure monarchy is the one that embodies the greatest inequality between governors and governed. The monarch rules and the rest obey.

* When the monarchy coexists with an aristocracy that tempers it by performing some of the duties of the royal power, the inequality between the king and the subjects is attenuated since some of them—the aristocrats—not only obey but participate in the royal power.

* The inequality is further attenuated when the royal power is exercised cumulatively with the aristocratic and popular powers. In this case, the people also exercise a portion of the public power, which is consonant with democracy.

* Finally, this enumeration must include the hypothesis of a State where no public power is held by a king or an aristocracy, in other words, a completely republican state. In it, political inequality is ipso facto nonexistent, at least in theory,[20] and the rulers, elected by the people, are supposed to exercise the power strictly in accordance with the voters' will.

Now, many are those today who prefer one of these forms of government on the basis of an abstract principle (actually condemned by Saint Pius X), namely, that monarchy and, implicitly, aristocracy are unjust forms of government because they admit a political and social inequality among the members of the same country. This principle, in turn, is derived from the metaphysical principle that every inequality among men is intrinsically unjust.

---

[20] See Part I, Chapter VII, 6 c.

2. The Position of Catholics Vis-à-vis the Forms of Government

When compared with the aforementioned pontifical texts and those of Saint Thomas, it becomes clear that both of these radically egalitarian principles are formally opposed to what Catholics ought to believe in this matter.

Indeed, monarchy (and implicitly aristocracy) is not only just and efficacious in promoting the common good, the Pontiffs teach, but it is also the best form of government, according to Pius VI and Saint Thomas.[21]

From this and everything expounded previously, it follows that:

* A Catholic who, mindful of the particular conditions of his country, prefers for it a republican and democratic form of government cannot be criticized. This form is not unjust or censurable in itself. It is intrinsically just and, depending on the circumstances, can efficaciously secure the common good.

* According to the right order of preferences, however, a Catholic who wants to be excellent in his fidelity to the Church's doctrine should admire and desire more what is excellent than what is simply good. He should thus be especially grateful to Providence when the specific conditions in his country permit or even call for the establishment of the best form of government, which, according to Saint Thomas, is monarchy.[22]

When a sound analysis of reality shows that the common good of his country can be furthered by a judicious alteration of its particular conditions, he will be worthy of praise if he is willing to take legal and honest action, within the framework of liberty of the democratic regime in which he lives, to persuade the electorate to change those particular conditions and establish (or restore) the monarchic regime.

* All this stems, as was said, from the more general moral principle that all men can and must reject evil, love and practice good, and reserve the best of their preferences for what is excellent. This principle, applied to the choice of a form of government, would result in the rejection of misgovernment, anarchy, and chaos; in the acceptance of a legitimate democratic or aristocratic republic; and in the decided preference for the best form of government, which is tempered monarchy, whenever it is propitious for the common good. Should the monarchic form be unsuitable in view of the country's specific conditions, the establishment

---

[21]   Another Doctor of the Church, Saint Francis de Sales, attests to the elevated degree of perfection in monarchy as a form of government more in accord with the order of Creation: "God, therefore, having a will to make all things good and beautiful, reduced the multitude and distinction of the same to a perfect unity, and, as man would say, brought them all under a monarchy, making a subordination of one thing to another and of all things to Himself the sovereign Monarch. He reduces all our members into one body under one head; of many persons He forms a family, of many families a town, of many towns a province, of many provinces a kingdom, putting the whole kingdom under the government of one sole king" (*Library of St. Francis de Sales*, Vol. 2 *Treatise on the Love of God*, transl. by Fr. Henry Mackey, OSB [London: Burns Oates & Washbourne, Ltd., n.d.], Book I, chap. 1, p. 19).

[22]   "Almost all the Scholastic authors, ancient and modern, together with a great number of non-Scholastic authors, declare that a tempered monarchy is the form to be preferred *in abstracto*" (Father Irineu González Moral, S.J., *Philosofiae Scholasticae Summa* [Madrid: Biblioteca de Autores Cristianos, 1952], Vol. 3, pp. 836-837).

of this more perfect good might be an act of inconformity with the designs of Providence, motivated by mere political sympathy.

* At any rate, one can conclude from this that the true Catholic must have a monarchic political mentality that coexists with a strong and penetrating grasp of reality and its possibilities.

3. Sociocultural Projection of the Aristocratic-Monarchic Political Mentality

These political principles shape the society, culture, and economy of a people. By the intrinsic and natural cohesion between these fields and the political field, the excellence of a certain aristocratic-monarchic spirit should be present—always in due measure—in all levels of society and all the manifestations of the activity of a people, whatever its form of government.

For example, in all societies, even when the State is democratic, a particularly strong respect for the father in a family, the schoolmaster at school, the professor or dean at the university, the owners and managers in the company, should reflect this aristocratic-monarchic spirit.

In this perspective, Pius XII taught that even in republican states society should have certain genuinely aristocratic institutions. He also praised the role of prominent families that "set the tone, as we say, for the village or the city, for the region or the entire country."[23] This deeply-mourned Pontiff reaffirmed this teaching in allocutions to the Roman Patriciate and Nobility pronounced both during Italy's monarchic period (1940 to 1946) and during the republic (1947 to 1952 and 1958). In other words, the change of government in no way diminished the social mission of the aristocracy.

When considering the relation between the aristocratic-monarchic mentality and the culture of a people, one should also take into account that this mentality may find expression in an art, literature, and, in short, a lifestyle characteristically popular in what concerns the lower classes, or characteristically bourgeois and aristocratic in what is specific to each of these categories.

The European states and societies prior to 1789 were rich in these varied manifestations. Each of them reflected in its own way the unity and variety of the nation's spirit. This spirit gave rise to magnificent works in each social level, many of which are carefully preserved today both in private collections and in first-rate museums and archives. This is the case, for example, with the homes and furnishings of working-class families and, naturally, with the cultural production of the upper classes. What earnest, what just, and even touching commentaries could be made in praise of the popular art of the periods prior to our egalitarian era!

Art and culture that are authentic and yet typically popular and suited to the condition of the common people displease our century's revolutionary spirit. So,

---

[23] RPN 1946, p. 340; see Part I, Chapter V, 1, 10.

when unforeseen economic growth considerably improves the living conditions of a working-class family or group, egalitarianism frowns on the family's refining itself within its own social level. Rather, the revolutionary spirit invariably impels the family or group to seek a higher social level immediately, a level for which it would often be prepared only after long decades of personal improvement. Whence arises the not uncommon disproportion and nonsense found among the parvenus.

These are but a few examples, among uncountable others, of the influence of abstract principles on the history of the immense cultural area that is the West.

4. The Legitimacy of Anti-egalitarian Principles

We have thus far analyzed the opposition between radical egalitarianism, which influences many of our contemporaries in their choice of governmental forms, and the Church's social doctrine on this matter. This egalitarianism is the principle that, like a hurricane or an earthquake, has produced the greatest and most evident transformations in the West.

Something should be said at this point about the legitimacy of anti-egalitarian principles as applied to forms of government. These principles are just when, inspired by Christian teachings, they not only contrast with radical egalitarianism, but also admit and favor political and social forms based on a harmonious and fair inequality of classes.

In synthesis, these principles acknowledge the equality of men in what concerns the rights they have from the simple fact of being human. But they also affirm the legitimacy of accidental inequalities stemming from differences in virtue, intellectual gifts, physical capacity, and so forth. These inequalities do not exist solely between individuals. They also exist between families in virtue of the beautiful principle enunciated by Pius XII: "Social inequalities, even those related to birth, are inevitable: Benign nature and God's blessing to humanity illuminate and protect all cradles, looking on them with love, but do not make them equal."[24]

According to the anti-egalitarian principles, inequalities tend to perpetuate and refine themselves—without becoming exaggerated—down through the generations and centuries. They even give rise to a strict legislation, customary or written, that excludes from the nobility those who become unworthy of it for any reason, and opens the doors of nobility to the authentically traditional analogous elites.

The existence of inequalities among persons, families, and social classes being legitimate, it is easy to deduce the legitimacy and excellence of the governmental forms in which these natural inequalities are preserved and favored in an organic and balanced way, namely, monarchy and aristocracy, both in the pure and tempered forms.

---

[24] RPN 1942, p. 347.

5. Reflections of the Political Mentality upon
the Intermediate Social Groups

We have considered the complex but beautiful subject of the forms of government in several of its most important aspects, as well as some reflections of the mentality inherent to these forms in the social, cultural, and economic life of nations.

It would be fitting to consider the reflections of this mentality on the social bodies between the State and the individual that made the nations of pre-revolutionary Europe vigorous ensembles of organic societies. However, the vastness and richness of the subject prevent its inclusion in this book.

If men today had an exact notion of what were—in the context of organic society—a region, a fief, a municipality, a great autonomous corporative entity, and so on, the premises of many reasonings about governmental forms would become clearer, and the discussions of the subject would gain in focus and practical application.

The subject of organic societies is far from being untimely. The speculations and efforts to unify Europe into a politico-socio-cultural-military-economic whole have been followed by an explosion of exacerbated regionalisms and centralisms. In the tumultuous news of the contemporary press, these seem like ships adrift on an ocean of indecision, vessels without compass, rudder, or ballast. From this fundamental lack results a lamentable fragility of cohesion that threatens to sunder the whole.

C. The French Revolution: The Prototypical
Model of a Revolutionary Republic

One could contrast the monarchic mentality discussed above with a republican mentality and even a revolutionary republican mentality, that is, the mentality born of a revolutionary movement in favor of the republic (the French Revolution, for example).

To understand this revolutionary republican mentality well, it is necessary to distinguish it from the mentality of the person who accepts the republican form of government for his country due to the circumstances but has a monarchic mentality.

It is necessary, therefore, to consider what the Revolution[25] is and how it differs from the republic in the Thomistic, objective, and speculative sense of a legitimate form of government.

This distinction was so clear at the time of the French Revolution that several of those who died on the steps of the throne fighting heroically for the French monarchy were citizens of republics, the Helvetian republics. These men, members of the famous Swiss Guard, saw no contradiction between their preference for the republican form of government in their small country and their defense of the throne of France. Nor did the King of France fear that he was jeopardizing the stability of his throne by having among his most faithful guards people who wanted a republic for their own country.

---

[25] The use of the word *Revolution* is explained in Part I, Chapter V, 3 b, note.

We shall now consider the relation between the Revolution and the form of government it generated: the revolutionary republic. This republic should not be confused with the non-revolutionary republic, which is a legitimate form of government, as described in pontifical documents and the writings of Saint Thomas.

We shall also see how public opinion can be led to accept this revolutionary republic by the action of pseudo-moderates who favor the Revolution. To illustrate this thesis, the French Revolution, a prototypical historical example, was chosen.

1. The Revolution in Its Essential Elements

a. An impulse at the service of an ideology

It is necessary to distinguish two elements in the Revolution:

The Revolution is an *ideology*. This ideology has at its service an *impulse*. Both in its ideology and in its impulse, the Revolution is *radical* and *totalitarian*.

As an ideology, this radical totalitarianism consists in taking all the principles that constitute its doctrine to their last consequences.

As an impulse, it invariably tends to transpose the revolutionary principles to events, customs, and institutions, thus applying its ideological elements to concrete reality. The goal of the revolutionary impulse may be defined in the slogan: Everything! Now! And forever!

The fact that one of the Revolution's essential elements is an impulse does not mean it should be understood as something impulsive in the popular sense of the term, that is, as something devoid of thought and moved by avidity and intemperance.

On the contrary, the model revolutionary knows well that he frequently encounters obstacles that cannot be overcome merely by force. He knows he will often have to temporize, to be flexible, to retreat and even make concessions in order not to suffer humiliating and extremely harmful defeats at the hands of the adversary. All these tactical retreats, however, are done to avoid greater evils. As soon as circumstances permit, the revolutionary will obstinately resume his advance, combining the greatest possible celerity with all the necessary slowness.[26]

The totalitarianism and radicality of the Revolution can also be seen from the fact that it strives to apply its principles to all the domains of the nature and action of man and society. This becomes evident whenever we analyze the transformations the world has undergone over the last hundred years.

Liberty, Equality, Fraternity. This trilogy gradually transformed individuals, families, and nations. There is hardly a sphere that does not bear in some way the victorious imprint of one of this famous trilogy's principles. Considering the aforementioned cautiousness of the Revolution, the revolutionary march has almost always resulted in an advance.

---

[26] A succinct and expressive description of this tactical flexibility of the Revolution is found in these words of Mao Tse-tung: "The enemy advances, we retreat; the enemy halts, we harass; the enemy tires, we attack; the enemy retreats, we pursue" (*Selected Works* [New York: International Publishers, 1954], Vol. 1, p. 124).

Take, for example, the transformation of the family during the last hundred years. Parental authority has continuously declined—*equality*. The bond between spouses has become weaker—*liberty*. Analyze the classroom environment at the elementary, secondary or college level. The formulas of respect students owe their teachers have been progressively reduced—*equality*. Teachers, in turn, tend to place themselves as much as possible on par with their students—*equality, fraternity*.

Analogous observations could be made regarding the most varied fields: the relations between rulers and those ruled, between employers and employees, or between members of the ecclesiastical hierarchy and the faithful. Actually, it would take forever to present a nearly complete list of all the transformations that have taken place in the world under the influence of this revolutionary trilogy.

b. One more element of the Revolution: its multitudinous character

It is the *multitude* that promotes or simply tolerates the unopposed and overwhelming offensive of the revolutionary propaganda, be it oral or written. It does this out of conviction, imitation, or the fear of the implacable assault of revolutionary slogans.

Were the Revolution merely an ideology served by an impulse, it would lack historical relevance. The Revolution's multitudinous character is the most important factor of its success.

2. The Opinion of Catholics Vis-à-vis the French Revolution: Dissensions

All this explains why almost from its inception the French Revolution was viewed by the great majority of people mainly as the action of a multitude psycho-intoxicated with the revolutionary trilogy and inebriated with the impulsive enthusiasm it unleashed. The inebriated multitude wanted to reach the trilogy's last consequences (the most violent, most despotic, most gruesome consequences) as quickly as possible. It therefore desired and undertook the overthrow of everything that signified Faith, authority, hierarchy, and political, social, or economic distinction.

In the last spasms of its bloodiest phase—after having broken statues and altars, closed churches, persecuted God's ministers, dethroned and executed the King and Queen, declared the nobility abolished, put countless aristocrats to death, and attained its goal of implanting a world new in "Everything! Now! And forever!"— the French Revolution was on the verge of accomplishing what Diderot, one of its most outstanding precursors, had written: "His hands plaited the entrails of the priest, making a rope for the last of the kings."[27]

---

[27] Diderot, *Les Eleuthéromanes*, quoted in Hippolyte Taine, *Les Origines de la France Contemporaine* (Paris: Robert Laffont, 1986), p. 165.

a. Different ways in which Catholics have viewed the French Revolution

Given the plurality of aspects in the revolutionary phenomenon—the revolutionary chaos—it is understandable that for many people the first and global aspect of the French Revolution was more noticeable than the Revolution considered only in light of the seemingly benign and equitable aspect of its trilogy, or merely in the subversive, bloody, and fanatic aspect that can also be discerned in the ambiguities of this trilogy.

It is not surprising, therefore, that in view of this panorama a great number of Catholics wondered what they should think, as Catholics, of the French Revolution.

Some, making a distinction between the revolutionary doctrine—expressed in the ambiguous trilogy—and the events to which it gave rise, tended to accept the benevolent interpretation of this trilogy as the only true one. This attitude made them sympathizers of the French Revolution, though categorical (if somewhat passive) critics of its crimes.

Others saw it above all as the nefarious cause of the cruelties and injustices just enumerated, giving the revolutionary trilogy the highly unfavorable interpretation to which it also lends itself. They denounced it as the criminal outcome of a satanic plot, planned and executed to mold individuals, nations, and even Christian civilization—which until recently had ruled them—according to the spirit and maxim of the first revolutionary, who had dared shout in the immensity of the heavens his *"Non serviam!"*[28]

According to these analysts of the French Revolution, the only attitude of a Catholic in face of such revolt was to proclaim the cry of fidelity of the angels of light who followed Saint Michael: *"Quis ut Deus?"* Following their example, the Catholic should wage a *"proelium magnum"* on earth analogous to the heavenly battle, destroying the tenebrous lairs where the Revolution was being plotted, punishing those responsible most severely, smashing the ranks of its conspirators, eliminating their pseudo-meritorious "conquests"; reconstructing the altars, reopening the churches, replacing the statues, reestablishing worship; restoring the throne, the nobility, and all the forms of hierarchy and authority; in a word, resuming the line of historic events vilely interrupted and deviated from its course.

---

[28]   Concerning the satanic character of the French Revolution, Cardinal Billot writes: "The essentially anti-religious character and impiety of the principle of liberalism will strike anyone who reflects on the fact that it was precisely this principle that informed the great Revolution; people say, and rightly so, that it presents a satanic character so expressly, so visibly, that it became distinguished, from that moment on, from anything that had taken place in the past.

"'The French revolution is unlike anything ever seen in past epochs. It is satanic in essence' (De Maistre, *Du Pape*, *Discours Preliminaire*).

"'In the French Revolution there is a satanic character that distinguishes it from anything ever before seen and perhaps from anything we shall ever see again' (De Maistre, *Considérations sur la France*, chap. 5)" (Louis Cardinal Billot, *Les Principes de 89 et leurs Conséquences* [Paris: Téqui], p. 30).

b. The French Revolution as seen by Pius VI

Consider the supernatural and prophetic grandeur of the analysis Pius VI made of the French Revolution in his allocution regarding the beheading of Louis XVI.

> By a conspiracy of unholy people, that Most Christian King Louis XVI was condemned to capital punishment and the judgment was executed.
>
> We will briefly tell you what sort of judgment it was and by what sort of reasoning it was carried out: On the basis of no authority and no right, it was carried out by the National Convention: for, having abolished the more excellent form of monarchical rule, that body placed all public power into the hands of the people....
>
> The more ferocious part of this people, not content with having pulled down the rule of their king by violence, since they wished to rip from him his life as well, ordered those to be judges who had made accusations and had openly declared themselves hostile to him;...
>
> Those men, now chanting this triumph as it were over a destroyed kingdom and a fragmented religion, are preaching the glory and the splendor of the name of impious writers, as if they were commanders of victorious forces. And then it was that, when they by these arts had seduced the greatest multitude of the people to their side, in order to dupe this same multitude more and more with help and promises, or rather in order to make a mockery of them, they discovered that specious name of liberty, and to its raised insignia and standards they called forth all men.
>
> Here, truly, is that philosophic liberty, which has as its goal that minds be corrupted, that morals be depraved, and that every order of laws and institutions be overturned....
>
> From this never-interrupted sequence of impieties begun among the French, to whom would it not be plainly evident that the first beginnings of those machinations that now shake and tear apart all Europe, and from which no one can deny that death was brought to Louis himself, are to be ascribed to a hatred for religion?
>
> Oh, France! Oh, France! called by our predecessors "the mirror of all of Christianity, inasmuch as in the fervor of Christian faith and the devotion to the Apostolic See thou didst not follow the others, but didst precede them!" (Gregory IX, in 1227). How thou art turned away from Us today, how hostile thy attitude toward the true Religion....
>
> Oh again, France! Thou who didst demand that a Catholic king be given to thee because the fundamental laws of the kingdom would not tolerate any king other than a Catholic one, behold today thou hast killed that Catholic king whom thou hadst, precisely because he was Catholic![29]

The revolutionary phenomenon is seen here in its ensemble: ideology, impulse, countless multitudes filling streets and squares, impious and unseen plotters, the

---

[29] *Pii VI Pont. Max. Acta*, Vol. 2, pp. 17-33 passim.

radical goals that attracted the revolutionaries from the outset to the outcome. In this terrible outcome could be seen, behind the initial and at times bland formulas, the radical goals toward which, more and more openly, the Revolution marched as a whole.

c. Connivance of the "moderates" with the radicalism of the Revolution

This way of seeing the Revolution does not ignore the existence of nuances of the revolutionary phenomenon.

Thus, one cannot equate the *Feuillants* of the early stage of the Revolution with the Girondins. The first were liberal monarchists who, in comparison with the unconditional enthusiasts of the Ancien Régime, were to a certain extent revolutionary figures; the latter were for the most part republicans hostile to the clergy and nobility but favorable to the conservation of a liberal socioeconomic regime that spared free enterprise, private property, and the like from the revolutionary hurricane. The Girondin position had all the elements to appear radically revolutionary not only to the manifest counter-revolutionaries (*émigrés*, *chouans*, and other royalist guerrillas) but also to the *Feuillants.* Yet it enraged the ultra-radicals of the Mountain, who besides demanding the abolition of royalty and the radical and bloody persecution of the clergy and nobility, frequently cast threatening glances upon the prominent fortunes of the bourgeois class.

Having seen this succession of nuances, from the *Feuillants* to the members of the Committee of Public Safety and their throngs of admirers, one perceives that each nuance or stage of the revolutionary march seems markedly leftist when compared to the preceding nuance or stage, and ultra-conservative in relation to the subsequent one. This continues until the Revolution's last breath, exhaled as it lay dying in 1795. This gasp was the communist revolution of Babeuf, to whose left one can conceive nothing save chaos and void, and to whose right a Babeufist would consign everything that preceded it.

A view of the Revolution that distinguishes its nuances, implicitly or explicitly presupposes the need to take into account that even the most moderate analysts of the Revolution manifested, along with their moderate designs, an inexplicable and contradictory indulgence toward and at times outright sympathy for the crimes and criminals of the Revolution.

The simultaneous presence of moderate inclinations and revolutionary connivances in the minds of "moderates" and throughout the Revolution's stages led one of the most fervent apologists of the revolutionary phenomenon—Clemenceau—to dodge the accusation of contradiction by the summary assertion that *"la Révolution est un bloc"* ("the Revolution is a block"),[30] in which cracks and contradictions are only apparent.

---

[30] Quoted in François Furet and Mona Ozouf, *Dictionnaire Critique de la Révolution Française* (Paris: Flammarion, 1988), p. 980.

In other words, the Revolution—the consequence of a miscellanea of propensities, doctrines, and agendas—cannot be praised or censured when identified with only one of its nuances or stages. It must be considered in the light of this evident miscellanea.

Clemenceau's expression may appear attractive to many minds; nevertheless, it is still an insufficient description of the historical reality.

In fact, in this apparent miscellanea, one notices an ordering principle of primary importance. From the outset, almost until Babeuf, each stage of the Revolution sought to destroy something and, at the same time, retain something of the old socio-politico-economic edifice. This may and must be admitted, but without ignoring that at each stage the destructive ferment acted with more efficacy, self-assurance, and victorious impetus than the conservative tendency did. In fact, the latter always appeared intimidated, insecure, and minimalist in what it wished to preserve and readily compliant in what it consented to sacrifice.

In other words, from beginning to end, the same ferment was active in each of these nuances or stages, making of each stage a fleeting marker in the march toward global surrender. Consequently, the Revolution was already entirely present in its ferment, just as a tree is entirely present in its seed. It was precisely this ferment that the unforgettable Pontiff Pius VI clearly saw first as a prisoner and later as a martyr of the revolutionary fury in 1799.

Two hundred years after the French Revolution, television polls taken to determine what people think of the King and Queen's guilt show that many French viewers—and even foreign viewers—still see the Revolution as "a block," in the manner of Clemenceau.[31]

Even many of those who today manifest support for the 1793 execution of the royal couple would presumably disapprove of it in and of itself. They endorse the regicide because they imagine it to have been—in the exuberant context of the aspects and counter-aspects of the revolutionary hurricane—the only way to save the Revolution, its "conquests," its "acts of justice," the deranged hopes it aroused, and, in short, the whole confused and effervescent "block" of ideologies, aspirations, resentments, and ambitions that were the soul of the Revolution.

Such people extend up to our days the "family of souls" that views the execution of the weak and benevolent King Louis XVI and Queen Marie Antoinette as acts of justice.

It is certain that a good number of these surprisingly numerous contemporary partisans of the regicide could not be adequately included in any of the nuances of the French Revolution. They represent an even more advanced stage of the

---

[31] On December 12, 1988, French television screened the trial of Louis XVI and asked viewers to give a verdict. Over 100,000 people phoned in: 55.5% voted for acquittal, 17.5% for exile, and 27% for the death penalty.

On January 3 of the following year, another television program presented a panel discussion on the trial of Marie Antoinette, with the participation of highly-renowned scholars and historians. This time the viewers were not asked if they agreed with her condemnation to death, but simply whether she was guilty or not: 75% of the viewers judged her innocent and 25%, guilty.

A painful complaint in the twilight of an unforgettable pontificate:

"For Us, having arrived at the evening of life, it would be too great a source of pain and bitterness to see disappear, without bearing fruit, Our good intentions toward the French nation and her government, to whom We have given repeated proofs not only of Our most scrupulous attentions, but also Our efficacious and special affection."

(Letter of Leo XIII to President Emile Loubet of France, June 1900)

revolutionary process, different but not disconnected from the stages of two hundred years ago. Intransigent ecologists are an example of this. They deem it unjust to kill a bird or a fish, yet show no indignation—but rather formal approval—at the execution of Louis XVI and Marie Antoinette, his gracious wife. An Austrian by birth, Marie Antoinette was so imbued with French spirit and culture that innumerable Frenchmen and non-Frenchmen continue to admire her matchless personification of the qualities which characterize France. With great discernment, the well-known British statesman Edmund Burke wrote:

> It is now sixteen or seventeen years since I saw the queen of France, then the dauphiness, at Versailles; and surely never lighted on this orb, which she hardly seemed to touch, a more delightful vision. I saw her just above the horizon, decorating and cheering the elevated sphere she just began to move in— glittering like the morning-star, full of life, and splendor, and joy. Oh! what a revolution! and what a heart must I have to contemplate without emotion that elevation and that fall! Little did I dream when she added titles of veneration to those of enthusiastic, distant, respectful love, that she should ever be obliged to carry the sharp antidote against disgrace concealed in that bosom; little did I dream that I should have lived to see such disasters fall upon her in a nation of gallant men, in a nation of men of honour, and of cavaliers. I thought ten thousand swords must have leaped from their scabbards to avenge even a look that threatened her with insult. But the age of chivalry is gone. That of sophists, economists, and calculators, has succeeded; and the glory of Europe is extinguished for ever. Never, never more, shall we behold that generous loyalty to rank and sex, that proud submission, that dignified obedience, that subordination of the heart, which kept alive, even in servitude itself, the spirit of an exalted freedom. The unbought grace of life, the cheap defence of nations, the nurse of manly sentiments and heroic enterprise is gone! It is gone, that sensibility of principle, that chastity of honour, which felt a stain like a wound, which inspired courage whilst it mitigated ferocity, which ennobled whatever it touched, and under which vice itself lost half its evil, by losing all its grossness."[32]

It would exceed the scope of this book to indicate and describe the links that, spanning the centuries, connect certain strains of ecologism to the Girondins, the Mountain, and even Babeufism. It will simply be mentioned in passing that more than one observer has identified in the extreme positions of environmentalism and similar currents a metamorphosis of the communism apparently "euthanatized" in the defunct U.S.S.R. and its satellite countries.

---

[32] Edmund Burke, *Reflections on the Revolution in France* (Harmondsworth, Middlesex: Penguin Books, 1969), pp. 169-170.

3. Leo XIII Intervenes

These considerations, so familiar to many readers, may be less so to others. Time has covered people, doctrines, schools of thought, disputes, and their respective history with the soothing veil of forgetfulness.

It was necessary to recall all this in order to understand the circumstances in which Pope Leo XIII launched the policy known as *"ralliement,"*[33] and tried to unite around himself the Catholics who were divided in their attitudes toward the revolutionary phenomenon.

In 1870, France inaugurated its Third Republic, which was confirmed in 1873 when the National Assembly refused to restore the legitimate pretender to the throne, the Count of Chambord, descendant of King Charles X. After the dismissal of General MacMahon in 1879, the republican regime showed itself more and more clearly inspired by the revolutionary and anti-Catholic principles that gave rise to the French Revolution.

Could the Vatican enter into an agreement with this regime? Or would this be tantamount to establishing a concordat with Satan? This was the burning question Leo XIII had to address when he ascended the Pontifical Throne in 1878. Unending polemics, which were not limited to doctrinal or historical issues, divided Catholics. The point in question was the assessment of the French Revolution, especially in its religious policy.

First, there were Catholics who staunchly defended the integrity of the age-old rights granted the Church by the tradition born of Saint Remigius and Clovis, King of the Franks.

Besides these Catholics, steadfast in their religious and counter-revolutionary positions, there were those who moderately adhered to the anti-religious policies of the Revolution. They considered that their position expressed the true thinking of the *Feuillant* revolutionaries or of the moderate Girondins.

Yet others felt an affinity with the more audacious anti-religious politics of the Girondins' leftist currents. Seldom, however, did a Catholic applaud the anti-religious extremes of the Mountain.

In many cases, these attitudes on religious policy were matched by analogous positions on strictly political questions.

On the extreme right were the Catholics who favored the royalty of the Old Regime and the restoration of monarchy in the person of the legitimate pretender, the Count of Chambord. They were, in a way, the successors of the people about whom Talleyrand had said, with clear intent to ridicule them, that they rejected the Revolution because they "have neither learned anything, nor forgotten anything."[34]

For their part, the moderates in religious matters were frequently so in political

---

[33] *Ralliement*: a policy that led militant French Catholics, following the appeal of Pope Leo XIII, to accept the republic in France (cf. *Le Petit Larousse* [Paris: Larousse, 1992], s.v. *ralliement*, p. 853).

[34] Jean Orieux, *Talleyrand ou le Sphinx Incompris* (Paris: Flammarion, 1970), p. 638.

matters as well. Their brand of monarchism was consistent with their Catholicism: They desired a pallid religion and a faded royalty.

There were also overt republicans, who advocated a State entirely or almost entirely separated from the Church. These pretended to be moderate republicans, as distinguished from those republicans—less numerous—who were spiritual sons of the Mountain.

These nineteenth-century *"montagnards"* were usually radical atheists as much as they were radical republicans. This position was described by Clemenceau: "Ever since the Revolution we have been in revolt against Divine and human authority, with whom, with just one blow, we settled a terrible score on January 21, 1793 [date of the beheading of Louis XVI]."[35]

The French Republic at the time of Leo XIII prevailed, thanks to the support it received from the partisans of a radical secularist State and also from those timorous Catholics who deemed it good policy to make friendly overtures to the Republic, and even to some demands of the secularist State, so long as the latter, in exchange, did not increase its hostility toward the Church.

These so-called centrist Catholics imagined that they could forge an agreement with the Republic. In exchange for minimal but guaranteed material conditions and freedom for the Church to conduct her affairs unhindered, these Catholics were prepared to pay a high price. Forgetting the past, including that of the Catholic royalty born from the anointing of Clovis, they were ready to contemplate the nobility's demise with an ill-humored indifference, and even to accept with resignation the laicist conquests already obtained.

Leo XIII, ascending to the Pontifical Chair, resolved to pursue this policy. In so doing, besides paying the aforementioned price, Leo XIII also sacrificed the support he could have obtained from those Catholics who, in the political arena, remained faithful to the legitimate monarchy of the Count of Chambord and, in the religious field, vindicated all or almost all the rights the Revolution had wrenched from the Church. Such Catholics, nostalgic for the political strategy of Pius IX, were the most fervent and enthusiastic partisans of the Papacy, the most intransigent defenders of dogmas. Leo XIII's policy disheartened and undercut the support of these courageous people who had suffered from the Revolution every sort of persecution and harm with a joyful heart, knowing well that they were sacrificing themselves for altar and throne, for God and for their king. In compensation, Leo XIII won the applause of the many Catholics who were heedless of the close interaction between temporal and spiritual problems, and of those willing to compromise.

Was it worth the price? This is what many people asked themselves.

Leo XIII decided to prove that it was. With the toast of Algiers[36] and the

---

[35] Cited in Louis Cardinal Billot, *Les Principes de 89 et leurs Conséquences*, p. 33.

[36] In November of 1890, the French Mediterranean war fleet anchored in the port of Algiers. Cardinal Lavigerie, Archbishop of that city and one of the main figures on whom Leo XIII counted to carry through his policy of *ralliement* in France, offered the officers a banquet in his residence.

Admiral Duperré, Commander of the fleet, was received to the sound of the revolutionary anthem, "La Marseillaise," played by students of the famous White Fathers (dedicated to missionary work in Algeria), which

encyclical *Au milieu des sollicitudes*, he sailed clearly and directly toward a compromise that—as he underlined carefully—did not imply renouncing any principle of Faith or morals taught by him or his predecessors.

As could be foreseen, discussions among Catholics, particularly on whether it was licit for a Catholic to be republican, became more frequent and heated.

Leo XIII defined the *doctrine* of the Church on the issue. But the heat of the discussions blurred the vision of many polemists, and so there appeared several erroneous positions among Catholics, some of which Leo XIII himself and, later, Saint Pius X rectified.

When resolving *in thesis* the question of the Catholics' position regarding the forms of government, Leo XIII did not delineate to the greatest possible extent the distinction between a revolutionary republic, born of the French Revolution, and the republican form of government considered exclusively in the abstract and capable of being legitimate according to the circumstances of each country. From what may have been Leo XIII's concern to be circumspect resulted a great part of the confusion surrounding this subject.[37]

---

was still not recognized as the national anthem by the flower of French monarchism.

During dessert, the Cardinal stood up, followed by his guests. He then raised a toast, reading a text prepared beforehand. After greeting his visitors, he began an exhortation in favor of acceptance of the republican form of government. He declared: "When the will of a people is clearly affirmed, when the form of government has nothing inherently contrary—as Leo XIII recently proclaimed—to the principles which alone can nourish Christian and civilized nations," this form of government deserves an "adhesion without mental reservation."

When the Cardinal concluded his toast, the officers, his guests, most of whom were monarchists, remained stunned and silent, without applauding. Everyone sat down again. The Cardinal then turned to the Admiral and asked, "Admiral, have you no answer to the Cardinal?" Admiral Duperré, an old Bonapartist, merely replied, "I drink to the health of His Eminence the Cardinal and to the clergy of Algiers."

This attitude of Cardinal Lavigerie, although encountering the approval and support of Leo XIII, was received very unfavorably in French monarchist and Catholic circles, and even among the French hierarchy, which did not grant the Cardinal the desired support (cf. Adrien Dansette, *Religious History of Modern France* [New York: Herder and Herder, 1961], Vol. 2, pp. 78-81).

[37] In his various teachings on the forms of government, Leo XIII did not abstain from considering the particular circumstances of France in his time. On the contrary, with greater or lesser clarity he manifested his belief that the republic was a form of government apt to promote the common good of France at the time.

Besides this, the Pontiff also evidenced his persuasion that the majority of the republican leaders were hostile to the Church not because of any animosity toward it, but only because they were irritated with the attacks against the Republic by numerous Catholics devoted to the monarchist cause. According to this view, so long as the Roman Pontiff, followed by an increasing number of faithful, seriously reconciled himself with the Republic, its leaders would reciprocate with a policy of conciliation toward the Church.

The facts did not justify the Pontiff's hopes, as he bitterly acknowledged in a letter to the President of France, Emile Loubet, in June of 1900:

"We would like, Monsieur le President, to open Our soul to you, confident that—with the nobility of your character, the loftiness of your views, and the sincere desire for religious pacification with which we know you to be endowed—you will set your heart on using the influence of your high position to fend off any cause for new religious conflicts. For Us, having arrived at the evening of life, it would be too great a source of pain and bitterness to see disappear, without bearing fruit, Our good intentions toward the French nation and her government, to whom We have given repeated proofs not only of Our most scrupulous attentions, but also Our efficacious and special affection" (in Emmanuel Barbier, *Histoire du Catholicisme Liberal et du Catholicisme Social en France* [Bordeaux: L'Imprimerie Yves Cadoret, 1924], Vol. 2, p. 531).

In a letter written to Cardinal François Richard, Archbishop of Paris, on December 23 of the same year, about the government's persecution of religious congregations, the Pontiff also manifested his disappointment on account of the ill success of the policy of the *ralliement*:

"Since the beginning of Our Pontificate We have spared no effort to realize in France this work of pacifica-

On the French political scene, the confusion led to a reduction in the number of those Catholics who, in keeping with the Church's doctrine and spirit, considered the monarchy tempered by some aristocratic and popular participation in the public power as the ideal form of government, even though resolved to accept without scruples of conscience the republican form so long as it proved necessary for the common good.

There was a concomitant increase in the number of Catholics who adhered to the republican form of government led not so much by the conviction that France needed a republic as by the false principle that equality is the supreme measure of justice in human relations. It seemed to them that only democracy, and therefore an integral republic, established perfect justice among men in the image of a perfect morality. This was precisely the error condemned by Saint Pius X in the apostolic letter *Notre charge apostolique*.[38]

This outcome was not restricted to France; it occurred throughout the West.

Such discussions reverberated around the world and, naturally, caused divisions and misunderstandings among Catholics of the most varied countries. These divisions continue to some extent, as does the great illusion of egalitarian radicalism, implacably anti-monarchic and anti-aristocratic.

This appendix was inspired by the desire to help increase, in the light of the pontifical documents, clarity of vision and union of soul in this matter. *"Dilatentur spatia veritatis"* [may room for truth be expanded] should be the desire of all sincere Catholic hearts. Consequently, *"dilatentur spatia caritatis"* [may room for charity be expanded].

---

tion, which would have resulted in innumerable advantages for her, not only in the religious sphere, but also in the civil and political spheres.

"We have not retreated in the face of difficulty. We have never ceased to give France special proofs of deference, solicitude, and love, hoping at all times that she would respond in a manner befitting a great and generous nation.

"We would experience extreme sadness if, having arrived at the evening of Our life, We should find ourselves disappointed in these hopes, frustrated by the cost of our paternal solicitudes and condemned to see, in the country We love, passions and factions struggling ever more desperately without being able either to measure the extent of their excesses or ward off misfortunes which we have done everything possible to prevent and the responsibility for which We disavow in advance" (*Actes de Léon XIII* [Paris: Maison de la Bonne Presse, n.d.], Vol. 2, pp. 190-191).

Many Catholics continued to behold with apprehension the policy the famous Pontiff pursued in France, since they believed that the majority of republicans were imbued with doctrinal errors inherited from the Enlightenment, namely radical egalitarianism and a phobia against the Catholic Church stemming from deism or atheism. In their opinion, Leo XIII's policy of appeasement with the Republic would not defuse the anti-Catholic animosity of most republicans. They were right. The republican offensive against the Church continued unabated into the reign of Saint Pius X.

With the outbreak of World War I, Frenchmen of every religious and political persuasion joined in a *"Union Sacrée"* against the invader. This truce in the political-religious conflicts continued, to some extent, after the Allied victory.

The subsequent facts will not be dealt with here so as not to overextend the matter.

[38] See the citation in section A, 4 of this appendix.

Aristocracy in the Thinking of a Controversial Twentieth-Century Cardinal Who Cannot Be Suspected of Bias in Its Favor

$\mathcal{T}$he comprehensive and erudite homiletic work *Verbum vitae—La palabra de Cristo*, comprising ten volumes written under the direction of His Eminence Angel Cardinal Herrera Oria, then Bishop of Málaga, Spain,[1] presents in its third volume (pages 720-724) an outline for sermons that includes some points of the Church's doctrine on aristocracy.

We will now transcribe and comment passages of this outline.[2]

---

[1]   *Verbum vitae—La palabra de Cristo: repertorio orgánico de textos para el estudio de las homilías dominicales y festivas*, prepared by a commission of authors under the direction of Angel Herrera Oria, Bishop of Málaga, 10 vols. (Madrid: Biblioteca de Autores Cristianos, 1953-59).

Angel Cardinal Herrera Oria was one of the remarkable figures of the Church in Spain in the twentieth century. He was born in Santander in 1886. In 1909, while still a layman, he founded the Asociación Católica Nacional de Propagandistas with Father Angel Ayala, S.J. In 1911 he founded the daily *El Debate*, which he directed until 1933, when he was nominated president of the Junta Central de Acción Católica. He played an outstanding part in movements such as Pax Romana and Acción Nacional.

In 1936 he travelled to Switzerland to pursue ecclesiastical studies and was ordained in 1940. Returning to Spain in 1943, he was consecrated a bishop in 1947 and was appointed to the Diocese of Málaga. During his prelacy there, he supervised the preparation of the important work that includes the outline commented herein. Paul VI raised him to the cardinalate in 1965. In 1966 he resigned his diocese on account of his age, and he died in 1968. (Cf. Enrique Florez, ed., *Diccionario de historia eclesiastica de España* [Madrid: C.S.I.C., 1972], s.v. Herrera Oria, Angel.)

As a thinker, writer, and man of action, Cardinal Herrera Oria was the focus of heated controversies. While his more enthusiastic admirers were for the most part situated in the center and on the left, those who disagreed with him were generally on the right.

This is not the place to take a stand regarding these controversies. We merely point out that the text on aristocracy we are about to quote received the unqualified approval, and perhaps even the collaboration, of a high prelate who is beyond suspicion of any bias in favor of the nobility.

As regards his participation in the preparation of this homiletic work, Cardinal Herrera Oria made the following remarks in the Prologue: "This work is not mine, even though the idea, the overall direction, and part of the text are mine. It is the result of the effort of a committee, whose members are named at the end of this prologue." He writes further on: "The work is the result of a common effort. I worked with a group of people who are very competent in their respective fields" (Bishop Herrera Oria, *Verbum vitae*, Prologue, pp. lxv, lxxi).

[2]   To facilitate this exposition, two small alterations were made in the order of the items. These changes in no way alter the thought of the outline's authors and preserve all their fluency and richness of expression. The first al-

Initially, aristocracy is considered in function of society and not of the State: "The aristocracy is a necessary element in a well-constituted society."

The outline then adds: "Let us recall the teaching of Christian philosophy, theology, and public law regarding the aristocracy."

1. Philosophical Sense

In the etymological sense of the word, "aristocrats are the best." The word "contains the idea of perfection, the idea of virtue."

In effect, "the aristocracy has virtuous habits." These habits are "of the understanding and the will," through which "the aristocracy excels."

"Considered individually, the sage is the aristocratic type engendered by ancient philosophy."

"Moral perfection and love for the people" are fundamental virtues of the aristocracy.

2. Theological Sense

  a. Theology sheds abundant light on this concept of aristocracy and provides solid bases for Christian public law.

  b. Aristocracy is perfection. A Christian is duty-bound to aspire to perfection.

    1) "Be ye therefore perfect, as also your heavenly Father is perfect" (Matt. 5:48).

    2) "He that is just, let him be justified still; and he that is holy, let him be sanctified still" (Apoc. 22:11).

    3) "Walk before Me and be perfect," God said to Moses (Gen. 17:1).

  c. In what does perfection consist?

    1) Saint Thomas teaches that:

      a) Perfection in Christian life consists mainly in charity [that is, the love of God].

      b) Indeed, it is said of each being that it is perfect in the measure that it attains its proper end, which is its ultimate perfection.

      c) Charity is what unites us to God, Who is the final end of the human mind, because "he that abideth in charity, abideth in God, and God in him" (I John 4:16). (Cf. *Summa Theologica*, II-II q. 184, aa. 1-3c; II-II q. 81, a. 7c.)

    2) Consequently, perfection in Christian life is reached especially through charity.

From this the authors of *Verbum vitae* deduced that:

  d. This luminous idea must be kept in mind, since it gives life to all the sociology and politics regarding the aristocracy.

    1) Aristocracy is perfection.

    2) Perfection is fundamentally Christian charity.

---

teration was the inversion of the items "Aristocracy in the Family" and "Political Aristocracy." The second was the inversion of the items "Aristocracy's Contemporary Social Mission" and "The New Aristocracy."

3. Christian Public Law

    a. Aristocracy and property.
        1) Not enough attention is paid to the fact that one of the foundations of private property is the duty to perfect oneself.
            a) However, Leo XIII makes mention of it in *Rerum novarum*.
            b) "Property should be held," he writes, "as though it were one's own, and managed as though it were common."
            c) That is, it should "satisfy the owner in that which is necessary, proper, and for his perfection," and what remains ought to be distributed as alms.
        2) Much is said about need and decorum, while perfection, which is a duty, is forgotten.

The outline then proceeds to some considerations that are being obscured by today's egalitarian atmosphere.

            a) Those who live in the world and have a family are bound to perfect the family and to promote in their children a sense of decorum and the social consideration of the family in the Christian sense.
            b) As long as they live under the influence of Christian charity, parents should strive, insofar as possible, to make their children better than themselves in science, the arts, technology, culture, in everything—not to raise them as vain persons, but to offer more perfect generations to society for the benefit of the people.
        3) In particular, aristocrats must keep abreast of any technical, social, or other advances that, assimilated and applied, may meet the needs of the more indigent classes.

These teachings show clearly that the aristocrats' endeavor to refine, in successive generations, their dwellings, furniture, apparel, and vehicles, as well as their bearing and manners, is an essential aspect of this journey toward global perfection, both for the glory of God and for the common good of temporal society.

This does not dispense the perfect Catholic aristocrat, in this promotion of the common good, from his duty to attend solicitously to the rights of the needy classes.

The aristocrats who act in this way constitute "the best," those who were termed earlier "a necessary element in a well-constituted society."

4. Social Aristocracy

Having considered the aristocrat as an individual, the outline goes on to deal with the aristocratic family.

    By perfecting himself and his family, the aristocrat creates an institution within society, the aristocratic family.

The outline makes it clear that the familial contexture of the aristocracy greatly enhances its capacity to be the source and thrust of this stimulus to perfection.

Family traditions are born in the bosom of families of every social class. In family life, parents and elders have the psychological environment and the occasions to communicate their convictions and the fruits of their experience to the younger ones. In this way, the thrust toward perfection finds optimum conditions. This thrust seeks not only the individual good of the family's members and the family as a whole, but also the common good of society.

Society is a collective entity that is more enduring than the family. The family, in turn, is more enduring than its individual members in the course of the generations. What is more enduring greatly benefits from the thrust of the aristocracy, inasmuch as the latter exerts a thrust that is, theoretically, as enduring as society itself.

Tradition assures the durability, paths, and characteristics of this thrust.

The outline continues:

> It could be said that the virtues and perfection itself tend to become hereditary.
>
> This institution cannot be egoistic. It must be eminently social and concerned for the welfare of others.

From these clearly enunciated principles is deduced the justification of one of the least understood aspects of the aristocracy: heredity.

Many people accept the idea that a person who performs arduous actions revealing superior personal qualities deserves a title of nobility, especially when these actions, besides serving as an example to all, have an important impact on the common good. But these same people feel that the transmission of such titles to descendants is not justifiable, since—they argue—great men often have average sons who do not deserve the reward their seniors received.

The application of this reasoning impedes the formation of noble families and eliminates their mission as a propelling force for the continuous perfecting of the whole social body. Now, this perfecting is indispensable for the continuous and inspiring march of a society and a country toward all the forms of perfection yearned for by individuals moved by love of God, Who is Perfection itself.

In other words, if to respect and reward great men is just, it is not just or realistic to deny the mission of great families in the propulsion of ascending countries.

> The historical aristocracy is based on human nature and is very much in accordance with the Christian view of life if it meets its requirements.
>
> There is no better school than the home of a lineage that is aristocratic in the authentic and Christian sense.
>
> When it knows how to fulfill its duties, society should allow it the means it needs for this supreme social magisterium.
>
> Palaces, paintings, manuscripts, works of art, masterpieces, travels, libraries, and the like: All of these belong directly and immediately to great families.
>
> However, the use of these goods must conform with the Church's ascetic and social doctrine.
>
> When used to form very carefully selected citizens for the benefit of the community according to the true Christian meaning of life, they can be considered a

type of public and collective property, since all society benefits from them.

The aristocracy is so much in accord with Christian society that a society can only call itself perfect when it has an aristocratic class. A wholesome aristocracy is the flower and cream of Christian civilization.

Such concepts are becoming rarer and rarer in Catholic literature about aristocracy. However, they were never disavowed by the Church's Magisterium. They could not, therefore, be omitted from this work, which analyzes aristocracy especially within Christian civilization, the shaper of all the Western nations.

5. Aristocracy in the Family

Still regarding the relationship between aristocracy and the family, the outline touches upon a delicate and elevated aspect of the life of an aristocratic class:

a. By analogy we can say that aristocratic power within the home is reserved to the wife.
   1) Authority resides in the husband.
   2) But within the family, the wife is an agent of restraint and counsel.
   3) She is a link in the relationship between father and children.
      a) The father's orders to the children are often better obeyed when they come through her.
      b) The children's needs and wishes reach the father through her.
b. Saint Thomas says that the father governs the children through "despotic" rule, in the classic sense of the word, and the wife through "political" rule.
   1) The wife is a counselor sharing in the father's power.
   2) The wife also represents charity within the family. She is a personification of mercy in the home.
   3) She should be keenly aware of the needs of the children and the servants, and ready to urge the father to attend them.
c. The Gospel offers a striking contrast between the absence of mercy, charity, and aristocratic spirit on the part of the apostles in the scene we are commenting on[3] and the ineffable aristocratic mission performed by the Blessed Virgin at the wedding feast at Cana.
   1) Aware of the others' needs, Mary approaches the One who can satisfy them and brings them to His attention.
   2) She then approaches the people, represented by the servants, and impresses upon them the necessity of their obedience.

The comparison of the aristocracy's mission in the State and the nation to the mission of the wife and mother in the home may be somewhat startling to the modern reader. Today's few popular works about the aristocracy have accustomed the public, and rightly so, to see in the aristocracy the military class par excellence— which hardly seems to be consonant with the mission of the wife and mother within

---

[3]   This outline is one of twenty concerning the multiplication of the loaves (John 6:1-15).

the family. Nevertheless, this in no way diminishes the wisdom of the comparison.

To see the comparison in its correct perspective, it is necessary to keep in mind that war is normally waged against a foreign power. Here Saint Thomas is discussing the mission of the aristocracy in the internal and everyday life of the country in times of peace, and not its mission of fighting external enemies in times of war.

In the Middle Ages, each aristocratic family gathered around itself other families or individuals of lesser rank, which were linked to it by work, vicinity, and so forth.

In medieval cities and also, to a certain extent, in those of the Old Regime, it was normal for palaces, mansions, and well-to-do homes to be adjacent to the more modest dwellings of the common people. This proximity of the great and the humble reflected the ambience of the aristocratic home, forming a discreetly luminous aura of affection and dedication around each aristocratic family.

In turn, work relations tended to expand from the professional sphere to the personal sphere as a consequence of Christian charity. Through the extended contacts of work, the noble inspired and oriented those below him. The latter, in their own way, inspired and oriented the noble, informing him of their aspirations and pastimes, their customs at church, in the guild, or at home, and also of the concrete circumstances of the people's lives and the needs of the unfortunate.

This created the fabric of interrelationships between greater and lesser that the post-1789 State sought to replace as much as possible with bureaucracy, that is, with bureaus of statistics and information and the always busy intelligence services. Through these bureaucracies, the anonymous State, using anonymous public servants, inspires, moves, and rules the nation, abetted by the likewise anonymous corporations that control the major means of mass communication. Reciprocally, the nation speaks to the State through the anonymous mouth of the voting booths. This anonymity reaches its ultimate sophistication with the secret vote, where the State does not know who voted one way or the other. This string of anonymities excludes as much as possible any human warmth from the interrelations of the modern State.

Countries blessed with an upright aristocracy had a different outlook. Relationships in these countries were as personal as possible. The influence of the greater over the lesser and, in its way, that of the lesser over the greater, was exercised within a relationship of Christian affection. This affection created mutual dedication and confidence, turning every human group—such as the manorial society—into something akin to the protoplasm around a nucleus. It suffices to read what authentic Catholic moralists say about manorial society to have an accurate notion of this type of relationship.

This relationship was repeated throughout the social body. In the guilds, for example, relations between masters, artisans, and apprentices mirrored to a great extent the serene atmosphere of the family. Such lively contact was much broader than what modern terminology coldly and pragmatically calls employer-employee relations. Through their servants and workers, the members of the higher classes, nobles or bourgeois, came to know the families of their subordinates, as these in turn knew the families of their superiors. To a greater or lesser extent, depending on the healthy spontaneity of society, these relationships were not only between individuals, but also between families. Sentiments of sympathy, benevolence, and charity proceeded from the higher to the lower classes, while gratitude, affection, and admiration ascended from the latter.

Good is by its nature diffusive. Through these intricate relationships the great became aware of the sufferings of people who otherwise would be unknown and isolated. Most of the time it was great men who, through their wives and daughters, remedied many pains that otherwise would have been left without care.

In this valley of tears, however, the great also have their bitter hours. At times their enemies surround them, threaten them, assault them, sometimes physically, sometimes politically. The strongest bastion for their assailed grandeur is the dedication of so many subordinates who disinterestedly rise up to protect them, even at the risk of their own lives.

So far our description has focused on urban life. At this stage of our exposition, it would be superfluous to do the same with rural life, which is so conducive to creating the atmosphere and relations described here.

Such was the case in the fief. Such, also, was the case in the farm when, after the disappearance of feudalism, the former relations between lord and vassal lost their political basis but conserved their social reality in the field of work. At times, even in the last grim decade of this century and the millennium, we still find this type of relationship here and there in one or another country.

In a monarchical State, tempered by elements of aristocracy and democracy as visualized by Saint Thomas, the aristocracy participates in the royal power as the wife participates in her husband's power in the home. Through a moderating action, consistent with the maternal instinct, it is up to the wife to transmit to the father an affectionate knowledge of the children's needs. By the same token, it is up to the aristocracy to consider the needs of the poor, the small, and the disfavored who live under the beneficial influence of their estates, and to bring them to the king's attention in order to obtain from him the needed assistance. Just as the mother softens the father's heart, so the aristocrat opens the monarch's heart.

From the same perspective, just as it is up to the mother to prepare the children's hearts to obey the father's commands, it is a duty of the nobility to dispose the spirits of the lower classes to filial obedience to the king's decrees.

6. Political Aristocracy

Until now, we have dealt with the aristocracy as a social class. We shall now deal with the mission of the aristocratic class in the political and social life of the country.

Those who find these teachings excessively conservative or even reactionary may be pleasantly surprised by the approach to the subject of political aristocracy adopted in the outline.

1) The social aristocracy
   a) Has a direct and immediate function to perform next to the people.
   b) Because of natural law, however, it will always perform a political function next to the power. It will participate in the power for the benefit of the people.

After referring in passing to the "mixed" government, "where the monarchy, the aristocracy, and the people each have roles," as being "the best government according to Catholic philosophy," the outline continues:

> 2) Placed between the supreme authority—monarchy in its philosophical sense, that is, government by one—and the people, the aristocracy is an agent for moderation, balance, continuity, and union. [In this perspective]:
>   a) The monarchy without an aristocracy easily leads to absolutism.
>   b) A people without an aristocracy is but a mass.
>   c) The aristocracy defends and restrains the monarchy.
>   d) The aristocracy is head of the people, its teacher, and an agent for channeling its energies.
>   e) An aristocracy without a people is an oligarchy, that is, hateful privilege for one caste in society.

7. The Aristocracy's Contemporary Social Mission

The outline then enumerates some characteristics that should be found in modern aristocracy:

> 1) Restraint on power.
> 2) Counsel.
> 3) Awareness of the people's needs.
> 4) Defense of the people before the supreme authority.
> 5) Education of the people.
> 6) Organization and orientation of the people's activities.
> 7) Use of all its technical resources and social progress for the benefit of the neediest classes in particular.

This list is not complete. It seems to have been made with the intention of sparing the aristocracy from the accusation, so frequently leveled at it, of being a minority class that monopolizes privileges to the detriment of the people.

In fact, the outline begins by pointing out the tendency of the aristocracy to pursue perfection in everything, guided by the love of the absolute Perfection, which is God. Aristocracy thereby becomes a powerful impetus for other people to pursue perfection, especially in virtue, but also in talent, good taste, culture, education, and even technology. This tendency toward perfection should appear in the decorum of life, in the arts, furniture, dwellings, and adornments. Spreading throughout the whole social body, it should elevate it, just as the aristocracy elevates itself.

The aristocracy is able to carry out the mission of elevating the whole social body because, as already pointed out, its members are the "best." When they share power as leaders of the nation, there exists an aristocratic form of government.

These considerations indicate the extent to which religious, moral, and other characteristics of a society can shape its form of government.

8. The New Aristocracy

The outline also deals with what is called "new aristocracy." A metaphor might help give an accurate idea of the necessary but prudent renovation of aristocracies.

In some pools, the water is constantly renewed, but in such a gradual way that the renewal goes unnoticed, or almost so. This is a true renewal, even though the water does not flow rapidly, let alone torrentially, impetuously, or even revolutionarily.

Any metaphor falls short of true description. The renewal of water in a pool, as slow as it may be, eventually replaces the whole mass of water. As for the nobility, a complete replacement is not exactly desirable. On the contrary, the slower the renovation the better. By its very nature, the nobility is so linked to tradition that, ideally, a majority of noble families should live on indefinitely, throughout the centuries. This conservation, however, should not produce stagnant and mummified castes incapable of participating relevantly in history's ongoing march.

This metaphor is in keeping with the subject of this work as a whole[4] and is consistent with the thinking of Angel Cardinal Herrera Oria.

1) Since the aristocracy is a necessary component of a well-ordered society, as a practical principle it would seem natural for historical aristocracies, which usually maintain great virtues, to endure, and for other aristocracies to be created at the same time.
2) The aristocracy cannot be closed. A closed aristocracy becomes a caste, which is the antithesis of aristocracy, because a caste as such ignores the principle of charity, which is the heart and soul of aristocracy.
3) Unfortunately, it is not infrequent for the worldly virus, infiltrating the aristocratic environment, to turn it into closed circles.
4) The great problem in this field today is precisely how to remake the aristocratic classes and create other forms of aristocracy.

A question naturally arises: What should be done when an aristocracy decays and its members are no longer the best but rather the worst?

In this case, it is necessary to create new aristocratic classes, without, however, neglecting to do everything possible to rehabilitate the old aristocracy. If the latter resists being saved it should be left aside. If the aristocracy declines, it befits the social body to find a new solution. This solution is more readily found when society seeks—usually in an instinctive and customary way—the help of its healthy elements. We say "instinctive" because, in such emergencies, the common sense and other qualities of the people normally achieve more than blueprints, however brilliant and enticing they may be. Drafted by dreamers or bureaucrats, constructors of "paradises" and "utopias," such blueprints lack a firm basis in reality and more often than not only bring failure and disappointment.

* * *

---

[4] See Part I, Chapter VII, 9.

A serious problem arises if 1) the "best" are not found among the aristocracy, 2) no one among the common people is willing to assume the mission of propelling society toward perfection, and 3) the clergy itself relinquishes this mission. Which form of government can save this society or nation from ruin?

There will never be a lack of people proposing political solutions. They will try to devise a government, supposedly composed of good men, to mechanically solve the problem from outside the ailing social body. When the whole social body is decadent, however, the problem is unsolvable and the situation desperate. The more one tries to remedy it, the more it gets entangled and precipitates its own ruin.

Desperate situations can only be resolved when a handful of people with Faith, who "against hope believed in hope"—"*contra spem in spem credidit*" (Saint Paul's eulogy of Abraham's faith [Rom. 4:18])—continue to hope and hope; in other words, when souls full of Faith have humble and insistent recourse to Providence to obtain a saving intervention. "*Emitte Spiritum tuum et creabuntur, et renovabis faciem terrae*" (Send forth Thy Spirit and they shall be created and Thou shalt renew the face of the earth [Pentecost antiphon]). Outside this perspective, vainly will one strive to save any form of government, society, or economy. "*Nisi Dominus custodierit civitatem, frustra vigilat qui custodit eam*" (Unless the Lord build the house, they labor in vain that build it [Ps. 126:1]).

The outline on aristocracy in the important work written under the direction of Cardinal Herrera Oria concludes with the following considerations:

1. Therefore, to say that aristocratic spirits are needed today is to say that there is need of a class that rises above the rest because of birth, culture, wealth, but especially because of its Christian virtues and boundless mercy.
2. An aristocracy lacking a bountiful reserve of perfect Christian virtues is an empty title, a lifeless history, a fallen social institution.
3. Its love, spirit, and life ought to be the spirit, charity, and life of Christ.
4. In sum, without Christian perfection, there will be de facto or titular aristocracies, but no aristocracies that are authentic through deeds and by right.

A possible interpretation of these final words is that they contain an assessment of the aristocracy of the time Angel Cardinal Herrera Oria published this work: "There is need of a class that rises above the rest because of birth." In other words, perhaps the aristocracy of those days was not fulfilling its mission.

If the outline of *Verbum vitae* had contained an unqualified eulogy of the aristocracy of the time, it would certainly have been assailed as one-sided. Critics would have said that the aristocracy has great qualities but also grave defects.

Perhaps the assessment is rather one-sided. For the sake of historical accuracy, it must be stated that if the aristocracy of the 1950s displayed numerous defects, it also undeniably possessed important qualities.

Part III

Pius XII

Allocutions of Pius XII to the Roman Patriciate and Nobility

Allocution of January 8, 1940

At the start of the New Year, a twofold gift has been given Us by the Roman Patriciate and Nobility by their gathering around Us: the most appreciated gift of their presence and the gift of their filial best wishes, adornments, as a flower, of the testimonial of their traditional loyalty to the Holy See, which was proved anew, beloved Sons and Daughters, by the devout and eloquent words just pronounced by your distinguished representative, thus providing Us with a much desired opportunity to confirm and add to the high esteem in which the Apostolic See has always held your illustrious class and which it has never ceased to manifest openly.

The history of centuries past rings in such esteem. Among those presently gathered round Us, more than a few bear names that for centuries have been intertwined with the history of Rome and the Papacy, in days of light and of darkness, in joy and in sorrow, in glory and in humiliation, sustained by that intimate sentiment arising from the depths of a faith inherited with the blood of their ancestors, surviving all trials and storms, and always ready, in its passing deviations, to take the path back to the house of the Father. The splendor and greatness of the Eternal City reflects and refracts its rays over the families of the Roman Patriciate and Nobility. The names of your forebears are indelibly etched in the annals of a history whose events have in many respects played a great part in the origins and development of so many peoples of today's civilized world. If indeed one cannot write the secular history of many nations and kingdoms and imperial crowns without mentioning Rome and her noble families, the names of the Roman Patriciate and Nobility recur even more often in the history of the Church of Christ, which rises to an even loftier greatness, surpassing every natural and political glory, in its visible Head, which, by the benign disposition of Providence, has his See on the banks of the Tiber.

Of your loyalty to the Roman pontificate and the continuity that honors you as the glorious appanage of your families, Our eyes can see around Us, in this select gathering, a living image in the simultaneous presence of three generations. In those of you whose brow is framed in white or silver, We hail the many merits gained in the long performance of duty, merits which you have brought here, like trophies of victory, to offer in homage to the only true Lord and Master, invisible and eternal. Yet most of you stand here before Us, bold with the flower of youth and the splendor of manliness, with that vigor of physical and moral energy that makes you ready and willing to devote your strength to the advancement and defense of every good cause. Our preference, however, goes to the serene and smiling innocence of the little children, the latest arrivals in this world, in whom the spirit of the Gospel allows us to see the fortunate first arrivals in the kingdom of God, and whose ingenuous candor, whose bright and vivid purity of gaze, an angelic reflection of the pureness of their souls, inspires Our love. They are innocent, and apparently defenseless, but in the charm of their ingenuousness, which pleases God no less than it pleases man, they conceal a weapon they already know how to use, like the young David with his sling: the tender weapon of prayer; while in the quiver of their still fragile but already free will, they keep a marvelous arrow, an unfailing, future instrument of victory: sacrifice.

For this panoply of the different ages of man, which We delight in recognizing in you, loyal custodians of chivalric traditions, We do not doubt, indeed We are certain, that the New Year will be good and happy in Christ Our Lord so long as you promptly receive it from the hands of Providence, though under the opaque veil in which the future has wrapped it, like one of those sealed envelopes, bearing an order for life's holy and virtuous struggles, which the officer, on a mission of confidence, receives from his chief and must not open until he is on his way. Day by day, God, Who has allowed you to begin this New Year in His service, will reveal its secret to you; and you are aware that everything this still mysterious sequence of hours, days, and months will bring you shall come to pass only by the will and with the permission of that heavenly Father, whose providence and governance of the world never fails or falls short in His designs. Could We, however, hide from you the fact that the New Year and the new age that it begins will also bring occasions of conflict and struggle, and, We hope, of merit and victory as well? Do you not see how, because the law of evangelical love has been disregarded, denied, and outraged, wars are raging today in certain parts of the world—wars that Divine Mercy has thus far spared Italy—in which we have seen entire cities transformed into heaps of smoking ruins and bountiful plains turned into necropoles of

battered corpses? Lonely on the deserted streets, in the shadow of a gloomy hope, peace wanders about, timidly; and in the wake of her footsteps, in the old and new world, her worried friends are looking for her, bent on bringing her back to the society of men by correct, solid, and lasting paths, and on preparing, in a brotherly effort of understanding, the arduous task of necessary reconstruction!

In this work of reconstruction, you, dear Sons and Daughters, can play an important role. For if it is true that modern society revolts against the idea and the very name of a privileged class, it is no less true that, like ancient societies, this society cannot do without a class of industrious people who, by this very fact, belong to the ruling circles. It falls to you, therefore, to openly prove that you are and intend to be a willing, active class. You have, moreover, well understood, and your children will understand and see even more clearly, that no one is allowed to avoid the original and universal law of work, however varied and multiple its intellectual and manual forms. Thus We are certain that in your magnanimous generosity you will know how to fulfill this sacred task no less courageously, no less nobly than you do your great obligations as Christians and gentlemen, being descended, as you are, from forebears whose industriousness is glorified and transmitted to our times by so many marmoreal coats of arms in the palaces of Rome and across the land of Italy.

There is, moreover, one privilege which neither time nor men will ever be able to take from you, if you yourselves do not agree to relinquish it, by becoming unworthy of it: that of being the best, the *optimates*, not so much by abundant wealth, sumptuous clothing, or opulent palaces, as by integrity of customs, uprightness in the religious and civil life; the privilege of being patricians, *patricii*, by the outstanding qualities of mind and heart; the privilege, finally, of being noble, *nobiles*, that is, men whose names are worthy of being known and whose actions deserve to be held up as examples to be emulated.

In acting and persevering in this manner, you shall make your inherited nobility more brilliant and lasting than ever; and from the tired hands of the elderly to the vigorous ones of the young shall pass the torch of virtue and action, the silent, calm light of golden sunsets that shall be reborn in new dawns with each new generation, with the radiance of a flame of generous and fruitful aspirations.

Such are, dear Sons and Daughters, the wishes We offer up to God for you, full of faithful hope, while imparting, as a pledge of the highest heavenly grace, to each and every one of you, to all your loved ones, and to all whom you bear in your minds and hearts, Our paternal Apostolic blessing.[1]

Allocution of January 5, 1941

A cause for deep, paternal joy in Our heart is granted Us, dear Sons and Daughters, by your welcome gathering around Us at the start of the New Year, a year no less fraught with fearful horizons than the one just passed. Here you have come to present to Us your filial good wishes through your excellent spokesman, whose devout and lofty expressions give your concordant and consenting presence a regard and affection that are especially dear to Us. In the Roman Patriciate and Nobility We see again and love an array of sons and daughters whose pride lies in the hereditary bond and loyalty to the Church and the Roman Pontiff, whose love for the Vicar of Christ arises from the deep root of faith and does not diminish with the passing of the years and the vicissitudes of the ages and of men. In your midst We feel more Roman by custom, by the air We have breathed and still breathe, by the very sky, the very sun, the very banks of the Tiber, on which Our cradle was laid, by that soil that is sacred down to the remotest bowels of the earth, whence Rome draws for her children auspices of an eternity in Heaven.

Although it is true that Christ Our Lord chose, for the comfort of the poor, to come into the world bereft of everything and to grow up in a family of simple laborers, He nevertheless wished to honor with His birth the noblest, most illustrious of the lines of Israel, the House of David itself.

Therefore, loyal to the spirit of Him whose Vicars they are, the Supreme Pontiffs have always held in high consideration the Roman Patriciate and Nobility, whose sentiments of unalterable devotion to this Apostolic See are the most precious part of the heritage they have received from their forebears and will pass on to their children.

The nature of this great and mysterious thing that is heredity—the passing on through a bloodline, perpetuated from generation to generation, of a rich ensemble of material and spiritual assets, the continuity of a single physical and moral type from father to son, the tradition that unites members of one same family across the centuries—the true nature of this heredity can undoubtably be distorted by materialistic theories. But one can, and must also, consider this reality enormously important in the fullness of its human and supernatural truth.

One certainly cannot deny the existence of a material substratum in the transmission of hereditary characteristics; to be surprised at this one would have to forget the intimate union of our soul with our body, and in what great measure our most spiritual

---

[1] *Discorsi e Radiomessaggi di Sua Santità Pio XII* (Tipografia Poliglotta Vaticana, January 8, 1940), pp. 471-474.

activities are themselves dependent upon our physical temperament. For this reason Christian morality never forgets to remind parents of the great responsibilities resting on their shoulders in this regard.

Yet of greater import still is spiritual heredity, which is transmitted not so much through these mysterious bonds of material generation as by the permanent action of that privileged environment that is the family, with the slow and profound formation of souls in the atmosphere of a hearth rich in high intellectual, moral, and especially Christian traditions, with the mutual influence of those dwelling under one same roof, an influence whose beneficial effects endure well beyond the years of childhood and youth, all the way to the end of a long life, in those elect souls who are able to meld within themselves the treasures of a precious heredity with the addition of their own merits and experiences.

Such is the most prized patrimony of all, which, illuminated by a solid faith and enlivened by a strong and loyal practice of Christian life in all its demands, will raise, refine, and enrich the souls of your children.

But, like every rich patrimony, this one brings with it some very strict duties, all the more strict as this patrimony is rich. There are two above all:

1) the duty not to squander such treasures, to pass them on whole, indeed increased, if possible, to those who will come after you; to resist, therefore, the temptation to see in them merely the means to a life of greater ease, pleasure, distinction and refinement;

2) the duty not to reserve these assets for yourselves alone, but to let them generously benefit those who have been less favored by Providence.

The nobility of beneficence and virtue, dear Sons and Daughters, was itself conquered by your ancestors, and bearing witness to this are the monuments and houses, the hospices, asylums, and hospitals of Rome, where their names and their memory bespeak their provident and vigilant kindness to the needy and unfortunate. We are

well aware that in the Roman Patriciate and Nobility this glory and challenge to do good, inasmuch as they have been in a position to do good, has not been lacking. Yet at this present, painful hour, in which the sky is troubled by watchful, suspicious nights, your spirit, while maintaining a noble seriousness, indeed a lifestyle of austerity that excludes all trifles and frivolous pleasures, which for every genteel heart are incompatible with the spectacle of so much suffering, feels all the more keenly the urge for charitable works impelling you to increase and multiply the merits you have already achieved in the alleviation of human misery and poverty. How many opportunities the New Year, with its new trials and events, will bring you, opportunities to do good not only within the walls of your homes, but also without! How many new fields of aid and succor! How many secret tears to dry! How many sorrows to allay! How much physical and moral distress to relieve!

Whatever be the course of the year just begun is the secret and decision of God, wise and provident, Who governs and guides the progress of His Church and the human race toward that end where His mercy and justice shall triumph. Yet Our yearning, Our prayer, Our wish is for just and lasting peace and the ordered tranquility of the world; a peace that would gladden all peoples and all nations; a peace that, bringing smiles back to all faces, would awaken in all hearts a hymn of the highest praise and gratitude to the God of peace whom we adore in the cradle of Bethlehem.

In this Our desire, beloved Sons and Daughters, there is also a wish for a year not ill-fated but happy for all of you, whose welcome presence offers Us an image of every human age, advancing under God's protection along the path of life, and making private and public virtues the highest commendation of its steps. To the elderly, custodians of noble family traditions and lights of wise experience for the young; to the fathers and mothers, teachers and exemplars of virtue for their sons and daughters; to the young as they grow up pure, healthy, and industrious, in the holy fear of the Lord, to the hopes of the family and of our beloved country; to the little ones, who dream of their future undertakings in the gestures and games of their childhood; and to all of you who savor and participate in the joy and sharing of family life, We offer Our paternal and heartfelt best wishes in response to the yearnings of each and every one of you, male and female, as you remember that all our longings are ever weighed and examined by God on the scales of our greater good, on which what we ask often has less weight than what He grants.

Such is the prayer which, at the start of this New Year, behind whose impenetrable veils the heavenly Providence Who dominates with love over the universe and the world of human events reigns, rules, and operates, We offer up to the Lord for you, invoking an abundance of heavenly favors for you, while, trusting in the immensity of God's goodness, We give to each and every one of you, to your loved ones, and to those you bear in your minds and hearts, Our paternal Apostolic blessing.[2]

Allocution of January 5, 1942

Beloved Sons and Daughters, the loftily worded message of greeting that your illustrious representative has communicated to Us, wishes, it seems to us, to manifest above all that filial attachment to the Apostolic See which spurs your faith and is the finest glory of the Roman Patriciate and Nobility. With great joy and exaltation, We thank you; and in return Our love bestows Our best wishes on you and your families, so as to bear witness to you once again, through such keen sentiment, of Our grateful and especial appreciation of your traditional loyalty to the Vicar of Christ.

This filial and paternal meeting in the house of the common Father, even if not a rarity, cannot be dimished in sweetness and enjoyment by the reign of habit, just as the recurrence of the Christmas holidays in no way diminishes their religious delight, nor the dawn of the New Year obscures the horizon of hope. Does the renewal of the sacred joy of the spirit not resemble indeed the repeated renewal of each day, of each year, of nature herself? The spirit, too, has its renewal and rebirth. We are reborn, we live again, when we commemorate the mysteries of our faith;

in the stable at Bethlehem we adore again the Infant Jesus, our Savior, light and new sun of the world, just as on our altars is reenacted the perennial Calvary of a God crucified and dying for our love.

You too, when remembering your ancestors, relive their lives in a way; and your ancestors live again in your names and in the titles they left you through their merits and their greatness. Are these not names weighty with glory and rich in meaning: *Patriciate* and *Nobility* of this *Rome*, whose name spans the centuries and shines over the world as a seal of faith and truth come down from heaven to exalt man?

In a human aspect, the name of the Roman Patriciate recalls to mind the memory of those ancient *gentes* whose origins are lost in the mists of legend but who in the clear light of history appear as minds and wills essential to the making of the power and greatness of Rome during the most glorious times of the Republic and the Empire, when the Caesars, in their commands, valued reason over will. The most ancient men were crude, yet all were instilled with a sense of the destiny of Rome, identifying

---

[2]   Ibid., January 5, 1941, pp. 363-366.

their own interests with those of the *res publica*, pursuing their vast and bold designs with a constancy, perseverance, wisdom, and energy that were never wanting. Even today they excite the admiration of anyone who remembers the history of those distant centuries. They were the *patres* and their descendants, *"Patres certe ab honore, patriciique progenies eorum appellati"* [they were called fathers certainly due to honor and their descent from the patriciates] (Liv. 1. I, c. 8, n. 7), who knew how to combine aristocracy of blood with the nobility of wisdom, valor, and civil virtue, toward a plan and process of world conquest, which God, against their purpose, would one day transform, in His eternal wisdom, into a ready and open field of holy battles and victories for the heroes of His Gospel, while making the Rome of the Emperors into the Rome of the peoples believing in Christ, and raising above the mute memories of the *Pontifice Massimi* of paganism the eternal Pontificate and Magisterium of Peter.

Wherefore it follows that, in a Christian supernatural light, the name "Roman Patriciate" awakens in Our mind even greater thoughts and visions of history. If the term patrician in pagan Rome, *patricius*, signified the fact of having ancestors and of belonging not to stock of common rank but to a privileged and dominant class, in a Christian light it takes on a more luminous aspect and deeper resonance in that it associates the idea of social superiority with that illustrious paternity. It is a patriciate of Christian Rome, which had its highest and most ancient splendors not in blood but in the honor of protecting Rome and the Church: *patricius Romanorum*, a title carried over from the time of the Exarchs of Ravenna to Charlemagne and Henry III. Through the centuries, successive Popes also had armed defenders of the Church, drawn from the families of the Roman Patriciate; and Lepanto marked and eternalized a great name in the annals of history. Today, dear Sons and Daughters, the Ro-

man Patriciate and Nobility are called upon to defend and protect the honor of the Church, using, as a weapon, the decorum of a moral, social, and religious virtue that should shine among the people of Rome and in the eyes of the world.

Social inequalities, even those related to birth, are inevitable: Benign nature and God's blessing to humanity illuminate and protect all cradles, looking on them with love, but do not make them equal. Look, for example, at the most inexorably leveled societies. No art has ever been able to work things so that the son of a great chief, the son of a great leader of the masses, should remain in the same condition as an obscure citizen lost among the common people. Yet, although such ineluctable disparities may appear, in a pagan light, to be the inflexible consequence of the conflict between social forces and the power acquired by some people over others, according to the blind laws believed to rule human activity and to make sense of the triumph of some and the sacrifice of others, on the other hand, to a mind instructed and educated in a Christian way these disparities can only be considered a disposition willed by God with the same wisdom as the inequalities within the family. Hence, they are destined to bring men more closely together on the present life's journey toward the Kingdom of Heaven, with some helping others in the way a father helps the mother and children.

And if this paternal conception of social superiority has sometimes, in the clash of human passions, driven souls to deviations in the relations between persons of higher rank and those of humbler station, it is no surprise to the history of fallen humanity. Such deviations in no way serve to diminish or obscure the fundamental truth that, for the Christian, social inequalities merge in the great human family; that therefore relations between unequal classes and ranks have to remain regulated by a fair and righteous justice and at the same time be informed by mutual respect and affection, which, while not abolishing the disparities, should diminish the distance and temper the contrasts between them.

In truly Christian families, do we not see perhaps the greatest of patricians being careful and solicitous to maintain toward their domestics and all those around them a comportment which, while surely in keeping with their rank, is always free of haughtiness and expressive of kindness and courtesy in words and actions that demonstrate the nobility of hearts that see these men as brothers and Christians and united to them in Christ by the bonds of charity, of that charity which, even in their ancestral palaces, between the great and humble, always comforts, sustains, gladdens, and sweetens life, especially in the hours of gloom and sorrow ever so abundant in this world?

You, beloved Sons and Daughters, as the Roman Patriciate and Nobility, you, here in this Rome, at the center of the Christian community, in the head and mother Church of all the Churches of the Catholic world, gathered round him whom Christ established as His Vicar and common Father of all the faithful, you are raised up by Divine Providence so that your dignity will shine before all the world in its devotion to the See of Peter, as an example of civil virtue and Christian greatness. If all social preeminence brings with it tasks and duties, that privilege which by the hand of God has fallen to your lot requires of you, especially in this grave and stormy hour—an hour dark with discord and with ferocious, bloody human conflicts,

an hour that calls us to prayer and penance, which should correct and transform the way of life of all and make it better conform to Divine Law, as the present hardships and the uncertainty of future perils clearly admonish us—a fully Christian life, an irreproachable and austere mode of conduct, fidelity in all your family duties, in all your private and public obligations, that they might never fall short but shine clearly and brightly in the eyes of all who look upon you and admire you. You must show them, in your acts and your footsteps, by the true path to good, that the finest ornament of the Roman Patriciate and Nobility is excellence of virtue.

While, then, We ask the humble and poor Infant Jesus, of royal lineage, the King of angels and men made Man, to be your guide in the fulfillment of the mission assigned to you, and to enlighten and fortify you with His grace, with heartfelt warmth We give you, beloved Sons and Daughters, Our paternal Apostolic blessing. We desire that it extend to and remain also upon all your loved ones, especially upon those fulfilling their duties far away from you and exposed to dangers, which they face with a courage equal to the nobility of their blood, and who perhaps have been lost, wounded, or taken prisoner. May this blessing come down upon you and be for you a balm, comfort, protection, and promise of the higher and more abundant favors and succors of heaven, and, for the restless and ravaged world, a hope for tranquility and peace![3]

Allocution of January 11, 1943

How, beloved Sons and Daughters, could the warm and heartfelt greetings that the lofty words of your illustrious representative conveyed to Us in your name fail to find their

response in the offerings We now raise to God on your behalf? Unvanquished by the sorrows of the present hour, We feel, at this moment, a sweet consolation and a pro-

---

[3] Ibid., January 5, 1942, pp. 345-349.

found joy, for in your persons We see before Us a kind of representation of Our beloved Rome. To such an eminent condition, the disposition of Divine Providence has seen fit to raise you in the course of history; you are aware of this and at the same time you feel thereby a sense of legitimate dignity and of weighty responsibility.

By privilege of birth, you have been placed by God in His wisdom like a city atop a mountain; you cannot therefore remain hidden (cf. Matt. 5:14). In addition, He has destined you to live in the middle of the twentieth century, now in a moment of great hardship and anguish. And though you are still highly placed and at a dominant position, it is no longer in the same manner as your ancestors. Your forebears, living in their strongholds and their lonely castles, formidably defended and of difficult access—with towers and manors scattered throughout Italy, including the Roman province—had therein a refuge against the incursions of rivals and malefactors and organized therein an armed defense, and from those heights descended to do battle on the plain. You too, and your progeny, attract the gaze of those from the valley below. Consider the great names that you bear, rendered famous in history by military valor, by social service worthy of every praise and benefit, by religious zeal and holiness; what crowns of glory surround them! The people have exalted them and sung their praises through the voices of their writers and poets and through the hands of their artists; but they have also judged, and still do judge, with implacable severity, at times to the point of injustice, their errors and faults. If you seek the reason for this, you shall find it in the high office, the weighty responsibilities to which even a common honesty or a simple and ordinary mediocrity, to say nothing of failures and downfalls, are unsuited.

The responsibilities which you, beloved Sons and Daughters, and which the nobility in general, bear in regard to the populace today are hardly less weighty than those which once weighed upon your ancestors in centuries past, as history tells us in no uncertain terms.

If, indeed, we look at the peoples who once univocally and harmoniously professed the Christian faith and civilization, we see today vast fields of religious and moral ruin; few are the regions of the ancient Christian West in which the avalanche of spiritual catastrophe has not left traces of its devastation.

Not that everything and everyone has been overwhelmed and oppressed; indeed, We do not hesitate to assert that rarely in the course of history have keenness and firmness of faith, dedication to Christ and readiness to defend His cause in the Catholic world been more open, manifest and strong as they are today—so much so, that in certain ways a comparison can be made with the early centuries of the Church. Yet in the very comparison, the other side of the coin also appears. Now, too, the Christian front is up against a non-Christian civilization; indeed, in our own case—and this makes the situation worse in comparison with the early centuries of Christianity—against a civilization that has strayed from Christ. This de-Christianization is so powerful and audacious today that it all too often becomes difficult for the spiritual and religious atmosphere to spread and remain entirely free and immune from its poisonous breath.

It is useful, however, to recall that this movement toward unbelief and irreligion found its starting point not from below but from above, that is to say, in the ruling classes, in the upper tiers of society, the nobility, the thinkers and philosophers. We do not, mind you, mean all the nobility, much less the Roman nobility, which has greatly distinguished itself for its loyalty to the Church and to this Apostolic See—and the eloquent and filial expressions We have just heard are yet another luminous demonstration thereof—but rather, the nobility of Europe in general. Does one not clearly perceive in the Christian West in the last few centuries a spiritual evolution which, horizontally and vertically, breadthwise and lengthwise, so to speak, has been progressively undermining and demolishing the

Faith, leading to that devastation visible to-day in the multitudes of men without religion or hostile to religion, or at least animated and confused by a profound and ill-conceived skepticism toward the supernatural and Christianity?

The vanguard of this evolution was the so-called Protestant Reformation, during whose vicissitudes and wars a large part of Europe's nobility broke away from the Catholic Church and appropriated her possessions. But unbelief properly speaking spread in the age that preceded the French Revolution. Historians note that atheism, even in the guise of deism, had become widespread at that time in high society in France and elsewhere; belief in a God who was Creator and Redeemer had become, in that world given over to all the pleasures of the senses, something almost ridiculous and unseemly for cultivated minds avid for novelty and progress. In the greater number of the salons of the greatest and most refined ladies, where the most arduous questions of religion, philosophy, and politics were tossed about, literati and philosophers, champions of subversive doctrines, were considered the finest, most eagerly sought ornaments of those worldly meeting-places. Impiety was fashionable in the high nobility, and the writers most in vogue would have been less audacious in their attacks on religion if they had not enjoyed the approval and incitement of the most elegant high society. Not that all the nobility and all the philosophers set their sights on the immediate de-Christianization of the masses. On the contrary, religion was supposed to remain, for the simple people, as a means of governance in the hands of the State. They, however, felt themselves and thought themselves to be above faith and its moral precepts, a policy that very quickly proved to be deadly and short-sighted, even when considered from a purely psychological perspective. With inexorable logic, the people, powerful in goodness and terrible in evil, always know how to draw practical conclusions from their observations and judgments, however well-founded or mistaken they may be.

Take the history of civilization of the last two centuries: It clearly reveals and demonstrates the damage to the faith and morals of nations wrought by bad examples being set and handed down from above, the religious frivolity of the upper classes, the open intellectual struggle against the revealed truth.

Now, what conclusion are we to draw from these lessons of history? That today salvation must begin there, at the place where the perversion had its origin. It is not in itself difficult to maintain religion and sound morals in the people when the upper classes set a good example and create public conditions that do not make a Christian education immeasurably onerous, but rather promote it as something sweet and to be imitated. Is your duty not the same, beloved Sons and Daughters, you who, by the nobility of your families and the offices you often hold, belong to the ruling classes? The great mission which to you and to very few others has been assigned—that is, first to reform and perfect private life in yourselves and in your homes, and then to apply yourselves, each in his place and in his share, to bring forth a Christian order in public life—does not admit postponement or delay. It is a most noble mission, rich with promises, especially at a moment when, in reaction to a devastating, demoralizing materialism, a new thirst for spiritual values has been emerging in the masses, and minds are opening up to religious things, in a move away from unbelief. These developments allow one to hope that the lowest point of spiritual decline has by now been left behind. To all of you, therefore, falls the glory, by the light and appeal of good examples raising themselves above all mediocrity, of working together to make these initiatives and aspirations to religious and social good achieve their happy fulfillment.

What can We say of the efficacy and power of those generous souls of your class who, convinced of the greatness of their vocation, have dedicated their lives in full to spreading the light of truth and goodness—

those "*grands seigneurs de la plume*," as they have been called, those great lords of intellectual, moral, and religious action? Our voice could never praise them too much. They have the high merit of being good and faithful servants of the Divine Master, and they put to excellent use the talents granted them.

We should like to add that the duty of the nobility must not remain satisfied with shining like a beacon that casts its beam for navigators but never moves. Your honor is also that of being on the lookout, from high atop the mountain on which you are situated, ever ready to espy in the valley below all the pain, suffering, and hardship, and to descend there, eager to alleviate these sorrows like compassionate comforters and rescuers. In these disastrous times, what a vast field offers itself to the devotion, zeal, and charity of the Patriciate and Nobility! How many examples of virtue by illustrious families come to comfort Our heart! Indeed, if responsibility in the face of need is great, the action of him who would take on such a burden is all the more glorious as the burden is heavy. You too, in this fashion, shall prove yourselves more and more equal to your rank, for the heavenly Father, who has in a special way destined you and raised you up to be the refuge, light, and succor to a world in distress, will not fail to reward you with superabundances of grace for worthily fulfilling your lofty vocation.

Yes, yours is a lofty vocation indeed, and in it Christian spirit and social standing unite and urge you to make that self-sacrificing goodness shine forth, winning for you praise and gratitude from your fellow men, and even greater and nobler praise from God, the just rewarder of good deeds done to one's neighbor, which He takes as having been done to Himself. Never cease, therefore, to do your utmost so that by your generous actions not only will your beneficent names be honored, but the people will honor the Christianity that animates your life, inspires your activity and raises you up to God. And now invoking God, beloved Sons and Daughters, to bestow His heavenly favor on your families, on your children with their sublime smiles, on the youngsters in serene adolescence, on the bold young men, confident and brave, on the mature men of virile resolve, on the old men of wise counsel who gladden and sustain your illustrious houses, and especially on the dear and valorous ones who are not here today, objects of your anxious thoughts and especial affection, We give you Our most deeply heartfelt paternal Apostolic blessing.[4]

Allocution of January 19, 1944

Little was your worry, beloved Sons and Daughters, that the present trials, which interrupt and disturb the calm continuation of family and social life, might prevent you from coming, as in past years, to offer Us, with filial devotion, the homage of your best wishes. This tragic, sorrowful time, so full of anxieties and cares, brings with it grave, imperative responsibilities, the moral resolve and steps to be taken toward the re-construction of human society upon the cessation and tranquilization, in a peaceful tomorrow, of this enormous worldwide cataclysm. Never before have prayers been more needed, nor offerings more opportune. We thank you, with the deepest emotion in Our heart, for those you have made to Us through the voice of your illustrious representative, and especially for the concurrence of intentions and actions that We are

---

4   Ibid., January 11, 1943, pp. 357-362.

ever certain of finding in you. When the house is afire, the first concern is to call for help to put out the flames; but after the devastation, one must repair the damage and rebuild the edifice.

We are witnessing today one of the greatest conflagrations in history, one of the profoundest political and social upheavals in the annals of the world; yet it shall be succeeded by a new order, the secret of which lies still concealed in the will and heart of God, Who providently rules the course of human events and their conclusions. Things of this earth flow like a river in the course of time: Of necessity the past gives way to the future, and the present is but a fleeting instant joining the former with the latter. This is a fact, a motion, a law; it is not in itself an evil. There would be evil if this present, which should be a tranquil wave in the continuity of the current, became a billow, upturning everything in its path like a typhoon or hurricane and furiously digging, by destruction and ravage, a gulf between what has been and what must follow. Such chaotic leaps as are made by history in its course constitute and mark what is called a crisis, in other words, a dangerous passage, which may lead to salvation, but whose solution is still wrapped in mystery amid the smoke of the conflicting forces.

Anyone who closely considers, studies, and ponders our most recent past, cannot deny that the existing evil could have been avoided and the crisis warded off by virtue of a natural manner of conduct: that is, if each and every one of us had decorously and bravely fulfilled the mission assigned him by Divine Providence.

Is not human society, or at least should it not be, like a finely tuned machine, in which all the parts work together toward the harmonious functioning of the whole? Each part has its own role, and each must apply himself toward the best possible progress of the social organism; each must seek to perfect it, according to his strengths and virtues, if he truly loves his neighbor and reasonably strives for the common good and welfare.

Now what part has been assigned in a special way to you, beloved Sons and Daughters? What role has been allotted particularly to you? Precisely that of facilitating this natural development, the role that in the machine is fulfilled by the regulator, the fly-wheel, the rheostat, which take part in the common activity and receive their part of the motive force so as to ensure the operational movement of the apparatus. In other words, Patriciate and Nobility, you represent and continue tradition.

This word, as we well know, resounds disagreeably in many ears, and it is justifiably unpleasant when pronounced by certain lips. Some misunderstand it, others make it the mendacious label of their inactive egotism. Amid this dramatic dissent and confusion, more than a few envious voices, often hostile and in bad faith, more often ignorant or deluded, ask you bluntly: What are you good for? To answer them, you must first come to understand the true meaning and value of this tradition, of which you must of necessity be the principal representatives.

Many minds, even sincere ones, imagine and believe that tradition is nothing more than memory, the pale vestige of a past that no longer exists, that can never return, and that at most is relegated to museums, therein preserved with veneration, perhaps with gratitude, and visited by a few enthusiasts and friends. If tradition consisted only of this, if it were reduced to this, and if it entailed rejection or disdain for the road to the future, then one would be right to deny it respect and honor, and one would have to look with compassion on those who dream over the past and those left behind in face of the present and future, and with greater severity on those who, spurred by less pure and respectable motives, are nothing but derelict in the duties of the now so very mournful hour.

But tradition is something very different from a simple attachment to a vanished past; it is the very opposite of a reaction mistrustful of all healthy progress. The word itself is etymologically synonymous with advancement and forward movement— synonymous, but not identical. Whereas, in fact, progress means only a forward march, step by step, in search of an uncertain future, tradition also signifies a forward march, but a continuous march as well, a movement equally brisk and tranquil, in accordance with life's laws, eluding the distressing dilemma: "*Si jeunesse savait, si vieillesse pouvait!*" [If youth knew, if the aged could]; like that Lord of Turenne of whom it was said: "*Il a eu dans sa jeunesse toute la prudence d'un âge avancé, et dans un âge avancé toute la vigueur de la jeunesse*" [In his youth he had all the prudence of advanced age and in his advanced age all the vigor of youth]- (Fléchier, *Oraison funebre*, 1676). By virtue of tradition, youth, enlightened and guided by the experience of elders, moves forward with a surer step, and old age can confidently pass on the plow to stronger hands, to continue the furrow already begun. As the word itself implies, tradition is a gift handed down from generation to generation, the torch that at each relay one runner places in and entrusts to the hand of the next, without the race slowing down or coming to a halt. Tradition and progress complement each other so harmoniously that, just as tradition without progress would be a contradiction in terms, so progress without tradition would be a foolhardy proposition, a leap into darkness.

The point, then, is not to go against the stream, to backstep toward lifestyles and forms of activity already eclipsed, but rather to take and follow the best of the past and go out to meet the future with the vigor of unfailing youth.

In this manner, your vocation, grand and laborious, is already radiantly defined, and should win you the gratitude of all and raise you above the accusations that might be leveled at you from either side.

As you prudently seek to help true progress advance toward a saner, happier future, it would be unjust and ungrateful to reproach you and dishonorably brand you for the cult of the past, the study of history, the love of sacred customs, and unshakeable loyalty to eternal principles. The glorious or unhappy examples of those who preceded the present age are a lesson and a light to guide your steps; and it has already been rightly stated that the teachings of history make humanity a man forever moving but never growing old. You live in modern society not like immigrants in a foreign country, but rather as exemplary and illustrious citizens, who want and intend to collaborate with their contemporaries toward the recovery, restoration, and progress of the world.

There are ills in society, just as there are ills in individuals. It was a great event in the history of medicine when one day the famous Laennec, a man of genius and faith, anxiously bending over the chests of the sick and armed with the stethoscope he had invented, performed auscultation, distinguishing and interpreting the slightest breaths, the barely audible acoustic phenomena of the lungs and heart. Is it not perhaps a social duty of the first order and of the highest interest to go among the people and listen to the aspirations and malaise of our contemporaries, to hear and discern the beatings of their hearts, to seek remedies for common ills, to delicately touch their wounds to heal them and save them from the infection that might set in for want of care, making sure not to irritate them with too harsh a touch?

To understand and love in Christ's charity the people of your time, to give proof of this understanding and love through actions: This is the art and the way of doing that greater good that falls to you, doing it not only directly for those around you, but also in an almost limitless sphere. Then does your experience become a benefit for all. And in this area, how magnificent is the example set by so many noble spirits ardently and eagerly striving to bring about and spread a Christian social order!

No less offensive to you, and no less

damaging to society, would be the unfounded and unjust prejudice that did not hesitate to insinuate and have it believed that the patricians and nobles were failing in their honor and in the high office of their station in practicing and fulfilling their duties and functions, placing them alongside the general activity of the population. It is quite true that in ancient times the exercise of professions was usually considered beneath the dignity of nobles, except for the military profession; but even then, once armed defense made them free, more than a few of them readily gave themselves over to intellectual works or even manual labor. Nowadays, of course, with the changes in political and social conditions, it is not unusual to find the names of great families associated with progress in science, agriculture, industry, public administration, and government—and they are all the more perceptive observers of the present as well as confident and bold pioneers of the future, since with a steady hand they hold firm to the past, ready to take advantage of the experience of their ancestors but quick to be wary of the illusions and mistakes that have been the cause of many false and dangerous steps.

As custodians, by your own choosing, of the true tradition honoring your families, the task and honor of contributing to the salvation of human society falls to you, to preserve it from the sterility to which the melancholy thinkers jealous of the past would condemn it and from the catastrophe to which the reckless adventurers and prophets dazzled by a false and mendacious future would lead it. In your work, above you and as it were within you, there shall appear the image of Divine Providence which with strength and gentleness disposes and directs all things toward their perfection (Wis. 8:1), as long as the folly of human pride does not intervene to thwart its designs, which are, however, always above evil, chance, and fortune. By such action you, too, shall be precious collaborators of the Church, which, even amid the turmoil and conflict, never ceases to foster the spiritual progress of nations, the city of God on earth in preparation for the eternal city.

Upon this your holy and fruitful mission, which, We are confident, you shall continue to fulfill with firm resolve, proceeding with a zeal and devotion more needed than ever in these very dark days, We pray for the most abundant heavenly grace, while with all Our heart We give to you and your families, to your loved ones near and far, to the sick and the healthy, to the prisoners, the lost, and those exposed to the bitterest sorrows and dangers, Our paternal Apostolic blessing.[5]

Allocution of January 14, 1945

Once again, beloved Sons and Daughters, amid the devastation, the mourning, the anxieties of every sort presently tormenting the human family, you have come to offer Us your devout best wishes, which your illustrious representative has presented Us with nobility of sentiment and delicacy of expression. We thank you for this with all Our heart, and for the prayers with which, in so troubled a time, you help us to carry out the formidable duties that weigh heavy on our feeble shoulders.

Just as after all wars and great calamities there are always wounds to heal and ruins to rebuild; so after great national crises a whole process of adjustment must be effected to put the troubled and damaged country back in general order, to make it win back the position

---

[5]   Ibid., January 19, 1944, pp. 177-182.

to which it is entitled and resume the journey toward the progress and well-being allotted to it by its standing and history, its material wealth and spiritual faculties.

This time the work of restoration is incomparably more immense, more delicate, and more complex. It is not a question of bringing one sole nation back to normalcy. One can say that the entire world must be rebuilt; the universal order must be re-established. The material order, the intellectual order, the moral order, the social order, the international order—all must be remade and set back in a regular, constant motion. That tranquil order that is peace, that is the only true peace, cannot be reborn and endure except by building human society upon Christ, so as to gather, recapitulate, reunite everything in Him: *Instaurare omnia in Christo* (Eph. 1:10)—with the harmonious union of the members and their incorporation in the sole Head which is Christ (Eph. 4:15).

By now, everyone generally admits that this reorganization cannot be conceived as a pure and simple return to the past. Such a step backward is not possible. The world, despite its often disorderly, disconnected, fragmented, and incoherent movements, has continued to move ahead; history does not stop, it cannot stop; it is forever advancing, following its course, whether straight and orderly or twisted and confused, toward progress or toward an illusion of progress. Nevertheless, it moves ahead, races on, and to wish simply to "go into reverse"—not for the purpose of reducing the world to immobility on ancient positions, but to bring it back to a point of departure unfortunately abandoned because of deviations and confusions—would be a useless, fruitless undertaking. Not there—as we saw last year on this same occasion—does true tradition lie. Just as one could not conceive of reconstructing a building required to serve modern-day needs in the same manner as one would conceive of an archaeological reconstruction, likewise such rebuilding would not be possible following arbitrary designs, even if these were theoretically the best and most desirable. One

must always bear in mind inescapable reality, the entire sweep and scope of reality.

By this We do not mean to say that one must be content with watching the stream flow by, much less with following it, drifting along according to its whims, at the risk of having the boat collide with the rocks or plunge into the deep. The force of torrents and waterfalls has been rendered not only harmless but useful, fruitful and beneficent by those who, instead of reacting against it or giving into it, knew how to harness it by means of sluices, dams, canals, and diversions. Such is the task of the leaders, who, with gazes fixed on the immutable principles of human functioning, must and will know how to apply these enduring laws to the contingencies of the present.

In an advanced society like our own, which will have to be restored and reordered after the great cataclysm, the responsibilities of the leaders are rather diverse: the leader is the man of State, of government, the politician; the leader is the worker, who, without resorting to violence, threats, or insidious propaganda, but through his own worth, is able to gain authority and standing among his peers; the leaders are all those in their respective fields, the engineer, the jurist, the diplomat, the economist, without whom the material, social, and international world would go adrift; the leaders are the university professor, the orator, the writer, all of whom aim at molding and guiding spirits; the leader is the military officer who infuses the hearts of his soldiers with a sense of duty, service, and sacrifice; the leader is the doctor carrying out his mission of restoring health; the leader is the priest who directs souls onto the path of light and salvation, providing them assistance for advancing safely along that road.

And what, in this multitude of leaderships, is your place, your function, your duty? It presents itself in dual form: the personal function and duty of every one of you individually, and the function and duty of the class to which you belong.

Personal duty requires that you, with your virtue and diligence, endeavor to become leaders in your professions. Indeed, we all know well that today the youth of your noble class, aware of the dark present and the even more uncertain future, are fully convinced that work is not only a social duty, but also a personal guarantee of livelihood. And We use the word *professions* in its broadest, most comprehensive sense, as We had occasion to point out last year—that is, technical or humanistic professions, but also political and social activities, intellectual occupations, works of every sort: the prudent, vigilant, hard-working administration of your property, your lands, following the most modern and tested methods of cultivation, for the material, moral, social, and spiritual good of the peasants or other populations who live on them. In every one of these situations you must make every effort to succeed as leaders, whether because of the trust placed in you by those who have remained faithful to the wise and still living traditions, or because of the mistrust of so many others, which you shall have to overcome by winning their esteem and respect, by dint of excelling in everything in the positions in which you find yourselves, in the activities you pursue, regardless of the nature of the position or the form of the activity.

In what, then, should this excellence of life and action consist, and what are its principle characteristics?

It manifests itself above all in the perfection of your work, whether it be technical, scientific, artistic, or anything else. The work of your hands and your spirits must bear that imprint of distinction and perfection that cannot be acquired from one day to the next, but rather reflects a refinement of thought, of feeling, of soul, and of conscience, inherited from your forebears and ceaselessly nurtured by the Christian ideal.

It also shows itself in what can be called humanism, that is, the presence, the intervention of the complete man in all the manifestations of his activities, even if specialized, in

such a way that the specialization of his ability should never hypertrophy, should never atrophy, never becloud the general culture, just as in a musical phrase the dominant should never break the harmony nor burden the melody.

It is also made manifest in the dignity of one's entire bearing and conduct—a dignity that is not imperious, however, and that, far from emphasizing distances, only lets them appear when necessary to inspire in others a higher nobility of soul, mind, and heart.

Lastly, it manifests itself above all in the sense of lofty morality, or righteousness, honesty, and probity that must inform every word and every deed. An immoral or amoral society that no longer distinguishes between right and wrong in its conscience or in its outward actions, that no longer feels horror at the sight of corruption but rather makes excuses for it, adapts to it indifferently, woos it with favors, practices it with no misgivings or remorse, indeed parades it without blushing, thereby degrading itself and making a mockery of virtue, is on the road to ruin.

The French high society of the eighteenth century was one tragic example of this, among so many others. Never was a society more refined, more elegant, more brilliant, more fascinating. The most varied pleasures of the mind, an intense intellectual culture, a very refined art of pleasure, and an exquisite delicacy of manners and language predominated in that outwardly so courtly and gracious society, and yet everything in it—books, stories, images, furniture, clothing, hair-styles—encouraged a sensuality that penetrated one's veins and one's heart, and even marital infidelity scarcely surprised or scandalized anyone anymore. Thus did that society work toward its own downfall, rushing headlong toward the abyss it had dug out with its own hands.

True nobility is another matter altogether: In social relations it lets shine a humility filled with greatness, a charity untouched by any egotism or concern for one's own interest. We are not unaware of the tremendous goodness, gentleness, devotion, and self-abnegation with which many, and many among your number, have in these times of endless suffering and anguish bent down to aid the unfortunate and have been able to radiate about themselves the light of their charitable love, in all its most progressive and efficacious forms. And this is another aspect of your mission.

For it is true that, despite the blind and slanderous prejudices, nothing is so contrary to Christian sentiment and to the true meaning and purpose of your class, in all countries but especially here in Rome, mother of faith and of civilized living, as the narrow spirit of caste. Caste divides human society into sections or compartments separated by impenetrable walls. Chivalry and courtesy are, above all, Christian in in-

spiration; they are the bond that unites, without confusion or disorder, all the classes. Far from forcing you into a proud isolation, your origins should incline you rather to penetrate all levels of society, to communicate to them a love of perfection, of spiritual cultivation, of dignity, that feeling of compassionate solidarity that is the flower of Christian civilization.

At the present hour of division and hatred, what a noble task has been assigned you by the will of Divine Providence! Carry it out with all your faith and all your love! With these wishes and as a token of Our paternal offerings for the New Year already begun, We give you and your families, with all Our heart, Our Apostolic blessing.[6]

Allocution of January 16, 1946

In past years, beloved Sons and Daughters, on this occasion—after having paternally welcomed the wishes that your illustrious representative usually offers Us in your name, with such noble expressions of faith and filial devotion—We usually accompanied Our expressions of thanks with some recommendations suggested by the circumstances of the moment. We spoke to you of your duties and your function in the tottering, tormented society of our modern times, though necessarily in a somewhat general manner, with the sense of a future in mind, a future whose time and aspect were indeed difficult to predict.

No doubt it remains obscure even today. Uncertainty persists, and storm clouds still loom heavy on the horizon. With armed conflict just ended, nations find themselves faced with the burdensome task of assuming responsibility for consequences that shall bear upon the course of the times and determine which way they turn. The time

has come, in fact, not only for Italy but for many other nations, to elaborate their political and social constitutions, either to create entirely new ones or to revise, retouch, and modify to a greater or lesser degree the already existing statutes bearing them up. What makes this problem all the more arduous is that all these constitutions will be as different and autonomous as you like, as autonomous and different as are the nations themselves which wish to draft them; but they will not be—in fact, if not by law—any less interdependent for all that. What we have before us, therefore, is an event of the highest importance, the likes of which have rarely presented itself in the history of the world. In it there is enough to make even the boldest tremble in their hearts, if they are even only slightly aware of their responsibility; enough to disturb the most clairvoyant of people, precisely because they see better and farther than others and because, convinced of the gravity of the

---

[6] Ibid., January 14, 1945, pp. 273-277.

task, they more clearly understand the need to devote themselves calmly and attentively to the mature reflections required by works of such great import. And now, all of a sudden, prompted by collective and mutual efforts, the event is upon us; it will have to be confronted very soon; in a few months, perhaps, solutions will have to be found and definitive decisions made, which will make their effects felt on the destinies of not just one nation, but of the entire world, and which, once made, will establish the universal condition of nations, perhaps for a long time to come.

In our democratic age, all members of human society must take part in this undertaking: on the one hand, the legislators, by whatever name they are designated, to whom shall fall the task of deliberating and drawing conclusions; and on the other hand, the people, whose task it is to make their will felt by voicing their opinions and exercising their right to vote. And you too, therefore—whether or not you shall belong to the future constituent assembly—have your own function to fulfill, which will have its bearing upon both the legislators and the people. What is this function, then?

You may have happened, more than once, to encounter, in the church of St. Ignatius, groups of pilgrims and tourists. You have seen them stop in surprise in the vast nave of the church, their eyes turned upward to the vault on which Andrea Pozzo painted his stunning triumph of the Saint in his mission, entrusted to him by Christ, of spreading the divine light as far as the remotest corners of the earth. Seeing the apocalyptic avalanche of architectonic figures colliding above their heads, they thought, at first, that they were witnessing the delirium of a madman. Then you politely led them toward the center. As they gradually drew nearer, the columns began to rise up vertically, supporting the arches soaring into space; and each of the visitors, when standing on the little disk indicating the best spot on the floor for viewing the fresco, then saw the material vault disappear before his eyes, allowing him to con-

template in astonishment, in that wondrous perspective, a vision of angels and saints, of men and demons, living and stirring around Christ and Ignatius, who form the center of the grandiose scene.

In the same way the world, to those who see it only in its complex and confused materiality, in all its disorderly proceeding, presents the appearance of chaos. Step by step the fine designs of the most skillful builders collapse and leave us thinking the ruins are irreparable, the construction of a new, balanced world on firm and stable foundations impossible. Why?

In this world there is a stone of granite laid by Christ; one must stand on that stone and turn one's gaze upward; thence originates the restoration of all things in Christ. Christ has revealed the secret thereof: *"Quaerite primum regnum Dei et iustitiam eius, et haec omnia adicientur vobis"* [Seek ye therefore first the kingdom of God, and his justice, and all these things shall be added unto you] (Matt. 6:33).

One cannot therefore draw up the healthy, vital constitution of any society or nation unless the two great powers—the legislator with his deliberations and resolutions and the people with the free expression of their opinions and the exercise of their electoral rights—are both firmly planted on this foundation so they can look upward and bring the kingdom of God upon their country and their world. But are things this way now? Alas, they are far from it.

In deliberative assemblies, as in mobs, there are always many who, unendowed with any consistent moral equilibrium, race ahead and lead the others haphazardly into the darkness, down the paths that lead to ruin! Others, feeling disoriented and lost, anxiously seek, or at least vaguely wish for, light, a hint of light, without knowing where it might be, without following the only "true light, which enlighteneth every man that cometh into this world" (John 1:9). They brush past it with each step, without ever recognizing it.

Even assuming the members of those assemblies to be competent in matters of a temporal nature—political, economic, and administrative questions—many of them are exceptionally less versed in matters concerning the religious realm, Christian doctrine and morals, and the nature, rights, and mission of the Church. At the moment of completing the edifice, they realize that nothing holds plumb, because the keystone to the vault is not in its place.

For its part, the numberless, anonymous multitude is easily provoked to disorder; it surrenders blindly, passively, to the torrent that carries it away or to the whims of the currents that divide and divert it. Once it has become the plaything of the passions or interests of its agitators, as of its own illusions, it is no longer able to take root on the rock and stabilize itself to form a true people, that is, a living body with limbs and organs differentiated according to their respective forms and functions, yet working all together for its autonomous activity in order and unity.

On another occasion, We spoke of the conditions necessary for a people to be ripe for a healthy democracy. Yet who can raise and nurture this state of ripeness? No doubt the Church could draw many lessons in this regard from the treasury of its experiences and its own civilizing activities. Yet your presence here today brings to mind one particular observation. As history will testify, wherever true democracy reigns, the life of the people is permeated with sound traditions, which it is not legitimate to destroy. The primary representatives of these traditions are the ruling classes, or rather, the groups of men and women, or the associations, which set the tone, as we say, for the village or the city, for the region or the entire country.

Whence the existence and influence, among all civilized peoples, of aristocratic institutions, aristocratic in the highest sense of the word, like certain academies of widespread and well-deserved renown. And the nobility is in that number too. Without claiming any privilege or monopoly, it is, or ought to be, one of these institutions. It is a tradi-

tional institution, founded on the continuity of an ancient education. Of course, in a democratic society, which our own wishes to be, the mere title of birth no longer suffices to command authority or esteem; therefore, in order to preserve in worthy fashion your elevated station and social rank, indeed to increase it and raise it, you must truly be an elite, you must meet the conditions and fulfill the indispensable demands of the epoch wherein we live.

You could well become this elite. You have behind you an entire past of age-old traditions that represent fundamental values for the healthy life of a people. Among these traditions, of which you are rightfully proud, you number religiousness, the living and working Catholic faith, as the most important of all. Has history not already cruelly proved that any human society without a religious foundation rushes inevitably toward its dissolution and ends up in terror? In emulation of your ancestors, you should therefore shine in the eyes of the people with the light of your spiritual life, with the splendor of your unshakeable faith in Christ and the Church.

Among these traditions is also the inviolate honor of a profoundly Christian conjugal and familial life. In all countries, or at least in those of Western civilization, there rises now a cry of anguish about marriage and the family, a cry so piercing it is impossible not to hear it. Here too, with your exemplary conduct you must put yourselves at the head of the movement for the reform and restoration of the domestic hearth.

And among these same traditions you also count that of acting for the people, in all the facets of public life to which you might be called, as living examples of an unwavering performance of duty, as impartial, disinterested men who, free of all inordinate lust for success or wealth, do not accept a post except to serve the good cause, courageous men unafraid of losing favor from above, or of threats from below.

Lastly, among these traditions there is also the calm, loyal attachment to all that which experience and history have validated and consecrated, that spirit unmoved by restless agitation and blind lust for novelty so characteristic of our time, but also wide open to all social needs. Deeply convinced that only the doctrine of the Church can provide an effective remedy to the present ills, set your hearts upon paving the way for Her, without reservations or selfish suspicions, with words and with works, and especially by guiding, in the administration of your estates, true model businesses from an economic as well as social point of view. A true gentleman never lends his participation to enterprises that can only sustain themselves and prosper at the expense of the common weal and to the detriment and ruin of persons of modest condition. On the contrary, he will put his virtue at the service of the small, the weak, the people—of those who, practicing an honest trade, earn their daily bread by the sweat of their brow. Only thus will you be truly an elite; thus will you fulfill your religious and Christian duty; thus will you nobly serve God and your country.

May you then, beloved Sons and Daughters, with your great traditions, with care for your progress and your personal, human, and Christian perfection, with your loving good works, with the charity and simplicity of your relations with all the social classes, may you then strive to help the people reestablish themselves on the foundation stone, to seek the kingdom of God and His justice. This is the wish We offer for you, the prayer We lift up, by the intercession of the Immaculate Heart of Mary, to the Divine Heart of Christ Our King, all the way to the throne of the Sovereign Lord of all peoples and all nations. May His grace descend abundantly upon you, and in this pledge We give to you all, with all Our heart, and to your families and all persons dear to you, Our paternal Apostolic blessing.[7]

Allocution of January 8, 1947

The homage of your loyalty and devotion, and the wishes of good tidings which you, beloved Sons and Daughters, come to offer Us each year by ancient custom, and which have been so beautifully expressed by your most excellent representative, always fill Our heart with sincere gratitude. Naturally, they usually reflect the thoughts and worries that to varying degrees trouble the human spirit in the face of the changeable conditions of the times. After the horrors of the war, after the unspeakable miseries that followed in its wake and the anxieties deriving from a suspension of hostilities that could not have been called peace, and indeed was not, We spoke to you more than once, on this same occasion, of the function and duties of the nobility in preparing the new state of things in the world and especially in this beloved country of yours. The characteristic tone at the time was one of complete uncertainty. We walked in total darkness: The deliberations, the manifestations of the popular will were forming and transforming constantly. What would come of it all? No one could predict it with any precision.

Meanwhile on the world stage, the year just ended presented a spectacle to our eyes, one which certainly did not want for activity, upheaval, and surprise. What was lacking, on the other hand, as in prior years, was the achievement of solutions that would let people breathe easier, definitively clarify the conditions of public life, and point out the straight road to the future, however arduous and harsh. Thus, despite some new progress

---

[7] Ibid., January 16, 1946, pp. 337-342.

that We pray will be lasting, uncertainty remains the dominant feature of the present moment, not only in international relations, where we hope for peaceful settlements that are tolerable at the very least, but also in the internal ordering of individual nations. Here too, there is as yet no way to foresee with any certainty what will be the final outcome of the meeting or clash of the various tendencies and forces, and especially of the different and discordant doctrines in areas of religion, politics, and society.

Less difficult, on the other hand, is the task of determining, from the various options open to you, what should be your mode of conduct.

The first of these modes of conduct is unacceptable: that of the deserter, of him who was incorrectly called the *"emigré à l'intérieur"*; it is the abstention of the angry, resentful man who, out of spite or discouragement, makes no use of his qualities or energies, participates in none of his country's and his epoch's activities, but rather withdraws—like Achilles in his tent, near the swift-moving boats, far from the battles—while the destinies of the fatherland are at stake.

Abstention is even less appropriate when it is the result of an indolent, passive indifference. Indeed, worse than ill humor, worse than spite and discouragement, would be nonchalance in the face of a ruin into which one's own brothers, one's own people, were about to fall. In vain would it attempt to hide behind the mask of neutrality; it is not at all neutral; it is, like it or not, complicit. Each light snowflake falling softly on the mountain's slope and adorning it with its whiteness plays its part, while letting itself be dragged along, in turning the little clump of snow that breaks away from the peak into the avalanche that brings disaster to the valley, crushing and burying peaceful homes. Only the solid mass, which is one with the rock of the foundation, can victoriously resist and stop the avalanche, or at least diminish its destructive course.

In this same way the man who is just and firm in his desire for good, the man of whom Horace speaks in a famous ode, who does not let himself be moved in his unshakeable thought by the furor of the citizens who give criminal orders nor by the tyrant's menacing scowl, but remains undaunted, even should the universe crumble over his head: *"si fractus inlabatur orbis, impavidum ferient ruinae" (Carmen Secularae*, III, 3). Yet if this just and strong man is a Christian, he will not content himself with standing erect and impassive amid the ruins; he will feel duty-bound to resist and prevent catastrophe, or at least to limit its damage. And if he cannot contain its destructive force, he will be there again to rebuild the demolished edifice, to sow the devastated field. That is what your conduct should rightly be. It must consist—without having to renounce the freedom of your convictions and your opinions on human vicissitudes—in accepting the contingent order of things such as it is, and in directing its efficiency toward the good, not of a specific class, but of the entire community.

Now this common good—that is, the realization of normal, stable social conditions so that it not prove too difficult for individuals and families with the right use of their powers to lead a proper life according to God's law, a worthy, orderly, and happy life—is the goal and the rule of the State and of its organs.

Men, as individuals and as a society, and their common good are always bound to the absolute order of values established by God. Now, in order to effect this bond and make it work in a manner worthy of human nature, man was given personal freedom, and the guardianship of this freedom is the goal of any judicial system worthy of the name. But from this it also follows that there can be no freedom or right to violate this absolute order of values. It would be tantamount to harming this order and to unhinging the defense of public morality—which is, of course, an essential element to the State's maintenance of the common good—if, to cite one example, one granted, with no regard for that supreme order, unconditional freedom to the press and cinema. In such a case one would not be recognizing the right to true and genuine freedom; rather, one would be legalizing license if one allowed the press and cinema to undermine the religious and moral foundations of the life of the people. To understand and admit such a principle, one need not even be Christian. One need only use reason and sound moral and judicial sense, without the interference of the passions.

It is quite possible that certain grave events that had been developing over the year just past had a sorrowful echo in the hearts of more than a few of us. Yet those who live in the richness of Christian thought do not let themselves be defeated nor discouraged by human occurrences, whatever they may be, and are always bravely turning their gaze to all that remains, which is indeed great and most worthy of their care. What remains is the country and the people: It is the State, whose highest end is the true good of all, and whose mission requires shared cooperation, in which each citizen has his own place; it is the millions of upright souls who love to see this common good in the light of God and to promote it in accordance with the orders of His eternal law.

Italy is on the verge of giving herself a new constitution. Who could fail to recognize the capital importance of such an undertaking? What the life principle is to the living body, the constitution is to the social organism, whose growth, moral as well as economic, is strictly conditioned by it. If, therefore, there are any who need to keep their gazes fixed on the orders handed down by God, if there are any obliged to have the true good of all forever before their eyes, then these are the men to whom is entrusted the great work of drafting a constitution.

Besides, what good are the best laws if they are to remain a dead letter? Their efficacy depends in large part on those who are supposed to apply them. In the hands of men who have not the spirit of the law within them, who perhaps in their hearts disagree with what it provides for, or who are not spiritually or morally capable of putting it into effect, even the most perfect work of legislation loses much of its value. A good constitution is without doubt a thing of great value. What the State is absolutely in need of, however, are men of competence and expertise in political and administrative matters, men wholly dedicated to the greater good of the nation, and guided by clear and sound principles.

Thus does the voice of your fatherland, prompted by the severe upheavals of recent years, call for the collaboration of all honest men and women in whose families and in whose persons reigns the best of the spiritual vigor, the moral categories, and the old and still living traditions of our country. That voice is exhorting them to make themselves available to the State with all the force of their most heartfelt convictions, and to work for the good of the people!

And thus does the road to the future open up for all of you as well.

Last year, on this same occasion, We showed how even in democracies of recent date that have no vestiges of a feudal past behind them, a kind of new nobility or aristocracy has been forming by force of circumstances. It consists of the community of families that by tradition place all their energies at the service of the State, its government, its administration, and whose loyalty it can always count on.

Your task is therefore far from being a negative one. It presupposes much study, much work, much self-abnegation, and above all, much love. Despite the rapid evolution of the times, it has not lost its value, it has not reached its end. What it also requires of you—something that ought to be the salient feature of traditional and family-oriented upbringing—is the noble sentiment and the will not to take advantage of your station—an often solemn, austere privilege nowadays—except to serve.

Go then with courage and with meek pride and meet the future head-on, beloved Sons and Daughters. Your social function, though new in form, is in its substance the same as in your past days of greater splendor. If at times it should seem difficult, arduous, perhaps even with its share of disappointments, do not forget that Divine Providence, which has entrusted it to you, will grant you at once the strength and the succor necessary to fulfill it worthily. For this assistance We pray to the God made

man, to raise human society from its fallen state, to reconstitute a new society on unshakeable foundations, to be Himself the cornerstone of the edifice, to restore it forever anew from generation to generation. With this, as a pledge of the highest heavenly favors, with paternal affection We give you, your families and everyone dear to your hearts, near and far, and especially your cherished young ones, Our Apostolic blessing.[8]

Allocution of January 14, 1948

Although the present difficult circumstances have advised Us this year to give your traditional audience an external form different from the custom, neither the reception of your homages and vows nor the expression of Our best wishes for you and your families has lost any of their intimate value and profound significance.

Just as the heart of the common Father needs few words to pour out into the hearts of the children so close to him, so your mere presence is in itself the most eloquent testimony and clearest confirmation of your undying feelings of loyalty and devotion to this Apostolic See and to the Vicar of Christ.

The gravity of the hour can only disturb and shake those who are lukewarm and hesitant. For ardent and generous souls accustomed to living in Christ and with Christ, it is, on the contrary, a powerful stimulus to overcoming it. And you, no doubt, wish to be among that number.

Therefore, what We expect of you is above all a strength of soul that even the harshest trials cannot vanquish; a strength of soul that should make you not only perfect soldiers of Christ for yourselves, but also, as it were, instructors and supporters

for those who might be tempted to doubt or give in.

What We expect of you is, secondly, a readiness to act that is not daunted nor discouraged by any anticipation of sacrifice that might be required for the common good; a readiness and a fervor that, in making you swift to carry out all your duties as Catholics and citizens, should keep you from falling into an apathetic, inert "abstentionism," which would be a grievous sin at a time when the most vital interests of religion and country are at stake.

What We expect of you, lastly, is a generous adhesion—not under your breath and for the mere sake of formality, but from the bottom of your hearts and carried out without reservation—to Christian doctrine and the Christian life, to the precept of brotherhood and social justice, the observance of which cannot fail to ensure you spiritual and temporal happiness.

May this strength of soul, this fervor, this brotherly spirit guide every one of your steps and reaffirm your path in the course of the New Year, which has been so uncertain in its birth and almost seems to be leading you toward a dark tunnel.

It will therefore probably be not only a

[8]   Ibid., January 8, 1947, pp. 367-371.

year of arduous trials for you, but also one of inner light, of spiritual joy, and beneficent victories.

With this expectation and with unshaken faith in the Lord and the Virgin who protects this Eternal City, We give you, with all Our heart, Our paternal Apostolic blessing.[9]

Allocution of January 15, 1949

The Christmas holidays and the renewal of the year are for Christian families a joyous occasion for strengthening the bonds of affection and for manifesting love of one another with good wishes and mutual promise of prayers. We feel this joy today, as in accordance with ancient tradition you have come, beloved Sons and Daughters, to offer Us your devout homage, so excellently expressed by your illustrious young representative.

Yet the members of a family worthy of the name are not content to exchange old and trite formulas of good wishes. Each year the father renews his customary recommendations, illustrating and complementing them with the kind of advice that the special demands of the hour suggest. For their part, the children examine their own conduct so as to be able, if necessary, to loyally affirm their obedience to the fatherly counsels.

We do the same. Every year We remind you of the fundamental and immutable duties, in all their variety and multiple aspects, imposed upon you by your station in society. Last year We delineated them for you with the brevity required by the circumstances. We do not doubt that, in examining your conscience, you have asked yourselves with what loyalty and in what practical, concrete, effective manner you demonstrated, over the course of the last year, your strength of soul, your readiness to action, and your generous adhesion to the precepts of Christian doctrine and the Christian life in accordance with your station.

No doubt this threefold task is required of all, in all ages. Nevertheless, it is graduated and differentiated according to the ever changeable events and special conditions of those whom it obligates.

Divine Providence has assigned everyone in human society a specific function; it has therefore also divided and distributed its gifts. These gifts and talents are supposed to bear fruit, and you know that the Lord will ask each to account for how they were administered, and according to the benefits gained He will judge and separate the good servants from the bad (cf. Matt. 25:14 ff.; Luke 16:2). The harshness of the times may even make it necessary for you to work, like so many others, to earn your living; yet even so, you will have, by virtue of your birth, special gifts and duties among your fellow citizens.

It is quite true that in the new Italian Constitution "titles of nobility are not recognized" (except, of course, in accordance with Article 42 of the Concordat, as pertains to the Holy See, those titles granted or to be granted by the Supreme Pontiffs); yet not even the Constitution can annul the past, nor the history of your families. Therefore even now the people—whether they are favorable toward you or not, whether they feel respectfully loyal or hostile toward you—look at you and see what sort of example you set in life. It is thus up to you to respond to such expectations and show how your conduct and actions are in keeping with truth and virtue, especially in the matters We have just discussed in Our recommendations.

---

[9]   Ibid., January 14, 1948, pp. 423-424.

All are in need of *strength of soul*, but especially so in our times, in order to bear the suffering bravely, to overcome life's difficulties victoriously, to constantly perform one's duty. Who does not have some reason for suffering? Who does not have some cause for sorrow? Who does not have something to fight for? Only he who surrenders and flees. Yet your right to surrender and flee is much less than that of others. Suffering and hardship today are commonly the lot of all classes, all social stations, all families, all persons. And if a few are exempt, if they swim in superabundance and enjoyment, this must spur them to take the miseries and hardships of others upon themselves. Who could find contentment and rest, who, rather, would not feel uneasy and ashamed, to live in idleness and frivolity, in luxury and pleasure, amid almost universal tribulation?

Readiness to act. In this moment of great personal and social solidarity, everyone must be ready to work, to sacrifice oneself, to devote oneself to the good of all. The difference lies not in the fact of obligation, but in the manner of fulfilling it. Is it not true that those who have more time and more abundant means at their disposal should be more assiduous and more solicitous in their desire to serve? In speaking of means, We are not referring only nor primarily to wealth, but to all the gifts of intelligence, culture, education, knowledge, and authority, which fate does not grant to certain privileged individuals for their exclusive advantage or to create an irremediable inequality among brothers, but rather for the good of the whole social community. In all that involves serving one's neighbor, society, the Church and God, you must always be the first. Therein lies your true rank of honor, your most noble preeminence.

Generous adhesion to the precepts of Christian doctrine and the Christian life. These are the same for all, for there are not two truths, nor two laws; rich and poor, big and small, noble and humble, all are equally expected to submit their intellects through faith in the same dogma, their wills through obedience to the same morals. Divine justice, however, will be much more severe toward those who have been given more, those who are better able to understand the sole doctrine and to put it into practice in everyday life, those who with their example and their authority can more easily direct others onto the road of justice and salvation, or else lose them on the fatal roads of unbelief and sin.

Beloved Sons and Daughters! The past year has shown how necessary these three inner forces are, and has demonstrated the results that can be obtained through their just application. Most important of all is that the activity not suffer any interruption or diminution, but rather that it be begun and carried out with constancy and steadfastness. This is why We were particularly pleased to learn from the words of your representative how deep your understanding of present-day social ills is, and how firm your offer to help remedy them through justice and charity.

You must therefore fortify in your minds the resolve to meet in full the demands that Christ, the Church, and society so trustfully make of you, so that you may hear, on the day of the great retribution, the blessed word of the supreme Judge: "Good and faithful servant,...enter thou into the joy of thy Lord" (Matt. 25:21).

With this ardent wish that, at the dawn of this New Year, We offer on your behalf to the Infant Jesus, with all Our heart We give you, your families, and all those dear to you Our paternal Apostolic blessing.[10]

---

[10]   Ibid., January 15, 1949, pp. 345-348.

Allocution of January 12, 1950

If, dear Sons and Daughters, following the example of Our Predecessors, We are accustomed to welcoming you at the start of the New Year to receive and exchange our good wishes, it is because Our heart, far from obeying worldly considerations or preferences, is moved by feelings of honor and loyalty. In you We hail the descendants and representatives of families long in the service of the Holy See and the Vicar of Christ, who remained faithful to the Roman Pontificate even when it was exposed to outrages and persecutions. Without doubt, over the course of time the social order has been able to evolve, and its center has shifted. Public offices, which once were reserved for your class, may now be conferred and exercised on a basis of equality; nevertheless, such a testimonial of grateful remembrance—which must also serve as an impetus for the future—must also command respect and understanding in modern man as well if he wishes to possess just and fair sentiments.

You find yourselves gathered around Us here today at the dawn of the year marking the division between the two halves of the twentieth century, a Jubilee Year inaugurated with the opening of the Holy Door. Considered in itself, the religious ceremony of striking three hammer-blows at the center of the Door has a symbolic value; it is a symbol of the opening of the great forgiveness. How then do we explain the vivid impression it made not only on the devoted children of the Church, who are able to fathom its inner meaning, but also on many others outside the Church who seem sensitive only to what can be touched, measured, and translated into numbers? Ought we to see in it perhaps the presentiment and expectation of a new half-century less fraught with bitterness and disappointment?

The symptom of a need for purification and reparation, the desire for reconciliation and peace among men whom war and social struggles have so divided? How indeed, with our humble and Christian faith, could we not see the hand of God in this so propitious beginning of the great Jubilee?

The power of benediction, which the Holy Year is called upon to spread over all humanity, will depend in large part upon the greatest possible cooperation of Catholics everywhere, especially through prayer and atonement. In this regard, however, the faithful of Rome indeed have special duties and responsibilities: Their mode of conduct, their way of living, will this year be particularly visible to the eyes of the Universal Church, as represented by the multitude of pilgrims who will pour into the Eternal City from every part of the globe. You yourselves, beloved Sons and Daughters, will not lack the opportunities to precede the others and lead them by your good example: by the example of fervor in prayer, of Christian simplicity in lifestyle, of the renunciation of comforts and pleasures, of true penance, of cordial hospitality, of zeal in good works for the humble, the poor, and the suffering, of intrepid strength in the defense of God's cause.

Moreover, the class to which you belong puts you more easily and more frequently in contact with persons of authority from other countries. Do your utmost, in such circumstances, to promote reconciliation and peace among men and among nations. May the face of this earth at the end of the Holy Year shine more serenely in tranquility and brotherly harmony!

With this wish and with all Our heart We give you and your families, especially those far away or sick, Our paternal Apostolic blessing.[11]

---

[11] Ibid., January 12, 1950, pp. 357-358.

Allocution of January 11, 1951

With all Our heart We extend Our paternal greeting to the members of the Roman Patriciate and Nobility who, true to an ancient tradition, have gathered around Us at the dawn of the New Year to offer Us their fervent best wishes, as expressed with filial devotion by their illustrious and eloquent representative.

One after another, each year enters history, handing down to the new year a legacy, the responsibility for which it bears upon itself. The year just ended, the Holy Year 1950, will remain one of the greatest in the moral and especially the supernatural order. Your family annals will note its more resplendent dates, like so many bright beacons to light the way for your children and grandchildren.

But will these annals be like a closed book? Will they count only the memories of a past dead and gone? No. On the contrary, they must be a message from the vanished generations to those of the future.

The celebration of the Holy Year came to a close for Rome, not like a spectacle that had reached its end, but rather as the program of a growing life purified, sanctified, and fecundated by grace, one that must continue to enrich itself with the endless contribution of the thoughts and feelings, the resolutions and actions whose memories your ancestors have passed on to you, that you yourselves might pass on their example to those who shall follow you.

The furious currents of a new age envelop the traditions of the past in their whirlwinds. Yet, more than this, these winds show what is destined to die like withered leaves, and what instead tends with the genuine force of its interior life to stand firm and live on.

A nobility and a patriciate that would, as it were, grow stiff and decrepit by regretting times gone by, would consign themselves to an inevitable decline.

Today more than ever, you are called upon to be an elite, not only by blood and by stock, but even more by your works and sacrifices, by creative actions in the service of the entire social community.

And this is not just a duty of man and citizen that none may shirk with impunity. It is also a sacred commandment of the faith that you have inherited from your fathers and that you must, in their wake, leave whole and unaltered to your descendants.

Banish, therefore, from your ranks all despondency and faint-heartedness; all despondency in the face of the age's evolution, which is bearing away many things that other epochs had built; and all faint-heartedness at the sight of the grave events accompanying the novelties of our age.

Being Roman means being strong in action, but also in support.

Being Christian means confronting the sufferings, the trials, the tasks, and the needs of the age with that courage, strength, and serenity of spirit that draws the antidote to all human fear from the wellsprings of eternal hope.

How humanly great is Horace's proud dictum: *Si fractus illabatur orbis, impavidum ferient ruinae* (*Odes*, III, 3).

Yet how much greater still, how much more confident and exalting is the victorious cry that rises from Christian lips and hearts brimming with faith: *Non confundar in aeternum*! [Let me not be confounded eternally] (*Te Deum*).

Thus beseeching the Creator of all good to grant you intrepid fortitude and the divine gift of an unshakeable hope founded on faith, with all Our heart We give you, beloved Sons and Daughters, your families, and all your loved ones, near and far, sick and in health, and all your holy aspirations and undertakings, Our Apostolic blessing.[12]

Allocution of January 14, 1952

Faithful to your ancient tradition, beloved Sons and Daughters, you have again come this year to present the visible Head of the Church with a testimonial of your devotion and your fond wishes for the New Year. We welcome them with keen and affectionate gratitude, and offer you in return Our warmest regards. We include them in Our prayers, so that the year just born may be marked by the seal of divine goodness and enriched with the most precious favors of Providence. To these wishes We should like to add, as usual, a few practical spiritual gifts, which We will summarize in a threefold exhortation.

1) First of all, you must look fearlessly, courageously, at the present reality. It seems superfluous to insist on recalling to your mind what, three years ago, was the object of Our considerations; it would seem vain and unworthy of you to veil it in prudent euphemisms, especially after the words of your eloquent representative have given Us so clear a testimonial of your adhesion to the social doctrine of the Church and to the duties stemming therefrom. The new Italian Constitution no longer recognizes you as possessing, as a social class, in the State and among the people, any particular mission, quality, or privilege. A page of history has been turned; a chapter has ended. A period has been placed, indicating the end of a social and economic past; a new chapter has begun, inaugurating very different lifestyles. One may think as one wishes, but the fact remains: It is the "irresistible course" of history. Some, perhaps, may painfully resent so profound a transformation; but what good can come of wallowing at length in the bitterness of that fact? All, in the end, must bow to reality; the difference lies solely in the "manner." While the mediocre can only wear a frown in the face of ill fortune, superior spirits are able, according to the classic expression, to prove themselves "*beaux joueurs*," imperturbably maintaining their noble and untroubled bearing.

2) Lift your gaze and keep it fixed on the Christian ideal. All those upheavals, those evolutions and revolutions, have left it untouched. They can do nothing against what is the inner essence of true nobility, that which aspires to Christian perfection, the same that the Redeemer pointed to in the Sermon on the Mount. Unconditional loyalty to Catholic doctrine, to Christ, and to His Church; the ability and the will to be also models and guides for others. Need We enumerate the practical applications of all this? You must present to the world, even to the world of believers and of practicing Catholics, the spectacle of a faultless conjugal life, the edification of a truly exemplary domestic hearth; you must build a dike against every infiltration, into your home and your circles, of ruinous ideas, pernicious indulgences and tolerances that might contaminate and sully the purity of matrimony and family. Here indeed is an exemplary and holy enterprise, well suited to ignite the zeal of the Roman and Christian nobility in our times.

As We present these reflections for your consideration, We are thinking especially of countries in which the devastating catastrophe struck the families of your class particularly violently, reducing them from power and wealth to forlornness and even to extreme poverty; yet at the same time it revealed and brought out the nobility and generosity with which many of them have remained faithful to God even in misfortune and the silent magnanimity and dignity with which they are able to bear their lot. These are virtues that are not improvised, but rather which flourish and ripen at the hour of affliction.

---

[12] Ibid., January 11, 1951, pp. 423-424.

3) Lastly, give your devoted and ready assistance to the common effort. Vast is the field in which your activities may prove useful: in the Church and in the State, in parliamentary and administrative life, in literature, in science, in the arts, in the various professions. Only one attitude is forbidden you—for it would be contrary to the original spirit of your station: We are referring to "abstentionism." More than an "emigration," it would be a desertion, since whatever may happen and however much it may cost, one must above all preserve, against the danger of even the smallest rifts, the strict union of all the forces of Catholicism.

It may well be that one thing or another about the present conditions displeases you. Yet for the sake and for the love of the common good, for the salvation of Christian civilization, during this crisis which, far from abating, seems instead to be growing, stand firm in the breach, on the front line of defense. There your special qualities can be put to good use even today. Your names, which resonate deeply in the memories even of the distant past, in the history of the Church and of civil society, recall to mind figures of great men and fill your souls with echoes of the dutiful call to prove yourselves worthy.

The inborn sentiment of perseverance and continuity, the attachment to a healthy notion of tradition, are characteristic features of true nobility. If you are able to combine them with a vast openness of views on contemporary reality, especially on social justice, and an honest and sincere collaboration, you will be making a contribution of the highest value to public life.

These, beloved Sons and Daughters, are the thoughts We deemed suitable to communicate to you at the dawn of this New Year. May the Lord inspire in you the resolve to carry them out and deign to fecundate your good will with the abundance of His grace, in hopes of which We now with all Our heart impart to you, and to your families, your children, your sick and infirm, and to all those dear to you, near and far, Our paternal Apostolic blessing.[13]

Allocution of January 9, 1958

With great satisfaction We welcome you, beloved Sons and Daughters, into Our house, which is still pervaded by the holy fragrances of the Christmas holidays. You have come to reconfirm your devout fidelity to this Apostolic See, and with the heart of a father anxious to surround himself with his children's affections, We comply most willingly with your desire to listen once again to a few words of exhortation in return, as it were, for the good wishes just communicated to Us by your distinguished and eloquent representative.

The present audience recalls to Our mind the memory of your first visit here long ago, in 1940. How many sorrowful absences there have been among your elect number since that time; yet, how many lovely new flowers have since blossomed in the same bed! The sad memory of the former and the happy presence of the latter seem to enclose in a single, broad frame an entire picture of life which, though past, never ceases to impart salutary lessons and shed hopeful light on your present and your future. While those "whose brow is framed in white or silver"—as We said back then—have moved on to the peace of the just, adorned with the "many merits gained in the long performance of duty," others, already "bold with the flower of youth and the splendor of manliness," have been assuming their positions, or have already as-

---

[13]   Ibid., January 14, 1952, pp. 457-459.

sumed them, driven by the irresistible hand of time, which is in turn guided by the provident wisdom of the Creator. In the meanwhile, those who at the time numbered among the children, those toward whose "serene and smiling innocence" Our preference went, whose "ingenuous candor, whose bright and vivid purity of gaze" We loved so much, have now entered the struggle themselves.[14] Well, to those children of that time, now become passionate youths and mature men, We wish to say a few words before anything else, as if to open a path deep into Our heart.

You, who at the start of each new year have never failed to come visit Us, must surely remember the careful solicitude with which We endeavored to smooth your way toward the future, which at that time promised to be harsh because of the profound upheavals and transformations in store for the world. We are certain, however, that when your brows too are framed with white and silver, you will yet be witnesses not only to Our esteem and affection, but also to the truth, the validity, and the timeliness of Our recommendations, which We hope are like fruits that have come to you and to society in general.

You will recall to your children and grandchildren how the Pope of your childhood and adolescence did not neglect to point you toward the new responsibilities that the new circumstances of the age imposed on the nobility; that, indeed, he explained many times how industriousness would be the surest and most worthy way of ensuring yourselves a permanent place among society's leaders; that social inequalities, while they make you stand out, also assign you certain duties toward the common good; that from the highest classes great boons or great harm could come to the people; that transformations of ways of life can, if one so wishes, be harmoniously reconciled with the traditions of which patrician families are the repositories.

Sometimes, in alluding to the contingency of time and events, We exhorted you to take an active part in the healing of the wounds caused by the war, in the rebuilding of peace, in the rebirth of the life of the nation, and to refuse all "emigration" or abstention. For in our society there still remained an ample place for you if you showed yourselves to be truly *elites* and *optimates*, that is, exceptional for serenity of mind, readiness to act, and generous adhesion. Also do not forget Our appeals to banish from your hearts all despondency and cowardice in face of the evolution of the times, and Our exhortations to adapt yourselves courageously to the new circumstances by keeping your gaze fixed on the Christian ideal, the true and indelible entitlement to genuine nobility.

Yet why, beloved Sons and Daughters, did We express then and do We now repeat these admonitions and recommendations if not to fortify you against bitter disillusionments, to preserve for your houses the heritage of your ancestral glories, and to guarantee for the society to which you belong the valid contribution that you are still capable of making to it? And yet—you may ask Us—what exactly must we do to achieve so lofty a goal?

First of all, you must maintain an irreproachable religious and moral conduct, especially within the family, and practice a healthy austerity in life. Let the other classes be aware of the patrimony of virtues and gifts that are your own, the fruit of long family traditions: an imperturbable strength of soul, loyalty and devotion to the worthiest causes, tender and generous compassion toward the weak and the poor, a prudent and delicate manner in difficult and grave matters, and that personal prestige, almost hereditary in noble families, whereby one manages to persuade without oppressing, to sway without forcing, to conquer the minds of others, even adversaries and rivals, without humiliating them. The

---

[14]   See Allocution of January 8, 1940, above.

use of these gifts and the exercise of religious and civic virtues are the most convincing way to respond to prejudices and suspicion, since they manifest the spirit's inner vitality, from which spring all outward vigor and fruitful works.

Vigor and fruitful works! Behold two characteristics of true nobility, to which heraldic symbols, stamped in bronze or carved in marble, are a perennial testimony, for they represent as it were the visible thread of the political and cultural history of more than a few glorious cities of Europe. It is true that modern society is not accustomed by preference to wait for your class to "set the tone" before starting works and confronting events; nevertheless, it does not refuse the cooperation of the brilliant minds among you, since a wise portion thereof retains an appropriate respect for tradition and prizes high decorum, whatever its origins. And the other part of society, which displays indifference and perhaps disdain for ancient ways of life, is not entirely immune to the seduction of glory; so much so, that it tries very hard to create new forms of aristocracy, some worthy of respect, others based on vanity and frivolity, satisfied with merely appropriating the inferior elements of the ancient institutions.

It is clear, however, that vigor and fruitful works cannot still manifest themselves today in forms that have been eclipsed. This does not mean that the field of your activities has been reduced; on the contrary, it has been broadened in the total number of professions and functions. The entire range of professions is open to you; you can be useful and excel in any sector: in areas of public administration and government, or in scientific, cultural, artistic, industrial, or commercial activities.

We would like, finally, for your influence on society to save it from a grave danger inherent in modern times. It is well known that society progresses and raises itself up when the virtues of one class are spread to the others; it declines, on the other hand, if the vices and abuses of one are carried over to the others. Because of the weakness of human nature, more often

it is the latter that are spread, with all the more rapidity nowadays, given the greater facility of means of communication, information, and personal contacts, not only among nations, but from one continent to the next. What happens in the realm of physical health is now happening in the realm of morals as well: neither distances nor boundaries can any longer prevent an epidemic germ from quickly reaching faraway regions. The upper classes, of which yours is one, could, because of their multiple relations and frequent sojourns in countries with different and sometimes inferior moral conditions, become easy conveyers of aberrations in customs. We are alluding in particular to those abuses that are threatening the sanctity of matrimony, the religious and moral education of the young, Christian temperance in pleasure, and respect for modesty. Your country's traditions regarding these values must be defended and kept sacred and inviolable, and protected from the dangers of the germs of dissolution, wherever they may happen to come from. Any attempt to violate these traditions, which is no sign of progress except toward decay, is an attack on the honor and dignity of this nation.

As for your own task, you must be vigilant and do your utmost to prevent pernicious theories and perverse examples from ever meeting with your approval and sympathy, let alone using you as favorable carriers and hotbeds of infection. May that profound respect for tradition that you cultivate and hope to use to distinguish yourselves in society give you the strength to preserve such precious treasures among the people. This itself may be the highest social function of today's nobility; certainly it is the greatest service that you can render to the Church and to your country.

To practice virtue and use the gifts proper to your class for the common good, to excel in professions and activities promptly embraced, to protect the nation from external contaminations: These are the recommendations We feel We must make to you at the start of this New Year.

Accept them from Our hands, dear Sons

and Daughters, and, transforming them by an act of will in a threefold commitment, offer them again in turn, as wholly personal gifts, to the Holy Infant, who will value them as He did the gold, frankincense, and myrrh offered Him a very long time ago by the Wise Men of the East.

That the Almighty may strengthen your resolve and fulfill Our desires, answering the prayers We have thus made to Him, We impart to all of you, to your families, and especially to your children, future successors to your worthiest traditions, Our Apostolic blessing.[15]

---

[15] *Discorsi e radiomessaggi,* January 9, 1958, pp. 707-711.

land disappear, it has become all the more imperative for the nobility to strive to restore to the intellectual patrimony those sacred notions that should guide them in their daily activities. In all ages have nobles been duty-bound to allow nothing indecent to enter their words and their actions, that their own license might not become an incitement to the vices of their subalterns, "*in integritate, in gravitate.*" Yet, this duty too, oh how urgent and weighty it has become, because of the bad habits of our time! Not just the gentlemen are beholden, however; the ladies, too, are obliged to join together in the holy struggle against the extravagancies and obscenities of fashion, distancing themselves from, and not tolerating in others, what is not permitted by the laws of Christian modesty.

And coming to the application of what Saint Paul advised directly to the nobles of his day, "*divitibus huius saeculi, praecipe...bene agere, divites fieri in boni operibus,*" to Us it is enough that the Patricians and Nobles of Rome continue, in peacetime, to shape themselves by that spirit of charity of which they have given such wonderful proof in times of war. The needs of the hour in which their actions will take place, and the specific conditions of place, may determine various and different forms of charity; yet if you, beloved Children, forget not that charity is due even yesterday's enemy who today languishes in poverty, you will show that you have done your "*bene agere*" by Saint Paul; you will enrich yourselves with the abundance promised by the Apostle him-self—"*divites fieri in boni operibus*" and you will continue to make the world appreciate what We have called the "priesthood of the nobility."

O how sweet it is for Us to contemplate the wondrous results of this continuity. Your nobility, then, will not be seen as a useless relic of times gone by, but as a leavening to resurrect corrupt society; it will be a beacon, a preserving salt, a guide for wanderers; it shall be not only immortal on this earth where everything, even the glory of the most illustrious dynasties, fades and vanishes, but will be immortal in heaven, where everything lives and is exalted in the Author of all things beautiful and noble.

Saint Paul the Apostle ends his admonitions to the nobles of his day by saying that treasures acquired by virtue of good works would open the doors of that heavenly abode where the true life is enjoyed—"*ut aprehendant veram vitam.*" And We, in Our turn, to return the good wishes that the Roman Patriciate and Nobility have expressed to Us at the start of the New Year, We pray the Lord to bestow His blessing not only on the members of the illustrious class here present, but also on those members far away and on the families of individuals, that each might cooperate with the priesthood proper to his class toward the elevation and purification of the world and, by doing good to others, ensure entry for himself as well into the kingdom of eternal life—"*ut aprehendant veram vitam!*"[1]

---

[1]   *L'Osservatore Romano*, January 5-6, 1920.

Special Duties of Society Toward the Impoverished Nobility

1. The Best Alms Is That Given to the Impoverished Noble

Saint Peter Damian (1007-1072), Doctor of the Church, points out the particular diligence that one should have in alleviating the needs of an impoverished noble:

> Although alms are praised throughout the pages of sacred eloquence, and compassion is superior to the other virtues and wins the palm among the works of piety, nevertheless, that compassion stands above the rest that extends aid to those recently fallen from abundance into want. For there are some indeed whom the rank of a rather exalted ancestry ennobles, but whom the poverty of their family constricts. Many are even adorned with knightly family titles but are depressed by a lack of domestic necessities. The demanding dignity of their ancestry compels them to be present at the gatherings of the noteworthy; in the assembly they are indeed equal, but they are very unequal when it comes to resources. Although the troubles of domestic poverty torture them, even if compelling necessity brings them to extreme circumstances, they know not how to seek for food as mendicants. For they choose to die rather than to beg publicly; they are embarrassed at being recognized; they are afraid to confess their want; and although others proclaim their poverty—indeed, sometimes exceed moderation by exaggerating their poverty in order to receive the consolation of a richer contribution—these people, insofar as they are able, pretend by concealing, lest some sign of their poverty should basely erupt into the sight of men.
>
> Their poverty, therefore, is rather able to be understood than to be seen; rather able to be conjectured from certain signs that break through than to be detected from manifest indications. How great is the return from those who are not manifestly but secretly paupers the Prophet indicates when he says: "Blessed is he that understandeth concerning the needy and the poor" (Ps. 40:2). Certainly when it comes to ragged and ulcerated paupers wandering through the streets, we have no need for understanding, for we see them indeed with manifest vision; as for those other paupers, however, we need to perceive what is in their interior, for we are not able to clearly see their misery externally.[1]

---

[1]   Migne, *Patrologia Latina*, Vol. 145, col. 214-215.

2. Solicitude of Saint Elizabeth, Queen of Portugal, Toward the Impoverished Nobility

In the life of Saint Elizabeth, Queen of Portugal (1274-1336), we read the following facts that manifest an edifying trace of her character:

> She took particular care in assisting people who, having lived under the norm of nobility with property, found themselves ruined, their necessity and misery increasing, and ashamed to beg. She aided these poor ones with great generosity and with no less secrecy and circumspection so that they enjoyed benefits without the counterpoise of shame.
>
> For the sons of poor nobles, she had in the palace special pouches that were prepared in accordance with their elevated position. She gave dowries for marriages to respectable poor maidens and took delight in dressing their hair for their weddings with her royal hands. She had gathered near her and educated many other orphans, daughters of her vassals; when they contracted a marriage, she dowered them abundantly, and she adorned them with her jewels on the wedding day. And so that her refinement of goodness would not end with her life, she established a trust in her monastery of Santa Clara for dowries for noble orphans and left instructions that part of the jewels she bequeathed to this convent be lent to these young ladies for their bridal adornment.[2]

---

[2] J. Le Brun, *Santa Isabel, Rainha de Portugal* (Porto: Livraria Apostolado da Imprensa, 1958), pp. 127-128.

Noble Lineage:
A Precious Gift of God

1. Nobility Is a Gift from God

From the allocution of Pius IX to the Roman Patriciate and Nobility on June 17, 1871:

One day a Cardinal, a Roman prince, presented his nephew to one of my Predecessors, who on that occasion made a very true statement: that thrones should be upheld principally through the nobility and the clergy. For there is no denying that nobility, too, is a gift of God, and although Our Lord chose to be born in a stable, in two Gospels we can read His and kings. You must use your privilege worthily, and keep the principle of legiti-

macy sacred.

Continue, therefore, to use this prerogative wisely; one truly noble use of it would be toward those who, though belonging to your class, do not subscribe to your principles. A few loving words from good friends could have a great influence on their minds, and a few prayers an even greater one. Tolerate with a generous heart the disagreements you may encounter. May God bless you your while life long, as I pray Him to do with all my heart.[1]

2. Our Lord Jesus Christ Willed to Be Born a Noble; He Himself Loved the Aristocracy

From the allocution of Pius IX to the Roman Patriciate and Nobility on December 29, 1872:

Jesus Christ Himself loved aristocracy; and if I am not mistaken, I expounded upon this idea on another occasion. He too chose to be of noble birth, of the House of David; and His Gospel shows us His family tree down

to Joseph and Mary, *"de qua natus est Jesus."*

Aristocracy, nobility, therefore, is a gift from God. Preserve it diligently, and use it worthily. You do so already with Christian and charitable works, to which you devote yourselves to the great edification of your fellows and to the great advantage of your souls.[2]

[1] *Discorsi del Sommo Pontefice Pio IX* (Rome: Tipografia di G. Aurelj, 1872), Vol. 1, p. 127.

[2] Ibid., Vol. 2, p. 148.

3. Nobility of Birth Seems a Fortuitous Fact, but It Results from a Benevolent Design of Heaven

From the allocution of Leo XIII to the Roman Patriciate and Nobility on January 21, 1897:

Our heart rejoices to see you here again, united by a concord of ideas and affections that honor you. Our charity knows no partiality, nor ought to know any, yet it is not to be blamed if it takes particular pleasure in you and in the very social rank that was assigned to you in what may seem a fortuitous manner, but was in truth the benign will of heaven. How can one deny special esteem to the prominence of a noble line if the Divine Redeemer manifested the same regard? Of course, during His earthly pilgrimage, He adopted a life of poverty and never wished for the company of riches, yet He chose His own lineage from royal stock.

We remind you of these things, beloved Children, not to flatter any foolish pride, but rather to give you comfort in works worthy of your rank. Every individual and every class of individuals has its function and its value; from the ordered accord of all is born the harmony of mankind. Nevertheless, it cannot be denied that in the public and private orders the aristocracy of blood is a special force, as are property and talent. And if it were somehow in contradiction to the will of nature, it would never have been what it has been in all ages, one of the moderating laws of human history. Wherefore, judging from the past, it is not illogical to infer that, however the times may evolve, an illustrious name will always have some validity to one who knows how to bear it worthily.[3]

4. Jesus Christ Willed to Be Born of Royal Stock

From the allocution of Leo XIII to the Roman Patriciate and Nobility on January 24, 1903:

And Jesus Christ, although He chose to spend His private life in the obscurity of a lowly dwelling, passing for the son of a laborer, and although in public life He so loved to associate with the common people, helping them

in every manner possible, still He chose to be born of royal stock, choosing Mary as a mother and Joseph as putative father, both of them scions of the Davidic line. And yesterday, the feast of their marriage, we were able to repeat with the Church the beautiful words, *"Regali ex progenie Maria exorta refulget"* [Mary shows herself to us all refulgent, born of royal stock].[4]

3   *Leonis XIII Pontificis Maximii Acta* (Rome: Ex Typographia Vaticana, 1898), Vol. 17, pp. 357-358.

4   Ibid., 1903, Vol. 22, p. 368.

5. Our Lord Jesus Christ Willed to Be Born Poor, but He Also Wanted to Have a Signal Relationship with the Aristocracy

From the allocution of Benedict XV to the Roman Patriciate and Nobility on January 5, 1917:

> Before God there is no preference of persons. Yet there is no doubt, writes Saint Bernard, that the virtue of nobles is more pleasing to Him, because it is more resplendent.
>
> Jesus Christ Himself was noble, as were Mary and Joseph, being descendants of royal lineage, even though their virtue eclipsed their splendor in His humble birth, which the Church has commemorated in the days just past.

Therefore, may Christ, Who chose to have such an illustrious relation to the earthly aristocracy, receive in the all-powerful humility of His cradle the ardent wish We express on your behalf today—that, just as in the manger the highest nobility was united with the most glorious virtue, the same may be true for Our own beloved children, the patricians and nobles of Rome. And may their virtue bring about the Christian regeneration of society and, with it, the graces that are inseparable therefrom: the well-being of all families and the longed-for peace of the world.[5]

6. Mary, Joseph, and, Therefore, Jesus Were Born of Royal Stock

From a sermon of Saint Bernardine of Siena (1380-1444) about Saint Joseph:

> Firstly, let us consider the nobility of the bride, that is, the Most Holy Virgin. The Blessed Virgin was more noble than any other creature that had been born in human form, that could be or could have been begotten. For Saint Matthew in his first chapter, thrice enumerating fourteen generations from Abraham to Jesus Christ inclusive, shows that she descends from fourteen Patriarchs, fourteen Kings, and fourteen Princes.... Saint Luke also, writing on her nobility in his third chapter, proceeds in his genealogy from Adam and Eve until Christ God....

> Secondly, let us consider the nobility of the bridegroom, that is, Saint Joseph. He was born of a Patriarchal, Royal, and Princely stock in a direct line as has been said. For Saint Matthew in his first chapter established a direct line with all the aforementioned fathers from Abraham to the spouse of the Virgin, clearly demonstrating that all patriarchal, royal, and princely dignity come together in him....

> Thirdly, let us examine the nobility of Christ. He was, as follows from what has been said, a Patriarch, King, and Prince, for He received just as much from His mother as others from father and mother.... From what has been said

---

[5] *L'Osservatore Romano*, January 6, 1917.

above, it is clear that the nobility of the Virgin and of Joseph is described by the aforementioned Evangelists so that the nobility of Christ be manifest. For Joseph, therefore, was of such no-bility that, in a certain way, if it be permitted to say, he gave temporal no-bility to God in Our Lord Jesus Christ.[6]

7. God the Son Willed to Be Born of Royal Stock in Order to Gather in His Person Every Kind of Grandeur

From the writings on Saint Joseph by Saint Peter Julian Eymard (1811-1868):

When God the Father resolved to give His Son to the world, He wanted to do it honorably, for He is worthy of all honor and all praise. He thus pre-pared Him a court and royal service worthy of Him: God wanted, even on earth, for His Son to enjoy, if not in the eyes of men, then at least in His own eyes, an honorable and glorious recep-tion. God did not improvise the mystery of grace of the Incarnation of the Word, and those who were chosen to play a role had been prepared by Him long in advance. The court of the Son of God is composed of Mary and Joseph: God himself could not have found more wor-thy servants for His Son.

Let us consider above all Saint Joseph. Charged with the education of the royal Prince of heaven and earth, charged with governing and serving Him, it was necessary that his service honor his divine pupil: God cannot be ashamed of His Father. And since He is king, of the blood of David, He has Joseph be born of this royal line; He wants Him to be noble, even of earthly nobility. In Joseph flows the blood of the Davids, the Solomons, and all the noble kings of Judah; if the dynasty still sat on the throne, he would be the heir and should have sat on the throne in turn. Pay no mind to his actual pov-erty; injustice had chased his family from the throne which was their due; he is no less a king for this, the son of these kings of Judah, the greatest, the most noble, the richest in the uni-verse. Thus in the census records of Bethlehem, Joseph will be registered and recognized as the heir of David by the Roman governor: therein lies his title; it is easy to recognize and bears the royal stamp.

What does the nobility of Joseph matter? you might ask. Jesus came only to humble Himself. I answer that the Son of God, who wanted to humble Himself for a time, also wished to unite in His person all types of greatness: He too is a king; through His birthright, He has royal blood. Jesus is noble; and when He chooses His apostles from the commonalty He ennobles them: He has that right, being son of Abraham and heir of the throne of David. He loves this honor of families: the Church does not judge the nobility in terms of de-mocracy; let us respect what she re-spects: nobility is a gift of God.

Must one then be noble to serve God? If you were noble you would bring Him further glory; it is not nec-essary, however, and He is satisfied with good will and nobility of the

---

[6] *Sancti Bernardini Senensis Sermones Eximii* (Venice: in Aedibus Andreae Poletti, 1745), Vol. 4, p. 232.

heart. Nonetheless, the Church annals show us that a large number of saints, and the most illustrious ones, had a blazon, a name, an illustrious family; many were even of royal blood. Our Lord loves to be honored by all that is honorable. Saint Joseph received a perfect education in the temple, and God thus disposed him to be a noble server for His Son, the knight of the most noble prince, the protector of the most august Queen of the universe.[7]

8. Nobility of Blood Is a Powerful Stimulus for the Practice of Virtue

From the magnificent sermon of Saint Charles Borromeo (1538-1584), Archbishop of Milan, on the feast of Our Lady, September 8, 1584:

The beginning of the Holy Gospel written by Saint Matthew, which was proclaimed to you from this place a short while ago by Holy Mother Church, inspires us above all to examine attentively the nobility, the remarkable lineage, and the magnificence of this Most Holy Virgin. For, if that person is to be considered noble who traces his origins from illustrious ancestors, how great is the nobility of Mary, whose filiation traces from kings, patriarchs, prophets, and priests of the Tribe of Judah, to the seed of Abraham, and to the royal stirp of David?

Moreover, although we are not ignorant of the fact that true nobility—the Christian nobility—is that which the Only Begotten of the Father conferred on all of us when "as many as received Him, He gave them power to be made the sons of God" (John 1:12), and that this dignity of nobility is common to all faithful Christians, nevertheless we believe that nobility according to the flesh ought not in any way be despised or re-jected. On the contrary, he who would not acknowledge this very nobility itself as a singular gift and blessing of God and would not also give special thanks for it to God, the Giver of all good things, would truly be utterly unworthy of the name noble, inasmuch as through the fault of an ungrateful soul, than which nothing could be more base, he would tarnish the splendor of his own ancestors. Indeed, nobility of the flesh adds much to true radiance of soul and bears no small benefits.

In the first place, the splendor of the blood and the virtue and famous deeds of the ancestors have a marvelous effect in disposing the noble, virile man to follow in the footsteps of those from whom he descended. And doubtless also it is that his own nature is more inclined to good and virtue, whether because of the conformity of his blood with that of his progenitors and, in consequence, the transmission of their spirits; or because of the perpetual memory of their virtues that he retains and on that account holds more dear—and knows how to value— for having shone forth in those of his own blood; or because, finally, of the sound rearing and formation he received from distinguished men. It is certainly

---

[7]   *Mois de Saint Joseph, le premier et le plus parfait des adorateurs—Extrait des écrits de P. Eymard*, 7th ed. (Paris: Desclée de Brouwer, n.d.), pp. 59-62.

recognized as true that the nobility, magnificence, dignity, virtue, and authority of the parents induce the sons the more to preserve zeal for the same things. Whence it follows that the nobles, as if by a certain instinct of nature, seek after honor, cultivate magnanimity, despise cheap gains, and finally abhor those things deemed unworthy of their nobility.

In the second place, nobility is equally a stimulus for holding fast to virtues. This differs from the first benefit we have described: the first predisposes the noble to embrace righteous works more easily; the second adds powerful stimuli to that which has been rendered easy and, as it were, is a kind of bridle that represses vices and actions unbecoming of the noble and that, should the noble fall into some fault, causes him to be overcome with an extraordinary shame so that he may, with all his strength, take care to purify himself of this stain.

Finally, the last benefit of nobility to consider is that, just as a precious rock glimmers more when it is set in gold than in iron, so also these virtues are more splendorous in the noble than in the common man; and nobility added to virtue is its greatest ornament.

It is not only true that we should value nobility and the luster of ancestors, but besides this we must most firmly hold these two theses:

Firstly, just as virtue is more splendid in the noble, so also is vice far more shameful. For just as dirtiness is more easily noticed in a bright place suffused with the sun's rays than in any obscure corner, stains are more noticeable on a golden garment than on a cheap and ragged one, and, lastly, moles and scars are more easily seen on the face than on another more hidden part of the body; thus, also, vices are more noticeable and offensive to the beholder and more dis-

figuring to the spirits of the sinners among the nobles than among men of vulgar condition. What is, in all truth, more disgusting than to see a young man sprung from illustrious, well-born parents who is corrupted and given over to taverns, gaming, drinking, and feasting?

Secondly, it is true that although someone may be exceedingly noble, nevertheless, unless he add his own virtues to the nobility of his ancestors, he straightaway becomes ignoble; for nobility ceases when virtue is discontinued, so that if there be any traces of splendor left in him, they are certainly useless: for they do not achieve their own aims in him, so that they might render him more disposed to outstanding deeds and might be a stimulus to virtues and a curb restraining him from sinning; and all his nobility is rather the highest reproach to him than even the slightest source of honor. And it is this very thing for which Our Lord Jesus Christ reproached the Pharisees when they boasted of being sons of Abraham, saying: "If you be the children of Abraham, do the works of Abraham" (John 8:39); for anyone at all can boast that he is the son, or the grandson, or a sharer of the nobility of the person whose life and virtues he imitates. And because of this Our Lord said to those same men: "You are of your father the devil" (John 8:44); nay, even by the most holy Precursor of Christ they were called "offspring of vipers" (Luke 3:7).

Who indeed would be so ignorant or thoughtless as to still find room for doubt concerning the supreme nobility of the Most Holy Virgin Mary? Who would not know that she not only equalled the virtues of her progenitors, but greatly surpassed them by far, and that she herself can and ought to be deservedly called most noble inasmuch as the splendor of so many illustrious patriarchs, kings, prophets, and priests, whose succession is described here in today's Gospel, received its greatest increase in her.

But someone or other will ask, how can the nobility of Mary be deduced from the enumeration of so many ancestors and great ancestors, when it is the origin of Joseph, Mary's husband, that is being described? But whoever shall diligently read the Sacred Scriptures will most easily resolve this doubt. Inasmuch as by Divine law it was prohibited that any virgin, especially one who was going to come into an inheritance, accept a husband from outside of her own tribe (Num. 36:6 ff.), therefore, it is most clearly evident that Joseph and Mary were of the same tribe and family, and one and the same nobility is obvious for both from this description of the human ancestry of the Son of God.

In addition to these reasons that impelled Matthew, at the urging of the Holy Spirit, to describe the lineage of Joseph, he himself was writing his Gospel to the Hebrews and they indeed would know that the Messiah was going to come from the seed of Abraham and from the stock of David; they also thought that Joseph was the father of Christ, though he was not His true father, but His supposed father; therefore, having learned from here that Joseph, whom they thought to be the true father of Christ, was descended from those from whom the Messiah was going to come, they could not possibly deny that Christ was the true Messiah promised to the races; wherefore, immediately at the beginning of the Gospel itself it is said: "The book of the generation of Jesus Christ, the son of David, the son of Abraham" (Matt. 1:1); for to each more expressly than to the others the great offspring of the Messiah had been frequently promised.

The Saint goes on to look at another aspect of this great theme of which he speaks.

Finally, in the third place, O most cherished Daughters (for this part is directed to you), the lineage of Joseph, but not of Mary, is described, in order that you might learn not to be haughty and not to say insultingly to your husbands: "I have brought nobility into your house; I brought you the brilliance of honors; to me, O Husband, you ought to ascribe whatever you have of dignity." But know this and inscribe it most constantly in your minds: the family, the glory, the nobility of the wife ought to be nothing other than that of the husband; and those wives are to be detested who in any way dare to place themselves before their husbands, or (what is even worse) are ashamed of the families of their husbands and pass over their names in silence, mentioning only those of their own ancestors. Truly, this spirit of haughtiness is diabolical. For what is the family of Mary? That of Joseph. What is the tribe, what the home, what the nobility of Mary? That of her husband, Joseph. This most becomes Christian spouses, truly noble and fearing God.[8]

---

[8] *Sancti Caroli Borromei Homiliae CXXII* (Augustae Vindelicorum [Augsburg]: Ignatii Adami & Francisci Antonii Veith Bibliopolarum, n.d.), editio novissima, cols. 1211-1214.

9. Our Lineage Greatly
Influences Our Actions

From the funeral oration for Philippe-Emmanuel de Lorraine, Duke of Mercoeur and Penthièvre, delivered in the metropolitan church of Notre-Dame in Paris on April 27, 1602, by Saint Francis de Sales (1567-1622), Bishop-Prince of Geneva and Doctor of the Church:

It is always God Who grants us salvation; He is its great architect, but He proceeds differently with His mercies, for He grants us certain favors unbeknownst to us, and others with the intervention of our desires, works, and will. Prince Phillippe-Emmanuel, Duke of Mercoeur, received an abundance of favors of the first order, upon which he built an excellent edifice of perfection of those of the second order; for in the first order God had him born of two of the most illustrious, ancient, and Catholic houses among the princes of Europe [the Houses of Lorraine and of Savoy].

It means a great deal to be the fruit of a good tree, metal of a good mine, river of a good source....

[He] was born, I say, for military glory and the honor of the Church, this deceased prince, worthy scion of two such great stocks, from which he inherited the blood as well as the virtues; and just as two streams join to make a great and noble river, so these two houses of paternal and maternal ancestors of this prince, having joined their noble qualities in his soul, made him accomplished in all the gifts of nature, which is why he could well echo the divine sage in saying, *"Puer autem eram ingeniosus, et sortitus sum animam bonam"* [And I was a witty child and had received a good soul] (Wisd. 8:19). It was good for his virtue to encounter so able an individual; it was a great boon for his ability to encounter a virtue such as this....

In such manner he was good enough to speak of his lineage, although to many it seems that nobility is a thing beyond our control, that only our actions are our own.

And in truth lineage accounts for a great deal, and has a great power in our destinies, even in our very deeds, either through the passionate sympathies we often borrow from our predecessors or through the memory of their prowess that we preserve, or through the good and most curious nourishment we receive from them.[9]

---

[9] *Oeuvres complètes de Saint François de Sales* (Paris: Béthune Éditeur, 1836), Vol. 2, pp. 404-406.

The Church's Doctrine
on Social Inequalities

The following pontifical texts show that Christian society, according to the Church's teaching, must be constituted by proportionately unequal classes that find their own good and the common good in a mutual and harmonious cooperation.

However, these inequalities can in no way injure the rights belonging to a man as a man, for, regarding these rights, human nature, which is the same in all, ipso facto makes all equal according to the most wise design of the Creator.

1. The Inequality of Rights and Power Proceeds from the Very Author of Nature

From Leo XIII's encyclical *Quod Apostolici muneris*, of December 28, 1878:

For, indeed, although the socialists, stealing the very Gospel itself with a view to deceive more easily the unwary, have been accustomed to distort it so as to suit their own purposes, nevertheless so great is the difference between their depraved teachings and the most pure doctrine of Christ that none greater could exist: "for what participation hath justice with injustice? or what fellowship hath light with darkness?" (2 Cor. 6:14). Their habit, as we have intimated, is always to maintain that nature has made all men equal, and that, therefore, neither honor nor respect is due to majesty, nor obedience to laws, unless, perhaps, to those sanctioned by their own good pleasure. But, on the contrary, in accordance with the teachings of the Gospel, the equality of men consists in this: that all, having inherited the same nature, are called to the same most high dignity of the sons of God, and that, as one and the same end is set before all, each one is to be judged by the same law and will receive punishment or reward according to his deserts. The inequality of rights and of power proceeds from the very Author of nature, "from whom all paternity in heaven and earth is named" (Eph. 3:15).[1]

---

[1] *Catholic World*, Vol. 27 (March 1879), p. 853.

2. The Universe, the Church, and Civil Society Reflect the Love of God in an Organic Inequality

In the same encyclical the Pontiff affirms:

> For, He who created and governs all things has, in His wise providence, appointed that the things which are lowest should attain their ends by those which are intermediate, and these again by the highest. Thus, as even in the kingdom of heaven He hath willed that the choirs of angels be distinct and some subject to others, and also in the Church has instituted various orders and a diversity of offices, so that all are not apostles or doctors or pastors (1 Cor. 12:28), so also has He appointed that there should be various orders in civil society, differing in dignity, rights, and power, whereby the State, like the Church, should be one body, consisting of many members, some nobler than others, but all necessary to each other and solicitous for the common good.[2]

3. The Socialists Declare That the Right of Property Is a Human Invention Opposed to the Innate Equality of Man

And he declares further on:

> But Catholic wisdom, sustained by the precepts of natural and divine law, provides with especial care for public and private tranquility in its doctrines and teachings regarding the duty of government and the distribution of the goods which are necessary for life and use. For, while the socialists would destroy the *right* of property, alleging it to be human invention altogether opposed to the inborn equality of man, and, claiming a community of goods, argue that poverty should not be peaceably endured, and that the property and privileges of the rich may be rightly invaded, the Church, with much greater wisdom and good sense, recognizes the inequality among men, who are born with different powers of body and mind, inequality in actual possession, also, and holds that the right of property and of ownership, which springs from nature itself, must not be touched and stands inviolate.[3]

---

[2] Ibid., p. 854.

[3] Ibid., p. 856.

4. Nothing Is So Repugnant to Reason as a Mathematical Equality Among Men

From Leo XIII's encyclical *Humanum genus*, of April 20, 1884:

> In like manner, no one doubts that all men are equal one to another, so far as regards their common origin and nature, or the last end which each one has to attain, or the rights and duties which are thence derived. But, as the abilities of all are not equal, as one differs from another in the powers of mind or body, and as there are very many dissimilarities of manner, disposition, and character, it is most repugnant to reason to endeavor to confine all within the same measure, and to extend complete equality to the institutions of civil life.[4]

5. Inequalities Are a Condition of Social Organicity

Leo XIII continues:

> Just as a perfect condition of the body results from the conjunction and composition of its various members, which, though differing in form and purpose, make, by their union and the distribution of each one to its proper place, a combination beautiful to behold, firm in strength, and necessary for use; so, in the commonwealth, there is an almost infinite dissimilarity of men, as parts of the whole. If they are to be all equal, and each is to follow his own will, the State will appear most deformed; but if, with a distinction of degrees of dignity, of pursuits and employments, all aptly conspire for the common good, they will present a natural image of a well-constituted State.[5]

6. Social Inequality Redounds to the Advantage of All

Leo XIII returns to the subject of social inequality in the encyclical *Rerum novarum*, of May 15, 1891:

> Let it, then, be taken as granted, in the first place, that the condition of things human must be endured, for it is impossible to reduce civil society to one dead level. Socialists may in that intent do their utmost, but all striving against nature is in vain. There naturally exist among mankind manifold differences of the most important kind; people differ in capacity, skill, health, strength; and unequal fortune is a necessary result of unequal condition. Such inequality is far from being disadvantageous either to individuals or to the

---

[4] Wynne, *The Great Encyclical Letters of Pope Leo XIII*, p. 98.

[5] Ibid., p. 99.

community. Social and public life can only be maintained by means of various kinds of capacity for business and the playing of many parts; and each man, as a rule, chooses the part which suits his own peculiar domestic condition.[6]

7. Just as the Diverse Members in the Human Body Are Arranged Among Themselves, So Also the Social Classes Should Integrate in Society

Further on the Pontiff declares:

The great mistake made in regard to the matter now under consideration is to take up with the notion that class is naturally hostile to class, and that the wealthy and the workingmen are intended by nature to live in mutual conflict. So irrational and so false is this view, that the direct contrary is the truth. Just as the symmetry of the human frame is the resultant of the disposition of the bodily members, so in a State is it ordained by nature that these two classes should dwell in harmony and agreement, and should, as it were, groove into one another, so as to maintain the balance of the body politic. Each needs the other: Capital cannot do without Labor, nor Labor without Capital. Mutual agreement results in pleasantness of life and the beauty of good order; while perpetual conflict necessarily produces confusion and savage barbarity.[7]

8. The Church Loves All the Classes and the Harmonious Inequality Among Them

Leo XIII teaches in his allocution to the Roman Patriciate and Nobility on January 24, 1903:

The Roman Pontiffs have always taken care to equally protect and ameliorate the lot of the humble, and to support and augment the honor of the upper classes. For they carry on the mission of Jesus Christ, not only in the religious order, but in the social order as well....

For this reason the Church, while preaching to humanity of the universal filiation from one Father in heaven, recognizes as being equally providential the distinction of classes in human society; for this reason does she impress upon her flock that only in the mutual respect of rights and duties and in charity to one another lies the secret of just balance, honest well-being, true peace, and flourishing peoples.

Thus We too, in deploring the present disturbances troubling peaceful human society, have turned Our gaze repeatedly to the lowest classes, the

---

[6]   Ibid., p. 217.

[7]   Ibid., p. 218.

ones most perfidiously menaced by iniquitous sects, and have offered them the maternal succor of the Church. Repeatedly We have declared that the remedy to their ills will never be a subversive equalization of the social orders, but rather that brotherhood which, without disparaging the dignity of rank, unites the hearts of all in a single bond of Christian love.[8]

9. In Society There Should Be Princes and Vassals, Proprietors and Proletarians, Rich and Poor, Learned and Ignorant, Nobles and Plebeians

In the motu proprio *Fin dalla prima*, of December 18, 1903, Saint Pius X summarizes the doctrine of Leo XIII on social inequalities.

1. Human society, as God established it, is composed of unequal elements, just as the members of the human body are unequal. To make them all equal would be impossible, and would result in the destruction of society itself (encyclical *Quod Apostolici muneris*).

2. The equality of the various members of society is only in that all men originate from God the Creator; that they were redeemed by Jesus Christ, and that they must be judged by God and rewarded or punished in strict accordance with their merits and demerits (encyclical *Quod Apostolici muneris*).

3. Wherefore it results that, in human society, it is God's will that there should be princes and vassals, proprietors and proletarians, rich and poor, learned and ignorant, nobles and plebeians, all of whom, united in the bond of love, should help one another to achieve their final end in Heaven, and their material and moral well-being here on earth (encyclical *Quod Apostolici muneris*).[9]

10. A Certain Democracy Goes So Far in Perversity as to Attribute Sovereignty to the People in Society and to Aim at the Suppression and Leveling of the Classes

From the apostolic letter *Notre charge apostolique* of Saint Pius X, August 25, 1910:

The Sillon, impelled by an ill-understood love of the weak, has fallen into error.

In effect, the Sillon puts forward as a programme the elevation and regeneration of the working classes. But in this matter the principles of Catholic doctrine are fixed, and the history of Christian civilization attests their beneficent fruitfulness. Our predecessor of happy memory reminded them of

---

[8] *Leonis XIII Pontificis Maximi Acta*, Vol. 22, p. 368.

[9] *Acta Sanctae Sedis* (Rome: Ex Typographia Polyglotta, 1903-1904), Vol. 36, p. 341.

this in masterly pages which Catholics occupied with social questions ought to study and keep always under their eyes. Notably he taught that Christian democracy ought "to maintain the diversity of classes which is assuredly a fitting characteristic of a well-constituted State, and to wish for human society the form and character that God, its Author, impressed upon it" [encyclical *Graves de Communi re*]. He denounced a "certain democracy which goes so far in perversity as to attribute in society sovereignty to the people and to aim at the suppression and the leveling down of the classes."[10]

11. Jesus Christ Did Not Teach A Chimerical Equality Nor Disrespect for Authority

Still in the same apostolic letter, Saint Pius X says:

Then, if Jesus was kind to those who went astray and to sinners, He did not respect their erroneous convictions, however sincere they might have appeared. He loved them all to instruct them, to convert them and to save them. If He called to Himself, in order to comfort them, those who were in trouble and suffering, it was not to preach to them jealousy of a chimerical equality. If He lifted up the humble, it was not to inspire them with the sentiment of a dignity independent and rebellious against the duty of obedience.[11]

12. Although Equal by Nature, Men Should Not Occupy the Same Position in Social Life

From Benedict XV's encyclical *Ad beatissimi Apostolorum*, of November 11, 1914:

Face to face with those to whom either fortune or their own activity has brought an abundance of wealth stand the proletaires and the workers, inflamed with hatred and jealousy because, although they share the same nature, they are not in the same condition. Infatuated as they are by the fallacies of agitators, to whose guidance they are ordinarily most docile, who should persuade them that it does not follow because men are equal by nature that all ought to occupy the same grade in society, but that every one holds that position which his qualifications, if circumstances permit, have procured for him? Wherefore when the needy struggle against those who are well to do, as if the latter had taken possession of property that belonged to others, they not only offend against justice and charity, but even against reason, because they also, if they desired, could by means of

[10] *American Catholic Quarterly Review*, Vol. 35 (October 1910), pp. 695-696.

[11] Ibid., p. 708.

honorable labor succeed in improving their condition. What consequences, not less inconvenient for individuals than for the community, this class hatred begets it is needless to say.[12]

13. Brotherly Treatment Between Superiors and Subordinates Should Not Eliminate the Variety of Conditions and the Diversity of Social Classes

Benedict XV continues:

Human fraternity, indeed, will not remove the diversities of conditions and therefore of classes. This is not possible, just as it is not possible that in an organic body all the members should have one and the same function and the same dignity. But it will cause those in the highest places to incline toward the humblest and to treat them not only according to justice, as is necessary, but kindly, with affability and tolerance, and will cause the humblest to regard the highest with sympathy for their prosperity and with confidence in their support, in the same way as in one family the younger brothers rely on the help and defense of the elder ones.[13]

14. Respecting Social Hierarchy for the Greater Good of Individuals and Society

From Benedict XV's letter *Soliti nos*, of March 11, 1920, to the Most Reverend Luigi Marelli, Bishop of Bergamo:

Let those who are of a lower station and fortune properly understand this: variety of rank in civil society originates from nature, and is finally to be traced back to the will of God, "for He made the little and the great" (Wis. 6:8), and indeed most fittingly for the advantage of both individuals and the community. Let these same people persuade themselves that however much they may progress toward better things, by means of their own industry and with good people helping them, there will always remain for them, as for other human beings, no small occasion for grief. Wherefore, if they are wise, they will not struggle vainly for what is above their reach, and they will quietly and steadfastly bear those evils that they cannot escape, in the hope of immortal advantages.[14]

---

[12] Ibid., Vol. 39 (October 1914), pp. 673-674.

[13] Ibid., p. 674.

[14] *Acta Apostolicae Sedis*, Vol. 12, no. 4 (April 1, 1920), p. 111.

15. One Should Not Excite Animosity Against the Rich, Inciting the Masses to the Inversion of Order in Society

In a letter of June 5, 1929, to the Most Reverend Achille Liénart, Bishop of Lille, the Sacred Congregation of the Council recalls principles of Catholic social doctrine and practical directives of a moral order, issued from the supreme ecclesiastical authority.

"Those who boast of the name Christian, be they taken in isolation or as groups or associations, should not, if they are conscious of their obligations, promote hostility or rivalries among the social classes, but peace and mutual charity" (Pius X, *Singulari quadam*, September 24, 1912).

"Catholic writers, in taking up the cause of the proletariat or the poor, should refrain from using language that might inspire in the people an aversion for the upper classes of society.... They should remember that Jesus Christ wanted to unite all men through the bond of reciprocal love, which is the perfection of justice and which entails the obligation to work mutually toward the good of one and all" (Instruction of the Sacred Congregation for Extraordinary Ecclesiastical Affairs, January 27, 1902).

"Those who preside over this type of institution (with the goal of promoting the good of the workers) should remember...that nothing will better assure the general well-being than peace and harmony among all classes, and that Christian charity is the best sign of unity. Thus he who would strive for the good of the worker would do so poorly indeed should he, in pretending to better the conditions of his existence, only help him in the acquisition of the ephemeral and fragile things of this world, neglecting to dispose his mind to moderation through the call to Christian duty, and much more so, should he go so far as to inflame animosity against the rich by indulging in the bitter and violent declamations with which men alien to our beliefs have the tendency to incite the masses toward the overthrow of society" (*Soliti nos*, letter of Benedict XV to the Bishop of Bergamo, March 11, 1920).[15]

16. The Inequality of Rights Is Legitimate

Pius XI affirms in the encyclical *Divini Redemptoris*, of March 19, 1937: "It is not true that all have equal rights in civil society. It is not true that there exists no lawful social hierarchy."[16]

---

[15] *Acta Apostolicae Sedis*, Vol. 21, no. 10 (August 3, 1929), pp. 497-498.

[16] Rev. Joseph Husslein, S.J., ed., *Social Wellsprings* (Milwaukee: Bruce Publishing Co., 1942), Vol. 2, p. 354.

17. Similarities and Differences Among Men Find Their Allotted Place in the Absolute Order of Being

From the 1942 Christmas message of Pius XII:

If the life of society involves inner unity, it does not, however, preclude differences which are upheld by reality and nature. Yet when one looks to God, the supreme regulator of all that concerns man, then men's similarities as well as differences find their proper place in the absolute order of being, of values and therefore also of morality. If, on the other hand, this foundation is shaken, then a dangerous breach is opened between the various areas of culture, and an uncertainty and instability of boundaries, limits, and values appears.[17]

18. Conviviality Among Men Always and Necessarily Produces a Scale of Degrees and Differences

Pius XII says in his allocution to Fiat workers on October 31, 1948:

The Church does not promise the absolute equality that others claim, for she knows that human society always produces, of necessity, a whole scale of degrees and differences in physical and intellectual qualities, in inner dispositions and tendencies, in occupations and responsibilities. Yet, at the same time she ensures complete equality in human dignity, as in the heart of Him who calls unto Himself all those who are weary and burdened.[18]

19. To Establish Absolute Equality Would Be to Destroy the Social Organism

Pius XII declares in a speech to a group of parishioners of Marsciano, Perugia, Italy, on June 4, 1953:

It is necessary that you truly feel like brothers. It is not a matter of mere appearance; you are truly sons of God, so you are really brothers to one another.

Now, brothers are not born equal, nor do they remain equal; some are strong, others weak; some are intelligent, others inept; sometimes one is abnormal or actually becomes a disgrace. A certain material, intellectual, and moral inequality is therefore inevitable even within the same family.

---

[17] *Discorsi e radiomessagi di Sua Santità Pio XII* (Tipografia Poliglotta Vaticana), Vol. 4, p. 331.

[18] Ibid., Vol. 10, p. 266.

To claim absolute equality for all would be like wanting to assign the exact same function to different parts of the same organism.[19]

20. Anyone Who Ventures to Deny the Diversity of Social Classes Contradicts the Very Laws of Nature

From John XXIII's encyclical *Ad Petri Cathedram*, of June 29, 1959:

The harmonious unity which must be sought among peoples and nations also needs ever greater improvement among the various classes of individuals. Otherwise mutual antagonism and conflict can result, as we have already seen. And the next step brings rioting mobs, wanton destruction of property, and sometimes even bloodshed. Meanwhile public and private resources diminish and are stretched to the danger point....

Anyone, therefore, who ventures to deny that there are differences among social classes contradicts the very laws of nature. Indeed, whoever opposes peaceful and necessary cooperation among the social classes is attempting, beyond doubt, to disrupt and divide human society; he menaces and does serious injury to private interests and the public welfare....

The various classes of society, as well as groups of individuals, may certainly protect their rights, provided this is done by legal means, not violence, and provided that they do no injustice to the inviolable rights of others. All men are brothers. Their differences, therefore, must be settled by friendly agreement, with brotherly love for one another.[20]

21. A Classless Society: A Dangerous Utopia

From John Paul II's homily in the Mass for youths and students, in Belo Horizonte, Brazil, on July 1, 1980:

I learned that a Christian youth ceases to be young, and has long ceased to be Christian, when he allows himself to be seduced by doctrines or ideologies that preach violence and hate....

I learned that the young dangerously begin to age when they are fooled by the adage, The end justifies the means, when they believe that the only hope of bettering society is by promoting conflict and hatred between social groups in the utopia of a society without classes that soon leads to the creation of new classes.[21]

---

[19]   Ibid., Vol. 15, p. 195.

[20]   *The Pope Speaks*, Vol. 5, no. 3 (Summer 1959), p. 16.

[21]   *Insegnamenti di Giovanni Paolo II*, Vol. 3, 2 (Libreria Editrice Vaticana, 1980), p. 8.

22. The Inequality of Creatures Is a Condition for Creation to Give Glory to God

Beside the pontifical texts transcribed above, it seems fitting to add some arguments from the Angelic Doctor to justify the existence of inequality among creatures. In the *Summa Theologica* he affirms:

> Hence in natural things species seem to be arranged in degrees; as the mixed things are more perfect than the elements, and plants than minerals, and animals than plants, and men than other animals; and in each of these one species is more perfect than others. Therefore, as the Divine Wisdom is the cause of the distinction of things for the sake of the perfection of the universe, so is it the cause of inequality. For the universe would not be perfect if only one grade of goodness were found in things.[22]

In fact, it would not be fitting to God's perfection to create only one being. For no created being, however excellent it may be imagined, can alone adequately reflect the infinite perfections of God. Thus, creatures are necessarily multiple, and not just multiple, but also necessarily unequal. This is the teaching of the holy Doctor:

> Furthermore, a plurality of goods is better than a single finite good, since they contain the latter and more besides. But all goodness possessed by creatures is finite, falling short of the infinite goodness of God. Hence, the universe of creatures is more perfect if there are many grades of things than if there were but one. Now, it befits the supreme good to make what is best. It was therefore fitting that God should make many grades of creatures.
>
> Again, the good of the species is greater than the good of the individual, just as the formal exceeds that which is material. Hence, the multiplicity of species adds more to the goodness of the universe than a multiplicity of individuals in one species. It therefore pertains to the perfection of the universe that there be not only many individuals, but that there be also diverse species of things, and, consequently, diverse grades in things.[23]

Inequalities, then, are not defects of the creation. They are excellent qualities of it, in which the infinite and adorable perfection of its Author are mirrored. And God takes pleasure in contemplating them.

> The diversity and inequality in created things are not the result of chance, nor of a diversity of matter, nor of the intervention of certain causes or merits, but of the intention of God Himself, who wills to give the creature such perfection as it is possible for it to have. Accordingly, in the Book of Genesis (1:31) it is said: "God saw all the things that He made, and they were very good."[24]

---

[22]   I, q. 47, a. 2.

[23]   *Summa Contra Gentiles*, bk. 2, chap. 45.

[24]   Ibid.

23. The Suppression of Inequalities Is a Sine Qua Non for the Elimination of Religion

God did not want these inequalities only among creatures of the inferior kingdoms—the mineral, vegetable, and animal—but also among men and, therefore, among peoples and nations. With these inequalities, which God created harmonious among themselves and beneficent for each category of beings as also for each being in particular, He wanted to furnish man with most abundant means to have His infinite perfections always present. The inequalities among beings are ipso facto a sublime and most ample school of anti-atheism.

The French writer Roger Garaudy (a communist later "converted" to Islam) seems to have understood this, for he highlights the importance of the elimination of social inequalities for the victory of atheism in the world.

It is not possible for a Marxist to say that the elimination of religious beliefs is a sine qua non condition for the establishment of Communism. On the contrary, Karl Marx demonstrated that only the full realization of Communism, by making social relationships transparent, would make the disappearance of religious concepts possible in the world. For a Marxist it is thus the establishment of Communism which is the sine qua non condition for the elimination of the social roots of religion, and not the elimination of religious beliefs which is the condition for the construction of Communism.[25]

To desire to destroy the hierarchical order of the universe is, then, to deprive man of the resources by which he can freely exercise the most fundamental of his rights, which is to know, love, and serve God. It is, thus, to desire the greatest of injustices and the most cruel of tyrannies.

24. By Nature, All Men Are in One Sense Equal, but in Another They Are Unequal

From the book *Land Reform: A Matter of Conscience*, by Archbishop Geraldo de Proença Sigaud, Bishop Antonio de Castro Mayer, Prof. Plinio Corrêa de Oliveira, and economist Luiz Mendonça de Freitas, in a topic composed and written by the author of the present work:

[All men] are equal because they are creatures of God, endowed with body and soul, and redeemed by Jesus Christ. Thus, by the dignity common to all, they have an equal right to everything that is proper to the human condition: life, health, work, religion, family, intellectual development, and so on. A just Christian economic and social organization thus rests upon a fundamental feature of true equality.

But, besides this essential equality, there are among men accidental inequalities placed by God: of virtue, intelli-

---

[25] Roger Garaudy, *L'homme chrétien et l'homme marxiste: Semaines de la pensée marxiste—Confrontations et débats* (Paris-Geneva: La Palatine, 1964), p. 64.

gence, health, capacity of labor, and many others. Every organic and living economic and social structure has to be in harmony with the natural order of things. This natural inequality must therefore be reflected in it. This reflection consists in this: that as long as all have what is just and deserved, those well endowed by nature can, by their honest labor and their economy, acquire more.

Equality and inequality thus compensate and complement one another, discharging diverse but harmonious roles in the ordering of a just and Christian society.

This rule constitutes, moreover, one of the most admirable characteristics of universal order. All of God's creatures have what befits them according to their own nature, and in this they are treated according to the same norm. But, beyond this the Lord gives very much to some, much to others, and to yet others, finally, only what is adequate. These inequalities form an immense hierarchy, in which each degree is like a musical note that forms part of an immense symphony to chant the divine glory. A totally egalitarian society and economy would, therefore, be anti-natural.

Seen in this light, inequalities represent a condition of general good order, and thus redound to the advantage of the whole social body, that is, of the great as well as of the small.

This hierarchical scale is in the plans of Providence as a means to promote the spiritual and material progress of mankind by the incentive given to the better and most capable. Egalitarianism brings with it inertia, stagnation, and, therefore, decadence, because everything inasmuch as it is alive, if it does not progress, deteriorates and dies.

The parable of the talents is thus explained (Matt. 25:14-30). God gives to each in a different measure and He demands from each a proportionate rendering.[26]

---

[26] *Reforma Agrária—Questão de Consciência* (São Paulo: Editora Vera Cruz, 1960) pp. 64-65.

The Necessary Harmony Between Authentic Tradition and Authentic Progress

1. The True Friends of the People Are Traditionalists

From the apostolic letter *Notre charge apostolique*, August 25, 1910, of Saint Pius X:

Let not the priests be led astray in the maze of contemporary opinions, in the mirage of a false democracy. Let them not borrow from the rhetoric of the worst enemies of the Church and the people an emphatic language full of promises as sonorous as they are unattainable. Let them be persuaded that the social question and social science were not born yesterday, that the Church and the State, acting in concert, have always created pro-ductive organizations with this goal in mind; that the Church, which has never betrayed the happiness of the people with compromising alliances, has no reason to break away from the past and that it is enough for it to reconstruct, with the co-operation of the true builders of social restoration, the organizations destroyed by the Revolution, and to adapt them, in the same Christian spirit that inspired them, to the new milieu created by the material evolution of contemporary society; for the true friends of the people are neither revolutionaries nor innovators but traditionalists.[1]

2. Respect for Tradition Absolutely Does Not Impede True Progress

From a speech of Pius XII to the professors and students of the Liceo Ennio Quirino Visconti of Rome, February 28, 1957:

It has been correctly noted that one characteristic of Romans, almost a secret of the timeless greatness of the Eternal City, is their respect for traditions. Not that such respect im-plies a fossilization in forms that time has left behind; rather, it means keeping alive what the centuries have proven to be good and fruitful. Tradition, in this way, does not in the least obstruct healthy and happy progress, and yet at the same time it is a powerful stimulus to persevere along the right path, a brake on the adventurous

---

[1]   *Acta Apostolicae Sedis* (Rome: Typis Polyglottis Vaticanis, 1910), Vol. 2, p. 631.

spirit inclined to embrace all novelty indiscriminately; and it is also, as we say, a warning signal against decadence.[2]

3. One of the Most Frequent and Most Grave Defects of Modern Sociology Lies in Underestimating Tradition

From the allocution of Paul VI to Slavic pilgrims of various countries, especially the United States and Canada, on September 14, 1963, the eleventh centennial of the arrival of Saints Cyril and Methodius in Greater Moravia:

It is characteristic of Catholic education to draw from history not only cultural material and reminders of events, but also a living tradition, a spiritual coefficient of moral formation, a constant direction for a direct and coherent progress in the march of time, a guarantee of stability and endurance, which gives to a people its dignity, its right to life, its duty to act in harmony with other peoples.

One of the defects of modern sociology, most frequent and most serious, is to underestimate tradition, that is, to presume that a firm and coherent society can be established without taking into account the historic foundation on which it naturally rests, and that the breaking away from the culture inherited from preceding generations can be more beneficial to the life of a people than the progressive development, faithful and wise, of its patrimony of thought and habits.

And furthermore, if this patrimony is rich with those universal and immortal values which the Catholic Faith instills in the conscience of a people, then to respect tradition means to guarantee the moral life of that people; it means to give them the consciousness of their existence, and to merit for them those divine helps which confer to the city of this world something of the splendor and perpetuity of the heavenly city.[3]

4. Detaching Oneself From the Past Causes Uneasiness, Anxiety, and Instability

From the homily of Paul VI during a Mass he celebrated in the patriarchal basilica of Saint Lawrence Outside the Walls on November 2, 1963:

We are accustomed to looking ahead, ignoring the merits of yesterday; we are not lavish in gratitude, in memory, in consistency toward our past, nor in the respect and fidelity

[2] *Discorsi e radiomessagi di Sua Santità Pio XII*, Vol. 18, p. 803.

[3] *The Pope Speaks*, Vol. 9, no. 2 (1964), p. 184.

due to history, to the actions that follow one another from one generation to the next. Often the sense of detachment from times past proves rather widespread; and this is cause for uneasiness, anxiety, and instability.

A healthy people, a Christian people, are much more faithful to those who have gone before; they look to the logic of the events in which their own experience must be formed, and they do not hesitate to give the necessary tribute of recognition and just appreciation.[4]

5. Tradition Is a Fertile Patrimony, an Inheritance That Must be Preserved

From an allocution of Paul VI to his fellow countrymen of Brescia, September 26, 1970:

Allow a fellow-citizen of yours from yesterday to render homage to one of the most precious values of human life, and one of the most neglected in our day: tradition. It is a fertile patrimony, a heritage to be preserved. Today the tendency of the new generations is entirely toward the present, indeed, toward the future. And that is fine, as long as this tendency does not obscure the real and total vision of life; since for enjoying the present and preparing the future, the past can be useful to us, and in a certain sense, indispensable. The revolutionary detachment from the past is not always a liberation; rather, it often means cutting one's own roots. To really progress and not decay, we must have a historical sense of our experience. This is true even in the area of external things, of techno-scientific and political matters, where the course of transformations is swifter and more impetuous; and it is even more true in the area of human realities and especially in the field of culture. And it is especially true for our religion, which is an entire tradition originating in Christ.[5]

---

4   *Insegnamenti di Paolo VI*, Vol. 1, pp. 276-277.

5   Ibid., Vol. 8, pp. 943-944.

Ancient Rome: A State Born From Patriarchal Societies

The classic work of Numa Denis Fustel de Coulanges,[1] *The Ancient City*, initially welcomed with enthusiasm, came under criticism over the course of time. Some, for example, faulted it for being too "systematic." Nonetheless, by its exemplary erudition, its lucidity of thought, and its clarity of exposition, *The Ancient City* still ranks among the true masterpieces of its genre.

1. The Word *Pater* Is Distinct from *Genitor* and Appears as a Synonym for the Word *Rex*

Thanks to the domestic religion, the family was a small organized unit, a small society that had its leader and its government. Nothing in our modern society can give us an idea of this paternal power. In this ancient time the father is not merely the strong man who protects and also has the power to make himself obeyed; he is the priest, heir of the home, continuer of the forebears and the line of descendants, the depositary of the mysterious rites of the cult and the secret formulas of prayer. All religion resides in him.

The very name by which he is called, *pater*, holds some interesting lessons. The word is the same in Greek, Latin, and Sanskrit, from which one can already conclude that this word dates from the time when the ancestors of the Hellenes, the Italians, and the Hindus still lived together in Central Asia. What did it signify and what was its meaning for the human mind then? This can be answered, for it has kept this first signification in the formulae of religious language and that of juridical language as well....

In juridical language the title *pater* or *pater familias* may be given to a man who has never had children, who has never married, who is not even old enough to be married. The idea of paternity is not related to this word. The ancient language had another word to designate father properly, which, being as ancient as *pater*, is also found in the languages of the Greeks, the Ro-

---

[1] A French historian (1830-1889), professor of medieval history at the Sorbonne and director of L'École Normale Supérieur. Besides *The Ancient City* he wrote other works, notably the *History of the Institutions of Ancient France*, in which he analyzes the formation of the feudal regime of that country. The excerpts below are translated from *La Cité Antique* (Paris: Librairie Hachette), book 2.

mans, and the Hindus (*gennetér, genitor, gânitar*). The word *pater* had another meaning. In religious language it was applied to all the gods; in the language of law, to any man who did not depend upon another and who had authority over a family and a domain, *paterfamilias*. The poets showed us that it was used to refer to all whom one wanted to honor. The slave and the client used it for their master. It was synonymous with the words *rex, hänas, basileús*. It contained not the idea of paternity, but that of power, authority, and majestic dignity.

The fact that such a word has been applied to the father of a family to the point of gradually becoming his most ordinary name is certainly very significant, and it will certainly appear important to anyone wishing to understand ancient institutions. The history of this word suffices to give us an idea of the power the father exercised in the family for a long time and of the sentiments of veneration which were attached to him, as to a pontiff or a king.[2]

2. The *Gens* of the Romans and the *Génos* of the Greeks

In the difficult problems that history often presents to us, it is good to seek all possible illumination in the terms of language. An institution is sometimes explained by the word with which it is designated. In Latin, the word *gens* is exactly the same as the word *genus*, to the point that one can be used in place of the other to say, indiscriminately, *gens Fabia* and *genus Fabium*; each corresponds to the verb *gignere* and the substantive *genitor*, just as *génos* corresponds to *gennäs* and *goneús*. All these words contain the idea of filiation.... Let us compare to all these words the ones we usually translate as family, the Latin *familia* and the Greek *oíkos*. Neither one nor the other contains the sense of generation or family relationship. The true signification of *familia* is property; it designates the field, house, money, and slaves, and it is for this reason that the Twelve Tables say, in speaking of the heir, *familiam nancitor*, the one who accepts the succession. As for *oíkos*, it is clear that it calls to mind no other idea than that of property or domicile. These are nonetheless the words we usually translate as family. In other words, is it admissible that these terms whose intrinsic sense is that of domicile or property could have often been used to designate a family and that other words whose intrinsic sense is filiation, birth, paternity, designated only an artificial association? Certainly this would not be consistent with the precision of ancient languages. It is beyond doubt that the Greeks and Romans attached the idea of a common origin to the words *gens* and *génos*.

Everything shows us that the *gens* is united by a tie of birth.

From all this it is evident that the *gens* was not an association of families, but the family itself. It could either designate a single line or produce numerous branches, but it was always a single family.

---

[2] *La Cité Antique*, book 2, pp. 96-98 passim.

It is in any case easy to understand the formation and nature of the ancient *gens* if one goes back to the old beliefs and old institutions analyzed in this work. One will even recognize that the *gens* is quite naturally derived from the domestic religion and private law of ancient times.... In observing of what authority in the ancient family consisted, we have seen that the son did not separate himself from the father; in studying the laws of the transmission of patrimony, we have ascertained that thanks to the principle of the community of the domain, younger brothers did not separate from the older brother. Home, tomb, patrimony, all this was indivisible in its origin.

Hence, the family was as well. Time did not break it up. This indivisible family, which developed throughout the ages, perpetuating its name and cult from century to century, this truly was the ancient *gens*. The *gens* was the family, but the family that had preserved the unity dictated by its religion and that had attained the level of development which ancient private law permitted it to attain.

Once this truth is acknowledged, what the ancient authors wrote about the *gens* becomes clear. The strict solidarity between the members, which we noticed earlier, is no longer surprising: they are related by birth.[3]

3. The Concept of Family in the Ancient World

One can then glimpse a long period during which men had no form of society other than the family....

Each family has its religion, its gods, its priesthood....

Each family also has its property, that is to say, its parcel of land inseparably attached to it through religion....

In short, each family has its leader, just as a nation would have a king. It has its laws, which undoubtedly are not written, but which religious belief etches in the heart of each man. It has its internal justice over which no other can prevail. The family contains in itself all that man rigorously needs for his material or moral life. He needs nothing from outside; it is an organized state, a self-sufficient society.

But this family of ancient times was not reduced to the proportions of the modern family. In the great societies the family scatters and becomes smaller, but in the absence of all other society it grows, it develops and branches out without breaking up. Many younger branches remain grouped around an older branch, near the only home and the common tomb.[4]

---

[3] Ibid., pp. 118-122 passim.

[4] Ibid., pp. 126-127 passim.

4. Family, Curia or Phratry, and Tribe

The study of ancient rules of private law allowed us to glimpse, beyond so-called historic times, a period of centuries during which the family was the only form of society. This family then contained many thousands of human beings within its large frame. But within this framework human association was still too narrow; too narrow for material needs, for it was difficult for this family to remain self-sufficient in the presence of all life's hazards; too narrow as well for the moral needs of our nature.

Religious ideas and human society would thus expand at the same time.

Domestic religion forbade two families to mix and join together. But it was possible for several families to unite at least to celebrate a cult they shared without sacrificing anything of their individual religions. And this is what happened. A certain number of families formed a group, which in Greek is called a phratry, and in Latin a curia. Did there exist a blood tie among the families of the same group? It is impossible to confirm. What is certain is that this new association was not undertaken without a certain expansion of religious ideas. At the very moment when they joined together, these families agreed upon a deity superior to their domestic deities, which

was shared among them and which watched over the whole group. They erected an altar to him, lit a sacred fire, and instituted a cult.

There was no curia, no phratry, which did not have its altar and its protective deity. The religious act there was of the same nature as in the family.

Each phratry or curia had a head, a curion or phratriarch, whose principle function was to preside over the sacrifices. Perhaps his duties were originally more extensive. The phratry had its assemblies and its deliberations and it could make decrees. In it, as in the family, there was a god, a cult, a priesthood, a tribunal, a government. It was a small society that was modeled exactly on the family.

The association naturally continued to grow larger, in the same manner. Many curiae or phratries grouped together and formed a tribe.

The new circle had its religion as well; in each tribe there was an altar and a protective deity.

The tribe, like the phratry, had assemblies and made decrees, to which all the members had to submit. It had a tribunal and the right to justice over its members. It had a head, *tribunus*, *phylobasiléus*.[5]

5. The City Is Formed

The tribe, like the family and the phratry, was set up to be an independent body, since it had a special cult from which strangers were excluded. Once formed, no new family could be admitted. Nor could two tribes merge into a single tribe; their religion was against it. But, just as

---

[5]   Ibid., pp. 131-135 passim.

several phratries united in a tribe, many tribes could join together, on the condition that the cult of each was respected. The day this alliance took place, the city was born.

It matters little to know the reason which prompted several neighboring tribes to unite. Perhaps the union was voluntary, perhaps it was imposed by the superior power of one tribe, or by the powerful will of one man. What is certain is that the bonds of the new association created yet another cult. The tribes which grouped together to form a city never failed to light a sacred fire and to give themselves a common religion.

Thus human society, in this race, did not grow larger in the manner of a circle which little by little grows bigger, by degrees. On the contrary, little groups, formed long beforehand, joined together. Many families formed the phratry, many phratries the tribe, many tribes the city. Family, phratry, tribe, and city are, moreover, perfectly similar societies, one born of the other

through a series of federations.

We must also point out that as each of these different groups joined together, they did not lose either their individuality or their independence. Although many families were united in a phratry, each family remained set up as in the time of its isolation; nothing was changed in it, its cult, its priesthood, its property rights, or its internal justice. Curiae then united, but each one kept its cult, its reunions, its holidays, its head. From the tribe we move to the city, but the tribes were not dissolved for this, and each one continued to form a unit, almost as if the city did not exist.

Thus the city is a grouping of individuals: It is a confederation of many groups which were formed beforehand and which continued to exist. In the Attic orators one sees that each Athenian was part of four distinct societies at the same time: He was a member of a family, a phratry, a tribe, and a city.[6]

6. *Civitas* and *Urbs*

Civitas and *urbs*, which we render as city, were not synonymous among the ancients. The *civitas* was the religious and political association of the families of a tribe; the *urbs* was the place of reunion, the domicile, and, above all, the sanctuary of this association....

Once the families, the phratries, and the tribes agreed to unite and have the same cult, they founded a city to be the sanctuary for the common cult. Thus the founding of a city was always a religious act.

We shall take Rome itself for our

first example.

When the founding day arrived, first he [Romulus] offered a sacrifice. His companions gathered around him; they lit a brushwood fire, and each jumped over the thin flame. The explanation of this rite is that for the act about to take place it was necessary that the people be pure; in other words, the ancients believed they purified themselves of all physical or moral blemish by jumping over the sacred flame.

When this preliminary ceremony had prepared the people for the great act of founding, Romulus dug a little

[6]   Ibid., pp. 143-145 passim.

ditch in the shape of a circle. Into it he threw a little heap of earth he had brought from the town of Alba. Then each of his companions approached in turn, throwing in a little piece of earth he had brought from whence he had come. This ritual is remarkable, and it reveals a consideration among these men which it is important to point out. Before coming to the Palatine, they lived in Alba or the neighboring towns. That was their home; that was where their fathers had lived and were buried. In other words, the religion prohibited them from leaving the land where the home had been fixed and where the divine ancestors lay. It was then necessary, to rid themselves of any impiety, that each man employ a fiction, bringing with him, symbolized by a clump of earth, the sacred earth where his ancestors were buried and to which their manes were attached. Man could not move without bringing his land and his ancestors with him. It was necessary for this rite to be accomplished for him to be able to say, in indicating the new place he had adopted: This is still the land of my fathers, *terra patrum*, *patria*; this is my fatherland, for here lie my family's manes.[7]

7. The Difficulty in Forming the State

One can easily imagine two things: first, that this religion proper to each city must have formed the city in a powerful and almost unshakeable way—it is, in fact, marvelous how this social organization has endured, in spite of its faults and chances of ruin; secondly, that this religion must have had the effect, over a period of centuries, of rendering impossible the establishment of a social form other than that of the city.

Each city, through the exigencies of its religion, had to be absolutely independent. Each had to have its own special code, since each had its religion and it was from the religion that the laws were derived. Each had to have its own sovereign justice and could have no justice higher than that of the city. Each had its religious holidays and calendar; the months of the year could not be the same in two cities, since the series of religious acts was different. Each had its own currency which, originally, was stamped with its religious emblem. Each had its weights and measures. No one believed that there should be anything in common between two cities....

Greece never succeeded in forming a single state; nor were the Latin cities, Etruscan cities, or Samnite cities ever able to form a compact unit. The incurable division of Greeks has been attributed to the nature of their country, and people say that the mountains that cross it created natural lines of demarcation between men. But there were no mountains between Thebes and Plataea, between Argos and Sparta, between Sybaris and Croton. Nor were there any between the cities of Latium, or between the twelve cities of Etruria. Physical nature no doubt plays some role in the history of a people, but man's beliefs play a more powerful role still. Between two neighboring cities there was therefore something more impassable than a mountain: It was a series of sacred obstacles, the differences of cults, the barrier each city erected between strangers and its gods....

For this reason the ancients could not establish nor even conceive of a social organization other than the city. Neither the Greeks nor the Italians, nor even the Romans for a very long period of time, had the idea that several cities could unite and live with equal rights under the same government. Between two cities there may well be an alliance, a temporary association with an eye toward a profit to be gained or a danger to repel, but never was there a complete union. For religion made of each city a unit which could not join to any other. Isolation was the law of the city.

With the beliefs and the religious practices that we have seen, how could several cities merge into a single state? People did not understand human association, and it did not seem right unless it was based on religion. The symbol of this association had to be a shared, sacred repast. A few thousand citizens could easily, if necessary, gather together around the same prytaneum, recite the same prayer, and share sacred foods. But just try, with these customs, to make a single state of the whole of Greece!

To join two cities into a single state, to unite the vanquished population with the victorious one and merge them under the same government, this is never seen among the ancients, with one exception [Rome]....

This absolute independence of the ancient city could only cease when the beliefs upon which it was based had completely disappeared. Only after the ideas had been transformed and many revolutions had taken place in ancient societies could one begin to conceive of and establish a larger state ruled by other laws. But for this it was necessary for men to discover other principles and a social bond other than those of ancient times.[8]

---

[8]   Ibid., pp. 237-241 passim.

Feudalism: Work of the Medieval Family

Frantz Funck-Brentano, a member of the Institute of France, describes the role of the family in the constitution of feudal society in his celebrated work *L'Ancien Régime*.

The Ancien Régime grew out of feudal society. Nothing contradicts this. As for the feudal system, it was produced, in that astonishing period which ran from the middle of the tenth century to the middle of the eleventh century, by the old French family transforming its private institutions into public institutions.

During the course of the ninth and tenth centuries, the succession of barbarian, Norman, Hungarian, and Saracen invasions plunged the country into an anarchy in which all its institutions collapsed. The peasant abandoned his devastated fields to flee the violence; the people hid in the depths of the forests or inaccessible places; they took refuge high in the mountains. The ties which served to unite the inhabitants of the country were severed; the customary or legislative rules were broken; society was no longer governed by anything.

It was within this anarchy that the work of social reconstruction took place, by the only organized force which had remained intact, under cover of the only shelter that nothing can upturn, for it has its foundations in the human heart: the family.

Under duress the family resists, fortifies itself; it becomes more cohesive. Forced into self-sufficiency, it creates the means necessary for agricultural and mechanical work, and for armed defense. The State no longer exists; the family takes its place. Social life closes in around the home; communal life is confined to the limits of the house and the domain; it confines itself to the walls of the house and its environs.

It creates a little society, near to, but isolated from other similar little societies based on the same model.

At the beginning of our history the head of the family is reminiscent of the ancient paterfamilias. He leads a group which gathers around him and bears his name; he organizes the common defense; shares out the work according to the abilities and the needs of each. He reigns—the word is in the texts—as an absolute master. He is called "sire." His wife, the mother of the family, is called "dame," domina.

A man's family became his fatherland, which the Latin texts of the time indicate with the word patria, a thing beloved with a tenderness all the stronger as it is always there, in full view of all, alive and concrete. It makes its presence, and its sweetness, immediately felt; it is a cherished and solid armor, a necessary protection. Without the family, a man could not survive.

Thus were formed the feelings of solidarity that united the members of the family to one another and that, under the influence of a sovereign tradition, would steadily grow and become more defined.[1]

---

[1]   Frantz Funck-Brentano, *L'Ancien Régime* (Paris: Americ=Edit., 1936), pp. 12, 14.

The Familial Character of Feudal Government—The King: The Father of His People

To illustrate well the familial character of the feudal government, it is advantageous to transcribe a passage from the substantial work *L'Esprit Familial dans la Maison, dans la Cité et dans l'Etat* [The Familial Spirit in the Home, in the City, and in the State], by Msgr. Henri Delassus, which describes the origins of that regime.

To give due distinction to this passage, it seems necessary to provide the reader with a biographical note on the author, a figure of great importance in the fight the Church in France undertook against the assaults of liberalism and modernism at the end of the nineteenth century and at the beginning of the twentieth.

1. Brief Biographical Note

Msgr. Henri Delassus (1836-1921), ordained a priest in 1862, served in parishes in Valenciennes (Saint-Géry) and Lille (Sainte-Catherine and Sainte-Marie-Madeleine). He was named chaplain of the basilica Notre-Dame-de-la-Treille (Lille) in 1874, an honorary canon in 1882, and domestic prelate in 1904. In 1911 he was promoted to protonotary apostolic. In 1914 he became canon of the recently erected diocese of Lille and dean of its cathedral chapter.

He authored the following published works: *Histoire de Notre-Dame-de-la-Treille, Patronne de Lille* (1891), *L'Américanisme et la conjuration antichrétienne* (1899), *Le problème de l'heure présente: antagonisme de deux civilisations* (2 vols., 1904), *L'Enciclique Pascendi dominici gregis et la démocratie* (1908), *Vérités sociales et erreurs démocratiques* (1909), *La conjuration antichrétienne: le temple maçonnique voulant s'elever sur les ruines de l'Eglise catholique* (preface by Cardinal Merry del Val) (3 vols., 1910), *Condamnation du modernisme dans la censure du Sillon* (1910), *La question juive* (extract from *La conjuration antichrétienne*) (1911), *La démocratie chrétienne: parti et école vus du diocèse de Cambrai* (1911), *La mission posthume de Jeanne d'Arc et le règne social de Jésus-Christ* (1913), *Les pourquoi de la Guerre Mondiale: réponses de la justice divine, de l'histoire, de la bonté divine* (3 vols., 1919-1921).

As a journalist, he began contributing to *Semaine religieuse du Diocèse de Cambrai* in 1872, and he became its proprietor, director, and editor in chief in 1874. He made of this publication "a bastion against liberalism, modernism and every form of anti-Christian conspiracy in the world." With the erection of the Diocese of Lille, this magazine assumed the name *Semaine religieuse du Diocèse de Lille*, becoming the official newspaper of the bishopric in 1919.

Msgr. Delassus, who had been ordained a priest under Pius IX, exercised the greater part of his priestly activities under Leo XIII and Saint Pius X, dying during the pontificate of Benedict XV.

Always moved by the great concerns that marked the pontificates of Pius IX and Saint Pius X, he had an outstanding role in the ardent polemics that marked the Church's life during these pontificates. Msgr. Delassus's way of facing the religious, social, and political problems of Europe and America of his time was very similar to that of Pius IX and Saint Pius X, whose policy he defended with intelligence, culture, and unrivaled prowess, both during the reign of these two Pontiffs and during that of Leo XIII.

As is known, many points of the interpretation given by Leo XIII (both when Cardinal-Archbishop of Perugia and when Pope) to the general religious, social, and political panorama of Europe and America during this period did not coincide—in the measure this may happen among Popes— with the interpretation of Pius IX and Saint Pius X. The fidelity of Msgr. Delassus to the line of thought and action that he had followed under Pius IX and continued to follow during the subsequent pontificates was bound to expose him to misunderstandings, warnings, and cautionary measures on

the part of the Roman Curia of Leo XIII's time. These were probably painful to him, but he bore them with all the reverence prescribed by the Church's laws while also using the full measure of liberty that these laws assured him.

Thus, he was admonished by local ecclesiastical authorities and by the Holy See itself on account of his attacks against the Ecclesiastical Congress of Rheims (1896) and the Congress of Christian Democracy (1897). In 1898 a letter from Father Sébastien Wyart informed him that his polemical articles displeased the Vatican. Immediately after, the Holy See asked Msgr. Delassus to cease "his refractory campaign and violent polemics." In 1902 Cardinal Rampolla asked Bishop Sonnois of Cambrai to admonish Msgr. Delassus's *Semaine religieuse*.

The ascension of Saint Pius X to the pontifical throne would considerably redress Msgr. Delassus for the displeasure he had suffered. The Holy Pontiff understood, admired, and clearly supported the valiant polemicist, who likewise unreservedly supported Saint Pius X's anti-liberal and anti-modernist fight. In recognition of the merit of his efforts, Saint Pius X elevated the valiant priest to domestic prelate in 1904 and to protonotary apostolic in 1911.[1]

During the war, Msgr. Delassus understandably suspended his polemics in favor of national unity against the external foe, as did the French polemists of all shades. At the dawn of peace, in 1918, Msgr. Delassus relit his polemical flame. This sacred flame was extinguished shortly thereafter with his death.[2]

---

[1] On the occasion of the golden anniversary of his priestly ordination, Msgr. Delassus received the following letter from the Pontiff: "With joy We learned that within a few days you will complete fifty years of priesthood. We congratulate you wholeheartedly, asking God for every kind of prosperity for you. We feel Ourselves brought to this act of benevolence which, We know well, you merit as much by your devotion to Our person as by the unequivocal testimonies of your zeal, be it by your defense of Catholic doctrine, by your maintenance of ecclesiastical discipline, or ultimately by your sustenance of all these Catholic works so needed in our epoch.

"Because of such holy works, it is with all Our heart that We bestow the deserved eulogies and grant you, with all good will, dear Son, the apostolic blessing, at once a pledge of heavenly graces and a testimony of Our benevolence.

"Given in Rome at the feet of Saint Peter on June 14, 1912, the ninth year of Our pontificate." (signed) Pius X, Pope (*Actes de Pie X* [Paris: Maison de la Bonne Presse, 1936], Vol. 7, p. 238).

[2] Cf. *Dictionnaire du monde religieux dans la France contemporaine*, Vol. 4, *Lille - Flandres* (Paris: Beauchesne, 1990).

2. Fatherland, the Father's Domain

After recalling in his book *L'Esprit Familial dans la Maison, dans la Cité et dans l'Etat* the thesis of Fustel de Coulanges on the family as the mother cell of ancient society, Msgr. Delassus shows that this thesis applies likewise to the origins of the present civilization.

We see social groupings forming in the same way in the beginnings of our modern world.

The family, in expanding, formed among us the *mesnie* (house, family, as in the *House* of France today), just as it formed the *phratry* among the Greeks and the *gens* among the Romans. "Relatives gathered around their leader," says Flach (*Les Origines de l'ancienne France*), "forming the core of an extended association, the *mesnie*. The texts, chronicles, and *chansons de geste* of the Middle Ages show us that the *mesnie*, extended through patronage and clientele, corresponded exactly to the Roman *gens*." Next Flach demonstrates how the developing *mesnie* in turn produced the fief, a more extended family, whose suzerain was still the father; so much so that to designate the ensemble of persons united under the suzerainty of a feudal lord, the word *familia* is frequently used in the texts from the twelfth and thirteenth centuries, the time when the feudal regime was in full bloom. "The baron," says Flach, "is above all the head of a family." And the historian cites texts in which the father is expressly compared to the baron, and the son to the vassal.

"A greater extension [of the family] creates the great baron." The small fief grew into the large fief. The agglomeration of the large fiefs formed kingdoms.

Thus was our France created. The language bears as much witness to this as history does.

The ensemble of persons placed under the authority of the father of the family is called *familia*. From the tenth century on, the ensemble of persons gathered under the authority of a lord, head of the *mesnie*, is called *familia*. The ensemble of persons gathered under the authority of the baron, head of the feudal fief, is called *familia*. And we shall see that the ensemble of French families was governed as a family. The territory over which these various authorities held sway, whether as the head of a family, the head of a *mesnie*, a feudal baron, or a king, is called *patria*, the domain of the father, in these documents. "The *fatherland*," says Funck-Brentano, "was originally the territory of the family, the land of the father. The word extended to the lordship and the entire kingdom, the king being the father of the people. The ensemble of the lands over which the authority of the king held sway was thus called 'fatherland.'"[3]

---

[3] Msgr. Henri Delassus, *L'Esprit Familial dans la Maison, dans la Cité et dans l'Etat* (Lille: Société Saint-Augustin, Desclée de Brouwer, 1910), pp. 16-17.

The Paternal Character of the Traditional Monarchy

1. Francis I's Reception in Vienna After the Withdrawal of Napoleon's Troops

The paternal character of the medieval monarchy was preserved in large measure by the sovereigns of the House of Austria until the dethronement of the Hapsburgs in 1918.

The speech of Vienna's burgomaster upon receiving the Emperor Francis I some time after the defeat at Wagram (1809) provides an expressive idea of the affection of this paternal character. For those modern readers not imbued with the spirit of class struggle, this speech will seem to be a page from a fairy tale rather than a historic document. A narrator of indisputable competence, the Austrian historian Johann Baptist Weiss (1820-1899), records this episode as follows:

> Most fervent support was shown [by the people of Vienna] in the reception for the Emperor, Francis I, after a devastating war and the departure of the French from Vienna on November 20, 1809, following an oppressive stay of six months, seven days....
>
> On November 26, the Austrian troops returned to Vienna, and on the 27th the Emperor arrived at four o'clock in the afternoon. Since daybreak thousands and thousands of people had been heading to Simmering to welcome their beloved Emperor. All of Vienna was standing by, pressing to-

gether like children awaiting their beloved father. He appeared at last, with no guards, in an open carriage and wearing the uniform of his Hussar regiment, with his chief steward, the Count of Wrbna, at his side. The air and ground virtually shook with cries of joy—"Welcome, Father!" Handkerchiefs waved incessantly.

The burgomaster addressed him in these words: "Beloved Prince, when a people, amid enormous sufferings and struggling against misfortune, thinks only of the woes of its Prince, their love is deeply rooted in strong, undying feeling. We are that people. When our sons were falling on the bloody battlefield, when incandescent balls were destroying our homes, when the foundations of Vienna trembled amid the thunder of battle, our thoughts were of you. O Prince and Father, our thoughts were then of you in silent love. For you did not seek this war. The fatal course of events forced it upon you. You wanted something better. You have not been the cause of our hardships. We know that you love us. We know that our happiness is your sacred, firm wish. We have often felt the blessings of your fatherly goodness; you have marked your return by new blessings. Fatherly Prince, accept these greetings filled with un-wavering love in our midst. It is true that the poor outcome of this war has taken away some of your subjects, but please forget the pain of these losses through close union with your loyal subjects. Not in numbers, but in the strong, constant wishes and the all-encompassing love are the sacred supports of the throne. And we are all filled with this spirit. We want to compensate you for your losses. We want to be worthy of our country, for no Austrian abandons his Prince where our country is concerned. Even though the walls surrounding your palace were to go to ruin, the strongest castle is the hearts of your people."

No monarch could have encountered a warmer reception. Francis I was able to move forward only a step at a time as the people kissed his hands, his garments, and the horses. When he reached the palace, they carried him up the grand staircase. At night the city and the outskirts were splendidly illuminated.[1]

2. The Welcome Given by the People of Paris to the Count of Artois Upon His Return from Exile

The festive and enthusiastic reception given by the people of another European capital to another princely victim of misfortune—that given by the populace of Paris to the Count of Artois, the future Charles X, on his return from exile—shows well the people's affection for the representatives of the ancient legitimate and paternal dynasties. It is narrated by the eminent contemporary historian Georges Bordonove.

Monsieur[2] made his solemn entrance into Paris on April 10, 1814, through the gate of Saint-Denis. The Baron of Frénilly testifies: "There were neither windows nor roofs enough to satisfy the enthusiastic crowds, which shouted themselves hoarse. Everything was decorated with flags, hangings, rugs, and flowers, and all handkerchiefs were waving. It was a touching sight."

The weather was splendid. The April sun lit up this profusion of white flags, flowers, and laughing faces....

Children and young people hung on the railings. Fine fellows, perched on the rooftops, waved their hats. Drums were beating. Horses caracoled on the pavement. Everywhere cries of "Long live the King! Long live Monsieur!" burst forth spontaneously. As one approached the center of Paris, the gaiety heightened, the enthusiasm changed into delirium.

Monsieur was such a handsome man! He maintained such an allure despite his fifty-seven years! He wore the embroidered blue uniform with silver epaulets so well! He rode the superb white horse procured for him so elegantly! His gaze was at once so proud and full of goodness! He responded so graciously to the greetings!... It had been so long since they had seen a real prince, charming and

---

[1] Johann Baptist Weiss, *Historia Universal* (Barcelona: Tipografía La Educación, 1932), Vol. 21, pp. 768-769.

[2] Title given to the king's oldest brother. The Count of Artois was Louis XVIII's brother.

chivalrous! Thus he approached Notre-Dame.... Monsieur allowed the crowd to come near, to touch his boots, his spurs, the withers of his horse. This forwardness was pleasing.

The marshals of the Empire followed him. Some of them presented themselves to him with the tricolor rosette. Others did not hide their hostility. All wished to remain in their positions. Monsieur greeted them. Little by little they allowed themselves to be overtaken by the general euphoria. The excitement and the joyful exclamations of the multitude disconcerted them. They did not understand why the Parisians were so infatuated with this prince whom they had not known the day before. A mysterious spark had electrified the hearts. Monsieur himself had ignited it. He had the gift of pleasing, of seducing crowds as well as individuals; he had what we would now call charisma. He conformed so well to the image people have of a prince, he had so much simplicity in his bearing, this supreme ease that cannot be learned, for it flows from the source. With difficulty a path was cleared for him to Notre-Dame, where a *Te Deum* was to be sung. Everything had happened so quickly that there had been no time to decorate the cathedral. He was seen kneeling, praying with fervor. He was thanking Providence for having granted him this joy of having restored France to the throne of the fleurs-de-lis.[3]

Perhaps the spark that fired the Parisians with such enthusiasm for the return of the legitimate monarchy had been caused by the general sentiment of the time, ingeniously expressed by Talleyrand in the closing words of a letter to the future Charles X on the occasion of Napoleon's first abdication: *"Nous avons assez de gloire, Monseigneur, mais venez, venez nous rendre l'honneur"* [We have had enough of glory, Sir, but come, come bring us honor].

---

[3] Georges Bordonove, *Les Rois qui ont fait la France—Charles X* (Paris: Editions Pygmalion, 1990), pp. 121-123.

What Popes, Saints, Doctors and Theologians Think Regarding the Lawfulness of War

The pugnacious and warlike manifestation of the medieval spirit, as well as the militant character of the Church, may amaze the radicals of contemporary pacifism, absolutely intolerant of any and every type of war, for to their ears the expressions "holy war" and "just war" sound radically contradictory.

It will not be superfluous to place at their disposition various texts of Roman Pontiffs and leading Catholic thinkers, so that they may see that no such contradiction exists.

1. War's Legitimate Purpose Is Peace in Justice

According to the entry *"Paix et Guerre"* in the *Dictionnaire Apologétique de la Foi Catholique*, the teaching of Saint Augustine regarding peace and war can be condensed into four topics.

First of all, there are wars that are just. These are the wars that attempt to repress a censurable enterprise on the part of an adversary.

But war should be considered an extreme remedy to which one resorts only after having ascertained the evident impossibility of otherwise safeguarding the legitimate right. Even if just, war in fact causes so many and such terrible sufferings—*mala tam magna, tam horrenda, tam saeva*—that one can only resign oneself to it through an imperious duty.

The legitimate goal of war is not precisely the victory, with all the satisfactions this entails. Rather, it is peace in justice, the durable reestablishment of a public order in which each thing would be restored to its rightful place....

Finally, the sufferings of war constitute one of the punishments for sin on this earth. Even when defeat humiliates those who believed themselves in the right, this painful test must be seen as the design of God for punishing and purifying the people of faults for which they must admit their guilt.[1]

---

[1] Yves de la Brière (Paris: Gabriel Beauchesne Editeur, 1926), Vol. 3, col. 1260.

2. Popes and Councils Confirm the Doctrine of Saint Thomas on War

Saint Thomas Aquinas, according to the same source, "sets forth the three conditions that legitimize in conscience the use of armed force."

> 1. When the war is brought on not by simple individuals or through some secondary authority,...but always through the authority that exercises the highest power in the State;
>
> 2. When the war is motivated by a just cause; that is to say, when the adversary is fought because of a proportionate offense that he really committed....
>
> 3. When the war is conducted with a right intention; that is to say, in faithfully making every effort to promote good and to avoid evil in all ways possible....

This doctrine of Saint Thomas is indirectly but strikingly confirmed in the papal Bulls, in the conciliar decrees of the Middle Ages concerning the "peace of God" and later the "truce of God," just as in the peaceful and arbitrated settlement of conflicts between kingdoms. These documents, in their concordance, interpret the authentic thought of the Church and the general spirit of its teachings on the subject of moral questions concerning the right of peace and war.... The practice of popes and councils corroborates and accredits the teachings of the Doctors [on the subject], whose three fundamental principles Saint Thomas puts into relief.[2]

3. To Die or to Kill for Christ Is Not Criminal, but Glorious

About the lawfulness of war against the pagans, Saint Bernard, the Mellifluous Doctor, has these glowing words:

> But in truth the knights of Christ fight the battles of their Lord with all tranquility of conscience, fearing neither sin by the death of their enemies nor the danger of their own death, because death inflicted or suffered for Christ's sake bears no trace of crime and often brings the merit of glory. In the former case, there is a gain for Christ; in the latter, Christ is gained, Who doubtless both willingly accepts

the death of an enemy for punishment and more willingly offers Himself to the soldier for consolation. The knight of Christ, I say, kills with tranquil conscience and dies even more tranquilly. In dying he benefits himself; in killing he benefits Christ. For he bears not a sword without cause; he is the minister of God for the punishment of evil and the exaltation of good. When he kills a malefactor, it is not homicide but, so to say, "malecide"; and he is clearly considered the avenger of Christ in the case of those who do evil, and the defender of Christians. Moreover, when

---

[2] Ibid., cols. 1261-1262.

he himself is killed, it is understood that he has not perished, but that he has arrived in eternal glory. The death, therefore, that he inflicts is a gain for Christ; the death that he receives is his own gain. The Christian glories in the death of a pagan, because Christ is glorified; in the death of a Christian, the liberality of the king is revealed, because the soldier is taken away to be rewarded. Furthermore, the just man will rejoice over the one when he has seen the punishment. Concerning the other, a man will say: "If indeed there be fruit to the just: there is indeed a God that judgeth them on the earth" (Ps. 57:12). Not that the pagans should be slain if by any other means they can be impeded from persecuting and oppressing the faithful. But presently it is better that they be killed so that, in this way, the just men do not bend to the iniquity of their hands, for on the contrary, certainly the sinners' rod will be upon the lot of the just.[3]

4. The Protection of the Faith Is a Sufficient Cause for the Lawfulness of War

From the Seraphic Doctor, Saint Bonaventure, we present the following judgment on the subject:

> For the lawfulness [of war] it is required...that the person who declares war be invested with authority, that the one who wages war be a layman,...that the one against whom war is waged be so insolent that he must be repelled by war. A sufficient cause is the protection of the homeland, or of peace, or of the Faith.[4]

5. Sacred Scripture Praises Wars Against the Enemies of the Faith

Francisco Suárez, S.J., a theologian of renowned authority in traditional Catholic thought, writes in *De Bello*, his famous compendium of the Church's doctrine on war:

> War, in itself, is not intrinsically evil, nor is it forbidden for Christians. This is a truth of Faith contained expressly in Sacred Scripture, for in the Old Testament the wars waged by very holy, virile men are praised: "Blessed be Abraham by the most high God, who created heaven and earth. And blessed be the most high God, by whose protection the enemies are in thy hands" (Gen. 14:19-20). One reads similar passages about Moses, Josue, Samson, Gedeon, David, the Machabees, and others, whom time and again God ordered to make war against the enemies of the Hebrews; and Saint Paul says that the saints conquered

---

[3]   Saint Bernard de Clairvaux, *De laude novae militiae*, in Migne, *Patrologia Latina*, Vol. 182, col. 924.

[4]   Saint Bonaventure, *Opera Omnia* (Paris: Vives, 1867), Vol. 10, p. 291.

empires by Faith. The same thing is confirmed by the witness of the Church Fathers cited by Gratian; and also Saint Ambrose in several chapters of his book on duties.[5]

6. The Church Has the Right and Power to Convoke and Lead a Crusade

In our days, a voluminous and very well documented study on the Church's right to promote war against infidels and heretics was published in 1956, by Msgr. Rosalio Castillo Lara, afterward elevated to the cardinalate. The work, *Coacción Eclesiástica y Sacro Romano Imperio*, furnishes data of the greatest interest to show how the Church in fact exercised this power, founded on juridical and doctrinal principles. We present here some passages of this study that well illustrate the combative attitude of the medieval popes:

> All the authors are in agreement in conceding to the Church a right to the *vis armata virtual*, without which any material coercion would be useless. This consists in the power to demand, under authority, that the State provide the service of its armed forces for purely ecclesiastical ends. This is commonly understood as invoking the help of the secular arm.[6]

Regarding the Crusades against the infidels and their convocation by the popes, one may read the following:

> The Bulls on the Crusades and conciliar canons always present as the first and foremost goal the reconquest of the Holy Land or, depending on the historical moment, the safeguarding of the Christian kingdom of Jerusalem, fruit of the First Crusade. To this one may add the release of captive Christians and, in consequence, the combat and confounding of the insolence of the pagans who offended the Christian name and honor. To the medieval mind, all these goals were completely religious. The motivations, for example, to induce the faithful to take part in the expeditions all had this character; they revolve around a central concept: the holiness of the places sanctified by the birth, life, and death of Our Lord Jesus Christ, which cannot continue to be profaned by the presence of the infidels. Christendom has an imprescriptible acquired right over those lands....
>
> This religious concept completely permeates all the expeditions of the Crusades and predominates, at least virtually, over all the other political or temporal motives that mingle with it....
>
> Celestine III makes it clear that fighting for the Holy Land is equivalent to serving Christ, something His followers are obliged to do: "*Ecce qui nunc cum Cristo non fuerit, juxta Evangelicae auctoritatis doctrinam ipse erit adversus*" [he who does not now declare himself with Jesus Christ will be, as the Gospel proclaims with authority, His enemy].

---

[5] Francisco Suárez, S.J., *De Bello*, I, 2, in Luciano Pereña Vicente, *Teoria de la Guerra en Francisco Suárez* (Madrid: C.S.I.C., 1954), Vol. 2, pp. 72, 74.

[6] Msgr. Rosalio Castillo Lara, *Coacción Eclesiástica y Sacro Romano Imperio* (Turin: 1956), p. 69.

The Bulls of Innocent III that deal with this subject are very numerous and the goal holds to the traditional line: the Crusade aims *"ad expugnandam paganorum barbariem et haereditatem Domini servandam ad vindicandam injuriam crucifixi, ad defensionem Terrae nativitatis Domini "* [to destroy the barbarism of the pagans, to guard the heritage of the Lord, and to avenge the injury made to the Crucified One, in the defense of the land in which Our Lord was born].

Innocent III prefers, however, more concrete grounds and provides a new formula for the traditional reasons, placing the Christian's obligation to participate in a crusade almost on a juridical plane: the duty of vassalage that links Christians to their King, Jesus Christ.

In an epistle to the King of France he explains: Just as it would be a crime of lèse-majesté for a vassal to fail to assist his lord were the lord expelled from his land and perhaps held captive, *"similiter Jesus Christus Rex regum et Dominus dominantium...de ingratitudinis vitio et veluti infidelitatis crimine te damnaret, si ei ejecto de terra quam pretio sui sanguinis comparavit et a Sarracenis in salutiferae crucis ligno quasi captivo detento negligeris subvenire"* [in a similar way, Jesus Christ, King of kings and Lord of lords...would condemn you for the sin of ingratitude and as a culprit of infidelity if, He being expelled from the land that He bought at the price of His Blood and retained as a slave by the Saracens on the salutary wood of the cross, you neglected to come to His aid].

Honorius III emphasizes the affront and dishonor to Christ and the Christians in consequence of the possession of the Holy Land by the impious and blasphemous Saracens. This motive is sufficient for taking up arms....

The duty of vassalage is so strict and the injury made to Christ should move Christians so strongly that one who is remiss might well fear for his eternal salvation....

Innocent IV considers the liberation of the Holy Land a strictly ecclesiastical work, particularly binding on prelates, since it will result in a large increase for the Catholic Faith....

Gregory X confessed that he longed for nothing save the liberation of the Holy Land, which he considered the principal objective of his pontificate....

In conclusion, in the Church's official thinking, the Crusades were a holy work of strictly religious character.... As a consequence, they fall within the ambit of the Church, which almost always took the initiative to promote, control, and direct them with Her authority.[7]

The military orders constituted the Church's armed force. In his valuable work, the erudite Cardinal says of them:

The military orders are a faithful expression of what could be considered the ecclesiastical *vis armata*. In fact, its members were at once soldiers and monks. As religious, they professed the three traditional vows under a rule approved by the Holy See. As soldiers, they formed a standing army prepared for battle wherever enemies of the Christian faith might threaten. The ecclesiastical objective, which was their sole aim, and the dependence on the Holy See created by their vow of obedience, made them soldiers of the Church.

Institutionally, they were lay religious [not priests] consecrated to war in defense of the Faith. Fitting a body of

---

[7] Ibid., pp. 85-89.

soldiers into the framework of purely ecclesiastical institutions bears witness to a strong awareness in the Church of possessing a supreme material coercive power, in which these warrior monks, as delegates, participated.

There is no other way of explaining the approval given these orders. In approving them, the Church made them strictly Her own and sanctified the goal toward which these knights, by profession, should aim, which was none other than war.[8]

And still on the lawfulness of war the Cardinal adds:

The Pontiffs, in sending out the appeal for the Crusade, motivating the soldiers and assuming their high command, never posed the problem of the war's incongruity with the spirit of the Church, nor did they wonder whether they had the right to organize armies and hurl them against the infidels.... Consequently, not only did the Popes not consider this illicit but, rather, they were consciously exercising a power that was specifically theirs: the supreme coercive material power. Nor did they view it even remotely as encroaching on the temporal sphere, which they knew to be reserved solely to the State.[9]

---

[8] Ibid., pp. 109-110.

[9] Ibid., p. 115.

Is Being Noble and Leading a Noble's Life Incompatible With Sanctity?

The current misunderstanding of nobility and the analogous traditional elites results largely from the adroit but biased propaganda spread against them by the French Revolution. Such propaganda, continuously disseminated throughout the nineteenth and twentieth centuries by ideological and political currents spawned by the French Revolution, has been challenged by serious historiography with growing efficacy. This propaganda, however, still clings to life in certain sectors of opinion. It is relevant, therefore, to say something about this.

According to the revolutionaries of 1789, the nobility was essentially constituted of pleasure seekers. Holding honorific and economic privileges, the nobles allegedly lived extravagantly off the merit and credit acquired by distant ancestors. This allowed them the luxury of enjoying earthly life, especially the delights of idleness and voluptuousness. This class of pleasure seekers was also highly burdensome to the nation and harmful to the poorer classes, which were hard-working, temperate, and beneficial to the common good. According to d'Argenson, *"La Cour était le tombeau de la nation"* (the Court was the nation's tomb).

This led to the notion that the life of a noble, with the station and wealth that normally accompany it, induces a moral negligence that sharply contrasts with Christian asceticism. This perception contains some measure of truth. The first signs of the terrible moral crisis of our day were already visible among the nobility and the analogous elites of the late eighteenth century. It is necessary, however, to stress that this perception is much more false than true and is harmful to the good reputation of the noble class.

Many aspects of the Church's history prove this, including the fact that she has raised a great number of nobles to the honors of the altar. She thus affirms that they followed the Commandments and the evangelical counsels to a heroic degree.

Saint Peter Julian Eymard has noted that "the Church annals show that a large number of saints, and the most illustrious ones, had a blazon, a name, an illustrious family; some were even of royal blood."[1] While several of these saints abandoned the world to more securely attain heroic virtue, others, such as the kings Saint Louis of France and Saint Ferdinand of Castile, remained amid the splendor of their lofty noble stations and therein attained heroic virtue.

To complete the refutation of this perception, which seeks to degrade the nobility, its customs and lifestyles, we thought it advisable to enquire about the proportion of nobles who were canonized by the Church.

A specific study on this subject could not be found. Some investigators have broached the subject without undertaking specific and

---

[1] *Mois de Saint Joseph*, p. 62.

exhaustive research. They based their calculations on registers that they themselves present as incomplete. University of Rouen professor André Vauchez published a study, *La Sainteté en l'Occident aux Derniers Siècles du Moyen Age,*[2] based on the processes of canonization and on medieval hagiographic documents, that merits particular attention. He analyzes the investigations *de vita, miraculis et fama* ordered by popes between 1198 and 1431. Of a total of 71 investigations, 35 concluded that the persons examined deserved to be elevated to the honors of the altar, which the Church did in the Middle Ages.[3]

The statistics furnished by Vauchez follow:

Processes of canonization ordered between 1198 and 1431 (71 cases)	
Nobles	62.0%
Middle Class	15.5%
People	8.4%
Social origin unknown	14.1%

Saints canonized by Popes of the Middle Ages (35 cases)	
Nobles	60.0%
Middle Class	17.1%
People	8.6%
Social origin unknown	14.3%

Even if very interesting, this data does not offer a complete picture, since it relates to a very small number of people and to a relatively short period. An investigation encompassing a larger number of people over a longer period was necessary—not that it would exhaust the subject. Nevertheless, some weighty difficulties arose.

First, there is no official list of the saints venerated in the Catholic Church. This is explicable and is related to the very history of the Church and the gradual perfecting of Her institutions. The veneration of saints had its start in the Catholic Church with the homage paid to the martyrs. Local communities honored some of their members who were victims of persecutions. Of the thousands of those who shed their blood in testimony of the Faith in the first centuries of the Church, only a few hundred names have come down to us. We know them through the acts of the Roman tribunals, which transcribed the oral processes, and through reports made by eye-witnesses of the martyrdoms. Many records of the martyrs were simply lacking. Of those that had existed—whose reading inflamed the souls of the first Christians and gave them the strength to bear new tribulations—many were destroyed during the persecutions, especially that of Diocletian.[4] Thus it is impossible to know all the martyrs venerated by the faithful in the first centuries.

After the persecutions, and for a long time, saints were venerated by restricted groups of faithful without prior investigation and pronouncement of an ecclesiastical authority. As the authority's participation in the organization of the Catholic communities grew, its role in deciding who should receive veneration also grew. The bishops began to sanction this or that cultus, and often ratified it at the request of the faithful. They even made the exhumation and translation of a new saint's relics.

Only at the end of the first millennium did the popes begin to intervene occasionally in the official recognition of a saint. As the Roman Pontiffs' power was affirmed and the contacts with Rome became more frequent, the bishops began to solicit

---

[2]   André Vauchez, *La Sainteté en l'Occident aux Derniers Siècles du Moyen Age* (Rome: Ecole Française de Rome, Palais Farnese, 1981), 765 pp.

[3]   Several others were canonized later.

[4]   Cf. Daniel Ruiz Bueno, *Actas de los Martires* (Madrid: Biblioteca de Autores Cristianos, 1951).

the popes' sanction of these cults. This occurred for the first time in 993. Between 993 and 1234 many bishops continued to translate relics and to confirm cults according to the ancient customs. Later, recourse to the Holy See was made compulsory by the 1234 *Decretals*, and the right of canonization was reserved to the Pontiff. From 1234 on, the processes for determining the veneration of a saint were gradually perfected.

From the end of the thirteenth century, the pontifical decisions were based on a prior investigation carried out by a college of three cardinals especially entrusted with this task. This remained the case until 1588, when the causes were confided to the Congregation of Rites, established the previous year by Pope Sixtus V. In the seventeenth century this development reached its term. In 1634, Urban VIII's brief *Coelestis Jerusalem cives* established the standards for canonization, which remain essentially the same to our day. The Constitutions of Urban VIII established the confirmation of cult, or equipollent canonization, for those servants of God whose public veneration had been tolerated after the pontificate of Alexander III (1159-1181). An equipollent canonization is a "decision by which the Sovereign Pontiff orders that a servant of God who is found in public veneration from time immemorial be honored in the Universal Church even though a regular process has not been introduced."[5] This procedure was valid also for similar cases occurring after the Constitutions of Urban VIII.

From 993 on (the date of the first papal canonization) it is possible to establish a list of saints designated by the Holy See. This list, however, is still not complete. Documents of extensive periods are missing. Furthermore, the list does not contain all the saints, for between 993 and 1234, as noted, the bishops continued to ratify cultus. For this reason, many individuals were objects of public veneration independently of Rome's intervention, which was often—but not always—requested only some centuries later.

Only with the beginning of the sixteenth century can one be certain that the list of saints and blessed (a distinction established by the legislation of Urban VIII) is complete.[6]

Apart from the difficulty in compiling a complete list of the saints, there is the problem of determining who among them belonged to the nobility. The certainty of a person's noble origin is not always easy to establish. On the one hand, the concept of nobility developed progressively and organically, conditioned by local characteristics. On the other hand, it is sometimes difficult to determine with precision the ancestry of a person, and thus to determine the social origin of a saint.

Having these difficulties in mind, we had to choose the most complete and trustworthy sources possible in order to determine the approximate number of nobles among the saints. The *Index ac Status Causarum*[7] was chosen because it is an official publication of the Congregation for the Causes of Saints, successor to the Congregation of Rites. This book is an "extraordinary and most ample edition" made to commemorate the fourth centennial of the Congregation and "contains all the causes that came before the Congregation from 1588 to 1988, even the rather ancient ones preserved in the Vatican's Secret Archives."

---

[5]   T. Ortolan, "Canonisation," in *Dictionnaire de Théologie Catholique* (Paris: Letouzey et Ané, 1923), Vol. 2, part 2, col. 1636.

[6]   Cf. André Vauchez, *La Sainteté en l'Occident*; John F. Broderick, S.J., "A Census of the Saints (993-1955)," *The American Ecclesiastical Review*, August 1956; Pierre Delooz, *Sociologie et Canonisations* (La Haye: Martinus Nijhoff, 1969); Ruiz Bueno, *Actas de los Martires*; *Archives de Sociologie des Religions,* published by the Group of Sociology of the Religions (Paris: Editions du Centre National de la Recherche Scientifique, January-June 1962).

[7]   Città del Vaticano: Congregatio pro Causis Sanctorum, 1988, 556 pp.

The work includes several appendices of which three are of special interest to this study. The first contains confirmations of veneration, some names of the blessed that were added, and those that were removed but later included in the catalogue of the saints. This appendix is based on the *Index ac Status Causarum* written by Father Beaudoin in 1975. The second appendix enumerates only those beatified since the institution of the Sacred Congregation of Rites but still not canonized. Lastly, the third appendix enumerates the saints whose causes were considered by the Sacred Congregation of Rites, including the cases of equipollent canonization.

With this list of names in hand, we consulted the respective biographies in the *Bibliotheca Sanctorum*[8] to discover which saints were nobles. This work, supervised by Pietro Cardinal Palazzini, former prefect of the Congregation for the Causes of the Saints, is considered the most complete catalogue of persons who have received veneration since the beginning of the Church.

The *Bibliotheca Sanctorum* does not focus its principal attention on the social origin of the listed persons, but rather on the problems related to their veneration. Thus, it is frequently impossible to know who was noble. To follow a strict criterion, we counted as nobles only those whom the work identifies as nobles or descendants thereof. Those whom the text merely depicts as belonging to "important," "known," "old," "powerful," or similarly-designated families were not included. In order to avoid doubtful cases, we further excluded persons whose noble origin could reasonably be presumed or even established with certainty through sources other than the *Bibliotheca Sanctorum*.

For yet greater precision, it also seemed convenient to distinguish the following categories, in accord with the *Index ac Status Causarum*:

* Saints canonized after a regular process;
* Those beatified after a regular process;
* Those whose venerability was confirmed;
* Servants of God whose processes of beatification are under way.

In the percentages presented in the table which follows, care was taken to discriminate, in each category, between those who were the object of an individual investigation and those who were part of a group, such as, for example, the Japanese, English, and Vietnamese martyrs.[9]

To correctly assess the appreciable percentage of nobles in these various categories, we must consider the percentage of nobles in relation to their respective country's population. We limit ourselves to two quite diverse and significant examples. According to the renowned Austrian historian J. B. Weiss, who drew on Taine's data, the nobility in France before the French Revolution comprised less than 1.5% of the population.[10] In his treatise on universal geography, *La Terra*,[11] G. Marinelli furnishes statistics on the nobility in Russia, basing himself on the work of Peschel-Krümel, *Das Russische Reich* (Leipzig, 1880). According to Marinelli, the sum of the hereditary nobility and personal nobility did not exceed 1.15% of the population. He also states that Rèclus, in 1879, and van Lëhen, in 1881, presented similar statistics, both arriving at the figure of 1.3%. Obviously these percentages varied slightly depending on time and place, but the variations are not significant.

The data presented above shows that in each of the categories (canonizations, beati-

---

[8] John XXIII Institute of the Pontifical Lateran University, 12 vols., 1960-1970; Appendix, 1987.

[9] *The Index ac Status Causarum* does not have the precise number of persons considered in some of these group processes, thus making it impossible to give an exact number. Our figures are, therefore, approximate.

[10] Cf. Weiss, *Historia Universal*, Vol. 15, p. 212.

[11] G. Marinelli, *La Terra—Trattato popolare di Geografia Universale* (Milan: Casa Editrice Francesco Vallardi), 7 vols.

fications, confirmations of cultus, and be-atification processes underway) the per-centage of nobles is considerably greater than in the total population of the coun-try.[12] This contradicts the revolutionary calumnies about the supposed incompati-bility between practicing virtue and being and living as a noble.

CANONIZATIONS	Total Number of Persons	Number of Nobles	%
Individual Processes	184	40	21.7
Collective Processes	364	12	3.3
Total	548	52	9.5
BEATIFICATIONS			
Individual Processes	182	22	12.1
Collective Processes	1074	46	4.3
Total	1256	68	5.4
CONFIRMATIONS OF CULTUS			
Individual Processes	336	107	31.8
Collective Processes	1087	10	0.9
Total	1423	117	8.2
BEATIFICATION PROCESSES UNDERWAY			
Individual Processes	1331	149	11.2
Collective Processes	2671	13	0.5
Total	4002	162	4.0

---

[12]   We notice, in the several categories, an appreciable difference between the percentage of nobles in the indi-vidual processes of beatification and in the collective processes. This can be explained by two main reasons. In many cases, the *Bibliotheca Sanctorum* only mentions the names without furnishing the biographical data that would permit one to know if they were nobles or not. Also, most of the collective processes refer to groups of mar-tyrs. Persecutions are usually directed against the whole Catholic population, regardless of social class. Thus, it is to be expected that among the martyrs the proportion of nobles would be similar to that within the population.

Bibliography

COLLECTED PONTIFICAL DOCUMENTS

Acta Apostolicae Sedis. Rome: Typis Polyglottis Vaticanis, 1920-1985. Vols. 12, 21, 36, 77.

Acta Sanctae Sedis. Rome: Ex Typographia Polyglotta, 1903-1904. Vol. 36.

Actes de Léon XIII. Paris: Maison de la Bonne Presse, n.d. Vol. 2.

Carlen, Sr. Claudia, IHM, ed. *The Papal Encyclicals, 1740-1878*. Raleigh, N.C.: McGrath Publishing Company, 1981.

Discorsi del Sommo Pontefice Pio IX. Rome: Tipografia di G. Aurelj, 1872. Vol. 1.

Discorsi e radiomessaggi di Sua Santità Pio XII. Vatican: Tipografia Poliglotta Vaticana, 1940-1958. Vols. 2-15, 18, 20.

Discorsi messaggi colloqui del Santo Padre Giovanni XXIII. Vatican: Tipografia Poliglotta Vaticana, 1960-1963. Vols. 2, 5.

Husslein, Rev. Joseph, S.J. *Social Wellsprings*. Milwaukee: Bruce Publishing Company, 1940, 1942. 2 vols.

Insegnamenti di Giovanni Paolo II. Vatican: Libreria Editrici Vaticana, 1980, 1984. Vols. 3, 7.

Insegnamenti di Paolo VI. Vatican: Tipografia Poliglotta Vaticana, 1963, 1964, 1968, 1970. Vols. 1, 2, 6, 8.

Leonis XIII Pontificis Maximii Acta. Rome: Ex Typographia Vaticana, 1898, 1903. Vols. 17, 22.

Pii VI Pont. Max. Acta. Rome: Typis S. Congreg. de Propaganda Fide, 1871. Vols. 1, 2.

Wynne, Rev. John J., S.J., ed. *The Great Encyclical Letters of Pope Leo XIII*. New York: Benziger Brothers, 1903.

Yzermans, Vincent A., ed. *The Major Addresses of Pope Pius XII*. St. Paul, Minn.: North Central Publishing Co., 1961. Vol. 2.

WORKS CITED IN PART I

Amerio, Romano. *Iota unum—Studio delle variazioni della Chiesa Cattolica nel secolo XX*. Milan-Naples: Riccardo Ricciardi Editore, 1985.

Augustine, Saint. *Epist. 138 ad Marcellinum*. In J. P. Migne. *Patrologia Latina*. Vol 2.

Benedict XV, Pope. Allocution to the Roman Patriciate and Nobility. *L'Osservatore Romano. January 5-6, 1920.*

Berville, M. *Mémoires de Rivarol*. Paris: Baudouin Frères, 1824.

Bordonove, Georges. *La Vie Quotidienne en Vendée*. Paris: Hachette, 1974.

Cadenas y Vicent, Vicente de. *Cuadernos de doctrina nobiliaria*. Madrid: Instituto Luis de Salazar y Castro, C.S.I.C. — Asociación de Hidalgos a Fuero de España, Ediciones Hidalguia, 1969, no. 1.

Claudel, Paul. *The Hostage*. In *Three Plays*. John Heard, transl. Boston: John W. Luce, Co. 1945.

Clinchamps, Philippe du Puy de. *La Noblesse*. Paris: Presses Universitaires de France, 1962.

Corrêa de Oliveira, Plinio. *Revolution and Counter-Revolution*. New Rochelle, N.Y.: The Foundation for a Christian Civilization, Inc., 1980.

Cowden-Guido, Richard. *John Paul II and the Battle for Vatican II*. Manassas, Va.: Trinity Communications, 1986.

Documents of Vatican II. New York: America Press, 1966.

Enciclopedia universal ilustrada. Madrid: Espasa-Calpe, n.d. Vols. 21, 23.

Fabro, Cornelio. *L'avventura della teologia progressista*. Milan: Rusconi Editore, 1974.

———. *La svolta antropologica di Karl Rahner*. Milan: Rusconi Editore, 1974.

Fustel de Coulanges, Numa Denis. *La Cité antique*. Paris: Librairie Hachette, n.d.

Graber, Rudolf. *Athanasius and the Church of Our Time*. Buckinghamshire, U.K.: Van Duren C.P. Ltd., 1974.

Holzer, Anton. *Vatikanum II: Reformkonzil oder Konstituante einer neuen Kirche*. Basel: Saka, 1977.

John Paul II, Pope. "Ad Patres Cardinales et Curiae Pontificalisque Domus Prelatos, imminente Nativitate Domini coram admissos," December 21, 1984. *Acta Apostolicae Sedis*. Vol. 77, no. 5 (1985).

John XXIII, Pope. Allocutions to the Roman Patriciate and Nobility, January 9, 1960; January 10, 1963. *Discorsi messaggi colloqui*. Vols. 2, 5 (1960-1963).

Leo XIII, Pope. Encyclical *Aeterni Patris*. *American Catholic Quarterly Review*. Vol. 4 (October 1879), pp. 733-745.

———. Encyclical *Au milieu des sollicitudes*. Wynne, *The Great Encyclical Letters of*

Pope Leo XIII. Pp. 249-263.

———. Encyclical *Immortale Dei.* Wynne. *The Great Encyclical Letters of Pope Leo XIII.* Pp. 107-134.

———. Letter to Cardinal Mathieu, March 28, 1897. In *La paix intérieur des Nations.* Paris: Desclée & Cie., 1952, p. 220.

Libro d'oro della nobiltà Italiana. 19th ed. Rome: Collegio Araldico, 1986-1989. Vol. 20.

Madelin, Louis. *Figures of the Revolution.* New York: The Macaulay Co., 1929.

Márquez de la Plata, Vicenta María, and Luis Valero de Bernabé. *Nobiliaria Española— origen, evolución, instituciones y probanzas.* Madrid: Prensa y Ediciones Iberoamericanas, 1991.

Mattoso, José. *A Nobreza Medieval Portuguesa.* Lisbon: Editorial Estampa, 1981.

May, Georg. *Der Glaube in der nachkonziliaren Kirche.* Vienna: Mediatrix Verlag, 1983.

Memórias da Irmã Lúcia. 3d ed. Fatima, Portugal: Postulação, 1978.

Moreno Vargas, Bernabé de. *Discursos de la nobleza de España.* Madrid: Instituto Luis de Salazar y Castro, C.S.I.C., Ediciones Hidalguia, 1971.

Oliveira, Luiz da Silva Pereira. *Privilégios da Nobreza e Fidalguia de Portugal.* Lisbon: Oficina de João Rodrigues Neves, 1806.

Paul VI, Pope. Allocution to the Roman Patriciate and Nobility. *Insegnamenti di Paolo VI.* Vol. 2 (1964).

———. Homily *"Resistite fortes in Fide"* of June 29, 1972. *L'Osservatore Romano* (English weekly ed.). July 13, 1972.

———. Speech to the Pontifical Lombard Seminary, December 7, 1968. *Insegnamenti di Paolo VI.* Vol. 6; *L'Osservatore Romano* (English weekly ed.). December 19, 1968.

Pius X, Pope Saint. Encyclical *Vehementer Nos. American Catholic Quarterly Review.* Vol. 31, no. 122 (July 1906), pp. 571-580.

Pius XII, Pope. Allocutions to the Pontifical Noble Guard. *Discorsi e radiomessaggi.* Vols. 1, 3, 4 (1939-1942).

———. Allocutions to the Roman Patriciate and Nobility, 1940-1952, 1958. *Discorsi e radiomessaggi.* Vols. 2-15, 18, 20 (1940-1958).

———. Christmas message, December 24, 1944. Yzermans. *Major Addresses of Pope Pius XII.* P. 81.

———. Christmas message, December 24, 1953. *Discorsi e radiomessaggi.* Vol. 15, pp. 517-531.

Raccolta di concordati su materie Ecclesiastiche tra la Santa Sede e le autorità civili. Vatican: Tipografia Poliglotta Vaticana, 1954. Vol. 2.

Ratzinger, Joseph Cardinal, with Vittorio Messori. *The Ratzinger Report.* San Francisco: Ignatius Press, 1985.

Rueda, Fr. Enrique. *The Homosexual Network.* Old Greenwich, Conn.: The Devin Adair Company, 1982.

Sanceau, Elaine. *The Reign of the Fortunate King.* Hamden, Conn.: Archon Books, 1970.

Siebel, Wigand. *Katholisch oder konziliar: Die Krise der Kirche heute.* Munich-Vienna: Langen Müller, 1978.

Siri, Joseph Cardinal. *Gethsemane: Reflections on the Current Theological Movement.* Chicago: Franciscan Herald Press, 1981.

Statuto del Regno. Annotated by Carlo Gallini. Turin: Unione Tipografico Editrice, 1878.

TFP-Covadonga. *España, anestesiada sin percibirlo, amordazada sin quererlo, extraviada sin saberlo: La obra de PSOE.* Madrid: Editorial Fernando III el Santo, 1988.

Thomas Aquinas, Saint. *On the Governance of Rulers.* Gerald Phelan, transl. London: Sheed and Ward, 1938.

———. *Summa Contra Gentiles.* Notre Dame, Ind.: University of Notre Dame Press, 1975.

———. *Summa Theologica.* London: R. & T. Washbourne, 1912.

Valdez, Dr. Rui Dique Travassos. "Títulos Nobiliárquicos." In *Nobreza de Portugal e do Brasil.* Lisbon: Editorial Enciclopédia, 1960. Vol. 2.

Von Hildebrand, Dietrich. *The Devastated Vineyard.* Chicago: Franciscan Herald Press, 1973.

———. *The Trojan Horse in the City of God.* Chicago: Franciscan Herald Press, 1967.

Weiss, Johann Baptist. *Historia universal.* Barcelona: Tipografía la Educación, 1931. Vol. 15.

WORKS CITED IN APPENDIX I
(ON THE UNITED STATES)

American Military History. Washington, D.C.: Center of Military History of the United States Army, 1989.

Acquaviva, Sabino S. *The Decline of the Sacred in Industrial Society.* New York: Harper & Row, 1979.

Adams, James T. *Provincial Society 1690-1763.* Vol. 3 in *A History of American Life.*

Arthur M. Schlesinger and Dixon Ryan Fox, eds. New York: Macmillan Company, 1927.

Ahlstrom, Sydney E. *A Religious History of the American People*. New Haven: Yale University Press, 1972.

Allen, Michael Patrick. *The Founding Fortunes*. New York: E. P. Dutton; Truman Talley Books, 1987.

Amory, Cleveland. *The Proper Bostonians*. New York: E.P. Dutton and Company, 1947.

——. *Who Killed Society?* New York: Harper & Brothers, 1960.

Andrews, Charles M. *The Colonial Period of American History*. New Haven: Yale University Press, 1934.

Auchincloss, Louis. Introduction to Dixon Wecter, *The Saga of American Society: A Record of Social Aspiration 1607-1937*. New York: Charles Scribner's Sons [1958] 1970.

Baltzell, E. Digby. *Philadelphia Gentlemen: The Making of a National Upper Class*. New York: The Free Press, 1966.

——. *Puritan Boston and Quaker Philadelphia*. New York: The Free Press, 1979.

——. "'Who's Who in America' and 'The Social Register': Elite and Upper Class in Metropolitan America." In *Class, Status, and Power: Social Stratification in Comparative Perspective*. Reinhard Bendix and Seymour Martin Lipset, eds. New York: The Free Press, 1966.

Bergel, Egon Ernest. *Social Stratification*. New York: McGraw-Hill, 1962.

Bierstedt, Robert. *The Social Order*. 4th ed. New York: McGraw-Hill, 1974.

Birmingham, Stephen. *America's Secret Aristocracy*. Boston: Little, Brown & Company, 1987.

Boorstin, Daniel J. *The Americans: The Colonial Experience*. New York: Random House, 1958.

Bowers, Claude G. *Jefferson and Hamilton: The Struggle for Democracy in America*. New York: Houghton Mifflin Company, 1925.

Bowes, Frederick P. *The Culture of Early Charleston*. Chapel Hill: University of North Carolina Press, 1942.

Brandt, Clare. *An American Aristocracy: The Livingstons*. New York: Doubleday & Company, 1986.

Bridenbaugh, Carl. *Cities in the Wilderness*. New York: Alfred A. Knopf [1938] 1966.

——. *Myths and Realities: Societies of the Colonial South*. Baton Rouge: Louisiana State University Press, 1952; reprint, Greenwood Press, 1981.

Brudnoy, David. "'Liberty by Taste': Toc-

queville's Search for Freedom." In *Modern Age: The First Twenty-Five Years: A Selection*. George Panichas, ed. Indianapolis: Liberty Press, 1988.

Bugg, James L., Jr. *Jacksonian Democracy: Myth or Reality?* New York: Holt, Rinehart and Winston, 1962.

Burch, Philip. *Elites in American History: The New Deal to the Carter Administration*. New York: Holmes & Meier, 1980.

Burt, Nathaniel. *First Families: The Making of American Aristocracy*. Boston: Little, Brown & Company, 1970.

——. *The Perennial Philadelphians: The Anatomy of an American Aristocracy*. Boston: Little, Brown & Company, 1963.

Burton, Michael G., and John Higley. "Invitation to Elite Theory: The Basic Contentions Reconsidered." In *Power Elites and Organizations*. G. William Domhoff and Thomas R. Dye, eds. Newbury Park, Calif.: Sage Publications, 1987.

Bushman, Richard L. *The Refinement of America: Persons, Homes, Cities*. New York: Alfred A. Knopf, 1992.

Cable, Mary. *Top Drawer: American High Society From the Gilded Age to the Roaring Twenties*. New York: Atheneum Books, 1984.

Cherry, Conrad. *God's New Israel: Religious Interpretations of American Destiny*. Englewood Cliffs, N.J.: Prentice-Hall, 1971.

Coleman, Richard, and Lee Rainwater. *Social Standing in America: New Dimensions of Class*. New York: Basic Books, 1978.

Cookson, Peter W., Jr., and Caroline Hodges Persell. *Preparing for Power: America's Elite Boarding Schools*. New York: Basic Books, 1985.

Corrêa de Oliveira, Plinio. *Revolution and Counter-Revolution*. 2d ed. New Rochelle, N.Y.: The Foundation for a Christian Civilization, 1980.

Curtis, Charlotte. *The Rich and Other Atrocities*. New York: Harper & Row, 1973.

Davies, Wallace Evan. *Patriotism on Parade: The Story of Veterans' and Hereditary Organizations in America 1783-1900*. Cambridge: Harvard University Press, 1955.

Davis, Kingsley. *Human Society*. New York: The Macmillan Company, 1949.

Dick, Everett. *The Lure of the Land: A Social History of the Public Lands from the Articles of Confederation to the New Deal*. Lincoln: University of Nebraska Press, 1970.

Domhoff, G. William. *The Higher Circles: The Governing Class in America*. New York: Random House, 1970.

——. *The Powers That Be: Processes of Rul-*

ing-Class Domination in America. New York: Random House, 1978.

———. *Who Rules America Now? A View for the 80's.* New York: Simon & Schuster, 1983; Touchstone, 1986.

Dowdey, Clifford. *The Virginia Dynasties: The Emergence of "King" Carter and the Golden Age.* Boston: Little, Brown & Company, 1969.

Dye, Thomas R., and L. Harmon Zeigler. *The Irony of Democracy: An Uncommon Introduction to American Politics.* 2d ed. Belmont, Calif.: Duxbury Press, 1972.

Eaton, Clement. *The Growth of Southern Civilization, 1790-1860.* New York: Harper & Brothers, 1961.

Family Associations and Societies and Reunions. Munroe Falls, Ohio: Summit Publications, 1991-1992.

Farber, Bernard. *Kinship and Class: A Midwestern Study.* New York: Basic Books, 1971.

Fichter, Joseph. *Sociology.* Chicago: University of Chicago Press, 1957.

Folsom, Michael Brewster, and Stephen D. Lubar, eds. *The Philosophy of Manufacturers: Early Debates over Industrialization in the United States.* Cambridge: MIT Press, 1982.

Glastris, Paul. "Where Americans Cheer the Rich." *U.S. News & World Report.* November 18, 1991, pp. 40-44.

Goodwin, Maud Wilder. *Dutch and English on the Hudson: A Chronicle of Colonial New York.* New Haven: Yale University Press, 1919.

Greene, Jack P. *Pursuits of Happiness: The Social Development of Early Modern British Colonies and the Formation of American Culture.* Chapel Hill: The University of North Carolina Press, 1988.

Grissom, Michael Andrew. *Southern by the Grace of God.* Gretna, Louisiana: Pelican Publishing Company, 1989.

Hammond, Bray. "The Jacksonians." In *Jacksonian Democracy: Myth or Reality?* James L. Bugg, ed. New York: Holt, Rinehart and Winston, 1962.

Harrington, Virginia D. *The New York Merchant on the Eve of the Revolution.* New York: 1935; reprint Gloucester, Mass.: Peter Smith, 1964.

Harris, Marshall. *Origin of the Land Tenure System in the United States.* Ames, Iowa: Iowa State College Press, 1953; reprint Westport, Conn.: Greenwood Press, 1953.

Hartz, Louis. *The Liberal Tradition in America: An Interpretation of American Political Thought Since the Revolution.* San Diego:

Harvest/Harcourt Brace Jovanovich, 1955.

Hereditary Register of the United States of America. Phoenix: Hereditary Register Publications, 1981; Yoncalla, Ore., 1986.

Hockett, Homer Carey. *Political and Social Growth of the American People, 1492-1865.* 3d ed. New York: The Macmillan Company, 1940.

Ingham, John. *The Iron Barons: A Social Analysis of an American Urban Elite, 1874-1965.* Westport, Conn.: Greenwood Press, 1978.

Jaher, Frederic Cople. *The Urban Establishment: Upper Strata in Boston, New York, Charleston, Chicago, and Los Angeles.* Urbana, Ill.: University of Illinois Press, 1981.

Kavaler, Lucy. *The Private World of High Society.* New York: David McKay Company, 1960.

Keller, Suzanne. *Beyond the Ruling Class: Strategic Elites in Modern Society.* New York: Random House, 1963.

Kim, Sung Bok. *Landlord and Tenant in Colonial New York.* Chapel Hill: The University of North Carolina Press, 1978.

Kirk, Russell. *The Conservative Mind: From Burke to Elliot.* 6th rev. ed. South Bend, Ind.: Gateway Editions, 1978.

———. *The Portable Conservative Reader.* New York: Penguin, 1982.

Klein, Milton M. "From Community to Status: The Development of the Legal Profession in Colonial New York." In *Business Enterprise in Early New York.* Joseph R. Frese, S.J., and Jacob Judd, eds. Tarrytown, N.Y.: Sleepy Hollow Restorations, 1979.

Lasch, Christopher. *The True and Only Heaven: Progress and Its Critics.* New York: W. W. Norton & Company, 1991.

Lerner, Max. *America as a Civilization: Life and Thought in the United States Today.* 30th. anniv. ed. New York: Henry Holt and Company, 1987.

Lewis, Jan. *The Pursuit of Happiness: Family and Values in Jefferson's Virginia.* Cambridge: Cambridge University Press, 1983.

Lidz, Victor M. "Founding Fathers and Party Leaders: America's Transition to the Democratic Social Condition." In *Social Class and Democratic Leadership: Essays in Honor of E. Digby Baltzell.* Harold J. Bershady, ed. Philadelphia: University of Pennsylvania Press, 1989.

Linton, Ralph. *The Study of Man: An Introduction.* Student's ed. New York: Appleton-Century-Crofts [1936] 1964.

Lipset, Seymour Martin. *The First New Na-*

tion: The United States in Historical and Comparative Perspective. New York: Basic Books, 1963.

——, and Reinhard Bendix. *Social Mobility in Industrial Society*. Berkeley and Los Angeles: University of California Press, 1967.

Lynch, William O. *Fifty Years of Party Warfare, 1789-1837*. Indianapolis: Bobbs Merrill, 1931.

McAvoy, Thomas. *The Americanist Heresy in Roman Catholicism, 1895-1900*. Notre Dame, Ind.: University of Notre Dame Press, 1963.

Maier, Pauline. *From Resistance to Revolution: Colonial Radicals and the Development of American Opposition to Great Britain, 1765-1776*. New York: Random House, 1972; Vintage Books, 1974.

Main, Jackson Turner. *The Social Structure of Revolutionary America*. Princeton: Princeton University Press, 1965.

Marcus, George F. *Elites: Ethnographic Issues*. Albuquerque: School of American Research, University of New Mexico Press, 1983.

Malone, Dumas, and Basil Rauch. *Crisis of the Union, 1841-1877*. New York: Appleton-Century-Crofts, 1960.

Merk, Frederick A. *Manifest Destiny and Mission in American History*. New York: Alfred A. Knopf, 1963.

Meyers, Marvin. *The Jacksonian Persuasion, Politics & Belief*. Stanford, Calif.: Stanford University Press [1957] 1960.

Miller, Douglas T. *The Birth of Modern America, 1820-1850*. New York: Pegasus, 1978.

——. *Jacksonian Aristocracy: Class and Democracy in New York, 1830-1860*. New York: Oxford University Press, 1967.

Mills, C. Wright. *The Power Elite*. New York: Oxford University Press, 1956.

Mott, Paul. *Organizational Integration and Change in American Society*. Englewood Cliffs, N.J.: Prentice-Hall, 1965.

Myers, Minor, Jr. *Liberty without Anarchy: A History of the Society of the Cincinnati*. Charlottesville, N.C.: The University Press of Virginia, 1983.

Nettels, Curtis P. *The Roots of American Civilization: A History of American Colonial Life*. New York: Appleton-Century-Crofts, 1963.

Newby, Idus A. *The South: A History*. New York: Holt, Rinehart and Winston, 1978.

Nisbet, Robert A. *The Present Age: Progress and Anarchy in Modern America*. New York: Harper and Row, 1988.

——. *The Quest for Community*. New York: Oxford University Press, 1953.

——. *The Social Bond: An Introduction to the Study of Society*. New York: Alfred A. Knopf, 1970.

——. *The Sociological Tradition*. New York: Basic Books, 1966.

——. "The Triumph of Status: Tocqueville." In *Status Communities in Modern Society. Alternatives to Class Analysis*. Holger R. Stub, ed. Hinsdale, Ill.: The Dryden Press, 1972.

——. *Twilight of Authority*. New York: Oxford University Press, 1975.

Ostrander, Susan A. *Women of the Upper Class*. Philadelphia: Temple University Press, 1984.

Packard, Vance. *The Status Seekers*. New York: David McKay Company, 1959.

Parsons, Talcott. "The Kinship System of the Contemporary United States." *American Anthropologist*. Vol. 45 n.s., 1943.

Pessen, Edward. *Riches, Class, and Power Before the Civil War*. Lexington, Mass.: D.C. Heath & Company, 1973.

——. "Status and Social Class in America." In *Making America: The Society and Culture of the United States*. Luther S. Luedtke, ed. Washington D.C.: United States Information Agency, 1988.

Peterson, Merrill D. *Thomas Jefferson and the New Nation: A Biography*. New York: Oxford University Press, 1970.

Potter, David. *Freedom and its Limitations in American Life*. Stanford, Calif.: Stanford University Press: 1976.

Powell, Michael. *From Patrician to Professional Elite: The Transformation of the New York City Bar Association*. New York: Russell Sage Foundation, 1988.

Prewitt, Kenneth, and Alan Stone. *The Ruling Elites: Elite Theory, Power, and American Democracy*. New York: Harper & Row, 1973.

Rabinovitz, Jonathan. "An Attempted Comeback for the Literary Salon." *New York Times*, April 13, 1992, p. C15.

Reichley, William. *Religion in American Public Life*. Washington, D.C.: The Brookings Institution, 1985.

Remini, Robert V. *The Legacy of Andrew Jackson*. Baton Rouge: Louisiana State University Press, 1988.

Schlesinger, Arthur Meier. *The Birth of the Nation: A Portrait of the American People on the Eve of Independence*. New York: Alfred A. Knopf, 1968.

——. *New Viewpoints in American History*. New York: Macmillan, 1922.

Schlesinger, Arthur M., Jr. "Jacksonian Democracy as an Intellectual Movement." In

Jacksonian Democracy: Myth or Reality? James L. Bugg, ed. New York: Holt, Rinehart and Winston, 1962.

Senior, Hereward. *The Loyalists of Quebec, 1774-1825.* Montreal: Price Patterson Ltd., 1989.

Sisson, Daniel. *The American Revolution of 1800.* New York: Alfred A. Knopf, 1974.

Stansfeld, Martin. "American Aristocracy Is Very Much Alive and Growing." *U.S. News and World Report.* December 12, 1983, p. 64.

Thomas, John L., S.J. *The American Catholic Family.* Englewood Cliffs, N.J.: Prentice-Hall, 1958.

Tindall, George Brown. *America: A Narrative History.* 2 vols. New York: W. W. Norton & Company, 1984.

Tocqueville, Alexis de. *L'Ancien Régime et la Révolution.* J. P. Mayer, ed. Paris: Gallimard, 1967.

——. *Democracy in America.* Henry Reeve translation, edited by Phillips Bradley. 2 vols. New York: Alfred A. Knopf [1945] 1972; reprint Vintage Books, 1990.

Tuveson, Ernest Lee. *Redeemer Nation: The Idea of America's Millennial Role.* Chicago: University of Chicago Press, 1968.

Van den Berghe, Pierre L. *Man in Society: A Biosocial View.* 2d ed. New York: Elsevier, 1978.

Van Tyne, Claude H. *The Loyalists in the American Revolution.* New York, 1902.

Von Borch, Herbert. *The Unfinished Society.* Transl. Mary Ilford. New York: The Bobbs-Merrill Company, 1963.

Ward, William R., ed. *A Guide to Hereditary and Lineage Societies, 1991.* Salt Lake City: Tradition Publications, 1991.

Warner, W. Lloyd. *American Life: Dream and Reality.* Rev. ed. Chicago: University of Chicago Press, 1962.

——. *Social Class in America: A Manual of Procedure for the Measurement of Social Status.* New York: Science Research Associates, 1949; Harper Torchbooks, 1960.

Weaver, Richard. *The Southern Tradition at Bay: A History of Postbellum Thought.* New Rochelle, N.Y.: Arlington House, 1968.

Wecter, Dixon, *The Saga of American Society: A Record of Social Aspiration, 1607-1937.* New York: Charles Scribner's Sons [1937] 1970.

Wertenbaker, Thomas J. *The Golden Age of Colonial Culture.* Ithaca, N.Y.: New York University Press, 1949; reprint Cornell University Press, 1967.

——. *The Old South: The Founding of American Civilization.* New York: Cooper Square Publishers, 1963.

——. *Patrician and Plebeian in Virginia: Or the Origin and Development of the Social Classes of the Old Dominion.* New York: Russell & Russell, 1959.

——. *The Planters of Colonial Virginia.* New York: Russell & Russell, 1959.

Whitehill, Walter Muir. "The New Aristocracies of Success." In *American Civilization.* Daniel J. Boorstin, ed. London: Thames & Hudson, 1972.

Williams, Robin M., Jr. *American Society: A Sociological Interpretation.* 2d ed. New York: Alfred A. Knopf, 1960.

Williams, T. Harry, Richard N. Current, and Frank Freidel. *A History of the United States (to 1876).* New York: Alfred A. Knopf, 1962.

Wilstach, Paul. *Potomac Landings.* Garden City, N.Y.: Doubleday, Page & Co., 1921.

Wood, Gordon S. *The Creation of the American Republic, 1776-1787.* University of North Carolina Press, 1969; reprint New York: W. W. Norton & Company, 1972.

Wright, Louis B. *The American Heritage History of the Thirteen Colonies.* New York: American Heritage Publishing Co., 1967.

——. *The Cultural Life of the American Colonies, 1607-1763.* New York: Harper & Row, 1957.

——. *The First Gentlemen of Virginia: Intellectual Qualities of the Early Colonial Ruling Class.* Henry Huntington Library, 1940; reprint Charlottesville, Va.: Dominion Books, 1964.

——. *South Carolina: A Bicentennial History.* New York: W. W. Norton & Company, 1976.

WORKS CITED IN APPENDIX II
(ON BRAZIL)

Abreu, J. Capistrano de. *Capítulos da História Colonial (1500-1800).* 4th ed. Sociedade Capistrano de Abreu, 1954.

Amaral Gurgel, L. *Ensaios Quinhentistas.* São Paulo: Editora J. Fagundes, 1936.

Andrade, Almir de. *Formação da Sociologia Brasileira.* Vol. 1. *Os primeiros estudos sociais no Brasil.* Rio de Janeiro: Livraria José Olympio Editora, 1941.

Azevedo, Fernando de. *Canaviais e Engenhos*

na Vida Política do Brasil. 2d ed. São Paulo: Ediçães Melhoramentos. Vol. 11.

———. *A Cultura Brasileira—Introdução ao Estudo da Cultura no Brasil.* 3d ed. São Paulo: Editora Melhoramentos. Vols. 1, 2.

Bastide, Roger. *Brasil Terra de Contrastes.* 4th ed. São Paulo: Edição Europeia do Livro.

Brandonio. *Diálogo das Grandezas do Brasil.* Quoted in Luis Palacin. *Vieira e a visão trágica do Barroco.* Rio de Janeiro: Hucitec/Pró-Memória e Instituto Nacional do Livro, 1943.

Calado, Fr. Manuel. *Valeroso Lucideno.* Lisbon, 1648.

Calmon, Pedro. *História do Brasil.* Rio de Janeiro: Livraria José Olympio Editora, 1959. Vols. 1, 2, 3, 7.

Cardim, Fr. Fernão. *Tratados da Terra e Gente do Brasil.* Belo Horizonte: Livraria Itatiaia Editora.

Clemenceau, Georges. "Notes de Voyage dans l'Amerique du Sud - XIII" *L'Illustration,* April 22, 1911.

Corrêa de Oliveira, João Alfredo. "O Barão de Goiana e sua Época Genealógica." in *Minha Meninice e Outros Ensaios.* Recife: Editora Massangana, 1988.

Cortesão, Jaime. *Raposo Tavares e a Formação Territorial do Brasil.* Rio de Janeiro: Imprensa Nacional, 1958.

Cunha, Rui Vieira da. *Estudo da Nobreza Brasileira (Cadetes).* Rio de Janeiro: Arquivo Nacional, 1966.

———. *Figuras e Fatos da Nobreza Brasileira.* Rio de Janeiro: Arquivo Nacional, 1975.

Duarte, Nestor. *A Ordem Privada e a Organização Política Nacional.* São Paulo: Companhia Editora Nacional, 1939.

Ellis, Alfredo, Jr. "Amador Bueno e seu tempo," *Colecção História da Civilização Brasileira,* Vol. 7. Boletim no. 86. São Paulo: Universidade de São Paulo, 1948.

Ellis, Alfredo, Jr. *Resumo da História de São Paulo.* São Paulo: Tipografia Brasil, 1942. Vols. 1, 3.

Ferreira, Manoel Rodrigues. *As Repúblicas Municipais no Brasil (1532-1820).* São Paulo: Prefeitura do Município de São Paulo, 1980. Vol. 1.

Fonseca, António José Victoriano Borges da. *Nobiliarchia Pernambucana.* Rio de Janeiro: Biblioteca Nacional, 1935.

Franco, Carvalho. *Nobiliário Colonial.* 2d ed. São Paulo.

Freyre, Gilberto. *Casa-Grande & Senzala.* 5th ed. Rio de Janeiro: Editora José Olympio, 1946. Vol. 1.

———. *Interpretação do Brasil.* Rio de Janeiro: José Olympio Editora, 1947.

Havighurst, Robert J., and J. Roberto Moreira. *Society and Education in Brazil.* Pittsburgh: University of Pittsburgh Press, 1969.

João III. *Regimento de Tomé de Sousa.* Lisbon: Biblioteca Nacional de Lisboa, Arquivo da Marinha, book 1, dispatches from 1597-1602.

Leite, Fr. Serafim. *História da Companhia de Jesus no Brasil.* Rio de Janeiro: Instituto Nacional do Livro, 1945. Vol. 5.

Melo Franco, Afonso Arinos de. *A Sociedade Bandeirante das Minas.* In AA. VV. *Curso de Bandeirologia.* São Paulo: Departamento Estadual de Informaçoes, 1946.

Morazé, Charles. *Les trois ages du Brésil: essai de politique.* Paris: Librairie Armand Colin, 1954.

Oliveira Lima. *O movimento da Independência, 1821-1822.* São Paulo: Companhia Melhoramentos de São Paulo, 1922.

Oliveira Vianna, F.J. *Instituições Políticas Brasileiras.* Rio de Janeiro: José Olympio Editora. 1st ed., 1949, Vol. 1; 2d ed., 1955, Vols. 1, 2.

———. *Populações Meridionais do Brasil.* 3d ed. São Paulo: Companhia Editora Nacional. Vol. 1.

———. *O povo Brasileiro e a sua Evolução.* Rio de Janeiro: Ministério de Agricultura, Indústria e Comércio; Directoria Geral de Estatística, Tipografia da Estatística, 1922.

Omegna, Nelson. *A Cidade Colonial.* Rio de Janeiro: Livraria José Olympio Editora, 1961.

Paes Barreto, Carlos Xavier. *Os Primitivos Colonizadores Nordestinos e seus Descendentes.* Rio de Janeiro: Editora Melso, 1960.

Palacin, Luís. *Sociedade Colonial, 1549-1599.* Goiânia: Editora da Universidade Federal de Goiás, 1981.

Pombo, Rocha. *História do Brasil.* Rio de Janeiro: W. M. Jackson Editores, 1942. Vol. 1.

Prado, Caio, Jr. *Evolução Politica do Brasil e outros estudos.* 7th ed. São Paulo: Editora Brasiliense, 1971.

Rodrigues, F. Contreiras. *Traços da Economia Social e Política do Brasil Colonial.* São Paulo: Ariel Editora, 1935.

Sodré, Nelson Werneck. *Formação da Sociedade Brasileira.* Rio de Janeiro: José Olympio Editora, 1944.

Vianna, Hélio. *Formação Brasileira.* Rio de Janeiro: Livraria José Olympio Editor, 1935.

Wiederspahn, Lt. Col. Henrique. "A Evolução da Nobreza Cavalheresca e Militar Luso-Brasileira desde o Descobrimento até a República." In *Boletim do Colégio de Armas e Consulta Heráldica do Brasil.* no. 1, 1955.

WORKS CITED IN APPENDIX III
(ON LIBERTY, EQUALITY, AND FRATERNITY)

Benedict XV, Pope. Allocution on the heroic virtue of Blessed Marcellin Champagnat, July 11, 1920. 2d ed. *L'Osservatore Romano.* July 12-13, 1920.

Furet, François, and Mona Ozouf. *Dictionnaire critique de la Révolution Française.* Paris: Flammarion, 1988.

John Paul II, Pope. Allocution to French pilgrims from Angers at the beatification of Guillaume Repin and companions, February 20, 1984. *Insegnamenti di Giovanni Paolo II.* Vol. 7, no. 1.

——. Homily at Le Bourget airport, Paris, June 1, 1980. *Insegnamenti di Giovanni Paolo II.* Vol. 3, no. 1.

Paul VI, Pope. On Saint Vincent Palloti's work in Frascati, Italy, September 1, 1963. *The Pope Speaks*, Vol. 9, no. 2.

Pius VI, Pope. Decretal to Cardinal de la Rochefoucauld and the Archbishop of Aix-en-Provence, March 10, 1791. *Pii VI Pont. Max. Acta.* Vol. 1 (1871).

——. Encyclical *Inscrutabile Divinae Sapientiae. Pii VI Pont. Max. Acta.* Vol. 2 (1871).

Soboul, Albert. *La Revolution Française.* Paris: Gallimard, 1962. Vol. 2.

WORKS CITED IN APPENDIX IV
(ON FORMS OF GOVERNMENT)

Billot, Louis Cardinal. *Les Principes de 89 et leurs conséquences.* Paris: Téqui. n.d.

Burke, Edmund. *Reflections on the Revolution in France.* Hammondsworth, Middlesex: Penguin Books, 1969.

Dansette, Adrien. *Religious History of Modern France.* New York: Herder and Herder, 1961, Vol. 2.

Documents of Vatican II. New York: America Press, 1966.

Francis de Sales, Saint. *Treatise on the Love of God.* Transl. by Fr. Henry Mackey, OSB. London: Burns Oates & Washbourne, Ltd., n.d.

Furet, François, and Mona Ozouf. *Dictionnaire Critique de la Révolution Française.* Paris: Flammarion, 1988.

Gonzalez Moral, Fr. Irineu, S.J. *Philosofiae Scholasticae Summa.* Madrid: Biblioteca de Autores Cristianos, 1952, Vol. 3.

John Paul II, Pope. Encyclical *Centessimus anos. Origins.* Vol. 21, no. 1 (May 16, 1991).

——. Encyclical *Solicitudo rei socialis. Origins.* Vol. 17, no. 38 (March 3, 1988), pp. 642-660.

John XXIII, Pope. Encyclical *Pacem in Terris. Peace on Earth.* Boston: Daughters of St. Paul, n.d.

Leo XIII, Pope. Encyclical *Diuturnum illud.* Husslein. *Social Wellsprings.* Vol. 1, pp. 47-62.

——. Encyclical *Au milieu des sollicitudes.* Wynne. *Great Encyclical Letters of Leo XIII.* pp. 249-263.

——. Encyclical *Immortale Dei.* Wynne. pp. 107-134.

——. Letter to François Cardinal Richard, Archbishop of Paris, December 23, 1900. *Actes de Léon XIII.* Vol. 2, pp. 190-191.

——. Letter to French President Emile Loubet, June 1900. In Emmanuel Barbier. *Histoire du Catholicisme liberal et du Catholicisme social en France.* Bordeaux: L'Imprimerie Yves Cadoret, 1924. Vol. 2., p. 531.

Mao Tse-tung. *Selected Works.* New York: International Publishers. Vol. 1.

Orieux, Jean. *Talleyrand ou le sphinx incompris.* Paris: Flammarion, 1970.

Pius VI, Pope. Allocution to the Secret Consistory, June 17, 1793. *Pii VI Pont. Max. Acta.* Vol. 2 (1871).

——. Encyclical *Inscrutabili Divinae Sapientiae.* Carlen. *The Papal Encyclicals, 1740-1878.*

Pius IX, Pope. Encyclical *Nostis et nobiscum.* Carlen. *The Papal Encyclicals, 1740-1878.*

Pius X, Saint. Apostolic Letter *Notre charge apostolique. American Catholic Quarterly Review.* Vol. 35. (October 1910).

Pius XI, Pope. Encyclical *Dilectissima Nobis. Catholic Mind.* Vol. 31, no. 13 (July 8, 1933), pp. 241-251.

Pius XII, Pope. Allocution to the Secret Consistory of February 14, 1949. *The Catholic Mind.* Vol. 47 (April 1949).

——. 1944 Christmas message. Yzermans. *Major Addresses of Pope Pius XII.* Vol. 2, pp. 78 ff.

Ratzinger, Joseph Cardinal. Interview. *El Mercurio* (Santiago, Chile), June 12, 1988.

Rodriguez, Fr. Victorino, O.P. *El Régimen Político de Santo Tomás de Aquino.* Madrid: Editorial Fuerza Nueva, 1978.

Taine, Hippolyte. *Les Origines de la France*

Contemporaine. Paris: Robert Laffont, 1986.

Thomas Aquinas, Saint. *On the Governance of Rulers*. London: Sheed and Ward, 1938.

———. *Summa Theologica*. London: R. & T. Washbourne, 1912.

WORKS CITED IN DOCUMENTS

Archives de Sociologie des Religions. Published by the Group of Sociology of Religions. Paris: Editions du Centre National de la Recherche Scientifique, January-June 1962.

Benedict XV, Pope. Allocutions to the Roman Patriciate and Nobility. *L'Osservatore Romano*. January 6, 1917; January 5-6, 1920.

———. Encyclical *Ad beatissimii apostolorum*. *American Catholic Quarterly Review*. Vol. 39 (October 1914), pp. 656-668.

———. Letter *Soliti nos*. *Acta Apostolicae Sedis*. Vol. 12, no. 4. (April 1, 1920).

Bernadine of Siena, Saint. Sermon on Saint Joseph. *Sancti Bernardini Senensis Sermones Eximii*. Venice: in Aedibus Andreae Poletti, 1745. Vol. 4. p. 232.

Bernard of Clairvaux, Saint. *De laude novae militiae*. In J. P. Migne, *Patrologia Latina*. Vol. 182, col. 924.

Bonaventure, Saint. *Opera Omnia*. Paris: Vives, 1867. Vol. 10.

Bordonove, Georges. *Les rois qui ont fait la France—Charles X: Dernier rois de France et de Navarre*. Paris: Editions Pygmalion, 1990.

Broderick, John F., S.J. "A Census of the Saints (993-1955)." *The American Ecclesiastical Review*, August 1956.

Castillo Lara, Msgr. Rosalio. *Coacción Eclesiástica y Sacro Romano Imperio: Estudio jurídico-histórico sobre la potestad coactiva material suprema de la Iglesia en los documentos conciliares y pontificios del período de formación del Derecho Canónico clásico como un presupuesto de las relaciones entre Sacerdotium e Imperium*. Turin: Augustae Taurinorum, 1956.

Charles Borromeo, Saint. Sermon on the Nativity of Mary. *Sancti Caroli Borromei Homiliae CXXII*. Augustae Vindelicorum [Augsburg]: Ignatii Adami & Francisci Antonii Veith Bibliopolarum, n.d. editio novissima, cols. 1211-1214. Delassus, Msgr. Henri. *L'Esprit familial dans la maison, dans la cité et dans l'état*. Lille: Société Saint-Augustin, Desclée de Brouwer, 1910.

Delooz, Pierre. *Sociologie et canonisations*. La Haye: Martinus Nijhoff, 1969.

Dictionnaire du monde religieux dans la France contemporaine, Vol. 4, *Lille-Flandres* (Paris: Beauchesne, 1990).

Francis de Sales, Saint. Funeral oration for Philippe-Emmanuel de Lorraine. *Oeuvres complètes de Saint François de Sales*. Paris: Béthune, Éditeur, 1836. Vol. 2, pp. 404-406.

Funck-Brentano, Frantz. *L'Ancien Régime*. Paris: Americ=Edit., 1936.

Fustel de Coulanges, Numa Denis. *La Cité antique*. Paris: Librairie Hachette n.d.

Garaudy, Roger. *L'homme chrétien et l'homme marxiste: Semaines de la pensée marxiste—confrontations et débats*. Paris-Geneva: La Palatine, 1964.

Index ac Status Causarum. Vatican City: Congregatio pro Causis Sanctorum, 1988.

John Paul II, Pope. Homily for youths in Belo Horizonte, Brazil, July 1, 1980. *Insegnamenti di Giovanni Paolo II*. Vol. 3.

John XXIII, Pope. Encyclical *Ad Petri Cathedram*. *The Pope Speaks*. Vol. 5, no. 3 (Summer 1959).

La Brière, Yves de. "Paix et guerre." *Dictionnaire apologétique de la foi Catholique*. Paris: Gabriel Beauchesne Éditeur, 1926. Vol. 3.

Le Brun, J. *Santa Isabel, Rainha de Portugal*. Porto: Livraria Apostolado da Imprensa, 1958.

Leo XIII, Pope. Allocutions to the Roman Patriciate and Nobility, January 21, 1897; January 24, 1903. *Leonis XIII Pontificis Maximii Acta*. Vols. 17, 22. (1898, 1903).

———. Encyclical *Humanum genus*. Wynne. *Great Encyclical Letters of Leo XIII*. Pp. 83-106.

———. Encyclical *Quod Apostolici muneris*. *Catholic World*, Vol. 27 (March, 1879), pp. 849-858.

———. Encyclical *Rerum novarum*. Wynne. *Great Encyclical Letters of Leo XIII*. Pp. 208-248.

Marinelli, G. *La Terra: trattato popolare di geografia universale*. Milan: Casa Editrice Francesco Vallardi. 7 vols.

Ortolan, T. "Canonisation." In *Dictionnaire de théologie Catholique*. Paris: Letouzey et Ané, 1923. Vol. 2.

Palazzini, Pietro Cardinal. *Bibliotheca Sanctorum*. John XXIII Institute of the Pontifical Lateran University, 1960-1970, 1987. 12 vols. & appendix.

Paul VI, Pope. Allocution to fellow countrymen at Brescia, September 26, 1970. *Insegnamenti di Paolo VI*. Vol. 8, pp. 943-944.

——. Allocution to Slavic pilgrims, September 14, 1963. *The Pope Speaks.* Vol. 9, no. 2 (1964).

——. Sermon at Saint Lawrence Outside the Walls, November 2, 1963. *Insegnamenti di Paolo VI.* Vol. 1, pp. 276-277.

Peter Damian, Saint. In J.P. Migne, *Patrologia Latina.* Vol. 145, cols. 214-215.

Peter Julian Eymard, Saint. *Mois de Saint Joseph, le premier et le plus parfait des adorateurs: Extrait des écrits de P. Eymard.* 7th ed. Paris: Desclée de Brouwer, n.d.

Pius IX, Pope. Allocutions to the Roman Patriciate and Nobility, June 19, 1871; December 29, 1872. *Discorsi del Sommo Pontefice Pio IX.* Vol. 1.

Pius X, Pope Saint. Apostolic letter *Notre charge apostolique. American Catholic Quarterly Review.* Vol. 35 (October 1910), pp. 693-711.

——. Letter to Msgr. H. Delassus. *Actes de Pie X.* Paris: Maison de la Bonne Presse, 1936. Vol. 7, p. 238.

——. Motu proprio *Fin dalla prima. Acta Sanctae Sedis.* Vol. 36 (1903-1904), pp. 339-345.

Pius XI, Pope. Encyclical *Divini Redemptoris.* Husslein. *Social Wellsprings.* Vol. 2, pp. 339-374.

Pius XII, Pope. Allocution to Fiat workers, October 31, 1948. *Discorsi e radiomessaggi.* Vol. 10, p. 266.

——. Christmas message, 1942. In *Discorsi e radiomessaggi.* Vol. 4, pp. 325-346.

——. Speech to parishioners of Marsciano, Italy, June 4, 1953. *Discorsi e radiomessaggi.* Vol. 15, p. 195.

——. Speech to professors and students of the Liceo Ennio Quirino Visconti, Rome, February 28, 1957. *Discorsi e radiomessaggi.* Vol. 18, p. 803.

Ruiz Bueno, Daniel. *Actas de los martires.* Madrid: Biblioteca de Autores Cristianos, 1951.

Sacred Congregation of the Council. Letter to the Bishop of Lille, June 5, 1929. *Acta Apostolicae Sedis.* Vol. 21, no. 10. (August 3, 1929).

Corrêa de Oliveira, Plinio, Archbishop Geraldo de Proença Sigaud, Bishop Antonio de Castro Mayer, and Luiz Mendonça de Freitas. *Reforma Agrária—Questão de Consciência.* São Paulo: Editora Vera Cruz, 1960.

Suárez, Francisco, S.J. *"De Bello"* I, 2, in Luciano Pereña Vicente, *Teoría de la guerra en Francisco Suárez.* Madrid: C.S.I.C., 1954. Vol. 2.

Thomas Aquinas, Saint. *Summa Contra Gentiles.* Notre Dame, Ind.: University of Notre Dame Press, 1975.

——. *Summa Theologica.* London: R. & T. Washbourne, 1912.

Vauchez, André. *La santité en l'occident aux derniers siecles du Moyen Age.* Ecole française de Rome, Palais Farnese, 1981.

Weiss, Johann Baptist. *Historia universal.* Barcelona: Tipografía la Educación, 1931, 1932. Vols. 15, 21.

Index

Credits

Preparation of Appendix I: under the guidance of Prof. Plinio Corrêa de Oliveira, by Dr. Murillo Maranhão Galliez, Julio Loredo de Izcue, Leo A. Horvat, J. Edward Parrot, Steven F. Schmieder, Matthew J. Carlson, Walter de León, Thomas B. Senior, Richard A. Lyon, Roberto Wasilewski, Arthur N. Hlebnikian, Michael P. McKenna, Brian Murphy, Gaspar Cruz, and André R. Dantas.

Research for Appendix II: under the direction of the author, by Dr. Murillo Maranhão Galliez, José Carlos Sepúlveda da Fonseca, Bernardo Glowacki, José Luis Ablass, Simão Pedro de Aguiã, and José António Dominguez.

Photography: Felipe Barandiarán Porta, Charles Preston Noell III, Thomas J. McKenna, and Todd F. Kamuf.

Credits not printed with photos: Vatican Museum (Giordani): Pius XII in *sedia gestatoria* (dust jacket front cover); TFP Archive (Felipe Barandiarán): Saint Peter's Square in the eighteenth century (front endpaper); Biblioteca Nacional de Madrid: knights (title pages); the author: Lucília Ribeiro dos Santos (dedication page); Arturo Mari (*L'Osservatore Romano*): Saint Peter's at dusk (facing title page); Olavo Corrêa Barbosa: tiara and keys (left side of foldout); Oporto Episcopal Palace (Felipe Barandiarán): The Good Shepherd, (right side of foldout); TFP Archive (Felipe Barandiarán): construction of a cathedral (30); TFP Archive (Sepúlveda da Fonseca): The Holy Family (56); TFP Archive (Preston Noell): West Point (64); courtesy of Columbia University, Columbiana Collection: Pierre Toussaint (136); courtesy of St. Joseph's Provincial House Archives: Saint Elizabeth Ann Seton (137); Europa Press: Cardinal Herrera Oria (419); Vatican Museum (Giordani): pontifical guards in formation (back endpaper); TFP Archive (Preston Noell): Iwo Jima Memorial, Arlington, Va. (dust jacket back cover).

Photos generously given for this book: Diputación Regional de Cantabria: oil by Utrillo, Leo XIII in *sedia gestatoria* (413); Hospital de la Santa Caridad, Seville: Saint Elizabeth of Hungary (60); Museu Paulista, São Paulo: discovery of Brazil (336), Martim Afonso de Sousa (340), founding of São Vicente (340), the *bandeirante* Antonio Raposo Tavares (348), Rua do Rosário (365); Editora Kosmos, São Paulo: passage of the Emperor by the Rua Direita (365), crowning of Dom Pedro I (369).